KU-255-334

Supplement to The Oxford Companion to Canadian History and Literature

Contributors

Alvine Bélisle
Université de Montréal

Carl Berger
University of Toronto

Jack Crompton
Arundel Comprehensive School, Liverpool

Frank Davey
York University

Kildare Dobbs

Sheila Egoff
University of British Columbia

Sheila Fischman

David Flint
A.Y. Jackson Secondary School, North York

Edith Fowke
York University

Wynne Francis
Sir George Williams University

Gary Geddes
University of Victoria

John Glassco

Michael Gnarowski
Carleton University

Monique Grandmangin
Bishop's University

David Hoffman
York University

Naim Kattan

L.W. Keffer
Bishop's University

Laurier LaPierre
McGill University

Laurent Mailhot
Université de Montréal

Joyce Marshall

Agathe Martin-Thériault
Université du Québec à Rimouski

C.R.P. May
University of Birmingham

Pierre Nepveu
Université de Sherbrooke

James Noonan
Carleton University

Jean-Louis Roy
McGill University

Donat Savoie
Department of Indian and Northern Affairs, Ottawa

Ben-Z. Shek
University of Toronto

Peter Stevens
University of Windsor

Norah Story

Philip C. Stratford
Université de Montréal

William Toye

Claude Trottier
University of Toronto

Maïr Verthuy
Sir George Williams University

Miriam Waddington
York University

Jack Warwick
York University

Sally M. Weaver
University of Waterloo

George Woodcock

Supplement to The Oxford Companion to Canadian History and Literature

General editor
William Toye

Toronto
London
New York
Oxford University Press
1973

PUBLICATION OF THIS BOOK WAS ASSISTED BY
THE HUMANITIES RESEARCH COUNCIL OF CANADA

ISBN 0-19-540205-7

2 3 4 – 6 5 4 3

Printed in Canada by
JOHN DEYELL COMPANY

Preface

Norah Story's invaluable and formidable *Oxford Companion to Canadian History and Literature* was published in 1967. The bibliographical articles in this *Supplement* discuss books that appeared between the beginning of 1967 and the end of 1972—a six-year period that gave rise to an unprecedented number of publications and a remarkable flowering of literary accomplishment in both English and French. (Detailed attention is given throughout the *Supplement*, for the first time in English, to the immense amount of literary activity in French Canada and to the intellectual environment that has surrounded it.) They include—besides the subject entries established in the original volume on anthologies, belles lettres, drama, Eskimos, fiction, folklore, Indians, literary magazines, literary studies, and poetry—articles on children's books, history studies (including biographies and art books), political writings, and translations. For such a productive six years, book reviews inevitably leave in retrospect a very vague impression of what has been accomplished and of what has become available. It is hoped that these surveys will provide a useful guide and record.

The author-entries include articles on those writers—mainly novelists, poets, playwrights, and historians—who have come into prominence in the 1967–72 period, as well as revised or new articles on writers who had entries in the original *Companion* and have continued to publish. To increase the usefulness of this *Supplement* as a reference work, entries on some important modern writers who died before 1967 (Grove, Pratt, Saint-Denys Garneau, and Wilkinson) or who did not publish in our period (Callaghan, Grandbois, Klein, and LePan) have been reprinted with slight revisions.

Unlike the 1967 *Companion*, which was the impressive achievement of one person, this *Supplement* is made up of articles by thirty-seven contributors—busy people for whom their undertakings amounted to a (usually inconvenient) labour of love. I am grateful to all of them for their willingness to assist in the project and for their informative articles. I owe special thanks to Professor Ben Shek, who supplemented his written contributions most generously and helpfully with various forms of editorial advice relating to the literature of French Canada.

WET

A

Abrahamson, Una. See FOLKLORE: BIBLIOGRAPHY.

Acorn, Milton (1923–). Born in Charlottetown, P.E.I., he described himself in his first book as a carpenter, a socialist, and a poet, and has lately added 'Canadian patriot'. He worked as a carpenter before selling his tools in Montreal and devoting himself to the writing of poetry. He supports himself partly from reading his poems aloud at poetry readings.

Acorn published his early poems privately: *In love and anger* (1956), a title that contains two of the principal subjects in his poetry, and *Against a league of liars* (1960), a broadsheet. They were followed by two books: *The brain's the target* (1960) and *Jawbreakers* (1963). In 1963 *The Fiddlehead* devoted an issue to Acorn's work. Much of his poetry of the 1960s was published in *I've tasted my blood* (1969) and some of it has been reprinted with new poems in *More poems for people* (1972). When the Governor General's Awards were announced in 1971 and *I've tasted my blood* failed to win, a group of Toronto poets gave a party for Acorn at Grossman's Tavern, awarded him 'The Canadian Poetry Award 1970', and dubbed him 'The People's Poet'.

Acorn's poetry is firmly fixed in love of people, sympathy for their predicaments, anger against the oppressive nature of society, and the recognition of human brotherhood. With these concerns at its centre, his poetry, particularly his work of the middle and late 1960s, became public and political. Acorn considers himself to be a revolutionary poet and sometimes his poetry is marred by a too directly propagandist tone; but in general it is tempered by his empathy for people. His political poetry exists side by side with tender love lyrics and nostalgic reminiscences of his life on Prince Edward Island and of the people there. While his early poetry tends to be straightforward in tone and language, his later work is at times diffuse, some poems developing by means of loosely connecting phrases and images rather than by the direct and somewhat hortatory style of his public poetry. PS

Adam, Marcel. See POLITICAL WRITINGS IN FRENCH 4.

Adams, Howard. See HISTORY STUDIES IN ENGLISH 6.

Adams, Ian. See FICTION IN ENGLISH 1.

Addison, Ottelyn. See HISTORY STUDIES IN ENGLISH 16.

Adler-Karlson, Gunnar. See POLITICAL WRITINGS IN ENGLISH 2.

Aitkin, Barbara B. See HISTORY STUDIES IN ENGLISH 17.

Allan, Iris. See CHILDREN'S BOOKS IN ENGLISH 3.

Allen, Richard. See HISTORY STUDIES IN ENGLISH 7.

Anderson, Doris. See CHILDREN'S BOOKS IN ENGLISH 1.

Anderson, J. W. See ESKIMOS: BOOKS IN ENGLISH.

Anderson, James D. See POLITICAL WRITINGS IN ENGLISH 8.

Anderson, Owen. See POLITICAL WRITINGS IN ENGLISH 8.

André, John. See HISTORY STUDIES IN ENGLISH 5.

Angers, F. A. See POLITICAL WRITINGS IN FRENCH 3.

Anthologies in English (see also DRAMA IN ENGLISH 4 and LITERARY STUDIES IN ENGLISH). The spectacular flowering of educational interest in Canadian literature has not unexpectedly produced a spate of anthologies in our six-year period. There has been a move away from the large, definitive compilation (e.g. A. J. M. SMITH's *Oxford book of Canadian verse* and the *Canadian anthology* edited by Carl

F. KLINCK and R. E. Watters), which featured writers of proven abilities, to smaller, more narrowly focused collections presenting work chosen on the basis of a very selective and personal taste. They are usually strengthened by highly attractive book design and are often embellished with drawings and/or photographs. There are numerous anthologies, usually of localized scope, that give a salutary first exposure to new writers, and several regional collections. The more traditional and solid approach is still in evidence, however, notably in *Fifteen Canadian poets* edited by Gary Geddes and Phyllis Bruce.

1. *Poetry*. The first important poetry anthology in our period was edited—appropriately enough—by the dean of Canadian anthologists, A. J. M. Smith. *Modern Canadian verse: in English and French* (1967) originally started as a revision of his famous *Oxford book of Canadian verse* of 1960 and soon turned into a book-length collection in its own right, devoted to twentieth-century poets beginning with PRATT. It is a strong anthology, infused with Smith's sound judgement of the lasting and good. Revised editions of two well-known anthologies were also published in 1967: *The Penguin book of Canadian verse* edited by Ralph GUSTAFSON and *The blasted pine: an anthology of satire, invective and disrespectful verse chiefly by Canadian writers* edited by Smith and F. R. SCOTT. For the New Canadian Library series Milton Wilson edited *Poets between the wars* (1967), containing work by Pratt, Scott, LIVESAY, Smith, and KLEIN; David Sinclair edited *Nineteenth-century narrative poems* (1972) devoted to Goldsmith, Howe, Sangster, Kirby, McLachlan, and Crawford; and Eli MANDEL edited *Poets of contemporary Canada 1960–1970* (1972), containing PURDY, ROSENBLATT, ACORN, COHEN, BOWERING, NEWLOVE, ATWOOD, BISSETT, MACEWEN, and ONDAATJE. Other Mandel anthologies—intended for college use, with interesting short notes on each poet—are *Five modern Canadian poets* (1970) (BIRNEY, LAYTON, Purdy, Atwood, Cohen) and *Eight more Canadian poets* (1972) (AVISON, SOUSTER, Mandel, Acorn, REANEY, WEBB, JONES, and MACPHERSON). Also for college use, Gary Geddes and Phyllis Bruce edited *Fifteen Canadian poets* (1970), a very sound collection with excellent critical notes on the poets: Birney, Purdy, Layton, Souster, Cohen, Jones, NOWLAN, Avison, Mandel, Atwood, MacEwen, Newlove, Bowering, COLEMAN, and Ondaatje. John Robert COLOMBO edited three anthologies that contain background material from the poets themselves on their work: *How do I love thee? sixty poets of Canada (and Quebec) select and introduce their own work* (1970); *Rhymes and reasons: nine Canadian poets discuss their work* (1971); and *New directions in Canadian poetry* (1971). Dennis LEE's *T.O. now: the young Toronto poets* (1968) and Peter Anson's *Canada first: a mare usque ad Edmonton: new Canadian poets* (1969) are devoted to the promotion of the younger writers. In the former the reader is introduced to thirteen Toronto poets, while in the latter the net is cast nationally with nineteen young poets but excludes representation from the west coast. Al Purdy edited *Fifteen winds: a selection of modern Canadian poets* (1969), which is a strongly subjective hodge-podge of established names, young poets, and some non-poets—and *Storm warning* (1971), which offers the work of thirty young poets. Another poet, Raymond Souster, with Douglas Lochhead, edited *Made in Canada: new poems of the seventies* (1970)—again very much a mixed bag, introduced rather too hopefully by Michael Macklem. *Soundings: new Canadian poets* (1970) was edited by Jack Ludwig and Andy Wainright and extended a claim for fourteen young and not-so-young writers of the day. *Mindscapes* (1971), edited by Ann Wall, contains the work of four new and developing poets. Mention should also be made of *Snowmobiles forbidden: personal statements of a computer age* (1971) edited by D. Chenoweth and C. Gurd, a collection of young poets centred on Montreal that contains a few prose pieces as well.

Of more specialized interest is *The broken ark* (1971) edited by Michael Ondaatje, an attractive anthology of animal poems, with drawings by Tony Urquhart. The appearance of such a book as *Forty women poets of Canada* (1972), edited by Dorothy Livesay, was perhaps inevitable at this time, even though it includes mostly poets who are already well known and have been frequently anthologized. *Three early poems from Lower Canada* (1969) edited by Michael Gnarowski contains the first poetic expressions about Canada, written in the eighteenth (and early nineteenth) century by English visitors. John GLASSCO's excellent *The poetry of French Canada in translation* (1970) was welcome, as were Fred COGSWELL's *One hundred poems of modern Quebec* (1970) and *A second hundred poems of modern Quebec* (1971). *Volvox: poetry from the unofficial languages of Canada—in English translation* (1971) edited by J. Michael Yates in collaboration with several translators is an unusual and entirely worthwhile effort. Yates is also the editor of *Contemporary poetry of British Columbia: volume 1* (1970). It is to be hoped that an American publication, *New American and Canadian poetry* (1971) edited by John Gill, will arouse interest south of the border in Acorn, Atwood, Bowering, Fetherling, Gasperini, JONAS, Patrick Lane, Layton, McFadden, Newlove, and Nowlan.

Finally it is worth mentioning that the first Canadian poetry anthology and the best of those that followed in the nineteenth century have been reprinted: E. H. Dewart's *Selections from Canadian poets: with occasional critical and biographical notes and an introductory essay on Canadian poetry* (1864)—still an interesting anthology, with an important introduction—and W. D. Lighthall's *Songs of the great Dominion: voices from the forests and waters, the settlements and cities of Canada* (1889), which was meant to appeal to the growth of national sentiment in Canada. It therefore contains much work that has only curiosity value today, but it is nevertheless an interesting reflection of the period and contains a useful introduction.

2. *Short stories.* Robert Weaver followed his *Canadian short stories*, a historical collection of 1960, with *Canadian short stories: second series* (1968), by now a well-established book that contains stories by GARNER, GALLANT, LAURENCE, RICHLER, HOOD, Ludwig, MUNRO, GODFREY, Faessler, and HELWIG. Alec Lucas's *Great Canadian short stories: an anthology* (1971), another historical collection (of twenty-seven stories) that begins with Haliburton, represents a breakthrough for the Canadian short story into the wide-distribution North American paperback market.

The belated though welcome interest in high schools, and even in many universities, in Canadian literature has produced numerous anthologies. Most of the short-story collections have general as well as educational interest, none is compendious, and the same writers—with exceptions, of course—crop up in all of them. *The narrative voice: short stories and reflections by Canadian authors* (1972), *Sixteen by twelve: short stories by Canadian writers* (1970), and *Kaleidoscope: Canadian stories* (1970)—the latter with decorative photographs by John de Visser—are all edited by John METCALF. *Contemporary voices: the short story in Canada* (1972), containing fifteen stories, is edited by Donald Stephens. *The Canadian short story* (1971) edited by Tony Kilgallin contains only five stories—by Hood, Helwig, Metcalf, Richler, and LOWRY—and is an unabashed teaching book, but in many ways it is an attractive introduction to the subject. *Tigers of the snow: eighteen Canadian stories* (1973)—which contains two stories by an Indian and an Eskimo, George Clutesi and Markoosie—is edited by James A. MacNeill and Glen A. Sorestad. *Canadian winter's tales* (1968) edited by Norman LEVINE is a trade book containing stories by Lowry, Moore, CALLAGHAN, Hood, Laurence, Gallant, Richler, Levine, and Wilson.

The regional compilation has not been very common in Canadian publishing, but there are two good recent examples of this kind of collection: *Stories from western Canada* (1972) edited by Rudy WIEBE and *Stories from Atlantic Canada* (1973) edited by Kent Thompson. Books devoted to younger or less well-known short-story writers are: *New Canadian writing, 1968, stories by D. L. Stein, Clark Blaise and D. Godfrey* (1968); and *New Canadian writing, 1969, stories by John Metcalf, D. O. Spettigue and C. J. Newman* (1969).

3. *General.* In commemoration of the centennial of confederation the Centennial Commission subsidized the publication of *A century of Canadian literature/Un siècle de littérature canadienne* (1967) edited by H. Gordon Green and Guy Sylvestre. Without employing very stringent literary standards—there is a disconcerting mixture of distinguished and undistinguished writers—the editors compiled short selections by many writers in both English and French that at least have variety and a period and regional representation to recommend them. Mordecai Richler's Penguin anthology, *Canadian writing today* (1970), contains stories, other prose, and poems by forty-six writers. *Creation* edited by Robert KROETSCH contains stories, a novel extract, poems, and a short two-act play by Kroetsch; stories, novel extracts, and poems by James BACQUE; and stories (in French) by Pierre Gravel. In addition there are conversations between these writers and Margaret Laurence, Milton Wilson, and J. Raymond

Brazeau. An anthology with a theme is *Marked by the wild: an anthology shaped by the Canadian wilderness* (1973) edited by Bruce Littlejohn and Jon Pearce, containing both prose and poetry. *The Oxford anthology of Canadian literature* (1973) edited by Robert Weaver and William Toye has only brief selections by the eighty writers included, but it is a good introductory survey of our prose and poetry that has as its earliest selections extracts from the *Jesuit relations*; it also contains useful notes on the English- and French-speaking writers. Brita Mickleburgh's *Canadian literature: two centuries in prose* (1973)—primarily intended, like the previous three books, for use in schools—is a more specialized introduction. GNAROWSKI

Anthologies in French. The sixties in Canada were a decade of self-discovery, self-appraisal, and self-affirmation. The list of events that were both cause and symptoms of this process is a long one: the Quiet Revolution; the centennial celebrations; Expo 67; the CEGEPS (Collèges d'enseignement général et professionnel); the expansion of university education and the aftermath of the events in Paris of May 1968; the growth of Canadian studies (eighteen universities were represented at a symposium in Ottawa in 1968 on the theme 'Recherche et littérature canadienne-française', the proceedings of which were published in Ottawa in 1969); the Royal Commission on Bilingualism and Biculturalism; and nationalist fears, doubts, and claims, both Canada's and Québec's, in response to the threat of cultural submersion.

It is no surprise, then, that the sixties should have been the decade of the anthology, which is the first step towards acquiring a sense of a cultural historical perspective. Its value in education is obvious. Guy ROBERT dedicated his *Littérature du Québec: poésie actuelle* (1970), an augmented edition of an anthology published in 1964, to the CEGEP generation, inviting them to draw from it breath for their contestation and meaning for their action. Jean-Guy PILON offered his *Poèmes 70* (1970), an attractive collection of verse by thirty-three poets selected from works published in 1969, to students both as a textbook and as a source of words and images. The anthology can serve too as cultural ambassador abroad. A special number of *Les Lettres nouvelles* (Dec. 1966 – Jan. 1967) presented Canadian writers of the sixties to the French public, twenty-two of the thirty authors included being French Canadian, and the review *Europe* (1969) followed a survey of the arts in Québec with an anthology of recent prose and verse. Auguste Viatte added to his literary history of 1954 an *Anthologie littéraire de l'Amérique francophone* (1971), representing the literature of Canada and the Caribbean. Alain Bosquet, whose *La poésie canadienne* (Paris, 1962) reappeared slightly enlarged as *Poésie du Québec* in 1968, has been fairly criticized in Canada for his rather patronizing attitude: it is far too convenient for the French critic to dismiss pre-1937 poetry as 'plus d'un siècle de pauvres et pesantes versifications'. Mordecai RICHLER included a dozen French Canadians in translation in his *Canadian writing today* (1970). The image of Québec that emerges from this collection is a particularly gloomy and unfavourable one. Richler's reason for including in an anthology with such a title the translation of a text on nationalism by Saint-Denys GARNEAU dated 1938 seems all too transparent.

The centenary of confederation was the occasion for several retrospective anthologies, the most important of which was *Un siècle de littérature canadienne/A century of Canadian literature* (1967), prepared under the editorship of H. Gordon Green and Guy Sylvestre, who were aided by committees in the selection of material in their respective languages. Eighty-two French Canadians appear, from Crémazie to Marie-Claire BLAIS, and the editors have interestingly represented early French-Canadian writing by orators, journalists, and essayists such as Arthur Buies, Lionel GROULX, Léon Gérin, Errol Bouchette, Olivar Asselin, Edouard Montpetit, and Jules Fournier—writing not readily available that creates an absorbing picture of the emerging French-Canadian national self-awareness. 1967 also saw the publication of an anthology of journalism, *Un siècle de reportage*, and Jacques Hébert's *Ah! mes aïeux! chronique de la vie sociale et politique des Canadiens Français de 1867 tirée des journaux de l'époque*. Reine Malouin's *La poésie il y a cent ans* appeared in 1968.

Of all the literary genres, it is poetry that lends itself best to anthologizing. In addition to the Pilon, Robert, and Bosquet anthologies already mentioned, Guy Sylvestre's *Anthologie de la poésie canadienne-française* went into a fifth edition in 1966. However, pride of place must still go to A. J. M. SMITH's *Oxford book of Canadian verse: in English and French* (1960), which was brought out in paperback in 1965. It is a sign of the times that when Smith came to revise his anthology there was so much good new material that what emerged was *Modern Canadian verse: in English and French* (1967), an equally elegant and authoritative selection of the best Canadian poetry of the last forty years. Where the two collections overlap, poets are represented mainly by different poems. A handy inexpensive anthology, *Poètes du Québec* (1969) edited by Jacques Cotnam, gives equal space to the poets of the nineteenth century, those of the thirties and forties, and to recent poetry. John Robert COLOMBO has followed his and Jacques GODBOUT's anthology of 1964 with *How do I love thee: sixty poets of Canada (and Quebec) select and introduce their own work* (1970), ten of the poets represented being French Canadian. John GLASSCO's *The poetry of French Canada in translation* (1970), forty-seven poets translated by several hands, goes back even to pre-conquest times. One must take issue with Glassco's contention, stated in his introduction, that Québec poets 'seem too often preoccupied by political and national ideas', as the reverse is, surprisingly, the case; but he is on safer ground when he deplores the effects of 'the dead hand of surrealism'.

Anthologies devoted to the French-Canadian short story are rarer than one would expect. Robert Weaver's *Canadian short stories* (1960; paperback, 1966) contains stories by Ringuet, Anne HÉBERT, and Roger Lemelin in translation. Adrien Thério has enlarged his *Conteurs canadiens français* in a new edition of 1970 and edited a further anthology, *L'humour au Canada français* (1968), another book that is valuable for the less-familiar examples it gives from the nineteenth century. The University of Ottawa plans to publish a multi-volume collection of nineteenth-century short stories; the first volume, *Contes et nouvelles du Canada français: 1778–1859* (1971), has been edited by John Hare, who provides a thorough scholarly introduction.

Other anthologies of use to specialists of French-Canadian literature include Gilles MARCOTTE's collection of recent literary criticism, *Présence de la critique* (1966), serving both as a panorama of Québec criticism and as a useful collection of critical essays, and Guildo Rousseau's *Préfaces des romans québécois du XIXe siècle* (1970), in which a disclaimer appears repeatedly that the works they preface are decidedly not examples of that frivolous luxury, the novel. The *Anthologie d'Albert Laberge* (1962), prepared by Gérard BESSETTE, is devoted to this author (1871–1960) of short stories and of a loosely constructed novel, *La Scouine*, the powerful grim realism of which contrasts sharply with the idealized portrait of rural life in Hémon's *Maria Chapdelaine*, roughly its contemporary.

Bessette has edited two other anthologies to introduce students to French-Canadian writing: a reader, *De Québec à Saint-Boniface: récits et nouvelles du Canada français* (1968), and, with Lucien Geslin and Charles Parent, *Histoire de la littérature canadienne-française par les textes* (1968) in which the texts, with notes and commentaries, are arranged in four sections by genres. Roger Duhamel edited a similar slighter work, *Manuel de littérature canadienne-française* (1967), and yet others were compiled by André Renaud: *Recueil de textes littéraires canadiens-français* (1969) and by Gérard Tougas: *Littérature canadienne-française contemporaine* (1969). The latter accompanies an attractive selection of texts with footnotes on particular words that reflect French-Canadian usage; the introductions to authors and passages are lively and informative and models of concision. Because Pierre de Grandpré's *Histoire de la littérature française du Québec* in four volumes (1967, 1968, 1969, 1969) is profusely illustrated with extracts from the works of the authors discussed, this valuable, thorough, and visually pleasing reference work by an impressive team of scholars might serve as final proof, if proof were needed, of the extraordinary vitality of Québec literature in French over the past decade and the interest it has aroused. CRPM

Appleton, Thomas E. See HISTORY STUDIES IN ENGLISH 12.

Aquin, Hubert (1929–). Born in Montreal, he studied political science in Paris and Switzerland. On his return to Canada, he worked in various capacities in radio and television as well as in real estate and with a stock brokerage firm. In 1964, while a member of the RIN (Rassemblement pour l'Indépendance nationale), he was arrested for suspected terrorism: his highly acclaimed first novel, *Prochain épisode*, was written while he was under detention in a psychiatric hospital. The charges were eventually dismissed. He was a founding editor of the literary quarterly, *Liberté*, with whose editorial board he has recently broken, and an occasional contributor to PARTI PRIS. In 1972 he was awarded the important Prix David, given for an author's entire work.

Aquin is a very idiosyncratic writer with a rapid nervous style that makes brilliant use of metaphor and word-play and an ability to handle very complicated forms. As a political and ideological novelist, he is more concerned with failure to act than with action itself. His most effective novel, *Prochain épisode* (1965), which was translated under the same title by Penny Williams in 1967, employs the device of the story within a story to illuminate the emotions of a young man, detained for an aborted subversive act, who is trying to lull his shame and sense of impotence by writing a classic detective story. The characters switch and refuse to behave as they should; like his creator, the detective cannot act or, at times, even distinguish the guilty from the innocent. In *Trou de mémoire* (1968), for which Aquin declined a Governor General's Award, the account of the murder of a young English-speaking woman by her lover, who is involved in Québec revolutionary politics, is constantly contradicted or changed by the characters involved. There is no final resolution to the mystery; some flaw in these people, or in the revolution itself, prevents the truth from being known. With *L'antiphonaire* (1969), Aquin leaves Québec politics to range contrapuntally between the sixteenth and twentieth centuries as a Montreal woman doctor married to an epileptic finds parallels to her own tragic dilemma in the life of the French scientist she is studying. The book, though technically skilful, is too melodramatic in its outcome to be wholly satisfying as fiction. *L'antiphonaire*, which won the Prix de la Province de Québec, was translated by Alan Brown as *The antiphonary* (1973).

Aquin is also the author of *Point de fuite* (1971), a collection of essays and other prose pieces. A brief discussion of his writing and politics is included in Malcolm Reid's *The shouting signpainters* (1972) and there is a detailed analysis of *Prochain épisode* in J. Raymond Brazeau's *An outline of contemporary French-Canadian literature* (1972). JM

Archambault, Germain. See BELLES LETTRES IN FRENCH.

Archambault, Gilles. See FICTION IN FRENCH 2.

Archambault, J. P. See POLITICAL WRITINGS IN FRENCH 6.

Archer, John. See HISTORY STUDIES IN ENGLISH 8.

Archibald, Kathleen. See POLITICAL WRITINGS IN ENGLISH 6.

Arès, Richard. See POLITICAL WRITINGS IN FRENCH 3.

Armour, W. T. See ESKIMOS: BOOKS IN ENGLISH.

Arthur, Eric. See HISTORY STUDIES IN ENGLISH 7.

Ashlee, Ted. See CHILDREN'S BOOKS IN ENGLISH 5.

Aspler, Tony. See FICTION IN ENGLISH 6.

Atwood, Mae. See HISTORY STUDIES IN ENGLISH 8.

Atwood, Margaret (1939–). Margaret Eleanor Atwood was born in Ottawa, and educated at Victoria College, University of Toronto, where she graduated in 1961, and at Radcliffe College. She worked as a cashier, a waitress, a writer for a market research firm, and at other casual occupations before teaching English at the University of British Columbia, Sir George Williams University, the University of Alberta, and York University. She was writer-in-residence at the University of Toronto in 1972–3 and is on the board of directors of the House of Anansi Press, Toronto.

After a quiet beginning with *Double Persephone* (1961), Margaret Atwood rapidly made a name as a poet with *The circle game* (1966), which won a Governor General's Award; *The animals in that country* (1968); *The journals of Susanna Moodie* (1970); *Procedures for underground* (1970); and *Power politics* (1971). These volumes established her in less than a decade as one of the leading contemporary Canadian writers, a reputation supported by two remarkable novels, *The edible woman* (1969) and *Surfacing* (1972), and by an original critical survey of Canadian literature, *Survival: a thematic guide to Canadian literature* (1972).

Margaret's Atwood's poetry is at once conceptual and perceptual. It combines extraordinary visual sensibility, a psychological realism like that of a French eighteenth-century novelist, and a spare and laconic intellectual discipline. So far as definitions count, Margaret Atwood is a classical poet, inclined to an almost Buddhist objectivity, though not to Buddhist impersonality, for it is hard to imagine a personality more astringently present than hers as she examines the cruel contradictions of human relationships and extends what she has found on an intimate human level to illuminate—in a way characteristic of poets in the sixties—the Canadian predicament of which she is intensely conscious.

What Margaret Atwood draws out of her observation of Canada, and of herself as a Canadian, is a poetic and a personal ethic defined in a phrase from one of her poems: 'Beyond truth/ tenacity . . .'. This concept is enlarged in *Survival* into a critical generalization about Canadian literature as a whole; she suggests that for our writers survival—or tenacity (i.e. to be)—is more important than truth (to know). One does one's best and shapes one's writing like one's life to the realities of existence. In this age and this land they are likely to be realities best expressed in poems that are spare, spiny, and defensive, as Atwood's are. Such an attitude Atwood develops with ironic wit in her two novels, *The edible woman* and *Surfacing*, in which the fantasy that has become a key element in contemporary fiction is finely handled. In both books the coming to self-realization of a central female character portrays not only the absurdities of our social world but also the layers of falsehood we have to strip down before we find our own true selves. All is shown with fine precision of language and a devastating but crystalline lucidity of psychological and especially motivational insight. More than any other novelist in Canada, Margaret Atwood approaches the French moralist tradition.

The poems in *The journals of Susanna Moodie* are read by Mia Anderson on a CBC recording. This collection is also the subject of a 15-minute film directed by Marie Waisberg and distributed by Universal Education and Visual Arts (Willowdale, Ont.), which also distributes a 5-minute film interpretation, directed by Paul Quigley, of Atwood's poem 'Progressive insanities of a pioneer'. GW

Aubry, Claude. See FOLKLORE: BIBLIOGRAPHY.

Aucoin, Peter. See POLITICAL WRITINGS IN ENGLISH 6.

Audet, Philippe. See HISTORY STUDIES IN ENGLISH 15.

Auf der Maur, Nick. See POLITICAL WRITINGS IN ENGLISH 1.

Avakumovic, Ivan. See HISTORY STUDIES IN ENGLISH 14.

Avison, Margaret (1918–). Born in Galt, Ont., she was educated at Victoria College, University of Toronto, from 1936 to 1940 and returned to do graduate work in English in 1963. She has been a librarian, a lecturer at Scarborough College, University of Toronto, and a social worker at the Presbyterian Mission in Toronto. In 1972–3 she was writer-in-residence at the University of Western Ontario. She has published two collections of poetry: *Winter sun* (1960), which won a Governor General's Award, and *The dumbfounding* (1966), containing poems written out of a profound religious conviction. She writes difficult poems whose metaphysical structure, shifting perspectives in time and place, and disparate images are brilliantly combined in a highly imaginative search for truth, for reality. She probes sensation and experience—visual and spiritual—and in minutely detailed steps of comprehension reveals new perceptions about them, to herself and to the reader. Collectively her poems are one of the most important achievements by a Canadian writer.

Margaret Avison has also translated poems from the Hungarian, some of which are included in *The plough and the pen: writings from Hungary 1930–1956* edited by Ilona Duczynska and Karl Polanyi. A brief selection of her poetry can be found in *Poets of mid-century: 1940–1960* (1964) edited by Milton Wilson for the New Canadian Library and in *Fifteen Canadian poets* (1970) edited by Gary Geddes and Phyllis Bruce. The complexities of many of her poems are examined with a good deal of illuminating insight by Ernest Redekop in a book on the poet's work in the Studies in Canadian Literature series (1970). WET

Ayre, Robert. See CHILDREN'S BOOKS IN ENGLISH 1.

B

Bacque, James (1929–). Born in Toronto and educated at the University of Toronto, he worked for three years as a stage hand for the Canadian Broadcasting Corporation. He has been assistant editor for *Saturday Night*; has edited two publications for Maclean-Hunter; and was the trade editor at Macmillan of Canada for seven years. He is one of the founders of New Press where he now works.

Bacque is a novelist whose style is characterized by the stripped-down phrase, eccentric punctuation, and the occasional effective compression of words: 'anymomenthate' in the context he uses covers a wide range of emotional intensities. His fiction treats of tight little groups, each mistrusting the others, and of lack of personal loyalty. Real or suspected treachery is the stumbling block of those who try to cross the tightly drawn lines of a consumer-oriented society that in Bacque's eyes must find means of self-reformation if the individual is to survive. *The lonely ones* (1969) is the phrase with which Bacque sums up the emotions of Québec separatists who feel isolated in a forest of 'Anglo' language and ideas, and who add to that isolation and defeat their own ends by the mistrust of one separatist cell for another and by lack of personal loyalty to their friends. His protagonists—wearied by talk, abortive plans, and some awareness that the remedy is social rather than political—find spiritual renewal in a Laurentian retreat. This novel has been reprinted as a paperback under the title *Big lonely* (1971).

The staccato narrative of *The lonely ones* gives way in *A man of talent* (1972) to a variety of styles that underscore the different attitudes and the disparate, mutually hostile groups that the wealthy, arrogant Jack Ramsay hopes to use to gain control of 'Simcoe College'—a course that ends in disaster. Jack's many good qualities come to the fore in his visits to Georgian Bay and to the Indian reserve at Manitoulin Island with an Indian girl, Anna, whom he vainly courts. The sections of the book that deal with those visits and with his father's death are truly lyrical.

Some of Bacque's fiction and poetry appears in *Creation* (1970), an anthology edited by Robert KROETSCH, which includes a conversation between Bacque and Milton Wilson. NS

Badgley, Robin F. See HISTORY STUDIES IN ENGLISH 8.

Bailey, A. G. See HISTORY STUDIES IN ENGLISH 7 and INDIANS 4.

Bailey, Douglas. See POLITICAL WRITINGS IN ENGLISH 2.

Baillargeon, G. E. See HISTORY STUDIES IN FRENCH 3.

Balawyder, Aloysius. See HISTORY STUDIES IN ENGLISH 11.

Baldwin, David A. See HISTORY STUDIES IN ENGLISH 12.

Baldwin, J. See HISTORY STUDIES IN ENGLISH 6.

Baldwin, R. M. See HISTORY STUDIES IN ENGLISH 6.

Bandi, Hans-Georg. See ESKIMOS: BOOKS IN ENGLISH.

Barbeau, Jean (1945–). Born in Saint-Romuald, near Quebec City, he studied at the Collège de Lévis and Université Laval. From 1966 to 1969 he experimented in various creative and collective forms of drama (all unpublished) that were put on in Collège de Lévis, at the Estoc Theatre in Quebec City, and at Université Laval: *Caïn et Babel*, *La Geôle*, *Et caetera* (which reached the finals of the Dominion Drama Festival in 1968), *Les temps tranquilles*, *Le frame all-dress*. 'To *write* drama is to limit it, to turn it away from its basic purpose,' Barbeau has said: he therefore sketches and improvises and refuses to be an 'author'. He became one in spite of himself, however, in *Le Chemin de Lacroix* (1971), produced by the Théâtre quotidien de Québec (of which Barbeau was a founder and resident playwright) in 1970, which presents the 'stations' and 'passion' of a young unemployed workman at a police station. Lacroix is a victim of circumstances; nevertheless Barbeau refuses to allow him to fulfil the expectations of the audience by radicalizing him at the play's end. *Ben-Ur* (1971) presents another victim—Benoît-Urbain—who searches in comic strips for the ritual, the formulas, and the gestures of the hero. The monologue *Solange* and the two-character *Goglu* (1970) express in a simple manner intense and pathetic solitude.

0-71 is a kind of historical fresco; it is also a number (unlucky?) in Bingo and 1971, year zero, when everything in Québec was beginning all over again. *Le théâtre de la maintenance* and *Le chant du sink* (1973) still owe something to the revue and to the initiation ceremony (to both theatre and life—which to Barbeau are one and the same thing). In *0-71* and several other published pieces—*Tripez-vous, vous? Lésés boys*, *Boursaille*, *L'herbe à puces*—Barbeau yields to situation comedy, or verbal comedy, that is a little facile, verbose, confusing. On the other hand *Manon Lastcall* and *Joualez-moi d'amour* (1970) are clearer and more lively. Manon is a waitress who has become a guide in the provincial museum, where she converts the curator to masterpieces of the flesh. In the second play the Parisian Julie and her Québec lover Jules are able to embrace only in *joual*. Here, as in *Le Chemin de Lacroix*, vulgarity is healthy and dramatically necessary; the author plays rapidly and effectively on the various levels of language and society.

Barbeau's language is more relaxed, less hard, broken and tragic than that of Michel TREMBLAY. His themes, structure, and style approach rather those of the experimental companies Les P'tits Enfants Laliberté and the Grand Cirque ordinaire (whose *T'es pas tannée, Jeanne d'Arc?* influenced *Ben-Ur*). His characters are naive young provincials. Dispossessed, bittersweet, given to moods of violence or calm, they still love life, dreaming, and joking. Barbeau believes that 'all the great québécois tragedies will be humorous ones because our greatest misfortune occurred in 1763 and nothing worse awaits us.' LM

Barbour, Douglas. See POETRY IN ENGLISH 2.

Barr, John. See POLITICAL WRITINGS IN ENGLISH 8.

Barré, George. See ESKIMOS: BOOKS IN FRENCH.

Barton, Carl. See CHILDREN'S BOOKS IN ENGLISH 6.

Basile, Jean (1934–). Jean Basile-Bezroudnoff was born in Paris of Russian parents and came to Québec as a young man. For a number of years he was a distinguished journalist, serving as editor of the 'Arts et lettres' section of *Le Devoir* and acting as that newspaper's rock music critic, using the pseudonym 'Pénélope'. Since 1970 he has directed a monthly underground magazine, *Mainmise*, which has had a remarkable commercial and popular success without benefit of grants from official or unofficial bodies.

Basile is one of the most North American of contemporary Québec writers—along with Raoul DUGUAY, Claude PÉLOQUIN, and Paul CHAMBERLAND—although he writes and works in an entirely different mode. Like many other writers he began as a rather conventional poet. His first novel, *Lorenzo*, was published in 1963. There followed a period of experimentation: his *Journal poétique* appeared in 1965 and a play, *Joli tambour*, in 1966. The latter has been performed in English, in Toronto, but Basile has not yet succeeded in having it produced in French in Montreal.

In 1964 *La jument des Mongols*, the brilliant first novel of a remarkable trilogy, appeared; it was followed by *Le grand Khan* (1970) and *Les voyages d'Irkoutsk* (1970). This trilogy is obviously influenced by Durrell's *Alexandria quartet*: each novel is narrated in the first person by one member of a trio—Jonathan, Jérémie, and Judith, who is one of the most real and unusual women in contemporary Québec fiction. Their lives are interconnected and their stories overlap. The characters are Québécois and they live in the most metropolitan part of central Montreal, but many of their preoccupations—drugs, rock, and the varieties of sexuality—know no boundaries. SF

Bates, Ronald. See LITERARY STUDIES IN ENGLISH 4 and POETRY IN ENGLISH 1.

Batten, Jack. See HISTORY STUDIES IN ENGLISH 13.

Bauer, Walter. See POETRY IN ENGLISH 4.

Bauer, William. See POETRY IN ENGLISH 2.

Bayley, Denis. See HISTORY STUDIES IN ENGLISH 3.

Beaglehole, J. C. See HISTORY STUDIES IN ENGLISH 3.

Beauchamp, Germain. See POETRY IN FRENCH.

Beaudry, René. See HISTORY STUDIES IN FRENCH 3.

Beaulieu, André. See HISTORY STUDIES IN ENGLISH 17; HISTORY STUDIES IN FRENCH 1; and POLITICAL WRITINGS IN FRENCH 1.

Beaulieu, Mario. See POLITICAL WRITINGS IN FRENCH 4.

Beaulieu, Michel. See FICTION IN FRENCH 3 and POETRY IN FRENCH.

Beaulieu, Victor-Lévy (1945–). Born in Saint-Paul-de-la-Croix—near Rivière-du-Loup, Qué.—Beaulieu is directeur littéraire of Éditions du Jour. A prolific writer, he is best known for his series of loosely related novels: *Mémoires d'outre-tonneau* (1968), *Race de monde* (1969), *La nuitte de Malcomm Hudd* (1970), *Jos Connaissant* (1970), *Un rêve québécois* (1972), and *Les grands-pères* (1972), which won the Grand Prix littéraire de Montréal.

In a book devised by himself, *Quand les écrivains québécois jouent le jeu!* (1970), in which forty-three Québec writers answer the Marcel Proust questionnaire, Beaulieu expresses his admiration for two writers in particular: Victor Hugo for his verbal power and his visionary quality and Jack Kerouac for what he symbolized. This preference is confirmed in essays devoted to these writers, *Pour saluer Victor Hugo* (1971) and *Jack Kérouac, essai-poulet* (1972). Beaulieu combines some of their qualities: the prolixity and the metaphysical restlessness of the Frenchman and the talent of the Franco-American for expressing the soul of the beat people (i.e. the poor and crushed). It is in this last accomplishment that Beaulieu excels, though his obsession with death, his quest for a truth that will transcend the absurdity of modern urban life, and the longing his characters express for lasting, satisfactory human relationships provide a serious backdrop to the saga of the Beauchemin family described in *Race de monde*, *Jos Connaissant*, and *Les grands-pères*.

Beaulieu combines form and content with apparent artlessness. The first-person monologue form he usually gives to his novels betrays the compulsive need of his characters to keep talking, talk being the life-support system these space-walkers need to survive in le Grand Morial Mort. Heavy drinking and masturbation are not merely facts of life for his characters but are also flagrant acts of defiance of bourgeois self-respect and symbols of moral and spiritual isolation, of the breakdown of fruitful human relations and of the alienating pressures of modern urban life. Beaulieu uses his own cranky spelling (*ouiquenne*, *gueurle*, *klinèxe*, *supermarquette*) and resonantly obvious puns, flaunting his contempt for the earnest sophistication of bourgeois art. The narrator of *Mémoires d'outre-tonneau* (the title itself is a play on one used by Chateaubriand) declares, for example, that elephants often say: 'Nous avons été trompés avec défense d'y voir.' While playing cornily on the words for trunk and ivory tusks, Beaulieu presents his recurrent image of man the dupe, prevented by a malicious trick of his condition from seeing clearly enough to shape his destiny.

Beaulieu seems to have inexhaustible inventiveness. *Jos Connaissant* is a long novel built around two events—Jos's pathetic affair with a forty-year-old whisky-drinking waitress and stripper and the death of his mother—that are handled with a perfect blend of social satire, psychological insight, poetry, and realism. Beaulieu goes further in exploring the nightmares and yearnings of the Québec 'cassé' than any other writer—with more control than Réjean DUCHARME, less conspicuous art than Marie-Claire BLAIS, and less gratuitous surrealism than Jacques FERRON.

CRPM

Beck, James Murray. See HISTORY STUDIES IN ENGLISH 12 and POLITICAL WRITINGS IN ENGLISH 5.

Bédard, Roger J. See POLITICAL WRITINGS IN FRENCH 3.

Beissel, Henry. See POETRY IN ENGLISH 2.

Bélanger, Henri. See LITERARY STUDIES IN FRENCH 3.

Bélanger, Marcel. See POETRY IN FRENCH.

Bélanger, René. See HISTORY STUDIES IN FRENCH 7.

Belford, Ken. See POETRY IN ENGLISH 2.

Bell, Don. See FICTION IN ENGLISH: SHORT STORIES.

Bellavance, Michel. See POLITICAL WRITINGS IN FRENCH 7.

Belles lettres in English. Reflective essays or other kinds of purely literary writing are not numerous in Canadian literature, though there were many collections of newspaper columns published in our six-year period—monotonous in rhythm, lacking any writerly 'music' or pacing—and of mechanical, contrived 'humorous' sketches. There were few books to rival the literary qualities of Hugh MACLENNAN's *Scotchman's return* (1960) and Robertson DAVIES' *A voice from the attic* (1960), both of which have recently appeared in paperback. Two books by Kildare DOBBS aspire to their company. The graceful essays in *Running to Paradise* (1962) and *Reading the time* (1968) are close to fiction in their blend of imagination, anecdotes, and a sense of the absurd. Like Davies, Dobbs shows a fondness for curious learning, or even—as in *The great fur opera* (1970), a travesty of the Hudson's Bay Company history illustrated by Ronald Searle—for pseudo-learning. John GLASSCO's *Memoirs of Montparnasse* (1970) is an unusual book of reminiscences that was completed from notes in 1932–3, not long after the events described. The author was eighteen when he arrived in Paris in 1928. His elegant record of a hectic pursuit of life and pleasure has the shape and dramatic detail of a novel. Yet another work of non-fiction that has some of the characteristics of fiction is Fredelle Bruser Maynard's *Raisins and almonds* (1972), which recalls her experiences as the only Jewish girl growing up in several prairie towns during the Depression. Like Glassco, she recreates her past with delicacy and affection. Each chapter of the book is skilfully poised between memoir and short story and Mrs Maynard commands a wide range of emotional effects from comic to sad.

The novelist Mordecai RICHLER in *Hunting tigers under glass* (1971) and *Shovelling trouble* (1972) has devised a form that might be called the impolite essay, combining personal reminiscence, moral concern, and sharp comedy. The articles collected in these books, however, reveal the unevenness of his satiric temper. At their best they are trenchant and imaginative; at their least successful they are ill-natured and unrepresentative of Richler's very real ability as a social critic. Robert Fulford's *Crisis at the Victory Burlesk: culture, politics and other diversions* (1968) contains some of the best writing of a sensitive and committed journalist whose critical interests embrace books, the visual arts, popular culture, and social issues. Fulford is perhaps Canada's ablest practitioner of a kind of journalism that presents serious comment, humour, and fresh observations of his time and place in a form that is always lively, and sometimes enduring. *The rejection of politics and other essays on Canada, Canadians, anarchism and the world* (1972) is a choice of George WOODCOCK's personal essays, written over a long and eventful literary career. They are fertile in ideas, strong and sensible, and lit everywhere by sympathy and insight. In *The short happy walks of Max MacPherson* (1968), a collection of columns that appeared in the Toronto *Star*, Harry Bruce turns his exploration of Toronto on foot into warm and companionable essays.

Two books of humour that stand out are by performers whose skills are mainly oral. Max Ferguson's *And now . . . here's Max* (1967) loses vitality in the transference to the printed page of the author's celebrated assembly of radio personae, but it is nevertheless a successful entertainment by a talented and consistently good-natured humourist. Donald Harron's *Charlie Farquarson's histry of Canada* (1972) presents monologues by the well-known Parry Sound farmer of radio and television, with their wonderfully distorted point of view and Joycean transformations of all the words ('Yer voyeurs', 'Yer repulsion of yer Excadians') that are mandatory in any re-telling of the nation's story. They are a little tedious only if read all at once.

The six essays that make up Naim Kattan's *Reality and theatre* (1972)—first published in French and translated with great expertise by Alan Brown—are quintessential *belles lettres*. Kattan was born in Baghdad, Iraq, studied at the Sorbonne, and has lived in Canada since 1954. He examines the East, where reality is viewed directly, without the mediation of symbols—which indeed 'is unable to separate theatre from life'—and the West, which he experienced as a multiplicity of theatres—where 'a thousand intermediaries were set up to link man to reality'. A spectator of cultures of unusual detachment who has 'one foot in both worlds', Kattan brings rich and unexpected insights to his meditations on the politics, art, languages, and religions of both East and West. KD

Belles lettres in French. If it was possible for Norah Story to say six years ago that 'few French Canadians have used the essay to express a personal philosophy' (*Companion*, p. 63), this claim could hardly be made today. Robert Vigneault—in an issue of *Études littéraires*, vol. 5, no. 1 (1972) devoted to the essay—traces what he calls 'la naissance d'une pensée' in the Québec essay in recent years. Drawing on the writings of men like Jean LE MOYNE, Father Ernest Gagnon (whose familiarity with the psychological truths available in the teachings of the Church and anthropology threw light on *L'homme d'ici* in influential essays of the 1950s, republished in 1963), Pierre TROTTIER, and Pierre Vadeboncoeur, he illustrates the way in which Québec thought, and particularly the French-Canadian's reflections on his own personality expressed in his culture, has gradually freed itself from the grips of a stifling orthodoxy. The effort this liberation called for can, incidentally, be felt as it betrays itself in the tetchiness and sardonic humour of men like Jean SIMARD and Le Moyne.

This emancipation can be traced back to the intellectual vandalism of the 'école automatiste' and the breath of fresh air it introduced. The seminal texts written by the group that gathered round Paul-Émile Borduas in the late forties—*Refus global* (1948) and *Projections libérantes* (1949)—have been republished: *Refus global* in book form in 1972 and the later text in a critical edition in *Études françaises*, vol. VIII, no. 3 (1972); both texts appeared in a number (janvier–août 1969) of *La Barre du jour* devoted to the automatists. In *Projections libérantes*, which is largely autobiographical, Borduas comments bitterly on his dismissal from the École du Meuble following the publication of *Refus global*.

Another republication, the enlarged edition of the *Journal* of Hector de Saint-Denys GARNEAU in his *Oeuvres* (1970), edited superbly by Benoît Lacroix and Jacques BRAULT, reminds us that Saint-Denys Garneau and the group of *La Relève*, to which he (and Jean Le Moyne) belonged, had tried a dozen years before Borduas to pose alternatives to the values and criteria embodied in that same stifling orthodoxy, whose influence they painfully experienced. Pierre Elliott Trudeau's collection of essays, *Le fédéralisme et la société canadienne-française* (1967), published in English as *Federalism and the French Canadians* (1968), shows him and his fellow contributors to *Cité libre* taking up a similar struggle in the 1950s.

In the last decade this process of intellectualization and self-discovery has proceeded apace. The historical, sociological, philosophical, and political essays of Gérard Bergeron and Marcel Rioux, of Jean Tétreau and Jacques Grand'Maison, are too technical to be included under the heading of Belles Lettres, but there is surely enough literature and personal philosophy in the calm reflections on rapid cultural change in his native province and in the modern world of Fernand DUMONT's *Le lieu de l'homme* (1968) and *La vigile du Québec* (1971) for these works to appear under this rubric.

In 1968 French Canada lost one of its chief spokesmen and intellectual leaders with the death of André Laurendeau. His life of action as editor of *L'Action nationale* in the 1930s, leader of the 'bloc populaire' in the 1940s, editor of *Le Devoir* in the 1950s, and co-chairman of the Royal Commission on Bilingualism and Biculturalism until his death, gave his writing a sense of urgency and realism. All the man's moods, from biting sarcasm and polemical anger to serene meditation, can be caught in *Ces choses qui nous arrivent: chronique des années 1961–1966* (1970), a selection, prefaced by Fernand Dumont, of the editorials Laurendeau wrote for *Le Magazine Maclean*. Pierre Vadeboncoeur shares the independence of mind of Dumont and Laurendeau and their calm lucidity. Vadeboncoeur was one of the team that founded *Cité libre* in 1950. The path of radical socialist thought and militant trade unionism he followed from the days of opposition to the obscurantism of Maurice Duplessis to public support for the principles and objectives of the Parti Québécois can be clearly traced in his collections of essays: *La ligne du risque* (1963; 1969), *L'autorité du peuple* (1965), *Lettres et colères* (1969), and *La dernière heure et la première* (1970). He was one of the first to say of Borduas that 'le Canada français moderne commence avec lui' and to salute his courageous gesture in the cause of freedom of thought. 'Un lyrique aventuré dans l'action' (Maurice Blain), he continues to stand for vigilance in the face of the opiates offered by the capitalist-political alliance, in a manner reminiscent of the prophetic stance of the Catholic Georges Bernanos in Europe in the 1930s.

Laurendeau refers to the opprobrium endured by those who had spent a year or two in Europe in the thirties (the 'retour d'Europe', he called them) on their return to their native Québec, but the experience of weaning oneself from Mother Orthodoxy and the consequent stimulus to one's thinking that travelling gave seemed until recent years an essential prerequisite to original thinking. Pierre Trottier, author of *Mon Babel* (1963), and the restless Jean Simard, and in poetry Alain GRANDBOIS, are obvious examples of men who, from their experience of a wider world, have helped to open up Québec's horizons. Naim Kattan's reflections on art, politics, languages, and religions in *Le réel et le théâtral* (1970)—translated by Alan Brown and published in English as *Reality and theatre* (1972)—range from Iraq where he was born in 1928 to London and North America. Contrasting his native Orient with the western world, Kattan sees the westerner as divorced from reality by his taste for the psychodrama, a constant act of self-dramatization through which he escapes from the problems reality poses by projecting them onto the stage of politics, public life, or the theatre itself. Another traveller, François HERTEL—back in Canada after almost thirty years in France—published *Souvenirs, historiettes, réflexions* (1972) and *Tout en faisant le tour du monde* (1972), which are portraits of the man as much as of his experiences around the world. Louis-Marcel Raymond gave us, just before his death in 1972, his much-admired *Géographies* (1971), containing memories of youth and portraits of friends mingled with descriptive writing. Jean Simard has added *Nouveau répertoire* (1965) to his *Répertoire* of 1961. Simard's fellow satirist of the fifties, Bertrand VAC, published in 1967 a collection of aphorisms entitled *Mes pensées 'profondes'*. An expatriate painter living in Paris, Gérald Robitaille describes his quest for a self through art in *Un Huron à la recherche de l'art* (1967), with an enthusiastic preface by Henry Miller whose secretary he once was. Fernand OUELLETTE, with an impressive blend of self-awareness and intuition in *Les actes retrouvés* (1970), retraces the steps by which he discovered himself through poetry and in the process reveals his compatriots to themselves.

Two sets of memoirs must count among the most important publications in this genre in recent years, poles apart ideologically and remote from each other in terms of generations. First, the three volumes of Lionel GROULX's *Mes mémoires* (1970, 1971, and 1972). These pages take us up to the year 1939 and remind us that the beginnings of French Canada's *aggiornamento* go back well before *La Relève* of the thirties to the early years of the century, beyond Groulx to Henri Bourassa, who figures prominently in volume II. Canon Groulx has written in his memoirs the history in fine detail, carefully and generously pieced together, of a faith, a commitment, and a pastoral concern that coincide in every respect with his life's work, the writing and shaping of the history of French Canada. The other important personal statement of recent years, Pierre Vallières's *Nègres blancs d'Amérique* (1968)—translated by Joan Pinkham and published in English as *White Niggers of America* (1971)—is half autobiography and half political pamphlet. In addition to having an impact in Canada, it was widely read in France and, in translation, made front-page literary news in New York. The incendiary nature of the book has been exaggerated. It will continue to be read for its glowing portraits of Vallières's friends Jacques FERRON, Gaston MIRON, and his fellow political militant of the 1960s Charles Gagnon, and for the description Vallières offers of 'la petite misère' in Québec. Autobiographical accounts of life in straitened circumstances are rare, compared with the fictionalized accounts readily available in novels from Gabrielle ROY and Roger Lemelin to Jacques RENAUD, Marie-Claire BLAIS, and Victor-Lévy BEAULIEU. Jean-Paul Desbiens, the Brother Anonymous of *Les insolences du Frère Untel* (1961), provides a moving account of a poor childhood in *Sous le soleil de la pitié* (1965). Vallières's latest essay, *L'urgence de choisir* (1971)—translated by Penelope Williams and published in English as *Choose!* (1972)—shows the former extremist re-evaluating political violence and opting for the democratic realization of his ideals through the program offered by the Parti Québécois.

Others pages are beginning to appear of that history of the French-Canadian people which, *pace* Léandre Bergeron, still remains to be written. Jean-Louis Roux recounts his experiences of strike action in a very racy, personal manner, along with Pierre Vadeboncoeur and other writers, in *En grève* (1963). Gérard Dion's *Les mémoires d'Alfred Charpentier* (1971) and Germain Archambault's *Le taxi: métier de crève-faim* (1964) paint pictures of the world of work and the evolution of organized labour from the days of the Confédération des Travailleurs catholiques du Canada to the Confédération des Syndicats nationaux, but a short personal account by Émile Boudreau in *Liberté* (1964) under the title 'De la rue des Anglais aux Métallurgistes-Unis' covers much the same ground with the liveliness that makes us wish for more from the same source. Across the spectrum of personal reflection from the Canon of the Church to Brother Anonymous, from the professor of philosophy to the shop steward, the picture of the Québec mentality is being filled out.

CRPM

Bennet, John W. See HISTORY STUDIES IN ENGLISH 8 and 14.

Benoit, Jacques. See FICTION IN FRENCH 3.

Berger, Carl. See HISTORY STUDIES IN ENGLISH 7.

Bergeron, Gérard. See HISTORY STUDIES IN FRENCH 2 and 11; POLITICAL WRITINGS IN FRENCH 3.

Bergeron, Léandre. See HISTORY STUDIES IN ENGLISH 12 and HISTORY STUDIES IN FRENCH 2.

Bériault, Raymond. See POLITICAL WRITINGS IN FRENCH 4.

Bernard, André. See POLITICAL WRITINGS IN FRENCH 5.

Bernard, Anne. See FICTION IN FRENCH: SHORT STORIES.

Bernard, Jean Paul. See HISTORY STUDIES IN FRENCH 4.

Bernier, Benoît. See HISTORY STUDIES IN FRENCH 1 and POLITICAL WRITINGS IN FRENCH 1.

Bernier, Hélène. See FOLKLORE: BIBLIOGRAPHY.

Bernier, Jovette. See FICTION IN FRENCH 1.

Berthelot, Brunet. See HISTORY STUDIES IN FRENCH 10.

Berton, Pierre (1920–). Pierre Francis de Marigny Berton was born in Dawson City, the Yukon, and was educated at the University of British Columbia. In 1942 he became city editor of the Vancouver *News-Herald*. He served in the army and then was a feature writer for the Vancouver *Sun*. He joined *Maclean's* in 1947 and was managing editor from 1952 to 1958, when he left to become a columnist and associate editor of the Toronto *Star*. In 1959 he was given the J. V. McAree

Memorial Award for the best daily newspaper column in Canada. Increasingly Berton's time became devoted to radio and television work. (He has appeared on television as a regular panelist on the CBC's *Front Page Challenge* and had his own interview program for many seasons.) In 1962 he left the *Star* and returned to *Maclean's* for a year.

Berton's *The royal family: the story of the British monarchy from Victoria to Elizabeth* (1954) contains gossipy and often humorous character sketches of the royal family. He received a Governor General's Award for *The mysterious north* (1956) in which graphic description is combined with an appraisal of the potentialities of the Canadian north, and for *Klondike: the life and death of the last great goldrush* (1958; rev. 1972) in which he vividly recreates the gaudy personalities who were attracted from the corners of the world in 1896–1903 by the possibility of discovering gold. (The American edition was entitled *Klondike fever.*)

Five books are products of the entertaining columns he wrote for the Toronto *Star*. *Just add water and stir* (1959)—awarded the Leacock Medal for Humour—examines everything from detergent salesmanship to shopping for a coffin. *Adventures of a columnist* (1960) contains anecdotes from behind the scenes of newspaper writing and current social comment—serious and humorous. *Fast fast fast relief* (1962) is personal in its sentiments and expresses Berton's liberalism. Exposés of the various confidence games played on unwary householders are offered in *The big sell: an introduction to the black art of door-to-door salesmanship and other techniques* (1964). *My war with the 20th century* (1965) was published for an American readership.

Berton attacks the myth of Toronto as materialistic, narrowminded, smug, dull old Hogtown in *The new city* (1961), a picture essay. The Anglican Church commissioned him to write *The comfortable pew* (1965) in which Berton, an agnostic, critically examines the public image of the church and attacks narrowness, complacency, and ineptness in church leadership in the face of change and social disorder. *The smug minority* (1968) is somewhat tedious in its condemnation of the Canadian 'establishment', which Berton identifies as an inbred Liberal/Conservative, Protestant/capitalistic minority reluctant to invest in education and the betterment of society.

The national dream: The great railway, 1871–1881 (1970) and *The last spike: the great railway, 1881–1885* (1971) dramatically portray the history of the Canadian Pacific Railway. While the political interpretation is traditional—yet widely criticized because the good of the nation is identified with central Canadian manufacturing and industrial interests—Berton provides captivating new anecdotal material and human interest in his descriptions of the politicians and financiers, surveyors and contractors who struggled to bring the project to fruition. *The last spike* won a Governor General's Award. *The impossible railway* (1972) is a one-volume edition published for the American market, while *The great railway illustrated* (1972) is a pictorial abridgement.

Berton is the editor of *Remember yesterday: a century of photographs* (1965) and *Historic headlines: a century of Canadian news drama* (1967) and co-author with Janet Berton of the *Centennial food guide* (1966)—all in the Canadian Centennial Library series. He is a contributor to *The arts as communication* (1962) and *Why the sea is boiling hot: a symposium on the Church in the world* (1965).

For young readers Berton has written *The golden trail: the story of the Klondike rush* (1954), which was reprinted under the title *Stampede for gold* (1955), and *The secret world of Og* (1963), an exuberant fantasy of childhood adventure. DF

Bertrand, Denis. See HISTORY STUDIES IN FRENCH 4.

Bessette, Gérard (1920–). Born in Sainte-Anne-de-Sabrevois, Qué., he was educated at the Université de Montréal. He has taught at Duquesne University, the University of Saskatchewan, and the Royal Military College. He is now professor of French and French-Canadian literature at Queen's University.

The failure of three university students to achieve intellectual purpose is the theme of Bessette's first novel, *La bagarre* (1958), which provides a forum for the discussion of French-Canadian culture and philology. Lebeuf, who wishes to write the great French-Canadian novel, reconciles himself to his proletarian life; Weston, an American who attempts a thesis on the French Canadians, tears it up and returns to Kentucky to become a journalist; and Sillery, defeated by his homosexual obsessions, goes to Africa to study anthropology. *Les pédagogues* (1961) lacks an adequate plot but is a powerful satire on clerical and political despotism in the field of education. Bessette's novella *Le libraire* (1960), which was translated by Glen Shortliffe as *Not for every eye* (1962), is a humorous satire on small-town book censorship in Duplessis Québec. In two more recent novels Bessette's range and penetration have deepened, his satire is more abrasive and his material more tragic. *L'incubation* (1965) uses the interior monologue as the witness to a suicide is haunted by images that reflect lack of purpose in life and the fleeting character of human relations. Winner of the first prize in the Concours Littéraires de la Province de Québec and of a Governor General's Award, *L'incubation* was translated as *Incubation* (1967) by Glen Shortliffe. *Le Cycle* (1971) also employs a stream-of-consciousness technique—this time to portray the frustrations of lower-middle-class life in Montreal as the relatives of a man who has just died ponder his life and their own sexual and other obsessions. There is a detailed analysis of Bessette's fiction, with particular attention to *L'incubation*, in J. Raymond Brazeau's *An outline of contemporary French-Canadian literature* (1972).

Some of Bessette's introspective poetry, expressed in traditional forms, has been published under the title *Poèmes temporels* (1954). Bessette is also the author of *Les images en poésie canadienne-française* (1960), *Une littérature en ebullition* (1968) and, in collaboration with Lucien Geslin and Charles Parent, of *Histoire de la littérature canadienne-française* (1968). He has edited two anthologies: *L'anthologie d'Albert Laberge* (1963) and *De Québec à Saint-Boniface* (1968), a selection for English-speaking students of French-Canadian short fiction from the late nineteenth century to the present day. NS/JM

Bhatia, June. See FICTION IN ENGLISH 2.

Bibaud, Michel. See POETRY IN FRENCH.

Bicha, Karel D. See HISTORY STUDIES IN ENGLISH 8.

Billon, Pierre. See FICTION IN FRENCH 3.

Bilodeau, Rosario. See HISTORY STUDIES IN FRENCH I.

Bird, Harrison. See HISTORY STUDIES IN ENGLISH 4 and 5.

Bird, Will R. (1891–). Born in East Mapleton, N.S., and educated at Amherst Academy, William Richard Bird won the Military Medal while serving in the First World War. For many years he was a member of the staff of the Nova Scotia Bureau of Information. A voluminous writer, he is best known for his historical romances about the Yorkshire settlers who came to the Chignecto area of Nova Scotia in the eighteenth century, and about their descendants. The best of these romances is *Here stays good Yorkshire* (1945). Others include *Judgment Glen* (1947), *The passionate pilgrim* (1949), *Tristram's salvation* (1957), and *Despite the distance* (1961). *The Earl must have a wife* (1969) is a historical romance about J.-F.-W. DesBarres, who was lieutenant-governor of Cape Breton (1784–7) and of Prince Edward Island (1805–12). He also played an important role in surveys of the Atlantic coast. Some of Bird's short stories have been collected in *Sunrise for Peter* (1946) and *Angel cove* (1972), which is concerned with the privations of people living in the Newfoundland outports.

Bird's works of non-fiction are *Done at Grand Pré* (1955), a moderate and sustained account of the Acadians in the eighteenth century until their expulsion in 1755; *A century at Chignecto: the key to old Acadia* (1928), a well-knit account of that area; *No retreating footsteps: the story of the North Nova Scotia Highlanders* (1954), the Second-World-War record of this regiment with which Bird's son was serving when he was killed; *The North Shore (New Brunswick) Regiment* (1963), a regimental history; three travelogues: *This is Nova Scotia* (1950), *Off trail in Nova Scotia* (1956), and *These are the maritimes* (1959); and *Ghosts have warm hands* (1968), reminiscences of his experiences during the First World War. Bird edited *Atlantic anthology* (1959), a collection of writings by maritime authors. NS

Birney, Earle (1904–). Alfred Earle Birney was born in Calgary, Alta, and brought up in Banff. He was educated at the Universities of British Columbia, Toronto, and California and taught English at the Universities of California and Utah before completing his studies at the Universities of

London and Toronto. In 1936 he was appointed lecturer in English at the University of Toronto. He served as personnel officer overseas during the Second World War. Upon his return in 1945 he joined the International Service of the Canadian Broadcasting Corporation and the following year was appointed professor of English at the University of British Columbia. In 1952 he was awarded the Lorne Pierce Medal for literature by the Royal Society of Canada and was elected to that society in 1953. While at UBC he was instrumental in creating the first Department of Creative Writing in a Canadian university. At this time he invited such American poets as Charles Olson, Robert Creeley, and Robert Duncan to teach there and they exercised a deep influence on the young writers studying in this new department. In 1965 Birney was writer-in-residence at the University of Toronto. He has also held this position at the University of Waterloo.

While a student at the University of Toronto, Birney became interested in left-wing politics. He was literary editor of the *Canadian Forum* from 1936 to 1940, and some of his poems were printed in that magazine. His first collection of verse, *David and other poems* (1942), won the Governor General's Award. The title poem, a narrative of mountain climbing in which the protagonist is faced with a dilemma, is also a parable of human life. In this, as in other poems, Birney shows his ability to suit his forms and language to philosophic thought, descriptive passages, and narration. This collection also contains poems that reflect the reaction of Canadians to war, as well as poems of a humorous and satirical nature. His second collection, *Now is time* (1945), also won the Governor General's Award. In it some of the poems from *David and other poems* are reprinted along with new verse, partly on war themes. His third collection, *The Strait of Anian: selected poems* (1948), contains poems strongly critical of many features of Canadian life. This criticism forms the substance of his poetic drama *Trial of a city and other verse* (1952) in which the city of Vancouver serves as a prototype for urban life.

The poems in *Ice cod bell or stone* (1962) graph responses to specific areas of Canada and to the more tropical landscape of Mexico. Birney places himself firmly in relation to people and places, using forms that vary from dramatic monologue, through typographic shape, to lyric; the writing ranges from colloquial through ironic and satiric to philosophic. This same mixture occurs in *Near False Creek mouth* (1964), a carefully structured book beginning with the long title poem that starts with a local reference and opens out onto a cosmic scale. The succeeding poems relate the poet's experiences of visits to the Caribbean, South America, and Europe before returning to focus once again on Canada. Revealing Birney's characteristic Canadianism in the broad context of universal human brotherhood, these poems also show his skilful handling of both open experimentation and formal control. His *Selected poems* was published in 1966. (A shorter American edition was issued under the title *Memory no servant* (1968).) A brief selection, *The poems of Earle Birney*, was published in the New Canadian Library in 1969.

Birney has always been a restless experimenter in his poetry and in the 1960s he showed a renewed interest in experiment: he moved into the new areas of concrete poetry. A package of his concrete and typographically adventurous poems, *Pnomes, jukollages and other stunzas* (1969), was issued by the press run by bp NICHOL, the leading Canadian concrete poet. Some of these poems were included in *Rag & bone shop* (1971), which shows the usual wide range of subject matter and contains some new long poems arising from memories of his younger days and his response to place. Some of Birney's experiments with graphics appear in *Four parts sand* (1972), a representative selection of concrete poetry by four Canadian poets.

Birney is also the author of two novels: *Turvey* (1949), a picaresque tale of the Second World War, and *Down the long table* (1955), which re-creates the hopeless feeling of the unemployed during the 1930s and satirizes the 'parlour pinks' of that period. He edited the anthology *Twentieth century Canadian poetry* (1953) and, with Margerie Bonner Lowry, *The selected poems of Malcolm Lowry* (1962). *The creative writer*, literary essays, was published by the CBC in 1966. He has explained the poetic process behind the writing of 'David' in *The cow jumped over the moon: the writing and reading of poetry* (1972), which also contains his comments on a few of his other poems.

Richard Robillard has written a brief critical

study of Birney's work for the Canadian Writers Series of the New Canadian Library (1972). Frank DAVEY, a student of Birney's at the University of British Columbia, has also contributed a critical monograph on Birney's poetry to the Studies in Canadian Literature series (1972). NS/PS

Bissett, Bill (1939–). Born in Halifax, he has lived most of his life in Vancouver. He has been a leading figure in the field of sound and concrete poetry and has published many books, including his own, under the imprint of the Blew Ointment Press, which he operates. His books are *Where is Miss Florence Riddle* (1966); *We sleep inside each othr all* (1966); *Fires in the temple* (1966); *Th Gossamer bed pan* (1967); *What poetiks* (1967); *Liberating skies* (1967); *Lebanon voices* (1968); *Of th land divine service* (1968); *Dragon fly* (1968); *Awake in th Red Desert* (1968), which includes a recording of the poet reading his own poetry; *Sunday work* (1969); *Lost Angel Mining Co.* (1969); *S th story I to* (1970); *Blew trewz* (1970); *Tuff shit* (1971); and *Drifting into war* (1971).

Many of these books are mimeographed and are often blurred and difficult to read. But Bissett maintains that the blur is part of the effect he wants to create by his work because he believes in breaking rigid systems, whether they be orthographical, metrical, grammatical, or political. Bissett often shapes his poems on the page in a non-linear way. (bp NICHOL has termed his poetic method 'typogeography'.) The poet brings the reader into his poetic world by using his own special method of spelling and phrase structure, crossing the borders between linear poetry and graphic design. His books often include line drawings—different designs for each copy of the book—and the poems are sometimes interleaved with artifacts, such as advertising from glossy magazines, as examples of the society Bissett condemns so rigorously in his writings. They also include some experimental prose.

Bissett can write lyrical, tender love poems and chant-like repetitions of phrases that seek to create a rhythmic extension of the senses. He also writes aggressively angry political poems, some arising from his own experience in prison, attacking what he considers the oppressive laws of Canadian society. Other poems express a fervent concern for a free and independent Canada, based on a return to the simplicities of nature and a reaction against ecological destruction and economic domination by outside forces.

The best representative selection of Bissett's work can be found in *Nobody owns th earth* (1971), edited by Margaret ATWOOD and Dennis LEE. PS

Blackburn, John H. See HISTORY STUDIES IN ENGLISH 8.

Blades, Ann. See CHILDREN'S BOOKS IN ENGLISH 5.

Blais, André. See POLITICAL WRITINGS IN FRENCH 4.

Blais, Marie-Claire (1939–). Born in Quebec City, she left school at fifteen to work in a shoe factory. Later she took courses in French literature at Université Laval, where she was encouraged in her writing by Jeanne Lapointe and the Rev. Georges-Henri Lévesque. After the publication of her first two novels, in 1962 she was awarded a Guggenheim Fellowship (which was sponsored by Edmund Wilson). This enabled her to spend a year in France. She lived on Cape Cod for several years and has recently settled in Brittany.

Marie-Claire Blais writes simply and directly of a world in which evil is simply a monstrous fact and there is neither guilt nor expiation. The central figures of her novels are all children and young people, more intelligent than those around them and so more aware of adult brutality and more appalled by it. They try to postpone growing up, which they see as a corruption; when forced to enter the adult world, they react with savagery or despair. The narcissistic mother of *La belle bête* (1959), which was translated by Merloyd Lawrence as *Mad shadows* (1960), neglects her plain daughter for her handsome imbecile son, then abandons both children for her lover; the son causes the lover's death and is in turn disfigured by his sister. (*Mad shadows* has been reissued in the New Canadian Library (1971) with an introduction by Naim Kattan.) In *Tête blanche* (1960), a slighter work translated without change of title by Charles Fullman (1961), an unloved child grows into an alienated adolescent. With *Une saison dans la vie d'Emmanuel* (1965), the fantasy-landscape of the earlier books becomes a nightmare caricature of rural Québec at its most clerical and rigid. The younger members of a large family must face not only parental neglect and cruelty but such tangible enemies as poverty, religious aberration, and disease. A sister, mistaking her adolescent sensuality for religious vocation, enters first a convent, then a brothel; two sons are the victims of a pederastic priest; and the most creative member of the family is so poorly equipped for life by an exclusively classical education that death from tuberculosis comes as a release. This novel, which was awarded the Prix France-Canada and the Prix Médicis of France, was translated as *A season in the life of Emmanuel* by Derek Coltman (1966). In *L'insoumise* (1966), the mother, father, and friend of an adolescent killed in an accident search for a clue to their lack of understanding of his character. The central figure of *David Sterne* (1967) also dies accidentally. Fatally ill, he decides to devote his remaining days to vice and, after corrupting his only two friends, is killed by the police; once again the adults are left to wonder where they failed. Their concern is handled ironically, almost with contempt. Recent novels present more robust, less destructive central characters and even a more positive sort of revolt. The heroine of *Manuscrits de Pauline Archange* (1968), winner of a Governor General's Award, *Vivre! Vivre!* (1969), and *Les apparences* (1970)—a series of novels about a girl growing up in Québec —is determined to live as a free individual despite the flaws in her upbringing and education. (The first two in the series have been translated by Derek Coltman in a single volume as *The manuscripts of Pauline Archange* (1969).) Even the homosexual youth in *Le loup* (1972), though aware that his particular sort of generous and charitable love is bound to bring out the worst in others, still feels that the mere capacity for love is good.

Marie-Claire Blais is also the author of *L'exécution* (1968), a play about a thrill-murder, and of two volumes of poetry: *Pays voilés* (1963) and *Existences* (1967). Two rather minor novellas—*Le jour est noir* (1962), a study of a group of children who see the death of their parents as betrayal, and *Les voyageurs sacrés* (1969), the story of a marital triangle in which disloyalty to a marriage is equated with disloyalty to childhood—have been translated in a single volume as *The day is dark* and *Three travelers* by Derek Coltman (1967). Marie-Claire Blais's fiction is analysed by J. Raymond Brazeau in *An outline of contemporary French-Canadian literature* (1972) and, more philosophically, by Philip Stratford in a study in the Canadian Writers and Their Work series (1970). JM

Blais, Martin. See POLITICAL WRITINGS IN FRENCH 2.

Blaise, Clark. See FICTION IN ENGLISH: SHORT STORIES.

Blake, Verschoyle B. See HISTORY STUDIES IN ENGLISH 5.

Blicker, Seymour. See FICTION IN ENGLISH 4 and 6.

Blicq, Anthony. See FICTION IN ENGLISH 7.

Bliss, Michael. See HISTORY STUDIES IN ENGLISH 11.

Blondahl, Omar. See FOLKLORE: BIBLIOGRAPHY.

Blower, James. See HISTORY STUDIES IN ENGLISH 8.

Blyth, J. A. See HISTORY STUDIES IN ENGLISH 11.

Boas, Franz. See INDIANS 5.

Bock, Philip K. See INDIAN LEGENDS AND ART.

Bodsworth, Fred (1918–). Born in Port Burwell, Ont., Frederick Bodsworth became a reporter for the St Thomas *Times-journal* and later joined the Toronto *Star*. His many articles in Canadian magazines won him an international reputation as an authority on birds, and he has led ornithological expeditions to many parts of the world. His greatest interest, however, has been in the arctic where he came to understand the life and customs of the native people. His knowledge of birds and their habitat is used effectively in three novels: *The last of the curlews* (1954), *The strange one* (1960), published in the United States under the title *The mating call*, and *The* *atonement of Ashley Morden* (1964). In *The last of the curlews* Bodsworth uses antiphonal chapters to contrast the simple beauty of the birds with the ugliness of man's wanton destruction of the species. In *The strange one* the fidelity of a Hebridean barnacle goose, which has been blown across the Atlantic, to the Canada goose with which it has mated is contrasted with the infidelity of a Hebridean-born Canadian scientist to the educated Indian girl who has been rejected by white people. In *The atonement of Ashley Morden*, a melodramatic story of war and northern adventure, the bird motif is introduced symbolically. Early in this novel a captured dove kills the bird with which it is caged; later Ashley Morden is broken by his revulsion to the bullying nature of man, the brutality of war, and the idea of chemical warfare. Unlike the dove, Morden eventually escapes to rebuild his life in the wilderness.

In *The sparrows fall* (1967) Bodsworth shows a unique ability to enter into the minds of a young Eskimo couple. Having fallen in love with each other, they allow themselves to be married by an inexperienced missionary who pays a short visit to their camp and does not understand that tribal taboos and marriage arrangements are techniques through which the Eskimos survive. Outcast by the tribe, and misunderstanding the commandment 'Thou shalt not kill', the couple meet disaster and near starvation.

Bodsworth is also the author of *Pacific coast* (1970), a history of British Columbia in The Illustrated Natural History of Canada series. *The last of the curlews* is in the New Canadian Library. NS

Boily, Robert. See POLITICAL WRITINGS IN FRENCH 1 and 5.

Boissonnault, Charles-Marie. See HISTORY STUDIES IN FRENCH 1.

Bolt, Carol. See DRAMA IN ENGLISH 3.

Bolus, Malvina. See HISTORY STUDIES IN ENGLISH 3.

Bonenfant, Jean Charles. See HISTORY STUDIES IN FRENCH 4.

Boorman, Sylvia. See HISTORY STUDIES IN ENGLISH 5.

Borden, Henry. See HISTORY STUDIES IN ENGLISH 7.

Borduas, Paul-Emile. See BELLES LETTRES IN FRENCH.

Bosco, Monique. Born in Vienna, she received her primary education in France and came to Canada in 1948, receiving her M.A. from the Université de Montréal in 1951 and her Ph.D. in 1953 with a thesis on 'L'isolement dans le roman canadien-français'. From 1952 to 1959 she was employed by Radio-Canada, and after two years' residence in Europe returned to Canada to engage in free-lance journalism and to work with the National Film Board and Radio-Canada. Since 1963 she has held the position of Professor in the Faculté des Lettres at the Université de Montréal. She has published one collection of verse, *Jéricho* (1971), distinguished by force of expression and command of technique, and three novels—*Un amour maladroit* (1961), *Les infusoires* (1965), and *La femme de Loth* (1970) which received a Governor General's Award. (*La femme de Loth* is at present being translated by John GLASSCO and will appear either late in 1973 or early in 1974 under the title of *Lot's wife*.) Her novels, dealing with the situation of women in contemporary society and particularly with regard to sex, are characterized by a trenchancy of observation that verges on misanthropy, and by the concise, masterly style in which she incorporates her basic attitudes of compassion and disgust. She is one of the most accomplished novelists of French Canada. JG

Bosquet, Alain. See ANTHOLOGIES IN FRENCH.

Bossé, E. See HISTORY STUDIES IN FRENCH 11.

Boston, Stewart. See DRAMA IN ENGLISH 4.

Boswell, Hazel. See FOLKLORE: BIBLIOGRAPHY.

Boulanger, Tom. See INDIANS 2.

Bourassa, Robert. See POLITICAL WRITINGS IN FRENCH 4.

Bourne, Kenneth. See HISTORY STUDIES IN ENGLISH 7.

Bourneuf, Roland. See LITERARY STUDIES IN FRENCH 4.

Bourque, Gilles. See HISTORY STUDIES IN FRENCH 4.

Bowering, George (1935–). Born in Penticton, B.C., and raised in the Okanagan Valley, he had a brief stint in the RCAF before enrolling at the University of British Columbia, where he completed a B.A. in history and an M.A. in English, and where he was an editor of the controversial magazine *Tish.* He has taught at Sir George Williams University and is now on the staff of Simon Fraser University. Bowering has published numerous books and chapbooks of poetry, including *Sticks & stones* (1963), *Points on the grid* (1964), *The man in yellow boots* (1965), *The silver wire* (1966), *Baseball* (1967), *Two police poems* (1968), and his two Governor General's Award books: *Rocky Mountain foot* (1969) and *The gangs of Kosmos* (1969). His most recent publications are *Sitting in Mexico* (1970), *Touch: selected poems 1960–1970* (1971), and *Autiobiology* (1972). Bowering has also published literary criticism, including a book on the poetry of Al PURDY in the Studies in Canadian Literature series (1970), and a novel, *Mirror on the floor* (1967).

Many readers think of Bowering as a west-coast primitive, a neo-Romantic who asserts the superiority of feeling over intellect, throws off the trappings of traditional verse, and advocates the language and rhythms of ordinary speech. Although he is concerned with the problem of 'how to get your own voice on the page', he is by no means an unconventional or anti-intellectual poet; in fact his academic career as teacher and critic, his attraction and subscription to poetic theory, and his chatty, low-key philosophizing suggest quite the opposite.

He subscribes to the poetic, if not the example, of William Carlos Williams and the Black Mountain poets—Olson, Duncan, and Creeley—aiming, as he says in 'For WCW', at 'Language lifted / out of the ordinary / into the illumination / of poetry'. At times Bowering is too easily satisfied, does not wrestle sufficiently with words so that they are lifted beyond the ordinary. Yet he is capable of a certain delicacy and lyricism in poems that arise from *felt* experience. In 'Circus Maximus' he speaks of style as a suit of clothes the poet inherits from his predecessors. His own best poems, in which there is a sense of *resistance* in the language, are his imitations of other poets, as in the Ginsbergian lines and rhythms of 'Grandfather'. In these poems, in the lyrics of childhood and memory or pure fancy, he escapes the introversion and easy generalization that engulf so many of the imitators of Olson and Creeley. By assuming a style, he gains a freedom to say what is closest not to his intellect but to his feelings. GG

Bowman, Charles A. See HISTORY STUDIES IN ENGLISH 15.

Bowsfield, Hartwell. See CHILDREN'S BOOKS IN ENGLISH 5 and HISTORY STUDIES IN ENGLISH 8.

Braithwaite, Max. See FICTION IN ENGLISH: SHORT STORIES.

Brandis, Marian. See FICTION IN ENGLISH 3.

Brault, Jacques (1933–). Born in the east end of Montreal, he worked as a labourer and longshoreman to pay for his education at the Collège Sainte-Marie and the Université de Montréal. He then studied in France at the Sorbonne and the Université de Poitiers. Since 1960 he has been a professor at the faculty of philosophy of the Université de Montréal. A renowned critic, he is equally at ease in such areas as literature, philosophy, and political science, and has published a critical edition of Saint-Denys GARNEAU's writings (1971) as well as an important study of Alain GRANDBOIS's poetry (1968).

Brault has published three collections of poetry. The poems in *Trinôme* (1957), which appeared with the work of two other poets, are sometimes overlooked by critics. They are elegiac poems on love and death and anticipate essential themes in his second book, *Mémoire* (1965), one of the most remarkable publications in recent Québec poetry that put Brault on a par with Gaston MIRON and Paul CHAMBERLAND. Here he attempts to exorcise the futility, frustration, and degradation of the human condition in the French-Canadian past by digesting and transforming the world of his personal past, particularly the memories of his family, their struggle against poverty, his father's failure to find employment, and his brother's futile death in the Second World War. His most recent collection, *La poésie ce matin* (1971), continues to find its inspiration in the everyday experiences of life in Québec, but it develops within a broader awareness of the universal human condition. Neither as hermetic as the first collection, nor as richly eloquent as the second, the poems here achieve an assured intensity. Short and incisive, they temper the philosophical sombreness of earlier volumes with a new emphasis on the promise of the immediate future, the world of beginnings and of the morning light; and they conclude, appropriately, with Mallarmé's 'Adieu, nuit, que je fus'. Brault's poetry has appeared in translation in *Ellipse 7* (1971). See also DRAMA IN FRENCH 4. MG

Bredin, Thomas. See HISTORY STUDIES IN ENGLISH 8.

Brett, K. B. See HISTORY STUDIES IN ENGLISH 7.

Brewin, Andrew. See HISTORY STUDIES IN ENGLISH 12.

Brewster, Elizabeth (1922–). Elizabeth Winifred Brewster was born in Chipman, N.B. She studied at the University of New Brunswick, continuing in postgraduate work at Radcliffe College and at King's College, University of London. She completed her Ph.D. at Indiana University and received a degree in library science from the University of Toronto Library School. She has worked in libraries in New Brunswick, Ontario, British Columbia, and Alberta, and has been a member of the department of English at the University of Saskatchewan, Saskatoon, where she lives.

Elizabeth Brewster's poetry first appeared in three chapbooks—*East coast* (1951), *Lillooet* (1954), a descriptive narrative poem of life in a New Brunswick village, and *Roads and other poems* (1957)—and poems by her were included in *Five New Brunswick poets* (1962) edited by Fred COGSWELL. Many of her poems were collected in *Passage of summer* (1969), though most of this book contains recent work. Her latest collection is *Sunrise north* (1972).

Much of Elizabeth Brewster's poetry is concerned with memories of her early life in New Brunswick, expressed in a direct and simple style. She deals with landscape and people in relation to their environment and to herself, her own memories and dreams. Though the poems record the process of change, the poet is constantly trying to find in her assessment of the people and places she has known some permanent values in the chaos and violence of modern society. The tone of her poetry is one of nostalgia touched with regret, for although she feels 'Civilization should tame barbarism/Decorum should control passion', behind many of the poems lies the conviction that man's barbaric instincts will outlast his civilized achievements. Her poetry is prevented from becoming too obsessively gloomy, however, by the honest attitudes she takes to the individuals she remembers, and it is enlivened at times by humorous understatement and self-mockery. Furthermore its simplicity of structure and diction express a disarming delight in ordinary objects and events. PS

Brichant, A. See POLITICAL WRITINGS IN ENGLISH 1.

Brillant, Jacques. See POLITICAL WRITINGS IN FRENCH 2.

Brochu, André (1942–). Born at Saint-Eustache, Qué., and educated in Montreal, he published his first collection of poems, *Privilèges de l'ombre* (1961), at the age of nineteen, and was acclaimed as one of the most gifted of the younger poets of Québec. With his second collection, *Délit contre délit* (1965), he announced that he would write no more poetry, and has since devoted himself to fiction and criticism. His poetry is fluent, felicitous and polished, especially in his light, satiric, and erotic vein; his more serious poems, imbued with the most fervent Québec nationalism, are more in the nature of rhetorical exercises and political effusions. He has also published some of his short stories in *Nouvelles* (1963), and a novel, *Adéodat I* (1973).

Brochu is highly regarded as a critic of Québécois literature. Two of his best-known articles are on Gabrielle ROY, reprinted in Gilles MARCOTTE's *Présence de la critique* (1968), and 'Yves THÉRIAULT et la sexualité', which he wrote for PARTI PRIS. JG

Brochu, Michel. See ESKIMOS: BOOKS IN FRENCH.

Brody, H. See INDIANS 6.

Brossard, Jacques. See POLITICAL WRITINGS IN FRENCH 3.

Brossard, Nicole. See FICTION IN FRENCH 3 and POETRY IN FRENCH.

Brown, Addison. See HISTORY STUDIES IN ENGLISH 4.

Brown, Cassie. See HISTORY STUDIES IN ENGLISH 10.

Brown, E. K. See LITERARY STUDIES IN ENGLISH 1.

Brown, George W. See HISTORY STUDIES IN FRENCH 11.

Brown, J. J. See HISTORY STUDIES IN ENGLISH 13.

Brown, Jim. See POETRY IN ENGLISH 2 and 3.

Brown, R. Craig. See HISTORY STUDIES IN ENGLISH 1 and 6.

Browne, G. P. See HISTORY STUDIES IN ENGLISH 7 and 12.

Bruce, Charles (1906–71). Born in Port Shoreham, N.S., Charles Tory Bruce was educated at Mount Allison University and became a journalist. In 1945 he was appointed head of the Canadian Press Bureau in Toronto. Nostalgia for the life of the farm-fishing community of the Nova Scotia coast is expressed both in his poetry and in his prose. The direct language and concrete images of his poetry evoke the life and character of the farmer-fisherman of Nova Scotia who by learning to understand the harsh terms of weather and tide develops courage and the ability to make decisions. Bruce's books of verse are *Wild apples* (1927); *Tomorrow's tide* (1932); *Personal note* (1942) and *Grey ship moving* (1945), both containing reflections on lives interrupted by war; and *The flowing summer* (1947), a narrative poem of an Ontario child's visit to his grandparents in Nova Scotia. *The Mulgrave Road* (1951), which won a Governor General's Award, is a collection of lyrics, some of which had appeared in *Grey ship moving*. His novel *The channel shore* (1954), set in a fishing village, brings out the frustration that leads young men in Nova Scotia to leave that province. *The township of time* (1959) is a chronicle of a Nova Scotia family told as connected short stories that date in their setting from 1786 to 1950.

Bruce is also the author of *News and the Southams* (1968), a lucid and free-flowing narrative history of a news empire and the men who made it and sustained its high reputation. NS

Bruce, Harry. See BELLES LETTRES IN ENGLISH.

Bruce, Phyllis. See ANTHOLOGIES IN ENGLISH 1 and POETRY IN ENGLISH.

Bruemmer, Fred. See ESKIMOS: BOOKS IN ENGLISH.

Brun, Henri. See POLITICAL WRITINGS IN FRENCH 5.

Brunet, Michel (1917–). Born in Montreal, he was educated at the Université de Montréal and at Clark University, Worcester, Mass., where he completed his Ph.D. with the financial help of the Rockefeller Foundation. Since 1949 he has been a professor at the Institut d'Histoire de l'Université de Montréal. In 1970 he was elected President of the Institut d'Histoire de l'Amérique française. He is a member of L'Académie canadienne-française and L'Académie des Sciences d'outre-mer de France. In 1972 he was visiting professor at the Sorbonne.

Brunet's contribution to the historical literature of Québec is very important: he was and still is the leading figure and interpreter of L'École de Montréal. In 1952, in collaboration with Guy FRÉGAULT and Marcel TRUDEL, he published a selection of texts: *Histoire du Canada par les textes 1534–1854* (2nd ed., 1967) and *1855–1960* (2nd ed., 1969). Four other publications express the nature of Brunet's position regarding Canadian history: *Canadians et Canadiens* (1954; rev. 1971), *La présence anglaise et les Canadiens: étude sur l'histoire et la pensée des deux Canadas* (1958; rev. 1969), *Québec—Canada anglais: deux itinéraires, un affrontement* (1968), and *Les Canadiens après la conquête 1759–1775: de la révolution canadienne à la révolution américaine*

(1969), which won a Governor General's Award. These studies focus the governing trend in Brunet's conception: the conquest represents the tragedy of a people socially beheaded, deprived of a bourgeoisie, a ruling class that could have secured a normal evolution for French-Canadian society. This historical fact implies a range of interpretations of the evolution of French-Canadian society that have had a fundamental influence on the recent history of Canada and of Québec.

Among other writings of Brunet, showing his constant interest in the social development of the Québec collectivity, his contributions to *L'université dit non aux Jésuites* (1961) and *La crise de l'enseignement au Canada français: urgence d'une réforme* (1961) should be mentioned. With J. Russell Harper he wrote *Un essai de gravures romantiques sur le pays du Québec au XIXe siècle* (1968).

More than seventy-five articles and brochures have also been published by this historian, whose influence on the intellectual and political history of Canada and Québec remains fundamental. J-LR

Buck, Tim. See HISTORY STUDIES IN ENGLISH 11.

Buckler, Ernest (1908–). Born in Dalhousie West, N.S., he was educated at Dalhousie University and at the University of Toronto. He has lived on the family farm near Annapolis Royal except for a short time when he worked in an actuarial firm in Toronto. A distinguishing feature of his novels are the vivid descriptions of the landscape of the Annapolis valley to which his eyes and ears are sensitively attuned. There is nothing bucolic or sentimental about them, however, as they reveal the feelings of people who are tormented by urban pressures, personal conflicts, or family disagreements. While his plots deal with specific cases, his novels can be read as allegories of man's need to come to terms with himself and to seek reconciliation with others.

In *The mountain and the valley* (1952) the lonely and sensitive protagonist, reflecting on the countryside, is able to heal his personal conflicts and find a sympathetic understanding of tangled family relationships. A second novel, *The cruelest month* (1963), also draws on landscape to enlarge the sympathies of a group of unhappy people from the city who stay at a summer hotel where the owner is facing a crisis. *Ox bells and fireflies* (1968) is a poetic fictionalized memoir of Buckler's childhood near Annapolis Royal. The colours, shapes, sounds, and smells of the countryside are faithfully recorded, and the conversations and attitudes of the people are vividly but gently recollected.

The mountain and the valley is available in the New Canadian Library. See *Ernest Buckler* (1972) edited by Gregory M. Cook in the Critical Views on Canadian Writers series. NS

Buell, John (1927–). Born in Montreal and educated there at Loyola College and the Université de Montréal, he is professor of communication arts at Loyola College. Buell's three novels *The pyx* (1959), *Four days* (1962), and *The Shrewsbury exit* (1972) are sympathetic studies of the plight of innocent people victimized by criminals and hoodlums. *The Shrewsbury exit* is set in the United States and gives a picture of life in prison from which the innocent man escapes and succeeds in getting the evidence that clears him. *The pyx* has been made into a film. NS

Buitenhuis, Elspeth. See LITERARY STUDIES IN ENGLISH 4.

Buitenhuis, Peter. See LITERARY STUDIES IN ENGLISH 4 and POETRY IN ENGLISH 1.

Bulien, Bernard. See LITERARY STUDIES IN FRENCH 1.

Bullock, Harry. See FICTION IN ENGLISH: SHORT STORIES.

Bumsted, J. M. See HISTORY STUDIES IN ENGLISH 4.

Burley, Kevin H. See HISTORY STUDIES IN ENGLISH 13.

Burnet, Jean. See HISTORY STUDIES IN ENGLISH 14.

Burnham, Dorothy K. See HISTORY STUDIES IN ENGLISH 7.

Burnham, Harold B. See HISTORY STUDIES IN ENGLISH 7.

Burns, E. L. M. See HISTORY STUDIES IN ENGLISH 12.

Burns, R. M. See POLITICAL WRITINGS IN ENGLISH 1.

Burroughs, Peter. See HISTORY STUDIES IN ENGLISH 6.

Burton, Thomas. See POLITICAL WRITINGS IN ENGLISH 2.

Butler, Juan (1942–). Born in London, Eng., of English and Spanish parentage, he came to Canada in 1942 and was educated to Grade 10 in various schools. He has travelled extensively in Europe and Morocco and now lives in Toronto where he has held a wide range of jobs.

Butler's two novels, *Cabbagetown diary: a documentary* (1969) and *The garbage man* (1972), reveal his talent for sustained but controlled emotional prose. He commands attention for his insights into the conflicting views of reality in modern society. *Cabbagetown diary*, while seemingly conventional, is fresh in its revelation of the falsity with which a callous and mischievous bartender relates his part in an affair with a mistress he has discarded and of the cynicism with which he encourages his radical friends. The book also exposes conditions in the poorer rooming-house districts of Toronto and the views prevalent among those who have been deprived of parental love and social security. In *The garbage man* Butler juggles time and place as he explores the horrible criminal fantasies of a man who may possibly have committed one murder, and whose insanity stems from revulsion to violence and mental cruelty. The insane protagonist, however, can still ask the serious question: What will become of a society if the violent prevail?
NS

C

Callaghan, Barry. See POETRY IN ENGLISH 1.

Callaghan, Morley (1903–). Born in Toronto, Morley Edward Callaghan was educated at the University of Toronto and Osgoode Hall; he was called to the bar in 1928. Except for brief periods he has lived in Toronto all his life. His distinguished career as a writer was recognized in 1970 when he received both the Molson Prize and the Royal Bank Award, given for 'work that serves humanity'.

While a student Callaghan worked as a reporter on the Toronto *Star* during the short time Ernest Hemingway was on its staff. Hemingway not only encouraged him in his writing but, after he had left Canada for Paris, was able to place some of Callaghan's stories in the 'little magazines' there. Meanwhile Callaghan, who had continued to write, had some stories accepted by *American Caravan*. Scott Fitzgerald saw them and drew them to the attention of his own publishers, Scribner's, who published Callaghan's first novel, *Strange fugitive* (1928), and his first collection of short stories, *A native argosy* (1929). Callaghan then spent some eight months in Paris where he renewed his acquaintance with Hemingway and became friends with Fitzgerald and James Joyce. He writes of this experience, not all of it happy, in *That summer in Paris* (1963), which also reveals the ideas and techniques that Callaghan has adopted in his writing. He states his purpose to describe things as he sees them, rejecting as 'literary' anything that distracts attention from the protagonist to the writer. This determination to employ direct and unvarnished description of persons and places is one of the strongest characteristics of Callaghan's work; his technique is particularly effective in the characterizations of the social misfits he writes about. In his short stories it is used to good advantage in sustaining interest in situations that are normally regarded as trivial, ridiculous, or exasperating. His short-story collections are *A native argosy*, *Now that April's here and other stories* (1936), and *Morley Callaghan's stories* (1959). He has also written a novella, *No man's meat* (1931).

In his early novels Callaghan gave little consideration to the solution of the moral problems implicit in the situations in which his characters placed or found themselves. His attitude changed after 1933 when, as the result of many conversations with the late Jacques Maritain (then at the Pontifical Institute of Mediaeval Studies, Toronto), he shaped and stiffened his conviction of the value of Christian doctrines dealing with the supreme importance of spiritual development through altruistic love.

In *Strange fugitive* (1928) a misfit who takes out his uncertainties and resentments by acting as a bully in a lumberyard is destroyed when drawn into the more deadly forms of violence used by hardened criminals of the bootlegging era. In *It's never over* (1930) the sister and friends of a criminal are unable to overcome the shock of his execution for murder. In *A broken journey* (1932) a mother competes for the affections of her daughter's faithful suitor, while the daughter impetuously abandons the suitor after bringing disaster upon him through her inability to resist the very promiscuity she had found so repellent in her mother.

In his more successful novels of the 1930s, Callaghan shows an awareness of contemporary problems; the depression and the discussions of Marxist philosophy that it engendered provided the background for his characters. In *Such is my beloved* (1934) a priest is broken by his attempt to force the wealthy and respectable to give assistance to two prostitutes with whom his sympathies have become deeply involved. In *They shall inherit the earth* (1935) the sense of guilt of Michael Aikenhead, who has allowed his hated step-brother to drown, becomes inextricably interwoven with the slow death-in-life imposed by the depression. *More joy in heaven* (1937) is the story of a paroled convict, Kip Caley, who is made a public hero until, abruptly disillusioned, he returns to his old companions and dies fighting for them when he knows they have been betrayed through their association with him. Caley is allowed to find personal salvation in the devotion of the girl who has accepted him for what he is. (This novel was inspired by the contemporary case of Red Ryan, a notorious gunman whose exemplary behaviour in the penitentiary led to an early parole, during which he was lionized, but who was killed ten months later while robbing a liquor store in Sarnia.) Even a satisfactory personal liberation is denied Peggy Sanderson who, in *The loved and the lost* (1951), pursues her obsession to be accepted by the black community to which she is a source of embarrassment and danger. This novel won a Governor General's Award. In *The many colored coat* (1960) Callaghan uses a tangled web of circumstances involving a public relations man (the professional glad-hander), a banker (symbol of solid respectability), and a tailor (the little man) to illustrate the prejudices and false values of society, its hasty judgements, as well as the futility of, and false impressions created by, attempts at self-justification. In *A passion in Rome* (1961) the death of Pope Pius XII and the election of his successor provide a background that symbolizes death and resurrection; against it, a photographer works out his own salvation and the rehabilitation of an alcoholic American singer with whom he has fallen in love. In the first issue of the magazine *Exile* (1972) there is an extract from a novel-in-progress, to be called *The dark and the light of Lisa*.

Callaghan is also the author of *The varsity story* (1948), a fictionalized portrayal of the federation of colleges that constitutes the University of Toronto; of *Luke Baldwin's vow* (1948), a novel for young readers; and of two plays 'Turn home again' and 'Just ask for George', written in 1939, which had short runs in Toronto in 1949 and 1950 under the titles 'Going home' and 'To tell the truth'.

There are two critical studies of Morley Callaghan: one by Brandon Conron in the Twayne World Authors Series (1966) and the other by Victor Hoar in the Studies in Canadian Literature series (1969).

Eight of Callaghan's books are available in paperback. *Such is my beloved*, *More joy in heaven*, and *They shall inherit the earth* have been reprinted in the New Canadian Library and *Morley Callaghan's stories*, *The loved and the lost*, *The many colored coat*, *It's never over*, and *Strange fugitive* are in the Laurentian Library. NS

Camp, Dalton. See HISTORY STUDIES IN ENGLISH 12.

Campbell, Marjorie Wilkins. See CHILDREN'S BOOKS IN ENGLISH 2.

Campeau, Lucien. See HISTORY STUDIES IN FRENCH 3.

Caouette, Réal. See POLITICAL WRITINGS IN FRENCH 4.

Cardinal, Harold. See INDIANS 1 and POLITICAL WRITINGS IN ENGLISH 3.

Cardinal, J. C. See POLITICAL WRITINGS IN FRENCH 4.

Careless, J. M. S. (1919–). James Maurice Stockford Careless was born in Toronto and educated at the University of Toronto and at Harvard University. He was appointed to the history department of the University of Toronto in 1945 and served as chairman of the department for eight years, from 1959. In 1962 he was elected to the Royal Society of Canada and was awarded the Tyrrell Medal for historical research. Careless has acted as co-chairman of the Archaeological and Historical Sites Board of Ontario and as president of the Canadian Historical Association. He is now a member of the Historical Sites and Monuments Board of Canada.

In common with Harold Innis and Donald Creighton, Careless has given careful consideration to the influence of the environment in Canadian history: his lectures and writings have stressed the importance of urbanism in the growth of government and society. His major publication is *Brown of the Globe: 1—The voice of Upper Canada, 1818–1859* (1959); *2—Statesman of confederation, 1860–1880* (1963), which won a Governor General's Award and also the University of British Columbia Medal for Popular Biography. Careless portrays George Brown, the founder of the Toronto *Globe*, as an enterprising businessman who was soundly schooled in the ideals and virtues of British liberal democracy. The biography illuminates the career of Brown, the politics of the era, the importance of Ontario in the confederation movement, and analyses the origins of Canadian liberalism. In *The union of the Canadas: the growth of Canadian institutions, 1841–1857* (1967)—volume ten of the Canadian Centenary Series—Careless shows that, although the Union of 1841 was designed to produce a unified Canada and to assimilate the French, in fact cultural duality became entrenched. As Toronto and Montreal sought larger hinterlands for their growing urban economies, and as they both sought to compete with the Americans, English- and French-speaking politicians found co-operation to be a necessity.

Canada: a story of challenge (1959; revised and enlarged 1970) is a clear and concise textbook that emphasizes political development. Careless is the editor and co-author of *The pioneers: the picture story of Canadian settlement* (1969); *Colonists and Canadiens, 1760–1867* (1971); and editor of *The Canadians, 1867–1967* (1967). The last two volumes are collections of essays by various historians of divergent backgrounds and viewpoints who examine a century of Canadian history for patterns of development. Careless is the author of numerous published essays and articles on urban, regional, and business growth in Canada. He contributed to *Nationalism in Canada* (1966) edited by Peter Russell and to *The New Romans* (1968) edited by Al PURDY. DF

Carrier, Roch (1937–). Born in Sainte-Justine-de-Dorchester, a small village in the Beauce region of Québec, he was educated at the Université de Montréal and at the Sorbonne, where he wrote a doctoral thesis on the poetry of Blaise Cendrars. For several years he combined a university teaching career with his real work as a writer. Since 1970 he has been secretary-general of the Théatre du Nouveau Monde in Montreal.

Carrier's earliest publications were poems and short stories and his first published book was *Jolis deuils* (1964), a collection of *contes*, fantastic and allegorical. *La guerre, yes sir!* appeared in 1968, followed by *Floralie, où es-tu?* (1969) and *Il est par là, le soleil* (1970). In a style and language that are deceptively simple Roch Carrier portrays lives that are turbulent, even violent, in their physical or psychological aspects. The characters and settings of the novels are more conventional than in the short stories, but they are pervaded by violence or by dreams that substitute for it. Briefly, the novels deal with approximately forty years of Québec history: *La guerre* is an account of personal and national tensions in a small Québec village in the early years of the

Second World War—a very human look at the Conscription Crisis; *Floralie, où es-tu?* goes back thirty years or so to the wedding night of the parents of *La guerre*'s central character, the young soldier Corriveau who died ignominiously and whose wake provides the setting for most of the first novel. *Floralie*'s mood and setting are more dreamlike and shadowy than in the previous novel, with its fights and feasts, and its possible interpretations are both more ambiguous and more ambitious. *Il est par là, le soleil* also has a wartime setting, but in Montreal rather than the isolated countryside: one of the characters from *La guerre*, the rebellious son of a grave-digger, moves into the city where he encounters the larger world. Taken together, the trilogy considers what Carrier has called 'Québec's dark ages', with specific attention given to religious, nationalistic, and even linguistic concerns. All of Roch Carrier's novels and a number of his short stories have been translated into English by Sheila Fischman: *La guerre, yes sir!* (1970), *Floralie, where are you?* (1971), and *Is it the sun, Philibert?* (1972).

Carrier adapted *La guerre, yes sir!* for the stage and it was performed at the Théâtre du Nouveau Monde in Montreal in 1970; it toured Europe in the summer of 1971 and an English version was produced at the Stratford Festival during the 1972 season.

In 1969 Roch Carrier published a series of short stories, *Contes pour mille oreilles*, in the Montreal review *Études françaises*. These are denser, more ambitious, and more poetic allegories that seem to be a natural development from the stories in *Jolis deuils*. SF

Carrière, Gaston. See HISTORY STUDIES IN FRENCH 11.

Carrigan, D. Owen. See HISTORY STUDIES IN ENGLISH 12 and POLITICAL WRITINGS IN ENGLISH 5.

Carter, Anthony L. See INDIAN LEGENDS AND ART.

Casanova, J. D. See HISTORY STUDIES IN ENGLISH 2 and HISTORY STUDIES IN FRENCH 3.

Casgrain, Thérèse F. See HISTORY STUDIES IN ENGLISH 11 and HISTORY STUDIES IN FRENCH 11.

Cashman, Tony. See HISTORY STUDIES IN ENGLISH 8.

Cass-Beggs, Barbara. See FOLKLORE: BIBLIOGRAPHY.

Caswell, Helen. See CHILDREN'S BOOKS IN ENGLISH 2.

Cell, Gillian T. See HISTORY STUDIES IN ENGLISH 2.

Chadwick, St John. See HISTORY STUDIES IN ENGLISH 12.

Chalmers, Floyd S. See HISTORY STUDIES IN ENGLISH 15.

Chalmers, John W. See HISTORY STUDIES IN ENGLISH 15.

Chalout, Rémi. See HISTORY STUDIES IN FRENCH 11.

Chamberland, Paul (1939–). Born in Longueuil, Qué., he was educated at the Collège de Saint-Laurent, the Université de Montréal, and at the Sorbonne. After leaving a religious community where he had spent three years, he became a co-founder of the Marxist-oriented PARTI PRIS and was one of its main driving forces until the magazine ceased publication in 1968. A professor of French and philosophy at the Université de Montréal, he abandoned the academic sphere in 1969 to set up and animate creative writing workshops.

Chamberland's poetic venture is that of an unorthodox theologian in his first collection, *Genèse* (1963), which, as its name implies, speaks of a personal and collective rebirth. He attains a new 'vision' of the world based on human action and the need for essential freedom, and this theme is pursued further in *Terre-Québec* (1964) through the imagery of the land—named, praised, loved, and possessed like the woman who is synonymous with it. In *L'afficheur hurle* (1965), his most dramatic collection, the naming becomes a cry, a howl of revolt for the political liberation of Québec. Marvellously cacophonous yet coherent, he writes 'the editorial of free men, of men to come', not only in Québec but in the universe, and protests against the darkness of accepted beliefs.

Throughout there is the feeling of solitude but also the possibility of harmony through love, and this continues in *L'inavouable* (1968), a long narrative poem where the 'unspeakable' daydreams become 'kill or be killed' and the hero comes to grips with this emotional cul-de-sac. *Éclats de la pierre noire d'où rejaillit ma vie* (1972) contains poems from 1966 to 1969 and appears as a transitional phase in his personal evolution. It ends with a 'revelation' whereby he sees himself as part of the 'eternal community of the living'; he says that he is no longer alone. From the black stone of absence, of blindness, he has come out into the light of the sensuous-divine.

A generous sampling of Chamberland's poetry, including extracts from *Demain les dieux naîtront* (yet to be published), appears in translation in *Ellipse 8/9* (1971). *L'afficheur hurle* is translated in Malcolm Reid's *The shouting signpainters: a literary and political account of Quebec revolutionary nationalism* (1972). Association coopérative des Éditions Parti Pris will soon publish Chamberland's *Écrits politikes (anciens & récents).* MG

Champagne, Antoine. See HISTORY STUDIES IN FRENCH 3.

Champagne, Maurice. See POLITICAL WRITINGS IN FRENCH 7.

Chance, Norman A. See INDIANS 5.

Chapais, Sir Thomas. See HISTORY STUDIES IN FRENCH 1.

Chapdelaine, Sylvain. See CHILDREN'S BOOKS IN FRENCH.

Chaput-Rolland, Solange. See HISTORY STUDIES IN FRENCH 2.

Charbonneau, Robert. See FICTION IN FRENCH 1.

Charyk, John C. See HISTORY STUDIES IN ENGLISH 15.

Châtillon, Pierre. See POETRY IN FRENCH.

Chavarie, Robert. See CHILDREN'S BOOKS IN FRENCH.

Chenoweth, D. See ANTHOLOGIES IN ENGLISH 1.

Cheshire, Neil M. See HISTORY STUDIES IN ENGLISH 2.

Chiasson, Anselme. See FOLKLORE: BIBLIOGRAPHY.

Children's books in English. Canadian children's literature in English is only about a quarter of a century old. Its nineteenth-century beginnings were a straight transplant from British culture; not until the late 1940s did it progress (and then only spasmodically) into something identifiably 'native' in character. It still bears some marks of its infancy, being largely based on our rugged landscape. The kind of adventurous outdoor life that Canada imposed upon its explorers and pioneers is still very much part of the Canadian imagination, even though only a small proportion of the population actually lives in our forests and mountains. However, the tradition has just enough living substance to put it at the centre of Canadian children's literature. So over the course of its development the basic character of that literature has been conservative and masculine in its appeal.

But significant changes have come within the last five years. These include a greater variety in themes and settings, a greater emphasis on the traditions of our native peoples, more successful ventures into fantasy (not easily attainable even in older cultures), more books with female characters, and more authentic biographies. And after years of dull-looking books, publishers have found the talent and/or the money to produce books that are visually attractive and even enticing. These are no mean achievements.

Equally significant have been changing attitudes towards a truly Canadian children's literature, brought about in part by a stronger feeling for things Canadian and a recognition of the importance of Canadian-based material; a greater understanding and appreciation of Canadian values; and an upsurge in writing, unpublished and amateurish though much of it is. On a more official level there is the show of government interest demonstrated by the Ontario Royal Commission on Book Publishing (1972) and the first exhibit of Canadian children's books by the National Library of Canada (1973);

an evident concern on the part of publishers; and most importantly the publication since 1967 of *In Review*, a journal devoted exclusively to reviews of Canadian children's books and published by the Provincial Library Service, Ontario Department of Education.

These flurries of concern have come none too soon. Canadian children's books have moved from infancy to adolescence, but they still need a great deal of attention to bring them to maturity. The forces operating against them are strong. There is competition from other English-speaking countries, particularly the United States. The themes of American books are regularly deemed more appealing—being more concerned with the impingement of the adult world upon the child and therefore less 'child-like' than the themes of Canadian children's books. Our newer books in particular do not easily become well known; they may be summarily reviewed or not reviewed at all. Our national media—newspapers, magazines, radio, television, the National Film Board—pay little or no attention to them, nor to their writers, which is a situation unheard of in other countries. Inadvertently, perhaps, some aspects of education contend against books and Canadian books in particular: the phenomenal rise of audio-visual materials in our school systems must inevitably operate against book budgets. Most alarmingly of all, the annual number of children's books published in the last five years has decreased. That quality has *increased* is a phenomenon as welcome as it is difficult to explain—but it may be temporary: good writing does not ordinarily spring up in isolation from other kinds.

Existing uneasily in all of this are the publishers. They have to justify publishing new children's books in the knowledge that there is an insubstantial market for them and without a backlist of bestselling Canadian children's classics, or indeed of many children's books that are even reprintable—a situation that is not imposed upon the publishers of any western European nation. Canadian publishers frequently find it impossible to sell an initial run of 3,000 copies of a worthy Canadian title—a figure that more often than not fails to allow even for basic expenses of production *if every copy is sold*. Yet if every public and elementary-school library (there are some 10,000) bought one copy of every 'good' Canadian children's book, the publishing of Canadian children's books would carry no risks—and more books would no doubt be written and published.

Most bookstore purchases of children's books are of acknowledged classics and these are rarely Canadian, although it is interesting to note that *Anne of Green Gables* has for a long time had average annual sales of more than 20,000 copies. (Publication rights are held in the United States!) Impulse buying usually leads the buyer to inexpensive 'quasi-books'—cut-up or colouring books, or other books to look at rather than to read. Finally there is buying on grounds of familiarity—for example the Sesame Street books of TV fame. But how much of our cultural familiarity is of things Canadian? The potential for increased retail sales rests on a better-educated public more aware of the value of gifts for the mind, and a gradual accumulation of Canadian titles that have paid off enough of their original investment to allow for republication in inexpensive reprint editions. The home-bookshelf market for good children's writing is being successfully invaded by British and American reprints selling at something like one dollar in Canada. When Canadian titles can be brought down to, say, $1.50, they will be competitive in this market, but not before. It will no doubt be a long time before there are many Canadian titles whose popularity can justify the large reprints this kind of price demands.

Certainly we haven't enough people (especially younger people) writing children's books, and much that is written is downright dull. But only in the last few years has the Canadian novel for *adults* generated any excitement. Children's literature follows adult literature and it can be expected that eventually some of the talent in this area will spill over into writing for children. Still, it is not impossible that the combination of our small population, regionalism, and inordinate competition from the United States will operate too strongly against so fragile and small a part of our national life as writing for children.

Some critics think the whole field of Canadian children's books in English is beyond help. In his background paper for the Ontario Royal Commission on Book Publishing (1972), George WOODCOCK says: 'This [writing for children] is a highly professional field of literary craftsmanship very much controlled by supply and demand, and it would seem that the decline is due less to the lack of writers than to the lack of interest in Canadian juveniles on the part of parents and perhaps also of children, who are inhabitants of microcosms rather than of nations. This may be one situation in which we should "not strive/Officiously to keep alive". '

Children do care little about the nationality of a writer whose book they like; but Canadian children of today are far more interested in their own country than were those of a generation or two ago. In spite of all difficulties it does not seem unreasonable for adults to want them to know about their country through lively, interesting, well-written books. The total potential Canadian market for children's books is unlikely to grow significantly for some time. Demographic predictions show little increase in the number of children under fourteen years of age for the next ten years or so. If a quantitative increase in sales is necessary, a market of the present size—particularly the school market—must be worked over more intensively and effectively. Considering the importation of books into Canada—the highest in the world—it may be helpful for us to seek foreign markets for more of our books to make our publishing viable. But this will improve only as Canadian writers become less selfconsciously regional and more universally relevant in the material they clothe in a Canadian setting. Children's books are more truly international than any other. Although it will be a long, long haul, it may be expected that Canadian books will ultimately take their place in the world if only their existence can be encouraged at home.

The six-year survey of Canadian children's books below is arranged primarily by year of publication; within each year the books are subdivided by age-group and genre. Thus each section begins with books for pre-school children (of which there are few) and/or picturebooks and moves on to books for older children. This record is confined to creative writing—fiction, legend, poetry, history, and biography—and to books that are Canadian in content and not just by circumstance of publication. Books that have received the medal of the Canadian Association of Children's Librarians are listed at the end.

1. *1967*. Folklore, that sturdy basis of literature and revelation of a nation's psychic energy, has been woefully lacking in Canada for various historical and geographical reasons. Our native peoples—the Indians and Eskimos—have vivid and living mythologies, but these have remained locked within the pages of anthropological studies almost until the present. The 1960s brought a few modern retellings of Indian legends for children, such as Dorothy Reid's *Tales of Nanabozho* (1963) and Kay Hill's *Glooscap and his magic: legends of the Wabanaki Indians* (1963). However, George Clutesi's *Son of Raven, son of Deer: fables of the Tse-Shaht people* (1967) was our first book of legends by an Indian—an 'insider's' record of this rich oral tradition. In contrast to the more stately Indian legends in Christie Harris's *Once upon a totem* (1963) and the cyclic approach of Robert Ayre's *Sketco the Raven* (1961), these are short, lively, humorous, and somewhat moral. Clutesi tells the adventures of the fool-hardy son of Deer and the greedy and thoughtless son of Raven, which have considerable links with the Anansi stories of Africa and the West Indies. The illustrations by the author are distinguished by their artistry, simplicity, bold colour, and design.

Another 'first' was Ronald Melzack's *The day Tuk became a hunter and other Eskimo stories* (1967), our first collection of Eskimo legends by a Canadian. Before this we were dependent upon American publications with their concentration on the Eskimos of Alaska. A reading of Knud Rasmussen's reports on his Thule Expeditions (published in the 1920s), with their anthropological and ethnological studies of Eskimo culture, shows Melzack's stories to be both accurate and central to the myth of our northern peoples. As retellings they reveal the kind of life imposed by one of the most inclement climates in the world, but they also show that the disparities of condition and life-style make little basic difference to human needs and deeply rooted life patterns. Eskimo legends belong to the world commonwealth of myth and folklore. James Houston, the man who helped bring Eskimo art to the attention of the world, found inspiration in the heroic story of an Eskimo youth cast adrift on a floating ice-pan. *Tikta'liktak* (1965) shows the training, experience, and fortitude that are necessary to conquer a hostile natural environment. Houston's *The white archer* (1967) conveyed, with passion and conviction, the inner turmoil of a young man training himself for an act of revenge but yielding in the end to the wisdom and love of an elderly Eskimo couple. The illustrations in both books, by the author, are modelled on Eskimo sculpture and achieve the appropriate simplicity and dignity.

Most of our children's books deal with the 'out-of-doors' in some form or another. The outstanding exponent of this type of story has been Farley MOWAT—naturalist, conservationist, and professional writer—who has a genuine feeling for the land combined with a sense of pace and an ability to create breathless suspense. Mowat's *Lost in the barrens* (1956) and *The black joke* (1962) are among our finest adventure stories. *The curse of the Viking grave* (1967) is a sequel to *Lost in the barrens*, but there the resemblance ends. The carelessness of the writing and the lack of conviction and integrity put this in the 'potboiler' class. To do Mr Mowat justice, however, almost everything he writes has an appeal for the young by virtue of his subject matter and his direct, forceful, often humorous style. Among his most popular books are *The dog who wouldn't be* (1957), *Never cry wolf* (1963), and the recent powerful and moving *A whale for the killing* (1972).

Historical fiction threads its inevitable way through our children's books. While the thread is strong, the texture and colours are all too frequently dull. Lyn Harrington's *The luck of the La Vérendryes* (1967) illustrates a flaw in much of our historical fiction—a thin line of fiction surrounded by a heavy dose of history. Such books lack both atmosphere and excitement. The opening of the prairies has become a favourite subject. In Lillian Pfeifer's *The wolfers* (1967) the son of a Montana trader follows a group of 'wolfers' or 'whisky traders' into what is now southwestern Alberta to avenge the murder of his father. Unfortunately the pedestrian writing is matched by a dull format. Another common theme is the friendship between white boy and Indian boy—as represented by Doris Anderson's *Blood brothers* (1967).

The emphasis on the outdoor tale and the historical novel has been achieved at the expense of stories with a modern and urban setting. Two books of this period redressed this imbalance partially but not distinctively. Both their authors had already established themselves as interpreters of early Indian life. Cliff Faulknor was well known for *The white calf* (1965) and its sequel *The white peril* (1966), stories of prairie Indian life. *The in-betweener* (1967) broke ground with a father-son conflict story set in Vancouver Island in the recent past and combined a study of personal relationships mixed with lively mystery and adventure. This is an interesting book that has been consistently ignored. Christie Harris—noted for her book of Indian legends, *Once upon a totem* (1963) and her historical novel about the impact of traders and missionaries upon the Haida Indians, *Raven's cry* (1966)—had already nudged children's books into a degree of 'modernity' with a light-spirited career story *You have to draw the line somewhere* (1964). In the same spirit, but with less charm, came *Confessions of a toe-hanger* (1967). Published in the midst of the new wave of American psychological novels for children, this story of the middle girl in a Canadian family who tries to 'find herself' is perhaps too ordinary and too mildly presented for it to make its way against the more sensational American competition. And, like most of those American books, it is not particularly well written.

Sound and lively biographies for children are difficult to write and so are not all that common: accuracy does not always promote readability. Josephine Phelan's *The ballad of D'Arcy McGee: rebel in exile* (1967), based on her award-winning adult biography *The ardent exile*, is smoothly written and covers the chief aspects of McGee's life and career. Yet the lack of a bibliography and some documentation and references does children an injustice; a book of fact should be shown as different from fiction. This book is volume 32 of the Great Stories of Canada series, which has provided since 1953 most of the non-textbook material on our famous figures and events in history with varying degrees of success.

2. *1968.* Canada is not a country where picturebooks are created for very young children; instead we import them. Our publications in this field are so minor and generally so thin and poor that the materials almost defy any reasonable analysis. However the University of Toronto Press's publication of *An alphabet book* (1968) showed that something could be done. This is only our third

Canadian alphabet book. (The first, *A Canadian child's ABC*, was published in 1931; and the second, *An illustrated comic alphabet*, although published in 1966, was first conceived by an English schoolteacher in Canada in 1859.) It was prepared by a group of Indian children on a reserve in southwestern Ontario and the child-like black-and-white drawings they created have far more appeal than many of the lavishly coloured American and British alphabet books. At any rate the text has distinctively Canadian touches—'M' is for 'Sir John A. Macdonald'. Hugh McClelland's *The bold bad buccaneers* (1968) is fairly typical of the picturebooks we do produce—a fairly good idea that was lost sight of somewhere along the line, and with no distinctive content, Canadian or otherwise. Here a gang of bloodthirsty pirates is horrified when it finds a boatload of children cast adrift by adults who have 'too many children'. It is a wry enough *volte-face*, but too incongruous a theme for a picturebook. The cartoon-like drawings—in black, white, and red—have a 'bold' look.

Eskimo folklore was strengthened by the publication of Helen Caswell's *Shadows from the singing house* (1968). Many of the stories have a starker and more authentic quality than those in *The day Tuk became a hunter* (1967), especially that of 'Sedna', the archetypal undersea figure who jealously guards the rules of the Eskimo world. James Houston's *Akavak: an Eskimo journey* (1968) continued his portrayal of life in the arctic with the moving account of an Eskimo boy who guides his ailing grandfather on what proves to be his last arduous journey.

Outside of books of folktales, chiefly Indian tales, there are very few Canadian books for children in grades three and four. Kerry Wood's *Samson's long ride* (1968) has as its hero an appealing ten-year-old Indian boy who runs away from a mission school to find his father's band before winter sets in. His tracking skill takes him 400 miles and his courage permits his survival against the onslaught of winter. Illustrations in colour and a more attractive format might have made this an outstanding book. Janet Lunn's *Double spell* (1968) is an attractively produced and well-written fantasy for the same age group. By means of a doll purchased in an antique shop on Yonge Street, Toronto, the twins are able to break a destructive spell that possesses their newly acquired family house on the shores of Lake Ontario.

Several books simply ring the changes on old themes. Cliff Faulknor's *The smoke horse* (1968) continued the adventures of the Indian boys he first wrote about in *The white calf* and *The white peril*. Perhaps because the boys are grown up in this book they have lost their freshness and ebullience. Christie Harris's *Forbidden frontier* (1968) was another novel of the past dealing with white-Indian relations, and Fred Swayze's *Fire over Huronia* (1968) was a rather factual story of a boy who learns the Huron language to become an interpreter for the French at Fort Ste Marie. Mystery stories were of more interest for their settings than for their pace, action, and credibility. Edmund Cosgrove's *The terror of the tar sands* (1968) had heroes and villains rushing around the northern woods in Ontario, while Nora Perez's *Strange summer at Stratford* (1968) was refreshing in its look at urban children in the setting of the Stratford Shakespearean Festival, if not for its plot. More firmly set in background and event was Lucy Berton Woodward's *Kidnapped in the Yukon* (1968). A more unusual book was Kay Hill's *And to-morrow the stars: the story of John Cabot* (1968), which combines fact and fiction. Cabot's early life is presented in fictional form, since the facts of his early life are unknown, and his later life is presented as biography. The result, while interesting, is overly long and crowded with unnecessary detail. Marjorie Wilkins Campbell's *The savage river: seventy-one days with Simon Fraser* (1968), although slightly fictionalized, is firmly based on Fraser's *Journals*. This is volume 33 in the Great Stories of Canada series and, as usual, one regrets the lack of source material references, a bibliography, and an index.

Considering that poetry is such a dynamic part of modern Canadian literature, it is both surprising and disappointing that we have not had some attempts at verse-writing for children in the mood of Robert Louis Stevenson's *A child's garden of verses* and A. A. Milne's *When we were very young*. Our one modern attempt at such writing by a single author is Jean Little's *When the pie was opened* (1968), which is unfortunately marred by inept versifying and a highly sentimental tone. (The tone especially is reminiscent of her novels for children, such as *Take wing*

(1968), the story of a ten-year-old girl who bears alone, almost to the end of the book, the burdens of a younger retarded brother.) However, 1968 saw the publication of two anthologies for children selected from the general stock of Canadian poetry. *The enchanted land: Canadian poetry for young readers* (1968) was compiled by Thelma R. Lower and Frederick W. COGSWELL and drew on a fairly wide range of poets, though the selections were obviously chosen for their 'niceness' rather than their vitality, and the overall content was not helped by a text-bookish format.

The high point of the year, and indeed of the years since, was the publication of *The wind has wings: poems from Canada* (1968) compiled by Mary Alice Downie and Barbara Robertson and illustrated by Elizabeth Cleaver. The compilers sought Canadian poems that might interest children and found seventy-seven of them—from Eskimo chants to poems by KLEIN, REANEY, and LAYTON, and including the good old 'Shooting of Dan McGrew'—that should do just that; or at least most children should be able to find *something* they like in this attractive collection. The collage illustrations, in four colours and black-and-white, have brought Elizabeth Cleaver both national and international fame.

3. *1969*. Elizabeth Cleaver's colourful and authentic collages for two of our outstanding Indian legends have given us our most distinguished picture-storybooks. These are the famous west-coast Tsimshian legend *The mountain goats of Temlaham* (1969) and an east-coast Micmac legend *How summer came to Canada* (1969), both retold by William Toye.

Collage, but with a humorous Victorian touch, was used by Alan Suddon for his illustrations in *Cinderella* (1969). The retelling of a single fairy tale with new illustrations has proved a lucrative business in the United States and Great Britain, but outside of the three books mentioned here, this market has hardly been touched in Canada.

Also in the realm of folklore is *Sally go round the sun* (1969), a collection of songs, rhymes, and games sung and chanted by Canadian children, brought together by the noted collector of folksongs, Edith Fowke. Lavishly illustrated and given a predominant note of gaiety, it is a feast for child and adult. Musical scores are included.

Romance and sentiment are not usual in Canadian children's books, but they are in the foreground of Luella Creighton's *The hitching post* (1969), set in a small Ontario town that seems to have a slight haze of unreality. This story of a little girl who befriends a recluse, inherits a cache of fifty-cent pieces, and as a result finds her mother (who has suffered from amnesia), is even more unreal; but somehow the reader suspends disbelief.

Genuine fantasy—rare in our literature—is the prerogative of a young British Columbian, Ruth Nichols, in *A walk out of the world* (1969). This is fantasy in the Tolkien sense—the creation of an 'other world'. A sister and brother, Judith and Tobit, become involved in high adventure with a rich and inventive host of characters and fight evil as Judith of the fair hair and green eyes becomes the talisman for restoring ancient royalty to its proper place. Though Miss Nichols did not write this, or her remarkable second novel—*The marrow of the world* (1972)—for children, they will certainly have a strong appeal for the intelligent, imaginative child.

The great majority of children's novels conform to a type that is vaguely defined as realistic fiction. The American children's novel leans heavily on subjects that would have been taboo about fifteen years ago—divorce, drugs, cruelty, mental illness, alcoholism, homosexuality, etc.—and tends to eschew characterization, plot, and descriptive settings. (An example of this kind of writing is Marilyn Sachs's *The bear's house*.) Practically all the above themes have been avoided by Canadian novelists for children, but this is not to say that they have avoided reality. David WALKER is perhaps our best example of a writer who is almost introspective in his search for the truth about his characters, but who also keeps to the traditional novel form. His *Dragon Hill* (1963) has an 'old-hat' theme—the crusty, terrifying, curmudgeon tamed by children—but it is rooted in the moral problems of the real world, not the storybook one—problems of friendship, prejudice, hatred, and sacrifice. *Pirate Rock* (1969) also has a conventional plot—a John Buchan-type spy story—set against the magnificent background of the Bay of Fundy. But the villain is not completely villainous; the boys who trap him feel also that they have betrayed him; and the adults in the story, especially the parents, exist as people outside of their parental role. Walker's sure hold on reality is seen even in his book for younger children, *Big Ben* (1969). Ben is a St Bernard, who finally proves that he is courageous as well as gentle. But this is a family story rather than a 'dog' story. Although a neighbour's accusation that Ben has killed a sheep brings the book to a climax, Walker gives his usual twist to the conventional, and so the real meaning of the story is to be found in the family relationships. Did the author really intend to make Ben a living example of the father's philosophy? No matter. He has shown again that he can deal with the complexities of human nature in a simple action story. There is less action and more didacticism in John Craig's novel for older children *No word for good-bye* (1969), although it stands up well in comparison with many American novels with a similar theme —race relations. A white boy discovers the degrading treatment of a band of Ojibways by the residents of a summer colony close to Winnipeg and the uncaring treatment of a large land-owning company. The boy and his father try to help the Indians, but fail. When the boy returns to his cottage at Thanksgiving to keep a fishing appointment with his Indian friend, the whole band has disappeared without leaving word of their whereabouts; there is no word for good-bye in Ojibway. John Craig's earlier book, *The long-return* (1959), was an equally thoughtful book about Indians, although set in the past. Here is a moving account of Indian family life in which a white boy reluctantly decides to escape from the tribe that has kidnapped him and a family that has adopted him and that he has come to love.

Career books, as a sub-section of the general umbrella group called realistic fiction, should come to terms with practicalities. In many ways Christie Harris's *Let X be excitement* (1969) does just that as she describes a young man's struggle (based on fact) to find out what he wants to be (a research engineer cum pilot) and eventually to fulfil his ambition. However, the protagonist is a curiously unsympathetic person. Far from experiencing a human confrontation with uncertainty and difficulty, he exhibits a cold, hard, logical drive and an ability to write letters to the right people at the right time.

Generally speaking, Canadian writers of history and biography for children have tended to eschew plain facts, no matter how dramatic and significant these may be, in favour of larding events with manufactured conversations—an in-between approach that juggles history and historical fiction all in the same book. Such is Iris Allan's *White Sioux: the story of Major Walsh of the Mounted Police* (1969). This biographical novel is detailed, accurate—and dull. Did Major Walsh, the great friend of the Indians, really address the famous Sitting Bull as 'Bull'? Once in a while the fictionalization technique can be successful, as is shown in Delbert A. Young's *Last voyage of the Unicorn* (1969), about Captain Munck's voyage of 1619 in search of the Northwest Passage. The story is told by a fifteen-year-old boy, Niels Olsen, who really did sail on the tragic voyage and was one of the three (out of a crew of sixty) who returned.

4. *1970. Wiggle to the laundromat* (1970) by the poet Dennis LEE is certainly our most 'mod'-looking picturebook to date. Great swirling drawings in black and white (by Charles Pachter) accompany Lee's nonsense verses, and all is contained in an outsize format. Some of the poems, containing many Canadian references, sound amusing when read aloud and there is the occasional perfect line, but the writer has forgotten that genuine nonsense is firmly rooted in sense. Ronald Melzack's second book of Eskimo tales, *Raven, creator of the world* (1970), tells of the great Eskimo hero in cyclic form. Both the simplicity of the telling and the lavishness of the illustrations by Laszlo Gal make this an outstanding picture-storybook for younger children. The vigorous coloured illustrations depict action and strength and are a sharp contrast to the more static native Eskimo drawings to which we are generally accustomed. Kay Hill's second volume of Micmac legends (the first was published in 1963), *More Glooscap stories: legends of the Wabanaki Indians* (1970), offers successful retellings for younger children. *Shogomac Sam* (1970) by Laurie McLaughlin also belongs to the legend tradition. It tells of the New Brunswick logging hero Main John Glazier (kin to Paul Bunyan) and his younger helper Shogomac Sam, 'and how he set out to find his name and found out somethin' more instead.' The cartoon-like drawings by Randy Jones add to the light-heartedness of the tale. The story is more properly described as a 'tall tale'—an art form that has flourished in the United

States where such western folk heroes as Davey Crockett, Johnny Appleseed, Buffalo Bill, and Pecos Bill have been exaggerated into modern legends. Canadians tend to say with Mr Gradgrind, 'Stick to the facts, sir', and so all extravagances have been culled from our approach to our famous figures. However, *Shogomac Sam* is great good fun.

As well as needing more 'tall tales', we could also use a few more pieces of creative historical writing for younger children, stories of the quality of William Toye's *Cartier discovers the St Lawrence* (1970). The text—which is partly based on passages in Toye's *The St Lawrence* and has many extracts from Biggar's *Voyages of Jacques Cartier*—is notable for combining simplicity and historicity. The emphasis on browns and yellows in Laszlo Gal's full-colour illustrations, and the clean, almost stylized lines of his drawings, give an overall impression that one is reading a story rather than a history book.

The disappointment of the year was Margaret LAURENCE's first book for children, an animal fantasy called *Jason's quest* (1970). Of all forms of writing, animal fantasy is the most difficult. A few fantasies are children's classics (*The wind in the willows*, *The jungle book*, and E. B. White's *Charlotte's web* are obvious examples), but great numbers of them never succeed in achieving suspension of disbelief in the reader and so fall into deserved oblivion. That *Jason's quest* is slow-moving and didactic is almost of less importance than the fact that the animals are completely anthropomorphic—we don't know they are animals until we are told. This genre is at its best when the writer is able to preserve the animals' innate characteristics while endowing them with human speech and emotions. Even the illustrations in this book are fuzzy—mere pale imitations of Ernest Shepard's famous drawings for *The wind in the willows*.

The more conventional Canadian children's novel was represented by W. Towrie Cutt's *On the trail of Long Tom* (1970). The story is set in the days of the Red River Rebellion. A boy is caught in conflicting loyalties between his Indian and Scottish backgrounds. As with most of our historical novels for children, the history in this book cannot be faulted, and it is more clearly fiction than most because the author does not depend completely on historical events to carry the plot.

Jean Little has a strong following among adults and children who like the simplistic and the sentimental. Her *Look through my window* (1970) describes how an only child learns to live with and love a larger family. The intent is laudable, but the machinery creaks and the language falters.

5. *1971*. Canadian publishers can rarely afford the high costs of colour and other production expenses necessary to produce the kind of colourful picturebooks that are issued in such numbers by English and American publishers—over-illustrated, many of them, with texts that are flat and cold. Chip Young's *The little hen of Huronia* (1971) is less pretentious and far more satisfactory than many of our imports. Light and humorous, it tells of the little hen's contribution to our history as she provides sustenance for Jesuit missionaries. Less successful is Mr Young's *Foxy grandpa* (1971), even though it deals with our national sport. Unfortunately it misses great opportunities for humour because the hockey-playing animals do not keep any of their animal characteristics and come out as mere parodies of players in any league. The drawings, with their daubs of colour, are cartoon-like. The colour illustrations are the outstanding feature of Ann Blades' *Mary of Mile 18* (1971). With a brief and gentle text they show us the daily round of a child's life in northern British Columbia, its harshness somewhat reduced when she is allowed to keep a pup that has proved its worth to the family. Also for younger children is an Eskimo story by James Houston, *Wolf run* (1971), more simply told than his previous books.

Many books written for adults have been 'taken over' by children. The classical examples, of course, are *Robinson Crusoe* and *Swiss family Robinson* and in our own time and country the animal stories of Roberts and Seton and Farley Mowat's *The dog who wouldn't be*. As these are books that initially defy categorization as being either for children or adults, all too often they remain unknown to both groups of readers. Two recent examples, both beautifully produced and illustrated, are Shizuye Takashima's *A child in prison camp* (1971) and Pitseolak's *Pictures out of my life* (1971). Takashima, now a distinguished artist (as the water-colour paintings in this book show), spent two years in an internment camp in British Columbia as a child during the Second World War.

Her book conveys very much a child's viewpoint with devastating objectivity and bewilderment but with no note of bitterness. Pitseolak (meaning Sea Pigeon in Eskimo) is also an accomplished artist. Older than Takashima, she makes us see what it was like to be young in an environment that was harsh, yet in which the simplicity of life was easier to handle than the complexities of the present imposed by the white man. The text is in both Eskimo and English and the illustrations, in black-and-white and stunning colour, are as satisfying as her memoir, which was recorded on tape, translated, and then adapted by Dorothy Eber.

These are unusual books. More regular offerings for children are *River of stars* (1971) by Jean MacKenzie, *Voyage into danger* (1971) by Ted Ashlee, and *Honor bound* (1971) by Mary Alice and John Downie. *River of stars* is a tough, outdoor, masculine, Indian/white-tension story set in northern British Columbia. With very little literary merit, it almost commands attention by its honesty and bluntness alone. *Voyage into danger* is a story of intrigue in B.C.'s coastal waters; it has a priggish hero (he is *so* good at everything), an unbelievable plot, and a cast of stereotyped heroes. The villains are almost a welcome relief. *Honor bound*, although set in the aftermath of the American Revolution and describing the trials of a hard-pressed Loyalist family who eventually reach a farm near Kingston, is a far gentler narrative than either of the books with a modern setting—perhaps because it has a more fully developed set of characters and a more plausible storyline. Jean Little's *Kate* (1971) is a dreary sequel to her *Look through my window* (1970). The problems of being a child of a Jewish father and a gentile mother are discussed in a manufactured and unchildlike way. Children are far less concerned with religious problems than most adults think.

The realistic Canadian animal story, which has its tradition in the works of Seton and Roberts, has continued to develop and forms a strong part of our literature. The wolf in Helene Widell's *The Black wolf of River Bend* (1971) doesn't meet the normal death in the wilderness: as he follows the children of a family he has adopted he is shot by drunken gun-happy hunters in front of the children. Cameron Langford's *The winter of the fisher* (1971) is a lyrical, almost mystical full-length animal biography that takes place completely in the forest, with the fisher escaping his fate for the time being and winning the respect of both Indian woodsman and white trapper.

Some children's books involve animals but are not, strictly speaking, animal stories. In many such cases the young heroes or heroines learn something about themselves through the training and care of their animals. In Adelaide Leitch's *The blue roan* (1971) the horse is the agent through which a boy comes to terms with himself.

Biographies for children have often suffered from both sins of omission and commission on the part of the biographer. Frequently facts are omitted that might detract from the subject's pristine image; even more frequently thoughts and conversations are invented to impose a 'story' format upon plain fact. Canadian Lives (1971) is a new series of biographies for older children that simply 'play it straight', giving the biographer's interpretation based upon findable evidence and not neglecting anecdotes and a fair amount of social background. To date the series includes: *James Douglas* by Dorothy Blakey Smith; *David Thompson* by James K. Smith; *John A. Macdonald* by Donald Swainson; *Wilfrid Laurier* by Barbara Robertson; *Louis Riel* by Hartwell Bowsfield; *William Lyon Mackenzie* and *John Strachan* by David Flint; and *Alexander Mackenzie* by Roy Daniells. All are by highly qualified experts on the man and the times; they are brief (up to 160 pages), have good contemporary photographs as illustrations, indexes, bibliographies; and are published in paperback.

6. *1972.* A musical mouse who inadvertently contributed to the composition of 'Silent Night' is the anti-hero of Jack Richards' *Johann's gift to Christmas* (1972). Len Norris's drawings, in full colour and sepia, are a surprising switch from his famous political cartoons. But his real land of mountainous Switzerland and his make-believe world of charming mice add up to a most satisfying picturebook. Chip Young's *Honky, the Christmas goose* (1972) is less successful. The text is a bit of a re-hash of 'Rudolf, the Red-Nosed Reindeer' and the illustrations by Louise Sheppard alternate in a bewildering manner between pastel in many colours and bold black, white, and red. Lyn Cook's *Toys from the sky* (1972) is another Christmas

book, but the suggestion of the Christmas story as it is conveyed in an Eskimo setting is not true to the Eskimo or to the real spirit of Christmas. *The Saturday party* (1972) by Anne McKechnie, for slightly older children, is a collection of three tales told by a perfectionist grandmother to her grandchildren—one tale for each child. The stories are pleasant enough, but they lack finesse and memorability.

It is perhaps gratuitous to point out that our children's libraries are exceptionally rich in folklore of all cultures. Leslie Quinton's *The lucky coin and other folk tales Canadians tell* (1972) brings together established tales—including Indian, Eskimo, and French Canadian—from the many nationalities that help make the 'Canadian mosaic'. Although the book does contain ethnic notes, only in one case is the source of a story acknowledged. The pen name 'Quinton' has been used for three Canadian writers of children's books—Madeline A. Freeman, Lyn Harrington, and Audrey McKim, the compilers of this anthology. A firmer pedigree and a more substantial achievement are shown in *Tales from the igloo* (1972), a collection of the traditional tales of the Copper Eskimos edited and translated by Father Maurice Métayer. The humour and drama of the stories are revealed both actively and symbolically in the brightly coloured drawings by Agnes Nanogak. The author of *Ningiyuk's igloo world* (1972), Anna Rokeby Thomas, spent several years among the Ekaluktuk tribe near St George's Mission on Victoria Island. Her story has a modern touch in the distress of a little Eskimo girl when she learns she has been adopted. A clash of cultures can be sensed as the old grandmother tells Ningiyuk stories similar to those in *Tales from the igloo*, while at Christmas and Easter the band journeys to the mission church for Christian services. However, it is refreshing to have a modern Eskimo story, and one about a girl at that. Both the Eskimo and the Indian world are brought beautifully and sensitively to life in *Songs of the dream people: chants and images from the Indians and Eskimos of North America* (1972), edited and illustrated by James Houston. The designs and drawings are perfect foils for the poetry, which is remarkably varied in mood and style and impact. This is a book for everyone. Houston's *Ghost paddle: a Northwest Coast Indian tale* (1972) is in the outstanding tradition of his Eskimo legends and has more of a story quality than his earlier Indian legend *Eagle mask* (1966). Less successful is Alex Grisdale's *Wild drums: tales and legends of the Plains Indians* (1972) as told to Nan Shipley. The material here is valid and interesting, but it is still in a raw state: it needed rewriting and refining to hold the attention of young readers.

Another unusual theme is a First-World-War story by Tom and Christie Harris, *Mule Lib* (1972). As a very young soldier Tom Harris was put in charge of 'The Big Gray', the most obstinate mule in the army. This picture of the life of an ordinary soldier has considerable authenticity, but it lacks the spark and cohesion to lift it above mediocrity.

Mrs Harris's *Secret in the Stlalakum wild* (1972) lies within the new stream of fantasy writing—that is, fantasy with a purpose above the traditional struggle between good and evil. Here a young girl is persuaded by Indian spirits—'the Stlalakum'—to join the battle for conservation. In the process she finds herself and her role within her family. Ruth Nichols' second fantasy, *The marrow of the world* (1972), takes us into a strange new world beneath a lake. The promise shown in her first book, *A walk out of the world*, is here more than fulfilled. Both *Secret in the Stlalakum wild* and *The marrow of the world* owe much to their Canadian settings—the former to the mountainous land of British Columbia and the latter to the 'autumn magic' of the Georgian Bay area where Ruth Nichols spent part of her childhood. W. Towrie Cutt's *Message from Arkmae* (1972), our most unusual fantasy to date, combines the major appeal of both the above books. Seals in the waters of the Orkney Islands are being hunted with guns and captured for scientific observation. The boys who are trying to protect them meet the Finman, survivor of a legendary race, who issues an awesome warning to mankind for their depredation of animal life. A marvellously told, haunting tale.

Robber's roost (1972) by Carl Barton is an example of our typical out-of-doors mystery tale. The setting is an island off the coast of British Columbia and the young 'detectives' learn not to judge people too quickly. It has an attractive paperback format. John Craig's *Zack* (1972) is thoroughly in the modern stream of writing for the young as an Indian boy, a black boy, and a white girl (artful conjunction!) search to find themselves and their place in the sun. While no better than most of its American counterparts, its itinerant look at Canada saves it from banality.

An interesting new publishing concept is represented by New Children's Drama (New Press, Toronto). The first three books in this attractively produced series are one-act musical plays by Dodi Robb and Pat Patterson, who have had great success in their work with Susan Rubes's Young People's Theatre in Toronto. *The dandy lion*, *The popcorn man*, and *Red Riding Hood* all appeared in 1972 and invite productions far and wide—with permission, of course. *The clam made a face* by Eric Nicol, which was also produced by the Young People's Theatre, was published in 1973.

7. *Book-of-the-Year medals.* This award, in the form of a bronze medal, is presented by the Canadian Association of Children's Librarians for the best children's book by a Canadian author. Only awards for English-language books are listed here. (See CHILDREN'S BOOKS IN FRENCH for the French-language awards of the Association canadienne des bibliothèques.) For several years the award was given two years after the date of publication.

1947 *Starbuck valley winter* by Roderick L. Haig-Brown. New York, Morrow, 1943.
1948 *Kristli's trees* by Mabel Dunham. Toronto, McClelland and Stewart, 1948.
1949 No award.
1950 *Franklin of the arctic* by Richard S. Lambert. Toronto, McClelland and Stewart, 1949.
1951 No award.
1952 *The sun horse* by Catherine Anthony Clark. Toronto, Macmillan, 1951.
1953 No award.
1954 No award.
1955 No award.
1956 *Train for Tiger Lily* by Louise Riley. Toronto, Macmillan, 1954.
1957 *Glooskap's country and other Indian tales* by Cyrus Macmillan. Toronto, Oxford University Press, 1955.
1958 *Lost in the barrens* by Farley Mowat. Toronto, Little, Brown, 1956.
1959 *The dangerous cove* by John F. Hayes. Toronto, Copp Clark, 1957.
1960 *The golden phoenix and other French-Canadian fairy tales* by Marius Barbeau. Retold by Michael Hornyansky. Toronto, Oxford University Press, 1958.
1961 *The St Lawrence* by William Toye. Toronto, Oxford University Press, 1959.
1962 No award.
1963 *The incredible journey: a tale of three animals* by Sheila Burnford. Toronto, Little, Brown, 1961.
1964 *The whale people* by Roderick L. Haig-Brown. London, Collins, 1962.
1965 *Tales of Nanabozho* by Dorothy M. Reid. Toronto, Oxford University Press, 1963.
*1966 *The double knights: more tales from round the world* by James McNeill. Toronto, Oxford University Press, 1964.
*1966 *Tikta'liktak: an Eskimo legend* by James Houston. Toronto, Longman Canada, 1965.
1967 *Raven's cry* by Christie Harris. Toronto, McClelland and Stewart, 1966.
1968 *The white archer: an Eskimo legend* by James Houston. Toronto, Longman Canada, 1967.
1969 *And to-morrow the stars: the story of John Cabot* by Kay Hill. New York, Dodd, Mead, 1968.
1970 *Sally go round the sun: 300 songs, rhymes and games of Canadian children* by Edith Fowke. Toronto, McClelland and Stewart, 1969.
1971 *Cartier discovers the St Lawrence* by William Toye. Toronto, Oxford University Press, 1970.
1972 *Mary of Mile 18* by Ann Blades. Montreal, Tundra Books, 1971.

AMELIA HOWARD-GIBBON AWARD (FOR ILLUSTRATION)

1971 *The wind has wings: poems from Canada* compiled by Mary Alice Downie and Barbara Robertson. Illustrated by Elizabeth Cleaver. Toronto, Oxford University Press, 1968.
1972 *A child in prison camp* by Shizuye Takashima. Montreal, Tundra Books, 1971. SE

*Two awards in the same year because of a change of policy in award procedure.

Children's books in French

Children's books in French. The sparse record of publication and the unoriginal and on the whole undistinguished quality of the books might very well lead us to believe that the publishing of children's books has not had much interest for Québec publishers and writers. This is in spite of the fact that since 1957 there has been the encouragement of three literary prizes for the writing of children's books—those of the Association canadienne des Éducateurs de Langue française, the Association canadienne des bibliothèques, and the Province of Québec.

A surprising number of the novels published in Québec for young people are detective- and science-fiction. Yves THÉRIAULT is a popular writer of the former—e.g. *Le secret du Mufjarti* (1965) and *Le château des petits hommes verts* (1966)—and Maurice Gagnon of the latter (*Unipax intervient* (1965) and *Les savants réfractaires* (1965).) Thériault's hero is a Canadian secret-service agent, Volpek, who bears a strong resemblance to James Bond. Gagnon's Unipax is an international organization that can on occasion step in between the great powers in the interests of world peace. Monique Corriveau also writes detective stories. *Le maître de Messire* (1965) and *Max* (1965) are two unpretentious, lively tales that take place in and around Quebec City.

In 1967 Thériault published a new Volpek exploit, *La bête à 300 têtes*, and Gagnon another Unipax adventure, *Alerte dans le Pacifique*. Henriette Major's fantasy *Le club des curieux* (1967)—about a little girl who can go through her mirror by saying her name backwards—is a story that brims over with fancy, surprise, and humour. The best book of 1967 was *Le drame au pays des Touareg* by Régine Delabit, an adventure in the African desert that is exotic and well written, though it would have benefited by a little more substance. Paule Daveluy's novel *Cet hiver-là* (1967) is a rather sentimental romance for teenaged girls.

1968 saw the publication of only nine books for young people, including four detective stories, and three novels of the future. Yves Thériault published his last two Volpek entertainments: *Les pieuvres* (1968) and *Les vampires de la rue Monsieur-le-Prince* (1968). Maurice Gagnon wound up the activities of Unipax in *Un complot à Washington* (1968) and *Servax à la rescousse* (1968). Monique Corriveau's *Max au rallye* (1968) is a further investigation by her young Québec doctor-hero (Mrs Corriveau also published a picture-storybook, *Cécile*, in 1968) and Rolande Lacerte's *Le soleil des profondeurs* (1968), set in the twenty-first century, is an imaginative account of what happens when scientists do away with night. Madeleine M. Des Rivières's *Ronde autour de mon pays* (1968) is a pleasing collection of French-Canadian folktales.

1969 saw the publication of Yves Thériault's *L'or de la felouque*, set in the Baie Comeau region of the north shore of the St Lawrence. The vigorous and highly coloured narrative is as much a portrayal of the lives of young adults today as a tale of a treasure hunt. The leading role is played by the St Lawrence itself. A new publishing house, Éditions Toundra, published *L'aïeule qui venait de Dworitz* (1969) by Ethel Vineberg (translated by Jacques de Roussan), the engaging story of a Jewish family that came from Europe in the last century and took root in Canada. Another novel set in Canada is Henriette Major's *A la conquête du temps* (1970) illustrated by Louise Roy-Kerrigan, which goes back in time to the year 1669 and offers a good guide to the life and customs of the first years of Ville Marie. The same author's picturebook *La surprise de Dame Chenille* (1970) combines charm, poetry, and humour, and is happily illustrated by Claude Lafortune and J. L. Frund.

Five novels by boys and girls of high-school age—none of them very good—were published in 1971: *Opium en fraude* by Robert Chavarie, *Crimes à la glace* by Pierre-Sylvain Fournier; *Feuilles de thym et fleurs d'amour*, a love story about rabbits by Michelle Jacob; *Au clair de la lune* by Marie Plante; and *La mystérieuse boule de feu* by Louis Sutal.

1972 was a somewhat more prolific year, with fourteen books published—four science fiction, two detective novels, five picture-storybooks, a biography, and two adventure stories. *Le trou* by Sylvain Chapdelaine is a poetic yet realistic illustrated story that is particularly worthy of mention. The biography is *Bernier capitaine à 17 ans* by Gilberte Tremblay, about Joseph-Elzéar Bernier (1852–1934), who made important arctic patrols in government and non-government vessels. It offers interesting and enjoyable reading. Three picturebooks published by Leméac are humorous, well illustrated, and atmospheric: *Petitou et les pommiers* and *Petitou et le printemps* by Louise Pomminville and *Le petit chocola cho* by Rita Scalabrini. Another recent and charming picture-storybook, illustrated in colour by Cécile Chabot, is the Christmas story by Simone Bussières: *Le petit sapin qui a poussé sur une étoile* (1972).

The Book-of-the-Year awards for French-language books given by the Association canadienne des bibliothèques are listed below.

1954 *Le vénérable François de Montmorency-Laval* by Emile Gervais. Montreal, Comité des Fondateurs de l'Église canadienne, 1952.
1958 *Chevalier du roi* by Béatrice Clément. Montreal, Éditions de l'Atelier, 1955.
1959 *Un drôle de petit cheval* by Hélène Flamme. Montreal, Leméac, 1957.
1960 *L'été enchanté* by Paule Daveluy. Montreal, Éditions de l'Atelier, 1958.
1961 *Plantes vagabondes* by Marcelle Gauvreau. Montreal, Centre de Psychologie et de Pédagogie, 1959.
1962 *Les Iles du roi Maha-Maha II: conte fantaisiste* by Claude Aubry. Quebec, Éditions du Pélican, 1960.
1963 *Drôle d'automne* by Paule Daveluy. Montreal, Éditions du Pélican.
1964 *Féerie: conte du jour de l'an* by Cécile Chabot. Montreal, Fides, 1962.
1965 *Le loup de Noël* by Claude Aubry. Illustrated by E. Perret. Montreal, Centre de Psychologie et de Pédagogie, 1962.
1966 *Le Wapiti* by Monique Corriveau. Quebec, Éditions Jeunesse, 1964.
1967 No award.
1968 *Légendes Indiennes du Canada* by Claude Melançon. Montreal, Éditions du Jour, 1967.
1969 No award.
1970 *La merveilleuse histoire de la naissance* by Lionel Gendron. Montreal, Éditions de l'Homme, 1969.
1971 *La surprise de Dame Chenille* by Henriette Major. Montreal, Centre de Psychologie et de Pédagogie, 1970.
1972 No award. AB

Chodos, Robert. See POLITICAL WRITINGS IN ENGLISH I.

Choquette, Robert (1905–). Born in Manchester, N.H., he came to Montreal with his parents in 1913. He was educated at the Collège Notre-Dame, the Collège de Saint-Laurent, and Loyola College. After being a reporter on the Montreal *Gazette* (1927), he became editor of *La Revue moderne* (1928–30) and secretary-librarian of the École des Beaux-Arts (1928–31). From 1932 to 1961 he was a free-lance playwright for radio and television and in 1963–4 was an associate commissioner of the Centennial Commission in Ottawa. In 1965 he was appointed Canadian consul-general in Bordeaux, France, and from 1968 to 1970 held the post of Canadian ambassador to Argentina, Uruguay, and Paraguay. From 1971 to 1972 he was special adviser to Information Canada.

Choquette's first collection of poetry, *À travers les vents* (1925), was regarded as revolutionary. Some critics were impressed by his vitality, picturesque imagery, and freedom of expression; others were shocked, particularly by his disregard for points of syntax. This work was awarded the Prix David in 1926. His *Metropolitan Museum* (1930), described by André Maurois in his preface as being of truly epic breadth and beauty and since then acclaimed as a veritable 'fresco of civilization', won the same award in 1932. *Poésies nouvelles* followed in 1933. Twenty years later his famous *Suite marine* (1953) appeared, and its place as the greatest collective poem of French Canada was at once recognized by the Académie française with the award of its Prix de Poésie; the same work received in 1956 both the Prix David and the Prix Edgar Poe (Paris). In 1954 the ensemble of his work was awarded the Prix Duvernay, and for his *Oeuvres poétiques* (2 vols, 1956) he once again received the Prix David; this definitive collection of his work marks the high point and the culmination of the classical poetic style in French Canada.

Choquette has also been outstanding as a novelist of manners. *La pension Leblanc* (1927), *Le curé de village* (1936), *Les Velder* (1941)—with a preface by André Maurois—and *Elise Velder* (1958) have been made into highly popular radio and television serials. His play *Elise Velder* was produced in 1940 and *Le curé de village* was made into a film in 1949.

Choquette is a member of P.E.N. International and one of the founding members and the present vice-president of the Académie canadienne-française. He is also president of the Société des écrivains canadiens and a member of the Société des poètes canadiens-français and of the Société des auteurs dramatiques. In France he is a member of the Académie Ronsard, the Société des poètes français, and many other literary associations. In 1959 he received the gold medal of the lieutenant-governor of Québec for his outstanding contributions to radio and television, and the Prix international des amitiés françaises (Paris) in 1962. He was proclaimed 'Prince des poètes du Canada français' for life by the Société des poètes canadiens-français in 1961. He was made a Companion of the Order of Canada in 1969 and received an honorary LL.D from the Université de Sherbrooke in 1972.

A bibliography and a representative selection of his poetry and prose are given in *Robert Choquette* (1959) by André Melançon. *Robert Choquette* (1972) by Renée Legris is a critical study of his work. Translations of his poetry are in *The poetry of French Canada in translation* (1970) edited by John GLASSCO.

JG

Cité libre. See LITERARY MAGAZINES IN FRENCH.

Clark, Andrew Hill. See HISTORY STUDIES IN ENGLISH 2.

Clark, Helen S. See INDIAN LEGENDS AND ART.

Clark, Jane. See HISTORY STUDIES IN ENGLISH 17.

Clark, Lovell C. See HISTORY STUDIES IN ENGLISH 7.

Clark, S. D. (1910–). Samuel Delbert Clark was born in Lloydminister, Alta, and educated at the Universities of Saskatchewan, McGill, Toronto, and at the London School of Economics. He was appointed a lecturer in sociology and political science at the University of Manitoba in 1937 and the next year joined the staff of the University of Toronto as a lecturer in sociology. In 1943–4 he was a Guggenheim Fellow at Columbia University and the University of Chicago. In 1954 he was promoted to the rank of professor and in 1963 became the first chairman of the department of sociology at the University of Toronto. He was a visiting professor of sociology at the University of California (Berkeley) in 1960–1, at Dartmouth College for the spring term of 1967, at the University of Sussex in 1970–1, and at Dalhousie University in 1972–3. In 1953 he was elected a fellow of the Royal Society of Canada.

Clark has been in the forefront of the growth of sociology as an academic discipline in Canada and a leading exponent of interdisciplinary studies—especially in the relationship between history and sociology. In *The social development of Canada: an introductory study with selected documents* (1942) he examined the role of the frontier in the development of Canadian society in an effort to show how change in new areas of growth had effects upon the whole society. Clark's emphasis on social change, examined within a historical context, involved a break from accepted modes of study in sociology—where the concern was with problems of order and the development of universal patterns of social behaviour—and from accepted modes of study in history, where the stress was upon the uniqueness of societies and generalizations were ignored. In *Church and sect in Canada* (1948), a study of the period 1760–1900, he theorizes that churches are successful only in stable, established societies where they act as a conservative, cohesive force, while on the frontier, sects spring up in dissatisfaction with the old social order and with formal religion. *Movements of political protest in Canada, 1640–1840* (1959)—in the ten-volume series Social Credit in Alberta of which Clark was the editor—attempts to show that there was no essential difference between American and Canadian frontier radical movements, that they originated on the North American continent, and that responsible government was a reaction rather than a positive response to the democratic spirit of the Canadian people. *The developing Canadian community* (1962; revised in 1968 with six additional chapters) contains a collection of essays, mostly published previously, illustrating the progression of Clark's thought over his thirty-year career. His theories on the frontier, religion, the formative influences in social change, and history's role in sociology are well represented. He cautions that, while sociologists must use history, theory should not be forgotten; the results of research must be judged on the merits of their theoretical significance.

Clark is editor of *Urbanism and the changing Canadian society* (1961)—seven essays by various University of Toronto sociologists on urban and suburban problems—to which he contributed an essay debunking the myth of the suburban stereotype. This theme is expanded in *The suburban society* (1966) where he emphasizes that suburbanism is a process essentially of the transformation of the country into the city, and that this process differs at different times and in different places. DF

Clarke, Austin C. (1932–). Born in Barbados and educated at the University of Toronto, he taught school in Barbados before immigrating to Canada in 1956. He has lectured at Yale, Brandeis, and Duke Universities. In 1973 he was appointed to the Metropolitan Toronto Library Board. He also writes scripts for the Canadian Broadcasting Corporation.

Clarke has reason for the underlying bitterness of his novels and stories. He writes vividly of the subsistence level to which the cane-sugar workers of his native island are reduced by seasonal labour, brutal overseers, and the way in which their own people, who have risen through politics, turn a deaf ear to their protests. These workers pin their hopes on education for their children and on an impression that Canada is a land of instant success. Clarke, however, is too good a writer to stop short at bitterness. His writing is leavened by humour, compassion, and generosity of spirit; his scenes and the idiosyncrasies of his characters are full of life.

The survivors of the crossing (1964), Clarke's first novel, is about a plantation worker, a born leader though illiterate, who sparks a strike. The leader is betrayed partly by a friend who can read and partly by his fellow workers who are threatened with the loss of their jobs. Escape to Canada seems the only solution for him. *Among thistles and thorns* (1965) covers two days in the life of a nine-year-old Barbadian boy for whom the poverty and degradation of his people are intolerable. Although he dreams of leaving the island, he seems to have all the characteristics of someone who will stay and eventually lead his fellows in a revolt. *The meeting point* (1967) portrays Bernice Leach, a Barbadian who comes to Toronto as a maid for an unhappy Jewish family; her lazy, self-centred sister who visits her for the summer; and various immigrant groups. Beatrice finds snobbery among the educated immigrants who get good jobs and growing materialism among others; she also discovers that the black men she knows, who are disadvantaged by lack of education, are drawn towards the violence of black groups in the United States.

Most of the tales in Clarke's collection of short stories, *When he was free and young and he used to wear silks* (1971), are taken from or related to his novels; the title story, however, is an experiment in impressionism. NS

Clarkson, Stephen. See HISTORY STUDIES IN ENGLISH 12 and POLITICAL WRITINGS IN ENGLISH 4, 7, and 8.

Cleaver, Elizabeth. See CHILDREN'S BOOKS IN ENGLISH 2 and 3.

Clément, Gabriel. See HISTORY STUDIES IN FRENCH 8.

Cloutier, Cécile (1930–). Born in Quebec City, she was educated there and at the Sorbonne in Paris. On her return to Canada she taught at the University of Ottawa and is now professor of French at University College, University of Toronto.

Mains de sable, her first book of poetry, which appeared in 1960, was awarded the silver medal of the Société des écrivains français by a jury headed by Jean Cocteau. This and *Cuivres et soies* (1964) established Cécile Cloutier as a highly disciplined poet, spare and sometimes elliptical in style, with a gift for sharp and very individual metaphors. Most of the poems are exceedingly brief. Some simply capture an instant of time; others deal with such themes as solitude and isolation and a longing for love. Two more recent collections, *Cannelles et craies* (1969) and *Paupières* (1970), strike a more sensual note; there are poems of fulfilment and delight and even a few expressions of nationalist feeling, all marked by the same meticulous phrasing and choice of metaphor and cadence. English translations of some of Cécile Cloutier's poems are included in John GLASSCO's *The poetry of French Canada in translation* (1970) and in John Robert COLOMBO's *How do I love thee? sixty poets of Canada (and Quebec) select and introduce their work* (1970). JM

Cloutier, Eugène (1921–). Born in Sherbrooke, Qué., he was educated at Université Laval and at the Sorbonne in Paris. He worked for three years as a journalist and, apart from two years spent as head of the Maison des Étudiants in Paris, has devoted the last twenty-five years to writing novels, radio and television plays, and travel books.

His first novel, *Les témoins* (1953), which was awarded the Prix David, makes skilful use of dialogue as a man who has just murdered his mistress is judged by his conscience, which speaks to him in four voices, each representing a facet of his personality. *Les inutiles* (1956), winner of the Prix du Cercle du livre de France, is also a novel of dialogue, this time between two men who have escaped from an asylum and are trying to re-establish themselves in the modern industrialized and impersonalized world. *Croisière* (1964) consists of two dream fantasies. 'De nuit' has all the fleeting and inconsequential qualities of the dream during sleep, whereas 'De jour' resembles the daydream in which the dreamer is vaguely aware of his surroundings. Cloutier is also the author of two plays, 'Le dernier beatnik' and 'Hotel Hilton, Pekin', which have been published in *Écrits du Canada français* (vols 14 and 28).

Cloutier's account of his journey across Canada, *Le Canada sans passeport* (2 vols, 1967), which was abridged and translated by Joyce Marshall as *No passport: a discovery of Canada* (1968), is notable for its freshness of approach, its openness to new impressions and experience, and its abundance of humorous and telling incidents. Cloutier's other travel books are *Journées japonaises* (1969) and—in a series that is to include three more titles—*Eugène Cloutier en Tunisie* (1970), *Eugène Cloutier en Suède* (1971), *Eugène Cloutier en Roumanie* (1971), *Eugène Cloutier à Cuba* (1971), *Eugène Cloutier en Californie* (1971), *Eugène Cloutier en pays basque* (1972), *Eugène Cloutier en Yougoslavie* (1972), and *Eugène Cloutier au Chili* (1972). JM

Clutesi, George. See ANTHOLOGIES IN ENGLISH; CHILDREN'S BOOKS IN ENGLISH 1; and INDIAN LEGENDS AND ART.

Coates, Robert. See HISTORY STUDIES IN ENGLISH 12.

Cockburn, Robert. See LITERARY STUDIES IN ENGLISH 3 and POETRY IN ENGLISH 2.

Cocke, Emmanuel. See FICTION IN FRENCH 3.

Codere, Helen. See INDIANS 5.

Cogswell, Fred (1917–). Born in East Centreville, N.B., Frederick William Cogswell served in the Second World War and then completed his education at the Universities of New Brunswick and Edinburgh. He teaches English at the University of New Brunswick where he also edits the poetry magazine *Fiddlehead.* He has made a modern adaptation of *The testament of Cresseid* (1957) and is the compiler of the anthology *Five New Brunswick poets* (1962). In his poetry Cogswell employs many traditional verse forms to express his sense of fallen man. He has been most effective in a group of sonnets, *The stunted strong* (1954), in which he portrays the ingrown and unpleasant characters whose narrow outlook he attributes to puritanism and to the harsh environment of his native province. Cogswell's other books include *The haloed tree* (1955), *Descent from Eden* (1959), which contains poems from earlier work, and *Lost dimension* (1960).

Cogswell's poetry has not changed radically through the years. His later volumes—*Star people* (1968), *In praise of chastity* (1970), and *The Chains of Liliput* (1971)—are written in mainly traditional forms, although at times he uses free verse, especially in his portraits of people. Increasingly he meditates on time, particularly in the poems in which his own aging is the subject. He has a neat epigrammatic touch and occasionally shows sardonic humour.

In recent years Cogswell's energies have been devoted to publishing many volumes of poetry by his own press, the Fiddlehead Press, which has performed a useful function in encouraging new poets (he is suspending his publishing program at the end of 1973). He has also turned to translation. *One hundred poems of modern Quebec* (1970) and *A second hundred poems of modern Quebec* (1971) demonstrate his sympathy for a wide range of French-Canadian poets. With Thelma Lower he edited an anthology of Canadian poetry

for elementary schools: *The enchanted land: Canadian poetry for young readers* (1968).
PS/NS

Cohen, Leonard (1934–). Born in Montreal, he grew up in its affluent Westmount district. Shortly after graduating from McGill University he published his first book of poetry, *Let us compare mythologies* (1956). In the next few years he attempted graduate study at Columbia University, worked in his family's clothing business, and wrote an unpublished novel, *Ballet of lepers.* He published a second book of poetry, *The spice box of earth*, in 1961, and after spending some time in England published a novel, *The favourite game*, in 1963. For about the next ten years he lived on the Greek island of Hydra, and commuted to New York and Montreal. During this period he published *Flowers for Hitler* (1964); *Parasites of heaven* (1966); a second novel, *Beautiful losers* (1966); *Selected poems* (for which he declined a Governor General's Award, 1968); and began a successful career as a popular composer-singer. Recently he has returned to Montreal and has announced his retirement as a popular entertainer. His most recent book of poetry is *The energy of slaves* (1972). His record albums are *Songs of Leonard Cohen*, *Songs from a room*, and *Songs of love and hate*.

Cohen's poetry and fiction have been extremely popular, particularly with high-school and college readers. The appeal of his poetry has been based chiefly on three elements: a traditional and recognizably 'poetic' prosody, suggestive imagery that the subjective reader can easily project himself into, and a theme of moral non-responsibility. George WOODCOCK has argued that Cohen has usually been conservative in poetic craft and escapist in theme. The poetry of his first two books draws heavily on Greek and neo-Hassidic mythology, not to reveal this mythology as alive in the present but to convert the present into the sepulchral figures of the mythology. Cohen's language here is highly decorative, reminiscent of the early Yeats. While the poems of his third book, *Flowers for Hitler*, adventure into both satire and experimental verse forms, those of the fourth, *Parasites of heaven*, return to the conventional and dispassionate measures of the earlier volumes.

A consistent theme in these books is the importance of reducing life to ceremony, of escaping from life by transmuting its slippery actualities into the reliable simplicities of myth and art. This theme is developed most clearly in Cohen's novels. It is the lesson by which Breavman 'comes of age' in *The favourite game*. In *Beautiful losers* it is the lesson 'I' must learn from 'F' and includes not only the transmuting of object and event but the self-reduction of one's identity into the anonymity of sainthood. The loser triumphs by escaping the desire to win. A clear extension of this belief appears in Cohen's latest book of poetry, *The energy of slaves*, a collection of fragments, failed poems, and anti-poems. On the surface the directness and self-deprecating cynicism of this book appear to mark a repudiation of the earlier poetry. In fact it represents a logical step in the saintly self-abnegation Cohen has always advocated: master becomes slave, poetic craftsman becomes his own beautiful loser—in his words 'only a scribbler'. Once again Cohen is working towards a kind of martyrdom.

Michael ONDAATJE has written a short critical study of Cohen's writings for the Canadian Writers Series in the New Canadian Library (1970).
FD

Cohen, Matt (1942–). Born in Kingston, Ont., and educated at the University of Toronto, he taught religion at McMaster University for one year before moving to a farm near Godfrey, Ont. He now lives in Toronto.

Cohen's experiments in the structure of the novel give additional interest to his treatment of the maladjusted individual as he moves towards self-destruction. Precision of vocabulary, a sense of pace, and the ability to manipulate tenuously related incidents distinguish the despairing novella *Korsoniloff* (1969), which deals with the mental deterioration of an unsuccessful schizophrenic professor of philosophy whose childhood trauma at his father's remarriage expresses itself in a feeling that he has killed his mother. His subsequent decline is expressed as a dialogue between 'I', the 'cold fish' who is unable to understand his one overt act of violence, and 'Korsoniloff', who can satisfy his sexual urges without a sense of guilt. The 'I' is finally replaced by 'you', permitting Korsoniloff to combine his matricide worry and his desire for revenge on his stepmother by fantasized murders of an old woman and his mistress. Interwoven into the narrative is a fable that leaves the searcher for truth with the cold black candle of despair.

In *Johnny Crackle sings* (1971) Cohen adapts the Greek drama form to reveal the fate of Johnny Harper, an Ottawa valley drop-out whose self-destructive urges are more powerful than his yearnings for the rural life to which he is better suited. The role of narrator is taken by Lew, who has overcome urban frustration by adapting to farming. The Messenger (or commentator) is a shrewd newspaper reporter. And Johnny meets his male Nemesis in an unscrupulous promoter who plays on Johnny's vanity. He contrives a local success for Johnny turned folk singer—'Johnny Crackle'—a success that does not deceive the sophisticated. Wrecked by gruelling practice sessions, drugs, and his tendency to flee under strain, Johnny is rehabilitated by Lew and his wife, though he returns in the end to the world of rock music that was his downfall. The second chapter, repeated at the end, is a chorus that presages the dénouement.

Cohen is not as successful in driving home a point or creating a mood in the compass of the short story. His collection *Columbus and the fat lady and other stories* (1972) falls between the impressionistic and the surrealist. Two of the stories are of interest in connection with *Johnny Crackle sings*: 'The toy pilgrim' and 'Country music' show that in his view not all unmerited success is ephemeral and rural life is not in itself a haven of salvation. The title story relates to a point raised in *Korsoniloff*, that modern education as a rehash of past values has little bearing on modern life. NS

Cohen, Sheldon. See HISTORY STUDIES IN ENGLISH 4.

Coleman, Victor (1944–). Born in Toronto, he grew up there and in Montreal. He dropped out of school and into the world of poetry, submitting poems to various magazines, editing *Island*, working at odd jobs (including periods as a production assistant at the Oxford University Press and as a linotype operator for *The Coast News* in Gibsons, B.C.), all the time corresponding with various American poets, including Ginsberg, Duncan, and Olson. Eventually his interest in poetry and his experience in printing and design brought him to The Coach House Press, Toronto, where he works as editor and production manager. He has published numerous books of poetry, including *From Erik Satie's notes to the music* (1965), *one/eye/love* (1967), *Light verse* (1969), *America* (1971), *Old friends' ghosts* (1971), *Strange love* (1972), and *Parking lots* (1972).

There is a poem in an early issue of *Island* called 'Peninsula' (section V) that seems to embody most of Coleman's poetic techniques. It is a meditation on the field of sound, idea, and image that surrounds the word 'peninsula'; it has no obvious structure but moves by a sort of associational logic, making surprising connections, tacking back and forth according to gusts of connotation or sound: 'sail/head on into what wind/there is/to move you'. The free-fall technique, which resembles the dadaists in its rejection of formal structures (anecdote, character, parable), argues a conception of poetry as an activity of discovery, a kinetic process. Coleman sees poetry as a *performance* that depends not on the assumption of symbiosis between poet and audience but on its own resources of movement and sound to sustain interest—on the quality of the poet's ear and his associative powers. Coleman is least successful where he tries to shock and to incorporate biographical detail into his free-flow poems: these elements are like dislodged cargoes or submerged rocks that often endanger the movement and stability of the poem. His improvisations, his sense of linguistic playfulness, and his resistance to the sirens of meaning and self-expression suggest that, in the long run, his contribution to the art of poetry will be considerable. GG

Colgrove, R.G. P. See HISTORY STUDIES IN ENGLISH 16.

Collard, Elizabeth. See HISTORY STUDIES IN ENGLISH 7.

Collie, Michael. See POETRY IN ENGLISH 1.

Colombo, John Robert (1936–). Born in Kitchener, Ont., he studied at the University of Toronto and has been an indefatigable entrepreneur of poetry since his student days. He organized poetry readings at the Bohemian Embassy, Toronto, and for a time was editor of the Hawkshead Press, which published pamphlets of poetry in the 1960s. He was an editor for the Ryerson Press and in 1963 became a free-lance editor: he has edited many books for McClelland and Stewart and other publishers. His other literary activities include teaching creative writing courses; writing art criticism and book reviews; and reading his own poetry at schools and universities. Since 1960 he has been the managing editor of *The Tamarack Review*. He has edited numerous books, beginning with *The Varsity chapbook* (1959), which contained some of his own poetry together with the poetry of other students at the University of Toronto. He also edited *Poetry 64/Poésie 64* (1964) with Jacques GODBOUT; *How do I love thee?: sixty poets of Canada (and Quebec) select and introduce their favourite poems from their own work* (1970); and two school anthologies, *New direction in Canadian poetry* (1971) and *Rhymes and reasons* (1972). He co-edited with Raymond SOUSTER *Shapes and sounds: poems of W. W. E. Ross* (1968).

Colombo is the leading Canadian exponent of 'found' poetry—written by taking another writer's prose and, without altering the wording or the grammatical structure, setting it down lined as poetry. Colombo himself calls this 'redeemed prose', by means of which he hopes to create a poetry of 'documentary realism'. Two of his collections of found poetry are based on the prose of two men famous in Ontario history, William Lyon Mackenzie and Bishop Strachan: *The Mackenzie poems* (1966) and *John Toronto: new poems by Dr Strachan* (1969). Two other of his books also include some 'found' poetry: *The great San Francisco earthquake and fire* (1971), a mosaic of recollections and responses to these events in the words of people who were there, and *The Great Wall of China* (1966), a collage of pieces, some original, some found, about the building and the history of the Great Wall. (This has been translated into French by Jacques Godbout.) Colombo has done some translations from other languages, including the poetry of Robert Zend, a Hungarian poet now living in Toronto. These versions of Zend, done in collaboration with the author, appear in *Volvox: poetry from the unofficial languages of Canada in translation* (1971).

Colombo published two small selections of his work—*Variations* (1958) and *Miraculous montages* (1967)—before publishing a fuller collection, *Abracadabra*, in 1967. Including original work as well as some found poetry, it focuses on a variety of subjects—painting, Canadian details, angels, and certain pop-culture figures like Fu Manchu and Dracula—in an attempt to present a view of the modern world in the widest context in order to fulfil one of Colombo's ideals. This is described in a later book of original poems, *Neo poems* (1970), as the inclusion in his poems of 'all other poems, all other places, all other things'. These neo-poems—not 'entirely prose' and not 'really poetry'—are deliberately plastic structures, aphoristic and open-ended. In his poetry Colombo seems to want to put down life as a continuing process; he is constantly rehabilitating the past within the framework of the present.

PS

Comeau, Robert. See HISTORY STUDIES IN FRENCH I.

Condemine, Odette. See POETRY IN FRENCH.

Conron, Brandon. See LITERARY STUDIES IN ENGLISH 4.

Cook, George M. See LITERARY STUDIES IN ENGLISH 4.

Cook, Lyn. See CHILDREN'S BOOKS IN ENGLISH 6.

Cook, Michael. See DRAMA IN ENGLISH 4.

Cook, Ramsay (1931–). George Ramsay Cook was born in Saskatchewan and educated at the University of Manitoba and Queen's University. In 1958 he was appointed to the history department of the University of Toronto, where he remained until 1968–9 when he became visiting professor of Canadian studies at Harvard University. He is now professor of history and social science at York University, Toronto. He was editor of the *Canadian Historical Review* from 1963 to 1968 and has been a frequent contributor to the *Canadian Forum*, *Saturday Night*, and other leading journals and magazines. He is often seen as a political commentator on national television.

Cook has stimulated the interest of historians and the public in the ideological ferment in Québec. Among his students he has encouraged the study of Canadian political ideas, the problems surrounding conflicting cultures, and a re-appraisal of the life and values of minority groups. In *The politics of John W. Dafoe and the Free Press* (1963) he examines the voluminous writings and political opinions of this nationally prominent Winnipeg journalist and editor. Dafoe is portrayed, throughout his forty-year career, as a nineteenth-century laissez-faire liberal thinker, a determined exponent of prairie agrarian political-economic ideas, and, in the twenties and thirties, a promoter of Canadian autonomy and international collective security. In *Canada and the French-Canadian question* (1966)—published in French as *Le Sphynx parle français* (1968)—Cook shows that confederation was meant to ensure the survival of Canada and the preservation of the French language and culture within it. Later French and English nationalists have misused history in their attempts to make over the country in their own image and to serve their own economic and political self-interest, thus encouraging separatism and national divisiveness. Cook feels that Canada would be better served by less nationalism, more tolerance, and a fuller expression of cultural duality. This theme is updated in *The Maple Leaf forever: essays on nationalism and politics in Canada* (1971), which furthers Cook's role as an opponent of traditional nationalism and as the major historian of Canadian political ideas. One of the first supporters of the prime ministership of Pierre Elliott Trudeau, Cook applauds Trudeau for his ability to combine political realism and an awareness of Canada's pluralistic, sectional, and federal nature with the demands of the modern, automated, technological state. In *Provincial autonomy, minority rights and the compact theory, 1867–1921/L'autonomie provinciale, les droits des minorités et la théorie du pacte, 1867–1921* (1969), the fourth volume in the Studies of the Royal Commission on Bilingualism and Biculturalism, Cook concludes that the compact theory was successfully developed and argued by provincial governments and political parties against the federal government in the heat of the provincial-rights controversies before 1896. Thereafter, when the compact theory—now revised as two founding peoples, Francophones and Anglophones—was used by the supporters of local religious and linguistic rights, the provinces viewed this as limiting their own power and did not support it.

Cook is also the co-author of two textbooks —*Canada: a modern study* (1964) with John Ricker and John Saywell and *Canada and the United States: a modern study* (1963) with Kenneth W. MCNAUGHT. He edited *The Dafoe-Sifton correspondence, 1919–1927* (1966); and *Confederation* (1967), *Politics of discontent* (1967), and *Constitutionalism and nationalism in Lower Canada* (1969), three booklets in the Canadian Historical Readings series. He also edited *French-Canadian nationalism: an anthology* (1969), a collection of twenty-five essays by sociologists, clergymen, journalists, historians, and professors. DF

Cooper, John Irwin. See HISTORY STUDIES IN ENGLISH 13.

Cooperman, Stanley. See POETRY IN ENGLISH 2.

Copithorne, Judith. See POETRY IN ENGLISH 3.

Copland, Dudley. See HISTORY STUDIES IN ENGLISH 10.

Corbett, Edward M. See HISTORY STUDIES IN ENGLISH 12 and POLITICAL WRITINGS IN ENGLISH 1.

Cornell, Paul G. See HISTORY STUDIES IN ENGLISH 1.

Cornish, John (1914–). Born in Vancouver and educated at the University of British Columbia, he has worked at a variety of occupations. He now lives in Toronto. Cornish's disciplined sense of the ridiculous invests the quite ordinary characters of his novels with an extra dimension that lifts them above the simple circumstances of their lives. In *The provincials* (1951) he satirized a wealthy British Columbia lumberman and his family. *Olga* (1959) is a comic, sometimes bawdy romance that brings together the ranchers and Doukhobors of the British Columbia interior. *Sherbourne Street* (1968) is set in Toronto following the Second World War when the overflow of the population lived in trailer camps. In one of these camps, Isabel Bailey and her husband, a viola player, together with their low-paid impractical friends, plan to reopen a music conservatory (the Hambourg Conservatory) that has become the home of Isabel's old uncle and his ninety-year-old housekeeper who dominates the house. Their blandishments and impractical schemes prove abortive. *A world turned turtle* (1969) is a tragedy that poses the question of whether a soldier's first loyalty is to the army or to humanity. Cornish treats the subject without sentimentality. NS

Corriveau, Monique. See CHILDREN'S BOOKS IN FRENCH.

Cosgrove, Edmund. See CHILDREN'S BOOKS IN ENGLISH 2.

Costisella, Joseph. See HISTORY STUDIES IN FRENCH 10 and LITERARY STUDIES IN FRENCH 2.

Cotnam, Jacques. See ANTHOLOGIES IN FRENCH.

Coulter, John (1888–). Born in Belfast, he studied at schools of art and technology there and later at the University of Manchester. Then he taught art and English at Coleraine, Ireland, and also worked as a textile designer. In 1914 Coulter moved to Dublin to be closer to the leaders of the Irish literary renaissance and to the Abbey Theatre; while there he wrote and taught school to support himself. In 1926 he was editor of *The Ulster Review*. From 1927 to 1930 he worked as an editor with John Middleton Murry on *The New Adelphi* in London. He also worked for the British Broadcasting Corporation from 1925 until 1936 when he married a Canadian, Olive Clare Primrose, and decided to live in Canada. One incidental result of that decision was the part he played in persuading his friend Tyrone Guthrie to come to Canada in 1952 to direct the first production of the Stratford Festival.

Besides writing for journals, magazines, and radio in Britain and Canada, Coulter has published plays, librettos, poetry, a novel, and a biography. His early plays reflect his Irish background in setting and theme. They are noteworthy for their local colour and careful construction, but their lack of the element of surprise or dramatic reversal detracts from their overall effect. *The house in the quiet glen* (1937), which won several prizes at the Dominion Drama Festival in 1937, is a one-act comedy about an Irish girl whose parents arrange to marry her to a widower, not knowing that she has designs on the widower's son. *The family portrait* (1937) is a full-length comedy about the reactions of a Belfast family to its playwrighting son and his successful play, which mirrors their own lives. *The drums are out* (1971) treats a more solemn theme: the effect of the Irish civil war on Protestant and Catholic alike. Set in Belfast in the early 1920s, it focuses on a family whose father is a policeman and whose daughter is secretly married to a member of the Irish Republican Army. The play was premiered at the Abbey Theatre in Dublin on July 12, 1948. An indication of the author's difficulty in providing totally satisfying endings for his plays is the inclusion of both the revised and the original versions of the third act in the published text of this play. *The family portrait* was not produced at the Abbey Theatre because of Coulter's inability to rewrite the final scenes to the satisfaction of Lennox Robinson, who nevertheless used the first act as a text for his acting classes there.

When he turned to writing plays with a Canadian theme, Coulter chose historical subjects. He became fascinated by the Métis leader Louis Riel and wrote three plays about him. *Riel* (1962) is a wide-ranging dramatization of events between the Red River Rebellion of 1870 and Riel's hanging in 1885. According to the author's note, it was 'designed for presentation in the Elizabethan manner'—a somewhat bold step to take four years before the construction of Stratford's revolutionary thrust stage. *The trial of Louis Riel* (1968) is a courtroom drama and a much more limited play; it uses transcripts from the trial itself, including some French dialogue with English translation supplied by an interpreter. Since its first (1967) production in Regina, where Riel was hanged, the play has become an annual attraction there. *The crime of Louis Riel*, which may be published soon, is perhaps the best of the trilogy, combining the expansiveness of *Riel* with the intensity of *The trial of Louis Riel*.

Coulter has written three opera librettos, all for the Canadian composer Healey Willan. *Transit through fire* (1942), a short play written in verse, conveys the bitter reflections of a young soldier on leave, and of his wife, about the society before the Second World War that gave its youth great hopes and then sent it to war. (Of this opera Coulter has said: 'I privately thought my collaborator had put fur-coat music on my hair-shirt libretto.') *Deirdre of the sorrows* (1944) is a retelling in verse and prose of the ancient Irish story of the foundling girl whose lovers are fated to die. *Deirdre* (1966), a slightly revised version of this work, was first staged in 1965 at the Macmillan Theatre, with performers from the Royal Conservatory of Music, Toronto; it was produced on stage again in 1967 by the Canadian Opera Company at Toronto's O'Keefe Centre. *Transit through fire* and *Deirdre of the sorrows* were the first two Canadian operas commissioned and broadcast by the Canadian Broadcasting Corporation, and *Deirdre* was the first Canadian work presented by the Canadian Opera Company.

The poems in *The blossoming thorn* (1946) are light, lyrical, romantic, elegiac, and sometimes humorous; they are Coulter's own alternative to what he considers to be the over-intellectual and unemotional qualities in modern verse and are superior to the verse in his three librettos. His novel, *Turf smoke: a fable of two countries* (1945), is the story of an Irish immigrant in New York who is unable to adapt to the American way of life but finally realizes he cannot return to Ireland either. While little attempt is made to explore character or situation, it is notable for its descriptive passages in which the immigrant recalls his native land. (It is an adaptation of an unpublished play, *Holy Manhattan*, that he wrote earlier.) Coulter also wrote *Churchill* (1945), which he calls a 'dramatic biography'; it is a short journalistic account based on the sources he used for an unpublished 'living-newspaper' play, *Mr Churchill of England*.

Coulter has written radio and stage plays that are unpublished and continues his productive career at the age of eighty-five. Some of his unpublished works can be found in the Metropolitan Central Library, Toronto, and in the Mills Memorial Library of McMaster University, which has a collection of Coulter's literary papers and plays. A personal account of his writing career can be found in the introduction to *The drums are out*. JN

Cox, David. See HISTORY STUDIES IN ENGLISH 12 and POLITICAL WRITINGS IN ENGLISH 7.

Craig, G. M. See HISTORY STUDIES IN ENGLISH 12.

Craig, John. See CHILDREN'S BOOKS IN ENGLISH 3 and 6; FICTION IN ENGLISH 3.

Creighton, D. G. (1902–). Donald Grant Creighton was born in Toronto and educated at the Universities of Toronto and Oxford. He was appointed to the history department of the University of Toronto in 1927 and served as its chairman from 1954 to 1959. He was Sir John A. Macdonald Professor of History from 1965 to 1968 and University Professor from 1968 to 1970. He was elected to the Royal Society of Canada in 1946 and was awarded the Tyrrell Medal for history in 1951. He was president of the Canadian Historical Association in 1956–7. He has received the National Award in Letters of the University of Alberta (1957), the first Molson Prize of the Canada Council for his outstanding contribution to Canada's cultural heritage (1964), and in 1967 became a Companion of the Order of Canada. Creighton is also the advisory editor of the eighteen-volume Canadian Centenary series. He is now retired and is a Fellow of Massey College, Toronto.

Creighton's clear, fluent, dramatic prose, his diligent research, and his discerning insight have made him English-speaking Canada's most accomplished historian. He has also brought forth exactness and thoroughness in his students. In his first major work, *The commercial empire of the St Lawrence: 1760–1850* (1937)—reprinted in 1956 as *The empire of the St Lawrence*—a volume in the Relations Between Canada and the United States series, Creighton made comprehensible and extended the theories of Harold Innis concerning Canada's economic history. Canada is portrayed as the product of the laws of nature; the political and economic life of the nation was determined by the St Lawrence-Great Lakes trading system and the country's survival has been dependent upon its continued existence. Those who would support continental trade policies and encourage competition from the United States work against nature and the best interests of Canada. *Dominion of the north: a history of Canada* (1944; rev. 1957) is an outstanding synthesis of Canadian history in Creighton's usual grand style. His more specialized study, *British North America at confederation* (1939; rev. 1963), prepared for the Royal Commission on Dominion-

Provincial Relations, is an examination of the allocation of financial and economic powers in 1867.

Creighton's mastery of his subject, his perceptions of character and events, and his vibrant prose are best revealed in his two-volume biography, *John A. Macdonald: The young politician* (1952) and *The old chieftain* (1955). Both volumes won the 1955 University of British Columbia Medal for Popular Biography and a Governor General's Award. To Creighton, Macdonald exemplified the Canadian politican *par excellence* when he recognized and acted upon the fact that the United States was a greater threat to Canadian independence than Great Britain. Creighton is also the author of *The road to confederation: the emergence of Canada, 1863–1867* (1964), which examines provincial politicians and concludes that confederation was the result of British-American initiative and the embodiment of British-American political experience.

Canada's first century, 1867–1967 (1970) is pessimistic about Canada's future. Creighton sees continentalism as the major threat to Canada's national independence and cultural identity. He believes that the growth of provincial autonomy and the rise of French-Canadian nationalism are serious dangers for Canadian national unity and obvious weaknesses in the national front against American pressures. He criticizes successive Liberal governments—particularly those of King and Pearson—for repudiating Canada's past, undermining the stability of its distinctive institutions, and increasing its dependence on the United States. *Towards the discovery of Canada* (1972) contains a selection of Creighton's essays and speeches from his distinguished forty-year career and includes an autobiographical introduction that confronts those who label him a 'conservative' historian with the actual record of his interests and opinions. He criticizes liberal historians because they assume that history is the onward march of progress and that progress is simply the unfolding of the present. The present—its interests, standards, and values—is the ideal, and the past should be interpreted so as to justify it. The old British imperial connection is impugned in order to vindicate a Canadian national independence that is, in fact, compromised by dependence on the United States. He sees the idea of a 'bicultural compact' at confederation as a myth invented to justify the pretensions of French-Canadian nationalists of the 1960s. DF

Creighton, Helen. See FOLKLORE: BIBLIOGRAPHY.

Creighton, Luella. See CHILDREN'S BOOKS IN ENGLISH 3 and HISTORY STUDIES IN ENGLISH 7.

Crémazie, Octave. See POETRY IN FRENCH.

Crispo, John H. G. See HISTORY STUDIES IN ENGLISH 13.

Cuff, R. D. See HISTORY STUDIES IN ENGLISH 7.

Cull, David. See POETRY IN ENGLISH 2.

Cumming, Peter A. See INDIANS 3.

Cummings, Richard. See HISTORY STUDIES IN ENGLISH 17.

Curtis, Edward. See INDIANS 4.

Cutt, W. Towrie. See CHILDREN'S BOOKS IN ENGLISH 4 and 6.

D

Dahlie, Hallvard. See LITERARY STUDIES IN ENGLISH 4.

D'Allaire, M. See HISTORY STUDIES IN FRENCH 8.

Dalton, Roy C. See HISTORY STUDIES IN ENGLISH 7.

Damas, David. See INDIANS 5.

Dandurand, Raoul. See HISTORY STUDIES IN FRENCH 11.

Daniells, Roy. See CHILDREN'S BOOKS IN ENGLISH 5 and HISTORY STUDIES IN ENGLISH 3.

Darios, Louise. See FOLKLORE: BIBLIOGRAPHY.

Dassonville, Michel. See LITERARY STUDIES IN FRENCH 4.

Datzell, Kathleen E. See HISTORY STUDIES IN ENGLISH 9.

Dauphin, Roma. See POLITICAL WRITINGS IN FRENCH 2.

Daveluy, Paule. See CHILDREN'S BOOKS IN FRENCH.

Davey, Frank (1940–). Frankland Wilmot Davey was born in Vancouver but lived in Abbotsford in the Fraser valley until 1958 when he returned to Vancouver to study at the University of British Columbia. While there he was managing editor of *Tish*, the influential magazine that brought into Canadian poetry concepts that were derived principally from such American poets as Robert Duncan, Charles Olson, and Robert Creeley. After completing his graduate studies in Los Angeles, Davey taught English at Royal Roads, Victoria, and was writer-in-residence at Sir George Williams University in Montreal (1969–70). He is now teaching at York University, Toronto.

In his introduction to Davey's first book of poems, *D-Day and after* (1962), Warren Tallman maintains that the poet uses the method of projective verse derived from Olson by attempting 'to project the body of his responses into the body of the poem'. These poems catch the anguish of a failing relationship in language that deliberately avoids rhetoric and in lines whose irregularities reflect the shifting disappointments and pain within the collapsing relationship. *Bridge force* (1965), which also uses projective verse, is concerned with the locale of the west coast. The sea is embodied in the poems as a symbol of flux, but woven into this presentation of a constantly changing world is the thread of a flourishing personal relationship. Locale is also important in *City of the gulls and sea* (1964), a short collection of lyric responses to the city of Victoria. The sea figures largely in *The scarred hull* (1966), a narrative poem that links shipping disasters to the experiences of a teacher with children in her school. The factual information about the disasters and the specific references to place give the poem a firmly realistic base. In *Four myths for Sam Perry* (1970)—lyrical meditations on a friend's death—the lines are longer, with none of the fragmentation of Davey's early work. Sam Perry's death is placed in a context of violence and death in the external world but is also seen within a frame of the ambiguities of light and growth. Growth is also a theme of *Weeds* (1970), a book of prose-poems that detail a reassessment of the poet's private life in a tone of muted desperation about the breaking down of a personal relationship. The same theme recurs in a series of short lyrics based on Tarot cards and some details from Arthurian legend, *King of swords* (1972). Davey published two other books of verse in 1972: *Griffon*, a poem about La Salle's first expedition on Lake Erie, which was issued in a small limited edition, and *L'an trentiesme: selected poems 1960–1970*.

Davey has written criticism, particularly as an apologist of projective verse. He is the editor of a critical forum of these poetic ideas, *Open letter*, and used them as the basis of his critical study of the Canadian poet who was his teacher at the University of British Columbia: *Earle Birney* (1972). Davey is also the author of a critical exegesis of certain elements in the poetry of Charles Olson, *Five readings of Olson's 'Maximus'* (1970). PS

Davies, Robertson (1913–). William Robertson Davies was born in Thamesville, Ont., and educated at Upper Canada College, Queen's University, and Oxford. He then joined the Old Vic Repertory Company where he did some acting, stage-managing, and directing, as well as teaching in the school attached to that theatre. He returned to Canada in 1940 and was literary editor of *Saturday Night* (Toronto) until 1942 when he became editor of the Peterborough *Examiner*, of which he was later the publisher. He was awarded the Lorne Pierce Medal for distinguished service to Canadian literature in 1960. He has taught English at the University of Toronto since 1960, and in 1962 became master of Massey College.

While editor of the *Examiner*, Davies wrote a syndicated column, 'The diary of Samuel Marchbanks', containing urbane, frank, and witty observations on life. Selections from this column were published as a book under the same title in 1947 and in *The table talk of Samuel Marchbanks* (1949). *Samuel Marchbanks' almanack* (1968), with a preface by Gordon Roper in the New Canadian Library, contains both selections from his original material and some later observations, commentaries, and 'correspondences' arranged under the signs of the zodiac. Another syndicated column, 'A writer's diary', which contained pointed comments on books, literature, and the art of reading, provided the genesis for *A voice from the attic* (1960), which is now in the New Canadian Library. Davies says he wrote the book for 'the clerisy', which he defines as 'people who like to read books', but this simple definition is later amplified until it approaches the exhortation to 'Read, mark, learn, and inwardly digest'.

The spirit of Samuel Marchbanks pervades Davies' plays. *Overlaid* (1948), an ironic comment on standards of values, was reprinted in the collection of comedies *Eros at breakfast and other plays* (1949), which also included *The voice of the people*, *Hope deferred*, and *At the gates of the righteous*. The position of the artist in Canada is dealt with in the comedy *Fortune my foe* (1949); it was reprinted in 1968 in the paperback collection *Four favourite plays*, which includes the previously published *Eros at breakfast*, *The voice of the people*, and *At the gates of the righteous*. In the historical comedy *At my heart's core* (1950) a slightly sinister figure is introduced to bring out the latent discontent and dissatisfaction of three well-educated women—Susanna Moodie, Catherine Parr Traill, and Frances Stewart—who are faced with cultural starvation in the Canadian backwoods in 1837. This play and *Overlaid* were reprinted together in paperback in 1966. In *A jig for the gypsy* (1954) radical principles are brought into contact with the occult powers of a gypsy during the British election of 1885. Davies' most recent collection, *Hunting Stuart and other plays*, appeared in 1972. He has also written *A masque of Aesop* (1952) and *A masque of Mr Punch* (1963), two plays for boys, and *Shakespeare's boy actors* (1939) and *Shakespeare for young players* (1942). He collaborated with Tyrone Guthrie and the artist Grant Macdonald in three books on the Shakespearean festival at Stratford, Ont.: *Renown at Stratford* (1953), *Twice have the trumpets sounded* (1954), and *Thrice the brinded cat hath mew'd* (1955).

A serious approach to culture as opposed to dilettantism underlies Davies' three serio-comic novels set in 'Salterton' (easily identified as Kingston), where a university, a cathedral, and a garrison accentuate the dominance of the social and cultural values of an old guard. All these elements are brought together in the first of these novels, *Tempest-tost* (1951), in which the local drama league stages *The tempest*. In *Leaven of malice* (1954) the gentle humour surrounding the task of editing a small-town newspaper is counter-balanced by the sardonic treatment of the vindictiveness and tyranny of the older generation, of the brashness of the half-educated 'specialist', and of the spite that is the only weapon of a weak and vain man. This book won the Leacock Medal for Humour. In his third novel, *A mixture of frailties* (1958), Davies starts with a farcical situation in which a gospel singer with no social or cultural background becomes the temporary beneficiary of a snobbish woman who made her will with the express purpose of perpetuating the family name and of dictating to her son. As the novel develops, the comic elements are replaced by serious contrapuntal themes: man's tendency to surrender to tyranny and his ability to endure the travail of mind and spirit required to transform the virtuoso into the artist. The work ends with a double affirmation: the birth of a son enables a young couple to enter into their inheritance and the gospel singer becomes a concert artist.

The sinister influence of a dead woman that pervades *A mixture of frailties* prepares the reader for the skill with which Davies uses Jungian psychology to examine the personalities of the oddly assorted characters of *Fifth business* (1970) and to establish interrelationships between them. He moves easily from a small town—with its long memory for scandal and its malicious cruelty to an innocent victim, Paul Dempster—to a wealthy, snobbish clique in Toronto that stultifies any possibility of moral growth in the successful and aggressive Boy Staunton. Davies parallels these environments with scenes set in Europe and Mexico where Dunstan Ramsay, having gone astray in his search for the meaning of sanctity, learns through the wit and wisdom of an erudite Jesuit, through the imagination of Paul Dempster, now a master illusionist, and through Liesel Vitzliputzli, an earth-mother figure, to 'shake hands' with his personal devil, thus becoming a whole man in the Jungian sense. Ramsay also becomes 'fifth business' (the person through whom the dénouement takes place) in a confrontation between Staunton and Dempster. In a companion novel, *The manticore* (1972), Staunton's alcoholic son, torn by a love-hate relationship with his father, whose mysterious death torments him, submits to Jungian analysis in Switzerland. He dreams of a sybil leading a manticore (a mythological figure with a lion's body, a man's face, and a barbed tail). He then meets Ramsay, Dempster, and Liesel who, in her earth-mother guise, gives him a rough introduction to bear mythology. This brings on a crisis that will no doubt be resolved in the third volume of Davies' projected trilogy. *The manticore* won a Governor General's Award. A lucid interpretation of Jungian psychology in *Fifth business* is given by Gordon Roper in the *Journal of Canadian Fiction*, Vol. 1, no. 1.

Davies is also the author of *Stephen Leacock* (1970), a brief study in the Canadian Writers Series of the New Canadian Library, and the editor of *Feast of Stephen* (1970), a short anthology of Leacock's writing.

Elspeth Buitenhuis has written a short critical study of Davies' writings for the series Canadian Writers and Their Work (1972). NS

Dawson, Nora. See FOLKLORE: BIBLIOGRAPHY.

Defries, R. D. See HISTORY STUDIES IN ENGLISH 15.

Delabit, Régine. See CHILDREN'S BOOKS IN FRENCH.

Del Grande, Louis. See DRAMA IN ENGLISH 3.

Dempsey, Hugh A. See INDIANS 2.

Denison, Merrill. See HISTORY STUDIES IN ENGLISH 13.

Deprez, Paul. See INDIANS 6.

Derome, Gilles. See DRAMA IN FRENCH 4.

Desbiens, Albert. See HISTORY STUDIES IN FRENCH 4.

Desbiens, Jean-Paul. See BELLES LETTRES IN FRENCH.

Désilets, André. See HISTORY STUDIES IN FRENCH 11.

Desjardins, E. See HISTORY STUDIES IN FRENCH 9.

Des Rivières, Madeleine M. See CHILDREN'S BOOKS IN FRENCH and FOLKLORE: BIBLIOGRAPHY.

DesRochers, Alfred (1901–). Born in Saint-Elie-d'Orford, Qué., he was educated at Trois-Rivières. He worked at several trades before becoming a sportswriter and translator for *La Tribune* in Sherbrooke of which he was made advertising manager in 1928. In 1927–8 he founded and edited *L'étoile de l'est* at Coaticook. Two years later he moved to Montreal where he became director of the International Service (short wave) of the Canadian Broadcasting Corporation.

DesRochers's most productive years as a poet were 1928 and 1929 when two volumes of his verse appeared. *L'offrande aux vierges folles* (1928) established his reputation as a master of strong rhythms in traditional forms in which, through the use of contrast in language and tone, he brings life and movement to his alexandrines. Various meanings have been read into this contrast: the deadening life of the town as set against the renewal of life in the countryside, or the life of the senses as opposed to the life of the spirit. He himself, however, stated in *Paragraphes* (see below) that the poems were intended as an expression of the conflict between the good and evil instincts in man, an explanation that clarifies his use of the parable of the wise and foolish virgins in the title. His second volume of poems, *À l'ombre d'Orford* (1929), is a magnificent appreciation of *le terroir* (Québec countryside) and won the Prix David of the Province of Québec in 1932. It includes a realistic sonnet sequence dealing with the annual departure, labour, and return of the lumbermen in a small village; it also contains a number of lyrics such as the powerful 'Hymne au vent du nord' and the self-revelatory 'Je suis le fils déchu'. A second edition (1948) includes 'Le cycle du village', a dozen sonnets full of humour and meticulous observation of village life. *Le retour de Titus* (1963) is a long poem in which the Emperor Titus (who was forced by the Roman Senate in A.D. 79 to choose between the throne and his love for Berenice) expresses his sorrow at the renunciation of love. DesRochers composed this poem in the difficult Spenserian stanza form and wrote it at intervals over many years. As he finished fragments of it he sent them to Jeannine Bélanger (Sister Marie-Joséfa) who put them together and wrote the preface. In 1967 he published *Elégies pour l'épouse en-allée*, a cycle of memorial sonnets characterized by intense personal emotion and perfection of form.

DesRochers stands alone in French-Canadian literature as the single first-rate poet of the rural scene and the rural soul, to the celebration of which he brings a rare combination of realism, profundity, sophistication, and grace. A representative selection of his poetry is in Guy Sylvestre's *Anthologie de la poésie canadienne-française* (4th ed. 1963). Translations of his poems are in *The poetry of French Canada in translation* (1970) edited by John GLASSCO. DesRochers is also the author of a prose work, *Paragraphes: entrevues littéraires* (1931), a series of commentaries on books. NS/JG

Desrochers, Clémence. See POETRY IN FRENCH.

Desrosiers, Léo-Paul. See HISTORY STUDIES IN FRENCH 3.

Dessaules, Henriette. See HISTORY STUDIES IN FRENCH 11.

Devirieux, C. J. See POLITICAL WRITINGS IN FRENCH 2.

Dewart, E. H. See ANTHOLOGIES IN ENGLISH 1.

D'Harcourt, Marguerite. See FOLKLORE: BIBLIOGRAPHY.

D'Harcourt, Raoul. See FOLKLORE: BIBLIOGRAPHY.

Diefenbaker, John. See POLITICAL WRITINGS IN ENGLISH 4.

Dion, Gérard. See BELLES LETTRES IN FRENCH.

Djwa, Sandra. See LITERARY STUDIES IN ENGLISH 4.

Dobbs, Kildare (1923–). Born at Meerut, India, Kildare Robert Eric Dobbs was educated at St Columba's College, Rathfarnum, Ireland, and Jesus College, Cambridge, where he graduated in 1947. Following a family tradition of imperial service, he was colonial officer in Tanganyika from 1948 to 1952. He immigrated to Canada in the latter year, and from 1953 to 1961 worked as editor to the Macmillan Company. In 1956 he was among the founders of *The Tamarack Review*, from 1965 to 1967 served as managing editor of *Saturday Night*, and in 1968 became literary columnist for the Toronto *Star*. His first book, *Running to paradise* (1962), which won him a Governor General's Award, was a series of embroidered autobiographical sketches drawn from his life in India, Ireland, Africa, and Canada; they set the tone of urbanity broken by wayward Celtic wit that has distinguished Dobbs from the Leacockian tradition of Canadian humour. In collaboration with the photographer Peter Varley, he next wrote a somewhat lyrical travel book on his adopted country, *Canada* (1964; rev. 1969). In *Reading the time* (1968) he collected a series of idiosyncratic literary essays. His sense of the incongruous, which tends to make or mar emphatically whatever he writes, reaches a surrealist level of fantasy punstership in *The great fur opera* (1970), a comic history of the Hudson's Bay Company, written in collaboration with the British caricaturist Ronald Searle, and one of the few good recent examples of humorous writing in Canada. GW

Dobell, Peter C. See HISTORY STUDIES IN ENGLISH 12 and POLITICAL WRITINGS IN ENGLISH 7.

Doern, Bruce. See POLITICAL WRITINGS IN ENGLISH 6.

Donaldson, Gordon. See HISTORY STUDIES IN ENGLISH 12.

Donnelly, Joseph P. See HISTORY STUDIES IN ENGLISH 2 and 4.

Donnelly, Murray. See HISTORY STUDIES IN ENGLISH 15.

Dor, Georges. See POETRY IN FRENCH.

Dosman, Edgar. See POLITICAL WRITINGS IN ENGLISH 3.

Douville, Raymond. See HISTORY STUDIES IN ENGLISH 2 and HISTORY STUDIES IN FRENCH 3.

Dow, Helen J. See HISTORY STUDIES IN ENGLISH 16.

Downie, John. See CHILDREN'S BOOKS IN ENGLISH 5.

Downie, Mary Alice. See CHILDREN'S BOOKS IN ENGLISH 2 and 5.

Doyle, Gerald S. See FOLKLORE: BIBLIOGRAPHY.

Doyle, Mike. See POETRY IN ENGLISH 2.

Drache, Daniel. See POLITICAL WRITINGS IN FRENCH 6.

Drama in English. The number of Canadian plays published in English increased remarkably in the last six years, and particularly after 1970. Much of this increase was due to the new vitality of Canadian theatre that came about largely through the efforts of various experimental and sometimes nationalistic groups and individuals throughout Canada. Encouragement was also given to Canadian playwrights by organizations that concentrate their efforts, sometimes exclusively, on the production of Canadian plays, and by the growing readiness of subsidized theatres to produce them as well. The renewed interest throughout Canada in its own literature also had its effects on the publication of plays, though this still lags behind the publication of poetry and fiction.

1. *Established playwrights.* James REANEY's best-known play, *Colours in the dark* (1969; rev. 1971), was produced at both the Stratford Festival and the National Arts Centre, Ottawa. A multimedia play, with forty-two scenes and some exquisite poetry, *Colours in the dark* relates the experience of growing up in southwestern Ontario to the universal themes of life and death, war and peace, youth and age, existence and man's place in the cosmos. *Listen to the wind* (1972), set in a southwestern-Ontario farmhouse in 1936, represents the vain efforts of a sick boy to reunite his parents. In his attempt to do this he gets them to act in *The saga of Caresfoot Court*, his adaptation of a Victorian novel (*Dawn* by Rider Haggard), which forms a play within a play and serves to highlight the child's concerns. Three of Reaney's plays were published in one volume under the collective title *Masks of childhood* (1972). It includes a rewriting of his already published play, *The killdeer*, a verse drama in which the survivors of a rural family feud are enabled through love and understanding to break the chain of hate that has affected their lives; *The Easter egg*, a macabre and sometimes farcical play, showing again how genuine love can overcome the forces of evil (in this case a boy who had been treated as retarded by his stepmother is led to normality); and *Three desks*, the least successful of these three plays, which examines, sometimes farcically, the frustrations and idiosyncrasies of professors at a small liberal-arts college on the prairies.

John COULTER's *Riel* was republished in 1972 after it had gone out of print. Coulter also wrote *The trial of Louis Riel* (1968), a one-act dramatization of the trial and condemnation of the Métis hero in a Regina courtroom in 1885, and a third play on the same figure, *The crime of Louis Riel*, which has been awarded drama-festival prizes and may soon be published. The three plays were conceived as a trilogy, and each examines a different aspect of Riel's significance for Canada. *The drums are out* (1972) is set in Coulter's native city of Belfast in the early 1920s, the 'time of the troubles'. It depicts with compassion and realism the strains and conflicts in the home of a Protestant constable whose daughter is secretly married to an IRA man on the run.

Robertson DAVIES' *Four favourite plays*, which contains the full-length *Fortune, my foe* and three one-act plays, appeared in paperback in 1968. A new volume of previously unpublished full-length works, *Hunting Stuart and other plays*, appeared in 1972; all three plays in this collection had been written some time earlier, but only the title play has been produced professionally. All the plays are characterized by neat construction, sharp wit, and sparkling dialogue. *Hunting Stuart* centres on the efforts of two New York doctors to convince a minor Ottawa official that he is a descendant of Bonnie Prince Charlie and thus the rightful king of England. *King Phoenix* has for its main character King Cole, living in pre-Roman Britain, who thwarts the efforts of his enemies to overthrow him and dies 'smiling' so that his daughter Helena and her fiancé Leolin may succeed him. *General confession*, written in the classic-romantic style of nineteenth-century melodrama, concerns the career of Casanova who, retired and acting as librarian to Count Waldstein in the Castle of Dux, is presented 'as a man of intellect, wit, and philosophy, and upon the whole very good-natured'.

Three of Norman Williams' one-act plays —*Don't touch that phone*, *Take to the trees*, and *He didn't even say goodbye*—were published in 1972. In somewhat absurdist style he dramatizes the frustrations and madness that can beset family life; only in the first two plays does he bring the chaos to a satisfactory resolution.

2. *Newly published playwrights*. The work of the new playwrights, who represent almost every region of the country, takes various forms: historical, social, absurdist, allegorical, realistic, and multi-media. In terms of popular success, John Herbert's *Fortune and men's eyes* (1967) has been the most spectacular. It is the first Canadian play to achieve international renown. Since its premiere in New York in 1967 it has had fifty-five professional productions in seven languages. Set in the dormitory of a boys' prison, it is a strong indictment of the Canadian reformatory system. It shows how violence and homosexuality are encouraged in such a system as it depicts the corruption of a newly sentenced seventeen-year-old by his three dormitory mates. While some of the play's success was due to its frank treatment of its subject matter and while it suffers from a certain claustrophobic and strident quality, it is nevertheless effectively constructed and inspired by a searing honesty. It was made into a film. Herbert's next major play, *Born of Medusa's blood*, opened in Toronto in December 1972 to generally unfavourable reviews.

One of the finest dramatic treatments of Canadian history to appear recently was John T. McDonough's *Charbonneau and le chef* (1968), an enactment of the conflict between the archbishop of Montreal and Premier Maurice Duplessis during and after the Asbestos strike of 1949. McDonough contrasts the leadership and heroism of the archbishop with the ruthlessness and opportunism of the premier, who was instrumental in having him removed from his office after Charbonneau had won the day for the strikers. The author describes his purpose in writing the play thus: 'To awaken the Canadian conscience to its own poetry and drama.'

George RYGA has recently emerged as one of the outstanding Canadian playwrights. His plays often deal with oppressed and downtrodden members of Canadian society. Three of them are published in *The ecstasy of Rita Joe and other plays* (1971). The title play depicts the sufferings of an Indian girl in a white man's world. *Indian*, which has also been printed in various magazines, dramatizes a confrontation between a casual Indian labourer and his employer as well as the local Indian agent. The last play in the volume, *Grass and wild strawberries*, which uses a very free dramatic form, shows the conflicts between a boy and girl who become part of the hippie culture and their parents who live in a middle-class world. *Captives of the faceless drummer* (1971)—which makes effective use of music, memory, dance, and poetry—pits a kidnapped Canadian diplomat against the commander of an anarchist group and in the process reveals much about the ambitions and frustrations of both. The refusal of the board of directors of the Vancouver Playhouse to produce this commissioned work in 1971 became a topic of great controversy in the Canadian theatre and highlighted the problems involved in the relationship between the artist and the administration of theatrical centres in Canada.

David Freeman's one-act play *Creeps* (1972) was the most talked-about theatrical production in Toronto in 1971 when it was produced at the Tarragon Theatre under the direction of Bill Glassco. It is a searing comedy about victims of cerebral palsy, set in the men's washroom of a workshop for people with this affliction. Written by a CP victim, the play has an authenticity and a sense of anger and revolt against a pitying society that only a person so afflicted could evoke. Freeman's next play *Battering ram* (1972) is a more ambitious work in both length and scope. It concerns a cripple invited into the home of a mother and her daughter. Like *Creeps* it is quite blunt in its language and in its treatment of sex, but it explores human relationships more deeply, especially the ways in which people exploit one another, and is a better-constructed work.

Crabdance (1969; rev. 1972), an absurdist and symbolic play by Beverley Simons, presents various incidents that occur during one day in the life of Sadie Golden, a middle-aged woman who lives in fear of 'the three o'clock terror'. Her death at that hour suggests the way in which the forces of human life are overcome by the impersonality of modern living. Simon Gray, a Canadian now living in England, is looked upon as one of the most promising dramatists on either side of the Atlantic. He is the author of *Wise child* (1968), which had Alec Guinness in the London production and suggests by its foreboding and mystery the work of Harold Pinter; *Sleeping dog* (1968), a play for television; *Dutch uncle* (1969); *Spoiled* (1971); *The idiot* (1971); and *Butley* (1971), which was acclaimed in both London and New York with Alan Bates in the title role.

Three plays by David HELWIG are contained in his book *Figures in a landscape*, which contains mostly poetry. Two of the plays are brief: one, *The dreambook*, is an allegory about a poet who has never committed any of his poems to paper and who cannot reveal his dreams even to win the girl he loves lest he die as Orpheus did; the other, *The dancers of Colbek*, is a poetic play based on the medieval legend about a group of young people condemned to dance for a whole year because of their merrymaking in the churchyard. *A time of winter*, Helwig's full-length play, depicts the disintegration of a family in a dying Ontario town on the banks of the St Lawrence River. Though it is neatly constructed and shows what happens when people live emotionally always in 'a time of winter', it does not probe the human relationships deeply enough and leaves too much about them unexplained. David Watmough has published three plays under the collective title *Names for the numbered years* (1967). All of them have macabre settings and absurd happenings. The action of *Friedhof*, a one-act play that has been adapted for radio, takes place in a graveyard that a man who recently died comes to accept as his rightful habitat. *My mother's house has too many rooms*, a play about a slightly mad family living in Uncover, B.C., is both violent and hilarious and is climaxed by a wedding at which the daughter stabs her new husband. *Do you remember one September afternoon?* is set in a ruined convent in England where three aging nuns, one of whom cannot speak, reflect on the past and the sad decline of their convent, and finally kill and bury their arrogant Mother Superior. It is unfortunate that the latter two plays have not had stage productions for they show an energy and a comic power that should make for successful theatre.

Arthur L. Murphy, a prominent surgeon in Halifax, has written a historical play based on events that took place in Ottawa during forty-eight crucial hours one week before the establishment of confederation. Entitled *The first falls on Monday* (1972) it focuses on the problem of cabinet representation for Québec and makes an educated guess at how that problem was solved so that the document could be signed as planned. The result is a skilful recreation of events, real and imagined, surrounding the formation of the first Canadian cabinet. The ambition and maneuvering of several of the Fathers of Confederation are combined with the charm and vitality of the wives of four of them. Dr Murphy also wrote *A virus called Clarence*

(1972), an imaginary tale of the discovery of the virus responsible for breast cancer. While sections of the play are somewhat technical for most readers, it blends the drama of the lives of people working in the laboratory of a university hospital with their dedicated search for a cure for the disease.

One of Len Peterson's early plays, *Burlap bags* (1972), originally produced in 1946, shows how this distinguished figure in Canadian theatre anticipated many of the techniques that were later associated with the theatre of the absurd. A one-act play, it emphasizes the horror of much of modern life through the actions of two roomers who discover the diary of a tramp who has just killed himself. The tramp appears on stage to convince them of the hypocrisy and misery of people, many of whom are shown wearing burlap bags so they will not see the realities of life. Peterson's full-length play *The great hunger* (1967) is a tragedy set in an Eskimo winter camp on an arctic island. In spare yet elegant language, it shows the working out of the ancient Eskimo law of retribution when, in fulfilment of that law, a father kills his adopted son in spite of the efforts by a white stranger to teach the people the forgiveness of Jesus Christ. A somewhat similar play but one with a more contemporary setting is Herschel Hardin's *Esker Mike and his wife Agiluk* (1969), which takes place in and near Aklavik in the Northwest Territories in the early 1960s. It contrasts the simplicity and primitivism of the northern natives with the corruption and bureaucracy of the white man's world. In order to prevent any more of her children from being taken from her, Agiluk, an Eskimo woman of impressive strength of will, refuses to bear any more and kills the two children she has.

3. *Playwrights Co-op.* An organization based in Toronto, Playwrights Co-op 'exists to serve the Canadian playwright and the Canadian theatrical community'. It was established in January 1972 with a grant from the Canadian government and publishes in script form (in English) the work of contemporary Canadian playwrights written for the stage. In 1972 it published seventy-five plays—full-length and one-act—by forty playwrights; twenty-five of these plays were produced in 1972. The first director of the Co-op was Daryl Sharp. He was succeeded by David Scollard in June 1973.

Some of the plays already mentioned in this article were published by the Co-op. These include plays by Norman Williams (all three), Arthur L. Murphy (*A virus called Clarence*), Len Peterson (*Burlap bags*), and David Freeman (*Battering ram*). Several noteworthy playwrights have been published almost exclusively by the Co-op. John Palmer is perhaps the most prolific and imaginative of the Co-op playwrights. Of the four full-length plays he has published, *A touch of God in the golden age* is probably his best. It explores in powerful and often beautiful dialogue the despair of two men who reject their past, have no hope for the future, and rely on alcohol and drugs for support in the present. David French's *Leaving home* was the most successful Canadian play of 1972. With local colour and background that mark it as distinctly Canadian, it deals with a Newfoundland family living in Toronto in the late 1950s. The action of the play takes place on the eve of the marriage of one of the sons. In the course of the evening we witness the breakup of the family as the painful truth about all their relationships, especially the father's with his wife and two sons, is revealed. *Leaving home* has had the most productions of any Co-op play—two on stage and one on television in 1972—and has several stage productions scheduled for 1973. It was published in book form by New Press in 1973.

Tom Hendry's *Fifteen miles of broken glass* is a warm, humorous, nostalgic dramatization of a romantic young man's gradual acceptance of the realities of his world in the Winnipeg of 1945. It has been performed on stage, radio, and television. Jack Winter's *Party day* was commissioned as the opening work in the Studio of the National Arts Centre, Ottawa, in June 1969. A multi-media presentation, it uses (the reason why is not always clear) Joseph Goebbels, Hitler's minister of propaganda, and the Nazi Party days of the 1930s to explore the relationship between politics and the arts. *Buffalo jump* is Carol Bolt's fast-moving dramatization of the depression years in western Canada and the role played in them by former prime minister R. B. Bennett and other leaders. It ends with the Regina riot of 1935 during which several strikers are attacked and imprisoned as communists. Ann Henry's *Lulu Street* is also located in a troubled moment of Canadian history, the time of the Winnipeg General Strike of 1919. But the emphasis here is not so much on the political and social crisis as on the lives of several people, especially a leader of the strikers and his daughter, living in a frame house on Lulu St in the midst of the turmoil. Jack Gray's *Chevalier Johnstone* delves much farther back into Canadian history to present in comic form the antics of a Scot, the Chevalier James de Johnstone de Moffat, who, after the battle of Culloden, joined the French against the English in the defence of the fortress of Louisburg on Cape Breton Island in 1758. Though somewhat drawn out, the play has a delightful and amorous hero and enlivens an important moment of Canadian history. George Walker subtitled his play *The Prince of Naples* 'a cerebral farce in one act'. (The title is the signature Neitzsche used late in his life.) It is marked by sharp dialogue between its two characters—one a young teacher, the other his elderly pupil—and incisive satire on the modern penchant for learning irrelevancies. *Maybe we could get some Bach* is a clever, gentle farce by Louis Del Grande about an insecure young man and a forward young woman living together in New York in the 1950s. The pace of the action, the comic situations, and the witty repartee remind one of the comedies of Neil Simon. Ben Tarver's *The savage dream* is a free adaptation of the Calderon classic *La vida es sueño*: in a manner reminiscent of Pirandello, it raises the question of just what the real world is when, at the end of the play, the main character Segismund reverts to the animal clothing he wore in the opening scene and suggests to the audience that all the previous action was only a dream. Fabian Jennings wrote *Charles Manson AKA (i.e., also known as) Jesus Christ*, 'a rock-musical tragedy' with music by Allen Rae. Centred on the spectacular trial of Manson and his 'family' for the Sharon Tate murders, with flashbacks into the family's way of life, the play asserts that American society is as responsible for the crimes as the individuals on trial. It had a very successful production at Theatre Passe Muraille in Toronto in 1971 under the direction of John Palmer. Martin Hunter's *Young hunting* is set in an old house in the Ontario countryside where a group of people attempt to live an unfettered life. In the course of this carefully structured and psychologically probing work they learn some hard truths about themselves, and Jeannie, who had organized the group on her return from thirteen years in Europe, decides that she must leave. Finally James Nichol, who has had several plays produced on radio and television, published *The house on Chestnut Street*, a play with an imaginary Canadian rural setting in 1900. Evoking as it does the rural domesticity of a small turn-of-the-century community, it is a moving study of a family whose mother becomes unhappy with her unambitious husband and makes a vain attempt at infidelity with his employer.

4. *Anthologies.* The first drama anthology to appear in some years was *A collection of Canadian plays* (1972) edited by Rolf Kalman. Attractively illustrated and designed, though somewhat overpriced for the average reader, the book contains six recent plays by five Canadian authors. They are written in various dramatic styles but the book makes no attempt to be distinctively Canadian in theme or subject matter. The failure to include a play from Québec in translation is an unfortunate omission. *Counsellor extraordinary* by Stewart Boston portrays the role played by Sir Francis Bacon in the conflict between Queen Elizabeth I and Essex. The dialogue is an elegant imitation of Elizabethan prose; the play is well constructed, though few relationships are much developed in its many short scenes. Monroe Scott's *Wu-Feng*, written for the open stage, contains much elaborate dancing and choral movement as it tells of an uprising in 1769 by a mountain tribe in Taiwan against Wu-Feng, the appointed governor, who thwarts their leader's plans by offering himself in sacrifice. The dialogue is a mixture of Oriental wisdom, poetry, and North American humour. The two one-act plays in the anthology are by Sheldon Rosen: *Love mouse* and *Meyer's room*, which have been produced on stage together. Both are farcical and surrealistic. *Love mouse* shows how a couple married eleven years become reacquainted when their diningroom floor is flooded and in the ensuing confusion they meet in succession a mouse, a rat, a fox, a wolf, and an insurance man—all played by a single mime. *Meyer's room* dramatizes the frustrations and limitations of three men—one of whom is called Rock Hudson, another Madeline—in the room of the third, Meyer. In the final scene of the play Meyer has been shot; Rock cries from inside the room, 'Let me out!', while Madeline cries from the outside, 'Let me in!'. *Colour the flesh the colour of dust* by Michael Cook is set in St

John's, Newfoundland, in the spring of 1762 when the English and French were fighting for possession of that town. The action is concerned mainly with the lives of the common people living there, who fare badly no matter who is in command. While the play effectively creates the precarious atmosphere in which they live, it suffers from a confusion of styles and language, and neither plot nor character is very fully developed. The last play in the collection is perhaps the best—*Exit muttering*, a comedy by Donald Jack. Cleverly constructed, with some brilliant dialogue, it illustrates the plight of a married man with three women in his life—one of whom he loves spiritually, one intellectually, and the other physically. Through a complicated set of circumstances he loses all three, only to find that he is happier alone. *A collection of Canadian plays* was especially timely in that it was the first anthology composed largely of full-length Canadian plays (if one excepts the second volume of Canadian plays from Hart House Theatre, Toronto, published in 1926). *Dialogue & dialectic: a Canadian anthology of short plays*, edited by the Alive Theatre Workshop of Guelph, Ont., contains nine one-act plays, each by a different author. The majority are non-realistic and the better ones are distinguished for theatrical rather than literary merits. They include a wide variety of themes, from American domination of the Canadian economy (*The subsidiary vice-president* by Jerzy Szablowski) to the nature of man and man's perception of himself (*A glass darkly* by S. R. Gilbert). There is also a mime play, *Hell's bells*, by Philip Spensley. With the growing support and awareness of Canadian drama and literature, and the desire to study more Canadian plays in schools and universities, it is hoped that other anthologies of full-length plays will appear (more reasonably priced) in the near future. JN

Drama in French. Until very recently, when English-language plays began to be published with some frequency, French-Canadian dramatists were more fortunate than their English-Canadian counterparts because publishers in Québec have been ready to print much of the good drama that has been produced in that province since the 1950s. Concentrated in one province and often in one city (Montreal), and with a common cultural background and a common concern for the preservation and enrichment of their culture, these dramatists have treated similar themes and subjects (unlike English-speaking Canadians). They have also worked more closely together in the theatre and have cooperated in the development of a distinctive québécois drama. Most prominent among the Québec publishers of drama has been the Montreal firm Leméac, which exercises what amounts almost to a monopoly on French-Canadian plays and publishes several paperback editions of individual playwrights each year. Leméac has two important series of plays—'Collection théâtre canadien' and 'Collection répertoire québécois'—and has recently taken over distribution of a series on Québec drama entitled 'Théâtre vivant', originally published by Holt, Rinehart and Winston. (The best-known play in this series is Michel TREMBLAY's *Les belles-soeurs* (1968).) French Canada has also been fortunate in that one of its leading annuals, *Écrits du Canada français*, has regularly published one-act and full-length plays.

Young dramatists have received encouragement from the Centre d'Essai des Auteurs dramatiques, a Montreal organization that fosters French-Canadian drama in both French- and English-speaking parts of the country. Noteworthy too is the encouragement Québec dramatists have received from Radio-Canada, the French-language section of the Canadian Broadcasting Corporation. Many of Québec's leading writers have had their plays adapted for television and radio, and many of them have made their mark as writers of television drama, either of series (téléromans) or of individual plays (téléthéâtre). This encouragement has been extended by Québec publishers, who have been ready to publish both television series (such as *Cap-aux-Sorciers* (1969) by Guy Dufresne) and television plays (such as *Entre midi et soir* (1971) by Marcel DUBÉ, *La mercière assassinée* (1967) by Anne HÉBERT, *Tuez le veau gras* (1970) by Claude JASMIN, and *Marie-Emma* (1970) by André Laurendeau).

1. *Plays by established writers.* Many of the established Québec writers continue to publish plays, most of which are in the realistic tradition. Gratien GÉLINAS published *Hier les enfants dansaient* (1968), the third and most contemporary of his full-length plays, which is a compassionate treatment of the father and son in a prominent Montreal family

that is divided on the issue of separatism. Marcel Dubé, the most prolific of Québec dramatists, had almost all his stage plays published or republished during our period. Republished were the early plays that dealt with the lower classes of east Montreal: *Zone* (1968), *Un simple soldat* (1967), *Le temps des lilas* (1969), and *Florence* (1970). Newly published plays with characters from this same class are *L'échéance du vendredi* and *Paradis perdu* (1970), and *Le naufragé* (1971). In most of his later plays attention shifts to a disillusioned middle class, often living in Montreal, and their ill-fated struggles to find happiness in an increasingly urbanized and technological world. Among these plays are *Les beaux dimanches* (1968), *Bilan* (1968), *Virginie* (1968), *Pauvre amour* (1969), *Le coup de l'étrier* and *Avant de t'en aller* (1970), and *Un matin comme les autres* (1971). What many consider to be Dubé's masterpiece, *Au retour des oies blanches* (1969), is written in an elegant style and is so carefully structured in its treatment of the relationships of an upper-class Québec family that it comes very close to Dubé's ideal of tragedy in the classical sense. (It was translated by Jean Remple and published as *The white geese* (1972).) Many of the plays that have appeared in the television series 'Le monde de Marcel Dubé' have been published as a separate collection by Leméac. The first title of the collection, *Entre midi et soir* (1971) is composed of eight episodes in the lives of a middle-aged couple, their family, and their friends, all affected by the 'noonday devil' of ennui and restlessness. The loose structure of the play and the sentimentality of some of the situations, dictated no doubt by the demands of the television-serial format, make it one of the less satisfying of his published works in spite of its insights into the lives of the characters.

Some of Françoise LORANGER's television plays were published, including *Un cri qui vient de loin* (1967) and *Jour après jour* (1971). While dealing often with themes and situations similar to Dubé's, Loranger presents them at a more troublesome psychological level and exposes their more shattering effects. (Dubé reminds us of Chekhov, while Loranger resembles Strindberg.) *Un cri qui vient de loin* juxtaposes past and present as a young married man, on the point of leaving his wife because of her supposed infidelity, realizes that he has been brought to this pass by the real infidelity of his own mother, which he witnessed as a boy. *Jour après jour* shows the effect an abandoned and overpowering mother has on the lives of her three grown daughters as she and two of them destroy the courtship of the third. *Encore cinq minutes* (1967), a play for the stage, bares the bitterness between a husband and wife whose daughter's elopement is seen as the wish fulfilment of the wife. When the daughter returns after the disillusioning affair, the mother decides that she herself will leave.

Yves THÉRIAULT's plays are usually spare in plot, language, and setting, and deal with the elemental forces of life in a family or a community. *Le marcheur* (1968) shows how the oppression of a tyrannical father can stifle the need of his children to develop and grow. Set in a country home in the course of one day, it dramatizes the rebellion of the children in the presence of the mother while the father, who is near death and never appears on stage, paces loudly upstairs. *Frédange* (1970), set 'somewhere in the world', is filled with foreboding as a husband returns to his wife after abandoning her for six years only to submit to the command of his paralysed mother (reminiscent of the mother in Zola's *Thérèse Raquin*) that he, and not the shepherd his wife has taken, must leave. *Les terres neuves* (1970) shows a poor and unhappy people from a miserable village on their way to a new village; as they approach this promised land they meet its inhabitants—also leaving for a promised land. 'The misery depicted here', says Thériault, 'is so transcendent that it has no language, no blood, no race, no geography.'

Jacques LANGUIRAND had two plays published in our period. *Les grands départs* (1970), first published in 1958, deals with a theme common to many Québec dramatists, that of a stifling family situation that various individuals try to leave but cannot; only the crippled grandfather in this play, disgusted when neither his daughter nor his granddaughter can do so, summons up the courage to depart. Though the action is melodramatic and unmotivated at times, the play is carefully constructed and psychologically probing. *Klondyke* (1971) is a spirited and light-hearted look at the gold rush of 1896, with dance, drama, poetry, and song. (The music was composed by Gabriel Charpentier.) It is followed by Languirand's essay, 'Le

Québec et l'américanité', which explains what he is saying in the play. By 'américanité' he means the American quest for adventure, manifested so strongly in the days of the gold rush. This spirit is seen as a suppressed part of the French-Canadian soul. He concludes by affirming: 'We must rediscover the America in us . . . render unto Dionysus the things that are of Dionysus.'

Claire MARTIN, who is best known as a novelist and writer of memoirs, wrote a play based on her novel *Les morts* called *Moi, je n'étais qu'espoir* (1972), While somewhat static and claustrophobic, it is a penetrating study of a woman, 'Elle', whose neglect has been responsible for the death of two of her lovers and who at the end is left alone and unrepentant with her novels and her writing. Marie-Claire BLAIS, also better known as a novelist, tried her hand at dramatic writing in *L'exécution* (1968), a macabre study of boys in a residential school who, in a Neitzschian desire for power, plan and execute the murder of one of their fellow students. The play shows the author's preoccupation with the evil and distortions of life, but it too often substitutes discussion for dramatic action.

Collections and revisions of previously published plays by three different authors appeared. André Laurendeau's *Théâtre* (1970) contains *Deux femmes terribles*, *Marie-Emma*, and *La vertu des chattes*. *Deux femmes terribles* was produced by the Théâtre du Nouveau Monde in Montreal in 1961; the other two were done on television. In spite of the refined and sometimes poetic dialogue of these works, the conflict and characters are not made sufficiently real for the reader. The best of the three, *Marie-Emma*, the story of a young Montreal girl in search (like her namesake Emma Bovary) of herself, includes a social and political dimension not found in the others. Anne Hébert's *Le temps sauvage* (1967) contains, besides the title play, *La mercière assassinée*, written for television, and *Les invités au procès*, written for radio. A distinguished poet and novelist, Hébert shows in these plays her facility with poetry, fantasy, and allegory. *Le temps sauvage*, though loose in structure, reminds one of Thériault in its fascination with an analysis of an elemental situation. The play is about a mother-dominated family that has been forced to withdraw from the world of the city to live in the wilderness and the mother's attempts to prevent any intrusion of that world into the lives of her children. Jacques FERRON republished three of his plays in his *Théâtre: Volume I* (1968). Two of them, *Les grands soleils* and *Le Don Juan chrétien*, are revisions of previously published plays; the third, *Tante Elise ou le prix de l'amour*, is a one-act play. *Les grands soleils*, called a 'cérémonial' in the 1968 version, is centred on the heroism of Jean-Olivier Chénier and his companions in the 1837 rebellion against the English forces under Colborne. Ferron dramatizes what he sees as the real birth of the people of French Canada and this play has been hailed as a rallying cry for a genuine patriotism on the part of the people of Québec.

2. *Plays of political, social, and historical content*. Several recently published Québec plays have treated political, social, or historical events of special concern to Canadians. Prominent among these events are those associated with Québec's identity and nationalism, including the traumatic crisis of October 1970. Jacques Ferron, the doctor and writer who played an important political role in that event, wrote a shorter and less optimistic work on French-Canadian identity after *Les grand soleils* entitled *Le coeur d'une mère* (1969). The theme is revealed in the subtitle—'le tragique refus d'être québécois'—and is dramatized through three characters playing multiple roles, and especially through Septime who, having sought the true meaning of Québec, is finally given it—after he has killed himself—in the form of his mother's heart in a jar. Guy Dufresne's *Le cri de l'engoulevent* (1969)—translated by Philip London and Laurence Bérard and published in English as *The call of the whippoorwill* (1972)—is a realistic drama in which a strongminded Québec farmer refuses to make a deal to sell his land to an American and as a result loses both money and his daughter to the American. The play can be seen as underlining both the necessity for Québec to accept the ways of the new and open industrial society and also the difficulties and dangers this entails. The date of the original production of the play, 1960—often considered the year in which Québec's 'Quiet Revolution' began — is important for an understanding of the impact of this play. Dufresne also wrote a historical drama, *Les traitants* (1969), based on an inquest in New France into the sale of intoxicating beverages to Indians in 1665. Dufresne calls the play a

'fresco' and attempts to depict a whole epoch in Canadian history; but while the dialogue is often moving, the action of the play is rather static. Jean-Louis Roux, better known as a director than a playwright, tried to do something similar in *Bois-brûlés* (1968), which he labelled an 'epic documentary' on the rise and fall of Louis Riel; it includes music composed by Gabriel Charpentier. But here again the dramatic action suffers; in the attempt at comprehensive historical recreation, little attention is given to the portrayal or development of character. Françoise Loranger turned her attention during this period from domestic drama to politically involved works. *Le chemin du Roy* (1969), subtitled a 'comédie patriotique', was written in collaboration with Claude Levac. In the best dramatic-workshop fashion, the play presents the conflict between Ottawa and Québec by means of a hockey game played at the Montreal Forum and against the background of the visit to Canada and 'Vive le Québec libre!' speech of French President Charles de Gaulle in 1967. The game pits federal politicians Pearson, Diefenbaker, and LaMarsh against Johnson, Lesage, and Lévesque. Québec wins 4 to 2. A more serious but less successful attempt by Loranger to combine drama and politics is her *Un si bel automne* (1971), which depicts the failure of a young Indian to win acceptance and love in a white man's world. The events take place during the October crisis, but since the main character has little interest in politics, the political crisis merely serves as a device to get him imprisoned and to destroy his romance with a white girl. *Médium saignant* (1970)—set at a meeting attended by a mayor, his council, and aroused citizens in one section of Montreal—revolves around the issue of language rights in the province of Québec and reminds one strongly of the recent embittered meetings on the same subject in the Montreal suburb of St Léonard. Though its claim to be considered drama has been questioned, the play aroused violent anti-English emotions on the part of some of the audience who attended it at the Comédie canadienne in 1970. Robert GURIK combines sharp satire and clever humour in his political dramas. *Hamlet, prince du Québec* (1968), using Shakespeare's play as a model, depicts the struggle between federalists and separatists in Québec: Laertes becomes Laertes-Trudeau and Horatio becomes Horatio-Lévesque. The hero dies in the arms of his separatist-counsellor, hoping that his death will bring freedom and independence to his people. *Les tas de sièges* (1971) is a series of three one-act plays, each concerned with issues raised during the October crisis. While the plays emphasize the need for Québec to separate and the alleged injustices committed during the crisis of October 1970, their lighter side is seen in the pun contained in the title, which can be understood to mean 'l'état de siège'—referring to the War Measures Act that was invoked by the Canadian federal government at that time. A more aggressive stance is taken by Dominique de Pasquale in his *On n'est pas sorti du bois* (1972), a fast-paced theatrical that includes music, lyrics, and dance. Taking his clue from Marshall MCLUHAN's statement that French Canadians make up one vast tribe thrust from the seventeenth into the twentieth century, the author depicts the Québécois as primitives who refuse to submit to the annihilation of their race, chanting 'We will not go to our burial . . .' and inviting the audience to join in. Novelist and critic Claude JASMIN published a television play, *Tuez le veau gras* (1970), that is an ironic though inconclusive statement about union organization and political corruption in Québec. In realistic fashion it dramatizes the futile efforts of a young intellectual to set up a union for workers in the town's biggest plant when he returns home after six years' study of sociology and industrial relations in Europe. When he leaves in the final scene, discouraged and physically beaten, to take a teaching position at a small college, the irony (suggested by the title) in the contrast between his reception and that of the prodigal son of the Bible becomes more clear.

The most imaginative of the dramatists to comment on the social and political situation in Québec is Jean-Claude Germain. His concern with basic issues of French-Canadian life and survival is combined with an ingenious theatricality that often calls to mind the techniques of Brecht. Though he does not provide any clear solutions to Québec's problems, he focuses attention on them by mocking satire. In 1969 he founded an organization called Le Théâtre du Même Nom. Its initials—TMN—are an ironic inversion of those of the established and more traditional Montreal group, Le Théâtre du

Nouveau Monde—TNM—and thus suggest its unconventional approach to theatre. First calling themselves Les Enfants de Chénier and then (in 1971) Les P'tits Enfants Laliberté, the actors of Le Théâtre du Même Nom performed several plays by Germain, of which three have been published. *Diguidi, diguidi, ha! ha! ha!* (1972) is a bitter commentary on the conflicts and oppressions that have existed in Québec family life, revealed through the relations between a father, mother, and son who regularly fall out of character to comment on their life in Québec. *Si les Sansoucis s'en soucient, ces Sansoucis-ci s'en soucieront-ils? Bien parler, c'est se respecter!* (1972), which Germain subtitles 'une sotie' (a farce), conjures up the past of an imaginary Québec family, the Sansoucis, through its three remaining members: Tharaise, Chlinne, and Farnand. Playing the roles of lawyers and actors at the trial of an accused musician who represents the vulnerability of the ordinary Québécois, the slightly mad Sansoucis are presented as types of those French Canadians who have been guilty of complicity with the English oppressors. (The one witness in the play, Madame Sansfaçon, lists Cartier, Saint Laurent, and Trudeau among the oppressors.) The fate of Farnand Sansoucis is followed up in *Le roi des mises à bas prix* (1972). Here we see him—and by extension all French Canadians who have accepted North-American culture unquestioningly—as the victim of the worst aspects of modern living. A note of hope is sounded at the end when 'le television man' leaves Farnand's apartment, the television ceases to function, and Farnand, who now feels that he is free, breaks into laughter.

Antonine MAILLET set her play *Les Crasseux* (1968) in Acadia. In a contemporary setting it contrasts the lives of the rich and the poor in a small village and shows how the latter, after years of subservience, manage by determination and shrewdness to take over the land of their rich neighbours. The play is marked by caricature and considerable humour, much of which is due to the dialogue spoken by the poor, whose speech is a survival of a sixteenth-century French brought to Acadia from central France and is still spoken among the poor in some regions of New Brunswick. This argot is the reason for much of the success of Maillet's *La Sagouine* (1971) ('The slattern'). (Like several recent popular plays in Québec, it is a monologue. Jacqueline Barrette's *Ca dit qu'essa-a-dire* (1972) is another.) La Sagouine is a charlady who appeared in *Les Crasseux* as a spy for the poor. In *La Sagouine* she is seventy-two years old (she was forty-five in *Les Crasseux*) and recalls various people and situations that she has observed in her life. Eight of the sixteen segments were adapted for the enormously popular stage presentation by Viola Léger, which has toured most provinces in Canada and has been presented at the Canadian Culture Centre in Paris.

3. *'Joual' in the theatre.* Perhaps the most significant development in recent French-Canadian drama has been the growing popularity of playwrights whose characters speak *joual*, the vernacular used by many Québécois today. *Joual* is a mixture of French, Anglicisms, slang, mispronunciations, and the elision or omission of words or syllables. (The word *joual* is derived from the way in which the French word for horse—*cheval*—is pronounced in some areas of Québec.) While Québec dramatists such as Gélinas and Dubé did not hesitate to put slang into the mouths of their characters drawn from the lower classes, they did not adopt *joual* as the standard form of speech in their drama. It was Michel Tremblay, currently the most popular dramatist in Québec, who began the assault of *joual* on the Montreal stage with his production of *Les belles-soeurs*, which was both produced and published in 1968. It is an evocation of the lives of lower-class women living in the east end of Montreal. Through the mouths of the all-female cast of fifteen, Tremblay presents the fractured speech that may be heard on the streets there. The slender plot tells of the winning of a million trading stamps by one of the women. When her neighbours come to help her lick and place the stamps on cards, the poverty, greed, pettiness, misery, backbiting, and hopelessness of all of them are revealed. As always with Tremblay, language and rhythm in the scenes are important techniques; the working-class women speak both as individuals and as a chorus. Tremblay's success and popularity, as well as the general acceptance of *joual* on the stage, continued as he presented a new play almost every year after his first triumph. *En pièces détachées* (1970) shows the material and spiritual poverty of a Montreal family struggling with themselves and with their

neighbours in a tenement section where no privacy is possible. *La Duchesse de Langeais* (1970) is a monologue by an aging homosexual from Québec as he gets intoxicated at a bar while vacationing in the tropics. His true origins are revealed as his attempts to speak refined French are belied by his constant falling back into *joual*. Tremblay's most moving play to date is *À toi, pour toujours, ta Marie-Lou* (1971), a harrowing picture of a Québec family whose two daughters, ten years after the violent death of their parents, reflect on the quality of life in their home and the lasting effects it has had on them. The influence of musical structure on Tremblay's work is seen here as the girls' conversation is intertwined with the bickering of their parents shortly before their deaths. Tremblay has used *joual* in adaptations of two plays by Paul Zindel: *L'effet des rayons gamma sur les vieux-garçons* (1970) and '*. . . et mademoiselle Roberge boit un peu . . .*' (1971); he also adapted Aristophanes' *Lysistrata* (1969). The opposition generated by plays that use *joual* was highlighted when an offer was made in 1972 by France's Jean-Louis Barrault to present *Les belles-soeurs* at the Théâtre des Nations in Paris. When Québec's minister of cultural affairs, Claire Kirkland-Casgrain, was approached for the necessary subsidy for the production, she refused to grant it on the grounds that the language of Tremblay's play made it an unworthy representation of Québec culture abroad. This attitude has been satirized in the *joual* plays of Jean-Claude Germain (see above), the title of whose *Si les Sansoucis . . .* ends with the words *Bien parler, c'est se respecter!*.

Roch CARRIER's *La guerre, yes sir!* (1970), which also uses *joual*, met with similar opposition. Because of the alleged impurity of its language it was removed from the libraries of all the secondary schools in a district south of Montreal and the author himself was prevented from giving a scheduled talk at one of the schools. The play is centred on a rural Québec community in 1942 and shows the misunderstanding and violence that arise when the body of a French Canadian killed in the war is accompanied to his home by a group of non-French-speaking English-Canadian soldiers. Based on Carrier's novel of the same title, the play toured Europe in 1971 after its successful run in Montreal the previous year. In 1972 it became the first Québec play to be produced (in translation) at the Stratford Festival in Ontario.

More traditional dramatists have not hesitated to use *joual* in some of their recent plays. Guy Dufresne's *Docile* (1972), a slight comedy about a palmist who reads people's fortunes in their toes and thighs, is one example; Françoise Loranger's *Le chemin du Roy* (1969) is another. One of the most inventive of the *joual* dramatists is Jean BARBEAU, who at twenty-eight is three years younger than Tremblay. Barbeau's best-known play is *Ben-Ur* (1971), whose title is a 'pop' version of the anti-hero's name, Joseph Benoît Urbain Théberge, and is a nickname that labels him for life. The play is an indictment of the superficiality of many aspects of North American society and shows how Ben-Ur's fantasies, fed by his constant diet of comic books, lead to tragedy when they become the basis for action in real life. In another of Barbeau's plays, *Le chemin de Lacroix* (1971), the main character has a friend from France who is constantly correcting his *joual* and urging him to speak proper French. The irony and humour involved in this situation exemplify the fact that in the eyes of many Québec dramatists and theatregoers the struggle for the acceptance of *joual* on the stage has indeed been won, in spite of the reluctance of some purists to admit the dramatic value of this form of spoken French.

4. *Avant-garde drama.* In their efforts to develop a distinctive Québécois drama, many playwrights have abandoned the realism of their predecessors and sought new forms for the expression of their culture and concerns. While these forms are often derived from avant-garde theatre in the United States and Europe, and while they have not always been successful on the stage, they are evidence of the continuing vitality of playwrights in French Canada. Robert Gurik has been one of the most innovative of the young writers. In a way that calls to mind Samuel Beckett's plays, he has often chosen a striking though absurd situation that he uses as the focus for his social or metaphysical statements. *Le pendu* (1970)—translated by Philip London and Lawrence Bérard and published in English as *The hanged man* (1972)—is an ironic statement of man's inhumanity. One of the characters poses as a 'hanged' man so that he and his father can make a living by the

sale of the rope by which he 'hangs': when he becomes world famous and his whole community profits by the ruse, they do hang him rather than reveal the deception. *À coeur ouvert* (1969) makes the same statement rather obviously and grotesquely: the ruling class of a futuristic society decides which other classes of people will 'donate' their hearts to the Heart Bank so that the rulers can live on; as each group of donors rebels in turn and assumes power, it becomes as inhumane as the group that preceded it. *Api 2967* (1971) creates a science-fiction world from which all human emotion and all growing things have been removed; after a vain attempt to break out of this world, the hero and heroine are subdued and forced to recite the slogan 'Life is not worth anything'. *La palissade* (1971), a more hopeful play, uses the image of a fence set on a street corner to examine the unhappiness of mankind and the prospect of its being happier 'on the other side'. *Le procès de Jean-Baptiste M.* (1972), a somewhat simplistic approach to a complex issue, uses multiple role-playing and choral dialogue to raise the question of the guilt of a little man, the victim of an impersonal world, who murders his employers. Barbeau uses the ritualism of the Catholic Way of the Cross in his *Le chemin de Lacroix* (1971), including chants between the fourteen stations, to emphasize the injustice of social systems. His *Goglu* (1971), a one-act play in which two friends meet in a park, is almost a monologue of despair and frustration by a rootless young man in an empty world. The play has many similarities in setting, theme, and technique to Albee's *The zoo story*. Alain Pontaut spells out his theme in the title of his play *Un bateau que Dieu sait qui avait monté et qui flottait comme il pouvait c'est-à-dire mal* (1970), which he subtitled 'a metaphysical operetta'. Though the play is too discursive in places, the central image of a ship stuck on a reef serves as a metaphor against which the three characters (two men and a woman) reflect on their values and relationships as they wait, try to dislodge the ship, and wonder what is beyond the horizon. Some of the later plays of Françoise Loranger mentioned above make her one of the few of the older dramatists who have enthusiastically moved from realistic drama to a more fluid and open type of theatre. This readiness is also manifested in her *Double jeu* (1969), which she describes as a 'psycho-drama', an attempt to involve the audience directly in the action. Indeed, members of the audience are invited on stage during the intermission to enact the story that the actors themselves have been trying to dramatize under the supervision of the sociology professor in whose class the play is set. Loranger has said that the play is an attempt to adapt the Living Theatre of New York to the Québec stage.

Gilles Derome's *Qui est Dupressin?* (1972) was one of the first stage plays to break with the traditional forms of French-Canadian drama when it was premiered in 1961. It combines farce and philosophical concern with identity in a manner reminiscent of Pirandello. A man and a girl working in a mental hospital, engaged to be married, adopt roles to cure a patient, Dupressin; but Dupressin also plays the role of their superior and is so changed at the end of the play that he and the engaged girl go off together, leaving her fiancé behind. Renald Tremblay's *Il suffit d'un peu d'air* (1971) has also been called a psychodrama. The four characters, two men and two women, who constitute in the author's mind one character, stand on a bare stage and recite their lines in mechanical fashion as they are gradually reduced from superficial chatter to harsh bickering and finally total passivity. More important perhaps than the characters, who become more tiresome as they become more indistinguishable, are the careful and detailed instructions on the use of lighting to reflect the many moods of the play. Roger Dumas has written two comic fantasies, *Les millionaires* (1967) and *Les comédiens* (1969). The first concerns a group of lovable rogues who execute their last robbery with the aim of passing the million-dollar mark in stolen money only to find on counting it that they are one dollar short. The second involves a disorganized family of actors and its entourage living on a desert island, and a director who tries unsuccessfully to get them to put on a play. Dumas contrives situations that are often genuinely funny, but his plots tend to be disconnected. He shows some advance from the abrupt, monosyllabic dialogue of *Les millionaires* in the more subtle and sometimes poetic speeches of *Les comédiens*. A more genuine poetic talent in the theatre is Jacques BRAULT. His *Trois partitions* (1972) contains two television plays, *La morte-*

saison and *Quand nous serons heureux*, and one radio play, *Lettre au directeur. La morte-saison*, a short work, juxtaposes poetry and prose, realism and fantasy, and the disillusionment of a long-married couple and the romantic love of Roméo and Juliette, whose names they happen to bear. *Quand nous serons heureux*, a more ambitious play, is a fairy-tale in a modern setting showing how beautiful dreams can triumph over ugly reality in the lives of Felix L'Heureux, a janitor, and his family. Just as engaging is *Lettre au directeur*, which depicts a second-class office clerk approaching retirement who is more disposed to recite poetry and write novels on the job than to run messages. He is dissuaded from sending his letter of early resignation by a charlady who tells him how much she enjoys hearing him recite when she comes to clean the office every Friday afternoon. In a *Post-script* to this play Brault emphasizes the importance of the French language for the identity of the people of Québec. Jacques Duchesne's comedy *Le quadrillé* (1968) is less successful than the work of either Dumas or Brault. It is a series of skits and songs hung loosely together in fifty-seven scenes on such topics as women, war, and terrorism. Nevertheless it was quite popular on stage in both Montreal and Paris. Finally the most unconventional play of the new Québec theatre is *Wouf wouf* (1970) by Yves Sauvageau, who died in 1970 at the age of twenty-four. Completely non-linear in its conception of time, the play is a violent rejection of the realistic theatre. Much of the dialogue is incomprehensible on the rational level; by the end several of the characters are reduced to adding the words 'wouf-wouf' to anything they say. The play is an attack on the frustration of the human spirit in a dehumanized world and manifests the deep sensitivity and outrage of an author faced with such a world. But it is difficult to see how a work that often has little communication with the mind and emotions of its audience can have much meaning for them. Though dramatist and critic Jean-Claude Germain entitled his introduction to the play 'The first spring of the québécois theatre', it would appear that a more fruitful direction for Québec theatre is that being taken by such writers as Michel Tremblay, Jean Barbeau, and Germain himself, who have shown a greater mastery of the language and craft of the theatre. JN

Draper, James. See POLITICAL WRITINGS IN ENGLISH 5.

Drucker, Phillip. See INDIANS 5.

Dubé, Jean Claude. See HISTORY STUDIES IN FRENCH 3.

Dubé, Marcel (1930–). Born in Montreal, he attended the Jesuit Collège Sainte-Marie and the Université de Montréal, which he left before completing his graduate studies to pursue a career of writing for the theatre. He also attended theatre schools in Paris in 1953–4. The most published and successful dramatist to emerge from Québec, he is probably the best Canadian dramatist writing in English or French. While he is primarily a playwright, he has also written poetry, short stories, radio and television scripts, adaptations and translations of plays written in English, and topical articles for such journals as *Perspectives*, *Le Magazine Maclean*, and *Cité libre*.

Dubé came into prominence as a dramatist with the successful production of *Zone*, which in 1953 was judged the best Canadian play at the Dominion Drama Festival in Victoria, B.C. In his stage and television plays he has been concerned with man's search for a happiness that is invariably fleeting or unattainable; with the fragility of human relationships; and with the emptiness of modern urban living. While the popular demand for Dubé's plays on television gave him much experience in dramatic writing, it may be responsible for the sentimental and melodramatic qualities that are found even in his stage plays. His dramatic technique has been influenced by Anouilh and by the realists of the modern American theatre, especially Miller, whose *Death of a salesman* Dubé adapted for French television. Like Miller, Dubé has consciously set out to write tragedy but in settings that are rooted in his native province. 'What is important to me,' he has said, is 'to arouse in people the tragic emotion.' While he uses the ordinary language of French Canadians, he rarely attempts to reproduce *joual*, as many other contemporary Québec dramatists have done. Especially in his later plays, he tends to write in an elegant, refined, and often highly poetic style.

Some seventeen of Dubé's plays have been

published to date. The early ones dealt with the lives of the lower classes, often in the east end of Montreal where Dubé grew up. These include *Zone* (1955), the story of a teenage gang of smugglers whose lives are restricted and frustrated by the very area or 'zone' in which they live, and *Un simple soldat* (1958; 1967), which depicts the dissolute and disheartening life of Joseph Latour, who returns from service in the Second World War, is unable to adjust to civilian life and the demands of his father and stepmother, and returns to the army to serve in the Korean war in which he is killed. *Le temps des lilas* (1958; 1969), a sad and moving play about the lives of a group of people in a Montreal boarding-house, is reminiscent of Chekhov, Dubé's favorite playwright, in the disillusionment of the characters and the quiet resignation of the old couple, Virgile and Blanche, at the end. *Florence* (1960; 1970) is a transitional work, showing Dubé's shift in interest to characters that belong to middle-class society, usually living in Montreal. *Bilan* (1968)—the title means 'balance sheet'—is an attempt to account for the human cost to William Larose, his wife and children, of financial success. *Les beaux dimanches* (1968) dramatizes the desperate efforts of four wealthy and unhappy couples to divert themselves in the course of one Sunday. (Their empty lives remind one of the characters in Fellini's *La dolce vita.*) *Au retour des oies blanches* (1969) is considered by many to be Dubé's best play to date. (It has been translated by Jean Remple and published as *The white geese* (1972).) It portrays an upper-class family in Quebec City and their gradual discovery of the truth about their relationships. The climax is reached when the central character, Geneviève, reveals that she conceived a child by Thomas, who was thought to be her uncle but is discovered to be her father. Not only the plot but also the structure and emotional impact of the play remind one strongly of *Oedipus the king*. *Pauvre amour* (1969) is a more optimistic play than many of its predecessors; while showing the breakdown of the marriage of Georges and Françoise, it ends on a note of hope as Georges begins working on the novel that he has put off writing for so long. Other plays by Dubé that have been published are *Octobre* (1964), *Virginie* (1968), *Le coup de l'étrier* and *Avant de t'en aller* (1970), *L'échéance de vendredi* and *Paradis perdu* (1970), *Un matin comme les autres* (1971), and *Le naufragé* (1971).

Dubé has written a great number of plays for television. One series, entitled 'La côte de sable', consisted of 68 thirty-minute episodes set in Ottawa during the war years; another, 'De 9 à 5', was made up of 108 thirty-minute dramas on the life of white-collar workers in Montreal. From the latter series a number of the programs were brought together under the title 'Le monde de Marcel Dubé' and repeated weekly on Radio-Canada. The Montreal firm Leméac, which publishes more plays than any other Québec publisher, has brought out most of Dubé's plays in French.

JN

Ducharme, Réjean (1942–). Born in Saint-Félix-de-Valois, Qué., he studied at the École Polytechnique in Montreal but left school to work in an office. He served in the arctic with the RCAF in 1962 and now lives in Montreal.

Ducharme's novels are notable for the dazzling pyrotechnics of their style and the blending of fantasy and realism with which they portray adolescents at war with an adult world they consider both menacing and empty. The half-Jewish, half-Catholic heroine of *L'avalée des avalés* (1966) reacts openly and savagely to the cruelty and neglect of her parents; she tries to 'swallow' the world by indulging in every possible experience, even the most sordid. *L'avalée des avalés*, which won a Governor General's Award as well as first prize in the Concours littéraires de la Province de Québec, was translated with the title of *The swallower swallowed* (1968) by Barbara Bray. *Le nez qui voque* (1967), which is written in journal form, describes the guilt-ridden sexual adventures of a sixteen-year-old who finally shuts himself up in a room with his girl friend to prepare for suicide. In *L'océantume*, published in 1968 but actually an earlier work, two young girls fantasize about journeys they will take to escape a reality they find unbearable. *La fille de Christophe Colombe* (1969) is pure satire—a mock epic in rhymed quatrains about some imaginary travels of Columbus.

See *Ducharme l'inquiétant* (1967), a literary study by Michel Van Schendel. JM

Duchesne, Jacques. See DRAMA IN FRENCH 4.

Duczynska, Ilona. See POETRY IN ENGLISH 4.

Dudek, Louis (1918–). Born in the east end of Montreal, of Polish immigrant parents, he attended McGill University from 1936 to 1940 and on graduation worked as an advertising copywriter and a free-lance journalist. In 1943 he moved to New York and enrolled for graduate study in journalism and history at Columbia University. Shortly afterwards he changed his major from journalism to literature. On completion of his doctoral course work, he accepted an English appointment at City College, New York. During his eight years in New York he became acquainted with writers Paul Blackburn, Cid Corman, and Herbert Gold, and began a correspondence with Ezra Pound. In 1951 Dudek returned to Montreal to teach at McGill University, where he lectures in modern poetry, Canadian literature, the art of poetry, and European literature.

Dudek began his career as a poet in the 1936–40 period, publishing social protest verse in *The McGill Daily*. In 1943 he joined John Sutherland and Irving LAYTON in editing *First Statement*, which Sutherland had founded in 1942, and contributed to it and its successor *Northern Review* throughout his New York years. On his return to Canada, Dudek became immediately a major force in Canadian small-press publishing and a major influence on the development of Canadian poetry. Instructed by the editorial activities of Americans such as Pound and Corman, he was convinced of the necessity for poets to take their means of publication out of the hands of commercial publishers and into their own. Throughout 1952–4 he was instrumental in shaping the editorial direction of Raymond SOUSTER's little magazine *Contact*. In 1952, together with Souster and Irving Layton, he founded Contact Press, which, between 1952 and 1967, would publish early books by most of the major poets of the sixties and early seventies. In 1956 he began another press, The McGill Poetry Series, which, despite its name, was entirely financed and edited by himself. In 1957 he began *Delta*, a personal literary magazine in which he attempted to promote further the urbane, realistic kind of writing his earlier editorial activities had encouraged. In 1966 he terminated *Delta*, but on the death of Contact Press in 1967 founded a new press, Delta Canada.

Dudek has been equally active as a poet, publishing *East of the city* (1946), *Twenty-four poems* (1952), *The searching image* (1952), *Europe* (1955), *The transparent sea* (1956), *En México* (1958), *Laughing stalks* (1958), *Atlantis* (1967), and *Collected poetry* (1971). His early poetry is almost all short lyrics that proceed from incidental observation and description toward a concluding insight or philosophical statement. Here Dudek employs few metaphors or elaborate images; his descriptions are direct and realistic. Although many of the scenes are from ghetto and working-class life, and many of the sentiments are Marxist in nature, a definite pessimism toward human accomplishment pervades these poems. Optimism is usually reserved for nature's powers—'the soon-rampant seed', 'the great orchestrating principle of gravity'.

With the publication of *Europe* and *En México*, Dudek moved from short, incidentally related lyrics to book-length meditations that are characterized by a prose-like rhythm and didactic tone. Unlike the lyrics, these long meditational poems interweave the general and particular so that their relationship is obscured. Thus, while some passages seem illustrated sermons, others seem to offer flashes of inspiration gained from particulars. Dudek has remarked in his one book of literary theory (*The first person in literature*, 1967) that because of our 'anarchically subjective' age, the egoist as writer must become a 'great moralist'. In *Europe*, *En México*, and *Atlantis* we see Dudek attempting to be the morally responsible egoist, to make his self universal, to come to terms with 'the enigma of human experience': 'the dichotomy of the self and the not-self, the I-myself and the mankind-to-which-I-belong'. Again Dudek is pessimistic about mankind's ability to reform and save itself. Joy, beauty, and eternity are certain residents only of nature. At the end of *Atlantis*, when the poet finally gains a vision of the lost continent, its 'palaces, and domes' are a North Atlantic iceberg—'a piece of eternity', 'a carved silent coffin', that promises only 'darkness' and 'infinite night'.

Dudek is also the author of *Literature and the press: a history of printing, printed media, and their relation to literature* (1960). In collaboration with Irving Layton he compiled *Canadian poems: 1850–1952* (1952), and in collaboration with Michael Gnarowski *The making of modern poetry in Canada* (1967), an extremely useful anthology of documents relating to the development of Canadian poetry since 1910. He is also the editor of *Poetry of our time: an introduction to twentieth-century poetry including modern Canadian poetry* (1965). FD

Duffy, Dennis. See LITERARY STUDIES IN ENGLISH 4.

Dufresne, Guy. See DRAMA IN FRENCH intro., 2, and 3.

Duguay, Raoul (1939–). Born in Val d'Or, Qué., he is a poet who has been a sculptor, painter, musician, composer, and a performer in films and on the stage. He has taught literature in a classical college and was a critic of Québec writing for PARTI PRIS from 1966 until the magazine's demise in 1968. He was also an editor of the short-lived review *Quoi*, which appeared twice in 1967.

Duguay has published five collections of poetry. In *Ruts* (1966) and *Or le cycle du sang dure donc* (1967), Duguay deals with erotic themes in an intoxicating manner that is also irreverent in its use of religious symbolism. From his first collection onward, he showed a great interest in rhythm and the phonetic aspects of language and its ambiguities, often following the approach of improvised jazz with words and sounds, rather than notes, as his material. *Manifeste de l'infonie* (1970), *Encyclopédie rien* (1970), and *Lapokalipsô* (1971) are all closely related to Duguay's activities as leader and inspirer of the group of musicians/poets/painters/composers known as *l'Infonie*, who wear Oriental robes and pronounce their names backwards to create a bizarre effect. These books resemble collages, containing, besides verse and prose poems, musical scores, drawings, photographs—even a facsimile of the author's baptismal certificate—and much typographical experimentation. Duguay is mainly an oral poet and his interest in the many registers of the human voice and in semantic and phonetic subtleties is evident in these three books. The poems of the *Infonie* period are full of humour and the joy of living. In them one finds a combination of elements of the 'new culture', with its relativist interest in distant peoples and religions and in spiritual transformation, and of the American 'Yippee' phenomenon, which combined the former with radical political commitment. This is seen especially in Duguay's poems inspired by the October 1970 political crisis. (*Lapokalipsô*). The poet creates neologisms (e.g. verbs based on Québec and *alléluia*), and combines standard French with *joual* words and popular speech (*toulmonde, toultemps, toutunchacun*), written to resemble their pronunciation. These latter become refrains stressing the importance of Everyman and universality in the poet's view of the world. Sometimes Duguay uses verse resembling the tone and content of the Bible, occasionally to satirize sententiousness. His most recent poems reflect on the relationships between nature and culture and project the vision of a fraternal and creative universe.

Duguay's theoretical views on writing are outlined in 'Le stéréo poème audio-visuel' (*Culture vivante*, 12 February 1969). English translations of two of his poems appear in *How do I love thee?: sixty poets of Canada (and Quebec) select and introduce their own work* (edited by John Robert COLOMBO, 1970) and in *Ellipse* (Issue 6, Winter 1971). B-ZS

Duhamel, Roger. See ANTHOLOGIES IN FRENCH.

Dumas, Evelyn. See POLITICAL WRITINGS IN FRENCH 6.

Dumas, Roger. See DRAMA IN FRENCH 4.

Dumont, Fernand (1927–). Born in Montmorency, near Québec, he studied at Université Laval, where he is now director of the Institut supérieur des sciences humaines and co-director of the journal *Recherches sociographiques*, and at the University of Paris. His attitude as a writer and teacher through the years of rapid change in Québec has been described by the epithet 'conscience vigilante', prompted by the title of his latest collection of essays, *La vigile du Québec* (1971). Dumont is, for Québec, what his fellow sociologists call 'un définisseur de la situation'. While poets and novelists around him display a consciousness still clouded by the taboos, superstitions, and false ideologies of the past, Dumont exhibits a serene lucidity and confidently grapples with the problems thrown up by the contemporary cultural revolution. The reconciling of tradition and experience has constantly engaged his attention over the past twenty years. His first sociological work, a study written with Yves Martin of the region of Saint-Jérôme just north of Montreal, *L'analyse des structures sociales régionales* (1963), examines the effect on traditional life in this town of the opening of the Laurentian autoroute, which both bypassed it and gave its inhabitants rapid access to the city. Leaving field-work behind in his later essays—*Pour la conversion de la pensée chrétienne* (1964), *Le lieu de l'homme* (1967), and *La dialectique de l'objet économique* (Paris, 1970)—he looks at the ways in which culture, defined as 'l'outillage mental d'une société', conceptualizes experience and allows members of a society to stand away from their experience and recognize the unfamiliar. He writes a balanced critique of conformism, which he sees as the sclerosis of the symbolical framework with which experience is processed. The portrait that emerges of a society ill-equipped to adapt suggests Québec, though the essays proceed with a minimum of reference to concrete situations and are fed by the widest, most eclectic erudition. His thoughts on the transformation of the anachronistic concept of a Christian culture in Québec, presented in *Pour la conversion de la pensée chrétienne*, are reflected in the report published in 1971 of the Commission d'étude sur les laïcs et l'Église that he headed.

The desire to 'define the situation' and to see clearly the process by which a society elaborates its culture—its 'mental tools'—can be traced in his teaching, in which he is examining with his students the ideological development of French Canada from the early nineteenth century, and in three colloquia organized by the review *Recherches sociographiques*, the proceedings of which appeared as *Situation de la recherche sur le Canada français* (1962), *Littérature et société canadiennes-françaises* (1964) and *Le pouvoir dans la société canadienne-française* (1966).

Dumont's definition of an ideology as 'la *justification* d'une définition de la situation d'un groupe en vue de l'action' allows him to see both the sociologist and the writer as concerned with the same collective vision. Dumont himself, through his limpid, orderly poetry—*L'ange du matin* (1952) and *Parler de septembre* (1970)—fits his own definition of both the sociologist and the writer: 'Un homme [qui], en pensant aux autres, ose tenter de définir son univers d'existence.'

In the moving conclusion to an essay entitled 'Vie intellectuelle et société depuis 1945: la recherche d'une nouvelle conscience', in Pierre de Grandpré: *Histoire de la littérature française du Québec*, vol. III (1969), Dumont describes a walk with his father that took him past the tenement block in which he was born. 'Mon père, qui ne sait griffonner que son nom, m'a interpellé: toi qui sais écrire, il faudrait que tu dises tout cela . . .' Dumont has done just that. CRPM

Duncan, James S. See HISTORY STUDIES IN ENGLISH 13.

Dunn, Marty. See INDIANS 2.

Durocher, Olivier. See POLITICAL WRITINGS IN FRENCH 1.

Durocher, R. See HISTORY STUDIES IN FRENCH 1.

Duval, Paul. See HISTORY STUDIES IN ENGLISH 16.

Dyck, Harvey L. See HISTORY STUDIES IN ENGLISH 1.

E

Eayrs, James (1926–). James George Eayrs was born in London, Eng., and educated at the University of Toronto, Columbia University, and the London School of Economics. He was appointed to the department of political economy of the University of Toronto in 1951 and teaches international relations. Eayrs, who believes that academics should be active in political and public life, also writes weekly columns on international affairs in the Toronto *Star* and other Canadian newspapers; broadcasts on CBC radio; and in 1972–3 was a television host and commentator on the national network program *Weekend.* He is a frequent contributor to the *Canadian Forum* and *Saturday Night*, and has been co-editor of the *International Journal* since 1959. He is a Fellow of the Royal Society of Canada. In 1967 he was named a John Simon Guggenheim Memorial Fellow.

Eayrs is unusual among writers in his field in being a fine literary stylist: his writing is pungent, incisive, and lucid. He has been critical of those who separate military and diplomatic history and stresses their integral relationship in his analyses of national safety policies. In *Canada in world affairs:* IX: *October 1955 to June 1957* (1959) he examines the response of the Canadian government to Suez and other international events and shows Lester Pearson as an ingenious conciliator and a symbol of Canada's more active role in the world. *The art of the possible: government and foreign policy in Canada* (1961) is a historical survey, from Laurier's prime ministership, of the origins of foreign-policy-making institutions, how they work and how they evolve. *Northern approaches: Canada and the search for peace* (1961) is a series of provocative essays on the principal issues confronting Canada in defence and foreign policy. Eayrs' most widely acclaimed work is *In defence of Canada. 1: From the Great War to the Great Depression* (1964); *2: Appeasement and rearmament* (1965), for which he won a Governor General's Award; and *3: Peacemaking and deterrence* (1972). Volume 1 depicts a military establishment confronted by a parsimonious government overly influenced by isolationists and pacifists who bickered among themselves in a power struggle. Volume 2 covers the period 1935–40 and is highly critical of Mackenzie King's 'do-nothingism' in foreign policy and his support of appeasement to the extent that the armed forces were grossly unprepared for the Second World War. Volume 3 studies policy-making in the forties and early fifties and includes an analysis of the leading political and military personalities, reorganization of the military after the Second World War, and Canada's early involvement with the United Nations. *Diplomacy and its discontents* (1971) includes *Fate and will in foreign policy* (1967), the text of seven half-hour CBC radio broadcasts, and *Right and wrong and foreign policy* (1966), comments on the relation of individual ethics to the exercise of political power, together with a selection of Eayrs' more recent writings. *Minutes of the sixties* (1968) contains articles from his columns in the *Family Herald* of the previous eight years, while *Future roles for the armed forces of Canada* (1969) is a booklet in the 'Headlines' series of the Canadian Institute of International Affairs. His most recent book, *Greenpeace and her enemies* (1973), is a selection from his journalism of 1968–72, and deals with international politics ('The cracked terrorism'), universities ('Alma Mater sleeps ground'), public figures ('Mutations of power'), and Canadian society ('Truncation of the north').

Eayrs edited and wrote introductory chapters for *The Commonwealth and Suez: a documentary survey* (1964), a collection of representative public statements from Commonwealth leaders to illustrate their attitudes towards the Suez crisis and their relationship to Britain. The two central topics of this book are Canada's finest hour in international politics and Lester Pearson's brilliant performance at the United Nations. Eayrs has also contributed essays to *The growth of Canadian policies in external affairs* (1960), *Canada: a guide to the peaceable kingdom* (1970), and *Contemporary Canada* (1967) edited by Richard H. Leach, and wrote seven talks for the CBC Learning Systems tape-recording series: 'The impermanence of power', 'The power to persuade', 'Why do nations so furiously rage together?', 'Words of world politics', 'The politics of balance', 'Face saving and the mask of the politician', and 'Fate and will in foreign policy'. DF

Eccles, W. J. (1917–). William John Eccles was born in Yorkshire, Eng., and educated at McGill University and the Sorbonne. He was on the staff of the history department of the University of Manitoba from 1953 to 1957 and of the University of Alberta from 1957 to 1963, when he was appointed to the history department of the University of Toronto.

Eccles has become the most distinguished Anglo-Canadian social historian of New France. As a historian he is anti-romantic, iconoclastic, and revisionist; as a writer he is lucid and erudite. His first major book, largely a result of archival work in Paris, was *Frontenac: the courtier governor* (1959), for which he received the 1959 Award of the Pacific Coast Branch of the American Historical Association. Eccles debunks the 'great man' myth established by nineteenth-century historians and portrays Frontenac's North American career as self-interested. What is perhaps more significant, he depicts a troubled and colourful era in a more meaningful light. In *Canada under Louis XIV: 1663–1701* (1964), in the Canadian Centenary Series, Eccles examines New France, not from the democratic assumptions of our time, but within the frame of reference of the era. He shows that Colbert's paternalism was justifiable and beneficial for the colony. The wider context of the French empire in North America to 1803 is examined in *France in America* (1972), a volume in the New American Nation series. Here Eccles challenges longstanding interpretations by claiming that after 1663 the clergy were subservient to the state, that the fall of New France was not inevitable, that the humane paternalism of the Old Régime withered away under British rule, and that the British, although they severely discriminated against the French after 1763, could not eradicate their will to survive as a social and cultural entity. *Canadian society during the French régime/La société canadienne sous le régime française* (1968) contains two public lectures Eccles gave at McGill University in 1967 in memory of E. R. Adair. In describing an affluent society with aristocratic and military values, he downplays the bourgeois nature of society in New France and stresses the establishment's concern with social welfare and the reckless, bouyant nature of the Canadians. *The Canadian frontier, 1534–1760* (1969)—in the Histories of the American Frontier series—reveals Eccles as an exponent of the 'metropolitan' thesis. In contrast to the American frontier, which moved westward with the advance of settlement, the Canadian frontier took the form of isolated military and fur-trade outposts far in the interior, its advance directed from France to further imperial and military aims rather than to expand settlement or trade. Eccles has also written *Frontenac* (1963), a short study that was translated into French; *The government of New France/Le gouvernement de la Nouvelle France* (1965), a booklet in the Canadian Historical Association series; *The ordeal of New France* (1966), thirteen radio talks published by the International Service of the CBC; and several articles in learned journals. He is co-editor of *Philip's historical atlas of Canada* (1966), and was general editor of the Canadian Historical Controversies series. DF

Edwards, Margaret H. See HISTORY STUDIES IN ENGLISH 17.

Edwards, Murray D. See HISTORY STUDIES IN ENGLISH 16.

Eggleston, Wilfrid. See HISTORY STUDIES IN ENGLISH 15.

Elliott, Jean L. See INDIANS 6.

Engel, Marian (1933–), *née* Passmore. Born in Toronto, she grew up in Galt, Hamilton, and Sarnia and was educated at McMaster and McGill Universities. She received a Rotary Foundation Fellowship in 1960 to study French literature in Aix-en-Provence and lived in Europe for several years. She has made her home in Toronto since 1964.

Mrs Engel's two novels are characterized by a fast-paced narrative style, excellent dialogue, wry humour, and vivid atmosphere. Her terse sentences have the force of explosives that shatter Canadian middle-class values and the fantasied escape route—a romantic life in Europe. In *No clouds of glory* (1968) the consciously Canadian, typically Ontario middle-class Sarah Porlock is so jealous of her beautiful unconventional sister whose marriage takes her to Venice that she throws herself into an academic career with the same stultifying industry that motivated her pioneer ancestors. Later, while spending a year in Europe, she revenges herself on her sister by an affair with her brother-in-law that ends in an abortion that revolts her to the point of emotional breakdown. Sarah's attempt to unite the pioneer myth with the myth of escape proves abortive and she must work out her salvation in a Montreal slum—the modern urban reality—where she finds romance in the fervour of the separatists who keep alive the spark of rebellion in 'this country of Zombies'.

Minn Burge, the protagonist of *The Honeyman festival* (1970), is the product of a small western Ontario town and the orderly existence impressed on her by a stern mother whose childhood had been work-oriented. Minn had escaped to Europe and a short career in Grade B films directed by Honeyman, who initiated her into love and then tired of her. She then married a Canadian foreign correspondent who brought her to Toronto. Here, with her husband away on assignment, she copes with a ramshackle house, a child of four, twins of two, and a baby due in six weeks; hippies who rent her attic; and a party to be given for a brittle crowd who are celebrating a revival of the Honeyman films. The only value from her past that can sustain her is the memory of her mother's strong character; in the present she is supported by love of her children. While she protects the hippies, she ponders on a generation without purpose or vitality, the boys more limp than the girls, who live by theft and drugs. In them she sees the collapse of middle-class values in a society that has provided no alternatives. NS

Epps, William. See FICTION IN ENGLISH 2.

Eskimos. Archaeological activity at primitive Eskimo sites has increased in recent years; especially important are the discoveries made by Father Rousselière at Button Point on Bylot Island. This is a Dorset site, first noticed by Mathiassen in 1923 but neglected until 1962, when Father Rousselière began to uncover the only midden in the arctic that has yielded any considerable quantity of the wooden sculptures made by the Dorset people. The most significant finds have been two complete life-sized wooden masks, and fragments of other similar masks, which arouse new speculations regarding the shamanistic practices and mortuary customs of the Dorset culture. Other finds at Button Point include wooden figures of animals and human beings evidently used in magical rites.

Since the middle 1950s there have been profound changes in the life of the Canadian Eskimos. Famines in that decade among the people of the Barren Lands resulted in the collapse of the inland cariboo-hunting culture and the initiation of a program of governmental paternalism that had major effects on Eskimo society throughout the arctic. Better medical attention and living conditions have brought a growth in population; at the same time there has been an inclination for many Eskimos, who in the past lived by hunting maritime animals, to join their inland congeners in the miniature urban centres that have been springing up all over the arctic—Rankin Inlet, Baker Lake, Frobisher Bay, Inuvik, etc. This has resulted in a weakening of the traditional balanced culture based on seasonal hunting that now survives only in the remoter communities, though even there it is considerably modified by the introduction of sophisticated merchandise in place of the simple trade goods of the past.

At the same time a new element has entered Eskimo life with the transformation of traditional Eskimo carving into an industry of considerable economic importance at a time when the fur trade is in decline. This development began in 1948 when James A. Houston, a young artist, returned from a trip to the arctic with a number of small stone carvings in which he was able to interest the Canadian Handicraft Guild. Up to then Eskimo carvings had been regarded mainly as curios that were occasionally made for interested visitors; they were not seriously considered in artistic terms. The movement Houston launched changed all this as, during the 1950s, the government began to encourage the production and subsidize the distribution of Eskimo artifacts. Workshops were set up in the new northern mini-towns, and elsewhere Eskimos were encouraged to work in their homes.

The result has been an output of extremely varied quality, ranging from the inferior carvings that are found in every shop catering to tourists to sculptures of power and originality that have been produced in surprising numbers. These show the rare phenomenon of a culture in traumatic change producing, at least for a period, an art of high quality and great vitality. The best pieces of contemporary Eskimo sculpture are now sought by art museums all over the world. The level and the sheer volume of achievement among Eskimo sculptors were dramatically shown in the definitive exhibition of Eskimo art, old and new, organized by the Canadian Eskimo Arts Council and first shown at the Vancouver Art Gallery in November 1971 before touring the major art centres of the world.

More recently, Eskimo artists have experimented in various forms of two-dimensional art, and have produced highly original work, adapting and developing traditional motifs, in both print-making and appliqué wall hangings.

Books in English. From the early 1960s the literature of the Eskimos developed in a number of directions. Archaeological-historical works began to appear that the research of recent years gave some pretensions to being definitive, among them *Eskimo prehistory* by Hans-Georg Bandi (1969) and *Ancient men of the Arctic* by J. L. Giddings (1967), and *Copper Eskimo prehistory* (1972) by Robert McGhee. These were complemented by studies of Eskimo culture changing under the impact of white influences, of which Nelson H. H. Graburn's *Eskimos without igloos* (1969) is perhaps the most valuable.

The rise of a modern school of Eskimo art has produced a number of books that consider either the traditional work of prehistoric and historic Eskimos or the new sculpture that—followed by prints and ceramics—has been reaching the art shops of southern Canada and the galleries of the world. These include W. T. Armour's *Innuit—the art of the Canadian Eskimo* (1968), Jorgen Meldgaard's *Eskimo sculpture* (1960), Beckman H. Pool's *Contemporary Canadian Eskimo art* (1964), and George Swinton's *Eskimo sculpture* (1965). Perhaps the best work of all in bringing the traditional and the new arts of the Eskimo together within a single horizon is Swinton's later and fuller work, *Sculpture of the Eskimo* (1972). An aspect of recent Eskimo art little noticed in the above works is treated in James Houston's *Eskimo prints* (1967). An important book, apart from its occasional significance, is *Sculpture/Inuit* (1971), the catalogue raisonné of the 1971–2 exhibition referred to above. To celebrate the same occasion *Artscanada* published a special issue (December 1971–January 1972) entitled 'The Eskimo World', containing an illuminating symposium of views by artists and scholars on Eskimo culture.

The interest aroused by modern Eskimo art has produced a complementary interest in the oral literature of the Eskimos and in the written literature that has just begun to emerge among them. *I breathe a new song: poems of the Eskimo* (1971), collected by Richard Lewis, gives an idea of the versatility of the Eskimo poetic sensibility, while two autobiographical books by Eskimos, Nugilak's *I, Nugilak* (1966) and Pitseolak's *Pictures out of my life* (the latter illustrated by Pitseolak who narrated the text to Dorothy Eber), give inside pictures of Eskimo life, which 'kabloona' writers continue to observe from the outside. Two of the most interesting examples of this kind of writing are by traditional traders: J. W. Anderson's *Fur trader's story* (1961) and Duncan Pryde's *Nunaga: my land, my country* (1971), which is interesting because it has aroused criticism among the younger Eskimos. More objective in the sense that they are not seeing Eskimo life primarily as a foil to their authors' own experiences, yet in their own way show a deep involvement, are Fred Bruemmer's *Seasons of the Eskimo* (1971) and Al PURDY's *North of summer* (1967). Combining evocative prose, a keen observational eye, and fine photographs, Bruemmer composes a sensitive threnody on a vanishing way of life among the remoter Eskimos. Purdy, in the only book of Canadian verse entirely devoted to the Eskimo north, evokes the long trajectory of a culture emerging out of prehistory as a perfect collective adaptation to a lethal environment and then sinking down into the dependence and the commercialism of the present. During the fifties and sixties, under the editorship of Malvina Bolus, *The Beaver* published many valuable and interesting articles on Eskimo archaeology, on the changing environment in which Eskimos now live, and on the art that has emerged from it. GW

Books in French. The documentation in French bearing on the Eskimo population of Canada is usually the fruit of research carried out by diverse groups and institutions in Canada and particularly in Québec. However, in Europe the Centre d'Études Artiques et Finno-Scandinaves, affiliated with the Sorbonne, has published since 1962 *Inter-Nord*, a bi-monthly international review of Eskimo and Nordic studies. It deals with the geo-economy of the North and publishes studies and discussions as well as an arctic bibliography (usually in the December issue) that lists the principal arctic publications of the past year. Among the publications of the Centre worth mentioning is a collection of texts, *Le Nouveau-Québec* (1964) compiled under the direction of Jean Malaurie and Jacques Rousseau. The Foundation Française d'Études Nordiques, which is associated with the Centre, has published the acts and documents of the 4ième Congrès International in the two-volume *Développement économique de l'Arctique et avenir des sociétés esquimaudes* (1972), of which the second volume, *Le peuple esquimau, aujourd'hui et demain*, deals mainly with the social and cultural changes that the Eskimo population is now experiencing.

Before listing the principal anthropological works in French on the Canadian Eskimo population it is important to identify briefly the main research groups that conduct these studies and publish them. The Centre d'Études Nordiques at Université Laval, founded in 1960, is indisputably the pioneer in the field. The CEN, whose activities are multidisciplinary and francophone, is devoted to research, teaching, and publishing. Its scientific publications can be found particularly in the series *Travaux et Documents*, *Travaux Divers*, *Bibliographie*, and *Mélanges*. In the department of anthropology at Laval a research group is working on a long-term project covering the whole Eskimo area of Nouveau-Québec. Finally the Groupe de Recherches Nordiques at the Université de Montréal, set up in 1966, is going ahead with various projects dealing with human problems in the arctic and sub-arctic regions. Along with these groups or institutes many others are doing research—missionaries, for example, whose contribution is far from negligible.

Few archaeological studies have been published in French. But André Leroi-Gourhan's *L'archéologie du Pacifique-Nord* (1946), which compares artifacts from America and Siberia, is notable. In 1970 the Société d'Archéologie Préhistorique du Québec published the thesis of George Barré, *Reconnaissance archéologique dans la région de la baie de Wakeham (Nouveau-Québec)* (1970), which contains a description of materials collected, and the structures of dwellings examined, on a field trip in the summer of 1968.

Two works of physical anthropology are Raoul Hartweg's *La dentition des Esquimaux de l'Ungava et des Indiens Wabema Kustewatsh de la côte orientale de la baie d'Hudson* and *L'adaptation des Esquimaux au froid* by Rollande Michaud and Jacques Leblanc.

The most important contribution to linguistic studies is without a doubt that of Father Lucien Schneider OMI, the author of *La grammaire esquimaude du sous-dialecte de l'Ungava* (1967) and *Le dictionnaire des infixes* (1968), both published by the Direction Générale du Nouveau-Québec du Ministère des Richesses Naturelles du Québec; *Le dictionnaire alphabético-syllabique du langage esquimau de l'Ungava* (1966; rev. 1970), published by the Centre d'Études Nordiques of Université Laval; and the two-volume *Dictionnaire français-esquimau du parler de l'Ungava et contrées limitrophes* (1970), published by Université Laval. Worth noting also is an essay on Eskimo grammar in the Ivujivik dialect, *Atii parlez esquimau* (1970) by Father Ernest Trinel OMI, published by the Centre Canadien de Recherches en Anthropologie of the Université Saint-Paul, Ottawa.

In the field of ethno-history Donat Savoie has edited all the ethnographic material collected by Father Émile Petitot OMI (1838–1917) when he was with the Tchiglit Eskimos in the Mackenzie region of the Northwest Territories some time after 1865: *Les Amérindiens du Nord-Ouest canadien au XIXe siècle selon Emile Petitot, Volume I: Les Esquimaux Tchiglit* (1971). It contains a list of all the works done by the missionary, including his *Vocabulaire français-esquimau* (1876) and his principal work *Les Grands-Esquimaux* (1887).

Concerning Nouveau-Québec, the Direction Générale du Nouveau-Québec du Ministère des Richesses Naturelles du Québec published a series of articles taken from *L'Annuaire du Québec* for 1964–5: *Aperçu sur le Nouveau-Québec* (1966).

Sanaaq (1970) is the name of the principal person in an account—edited and translated by Bernard Saladin d'Anglure—of a young Eskimo widow, Mitiarjuk, from Kangirsujuak (Maricourt-Wakeham). From information she gives and stories she narrates, Mitiarjuk reveals to us the daily life of a small group of Eskimo hunters and fishermen before Euro-Canadians had come to stay in Eskimo territories.

Saladin d'Anglure used *Sanaaq* as one source of information for *L'organisation sociale traditionelle des Esquimaux de Kangirsujuak (Nouveau-Québec)* (1967), an ethnographic reconstruction of the traditional social organization of the Kangirsujuaamiut (Maricourt-Wakeham). It was published by the Centre d'Études Nordiques at Université Laval.

In *L'adoption chez les Esquimaux Tununermiut (Pond Inlet) T.N.-O.* (1970) Jérôme

Rousseau attempts to describe and analyse, from data collected during two sojourns with the Tununermiut in the north of Baffin Land, their surprising system of adoption, which has a major place in the social organization of Eskimos.

Various authors have shown ethnological interest in Eskimo string games, to which Franz Boas, Kathleen Haddon, and Diamond Jenness were not above devoting studies and monographs. In 1969 the Queen's Printer published *Les jeux de ficelle des Arviligjuarmiut* (of Pelly Bay) by Guy Mary-Rousselière OMI.

Esquimaux, peuple du Québec (1966) is the title of a catalogue published by the Ministère des Affaires culturelles du Québec devoted to a collection of art and tools of the Eskimos in Nouveau-Québec. The text is by Michel Brochu.

We have mentioned above only a few of the principal works in French on the Eskimo population of Canada. Francophone scholars often publish the results of their research in Canadian and European journals. It is worth noting, however, that there is a large amount of research material that is unpublished. Let us hope that a systematic effort of publication will soon be launched that will make known to all scholars of the North the research that has already been done by scholars in francophone Canada and especially in Québec. DS

Ethier-Blais, Jean (1926–). Born in Sturgeon Falls, Ont., he was educated at the Jesuit College in Sudbury, at the Université de Montréal, and in Munich and Paris. He received his Ph.D. from Laval with a thesis on the painter Paul-Emile Borduas. After serving in the diplomatic corps for seven years—in Paris, Warsaw, and Hanoi—he turned to university teaching and literary criticism. He taught at Carleton University and is now at McGill, where he was head of the department of French until his resignation in 1973. He has contributed literary criticism to *Le Devoir* since 1960. Some of his articles from this newspaper were published in *Signets* (1967), the first volume of which is devoted to French literature, the second to the literature of French Canada. It received the Prix France-Canada and the Province of Québec literary prize for non-fiction. In 1969 he published a collection of short stories, *Mater Europa*. A collection of poems, *Asies*, appeared in 1969. He is the Editor of *Émile Nelligan: poésie rêvée—poésie vécue* (1969).

As a critic Ethier-Blais is generous in his praise and severe in his criticism. His essays, which offer penetrating reflections and precise analyses, are lightened by anecdotes and humour. In his poetry and novel he is a moralist in the great tradition of France—a man who observes the world with affection and is distressed by its imperfections and shortcomings. NK

Evans, G. N. D. See HISTORY STUDIES IN ENGLISH 4.

Evans, Cecily Louise. See FICTION IN ENGLISH 6.

Everson, R. G. (1903–). Born in Oshawa, Ont., Ronald Gilmour Everson was educated at the University of Toronto. After practising law for several years, he took up a public relations career in Montreal and continued in that work until his retirement.

Everson started writing poetry in the 1920s, during which time he was published in magazines both in Canada and the United States, but it was not until 1957 that he published his first book, *Three dozen poems*. Much of the verse in his subsequent books—*A lattice for Momos* (1958), *Blind man's holiday* (1963), and *Wrestle with an angel* (1965)—was revised for its appearance in *Selected poems 1920/1970* (1970). This book, together with *The dark is not so dark* (1969), contains the best representative selection of his poetry.

Everson's poems are often simple fragments about incidents in his life, short impressions in an imagist vein. The language is direct, alternately sardonic and gentle. In some poems the matter-of-fact, almost prosaic tone is played off against sudden intrusions of grotesque images that occasionally jar by being too obtrusive within the realistic context. His poetry moves easily through a wealth of literary and artistic references and through allusions to historical personages and events, but his writing is tough-minded and realistic and rarely loses its sense of immediacy as he meditates on the country around Oshawa, on rural Ontario and Montreal, and on his travels in other parts of Canada. PS

Ewers, John. See INDIANS 5.

F

Faessler, Shirley. See FICTION IN ENGLISH: SHORT STORIES.

Falardeau, Jean Charles. See LITERARY STUDIES IN FRENCH 2.

Faribault, Marcel. See POLITICAL WRITINGS IN ENGLISH 1 and POLITICAL WRITINGS IN FRENCH 3.

Farmiloe, Dorothy. See POETRY IN ENGLISH 2.

Farr, D. M. L. See HISTORY STUDIES IN ENGLISH 1.

Farrell, Barry. See POLITICAL WRITINGS IN ENGLISH 7.

Faucher, Albert. See HISTORY STUDIES IN FRENCH 7.

Faulknor, Cliff. See CHILDREN'S BOOKS IN ENGLISH 1 and 2.

Feldman, Lionel. See POLITICAL WRITINGS IN ENGLISH 8.

Fenton, W. N. See INDIAN LEGENDS AND ART.

Ferguson, Max. See BELLES LETTRES IN ENGLISH.

Fergusson, G. Bruce. See HISTORY STUDIES IN ENGLISH 4 and 7.

Ferron, Jacques (1921–). Born in Louiseville, Qué., he was educated at the seminary in Trois-Rivières and at Université Laval. He practised medicine in the army and later in the Gaspé. Since 1949 he has been a general practitioner in Ville Jacques-Cartier, a working-class suburb of Montreal. Thus, as well as being a man of letters he is also a man of action. In fact Doctor Ferron is a well-known figure in the Québec independence movement. From the separatist RIN (Rassemblement pour l'Indépendance nationale) he went on to form his own satirical political movement—the Rhinoceros Party. More recently he became a member of the Parti Québécois. In December 1970 he negotiated the surrender of the Rose brothers and Francis Simard, the presumed kidnappers and killers of Pierre Laporte.

Yet Dr Ferron's imaginative works are anything but dogmatic: despite the seriousness of his ideas, his sense of humour ensures that his books are always highly entertaining. He mocks the French-Canadian bourgeoisie, the 'Angluche', and anachronistic religious ideas: a spirit of anarchy pervades his work. At the same time this humour has its basis in an accurate and profound observation of human behaviour. His treatment of poverty, injustice, and death is often very touching.

One of Québec's most prolific novelists and short-story writers, Ferron has had eight plays published and contributes articles to many magazines. *Contes du pays incertain* (1962), a collection of stories, immediately established his reputation and won him a Governor General's Award. In a second collection, *Contes anglais et autres* (1964), he focuses his wit on some aspects of life in Ontario. *Contes* (1968) combines the two collections, augmented by four new stories. A selection of his short stories, many of them from *Contes du pays incertain*, was translated by Betty Bednarski and published in English under the title *Tales from the uncertain country* (1972). Reviewing this book, William French wrote: 'The uncertain country of the title is usually Quebec, sometimes all of Canada, but just as often it is the boundless geography of Ferron's fertile imagination.'

Ferron's first novel, *Cotnoir* (1962), is the seemingly simple story of Emmanuel, a mental patient, and the unusual treatment administered to him by Dr Cotnoir. The latter's young colleague, who acts as narrator, attempts, at a distance of ten years, to discover the meaning of this venture. Cotnoir himself represents a favourite type of Ferron hero: an old alcoholic doctor whose unassuming humanity is considered to be eccentricity by other members of the community. *Le ciel de Québec* (1969) is a novel that typically mixes history and folklore, the individual and the collectivity, to provide a panorama of the long march of the Québec people. This is in fact the central theme of all Ferron's work. In *Le ciel* we are shown, side by side, two irreconcilable worlds: that of the Chiquettes, regarded as savages, and that of the bourgeoisie, who, beneath their pretensions, are shown to be shallow and hypocritical. Instead of trying to teach a lesson, however, Ferron devises numerous zany situations that leave the reader with a clear image of the inner spirit of the Québec nation. *L'amélanchier* (1970) is named after a little-known species of fruit-tree, the first tree to blossom after the winter and the first to die in the fall. We can take this tree to stand for the mystery of childhood. This is perhaps Ferron's most poetic novel. In it he gently mocks human cruelty and stupidity through the eyes of his young heroine, Tinamer. His next novel, *Le salut de l'Irlande* (1970), also has a young protagonist, Connie Haffigan, the boy who is to save Ireland—though in fact the book is as much about Québec as about Ireland. The other central 'characters' include a dilapidated house and a talking fox. As in much of his work Ferron is here using fantasy to express a political reality. *Les roses sauvages* (1971) is a difficult symbolical novel. The wild roses grow in the shadow of a bungalow in the suburbs of Montreal. Its owner, Monsieur Baron, may represent the older generation of French Canadians: unable to reconcile national consciousness with the overwhelming pressures of individualism, he kills himself. His daughter, Rose-Aimée, who has been brought up in Acadia, is in the mould of Ferron heroines: uncomplicated and well balanced, she marries a young Acadian lawyer and goes to live in New York. The novel offers no solutions but shows that the new generation is unhindered by the complexes that have haunted Québécois up to the time of the 'Quiet Revolution'. At the end of the novel the wild roses are uprooted. *Le Saint-Elias* (1972) is a three-master, built at Batiscan, a symbol of the Québécois's new-found identity. Once again a sympathetic doctor appears—Dr Fauteux, whose funeral service must take place outside the church because he was not a practising Catholic. As in previous novels Dr Ferron demonstrates his intimate knowledge of the history and geography of Québec. His other novels are *La nuit* (1965), *Papa Boss* (1966), *La charrette* (1968), and *La chaise du maréchal-ferrant* (1972).

Ferron has had less success in the theatre, only one of his plays having been professionally produced in Montreal. *Les grands soleils* (1958), which treats of the 1837 revolt as a turning-point in French-Canadian history, was performed in its revised version by the Théâtre du Nouveau Monde in 1968. It is an exercise in 'epic theater' in the Brechtian sense. Unfortunately Ferron's uncompromising political and social views proved too strong for the palate of the TNM's public and the play was sparsely attended. *La tête du roi* (1963) also uses history, in this case the figure of Louis Riel, to suggest reasons for the explosions perpetrated by the FLQ. *Le coeur d'une mère* (1969), another historical play, is almost a medical analysis of the condition of the 'old lady', Québec. Most of Ferron's plays were written before he turned to novel-writing: *L'ogre* (1949), *La barbe de François Hertel* and *Le licou* (1951), *Le dodu; ou, le prix du bonheur* (1956), *Tante Elise; ou, le prix de l'amour* (1956), and *Le cheval de Don Juan* (1957). *Le licou* was republished in 1958 and *La barbe de François Hertel* was reissued with *Cotnoir* in 1970. Ferron's other plays are *Cazou; ou, le prix de la virginité* (1963) and *La sortie* (1965). The first volume of his collected *Théâtre*, which appeared in 1968, contains *Tante Elise*, the revised version of *Les grands soleils*, and *Le Don Juan chrétien*, a reworking of *Le cheval de Don Juan*.

Historiettes (1969) is a collection of Dr Ferron's essays. He is the subject of a book by Jean Marcel, *Jacques Ferron malgré lui* (1970).

JC

Ferron, Madeleine. See FICTION IN FRENCH 3 and SHORT STORIES.

Fetherling, Doug. See LITERARY STUDIES IN ENGLISH 4 and POETRY IN ENGLISH 2.

Fiamengo, Maria. See POETRY IN ENGLISH 2.

Fiction in English. The fiction in our period shows a new sophistication not only in writing styles but in attitudes towards Canada, the outside world, society in general, and individual characters. Novels have become more complex, with a greater development of the roles of supporting characters; the many facets of a personality have been emphasized by role reversal, as in Graeme GIBSON's *Five legs* where the distraught Felix Oswald is the only person to act responsibly at the scene of an accident; increased attention is given to disadvantaged ethnic groups and the urban subculture; and the national whipping boy, formerly the Anglican tory, is now the middle-class Presbyterian who, it sometimes seems, is thought to be the *only* believer in sin, guilt, and retribution.

While all authors are aware of the pressures of a society geared to mass consumption, of the sexual revolution, and of growing violence and its concommitants, there is a fundamental split in their attitudes towards these problems. Those who believe in the dignity of the human spirit may hit out at society in general but are tolerant of human frailty. In the words of Robertson DAVIES, they show man's need to 'shake hands' with his personal devil and do so without offensiveness. Other writers, concentrating heavily on man's sexual nature, or who have not yet learned to accept the newer freedom, overwork the meagre vocabulary of sex and play-by-play descriptions, which have become so similar in effect that they tend to be boring.

This article discusses the novels according to the dominant themes. Any such arrangement must be subjective, but it is hoped that it will be more useful than a purely chronological or alphabetical arrangement.

The categories used are: 1. Political and international novels; 2. Regional novels; 3. Native peoples; 4. Man and society: the general picture; 5. Individual character: problems of growth and understanding; 6. Personal problems and solutions; 7. The subculture.

1. *Political and international novels.* In Hugh MAC LENNAN's *The return of the Sphinx* (1970), Alan Ainslie of Montreal, a member of the federal cabinet, tries to bring about a lasting reconciliation between Québec and the rest of Canada in the face of a common threat of American domination. His failure is partly due to the intransigence of his colleagues and partly to the separatist activities of his son, a vain and weak young man who is pushed into the foreground by a clever anarchistic leader. The novel is also a sequel to MacLennan's *Each man's son*, for Ainslie's urge to prevent violence is motivated by the memory of his own childhood. James BACQUE in *The lonely ones* (1969) deals with the pitiful plots of Québec separatist cells, the mistrust between the cells and even between individuals within the same cell who betray their trust in each other with little or no compunction. Bacque's conclusion that Québec would get little but fine speeches from France should she gain independence is also the theme of Eric Koch's witty political fantasy *The French kiss* (1968). Koch juggles time so that General Charles de Gaulle's 'La francophonie' parallels Napoleon III's flirtations over the liberation of Italy. Both affairs are conducted by secret agents who are continually being put into false positions by the whims of their erratic masters. Koch concludes that there was and is political blackmail on both sides. Brian Moore, who was in Montreal in October 1970, wrote *The revolution script* (1972), a fictionalized account of the kidnapping of James Cross, the British Trade Commissioner, by one FLQ cell, and of the murder of Pierre LaPorte, Québec labour minister, by another. Ian Adams' *The Trudeau papers* (1971) and David WALKER's *The Lord's pink ocean* (1972), both science fiction, are included here because they deal with problems that disturb us all. Adams focuses on an atomic explosion that might enable the United States and the Soviet Union to fight it out in our rather than their own backyards. Walker foresees destruction through careless storing of noxious biochemicals, and feels that any survivors would learn nothing from the experience.

The kaleidoscopic situation in Africa has provided material for three noteworthy novels. Hugh HOOD's *You can't get there from here* (1972) is a compact and shrewd satire on the devious methods of the Great Powers in their dealings with emerging African nations. It also reflects the Canadian situation, for 'Leofrica' is a federation of two states that differ in language, customs, and economic development. Hood evokes sympathy for his very human characters, who are caught in tragic situations that he lightens with a number of comic scenes. In Dave GODFREY's *The new ancestors* (1970) chronology, language, and political and religious beliefs are manipulated to convey the paradoxes and ironies of life in 'Lost Coast' (Ghana, with a part of Mali), a state subject to the whims of a dictator, seething with revolt, and suspicious of foreigners, particularly Americans. Though it is a brilliant novel, readers may be sickened by some gratuitously sadistic and lecherous scenes. A powerful novel by David KNIGHT, *Farquharson's physique and what it did to his mind* (1971), gives insight into the criminal mind. His protagonist, a strong and amiable man whose human relationships have been superficial, cracks under the strain and racial tension of life in Nigeria, becomes a murderer (and finds that he enjoys committing murder), a prey to lust, and finally the victim of his own arrogance. Nigel Foxell's *Carnival* (1968) records the shock and disgust with which a German-Canadian, who has returned to Germany to teach, finds that he is being used as a pawn in the neo-nazi movement. David HELWIG's *The day before tomorrow* (1971) deals unconvincingly with the psychological reasons behind the temporary defection of a hitherto eminently respectable Canadian foreign-service officer, who lacks both nerve and access to really secret information, and with his brash and anarchistic young brother. Rudy WIEBE, whose *Peace shall destroy many* (1962) dealt with the breakdown of Mennonite communal life under the pressures of the Second World War, returned to this subject in *The blue hills of China* (1970), a saga of Mennonites who escape from persecution in Russia to join relatives or connections in Western Canada or Paraguay. Some of them adapt to North American ways, others hold to the old way, and Wiebe draws a clear distinction between faith and fanaticism. The title refers to one of the routes by which the Mennonites escaped from Russia. *Graves without crosses*, Arved Virlaid's powerful novel of the Estonian struggle for independence from Russian domination, was published in England in 1951 in Estonian. Virlaid is now a Canadian citizen and his book has been translated by Ilse Lehiste (1972). In John CORNISH's *A world turned turtle* (1969), Emm Kroot, an Estonian Canadian, a sergeant in the Canadian provost corps on service in England during the Second World War, must ask himself whether his true loyalty is to his superior officers or to humanity. Set to guard a former schoolteacher, an Estonian refugee who is about to be turned over to the Russians, facing death or Siberia, Kroot chooses humanity, with tragic consequences for both men. In *Goddam gypsy* (1971) Ronald Lee fictionalizes his experiences of wandering for some years with the Canadian coppersmith gypsies. Lee, a gypsy who was born in Montreal and is a leading authority on ship models, tells an excellent story about his experiences, but sometimes breaks into a tirade against modern society that no longer uses the skills of the tinsmith and relies for entertainment on syndicates that have little use for real gypsy music.

2. *Regional novels—the West.* Modern technology, the increasing development of oil and minerals, and the growth of towns and cities have given the westerner greater confidence in his ability to meet the difficult terrain of British Columbia and the vast prairie, a land alternately beneficent and hostile. Robert KROETSCH reflects this new confidence and is also close enough to the past to convey a sense of continuity with the harsh life of the depression years. In *But we are exiles* (1965) the hostile environment is reflected in a story of men trapped by a winter storm on a vessel in the Mackenzie River and facing the added stress of a corpse on board while the main protagonist must struggle with his sense of guilt. In *The words of my roaring* (1966) Kroetsch combines compassion with an exuberant tall tale of rivalry between two candidates in a rural constituency during the Alberta election of 1935, in which the tone was set by the Bible-thumping William Aberhart. The vastness of the prairies and the vision they beget are apparent in Kroetsch's *The studhorse man* (1969) in which the poignant, sometimes boisterous fantasies of an inmate of a mental hospital centre on a horse, the symbol of the beauty and power that disappear in a mechanical age. This novel won a Governor General's Award. Sinclair ROSS's *Whir of gold* (1970) uses the horse as the symbol of qualities that are required for prairie life but, when unrestrained, are a disaster in an urban setting. Herbert Harker's *Goldenrod* (1972) is an absorbing novel that strips the glamour from bronco-busting to reveal not only cruelty to animals but also the suffering and despair of a man who, knowing no other skill, is broken by continuous injuries early in life. In *Wandering Rafferty* (1972) Ken Mitchell presents a romantic drifter who wanders through British Columbia and the prairies making a precarious living. Robert Harlow's *Scann* (1972) is an interesting attempt to recreate the first fifty years (1910–60) of a British Columbia town that grew round a trapping post and railway

cache. Harlow has a good vocabulary and a sense of time and place but tends to become confused as he ponders man's need to create myths about himself and others and discusses the differences between men of action and men of sloth. He also fails to establish proper backgrounds for the characters and problems introduced from his earlier novels, *Royal Murdock* (1962) and *A gift of echoes* (1965). June Bhatia's *The latchkey kid* (1971) is a scathing satire on social climbers in an Alberta city that has mushroomed from the oil boom. It seems strange, however, that during her residence in Canada Mrs Bhatia could not find a Canadian type with sufficient sophistication and grace to act as a mentor for the uncouth young protagonist; the heavy stress on British manners, bearing, and speech becomes at times invidious. Paul G. Hiebert's *Willows revisited* (1967) is a sequel to his pseudo-biography *Sarah Binks* (1947), a satire on would-be poets in rural Saskatchewan of the 1930s.

The East. James Bacque's urban protagonists seek healing for frayed nerves and cramped muscles in the hinterlands of Montreal and Toronto. In *The lonely ones* (1969) shooting rapids and swimming and sunning in the Laurentians influence the outlook of Harry Summers and André Raincourt, both as painters and as Québec patriots who commit themselves to mismanaged separatist cells. Tragedy follows from mistrust between the cells and betrayals of personal loyalties. In Bacque's *A man of talent* (1972) Jack Ramsay's visits to Georgian Bay and the Indian reserve on Manitoulin Island bring out fine qualities in his character that indicate his ability to rise above the disaster into which his arrogance leads him.

Canadian fiction has not been generous in its treatment of the Scots. It is therefore a joy to read William Epps's *Pilgaric the death* (1967), set in the Eastern Townships of Québec. It is full of lifelike characters who take time out to toss their caps over the windmill. A sprinkling of dour Scots is not allowed to disturb the general gaiety, and indeed adds to the reality of this eccentric community.

Edward B. Jolliffe's conventional historical novel *The first hundred* (1972) recalls the Orange-Catholic riots among the pioneers in Ontario townships (1846–62), subtly indicating that much of the trouble and the slipshod farming methods of the Catholic newcomers were due to the insulting way in which the Orangemen rejected the proffered help of the Catholics at bees and harvesting. Ernest BUCKLER's *Ox bells and fireflies* (1968) is a fictionalized memoir of his childhood and of village life in Annapolis Royal, N.S. The sights and sounds of the countryside are faithfully recorded, along with the habits, peculiarities, and simple dialogue of the people, which are recalled with nostalgia. Will BIRD's *The Earl must have a wife* (1969) is a historical romance based on the career of J.-F.-W. DesBarres, who was lieutenant governor of Cape Breton (1784–7) and of Prince Edward Island (1805–12). He also played an important role in surveys of the Atlantic coast.

3. *Native peoples.* Fred BODSWORTH in *The sparrows fall* (1967) enters into the minds of his Eskimo characters, Jacob and Nika, who, confused by the preaching of an inexperienced flying missionary, court disaster as outcasts. Bodsworth's descriptions of people torn between old and new ideas, of a hungry winter and an agonizing search for caribou, are powerful and convincing. James Houston, an artist who spent twelve years among the Eskimos, nine of them as the first civil administrator of Baffin Island, looks back to the nineteenth century to examine the early confrontation of white and Eskimo cultures in *The white dawn: an Eskimo saga* (1971). He gives an indication of ill will between Eskimo groups, but the main story is that of three survivors from a wrecked American whale boat who are cared for by Eskimos who had never seen a white man. One of the survivors makes an attempt to understand and respect Eskimo culture, but Eskimos and white men alike create a situation in which tribal customs break down. During a lean winter the intruders are executed by tribal decree. Harold Horwood, who represented Labrador in the Newfoundland legislature for many years, has written *White Eskimo* (1972), a novel set (with some anachronisms) in the 1930s. It gives a lively account of the fur trade and of the excitement and vicissitudes of travel in the far north. Unfortunately Horwood echoes the propaganda of many of the St John's fur-trade and merchant interests against the work of the Moravian missions and the International Grenfell Foundation—work that is too well documented to be denigrated.

Among novels about Indian life, none has surpassed Rudy Wiebe's *First and vital candle* (1966) for penetration of Indian reliance on myth and for understanding the role of the medicine man. But Wiebe's independent fur trader is too evil and his missionaries too good to be lifelike. The unadorned style used by R. D. Symons in *Still the wind blows: a historical novel of the northwest 1860–1916* (1971) points up his careful research and balancing of evidence about the parts played by Poundmaker, the Crees, and the Blackfoot during the North West Rebellion (1885), but neither John Curtis, the white boy who grows up to become a police inspector, nor Arrow Boy, John's Cree foster brother who declines into poverty with his people, has enough individuality to spice this readable social novel. E. G. Perreault's conventional *The kingdom carver* (1968) gives a lively description of logging operations in a remote part of Vancouver Island and the building of a settlement there through the joint effort and mutual respect of Indians and whites. It is a tale of courage and common sense among whites and Indians, both of whom have human weaknesses. Alan Fry, who has been an Indian agent in the Yukon, maintains a good narrative pace in *Come a long journey* (1971), a fictionalized account of a leisurely hunting trip down the Yukon River in which the white narrator and his Athapascan companion, Dave, bridge the gulf that separates Indian and white cultures. Dave's campfire stories show how Indian customs were geared to survival in the boreal forest and were broken down by fur traders and the Klondike gold rush. Pearl Packard's *The reluctant pioneer* (1968) is a good-humoured account of the hardships faced by the wife of a Hudson's Bay Company trader as she makes the long canoe journey from Lachine to Brunswick House in the mid-nineteenth century. There, thrown on her own resources and on Indian goodwill, she bears eight children, educates them as best she can, and comes nearly to the end of her courage before her husband is removed to the more congenial post of Fort William. Two slight novels without depth but that illustrate the modern trend towards mutual understanding are John Craig's *Zach* (1972) and Marian Brandis's *The spring sowing* (1970). Craig's tendency to moralize and his contrived situations leave the reader confused about whether he finds hope for outcasts through communes or whether they are doomed to extinction. Marian Brandis creates some lively ironic moments in her tale of a teacher who, with only a few months to live, goes to a northern cabin where she takes a halfbreed lover. Peter Such's *Fallout* (1969) gives poetic glimpses of mixed nationalities working at the Elliot Lake uranium refinery at the time of the shutdown. He treats Indian myth and custom sympathetically as he centres attention on the successful marriage of Robert, an Indian, to the daughter of the white foreman.

Mort Forer, who spent many years as the only social worker in southeastern Manitoba, assembles a large cast of lively characters in *The Humback* (1969), a novel of the dispossessed Métis who, with the passing of the buffalo and the filling up of prairie lands, transferred their activity to the forest where they cut pulpwood, working during the season with all the disciplined activity that had distinguished their ancestors on the annual buffalo hunt. Seasonal work and the truck system by which they turn in their wage books to the local merchant who holds the logging permit account for the between-season drunkenness, violence, and amorality that place their women and children in an anomalous position: their pride forbids them to accept public relief.

4. *Man and society: the general picture*. In two novels, each stylistically different—*Five legs* (1969) and *Communion* (1971)—Graeme Gibson looks at modern society and sees repressed man threatened by a waiting conflagration. His thesis is that since modern society has identified the 'elect' with the successful and respectable, the social failure is apt to identify himself with the maimed and hunted animal. In *Communion* the man-animal identification is carried out through a series of fantasies that bind the unfulfilled in a communion of the damned. Gibson, however, does not overlook the possibility of spiritual and natural salvation. This concept is held by Lucan Crackell, one of Gibson's anti-heroes in *Five legs*. Crackell is the type of man for whom the conflagration could be purgative.

For his social satire *The assignment* (1971) Martin Myers created the unforgettable dialectitian Spiegel, chief (and sole) collector for The Universal Junk Foundation, and its wealthy and devious one-eyed president, J. J. Jonas. Myers includes a host of supporting characters who enliven this comic fantasy of man in a decaying civilization. Spiegel's likeable *alter ego* is Alvin H. Gunnarson, an overworked professor of philosophy who, in moments of stress, likens the world to a junk heap. Myer's optimistic view that an individual's destiny lies in his own hands is not shared by Leo Simpson, author of *Arkwright* (1971). After many comic adventures, some of them with weird characters, Simpson's anti-hero, Addison Arkwright, concludes that modern society is becoming a monster with a thousand mouths and no inward eye. As he reflects on modern trends that mirror the decay of previous civilizations, he carries off his nine-year-old daughter to Crete, hoping for a new start in the place from which our known civilization began. Society is ridiculed by John Mills in *The land of is* (1971), a parody of the modern suspense novel in an eighteenth-century format. The characters are either grotesque or vapid and the situations farcical, but both form and pace are suited to Mills' analysis of 'a marshmallow world . . . shrunk to a pin-head on which angels have ceased to dance' and where men and women sink into depravity under the shadow of the atom bomb. Chris Scott's *Bartleby* (1971) is a brilliant comic fantasy in which all literary styles from that of the bible to those of the modern age are combined to depict a world in anarchy where the unruly and volatile characters take matters into their own hands, frustrating the would-be author at every turn. Rachel Wyatt's *The string box* (1970) satirizes the plastic world of Hollywood, the obsession with public images, and the snobberies of self-appointed dictators of writing standards. Her protagonist, the writer of a successful but appalling soap opera who has also been commissioned to write the biography of a sex-crazy woman, is regarded as worthy to be initiated into the zany string-box club, the status of whose members is decided by the number of pieces of string each member contributes to be distributed among the Indians. This is one round the Indians do not lose. Timothy FINDLEY's *The butterfly plague* (1969) draws a parallel between the Nazi persecution of the Jews in 1936–8 and the ruthless manner in which Hollywood stars were made and unmade. Hugh Hood's *The camera always lies* (1967) contrasts the ruthlessness and sex-orientation of the American film industry with the artistic integrity of French film producers. David Lewis Stein overloads his plot with motivations and characters in his satire *Scratch one dreamer* (1967). His bitter and cynical protagonist is Joe Fried. He hates his uncle, who brought him up, for personal and philosophical reasons and because of his contempt for the labour movement of the 1940s (satirized by Stein) of which his uncle is a dethroned leader. Later, Joe's outlook changes as he becomes conscious of each man's social responsibility. The social criticism of *Scratch one dreamer* is stronger in Stein's *My sexual and other revolutions: the memoirs of Daniel Johnson* (1971), a vitriolic attack on all classes of society except the bagel makers. Stein's characters include the weak and the ugly, as well as beautiful women and strong men. The treatment of sex is overpowering and includes abberations. Stein can foresee only anarchy followed by tyranny for the world he portrays.

The necessity for a balance between idealism and pragmatism in society shines through Gwendolyn MACEWEN's historical novel *King of Egypt, king of dreams* (1972), a poetic presentation of Akenaton, Pharoah of Egypt (1380–62 B.C.), the first-known monotheist, whose hymn to the sun she translates into verse. Akenaton's passion for the sun god and his absorption in his short-lived religious revolution were so consuming that the great Egyptian empire perished through neglect. Akenaton and the characters arrayed against him for political, social, or religious reasons have a dreamlike quality: the most real of them is his uncle, Ay, the skeptic who provides a correlation between the old and new religions. Behind Miss MacEwan's pellucid style lies careful historical research in a difficult period. A surrealistic novella that deals with modern society is Claudio Ianora's *Sint Stephen Canada, Polyphemus cave, and the borderland express* (1970). It portrays a young man's bewildered attempt to reconcile life as it is lived in a commercialized world and the idea of holiness in its ancient sense of wholeness, or, as he puts it, the role of sint versus saint. The fantasies follow each other in good rythmic prose that is laced with outbursts of raw humour.

Austin C. CLARKE, a native of Barbados, writes vividly of the plantation workers on that island who live at subsistence level. His *Survivors of the crossing* (1964) deals with an abortive strike in which the illiterate but able leader is betrayed by his followers, who fear for their jobs, and then dreams of escaping to Canada, misled by a false report about the success of a friend who had gone there. A similar dream is held by a nine-year-old-boy in Clarke's *Among thistles and thorns* (1965), but it seems more likely that this child will grow up to become a revolutionary leader. In both books Clarke shows how much Barbadian workers hope for from the education of their children. In *The meeting point* (1967) Clarke reveals how the fate of Barbadian immigrants depends on their education. Starting with a Barbadian maid in a Jewish household in Toronto, he assembles his characters from various economic brackets, pointing out that the uneducated black is the most disadvantaged of all immigrant groups. Clarke has a delicate hand with both humorous and tragic situations.

Seymour Blicker, a graduate of Loyola University and a business executive in Montreal, made a tour of the United States as a wandering folk singer so that he could examine conditions there for himself. In *Blues chased a rabbit* (1969) his protagonist, Jason Defoy, who had made a successful career in New York, is so shocked by the accidental death of his wife that he roves restlessly through the southern states. Arrested on a vagrancy charge in Mississippi, he is bound into virtual slavery and forced to live in degrading conditions. His ability to endure rings true, as does his decision to kill in order to regain his liberty.

Harold Sonny Ladoo, a twenty-seven-year-old native of Trinidad now living in Toronto, shows himself to be a talented writer in his first novel, *No pain like this body* (1972). It has for its background the deplorable conditions among East Indians living on 'Carib Island' in 1905—semi-starved, a prey to water snakes and scorpions, their superstitions fed by fakirs masquerading as Hindu priests. The story is artfully told as it was experienced by a terrified eight-year-old boy, Panday, whose brutal and depraved father has been largely responsible for the death of Panday's twin, Rama. The weather is a major character as violent storms highlight the dramatic events in the story. The narrative is in dialect for which Ladoo supplies a glossary.

5. *Individual character: problems of growth and understanding.* Robertson Davies' *Fifth business* (1970) and its companion *The manticore* (1972), written with his customary grace and wit, hinge on the Jungian concept of the whole man, the person who has reconciled his outward image with the elements of his personality that lie below the surface, elements that he may not recognize without some guidance from others. In the dramatic events of *Fifth business* a large cast of characters and several changes in environment illustrate that wit, wisdom, intelligence, imagination, and the earthy aspects of life must all be harmonized. In *The manticore* Davies adheres more closely to Jungian analysis in which the patient is made to recognize an archetype, the manticore, and is also introduced to bear mythology.

While Davies dissects character, Margaret LAURENCE in *A bird in the house* (1970) and Alice MUNRO in *Lives of girls and women* (1971) follow the development of a girl from childhood through adolesence. Vanessa MacLeod, Margaret Laurence's protagonist, is an only child growing up in a western town in a household of adults who can barely save their individuality from her tyrannical grandfather. In a series of secret observations among her elders, Vanessa learns to manage grief and frustration and to emerge safely from ironical situations. This book is distinguished by Mrs Laurence's customary mastery of characterization. Alice Munro is one of the few writers who have affection for small towns. 'Jubilee', the town in which Del Jordan spent a happy childhood, is a lovingly depicted background for Del's experiences of growing up, of dealing with her mother and other eccentric characters and with the consequences of her own escapades. How easy it is to destroy a child is shown by Ruth Nichols in *The ceremony of innocence* (1969) in which the motherless Marjorie Baldwin is drawn into a situation where adult tensions are given full reign. Terrified and shocked, Marjorie shows a potential viciousness from which she is saved by adults who awake to their responsibilities. The setting, an archaeological dig, is well drawn and the characters are vivid. In *Pandora* (1972) Shirley Fraser shows a warm understanding of the mores of a working-class district during the depression. In her pre-school and early-school days, Pandora learns to adjust to the snobberies, injustices, and cruelties of life without letting them affect her natural gentleness.

Over Richard Wright's *The weekend man* (1970) hangs the heavy pall of emotional immaturity that will give many readers a shock of recognition. Unstable in his marriage and in his attitude towards earning a living, he seeks constant diversion in sex, television, and as a spectator of the ironies of life, the greatest of which is a sudden business success that arises despite his ineptness. His one redeeming feature is love for his mongoloid son, for whose sake he will make an attempt to salvage his marriage. (The prognosis is not good.) Blanche Howard's *The manipulator* (1972), though over-contrived in parts, captures the psychology of Bill Wentworth, a ruthlessly ambitious architect, and that of the weak John Phillips who cannot quite blind himself to the fact that his own ambition has made him the butt of Wentworth's contempt. In *Above ground* (1968) Jack Ludwig gives a good portrait of the philanderer whose main object in life is the pursuit of all types of women. Ludwig reflects his protagonist's emotional instability by a disjointed style that varies from clipped expressions to extravagant language.

6. *Personal problems and solutions.* Two posthumous novels by Malcolm LOWRY, edited by Mrs Lowry, poignantly express the anguish of a man who, in spite of repeated failure, believes that he can find a haven where he will be able to come to terms with life and with himself. Each is the record of a journey during which the sights, sounds, and encounters of travel serve as signposts on the interior quest. On both journeys the protagonist is accompanied by his wife, his only fixed star after the destruction of his home by fire—a recurrent theme in both novels. In *Dark as the grave in which my friend is laid* (1968) the journey is to Mexico where Sigbjorn Wilderness (sea-born wanderer) travels from Vancouver only to find that his friend (the model for the consul in *Under the volcano*) is dead. In *October ferry to Gabriola* (1970) Ethan Llwelyn and his wife make a tiring journey from Vancouver, where they face eviction, to a remote place where they hope to escape urban life. This novel ends on a note of anticipation that is rare in Lowry's work.

Wry humour lightens Margaret Laurence's *The fire-dwellers* (1969), a revelation of the steps by which a woman raging against the emotional problems of middle age reaches maturity when faced with a real tragedy—the advancing blindness of her father-in-law. Jane RULE shows delicacy and sophistication in handling various types of sexual relationships, stressing particularly the sense of loss among lesbians who realize that they are condemned to barrenness because their affliction bars them from consummating a marriage. *This is not for you* (1970) is written as an unposted letter by a woman who has restrained her passion in the vain hope of protecting a young girl. In *Against the season* (1972) Miss Rule uses a large cast of characters who, taken together, form a commentary on all forms of love in a decaying American seaport town. Joan Haggerty's *Daughters of the moon* (1971) gives a realistic account of two women of very different character who meet in the Balearic Islands; both fail in marriage, love affairs, and a lesbian relationship: it is perhaps a weakness in the novel that both should die in childbirth. Cecily Louise Evans gives a convincing analysis of the respective contributions a man and woman must make to a successful marriage. In her first novel, *The newel post* (1968), a couple in late middle age and victimized by previous marriages, reach an understanding in a marriage that suits their psychological needs. Mrs Evans' *Nemesis wife* (1970) is a ghost story, set in England, in which a strong-minded woman is able, at great psychological strain to herself, to unravel entangled conflicts that have wrecked the marriages of two generations and threaten the children of the third generation.

Both Mavis GALLANT and Marian ENGEL disabuse Canadian women of the romantic notion that they can escape adult responsibilities by seeking a glamorous life in Europe. With her usual wit and her flair for describing life styles in cool and telling detail, Mrs Gallant in *A fairly good time* (1970) tells of a well-meaning but awkward and alienated Canadian girl and her marriage into a middle-class Parisian family and describes her response to its inevitable breakup. In *The Honeyman festival* (1970) Mrs Engel portrays Minn Burge, a beauty from a small town who, having had a European fling with a producer of Grade B movies, matures back home in Toronto as she copes during pregnancy with three small children and a ramshackle house whose attic is rented to hippies. The most forthright of the younger women novelists, Mrs Engel relieves tension with elements of farce and subtle humour. In

No clouds of glory (1968) Sarah Porlock's sibling jealousy makes her an easy prey for her brother-in-law during a chance encounter in Europe. The affair ends in the psychological shock of an abortion and then in Sarah's flight towards the kind of violence she associates with the Montreal separatist. Audrey THOMAS's *Mrs Blood* (1970) is a study of the inner turmoil of an Englishwoman hospitalized in Ghana and near death; it elaborates on material she used more effectively in 'If one green bottle . . .', one of the short stories in her collection *Ten green bottles* (1968). The two interlocking novellas that make up Mrs Thomas's *Munchmeyer and Prospero and the island* (1972) are set in British Columbia. The first portrays a modern Caliban; in the second, Miranda, while writing *Munchmeyer*, finds comfort and moral support from an artist whom she calls Prospero. Brian Moore's *I am Mary Dunne* (1968) deals with a day in the life of a nerve-wracked Nova Scotia woman, now married to an American in New York, whose poltroon of a husband sits by while one of her former friends tells tales of her unfortunate affairs in Montreal. In Margaret ATWOOD's well-knit double-edged comedy *The edible woman* (1969), Marian McAlpin, who works at consumer research while she plays the mating game, is so shocked by her lover's disgusting hunting story that she relates it to the fraudulent pressures of the world geared to mass consumption: she gradually becomes revolted by all food. She is near starvation before she pulls herself together to seek comfort with a graduate student who has experienced a similar revolt against sex-oriented trivia in which his academic career has enmeshed him. Miss Atwood's *Surfacing* (1972) is set in northern Québec, and nature, one of the novel's characters, is vividly described. The novel explores a girl's gradual psychic retreat—from her tawdry companions, from her past, from forces that can only be described as 'Americanism'—into nature until, finding her true identity, she is able to surface and resume her life. Joy Fielding's *The best of friends* (1972) treats the psychological shock of abortion (which also has a place in *Surfacing*) from a clinical point of view, but it is interesting only to those who have a strong stomach.

Ronald Sutherland's *Lark des neiges* (1971) is a thesis novel that attempts to portray conflicts among disadvantaged English- and French-speaking Montrealers. Suzanne Laflamme, born of French-Scots parents and now married to a Québécois schoolmaster, reflects that the emotions of love and hate are intensified when people live in overcrowded conditions where hatred breaks out in racial and religious violence.

In John Reid's *Horses with blindfolds* (1968) a Canadian on holiday in Andalusia recovers his health once he admits that he has been wrecked by his unresolved resentments. In Leslie Stevenson's *Civil servant* (1970) John Osborn's naiveté gives credibility to the open ruthlessness that brings about his downfall. John Peter and John Metcalfe examine the grounds for Canadian prejudice against British immigrants. Both authors bring two such immigrants to Canadian educational institutions. One man acts with obnoxious lordliness while the other shows adaptability and the best British characteristics. Peter's *Shake hands at winter* (1967), set in a western college, ends ironically, but Metcalfe's *Going down slow* (1972) leaves some hope for the arrogant Montreal high-school teacher who reaches almost rock bottom before realizing that his position and even his health require that he come to terms with North America. Seymour Blicker's '*Shmucks*' (1972) is a delightful tale of a farcical confrontation between two frustrated and stubborn men, a Rumanian immigrant taxi driver and the manager of a real-estate agency, neither of whom will back out of a narrow alley in Montreal. Neither man is basically violent and each becomes a bit ashamed of his childishness. Blicker's controlled amusement and economy of words show his sympathy for human frailty. Tony Aspler's *The streets of Askelon* (1972) deals humorously with the Montreal engagement of a drunken Irish poet, a figure reminiscent of Brendan Behan. Hugh Hood's *A game of touch* (1970), while satirizing politics and the big company, is also a telling exposition of the way in which individuals of different backgrounds and interests are temporarily brought together by sport and other recreations, which they gradually abandon as they become aware of their social responsibilities.

Mordecai RICHLER uses Jewish protagonists in two satirical novels, each with a rich and varied cast of characters. *Cocksure* (1968) is an embittered and pornographic farce about the film and publishing worlds and *St Urbain's horseman* (1971) delves deeply into the ambivalent and irresponsible attitudes of Jake Hersch, a frustrated television and film director who seeks relief from his inner anguish by a fantasy that his scoundrely cousin Joey will murder a Nazi war criminal who has escaped to Paraguay. Both novels won a Governor General's Award. Norman LEVINE makes a happy Jewish-gentile marriage central to his novel *From a seaside town* (1970), which is set in England, and shows both nostalgia for and impatience with the Jewish-Canadian background of his protagonist, Joseph Le Grand. The novel gains much from the humorous treatment of Le Grand's financial difficulties, the variety of Canadian and English characters, and its polished style. Phyllis GOTLIEB's *Why should I have all the grief?* (1969) is a compassionate treatment of a troubled and withdrawn adult—the survivor as a child of a Nazi concentration camp—who learns from the sufferings of others to come to terms with life. The author's poetic skill adds poignancy. Hilda Shubert in *They came from Kernitz* (1969) combines a novella and two short stories into a comic novel that contrasts the values, successes, and failures of a number of Jewish families who, having escaped from a Russian village run on ritualistic lines, establish themselves in Montreal. The Jewish genius for self-mockery heightens the comedy by emphasizing the ideals of love and generosity that underlie the old rituals but have little significance in North America. Charlotte Fielden's *Crying as she ran* (1970), while at times sentimental, contains an excellent portrayal of a family of Jews that came to Canada from Eastern Europe and began life in slum conditions. When the father is tempted to front for a dishonest construction company, he brings wealth and then disaster upon them all.

7. *The sub-culture.* In *The rise and fall of married Charlie* (1970) Anthony Blicq moves his assorted parasites through the luxury hotels and apartments of London, New York, Athens, and the slums of London. Their motives and conduct vary, but all believe that Bertha Swan exists only to supply them with money. Bad though they may be, Blicq's characters can still be momentarily touched by love and sympathy.

Some authors write about people who are so inhumane or so victimized by drugs and/or insanity that only a psychiatrist could evaluate their credibility. The most recognizable of these characters is the young alienated bartender, Michael, the diarist of Juan BUTLER's *Cabbagetown diary: a documentary* (1969). Born and still living in Toronto's shabby rooming-house district, which Butler effectively brings to life, Michael decides after his early reform-school experience to remain within the law but works out his hostility by encouraging and remaining safely on the edge of the activities of his anarchistic friends. His diary is a patent attempt at self-justification for his callous treatment of his mistress. Butler's novella *The garbage man* (1972) describes a mental patient who committed or fantasized at least two revolting murders and causes as much trouble as he can in the hospital. Timothy FINDLEY's suspenseful *The last of the crazy people* (1967) is pervaded by a Greek sense of doom that gives inevitability to the horrible fate of the child Hooker, a victim of his mother's insanity, the crazed alcoholism of his brother, and the scorn of society. Matt COHEN's *Korsoniloff* (1969) is a brilliant study of the degeneration of a schizophrenic professor of philosophy whose childhood trauma leads him to imagine that he has committed murders. Cohen also wrote *Johnny Crackle sings* (1971), about a weak, untalented rock singer who is ruined by an unscrupulous promoter who drives him too hard and by his own flight from reality with the use of drugs. Robert Hunter's *Erubus* (1968) lacks unity and a precise use of language, but it succeeds in portraying a man who regards himself as uncommitted, although he is actually a slave to women and alcohol, and who, while demanding complete freedom of action for himself, becomes outraged when women play the same game. Roy MacSkimming's *Formentera* (1972) is a vivid but dispiriting account of the wasted lives of expatriates living on one of the Balearic Islands where they become preys to drugs and drink. George BOWERING's *Mirror on the floor* (1967) is an even sadder commentary on the tragedies to which lack of purpose and excessive reliance on alcohol and drugs can lead. The most outré of significant avant-garde novels is Russell Marois's *The telephone poll* (1967), the rambling fantasies of a man who is criminally insane. They have the same effect on the nervous system as the jarring and flashing commercial messages of television. In *Place d'armes* (1969) and *Civic square* (1972) Scott Symons catches the rhythms of the obsessive-compulsive syndrome and in both novels male genitalia are glorified. In the former, the afflicted narrator, fascinated by the historical architectural mixture of Place d'Armes, Montreal, is compelled to circle the area endlessly while impugning the motives of tourists and shoppers who look at its treasures. In the epistolary *Civic square*—848 pages of printed typescript in a box—a man pours out abuse of Torontonians who are not homosexual in between his erotic effusions. The reader is not enlightened about any real grievance but is rather stupefied. John BUELL's *The Shrewsbury exit* (1972) points out the difficulty of securing evidence in crimes committed by motorcycle gangs and gives a vivid account of the hardships of prison life in the United States.

Harry Boyle's *The great Canadian novel* (1972), written in the popular vein, deals with the regeneration of an alcoholic drug addict who goes to Mexico where he is reformed by the care of simple peasants and a Spanish ex-loyalist. As part of his cure, he proceeds to write a novel that will create truly Canadian characters.

Short stories (see also ANTHOLOGIES IN ENGLISH). In 1971 Hugh GARNER brought out his fifth collection of short stories, *The violation of the virgins*. As in his previous books, the characters are frequently misfits or unsettled persons, but Garner shows no sympathy for hippie violence. The title story, with its surprise ending, follows the adventures of two women teachers on a holiday in Mexico. In Hugh HOOD's *Around the mountain: scenes from Montreal life* (1967) the individual stories catch many varied aspects of life in a large city where there is much development and redevelopment and a mixed population. Hood's *The fruit man, the meat man, and the manager* (1971) contains very sophisticated tales of ordinary people, some of whom are caught in extraordinary circumstances.

The stories in *Ten green bottles* (1967) by Audrey THOMAS are powerful expressions of grief that grow out of such situations as the impotence of a child, the sense of inadequacy in a woman, and a tragedy of colour, as in one of the stories set in Ghana where Mrs Thomas lived for some years. The stories of Dave GODFREY, while often concerned with the sadness and inexorability of death, have a wide range of emotion and can be humorous and sardonic. *Death goes better with Coca Cola* (1967) is composed chiefly of hunting and fishing stories that illustrate both man's instinct to kill and his revulsion by that act. In 'The hard-headed collector' he castigates Canadians for their lack of a common creative purpose, a characteristic that he blames partly on provincialism and partly on the wealth and dominance of the United States. In 1968 Godfrey joined David Lewis Stein and Clark Blaise in a collection of their stories called *New Canadian writing* (1968). Godfrey's contributions to this work deal with death and loneliness and include a story he later incorporated in his novel *The new ancestors*. Godfrey as a humorist is revealed in 'River Two Blind Jacks', which appears in Robert Weaver's *Canadian short stories: second series* (1968). Stein's contributions to the joint collection reflect his disgust with modern manifestations of greed, hatred, and violence, while his 'The night of the little brown men' is a despairing restatement of the age-old question 'Am I my brother's keeper?'. Clark Blaise, the third contributor, is of French-Canadian parentage but was brought up in poverty in various parts of the United States and now teaches in Montreal. In 1973 he published *A North American education* in which he transforms his experiences as an outsider—growing up in the U.S., travelling in Europe and Sweden, flying to India, teaching in Montreal—into what he calls 'short fiction' that is assured, sensitive, and true.

Another of Canada's talented short-story writers in Alice MUNRO, who has created a memorable small-town world in *The dance of the happy shades* (1968), a distinguished collection of stories that won a Governor General's Award, and in her novel *Lives of girls and women* (1971), which is composed of linked short stories. Other authors who have built short stories into novels are Margaret LAURENCE in *A bird in the house* (1970) and Mavis GALLANT, most of whose *A fairly good time* (1970) appeared as stories in the *New Yorker*. The title story of Austin C. CLARKE's *When he was free and young and he used to wear silks* (1971) is an experiment in impressionism; the other stories are taken from or are possibly drafts for his published novels. A revised edition of Malcolm LOWRY's story

Lunar caustic was published by Margaret Bonner Lowry in 1968. This tragic story, based on Lowry's experiences in Bellevue mental hospital, was published in draft form in the *Paris Review* in 1956.

David HELWIG, whose *The streets of summer* appeared in 1969, writes with singular grace and versatility. Some of his stories convey the delicate stillness of a cameo and yet convey fluidity of movement; others are brisk narratives told in a casual manner; while 'Something for Olivia's scrapbook I guess', depicts the colours, sounds, and smells of Toronto's hippie community and is saved from melodrama by the sarcastic tone of the narrator.

John METCALF is another writer who has command over varied moods and styles. In his *The lady who sold furniture* (1970), the title story is an amusing tale of a confidence trickster that reveals a perceptive understanding of the mind of a child and a love of the English countryside. The other stories in this collection deal with children who face horror and with the anguish of an old man who realizes that he is slipping into senility. Sympathy predominates but Metcalf can also be sardonic and can combine love of beauty with bitter secret resentments. An instance of the last type of story is 'The estuary', which won the President's medal of the University of Western Ontario in 1969 and is reprinted in Metcalf's anthology *Sixteen by twelve: short stories by Canadian writers* (1970).

Norman LEVINE combines both Canadian and British stories in *I don't want to know anyone too well and other stories* (1971). The title is well chosen, for Levine maintains an air of aloofness in most of these stories; however the patina of his polished style commands attention. 'On the Richelieu', a Canadian story, is touched with genuine pathos, but in many of his English stories his stock village characters lack vitality.

Between 1968 and 1972 a number of regional collections were published. Sinclair ROSS's *A lamp at noon and other stories* (1968), with an introduction by Margaret Laurence, and Frederick Philip GROVE's *Tales from the margin* (1971) edited by Desmond PACEY are two impressive collections that feature the prairies in the depression years. Ross's stories were originally published in *Queen's Quarterly* and were admired for their stark realism. During his life Grove had collected a number of his stories under the title used by Pacey but the book was not published. While stressing the hardships of prairie life, Grove here gives more emphasis to the joys and beauty of the countryside and shows more sympathy with human folly than in his novels. Max Braithwaite, who faced all the hardships of poverty on the prairies where he taught school for a pittance, is able to look back on his experiences with laughter. To his collection *Why shoot the teacher?* (1965) he has added *Never sleep three in a bed* (1969), which includes stories of growing up first in a small prairie town and then in Prince Albert, and *The night we stole the Mounties' car* (1971). Alden NOWLAN's *Miracle at Indian River* (1971) gives short but penetrating glimpses of life in a depressed area of New Brunswick. Some of the stories are frightening, others are hilarious. In one story, 'The innermost one', Nowlan leaves New Brunswick to give an unusual twist to an imaginary interview with the Dalai Lama. Will R. BIRD's *Angel cove* (1972) contains stories that reflect the hard life of the Newfoundland outports before that province joined confederation. Don Bell's *Saturday night at the bagel factory* (1972) contains journalistic exaggerations of various types of characters in Montreal, some of them quite amusing. In 'The four Mondays of Abdullah the butcher' Bell vividly catches the fever of those who crowd into the Montreal Forum for wrestling matches.

An exceptionally fine collection is *The stone cross* (1971), an English translation of twenty-two stories by the Ukrainian writer Vasyl Stefanyk (1871–1935), whose tales of the joys, sorrows, poverty, and ignorance of oppressed Ukrainian peasants have long been valued by the Canadian Ukrainian community. The translation was made by the Rev. Joseph Wiznuk and Dr C. H. Andrusyshen for the Stefanyk Centennial Committee.

In *Noman* (1972) Gwendolyn MACEWEN's forceful, imaginative writing and her use of myth and allegory enliven stories on a variety of subjects, from the pathetic 'House of the whale' through the hectic fever of 'Fire', to the allegorical title story, which reveals a low opinion of Canadian life. Harry Bullock has a masterly directness of style and a lightness of touch that command attention in his surrealistic tales. His *Sixteen stories as they happened* (1969) is less varied than his second collection, *Green beginning: black ending* (1971), in which there is an effective fluctuation from light to heavy themes. The stories in Matt COHEN's *Columbus and the fat lady* (1972) are not such successful experiments in form as his novels. With the notable exception of 'Country music', which realistically describes a band of 'welfare drunks', most of Cohen's stories waver between impressionism and surrealism. An unusual collection is Ray Smith's *Cape Breton is the thought control centre of Canada* (1969), with its uproarious 'Galoshes', which pits a proper young man from Toronto against a witty and uninhibited Cape Bretoner. Most of this book is what one of the characters describes as 'combined fiction'—Joycean skits on conventional literary forms and vocabularies in which 'the medium is the message'. Like most of such writing, not all of it comes off and it is best taken in small doses.

Some well-known short-story writers have not yet prepared collections. Shirley Faessler, whose wryly humorous stories of first- and second-generation Romanian Jewish immigrants have been published in the *Atlantic Monthly*, gives her widest insight into the life of this community in 'Henye'. This story, reprinted in John Metcalf's anthology *The narrative voice* (1970), not only creates a redoubtable character but also follows the picaresque activities of her husband and his cronies. Rudy WIEBE's stories about Indians, although not always historically correct, are sympathetic to them. More impressive are his chilling tales of fundamentalist fanaticism, the most frightening of which is the allegorical 'Millstones for the sun's day', also reprinted in *The narrative voice*. Kent Thompson deals chiefly with adolescents and the alienated. His stories move slowly and gain much of their impact from his careful eye for the relevant details of the setting and from his ear for dialogue. A good example is 'Professor Kingblatt's profession' in the anthology *Kaleidescope* (1972) edited by John Metcalf. Both James BACQUE and Robert KROETSCH contributed short stories to *Creation* (1970), edited by Kroetsch, whose 'That yellow prairie sky' is a moving tale of the bitter hazards of prairie farming. NS

Fiction in French. The period under review, 1967–72, follows immediately a very fruitful harvest in French-Canadian fiction. In 1965 Marie-Claire BLAIS gave us the beautifully tragicomic *Une saison dans la vie d'Emmanuel*; Hubert AQUIN published his first novel, *Prochain épisode*—full of poetry and psychological insight into the new Québec nationalism; Gérard BESSETTE made evident his shift from social to metaphysical satire in his labryinthine *L'incubation*; Jacques GODBOUT offered his symbolic-realistic quest of identity, *Le couteau sur la table*. The following year came Réjean DUCHARME's bizarrely explosive childhood odyssey, *L'avalée des avalés*. The same year Gabrielle ROY produced the third, and perhaps most moving, literary transposition of her formative years in Manitoba, *La route d'Altamont*. Claire MARTIN created an outstanding non-fiction novel with her two-part *Dans un gant de fer*.

In our six-year period, established writers continued to produce works of interest; developing writers added to their publications; and a group of new writers emerged. These three groups will be examined in turn. (English translations, where they exist, are referred to in the separate author entries.)

1. *Established writers.* The most prolific of these authors during the period were Yves THÉRIAULT and Jacques FERRON. Thériault, with nine entries in the novel category, has continued to examine man's primitive passions; Canada's aboriginal peoples and their cultural interaction with those of European origin; the struggle between man and beast, or man and the elements, as well as between archetypal men and women. The best recent novels by Thériault are probably *La mort d'eau* (1968), dealing with a girl from the Madeleine Islands who is torn between her desire to settle in Montreal and the contrary pull of her birthplace; *Le dernier havre* (1970) about a Gaspé fisherman who, in advanced old age, voluntarily goes to his death in the sea, unable to reconcile life with decrepitude; and *La Passe-au-Crachin* (1972), in which a Breton fisherman settles in northern Labrador with his wife, and the two are torn apart by the hero's pull towards the isolated, free life of his Montagnais companion. None of these works, however, matches the force and attraction of Thériault's 'classics': *Aaron* (1954), *Agaguk* (1958) and, to a lesser extent, *Ashini* (1960).

Jacques Ferron seems to have abandoned writing plays and the short *conte*, which brought him into the forefront of French-Canadian letters, in favour of the longer novel form. Seven of his works in this category were published in the period under review, and these are of unequal value. In *La charrette* (1968) he returns to the framework of *La nuit* (1965) with its combination of realism and fantasy, and the counterpoising of good and evil, day and night, the south shore and Montreal. The mixture is unstable, wordy. The same can be said of *Le salut de l'Irlande* (1970), a Québec/Irish allegory, which has its moments of interest, however, especially in the development of a theme of importance to Ferron since his excellent *Cotnoir* (1962)—that of individual and collective salvation. Yet the believability of two key characters, Frère Thadéus and the narrator's father, is wanting, as are aspects of narrative point of view. The salvation theme is much more successful in *L'amélanchier* (a rare Québec tree with a purple pear-like fruit), published the same year. The fantasy of a childhood garden merges smoothly (for the most part) with the efforts of the narrator and her jailer-father to save an emotionally deprived young prisoner. The image of the tree could be a metaphor for the author's search for solid and distinctive roots. The author's interest in mental illness, probably derived from his recent experience as physician in the Montreal Saint-Jean-de-Dieu hospital, is evident also in *Les roses sauvages* (1971), where this theme is combined with a denunciation of strident English unilingualism in Moncton and the resulting French assimilation. This work, however, is plagued by clumsy omniscient third-person narration, the unbelievably quick politicization of the businessman-hero, and numerous examples of faulty English transcription. It is eclipsed in interest by the appended barely fictionalized story of a schizophrenic, *Lettre d'amour*. Ferron's longest book, the 400-page tome *Le ciel de Québec* (1969), is less a novel than a collection of incidents and anecdotes involving real people (Cardinal Villeneuve, the Hon. C. G. Power, Camille Roy, Saint-Denys-GARNEAU), often placed in highly imaginary situations, and fictional ones taken from other Ferron writings (Dr Cotnoir, Biouti Rose). The result is a dislocated social satire. In Ferron's two most recent novels, both published in 1972—*La chaise du maréchal ferrant* and *Le saint Elias*—the author draws on French-Canadian folklore and history. The first has the material for several good *contes* based on popular devil legends; but stretched out to include journalistic chunks of Canadian political history, it ends in a boring hodge-podge. Much more readable is the second, also a mixture of real and imaginary characters. Monseigneur Laflèche, the ultramontane bishop of Trois-Rivières, appears in the book as himself; Pierre Maheu (editor of PARTI PRIS) is the intrepid captain of the ship *Le saint Elias*, which symbolically breaks with the isolationist past of French Canada, plying the western and eastern Atlantic; and Philippe Cossette (the Créditiste functionary) is the founder of a new, proud dynasty in what has been called a novel of Québécois reconciliation.

Jean-Jules Richard is third in the list of veteran writers with three quite different novels to his credit. In *Faites-leur boire le fleuve* (1970) the setting is the Montreal waterfront; *Carré Saint-Louis* (1971) is a drama of young drug-users and pushers; *Exovide Louis Riel* (1972) is a historical novel based on the second (North West) Riel rebellion. Richard is a populist writer who influenced younger novelists of the late 1950s and 1960s. Ostracized for political radicalism during the Duplessis years, he was inactive for some time. He has recently taken pen in hand again, usually to write works that are just short of first-rate. This is certainly the case in the gripping story of the docks, with its original milieu, its mores, argot, and moments of violent high drama. It is marred only by a melodramatic tendency towards unbelievable coincidence and hidden identity, as well as by occasional stereotyped characterization. In the second novel the intense worlds of the drug-addict and the 'hippie' culture are interestingly presented, but characterization is again, and more pervasively, faulty. The novel based on Riel has merit in humanizing the French-Canadian folk-hero and giving us a rational explanation for his 'visions'. One or two mass scenes are colourful; the author might have used this technique more extensively to give greater force to the intermingling of Métis, Amerindians, the Anglo-Saxon settlers. Also, the omniscience of the author is irritating at times.

Three women and a man—Anne HÉBERT, Jovette Bernier, Claire Martin, and Jean SIMARD—have tackled the novel of love, with varying results. Anne Hébert's *Kamouraska* (1970), clearly superior to her earlier *Les chambres de bois* (1958), is one of the finest literary creations of recent years. A richly woven work based on an actual crime of passion committed in 1838, *Kamouraska* places Anne Hébert in the front rank of French-Canadian novelists. At the bedside of her dying second husband, Elisabeth d'Aulnières, in a state of semi-consciousness, tries to piece together the fragments of her turbulent life. In visions dominated by red, green, and white images, she retraces her fervent will to live and love in a society in which women must conform to a rigid social role. This 'period' novel of Québec treats two very contemporary preoccupations: the inferior position of women and the influence of class on justice. Could the title, *Kamouraska*—typical of the many sonorous and evocative place-names in the story—be an anagram for *Qu'est-ce que (l')amour?* Jovette Bernier, probably the oldest active creative writer in Québec, returned to the novel after an absence of nearly forty years with her successful *Non monsieur* (1969). In folksy, earthy language, and a style that mixes laughter and tears, Mme Bernier recounts the frustrating love of Puce, a young rural schoolteacher, for her ever-evasive Noc. The title signifies a series of refusals by the narrator to submit to various constraints, but the novel also suggests 'Oui, monsieur' because she tolerates her flighty lover. Claire Martin's *Les morts* (1970) is a dialogue between a woman writer and an unnamed person (her publisher?) in which she painfully reminisces about two bereaved lovers as well as another dead loved one (her mother) and a lost object (an unfinished manuscript). War is passionately denounced for having snatched the first lover away. The novel's effectiveness is reduced by a certain abstractness and the occasional artificiality of the interlocutor, which makes one appreciate all the more the totally convincing *Dans un gant de fer*. Jean Simard too has dealt with the vicissitudes of love in his epistolary novel, *La séparation* (1970). Two lovers separated for a year on either side of the Atlantic write endless letters that are monotonous, unvaried declarations of fidelity.

Gabrielle Roy has published only one novel in the last six years, *La rivière sans repos* (1970), which was translated by Joyce MARSHALL as *Windflower* (1970). (This book also contains three short stories.) It is set in the Far North, in the region of Fort Chimo and the Koksoak River. In the story of Elsa, the Eskimo girl whose illegitimate child, fathered by a U.S. serviceman, becomes a bomber pilot in Viet Nam, Gabrielle Roy returns to some of her important themes. In what may be a symbolic setting, she probes the respective merits of '*la primitive insouciance*' and civilization; cultures in contact (and in conflict); the search for identity. Like *La montagne secrète* (1961), however, this interesting work does not totally absorb the reader as do the writings based on the author's formative years in Manitoba, or her two novels set in Montreal.

Gérard Bessette's *Le cycle* (1971) is probably the most audacious French-Canadian novel using internal monologue. In its seven parts the grandson, widow, and five children of a dead man reflect on the deceased and on their own lives and obsessions. In each monologue the author uses single and double parentheses to reveal subconscious and unconscious thoughts respectively, and also notes the physiological reactions engendered by these thoughts. Sexual obsessions dominate, and there are also flashes of ethnic prejudice and political and economic concerns. Fascinating reading for the most part, *Le cycle* errs in introducing quite inappropriate imaginative content into the monologues of some of the characters; for instance the simple widow Vitaline evokes Cro-Magnon man at one point. There is also a gratuitous totalitarian vision of the Québec independence movement. André LANGEVIN, one of Québec's most respected writers, published his fourth novel, *L'élan d'Amérique* (1972), after an absence of sixteen years. The author uses 'description of consciousness'—a modified third-person variant of the internal monologue—for the two main characters, Claire Peabody, a young Franco-American, and Antoine, a middle-aged French-Canadian woodsman. In addition there is omniscient third-person narration in sections of the novel, as well as authorial intervention into the 'stream-of-consciousness' portions, all of which adds to the confusion of an already disjointed story-puzzle. The book suffers, too, from melodramatic characterization and thematic diffusion; it lacks the 'classical' economy of *Poussière sur la ville* (1953), Langevin's best achievement. Nevertheless this profoundly pessimistic look at the survival of French Canada is intriguing in its linking of the various doomed elements (Claire, Antoine, the Indian, the symbolic moose—all to a certain extent '*nègres blancs d'Amérique*'), and for its archetypal and generational conflicts. Finally, brief mention should be made of the late Robert Charbonneau's *Chronique de l'âge amer* (1967), which is a fictionalized autobiography dealing with the author's involvement in the editorship of the Catholic intellectual journal *La relève*—later *La nouvelle relève* (1934–48).

2. *Developing writers.* A number of novelists who had already published at least one work before 1967 are grouped in this category—some fifteen in all.

Réjean Ducharme dazzled the literary world in both France and Canada with his *L'avalée des avalés* (1966), which was followed, respectively, by the publication of two other prose novels and one novel written in rhymed quatrains: *Le nez qui voque* (1967), *L'océantume* (1968), and *La fille de Christophe Colomb* (1969). *L'océantume* was actually written before *L'avalée des avalés* and one feels that the author has not yet refined his style—its verbal magic and child-like poetry. As in the other Ducharme prose works, the parents are of different ethnic origin—in both cases they have come from a small nation. The same lack of polish and surprise is found in the quatrains of *La fille de Christophe Colomb*. On the other hand *Le nez qui voque*, somewhat reminiscent of French writer Boris Vian's *L'écume des jours*, is a convincing and moving eulogy on the quest of two adolescents for meaning and wholeness in the fragmented, dehumanized '*royaume du mal*' of adults. In addition, in this work more than in any other Ducharme not only treats the conflicting universal themes of innocence, sexual obsession, and moral cowardice, but also fully assumes his Québécois identity. His heroes, Mille Milles and the 'blonde' Eskimo girl whom he calls 'Chateaugué', reveal—through their speech patterns, their identification with Emile Nelligan, and their references to specific social woes—that their cultural alienation and humiliation are rooted in a specific time and place. This condition, whether inflicted by Anglophones or continental Frenchmen, is summed up by the narrator's vision of himself: 'Pauvre Mille Milles! qui, en plus d'être tout sale, est Canadien français.'

Marie-Claire Blais is a spiritual cousin of Réjean Ducharme, and in fact both have dedicated works to each other. In the period under study Blais published five novels, three of which form parts of a series centred on Pauline Archange, first as a child and then as an adolescent in Lower-Town Quebec City: *Les manuscrits de Pauline Archange* (1968), *Vivre! Vivre!* (1969), and *Les apparences* (1970). In these works the author is very sensitive to the experience of poverty, to the sights and sounds of her native city, to the rare gesture of tenderness, which she renders in fine poetic prose. As in *Une saison dans la vie d'Emmanuel* (1965), she treats the theme of the cultural wasteland that stultifies the young shoots of creative expression. Yet unlike that of her excellent achievement in *Emmanuel*, the atmosphere is too monotonally dark. These novels are nearly totally naturalistic, stressing ugliness, cruelty, and suffering with only occasional relief. In the second and third novels this exaggerated sombre fatalism is sometimes relieved by sparks of revolt, by objective insight into causes of crime and depravity, and by the presence of the positive, self-assertive nurse and journalist, Germaine Léonard. In Blais's *David Sterne* (1967) the hero is an eighteen-year-old student from a comfortable family who tries to embrace all the vices before being shot dead by police bullets. Two of his friends take their own lives, one setting himself on fire after losing faith in his crusade against nuclear weapons. The homosexual theme, touched on in this novel, dominates in *Le loup* (1972). Sébastien, the narrator, is a young man obsessed with a love of the strong for the weak, of men for boys. He analyses drily and minutely the causes of erotic failure. There are touches of grandeur in all of Blais's novels, but none of those discussed above has the fullness and enchantment of *Une saison dans la vie d'Emmanuel*.

The following novels dealing with the love theme are invariably concerned with the breakdown in erotic relationships, be they heterosexual or homosexual. Louise Maheux-Forcier weaves a complex and poetic plot around the vicissitudes of female homosexuality in *Une forêt pour Zoé* (1969). As in *Amadou* (1963) and *Triptyque* (1965), she develops the related themes of childhood, love, and creativity. In *Une forêt pour Zoé*, the narrator-writer, attempting to compose a book about her childhood friend, Zoé, is haunted by visions of the girls and women—

all red-headed and green-eyed—to whom she has been sexually attracted. Her escapist behaviour is motivated by the brutal or indifferent men she has known. In Monique BOSCO's *La femme de Loth* (1970) and Gilles Archambault's *Le tendre matin* (1969) the narrators are able to compensate for unrequited love, in the first instance by writing and in the second through friendship and renewed love. In both novels the narrator-heroes retrace their entire lives in retrospect. The tragic impact of Monique Bosco's work resides in the narrator's decision to resist the temptation of suicide, engendered by a string of sentimental failures in and out of marriage. The narrator in Adrien Thério's *Soliloque en hommage à une femme* (1968) also finally rejects suicide after tracing in his mind the ups and downs of a tumultuous love affair and making painful confessions about his own past.

The love theme is not fundamental to but is certainly present in the novels of Jean BASILE, where its particular tone reflects the bohemian attitudes of 'Beatniks' on the way to becoming part of the new drug culture. While it is treated in a mocking, blasé way, underneath there is tragedy, as in Armande's suicide at the end of *La jument des mongols* (1964) or the murder of the harelipped child in *Le grand khan* (1967). In this second part of a trilogy, the author again captivates the reader with his sinuous, ceaseless flow of sense impressions and prose poems on nihilistic aspects of Montreal life that have been untouched by other writers. In the second novel the characters who were in their late twenties in *La jument des mongols* are now into their thirties and conscious of their fleeting youth. Jonathan, narrator of *Le grand khan*, turns out to be the 'author' of the first! He is cynically existentialist, is both attracted to and repelled by fascist ideas, and mocks all forms of political commitment, especially the Québec independence movement. The third volume of what was to be a tetralogy, *Les voyages d'Irkutsk* (1970), is disappointing, without the allure of the earlier novels and overburdened with pharmacological descriptions of drugs and drug-taking. The author himself seems conscious of this novel's weaknesses when he has the 'novelist' Jonathan flay his own writing.

Under the thematic heading of 'search for identity' there are novels that deal with the French Canadian's past and present, in both a personal and collective sense, and that draw on aspects of history, social transformation, or folklore. Jacques Godbout has followed a geographical and psychological odyssey in his four novels. *L'aquarium* (1962) is set in a vaguely oriental country, and the French-Canadian hero is one of a group of international technocrats; in *Le couteau sur la table* (1965), the narrator-hero traverses Canada from west to east, travels throughout the United States and Mexico, and returns to Montreal where he is torn between an Anglophone and a Francophone woman; in *Salut Galarneau!* (1967) the semi-educated hotdog vendor who is both narrator and prospective author lives his adventures and defeats in the Montreal region, Lévis, and (through his mother) Francophone New England; all of the action of *D'amour P.Q.* (1972) takes place in Montreal, and the protagonist, Mireille, is a *joual*-speaking stenographer. The trajectory, then, is mainly from the universal in the first novel, through the pan-Canadian and American contexts, to the Québec and Montreal one, including its anglicized sub-language. In *Salut Galarneau!* the hero suffers a broken marriage and the loss of his beloved to his brother, a professional writer. He isolates himself from the world by building a concrete wall around his home and spends his days being bombarded by television commercials. Galarneau finally decides to assume his true self and symbolically leaves behind his walled barrier (like Québec) to offer the world his manuscript, which become the novel itself. He reaches out towards the sun, his namesake in Québec folklore. In his most recent novel, *D'amour, P.Q.*, Godbout pursues the writer's search for identity, but with less spontaneity and aesthetic conviction than in *Salut Galarneau!*. This book is dedicated to and inspired by Raoul DUGUAY and his poetic call for Everyman to be given centre-stage and for Quebeckers to create 'love cells' and 'bombs of love' in the wake of the 1970 October crisis. Like *Salut Galarneau!*, it is a novel about a novel. Thomas D'Amour, in the midst of creating a novel, is rebuked by his typist, who ridicules his attempts at exoticism and universality and finally dictates to *him* a novel rooted in Québec and its popular speech, claiming that the word-fund is a natural resource belonging to the masses. In a transposition of the crisis of October 1970 Godbout proposes a fraternal Québec utopia in opposition to the present 'plastic civilization', but is unable to sustain reader interest. The gratuitous vulgarity is a flaw in a novel that is often witty.

Hubert Aquin's *Prochain épisode* (1965) transposes certain aspects of the author's own life (e.g. his involvement in the independence movement, his arrest and confinement to a psychiatric prison, his travels throughout Switzerland). It uses a double or mirror structure (the novel within the novel) to emphasize the narrator's failure to live the coveted role of political terrorist. There is also a muted mock-melodramatic aspect as well as ambivalence in relation to English-speaking Montrealers. The narrator's identification with the Third World via the Cuban revolution in this first novel is extended in the second, *Trou de mémoire* (1968), to Black Africa, evoking the idea of '*nègres blancs d'Amérique*'. The mirror structure of the second novel becomes much more complicated than in the first, with auxiliary narrators and editors intervening in the story of the self-styled revolutionary pharmacist, P.-X. Magnant, and his murder of Joan Ruskin. The resulting confusion has been labelled a baroque exercise, the Québec political themes being drowned in a flood of pharmacological and ethnographic erudition and lost in structural mazes. For other critics, the very confusion is politically significant, for Magnant writes: 'je n'ai sûrement pas la force qu'il faut pour entreprendre ce roman policier inconcevable qui sera à l'image du Québec secoué par ses propres efforts pour obtenir un spasme révolutionnaire qui ne vient jamais. Cher pays déboussolé, comme je te ressemble . . .' In Aquin's third novel, *L'antiphonaire* (1969), the title itself reflects the mirror approach in its reference to a book containing the musical accompaniments to religious services. The narrator, Dr Christine Forestier, is preparing a thesis on a sixteenth-century medical scholar, and the intertwining of this task and her own tumultuous life shared with an epileptic husband and a demanding lover(s) constitutes the novel. This work is more baroque than ever, with the juxtaposition of two stories four hundred years apart, the dazzling array of erudition and pseudo-erudition, the propensity of the narrator to fall victim (?) to rape, etc. The political allusions to Québec are reduced to a single vague reference: Robert, Christine's lover, undertakes a speaking tour of the province for an otherwise undefined group or movement. Again it has been claimed that the disorder of the narration and its fragmentation (self-critically remarked on by Christine) have a profound social significance. This time, though, the argument is much less convincing and the book seems to be primarily a brilliantly conceived toy for the amusement of the author and readers.

Claude JASMIN tried his hand at regional history in his *L'outaragasipi* (1971) (the Indian name for the river L'Assomption) in an attempt to link past and present. This book is not called a novel but rather a 'saga', although in fact it is neither. It is a very sketchy account in which Jasmin has put neither his heart nor his thought. And yet in the *libertins*, along with the worker-priest Pierre Le Sueur and the town crier, among others, the author had ample novelistic material. Far superior are Jasmin's personal monologues and reminiscences, *Rimbaud mon beau salaud!* (1969) and *La petite patrie* (1972). The late Jean Hamelin, a respected drama critic, was also concerned with the search for identity. In *Les occasions profitables* (*Écrits du Canada français*, x, 1961) he told the story of a union struggle in a textile mill during the reign of Premier Maurice Duplessis. His second novel, *Un dos pour la pluie* (1967), is a more substantial work, in some ways an extensionof *Trente arpents*. With earthy realism, and using the style of a sly and ironic oral narrator, Hamelin recounts the life of a couple who move to Montreal during the crisis years of the 1930s, and how they get tragically caught up in the events of the Second World War. The roots of Acadian folklore are evident in Antonine MAILLET's allegory *Don l'Orignal* (1972). There is charm in her use of the particularisms of Acadian French (especially in proper names and curses) and its quaint morphology. The gentle social satire and designation of the Acadians as *nègres blancs* are convincing. And yet the author seems to run out of wind about two thirds of the way through her short work. *Don l'Orignal* does not have the memorable poignancy of Maillet's very successful dramatic monologue, *La Sagouine* (1971).

3. *New writers.* In this category we shall discuss writers who first published novels

in 1967 or after or, if their first novels appeared earlier, had not yet imposed themselves on the reading public.

A number of writers, usually in their twenties, have chosen the theme of political terrorism, obviously inspired by some of the explosive events that Québec lived through from 1963 to 1970. Gilbert La Rocque's *Corridors* (1971) and Pierre Gravel's *À perte de temps* (1969) are both based on transposed events of the first wave of FLQ bombings in the spring of 1963. La Roque's novel is the work of a talented and sensitive writer who uses a usually harmonious mixture of third-person narration for the dramatic episodes seen in retrospect and the first person for the hero recalling his childhood and for the diary of his younger sister. The hero, Clément, has joined an FLQ auxiliary group, the main task of which is to seek out and punish turncoat informers. Clément joins the group following his desertion of his pregnant lover, Céline, partly because of his beliefs and partly to fill the emptiness of his life; he breaks with it because he cannot tolerate its violent methods of retribution. The hero's development as a human being passes through a series of corridors at the end of which he renews his ties with Céline and his child, although his ideological confusion seems to persist. Pierre Gravel lacks the finish and style of La Rocque. His hero, Robert, is in a terrorist group that has been betrayed and he is the last member still at large. The entire novel traces—sometimes naively, with repetition and blurring of point of view—two days in his life before his arrest. Like Clément, Robert recalls the mediocrity of his home and especially the spiritual absence of his father. While a committed revolutionary able to accept responsibility for his act, he is constantly haunted by memories of Victor, a former comrade who broke with the terrorists on moral grounds. In both books, then, doubts are raised about the ideology and tactics of political violence. Gilbert La Rocque has also published *Le nombril* (1970) and *Après la boue* (1972), both dealing with young Québécois growing up in an alienating milieu who are in search of themselves; both, however, are inferior to *Corridors*. The terrorist theme also appears in Jean Somcynsky's rather unbelievable *Les rapides* (1967), in which a group bent on armed revolution in Québec and Canada as a whole is led by an Anglophone; and in Michèle Mailhot's *Le fou de la reine* (1969). In the latter the author's psychological insight is evident as she relates the monologue of a man who had turned to revolutionary politics after an unhappy love affair, all the while blaming society for his chronic failure to face reality. Another woman novelist, Yvette Naubert, attempted to paint a broad canvas dealing with the main preoccupations of Québec's neo-nationalism in *Les Pierrefendre* (1972). This book follows her successful *L'été de la cigale* (1968), in which she probed the reaction of a white racist family in the U.S. to an interracial marriage. Mme Naubert ambitiously constructed her second novel along the lines of a fugue, using musical terms for its various components. Equally ambitious are her four time schemes: the fictional present, centred on Françoise Ridgewood (née Pierrefendre) and her twin brother François; the previous thirty or so years, as reviewed by Françoise's parents and through letters sent her father by his soldier friend, Hubert, who was to die in the Second World War; the immediate past, as seen through the Mickiewicz family who immigrated to Montreal; and finally the real or imagined future, fifteen years hence, as reflected upon by Françoise's Anglophone husband Charles. Through these various 'narrators' we live through the pre-war nationalist movement and its fight against conscription, the conflict over the French language in Québec as it affects New Canadians, the rise of the post-war independence movement, and terrorism, etc. Unfortunately this task was too much for the author, who is most successful with Françoise's conflicting thoughts on the eve of, and through, childbirth. Large portions of the novel degenerate into a *roman à thèse*, with its rhetoric and stereotyped characters.

The theme of violence also appears in the works of young novelists who do not link it directly to social or political causes. Such is the case of Jacques Benoit, whose *Jos Carbone* (1967) won the literary prize of the Province of Québec and revealed a storyteller with unusual talents. He followed it with *Les voleurs* (1969) and *Patience et Firlipon* (1970). His first work is set in a forest where the primitive instincts of the characters are given full play. Apart from melodramatic moments, the attempts at rape, ambushes, violent struggles, betrayals, and the tender fidelity of the two main characters are the stuff of suspenseful drama. The strange county of Gagourouge and the village of St-Forficule give way to real streets in east-central Montreal in Benoit's second novel. Because of confusion in narrative voice, considerably more melodrama, and a rather abrupt ending, this longer work is not as convincing as his first. There is, however, good psychological insight into the women characters and a mostly interesting story of the combined efforts of ex-convicts, an unemployed truckdriver, and a bishop to help 'steal' an election for the cleric's political friends. In Benoit's most recent novel he seems to return to the dreamlike atmosphere of the first. Firlipon is a mobster who is saved from his life of violence by the love of Patience in a fantasy set in Montreal in 1978. Another young writer who has placed her novel in a pitiless rural milieu is Hélène Ouvrard. In *Le coeur sauvage* (1967) the young hero and heroine fail in their attempt to achieve a libertarian environment by shaking off the taboos and prejudices of their miserable village.

In the area of the social novel two writers, Victor-Lévy BEAULIEU and Roch CARRIER, have adopted the form of the *roman-fleuve* and both have attracted public attention by their original handling of naturalist themes. Each published his first novel in 1968. For Beaulieu it was *Mémoires d'outre-tonneau*, a punny, often boring mixture of realism and fantasy, dealing with the disturbed public masturbator, Satan Belhumeur, who reappears episodically in *La nuitte de Malcolm Hudd* (1969). In this work, too, the fantasies and phantasms of the narrator, another mentally ill character, are hard to distinguish from objective events. The vital language question is raised both here and in Beaulieu's other novels by the frequent use of highly anglicized *joual* expressions and by reflections on bilingualism in Montreal. Beaulieu didn't really approach a style until he began the Beauchemin saga with *Race de monde!* (1969). This novel is narrated by twenty-year-old Abel, sixth of the twelve Beauchemin children. (This and other biographical details, as well as his reflections on literature, clearly indicate that Beaulieu himself was the model.) There is still an extravagant use of puns; a somewhat gratuitous delectation with physical ugliness, putrefaction, genitalia (Beaulieu flays the enduring Québec taboos with a vengeance!); boring passages; and fragmentary characterization. More appealing to the reader is a thread of ironic humour, a demystification of literary sacred cows, and a demythification of traditional institutions. In *Jos Connaissant* (1970) Beaulieu further develops his command of subject matter and creates a poignant and pathetic character in his narrator, the eldest of the Beauchemin children, who capitalizes adjectives, adverbs, and nouns according to the emphasis desired. The mother emerges in strongly visual and emotive images, as does the suburb of Morial-Mort (read Montréal-Nord) with its squalor and multi-ethnic population. But some earlier flaws persist. In *Les grands-pères* (1971) the story centres on Mme Beauchemin's father, Milien (*le Vieux*), through whose eyes we perceive the human drama of aging. Here death dominates—that of the old man's two wives, of his children, or his own, which is very near at the book's end, and that of the barren, stump-covered Bas-du-Fleuve area where Milien has eked out an existence. The flow of remembrances, dreams, and hallucinations in an interplay between past and present is sometimes confusing, but on the whole it is a creative device. The use of the generalized plural in the title and the pluralizing of proper nouns and adjectives ('les Miliens', 'les Vieux') effectively emphasize the derisively repetitious resemblance between named and unnamed characters. In 1972 Victor-Lévy Beaulieu set aside the Beauchemin saga (temporarily?) to write *Un rêve québécois*, a less successful hallucinatory novel about a gruesome, ritualistic murder in which the deranged hero kills and seemingly mutilates the body of his wife to avenge his own misery and humiliation. This violent gesture takes place on the Rue des Récollets while James Cross is being held in another house on the same street. The rare references to the events of October 1970 suggest that out of individual and social violence there may emerge the possibility of Québécois survival.

Roch Carrier's first novel, *La guerre, yes sir!* (1968), launched a popular trilogy based on transposed and transfigured reminiscences of his childhood and youth in Ste-Justine, south of Quebec City. It was followed by *Floralie, où es-tu?* (1969) and *Il est par là, le soleil* (1970). Like Beaulieu, Carrier writes in the naturalist tradition, which has a short history in French

Canada. But Carrier is less extreme. His novels contain echoes of Rabelaisian humour and in the first there is the same mixture of pathos and satire found in Marie-Claire Blais's *Une saison dans la vie d'Emmanuel*. Like the latter, Carrier's *La guerre, yes sir!* runs totally counter to the traditional *roman de la fidélité*. In fact, in aiming to destroy the exaggerated 'saints' of the pastoral idyll, Carrier seems to go to the opposite extreme, creating a village of brutes and ignoramuses. True, the count is even at the end of the novel, with one dead on the side of the stereotyped, ramrod English-speaking soldiers and one on that of the folkloric *habitants* and their equally stereotyped cleric. Carrier has a strong gift for antithesis: at the wake that is the setting for most of the novel the grief surrounding the return of the ludicrously killed village soldier, Corriveau, gives way to a raucous and earthy spree of eating and drinking. The most convincing character is Bérubé, another village soldier and outhouse cleaner at Gander with other 'lesser breeds', who is torn asunder in his quest for identity between his emotive loyalty to his own folk and his obligatory duty to his English-speaking sergeant. It is he who gives meaning to the novel's title as he teaches the butcher-gravedigger Arsène a lesson in what war is all about. The war that is most palpable to the villagers is, in fact, '*la petite guerre*' between themselves and the Anglophone soldiers—an extension of a historic conflict that is far from over. This political overtone is present also in Carrier's third novel, in the string of failures suffered by Philibert at the hands of exploiters who more often than not are Anglophones. Critic Jean-Cléo Godin has suggested that central to the trilogy is the dialectical opposition between life and death. The characters are dazzled by a duo of 'suns', divine and diabolical, both of which must be rejected in order to attain a liveable, sensual, and natural existence, as do Floralie and Anthyme at the end of the second novel. In the third, Philibert, who has fled his violent father and the village with its death images, never really leaves behind his own symbolic occupation of apprentice grave-digger when he goes to Montreal. He dies (is it a self-fulfilling prophecy?) just on the eve of prosperity, and within grasp of the 'sun'.

Brief mention can be made here, under the rubric of the social novel, of Marcel Godin's *Ce maudit soleil* (1965) and *Une dent contre Dieu* (1969). The first novel is set in a lumber camp, and is full of violence, sexual turmoil, and fear of the 'civilisés'—the New Canadians who threaten the lumberjacks' jobs. The second, largely autobiographical, is an attempt to exorcise all the social, religious, and sexual taboos of the narrator's youth. Godin also wrote *Danka* (1971) in which the narrator relates, through a journal, his misadventures with a Yugoslav-born dancer for whom he unhappily gave up wife and mistress. Godin has yet to find an original and satisfying style.

One of the revelations of the past few years in Québec writing is the work of Jacques Folch-Ribas, Spanish-born architect and member of the editorial board of the literary review *Liberté*. He has set out to produce a vast fresco under the general title *La horde des Zamé*, of which two volumes have appeared: *Le démolisseur* (1970) and *Le greffon* (1971). The second novel, more ample and richer than the first, is the chronicle of an adolescent growing up with remnants of his family in a Flemish village after their exile from Spain following the Civil War. Jaume, through whose eyes we see most of the action, is like the *greffon*, the cherry tree grafting that his father and grandfather optimistically transplant. Torn between an 'unpronounceable' Catalonian label and his French name (Jacques), and between two languages, he undergoes an identity crisis not unlike that of the Québécois that is resolved by a positive acceptance of himself and his roots. The constant interchange between past and present and the flow of humanity through its pages make *Le greffon* a captivating work of art. *Le démolisseur* is a drier, more abstract novel whose central character, Amsterdam Zamé, cousin of Jaume, is the head of a wrecking firm in a vague north-European country. He is imbued with anarchistic ideas of creative destruction and is ferociously independent and fearful of tenderness and enclosures, perhaps because of the same Civil War that exiled him.

Another novel of *dépaysement* in which the Second World War is seen through the eyes of a child is *L'ogre de barbarie* (1972) by Pierre Billon. A pre-adolescent girl recounts her involvement in helping to smuggle French refugees into Switzerland, where Nazi sympathizers are also active. The plot of Madeleine Ferron's *Le baron écarlate* (1971) is situated closer to home. A mature woman recounts her childhood and youth in the Beauce area, where she was brought up from the age of six by a driving, unscrupulous uncle. The contrast between his growing wealth and the surrounding misery revolts the narrator, who deserts the disoriented uncle in search of independence. One of the most lauded books on the theme of childhood is essayist and trade-unionist Pierre Vadeboncoeur's *Un amour libre* (1970), a poetic 'dialogue' between the author and his child, the development of whose sense perceptions and apprehension of the world are sources of wonderment to his parent and chronicler.

A number of young writers have tried their hand at formal experimentation, some more successfully than others. Jacques POULIN is the most appealing novelist to come out of Quebec City since Roger Lemelin, and his *Le coeur de la baleine bleue* (1970) is a fine example of the *roman-poème*. It is a work in which the author plays verbally and thematically on the expression '*une histoire de coeur*'. Tension is created between the struggle of the apprentice-novelist Noël to create fiction and his fear of the rejection of his transplanted heart, the donor of which was a young girl. In spite of a certain amount of diffusion and lack of control over his material, Poulin is a promising and natural writer. These pluses and minuses are evident also in his first novel, *Mon royaume pour un cheval* (1967), and in *Jimmy* (1969). The first deals in a semi-realistic fashion with a terrorist interned in a psychiatric prison and presents the intriguing character Simon, a calèche driver (who reappears in *Le coeur de la baleine bleue*); the second juxtaposes the boundless imagination and innocence of the eleven-year-old narrator with the reality of his parents' imminent marriage breakdown. The theme of the 'decrystallization' of love is present in all three novels, as is the background of the old Quartier latin of Quebec City.

Another good example of the technique of the *roman-poème* is Louis Gauthier's *Anna* (1967) in which objective reality is transformed into a world of fantasy in the mind of a deserted lover. Emmanuel Cocke is in the general lineage of Réjean Ducharme's verbal revolution. His two novels, *Va voir au ciel si j'y suis* (1971) and *L'emmanuscrit de la mer morte* (1972)—with their droll characters, Jésus Tanné and Dieuble respectively, inverted spellings, and other juggling—are a futuristic search for meaning in a mechanized world. Experimentation with point of view by using two parallel columns with different type faces is the approach chosen by Michel Beaulieu in *La représentation* (1972). The stepfather's uttered words are in boldface on the left, the stepson's thoughts and 'corrections' in parentheses and lighter type on the right. Poet Nicole Brossard's fervid rejection of traditional narrative techniques did not suffice to make a novel out of the amorphous matter of *Un livre* (1970).

If one has Luc Granger's gift for irreverent humour and his ability to mix imaginatively *joual*, English, and French, the non-fiction *récit* can be as much of a creative endeavour as a novel. His *Ouate de phoque* (1969), which recounts his longlasting battle with Radio-Canada bureaucrats in several centres, is a total success. B-ZS

Short Stories (see also ANTHOLOGIES IN FRENCH). An index to recent work in the short story in Québec is the revised edition of Adrien Thério's *Conteurs canadiens-français (époque contemporaine)* (1965). The 1970 edition includes stories by five new writers: Roch CARRIER, Madeleine Ferron, François HERTEL, Suzanne PARADIS, and Jacques RENAUD. Comment on new trends and developments can be grouped around these names.

François Hertel, born in 1905, is hardly a new writer, but his inclusion corrects an oversight, for his two volumes of short stories, *Six femmes, un homme* (1950) and *Jérémie et Barrabas* (1959), display a brand of sardonic humour quite uncommon in Québec. In the same vein, though more actively satirical, are Jacques FERRON's stories, two of which were included in Thério's first anthology (though his name was omitted from the 1967 *Companion*'s list of contributors). In the past six years Ferron has come into prominence as one of the most original and productive literary figures of his time. His stories are earlier work. *Contes du pays incertain* won a Governor General's Award in 1962 and was followed by *Contes anglais et autres* in 1964. His collected stories, *Contes—édition intégrale* appeared in 1968, and a selection of them was translated by Betty Bednarski as *Tales from the uncertain country* (1972). Among Ferron's stories one should probably include *Historiettes* (1969), highly personal and often farcical interpretations of some thirty episodes in Québec history. While Ferron's novels and plays tend to be rambling and unfinished, his stories are neat and pointed and represent well the mixture of fantasy, malicious wit, and rural realism that has made him famous.

None of the new contributors to Thério's anthology is principally a short-story writer. Roch Carrier, for example, began his novelist's career with *Jolis deuils* (1964), a series of brief excursions into the absurd through the door of the just-possible. In 1969 he published *Contes pour mille oreilles*, a selection of the same kind of elusive miniature allegories, in *Écrits du Canada français*, the review that is the best source of new work in short fiction in Québec. Dramatist Michel TREMBLAY is another writer whose first published work was a book of short stories, *Contes pour buveurs attardés* (1966). These grotesque little fantasies relate back to the tradition of folk-tale or fairy story rather than to the realistic North American short story. In the same style one might include chansonnier Gilles VIGNEAULT's *Contes sur la pointe des pieds* (1961), short short stories that deftly serve up a character or a situation by using poetic rather than analytical logic. The book was published in a bilingual edition, *Tales sur la pointe des pieds*, in 1972. Also in the category of the fantastic, though more anecdotal and conventional, are stories by Jean Tétreau in *Volupté de l'amour et de la mort* (1968) and *Treize histoires en noir et blanc* (1970) in which the author gives a gothic twist to adventures in metropolitan and international settings.

Madeleine Ferron and Suzanne Paradis represent in Thério's 1970 anthology some of Québec's distinguished women writers. Madeleine Ferron (sister of Jacques Ferron) is a novelist whose collection of stories, *Coeur de sucre* (1966), portrays the lives of country people with a deep feeling for their unconscious kinship with natural forces. Suzanne Paradis—poet, essayist, and novelist—has published one volume of stories, *François-les-oiseaux* (1967), that are experimental in style and influenced by her poetry. Other women, also professional novelists, who have published books of short stories but in a more traditional vein are Yvette Naubert (*Contes de la solitude*, 1967) and Anne Bernard (*Le soleil sur la façade*, 1967).

The fifth new writer to be included in *Conteurs canadiens-français* also represents a group. Jacques Renaud's *Le cassé* (1964) is a key work in the PARTI PRIS/*joual* school of writing. Written in popular dialect, set in the slums of Montreal, these interconnected naturalistic stories, told with a kind of desperate savagery, strike the note for a whole generation of angry young writers. Among those who have written collections of short stories in variants of this style, one can cite Marcel Godin (*La cruauté des faibles*, 1961), André MAJOR (*La chair de poule*, 1965), and Claude JASMIN (*Les coeurs empaillés*, 1967).

Thério's revised edition of *Conteurs canadiens* does, then, touch the major developments of the last few years in a representative way. No new trends have declared themselves since, though one might single out three of the most interesting recent collections that do not fall into any of the above categories. Paul Roussel's *La dame en coup de vent* (1970) gives in a clipped, objective style biographical sketches of characters, mainly children, whose affective lives have cruelly atrophied. Claude Robitaille's stories in *Rachel-du-hasard* (1971) take place in the inter-zone where desires, obsessions, inhibitions, dreams, and fantasies float freely round insignificant actions, giving them a kind of Proustian depth. And Antonine MAILLET, the Acadian writer who came to notice with her very effective monologues in *La Sagouine*, has published a book of short stories, *Par derrière chez mon père* (1972), that tells of the hard life of the New Brunswick fishing village in the same savoury language.

Gabrielle ROY supplemented her novella, *La rivière sans repos* (1970), with three short stories that are also about Eskimos. Her *Cet été qui chantait* (1972) is a collection of nineteen stories and sketches—delicate, impressionistic, and evidently autobiographical—that grew out of a summer spent in Charlevoix County.

Two recent anthologies should also be mentioned. *De Québec à Saint-Boniface* (1968) edited by Gérard BESSETTE includes stories by sixteen writers, all but three written after the Second World War. The writers chosen are nearly all represented in Thério's collection but most of the stories are different. *Contes et nouvelles du Canada français: 1778–1859* (1971) edited by John Hare presents ten little-known nineteenth-century tales. Several additional volumes are planned for this historical series.

Finally *Quebec short stories in translation* edited by Philip Stratford—the first anthology of its kind—will be published in 1973 and will include thirty stories by eighteen contemporary writers. PCS

Fielden, Charlotte. See FICTION IN ENGLISH 6.

Fielding, Joy. See FICTION IN ENGLISH 6.

Findley, Timothy (1930–). Born in Toronto, he became an actor in his teens and appeared in a London production of *Hamlet* and the London and New York productions of Thornton Wilder's *The Matchmaker*. He was also in the first season (1953) of the Stratford Festival (Ont.). Besides his novels and short stories, Findley has written for television—notably episodes in the CBC *Jalna* series. He lives in a farmhouse at Cannington, Ont.

Findley's mastery of theatre techniques lends great affectiveness to his two novels, *The last of the crazy people* (1957) and *The butterfly plague* (1969), in which action, dialogue, and interior monologue are highlighted by the carefully constructed backgrounds in which the protagonists play out their parts. His themes juxtapose the life force and the death wish as shown by people who must live as opposed to those who either cannot or will not live. In *The last of the crazy people*, Hooker, a child condemned to a living death by the insanity of his mother, the alcoholism of his brother, and the scorn of society, kills to secure interior freedom. *The butterfly plague* is a more complex novel, set partly in Germany and partly in Los Angeles. In it Findley draws a successful parallel between the Nazi persecution of the Jews and the ruthlessness with which Hollywood stars are made and broken. The author fails, however, in an attempt to equate the Nazi-Jewish problem with the well-cushioned deaths or refusals to live of wealthy Americans. NS

Fingard, Judith. See HISTORY STUDIES IN ENGLISH 4.

Finnigan, Joan (1928–). Born in Ottawa, Joan Finnigan studied at Carleton University in Ottawa and at Queen's University in Kingston, where she has lived for several years. Her first two books, *Through a glass darkly* (1957) and *A dream of lilies* (1965), contain a personal poetry, often forlorn in tone, about friends and neighbours, her family, lovers, and the joys and anguish of human relations. In *It was warm and sunny when we set out* (1970) the elegiac note of loss is sounded strongly and in a more openly confessional way, but it is framed by a belief in the persistence of love and the renewal of life. Many of these poems are placed specifically in the area around Kingston and through the Ottawa valley and continue her examination of personal relationships in nostalgic memories of her past and her family. Her poetry in this volume loses some of the overt melancholy of her previous books by emphasizing contentment, but the nostalgia is contained within realistic and direct statement that prevents the poetry in general from dropping into merely sentimental reminiscence. The two poles of Joan Finnigan's poetry are love and death and to some extent her other two books deal respectively with these themes. *Entrance to the green-house* (1968) is a series of almost haiku-like lyrics about the approach of summer; they link her feelings to the sudden outgrowths of life in nature. The large page size of *In the brown cottage on Loughborough Lake* (1970), an affecting poem describing her 'limbo all summer long' as she reflects on the death of love, allows for a visually appealing marriage between the text and complementary nature photographs by Erik Christensen.

Joan Finnigan wrote the script for the National Film Board movie, *The best damn fiddler from Calabogie to Kaladar*. PS

Firestone, O. J. See HISTORY STUDIES IN ENGLISH 15.

Firth, Edith. See HISTORY STUDIES IN ENGLISH 7.

Flanagan, Eileen C. See HISTORY STUDIES IN FRENCH 9.

Flanagan, Robert. See POETRY IN ENGLISH 2.

Fleming, W. G. See HISTORY STUDIES IN ENGLISH 15.

Flint, David. See CHILDREN'S BOOKS IN ENGLISH 5 and HISTORY STUDIES IN ENGLISH 5.

Folch-Ribas, Jacques. See FICTION IN FRENCH 3.

Folklore: Bibliography. Two of the most important folklore books of the last five years come from eastern Canada. Helen Creighton's *Bluenose magic: popular beliefs and superstitions in Nova Scotia* (1968) is a Canadian contribution to a continental survey of popular beliefs being conducted by Wayland Hand of the University of California. *Christmas mumming in Newfoundland: essays in anthropology, folklore, and history* (1969), edited by Herbert Halpert and G. M. Story, studies the mumming tradition in widely scattered areas of Newfoundland and Labrador, and provides insights into the rural communities and their folk customs.

New Brunswick has also been represented by several important folklore collections in recent years. Louise Manny and James Reginald Wilson produced the first major volume of New Brunswick songs, *Songs of Miramichi* (1968), selected from Miss Manny's extensive collection made under the auspices of Lord Beaverbrook. Where that volume emphasized the native songs, particularly those of the lumberwoods, Helen Creighton's *Folksongs of southern New Brunswick* (1971) deals mainly with versions of British songs and ballads. Earlier Helen Creighton had collaborated with Edward D. Ives in editing a collection of *Eight folktales from Miramichi, as told by Wilmot MacDonald* (1962).

Edward D. Ives followed up his study of Larry Gorman, the folk composer of the eastern lumberwoods, with another volume about *Lawrence Doyle: the farmer-poet of Prince Edward Island* (1971), and in *Folksongs and their makers* (1970)—written with Henry Glassie and John F. Szwed—Ives discusses still another Maritime singer-composer in 'A man and his song: Joe Scott and "The plain golden band"'. The same volume also contains John F. Szwed's 'Paul E. Hall: a Newfoundland song-maker and his community of song'. Then there is an extensive volume of *Folk songs from Newfoundland* (1971) edited by Maud Karpeles. This has the same title as her smaller collection issued in 1934, and gives 150 of the tunes she noted when she visited the island in 1929 and 1930. Two smaller song collections are the fourth edition of Gerald S. Doyle's *Old-time songs and poetry of Newfoundland* (1966) and *Newfoundlanders, sing!* (1964) by Omar Blondahl.

The first book devoted to songs from Ontario was Edith Fowke's *Traditional singers and songs from Ontario* (1965) which introduces ten singers with some of the songs they sang, most of which came originally from the British Isles. She followed this with *Lumbering songs from the northern woods* (1970), which deals specifically with native Canadian songs about lumbering and lumbermen. She also produced a book of children's lore drawn largely from Ontario, *Sally go round the sun: 300 songs, rhymes, and games of Canadian children* (1969), and collaborated with Richard Johnston to prepare *More folk songs of Canada* (1967), an anthology covering the whole country.

Very little folklore has been published in the four western provinces, although Barbara Cass-Beggs produced two small booklets: *Eight songs of Saskatchewan* (1963) and *Seven Métis songs of Saskatchewan* (1967).

Three more general books that are not strictly folklore but deal with folklife are Una Abrahamson's *God bless our home: domestic life in nineteenth century Canada* (1966), Jeanne Minhinnick's *At home in Upper Canada* (1970), and Eustella Langdon's *Pioneer gardens at Black Creek Pioneer Village* (1972).

The National Museum of Man continues to produce many valuable folklore items. Carmen Roy, chief of the folklore division, published *Saint-Pierre et Miquelon: une mission folklorique aux îles* (1962) and *Littérature orale en Gaspésie* (1955, 1962). Kenneth Peacock followed his massive three-volume *Songs of the Newfoundland outports* (1965) with *Twenty ethnic songs from western Canada* (1966), *Songs of the Doukhobors* (1970), and *A garland of rue: Lithuanian folksongs of love and betrothal* (1971). Robert B. Klymasz has published *An introduction to the Ukrainian Canadian immigrant folksong cycle* (1970) and *The Ukrainian winter folksong cycle in Canada* (1970), as well as a *Bibliography of Ukrainian folklore in Canada, 1902–1964* (1969).

Robert-Lionel SÉGUIN, who specializes in various aspects of French-Canadian folk life, has published *Les moules du Québec* (1963), *Les granges du Québec* (1963), *Le costume civil en Nouvelle-France* (1968), *La maison en Nouvelle-France* (1968), and *Les divertissements en Nouvelle-France* (1968) in the National Museum's series of Bulletins, and *Les jouets anciens du Québec* (1969) with another publisher.

The major studies of French traditions in America are in Université Laval's series 'Les archives de folklore' published under the direction of Luc Lacourcière. The first four numbers, which appeared between 1946 and 1949, contained miscellaneous articles by various folklorists; then the pattern changed to volumes presenting a single extensive study. In a double issue Soeur Marie-Ursule surveyed *Civilisation traditionnelle des Lavalois* (1951). Two more issues followed at four-year intervals: *Vieilles chansons de Nouvelle-France* (1956) by Russell Scott Young, and *La vie traditionnelle à Saint-Pierre (Île d'Orléans)* (1960) by Nora Dawson. No further issues appeared for nine years, and then the series gained momentum, with seven numbers in the last four years: *Étude linguistique de quatre contes folkloriques du Canada français (morphologie et syntaxe)* (1969) by James E. La Follette; *Placide-Eustache, sources et parallèles du conte-type 938* (1970) by Germain Lemieux; *Le vaisseau fantôme, légende étiologique* (1970) by Catherine Jolicoeur; *La fille aux mains coupées (conte-type 706)* (1971) by Hélène Bernier; *Rabelais et les traditions populaires en Acadie* (1972) by Antonine MAILLET; and *La mensongèrie, conte-type 710* (1972) by Nancy Schmitz. In addition, Laval has published several separate collections of French-Canadian folk songs, the most extensive being *Chansons folkloriques françaises au Canada* (1956) by Marguerite and Raoul d'Harcourt, and the more recent *Le chant de l'alouette* (1969) by Raoul Roy.

The other major source of French-Canadian folklore publications is the University of Sudbury where Germain Lemieux heads an Institut de Folklore. In the series of 'Documents historiques' issued by La Societé historique du Nouvel-Ontario he has published two booklets of songs: *Folklore franco-ontarien: chansons* (1949, 1950); two booklets of tales: *Contes populaires Franco-Ontariens* (1953, 1958); and three more extensive studies: *Chanteurs franco-ontariens et leurs chansons* (1963–1964), *De Sumer au Canada français: sur les ailes de la tradition* (1968), and *Les jongleurs du billachet* (1972). In the same series Mary Ann Griggs published *La chanson folklorique dans le milieu canadien-français traditionnel* (1969), which also appeared in English as *The folk song in the traditional society of French-Canada.*

The books so far mentioned deal with authentic folktales and songs collected from oral tradition. There are also a number of books in which folktales have been rewritten for popular consumption. The handsomest of these is *Le violon magique et autres légendes du Canada français* (1968), with text by Claude Aubry and illustrations by Saul Field. Alice Kane provided the translation for the English version, *The magic fiddler and other legends of French Canada.* Hazel Boswell produced another illustrated collection, *Legends of Quebec* (1966); Madeleine M. Des Rivières told tales typical of the different provinces in *Ronde autour de mon pays* (1968); Anselme Chiasson recounts *Les légendes des îles de la Madeleine* (1969); and Louise Darios wrote *Contes étranges du Canada* (1962), which also appeared as *Strange tales of Canada* (1965). From Newfoundland come two undated collections: *The treasury of Newfoundland stories* by L. W. James, and *Newfoundland wit, humor and folklore* by H. J. Reader; and F. H. MacArthur told *Tales of Prince Edward Island* (1966). Three Canadian writers using the nom-de-plume of Leslie Quinton collaborated in producing *The lucky coin* (1972), an anthology of tales representing Canada's various ethnic groups. EF

Ford, R. A. D. (1915–). Robert Arthur Douglass Ford was born in Ottawa and educated in London, Ont. He is a graduate of the University of Western Ontario in English and history and pursued postgraduate work in history at Cornell University, where he worked as an assistant in the history department from 1938 to 1940. He was employed briefly by the Montreal *Gazette* in 1938. From 1940 he has worked for the department of external affairs and has held a variety of diplomatic posts in South America, England, Russia, and the United States. He returned to Ottawa in 1954 to become head of the European division of the department of external affairs. Since that time he has been Canadian ambassador to Colombia, Yugoslavia, and the United Arab Republic. From 1964 he has been ambassador to the U.S.S.R.

Ford's first book of poems, *A window on the north* (1956), won a Governor General's Award. As its title suggests, much of the poetry focuses on the northern landscapes of Canada and Russia. This emphasis is heightened by his inclusion of some translations by three Russian poets—Akhmatova, Pasternak, and Yessenin. There is a tone of resignation to violence as the poet sees man's violent instincts in a hostile environment as being related to the general disquiet of the post-war world. The cold northernness of the poetry is leavened by some poems of southern landscape in Ford's translations of South American verse. His interest in the two polarities of north and south, in the mysteries of place, in political necessities, are drawn together in the long poem that closes the book, 'Luis Medias Pontual in Red Square'.

The solitary city (1969) includes poems about the Canadian winter and about Ford's travels in South America. The tone of this volume is darker, as the poet finds no solace in the historical past, seeing the pressure of land and place as the one continuing entity and himself as being only marginal in relation to 'the barren/Truth at the dead centre'. His poetry is grounded in regular metres and rhyme, though he adopts freer structures in some of his translations, which in this collection range from Russian and Serbo-Croat to Portuguese and French. PS

Forer, Mort. See FICTION IN ENGLISH 3.

Forman, Werner. See INDIAN LEGENDS AND ART.

Forster, Donald F. See HISTORY STUDIES IN ENGLISH 12.

Fortin, Gérald. See POLITICAL WRITINGS IN FRENCH 1.

Fournier, Pierre-Sylvain. See CHILDREN'S BOOKS IN FRENCH.

Fowke, Edith. See CHILDREN'S BOOKS IN ENGLISH 3 and FOLKLORE: BIBLIOGRAPHY.

Fox, Gail. See POETRY IN ENGLISH 2.

Foxell, Nigel. See FICTION IN ENGLISH 1.

Franchère, Gabriel. See HISTORY STUDIES IN ENGLISH 3.

Frankfurter, Glen. See HISTORY STUDIES IN ENGLISH 1.

Fraser, Blair. See HISTORY STUDIES IN ENGLISH 12.

Fraser, Esther. See HISTORY STUDIES IN ENGLISH 9.

Fraser, Frances. See INDIAN LEGENDS AND ART.

Fraser, Graham. See HISTORY STUDIES IN ENGLISH 12 and 13.

Fraser, John. See HISTORY STUDIES IN ENGLISH 12.

Fraser, Shirley. See FICTION IN ENGLISH 5.

Freeman, David. See DRAMA IN ENGLISH 2 and 3.

Freeman, Madeline A. See CHILDREN'S BOOKS IN ENGLISH 6.

Frégault, Guy (1918–). Born in Montréal, he was educated at the Université de Montreal and at Loyola University, Chicago. He was professor of history at the Université de Montréal from 1950 to 1959 and then at the University of Ottawa until 1969, when he became deputy minister in the department of cultural affairs of the province of Québec.

Frégault is the author of *Iberville le conquérant* (1944); *La civilisation de la Nouvelle-France (1713–44)* (1944; 2nd ed., 1969); *François Bigot: administrateur français* (2 vols, 1948); *Le grand marquis: Pierre de Rigaud de Vaudreuil et la Louisiane* (1952); *La société canadienne sous le régime français* (1954); *La guerre de la conquête* (1955), which was published in an English translation by Margaret Cameron as *Canada: the war of the conquest* (1969); *Pierre LeMoyne d'Iberville* (1968); *Le 18e siècle canadien* (1968); and *Histoire du Canada par les textes. Tome I (1534–1854)* (2nd ed., 1967), with Marcel TRUDEL and Michel BRUNET.

Frégault views the French régime as an *épopée*—the formation of a nation, the birth and development of a culture. The titles of his works have great importance in terms of his dynamic conception of the first age of the Canadian people and society. For him the fundamentals of French-Canadian culture were first established before the conquest and the challenge for survival rests in a concept deeply rooted in the intellectual and political history of Québec: the notion of fidelity.

Frégault was awarded the Prix David in 1969 and the Prix de l'Académie française for *Pierre LeMoyne d'Iberville*. J-LR

Fremont, D. See HISTORY STUDIES IN FRENCH 11.

French, David. See DRAMA IN ENGLISH 3.

French, Doris. See HISTORY STUDIES IN ENGLISH 15.

French, William. See LITERARY STUDIES IN ENGLISH 4.

Friesen, J. W. See INDIANS 6.

Frost, Leslie M. See HISTORY STUDIES IN ENGLISH 7.

Fry, Alan. See FICTION IN ENGLISH 3 and INDIANS 6.

Frye, Northrop (1912–). Herman Northrop Frye was born at Sherbrooke, Qué. He began his education in Moncton, N.B., and went on to Victoria College and later to Emmanuel College in the University of Toronto. In 1936 he was ordained to the ministry of the United Church and served briefly in Saskatchewan before returning to his studies at Oxford University. In 1939 he began to lecture in the English department of Victoria College, and, after serving as chairman of that department from 1952 to 1959, he became principal of the college in 1959. In 1966 he became the first University Professor of English at the University of Toronto.

Apart from his distinguished academic career, Northrop Frye has taken an active part in the development of a Canadian tradition of public as well as academic criticism. He began in 1936 to contribute articles to the *Canadian Forum*, and for a period after the Second World War he was editor of that journal, encouraging the new poets who began to emerge in Canada during the later 1940s. This role he deepened during the next decade when, from 1950 to 1960, he wrote the section on Canadian poetry in English for the annual 'Letters in Canada' feature of the *University of Toronto Quarterly*. In doing this he contributed more than any other single critic to establishing the criteria according to which Canadian writing might be judged.

Frye's interests have led him to combine several roles in a single career. He is the loyal academic, seeking to sustain a scholarly community that will play an active role in national intellectual life. His activities as a university teacher and administrator, as well as many of his essays and lectures, have been devoted to this end.

In the main body of his writings, however, Frye's achievements can be divided into two quite different categories. On one side he proceeds from the essential universalism of intellectual pursuits towards the works by which he has established an international repute as a theorist of the nature of criticism and the character of literary genres. These works are *Fearful symmetry: a study of William Blake* (1947), which goes far beyond Blake himself to a consideration in depth of the role of myth and symbol in the various literary genres, and *Anatomy of criticism* (1957), in which Frye analyses the principles and techniques of criticism, isolating its various modes: the historical, the ethical, the archetypal or mythopoeic, and the rhetorical or classificatory.

Up to the present, these works stand alone as Frye's masterpieces, monumentally self-contained and self-consistent in their systematization of literary theory. His other books are mainly collections of lectures, sometimes delivered as series, and of articles, gathered in such ways as rather unevenly to illuminate certain common themes. Four volumes are concerned with great English poets: *T. S. Eliot* (1963); *The return of Eden: five essays on Milton's epics* (1965); *A natural perspective: the development of Shakespearean comedy and romance* (1965); and *Fools of time: studies in Shakespearean tragedy* (1967). *A study of English romanticism* (1968) returns to the period and many concerns of *Fearful symmetry*. Other more general volumes published over the last two decades include *Culture and the national will* (1957), *By liberal things* (1960), *The well-tempered critic* (1963), *The educated imagination* (1963), *The modern century* (1967), *The stubborn structure* (1970), and *The critical path* (1971). The most important of his collections is undoubtedly *The bush garden: essays on the Canadian imagination* (1971), in which Frye gathered his fugitive writings over a quarter of a century on Canadian literature and its creators. *The bush garden*, with its penetrating but endlessly patient judgements on individual writers and its development of seminal attitudes towards the function of a writer in a society emerging from colonialism, helps to explain the influence Frye has wielded not only on academic and public critics alike, but also on poets. *The bush garden* includes not only the chronicles on Canadian poetry from 'Letters in Canada', but also the 'Conclusion' that Frye wrote to the *Literary history of Canada* (1965) in which he traced the liberation of Canadian culture from the 'garrison mentality' of colonial days. Frye has been the pioneer of systematic criticism in Canada and up to the beginning of the 1970s he has been Canada's most significant critic.

Criticism of critics is never adundant, and, apart from individual essays in periodicals, the only studies of Frye are *Northrop Frye* (1972) by Ronald Bates in the Canadian Writers Series and *Northrop Frye in modern criticism: selected papers from the English Institute* (1966).

GW

Fulford, Robert. See BELLES LETTRES IN ENGLISH and HISTORY STUDIES IN ENGLISH 17.

G

Gadd, Maxine. See POETRY IN ENGLISH 3.

Gagan, David P. See HISTORY STUDIES IN ENGLISH 8.

Gagnon, David T. See POLITICAL WRITINGS IN ENGLISH 8.

Gagnon, Jean-Louis. See POLITICAL WRITINGS IN FRENCH 2.

Gagnon, Marcel-Aimé. See LITERARY STUDIES IN FRENCH 4.

Gagnon, Maurice. See CHILDREN'S BOOKS IN FRENCH.

Gaida, Pr. See HISTORY STUDIES IN ENGLISH 14.

Galarneau, Claude. See HISTORY STUDIES IN FRENCH 4.

Gallant, Mavis. Born and educated in Montreal, she has travelled extensively. She has lived in Europe since 1950 and makes her home in France.

The effectiveness of Mrs Gallant's short stories and novels rests on her penetrating, witty, detached examination of character, life styles, and human relationships. The climax in her short stories occurs when her characters are forced by circumstances to see some irreparable crack in the façade they have erected to cover their weakness or folly. To achieve this point, relevant details about their looks, dress, mannerisms, and habits are combined with acutely observed descriptions of their rooms, their furniture, and the sights, sounds, and smells of the cities they live in and the resorts they frequent. Since most of her characters are English-speaking people attempting to live in Paris or on the Riviera on very little income, there is no glamour in their lives. Financial crises are so real that their follies and foibles are pathetic rather than merely ludicrous. Some of her stories, which are usually first published in the *New Yorker*, have been collected in *The other Paris* (1957) and *My heart is broken* (1959).

Mrs Gallant is more caustic in her novels in which her characters cannot free themselves from their stifling middle-class background or from limpet mothers and sibling jealousy. In *Green water, green sky: a novel in which time is the principal actor* (1959)—set in Venice, Cannes, and Paris—a clinging, foolish mother wrecks her daughter whom she has dragged about Europe since she was thirteen. 'Its images in a mirror: a short novel', which is included in *My heart is broken*, follows Jean Price (a jealous child grown into a parasite) in her vain efforts to twine herself round the life of her beautiful and unconventional sister. Defeated, Jean comforts herself with reflections on her own middle-class obsession with order and the solidity of her marriage from which she gets a shaky feeling of victory. This novel is set chiefly in Montreal. In *A fairly good time* (1970), an awkward Canadian girl living in Paris who is 'comfortable in chaos' marries a well-to-do Frenchman whose family revolves round a matriarch. Ill-prepared for this marriage by education and temperament, she does not understand what is required of her. Stunned when her husband leaves her, she ploughs about Paris with friends whose difficulties are similar to her own.

In 1973 Mrs Gallant published *The Pegnitz Junction*, a novella and five linked short stories about Germany and Germans at home and abroad. *The end of the world and other stories* with an introduction by Robert Weaver will be published in the New Canadian Library early in 1974.

In the realm of non-fiction Mrs Gallant wrote a long report of the ordeal of a thirty-year-old French school teacher who had an affair with a sixteen-year-old boy that was published as the introduction to *The affair of Gabrielle Russier* (1971) NS

Garcia, Juan. See POETRY IN FRENCH.

Garigue, Philippe. See HISTORY STUDIES IN FRENCH I.

Garneau, F.-X. See HISTORY STUDIES IN FRENCH I.

Garneau, Hector de Saint-Denys (1912–43). Great-grandson of François-Xavier and grandson of Alfred Garneau, he was born in Montreal and spent most of his childhood in Sainte-Catherine-de-Fossambault, twenty-five miles north of Quebec City. In 1923 his family returned to Montreal and Garneau was sent to the Jesuit Collège Sainte-Marie. The next year he attended the École des Beaux-Arts but returned to the Jesuit school in 1925. An attack of rheumatic fever in 1928 left him with a damaged heart, and a serious illness in 1933 put an end to his studies. In 1934 he exhibited two canvases in the Montreal Art Gallery and became one of the founders of *La Relève*, an art magazine founded in sympathy with the Christian revival movement in France. During the next three years he wrote art criticism for *La Relève*, but he had already begun to withdraw from human companionship for long periods. This self-isolation became complete by 1941 when he retired to Sainte-Catherine-de-Fossambault, where he remained with his parents until his death.

Products of Garneau's solitude are his collection of poems *Regards et jeux dans l'espace* (1937); the posthumous *Poésies complètes—Regards et jeux dans l'espace, Les solitudes* (1949; rev. 1972) with a preface by Robert Élie; and the stark, intimate *Journal* for the years 1935 to 1939, with a preface by Gilles MARCOTTE, which was edited by his friends Robert Élie and Jean LE MOYNE, and published in 1954 (3rd ed. 1964) through their efforts. (The *Journal* was translated into English by John GLASSCO in 1962.) *Lettres à ses amis* (1967) contains Garneau's letters to Jean Le Moyne, Robert Elie, André Laurendeau and others, to August 1943, and shows his increasing withdrawal from the world.

Garneau's poetry and journal complement each other in that they are concerned with the same obsessions. Some of the entries in the journal show that his withdrawal from the world came from the inner pressure of a puritan conscience coupled with an excessive shyness that amounted to a fear of a loss of identity. Other entries record the conception and development of the symbols Garneau used in his poetry and the complete absorption in the reality of an imaginary world that characterizes a child at play. The meditations on death and suicide found in the *Journal* are reflected in poems with tragic analogies such as the image of the poet stripped of the flesh and then dismembered bone by bone. Garneau spent much time listening to music, and his understanding of it is reflected in the rhythms of his poetry.

A representative selection of Garneau's poetry is found in Benoît Lacroix, *Saint-Denys-Garneau* (1956; rev. 1969). See also *Poèmes choisis: précédés d'une chronologie, d'une bibliographie et de jugements critiques* (1970). The *Oeuvres* of Garneau edited by Jacques BRAULT and Benoît Lacroix was published in 1971. Some of his verse in English translation can be found in F. R. SCOTT, *St-Denys Garneau & Anne Hébert: translations/traductions* (1962). In *De Saint-Denys-Garneau: art et réalisme* (1949) M. B. Ellis provides an enthusiastic appreciation of the spiritual content of Garneau's poetry but passes lightly over the morbid tendencies. Brother Lévis Fortier has given a more solid critical analysis of the poetry in *Le drame spirituel de Saint-Denys-Garneau* (1952) and *Le message poétique de Saint-Denys-Garneau* (1954), and Romain Légaré's *L'aventure poétique et spirituelle de Saint-Denys-Garneau* (1957) is a documented critical study. Recent publications on the poet are *Saint-Denys Garneau* by Eva Kushner (1967)—a psychological study followed by selections from the poetry, journals, and letters—and *De St Denys Garneau* (1971) edited by Jacques Blais in the series Dossiers de Documentation sur la littérature Canadienne-française. See also *Saint-Denys Garneau et ses lectures européennes* (1969) by Roland Bourneuf. NS

Garneau, Michel. See POETRY IN FRENCH.

Garneau, Sylvain (1930–53). Born in Montreal and educated at the Collège Stanislas, he began publishing poetry in newspapers and in the review *Amérique française* at the age of sixteen. After graduating he made an extended European cruise as a cadet-officer in the Merchant Marine, returning to Montreal to work as a construction labourer, then as a reporter and a radio announcer. He died in Montreal, aged twenty-three, from a head wound inflicted by his own rifle. His two collections of poems, *Objets trouvés* (1951) and *Les trouble-fête* (1952), the latter with an important foreward by Alain GRANDBOIS, display an alternation of sombre depth and delicate playfulness which, always expressed with a dazzling mastery of traditional verse-forms, has elicited comparisons to Villon, Verlaine, and Rimbaud. His long story, 'La bleue', recaptures a country childhood with nostalgia and humour. A collection of his verse and prose, *Objets retrouvés*, with an introduction and bibliographical notes by Guy ROBERT, appeared in 1965. English translations of several of his poems are in *The poetry of French Canada in translation* (1970) edited by John GLASSCO. JG

Garner, Hugh (1913–). Born in England, he came to Toronto as a child and was educated there. He fought as a volunteer in the Mackenzie-Papineau brigade in the Spanish Civil War. During the Second World War he spent a short time in the army and then transferred to the navy. His naval experiences provided the background for his realistic novel *Storm below* (1949), which deals with four tense days on board a corvette doing convoy duty on the Atlantic. Garner's difficulties during the depression gave him the deep understanding of the 'little man' in the pre-welfare industrial society, an understanding that permeates his novels of Toronto: *Waste no tears* (1950), which was published under the pseudonym 'Jarvis Warwick'; *Cabbagetown* (1950; rev. 1968), a story set in a slum area of the east end of Toronto that brings out the shifts to which the poor are reduced; and the more literary *The silence on the shore* (1962), set in a Toronto boarding house. (The last two novels are part of a Toronto trilogy, of which the middle volume is in progress.) *Present reckoning* (1951) is a slight tale of the affairs of a bad-tempered philanderer.

Garner's skills as a storyteller and the development of his social attitudes are best revealed in his short stories, beginning with those published in the *Canadian Forum* in 1936–7 in which the emphasis is on the unfortunate. While he has never lost sight of the victims of society, he has given increasing attention to human failings, the deterioration of character, alcoholism, and the current wave of violence. These themes, lightened with flashes of wit and irony, pervade his collections of short stories: *The yellow sweater and other stories* (1952); *Hugh Garner's best stories* (1963), which won a Governor General's Award; *Men and women* (1966); and *The violation of the virgins and other stories* (1971), in which the title story centres on a Mexican village's annual fiesta to commemorate the rape of young girls by Spanish *conquistadores*.

The sin sniper (1970), a police thriller set in Toronto, and *A nice place to visit* (1970), about a sensational criminal case, are two suspense stories in which alcoholism and violence are the key notes. *Author! author!* (1964) is a collection of humorous essays.

In 1971 five of Hugh Garner's novels and *Hugh Garner's best stories* were published as paperback reprints by Pocket Books.

Doug Fetherling has written a brief study of Garner's books for the Canadian Writers and Their Work series (1972). NS

Garner, John. See HISTORY STUDIES IN ENGLISH 6.

Garon, Yves. See LITERARY STUDIES IN FRENCH 4.

Garrett, F. V. See HISTORY STUDIES IN ENGLISH 15.

Gasparini, Len. See POETRY IN ENGLISH 1 and 2.

Gates, Lillian F. See HISTORY STUDIES IN ENGLISH 5.

Gauthier, Louis. See FICTION IN FRENCH 3.

Gauvreau, Claude. See POETRY IN FRENCH.

Gay, Paul. See LITERARY STUDIES IN FRENCH 1.

Geddes, Gary. See ANTHOLOGIES IN ENGLISH 1; LITERARY STUDIES IN ENGLISH 4; and POETRY IN ENGLISH intro. and 2.

Gélinas, André. See POLITICAL WRITINGS IN FRENCH 5.

Gélinas, Gratien (1909–). The first important figure in the modern French-Canadian theatre, he is the person most responsible for the emergence of theatre as a popular form of art in Québec today. Born in Saint-Tite de Champlain, Qué., he was brought up in Montreal and educated at the Collège de Montréal, the École des Hautes Études commerciales, and the Université de Montréal. While working as an accountant with an insurance firm in Montreal, he began writing and acting on radio and in a revue featuring a simple, sensitive, Chaplinesque character named Fridolin. First presented on stage in 1938, *Fridolinades* was immensely popular in Montreal. Nine more such revues were produced annually thereafter. (A collection of these revues is shortly to be published in three volumes.)

Gélinas has written three plays, all of which have been produced and published in both English and French. The title character of *Tit-coq* (French edition 1960; English edition translated by Mavor Moore, 1967) bears many resemblances to Fridolin of the revues. It depicts the desperate search for love and acceptance of an illegitimate young soldier. Gélinas created the role in 1948 and the play ran in Montreal for over 500 performances over a period of two years. It was also made into a film. His next play, *Bousille et les justes* (1960) in which Gélinas also played the leading role, was first produced in 1959. It presents a naive and honest man who is victimized by the intrigue of his relatives who want to avoid a family scandal. An English translation by Kenneth Johnson, *Bousille and the just*, was published in 1961. Gélinas's third play, *Hier les enfants dansaient* (1968), which was published in an English translation by Mavor Moore as *Yesterday the children were dancing* (1967), is about a family divided by the issues of federalism and separatism in Québec. While it is highly topical, its chief interest lies in the exploration of family relationships rather than in the resolution of political issues.

Gélinas's output of creative writing has not been great but he has also done much organizational work for the development of Canadian theatre. This has included the foundation in 1958 of the Comédie canadienne, a theatrical company, and of a theatre in Montreal with the same name (recently taken over by, and named after, another dynamic Montreal acting company, Le Théâtre du Nouveau Monde). In 1969 Gélinas was appointed chairman of the Canadian Film Development Corporation; this put him in a position to contribute much to the development of Canada's burgeoning film industry. Some Québécois today feel that Gélinas's plays, especially *Tit-coq* and *Bousille et les justes*, are outdated; and some claim that recent studies of Québec show that the type of simple, ineffectual, and somewhat pathetic victim at the centre of each of these plays was never typical of French Canada as it was often considered to be. Nevertheless, Gélinas remains an influential figure in the cultural life of Québec and of the whole of Canada. JN

Gellner, John. See HISTORY STUDIES IN ENGLISH 12 and 14; POLITICAL WRITINGS IN ENGLISH 7.

Germain, Jean-Claude. See DRAMA IN FRENCH 2.

Gervais, C. H. See POETRY IN ENGLISH 2.

Geslin, Lucien. See ANTHOLOGIES IN FRENCH.

Gibbs, Robert. See POETRY IN ENGLISH 2.

Gibson, Dale. See HISTORY STUDIES IN ENGLISH 8.

Gibson, F. W. See HISTORY STUDIES IN ENGLISH 12.

Gibson, Graeme (1934–). Born in London, Ont., he studied for a year at the Collège Militaire de St-Jean, Qué., and then at the University of Western Ontario. He has travelled extensively in England, France, and Mexico. He now lives on a farm near Tottenham, Ont.

Gibson's mastery of different styles is used effectively in his two novels *Five legs* (1969) and *Communion* (1971). Both novels, with their impressive use of fire and animal symbols, challenge the perceptiveness and imagination of the reader, and each ends with a conflagration. They suggest a parallel between modern society headed towards self-destruction and the unfulfilled man who is unable to reconcile his spiritual aspirations and his animal instincts with the repressive canons of the modern 'elect'.

In *Five legs*, which maintains a good narrative pace, human failure is personified by Lucan Crackell, a professor whose misfortune is to be caught in situations brought about by indiscrete self-indulgence. Crackell hopes for salvation through attrition, but his hopes are jeopardized by Felix Oswald, a student so crushed by academic and sexual failure that he identifies himself first with an animal freak and then with all hunted animals. In his agony, Oswald flees to nature and the teeming life of the woods, swerving from man and rushing towards a fire that could either purify or destroy him.

In *Communion* Gibson clarifies the purgative and destructive properties of fire. Oswald pursues his man-animal identification in a series of fantasies as he is being roused from a catatonic state by the forced inhalation of cigarettes. Each fantasy is separated by the repetition of key paragraphs or sets of phrases. Oswald sees himself as an assistant to a veterinarian and he accidently kills a sick husky that he hopes to cure by restoring it to life-giving nature. His sexual urges are expressed in fetishism, voyeurism, and other aberrations. His flight from Canada cannot save him—he is burned by vicious adolescents who symbolize both American violence and the bomb that threatens us all. This is the communion of the unfulfilled and spiritually damned—lover and pervert, healer and murderer, hunter and hunted.

Gibson edited *Eleven Canadian novelists* (1973), a collection of his interviews. NS

Gibson, Lee. See HISTORY STUDIES IN ENGLISH 8.

Giddings, J. L. See ESKIMOS: BOOKS IN ENGLISH.

Giffard, Ann. See HISTORY STUDIES IN ENGLISH 13.

Giguère, Roland (1929–). Born in Montreal, he was educated at the École des Arts graphiques, Montreal, and the École Estienne, Paris. He lived in France from 1955 to 1963, working in Paris and spending the summers at Châteaunoir, Aix-en-Provence, where Cézanne once lived. He was closely associated with the Surrealists and was an intimate friend of André Breton. He conducts a studio in Montreal where he produces 'Éditions Erta', booklets of poems. One of the French-Canadian poets whose anger has been inspired by world conditions of declared and undeclared war and the threat of the atomic bomb, as well as by the turmoil of the revolutionary currents in Québec, Giguère has shown a growing tendency to come to terms with his age and with the pace of change in his province. This tendency can be traced from the tempestuous thought and language of his first poems in *Faire naître* (1949), through the more disciplined collections *Yeux fixes; ou, L'ébullition de l'intérieur* (1951), *Les armes blanches* (1954), and *Le défaut des ruines est d'avoir des habitants* (1957). An optimistic attitude is apparent in the long poem 'Adorable femme de neige' and in 'Dialogue entre l'immobile et l'éphémère', both published in *Écrits du Canada français* (vol. XVI, 1963). In the former the 'femme des neiges' is a symbol of Giguère's ideal picture of Québec in which reconciliation can be achieved; the latter might be translated freely as 'thoughts during a period of change'. When he returned to Montreal, Giguère worked as a graphic designer for the Théâtre du Nouveau Monde and for Gaston MIRON's Éditions de l'Hexagone. (The latter publishes some of the most beautifully designed and best-printed books of poetry in North America.) In 1965 Hexagone published Giguère's *L'âge de la parole*, a collection of poems written between 1949 and 1960. In 1968 Erta published *Naturellement*, a stunningly beautiful portfolio of eight poems and eight silkscreen prints, published in a limited edition of forty copies. Various aspects of nature serve as themes for both poems and prints. Another collection of prose-poems and unpublished material is due to be published by Hexagone at the end of 1973.

Some of the poems of Roland Giguère have been translated into English by John GLASSCO, F. R. SCOTT, D. G. JONES, Francis SPARSHOTT, and others. NS/SF

Gilbert, Marcel. See POLITICAL WRITINGS IN FRENCH 4 and 7.

Gilbert, S. R. See DRAMA IN ENGLISH 4.

Gill, John. See ANTHOLOGIES IN ENGLISH 1.

Gill, M. Lakshmi. See POETRY IN ENGLISH 2.

Gipson, Lawrence Henry. See HISTORY STUDIES IN ENGLISH 4.

Giraud, Marcel. See HISTORY STUDIES IN FRENCH 1.

Giroux, Maurice. See POLITICAL WRITINGS IN FRENCH 3.

Giroux, Suzanne. See HISTORY STUDIES IN FRENCH 9.

Glassco, John (1909–). Born in Montreal, he was educated at Bishop's College School in Lennoxville, Qué., and at McGill University, which he left in 1928, without graduating, to complete in Paris his education in sensibility, described in his *Memoirs* (see below). In 1935 he elected for rural existence in the Eastern Townships of Québec, and now divides his time between his house in Foster and Montreal. Best known as a poet (his first book of verse, *Conan's fig*, appeared in 1928), John Glassco claims with justification that he is 'as much a novelist, anthologist, translator and pornographer'. His poignantly evocative recollections of literary and expatriate Paris in the late 1920s, *Memoirs of Montparnasse* (1970), suggest the protean sensibility that produced *Under the hill* (1959), a brilliant completion of Aubrey Beardsley's unfinished romance of the same title, and such pseudonymous works as *The English governess* (by 'Miles Underwood', 1960), a novel; 'A season in Limbo' (by 'Silas Gooch', *The Tamarack Review*, Issue 23, 1962), a novella; and the early *Contes en crinoline* (by 'Jean de Saint-Luc', 1930).

The irony, elegance, and deliberate decadence of such works seem remote from the elegiac tone and rural preoccupations of many of the poems contained in *The deficit made flesh* (1958), *A point of sky* (1964), and *Selected poems* (1971), which won a Governor General's Award. But the sophistication of one part of Glassco's work and the sensitive simplicity of the other can be considered as two aspects of a neo-classical mood that echoes to the nineties and the Augustan age, yet also evokes faithfully the nostalgia and the sense of loss stirred by his reading of history and literature and his experience of a rural Québec that time has passed over and left neglected. The versatility of technique and the degree of empathic understanding Glassco can evoke are admirably shown in this collection of his own renderings into English of Québec poets from the seventeenth century to the present, *The poetry of French Canada in translation* (1970) and in his brilliant translation of *The journal of Saint-Denys-Garneau* (1962). He is the editor of *English poetry in Quebec* (1963). GW

Glassie, Henry. See FOLKLORE: BIBLIOGRAPHY.

Glazebrook, G. P. deT. (1899–). George Parkin deTwenebrokes Glazebrook was born in London, Ont., and educated at the Universtiy of Toronto and at Oxford. He was on the staff of the history department of the University of Toronto from 1924 to 1941, when he became special assistant to the under-secretary of state for external affairs. He was a professor again at Toronto from 1946 to 1948, and then returned as a counsellor to the department of external affairs until 1953 when he was appointed minister in the Canadian embassy at Washington. After three years he came back to work in Canada and from 1959 until his retirement in 1963 he was an assistant under-secretary of state for external affairs. He was a special lecturer in history at the University of Toronto until 1967 when he again retired to devote more time to writing. In 1954 he was awarded the Tyrrell Medal of the Royal Society of Canada.

Glazebrook's writings have been mainly political but in his later years he has turned his attention to social history. *Sir Charles Bagot in Canada: a study in British colonial government* (1929) explains that under the administration of this governor-general the foundations of an orderly government were formed and better Canadian-British relations were developed. Bagot accepted the French-speaking Canadians as citizens and ignored previous plans to assimilate or segregate them. The biography of *Sir Edmund Walker* (1933)—one-time president of the Bank of Commerce and governor of the University of Toronto—demonstrates the man's distinctive service to his country and to his community. *A history of transportation in Canada* (1938)—reprinted in the Carleton Library as volume 1: *Continental strategy* and volume 2: *National economy* (1964)—claims that the formation of the northern half of the continent into a single economic unit by Canadian businessmen and politicians was in reaction to British North America's failure to compete with the United States on a continental basis. The Canadian Institute of International Affairs sponsored publication of *Canadian external relations* (1942; 2nd ed. 1950, *A history of . . .*; rev. 1964), which has been reprinted in the Carleton Library. Volume 1: *An historical study to 1914* states that there is a pattern of foreign policy that has been held consistently by Canadians (depending upon internal and external conditions) and that involves three alternatives: independence, annexation to the United States, or absorption within the British empire; volume 2: *In the empire and the world, 1914–1939* asserts that Canada shared, with many other nations, a parochial outlook and wanted no international commitments, especially collective force, to maintain the status quo. This theme had been developed more extensively in *Canada at the Paris Peace Conference* (1940), in which Glazebrook maintained that the Canadian delegation mainly sought a recognition of Canada's independent voice in world affairs apart from Great Britain's policies and actions and that world responsibility and wider commitments, especially on collective security, were far from their minds. *A short history of Canada* (1950) describes the nation as a new society formed from her European background and the adaptations made necessary by the North American environment. It is somewhat romantic, however, in portraying Canada as a world power and in claiming that Canada's actions in siding with her three traditional partners—France, Great Britain, and the United States—to save freedom in the world were a mark of her maturity. *A history of Canadian political thought* (1966) studies the flexibility of confederation. Glazebrook notes that, while religious animosities have faded away, regional and economic disparities now demand solution. Changing social conditions and their effects on the people are considered in *Life in Ontario: a social history* (1968); while *The story of Toronto* (1971) describes the growth of this metropolitan area. Glazebrook admits the difficulty in generalizing about the nature of this cosmopolitan community but suggests that old Toronto slumbers on beneath the outward changes. He is also co-editor of *A shopper's view of Canada's past: pages from Eaton's catalogues* (1969) and has edited the Champlain Society publication, *The Hargrave correspondence: 1821–1843* (1938), a valuable contribution to the study of the fur trade.

DF

Gnarowski, Michael. See ANTHOLOGIES IN ENGLISH 1 and LITERARY STUDIES IN ENGLISH 2 and 4.

Godbout, Jacques (1933–). Born in Montreal, he was educated at the Collège Jean Brébeuf and the Université de Montréal. He taught literature at University College, Addis Ababa, from 1954 to 1957 and has travelled extensively. In 1958 he joined the staff of the National Film Board. He has been a contributor to PARTI PRIS, the influential revolutionary literary and political review of the 1960s, and to *Liberté*, the literary magazine of which he was one of the founders.

Godbout expresses a wide range of emotion in both poetry and prose. *Carton-pâte* (1956) is a volume of imagist poems that associate colour and warmth with love, bleakness and cold with deprivation of hope and affection. The ironic tone of *Carton-pâte* is replaced by a sardonic note in *Les pavés secs* (1958). In his third collection, *C'est la chaude loi des hommes* (1960), Godbout is an angry poet denouncing the sterility and emotional paralysis of man who lives in fear of the atomic bomb.

In his first novel, *L'aquarium* (1962), Godbout employs symbolism to develop the theme that modern man has become emotionally sterile in the face of constant danger. In this novel Godbout uses his African experiences in his setting and applies the shifting techniques of the film. From the passive world of *L'aquarium* he moves to the other extreme in the novel *Le couteau sur la table* (1965) in which he conveys the idea that the French Canadians may have to resort to violent revolution in order to establish their identity and to sever themselves from the modern world and from the Anglo-Saxon majority by whom they are surrounded. His third novel, *Salut Galarneau!* (1967), is the story of a 'marginal man'—almost a writer, almost a committed Québécois, almost a failure—and his attempts to come to terms with and to reconstruct the reality that surrounds him. It has been admirably translated into English by Alan Brown and published as *Hail Galarneau!* (1972).

For several years Godbout devoted more time to film-making than to fiction; then in 1972 he published his most ambitious novel to date, *D'amour, P.Q.* This is about a novel and its author and is a kind of bawdy celebration of *joual* and those who speak it. *D'amour, P.Q.* might be considered a political landmark for Godbout, as it seems to be characterized by an unequivocal *engagement* to the political future of Québec.

Jacques Godbout is probably the only Québec writer who has translated into French an entire book of English-Canadian poetry: John COLOMBO's *The Great Wall of China* (*La grande muraille de Chine*, 1969).

Godbout edited with Colombo the anthology *Poetry 64/Poésie 64* (1963). NS/SF

Godfrey, Charles M. See HISTORY STUDIES IN ENGLISH 5.

Godfrey, Dave (1938–). Born in Toronto, he was educated at the Universities of Toronto and Iowa and at Stanford University. He spent about eighteen months in Ghana where he was employed by the Canadian Universities Overseas Service. Returning to Toronto, he became one of the founders of two publishing firms, first the House of Anansi, then New Press. He teaches English at Trinity College, lives in Mississauga Township, and plays with a jazz band in Toronto.

Godfrey's novel *The new ancestors* (1970), which won a Governor General's Award, is set in 'Lost coast', Africa (Ghana and Mali, just prior to the revolution of 1966 during which President Kwame Nkrumah was exiled). It has been the subject of differences of opinion. Some people with African experience claim that Godfrey gives a distorted picture of Ghana; others think that it is a fair assessment of the forces behind the revolution of 1966. Whatever the political facts may be, Godfrey has brilliantly juggled time and mixed idiomatic speech, dialect, and untranslated African phrases to give a powerful impression of seething undercurrents in an emerging African nation, confused by conflict between indigenous mythology and imported Christian dogmas and between tribal customs and imported political philosophies and institutions. The Africans have a justifiable distrust of nations that had exploited and enslaved them in the past and now come bearing gifts. Althouth all nations are suspect, hatred is directed against the United States, whose CIA agent, Rusk, is murdered six times. Unity in the novel is obtained through three principal characters: Michael Burdener, a shabby English representative of colonial days; his mission-educated native wife, Ama, who is torn between love and pity for her husband, her Christian ideals, and the tribal orgiastic rites in which the 'Redeemer' (political leader) indulges; and First Samuels, principal agent of the Redeemer, whose foreign education consists of time spent playing with a jazz band in the United States.

Godfrey is an accomplished writer of short stories, some of which are collected in *Death goes better with Coca Cola* (1968). Most of them deal with hunting and fishing as activities typifying man's instinct to kill. The final story, 'The hard-headed collector', makes use of myth and allegory to symbolize the lack of a common creative purpose in Canada, a lack that he attributes to provincialism and to subservience to the United States. Differing types of Godfrey stories are 'Newfoundland night', a poetic recollection of young love, and 'River Two Blind Jacks', a tall tale of lumberjacks, each of whom, while plotting the death of the other, encompasses his own death. Both these stories have been anthologized by Robert Weaver in *Canadian short stories: second series* (1968). 'On the river' reflects the loss of human feeling by an old man living in isolation and poverty. It is included in *New Canadian writing 1969: stories by Lewis Stein, Clark Blaise, and Dave Godfrey* (1969).

Godfrey edited with William M. McWhinney *Man deserves man: CUSO in developing countries* (1968), an account by *CUSO* volunteers of their work in developing countries; with Melville Watkins *Gordon to Watkins to you: a documentary of the battle for control of our economy* (1970); and with Robert Fulford and Abraham Rotstein *Read Canadian: a book about Canadian books* (1972). NS

Godin, Gérald (1938–). Born in Trois-Rivières, he dropped out of school to work as a proof-reader for the newspaper *Le Nouvelliste*. Later he was employed as a reporter for *Le Nouveau Journal* in Montreal and as a researcher for the Radio-Canada daily news-commentary program, *Aujourd'hui*. An early contributor to PARTI PRIS, he was for a time editor of the magazine and at present directs Les Éditions Parti Pris.

As well as satirical short stories and polemical articles contributed to *parti pris*, Godin has published four volumes of poetry: *Chansons très naïves* (1960), *Poèmes et cantos* (1962), *Nouveaux poèmes* (1963), and *Les Cantouques* (1967). He was one of six young French-Canadian poets chosen by Jacques GODBOUT and John Robert COLOMBO for inclusion in the bilingual anthology, *Poésie/poetry* (1964). Like other writers of the *parti pris* group, he makes considerable use of *joual*; he has called this 'a sort of literary sit-in'—a way of using what he sees as the degradation of the French language in Canada as an instrument of revolution. Most of his poetry, however, is personal rather than political in the narrow sense. There are ironic or wrily tender love-poems, mocking glances at some of his fellow-revolutionaries and at the contradiction of his own mental processes, much gaiety and exuberance, and a sheer delight in words; his rage on behalf of such victims of social unjustice as lumberjacks and city slum-dwellers is never brutal. A true poet with a marvellous sense of language and its possibilities, he is unique among younger French-Canadian writers for his balance and good humour.

English translations of some of his poems have been published in *Ellipse 1* and in John GLASSCO's *The poetry of French Canada in translation* (1970). Malcolm Reid's discussion of Godin as poet and political thinker in *The shouting signpainters* (1972) includes English renderings of two poems. JM

Godin, Jean-Cleo. See LITERARY STUDIES IN FRENCH 3.

Godin, Marcel. See FICTION IN FRENCH 3 and SHORT STORIES.

Goheen, Peter G. See HISTORY STUDIES IN ENGLISH 13.

Golden, Aubrey E. See HISTORY STUDIES IN ENGLISH 12 and POLITICAL WRITINGS IN ENGLISH 1.

Goldrick, Michael. See POLITICAL WRITINGS IN ENGLISH 8.

Gooderham, Kent. See INDIAN LEGENDS AND ART.

Goodspeed, D. J. See HISTORY STUDIES IN ENGLISH 7.

Gosselin, André. See HISTORY STUDIES IN FRENCH 1.

Gotlieb, Phyllis (1926–). Phyllis Fay Gotlieb (*née* Bloom) was born in Toronto, where she still lives, and educated at Victoria and University Colleges in the University of Toronto. Her first published work was a pamphlet of poems, *Who knows one* (1961), some of which were reprinted in her next book, *Within the zodiac* (1964), in which she uses flamboyant language, sometimes with humorous effect, to explore her childhood, her Jewish background, and her family life. She developed this style with more control in *Ordinary, moving* (1969), a loose sequence of poems growing from her sense of Jewishness and drawing on memories fixed in fragments remembered from her childhood and adolescence. This collection makes exuberant use of childhood rhymes, old phone numbers, persons and places of school and street life—images and remembrances that are gathered together in the moving title poem that closes the collection.

Her novel *Why should I have all the grief?* (1969) concerns an Auschwitz survivor who is involved for an agonizing three days in the ceremonies surrounding the death of a distant relative. He meets other relatives and painfully arrives at a reassessment of his identity and a sense of commitment to his recent but foundering marriage. These relevations from the past are managed with growing suspense and a masterly command of dialogue. Mrs Gotlieb also writes science-fiction stories that have been published in the leading American SF magazines; her novel *Sunburst* (1964) describes how a group of adolescents, after a thermonuclear disaster, become a pack of violent psychopaths with telepathic and supernatural powers.

Her 'Dr Umlaut's earthly kingdom', commissioned by the CBC, was broadcast in 1970 and can be found in the CBC publication *Poems for voices* (1970). PS

Gough, Barry M. See HISTORY STUDIES IN ENGLISH 9.

Goulson, Cary. See HISTORY STUDIES IN ENGLISH 2.

Graburn, Nelson H. H. See ESKIMOS: BOOKS IN ENGLISH.

Granatstein, J. L. See HISTORY STUDIES IN ENGLISH 7, 12, and 15; POLITICAL WRITINGS IN ENGLISH 7 and 9.

Grandbois, Alain (1900–). Born in Saint-Casimir de Portneuf, Qué., he studied law at Université Laval. An inheritance made it possible for him to travel extensively in the years between the two world wars—in Western Europe, Africa, India, Russia, China, and Japan. His home during this period was in France, where he met fellow-expatriates Hemingway, Cendrars, and Supervielle. His prose writings, close in theme and style to his poetry, reflect his love of travel. They are biographies of explorers who, on their journeys in search of earth's 'éblouissants secrets', courted danger and death: *Né à Québec: Louis Jolliet* (Paris, 1933; Montreal, 1949, 1969), which was published in an English translation by Evelyn Brown as *Born in Quebec* (1964), and *Les voyages de Marco Polo* (1942). *Avant le chaos* (1945), a collection of short stories, republished with four additional tales in 1964, recalls with a mixture of elegant detachment and suppressed passion the 'monde insouciant et frivole' that the 'chaos' of the Second World War had destroyed irrevocably—a world of small bars and glittering salons from Paris to Djibouti, Canton to Cannes, in which charming people whiled away eternity over cards and a glass of spirits. Further personal reflections by Grandbois on the interwar years, written for Radio-Canada in 1951, have been published in an edition presented by Léopold Leblanc: *Visages du monde: images et souvenirs de l'entre-deux-guerres* (1971). Grandbois translated Merrill Denison's *The barley and the stream: the Molson story* (1955) under the title *Au pied du courant* (1955).

Grandbois is justly renowned as a poet. A casual acquaintance published seven of his poems in Hankow (China) in 1934. These, with minor variants, were included in *Les îles de la nuit* (1944). *Rivages de l'homme* followed in 1948 and *L'étoile pourpre* in 1957. An anthology of his verse and prose, *Alain Grandbois* (Paris, 1968), ably presented by Jacques BRAULT, contains three poems previously unpublished. (In *Selected poems* (1965) the French originals are accompanied by translations by Peter Miller.) Grandbois's influence on post-war poetry in French Canada has been acknowledged by the poets of the fifties and sixties: by Jean-Guy PILON and Gaston MIRON in the review *Amérique française* in 1954, in a special number of *Liberté* (1960), and by the publication by Éditions de l'Hexagone of Grandbois's collected *Poèmes* (1963). He has three times been awarded the Prix David; he has also received the Prix Duvernay and the Lorne Pierce medal, and an honorary doctorate from Université Laval.

Grandbois appears in his poetry as a solitary figure in a harsh, implacable universe. The human tragedy is played out against a vast, dark backcloth with cosmic dimensions. There is a humiliating disproportion between the grim permanence of the natural world and the mortality of man. The poet's endless journey takes him in search of those rare moments of joy that come from the fleeting experience of communion with his fellows, like points of light in the darkness of night or tiny islands on a vast sea. The beauty of the world is revealed at its most vulnerable and enchanting in the body of a woman, but the experience of love is not only the justification of life but also the vivid illustration of the absurd. Nothing so reminds man of his impermanence as the fall from a timeless moment of ecstasy to the realization of the finality of separation in a world where life ebbs away and the heavy doors of forgetfulness are constantly closing. Faced with the reality of death, the poet finds comfort in a stoical obstinacy. After rehearsing the litany of death he repeats frequently the words 'et pourtant', which express his insistent refusal of the inevitability of his condition. CRPM

Grand'Maison, Jacques. See POLITICAL WRITINGS IN FRENCH 2.

Grandmont, Eloi de (1921–71). Born in Baie-du-Fèvre, Qué., he was educated at the Collège de Nicolet, the École des Beaux-Arts in Montreal, and in France. He was one of the founder-members of the Théâtre du Nouveau Monde and acted with the company in its early years. His play *Un fils à tuer* (1950), written in Paris, was staged with the collaboration of Jean-Louis Roux in 1949. It chronicles a family conflict that takes place in Nouvelle-France before the conquest. It was one of the first French-Canadian plays to express the contemporary theme of man's inability to find individual expression within society. The father, a French immigrant proud of his new country, opposes his son's stubborn desire to return and settle in France. Rather than being a historical drama, however, *Un fils à tuer* explores complex moral, psychological, and social issues and maintains a certain contemporaneity. *La fontaine de Paris* (1955) was the first Canadian play to be produced by the TNM—in a double-bill with André LANGEVIN's *Une nuit d'amour*. It is a slight piece, a medieval-style farce. Subsequently Grandmont concentrated on writing adaptations, many of them for the TNM: *Lysistrata, Les Fantasticks,* and *Un coup de fil pour te pendre* (*Dial M for Murder*) are three notable examples. He also wrote *Soif d'aimer* and *Doux temps des amours,* the latter a musical, in collaboration with Louis-Georges Carrier. His greatest success, however, was undoubtedly his adaptation of Shaw's *Pygmalion* (1968). This broke all box-office records for the TNM. Although Elise Lacroix (i.e. Eliza Doolittle) speaks *joual* in the play, Grandmont had little sympathy for this popular form of speech. His declaration that 'The Québécois don't know how to speak French' would be considered irrelevant by the modern artists of Québec, who are seeking to stimulate a truly indigenous culture. A first volume of his *Théâtre* was published in 1968, consisting of *Un fils à tuer*, *La fontaine de Paris*, and *Le temps des fêtes*, an early one-act play.

As a poet, Eloi de Grandmont is less well known. He wrote simply, often movingly, of everyday subjects: the countryside, the woods, sunshine, and sleep. Occasionally there are signs of adolescent revolt, against the restraints of society in particular, but his poetry never loses its charm and grace. His imagery is often reminiscent of Alain GRANDBOIS's, though Grandmont's favourite poet was Émile Nelligan. *Le voyage d'Arlequin* (1946) is an elegy for a friend killed in the war. *La jeune fille constellée* (1948), a slim volume, is a far more mature work that still evinces the poet's delight in simple things. This was followed by *Premiers secrets* (1951) and *Plaisirs* (1953). Of these two books Gilles MARCOTTE has written: 'There is an underlying revolt [in *Plaisirs*], but though this had a certain bitterness in *Premiers secrets*, here everything resolves into good humor and the rather naive desire to scandalize.' *Dimanches naïfs* (1954) is a selection of Grandmont's poetry compiled by Louis Guillaume. Later collections are *Une saison en chansons* (1963), *Voyageurs ou touristes* (1970), *Je n'aurais jamais cru!* (1971), and *Vernousses!* (1971). Grandmont also wrote a guide to Montreal with the journalist Louis-Martin Tard, *Montréal-Guide* (1967). JC

Grandpré, Pierre de. See ANTHOLOGIES IN FRENCH; HISTORY STUDIES IN FRENCH 10; and LITERARY STUDIES IN FRENCH 1.

Granger, Luc. See FICTION IN FRENCH 3.

Grant, G. P. (1918–). George Parkin Grant was born in Toronto and attended Upper Canada College, where his father had been principal. His paternal grandfather—George Munro Grant, one-time principal of Queen's University—and his maternal grandfather—Sir George Parkin, one-time principal of Upper Canada College and later head of the Rhodes Trust—were both prominent theologians, moral philosophers, and advocates of imperial federation before the turn of the century. G. P. Grant was educated at Queen's and, as a Rhodes scholar, at Oxford. He worked for the Canadian Association for Adult Education, 1944–5, and in 1947 joined the staff of Dalhousie University, later to be professor and head of the department of philosophy. He left Dalhousie in 1960 and in 1961 became chairman of the department of religion at McMaster University in Hamilton. He is well known for his radio and television work and for his contributions to scholarly publications.

Grant is one of Canada's most published intellectuals and is able to combine his understanding of philosophy, history, and Christian belief with a penetrating analysis of contemporary social and political behaviour. *The empire, yes or no?* (1945), a booklet in the Canada Must Choose series, decries the influence that Marxian economics and Freudian sex have had upon the world, revealed in the brutality, irrationality, and ruthlessness of war-torn Europe. Only British nations have been able to work out a political and social compromise between order and unrestrained liberty, and within this Commonwealth Canada must remain.

Philosophy in the mass age (1959), originally a provocative series of half-hour CBC radio talks, depicts ancient man being freed from the bonds of nature by Judeo-Christian understanding. Man, according to Grant, is not the measure of all things and there is a limit to his capabilities. A paradox remains: man is free and yet he has moral obligations; there are laws of nature that must be obeyed or mankind will be destroyed. Order and limitations on social and personal behaviour are in the nature of things.

In *Lament for a nation: the defeat of Canadian nationalism* (1965) Grant proclaims the death of Canada—a victim of continentalism and technology. American corporation capitalism, aided by the Canadian business establishment and the federal Liberal party, has insidiously destroyed Canadian culture. The culprit is the political philosophy of liberalism in that its preoccupation with progress and the overturning of past values has played into the hands of the exponents of the American concept of freedom—that there are no limits; that man has unbridled freedom to reshape the world as he wishes. The reshaping is carried out by American technology and, sad to say, no other life is now possible, for to survive and make a living one must work within the American economic framework that controls Canada. *Lament for a nation* has been reprinted in the Carleton Library, with a new introduction by the author.

Grant draws upon the work of the American political philosopher Leo Strauss and the French sociologist Jacques Ellul for his *Technology and empire* (1969). Here he maintains that liberalism and technology have so imbedded themselves within our culture that the nature of existence, rather than nationalism, is the main challenge. The abyss into which political philosophy has fallen is signified by the common meaning of 'conservative' as free-enterprise capitalism—a term describing those who have emancipated greed and enshrined it as a virtue. Somehow the conscience of man must be retrained—perhaps by a systematic study of values other than our own. We must move outside our present frame of reference by memory or by thought.

In *Time as history* (1969), originally presented by the CBC as the Massey Lectures, Grant studies the philosophy of Nietzsche and the concept of time in relation to history. He concludes that modern man has realized that he is the source of his own values but is perplexed and paralysed by the implications for potential freedom of choice that self-knowledge brings. Some refuse to acknowledge freedom of will and strike out against those who are attempting to use the full potential of their humanity; others lash out because, in their nihilism, they cannot tolerate the thought that a joyful world can be produced. Grant poses the question: Will there be men who realize their potential and carry it through to bring joy as masters of earth?

Grant has also contributed essays to *The new Romans* (1968) edited by Al PURDY and to *A social purpose for Canada* (1961) edited by Michael Oliver. DF

Grant, John Webster. See HISTORY STUDIES IN ENGLISH 5 and 7.

Grant, Madeline. See HISTORY STUDIES IN ENGLISH 17.

Gravel, Pierre. See FICTION IN FRENCH 3.

Gray, Jack. See DRAMA IN ENGLISH 3.

Gray, James H. See HISTORY STUDIES IN ENGLISH 8.

Gray, Simon. See DRAMA IN ENGLISH 2.

Graymont, Barbara. See HISTORY STUDIES IN ENGLISH 4 and INDIANS 5.

Grayson, L. M. See HISTORY STUDIES IN ENGLISH 11.

Green, H. Gordon. See ANTHOLOGIES IN ENGLISH 3 and ANTHOLOGIES IN FRENCH.

Greene, Alma. See INDIAN LEGENDS AND ART.

Greenhill, Basil J. See HISTORY STUDIES IN ENGLISH 13.

Greenhill, Ralph. See HISTORY STUDIES IN ENGLISH 5.

Grégoire, Gilles. See POLITICAL WRITINGS IN FRENCH 4.

Gregorovich, Andrew. See HISTORY STUDIES IN ENGLISH 17.

Gregson, Harry. See HISTORY STUDIES IN ENGLISH 9.

Grier, Eldon (1917–). Born in London, Eng., while his father was serving in the Canadian army, Eldon Grier received his schooling in Montreal, Ottawa, and Toronto. A painter, he went to Mexico in 1945 to study and eventually worked under Diego Rivera. When he returned to Canada he taught at the Montreal Museum of Fine Art. Between 1955 and 1965 he travelled widely in Europe. It was during his stay in Spain in the mid-1950s that he began to write poetry. He published four small collections at this time: *A morning from scraps* (1955), *Poems* (1956), *The ring of ice* (1957), and *Manzanillo and other poems* (1958). These early poems are relatively direct in their language; there are some short lyrics that are strongly visual. This painterly response becomes more emphatic in his later books. *A friction of lights* (1963) has a long sequence that is filled with colour and references to design; it closes with a poem about Apollinaire who has been one of the influences on Grier's poetry, for in his writing he tries to break through the rationality and order of social existence to reach what he himself calls 'a psychic-state-progressing which can never quite confirm the object it creates'. This search for the irrational, and the curiously unfixed process of living that lies beyond the surface of life, emerge in *Pictures on the skin* (1967). Here the surrealistic elements are juxtaposed with direct statement and image to give an exotic flavour that effectively breaks down the normal responses of the reader—an effect that is enhanced by the interleaving of the poems with photographs taken by Grier and drawings, graphics, and collages contributed by his wife, Sylvia Tait. Grier's *Selected poems 1955–1970* (1971) contains most of the poems from these last two books, some from his early work, and new poems from the 1960s. While showing a continuation of his interest in painting and place, this collection also contains poems about movies, poets, and politics. PS

Griffin, J. A. See HISTORY STUDIES IN ENGLISH 12.

Griggs, Mary Ann. See FOLKLORE: BIBLIOGRAPHY and HISTORY STUDIES IN FRENCH 10.

Grisdale, Alex. See CHILDREN'S BOOKS IN ENGLISH 6.

Grosskurth, Phyllis. See LITERARY STUDIES IN ENGLISH 4.

Groulx, Lionel-Adolphe (1878–1967). Born in Chenaux, near Montreal, he was educated at Sainte-Thérèse-de-Blainville and at the Seminary of Montreal and was ordained a priest in 1903. After teaching at Valleyfield Seminary from 1901 to 1906, he completed his studies in Rome, at the University of Fribourg, Switzerland, and in Paris. He then returned to Valleyfield where he remained until 1915 when he was appointed professor of Canadian history at the Université de Montréal. In 1920 he became director of the Action française nationalistic movement and wrote extensively to publicize it. He was elected to the Royal Society of Canada in 1918—he was awarded its Tyrrell Medal in 1948—and resigned in 1952. He was one of the early members of the French Canadian Academy (1944), founded the Institut d'Histoire de l'Amérique française in 1946, and established the *Revue d'histoire de l'Amérique française* in 1947.

In *Croisade d'adolescents* (1912) Groulx tells how he assumed leadership of a religious and nationalist movement founded among the students at Valleyfield in 1901. This movement, l'Action Catholique, spread to other schools and colleges. Similar groups were formed and were later organized as l'Association de la Jeunesse, which also accepted Groulx's leadership and adopted the slogan '*Notre maître le passé*' ('our master the past'). His *Les rapaillages—vieilles choses, vieilles gens* (1916) is a series of essays in praise of folkways that had survived from the French régime. *Chez nos ancêtres* (1920) emphasizes the religious, feudal, and parish customs, and the pioneer virtues of the *habitant*.

Groulx had by this time begun his series of public historical lectures in which he sought to reverse the tendency of French-Canadian historians to adopt a moderate attitude, and he took advantage of a revival of interest in Dollard des Ormeaux to uphold this French hero as an inspiring symbol for contemporary nationalists of the willingness of French Canadians to fight to the last for their culture. The accuracy of his *Si Dollard revient* (1919) was challenged, notably by Gustave LANCTOT and Marius Barbeau. He defended his position in *Le dossier de Dollard: la valeur des sources, la grandeur du dessein, la grandeur des résultats* (1932) and in *Dollard, est-il un mythe?* (1960). His advocacy of the cult of Dollard found full expression in *Paroles à des étudiants* (1941) in which he urged students to pray for the coming of a great champion through whom French Canada would achieve its messianic destiny as leader of a French and Catholic culture centred on the banks of the St Lawrence River. He did not, however, directly espouse separatism.

Groulx's passionate historical writing is based on the thesis that the history of French Canada has been one of constant struggle to survive in the face of a relentless British determination to crush her. His formative years, 1890–1917, were filled with racial conflict and Groulx saw that the struggle for survival was far from over. Confederation had lulled French Canada into false security. He began to re-interpret history to awaken his people to their danger and looked to the past to explain French Canada's future. His main works are *Nos luttes constitutionnelles* (5 parts, 1915–16); *La confédération canadienne, ses origines* (1918); *La naissance d'une race* (1919) in which he develops the theme that the French and English races are incompatible and that conflict was inevitable—only the unity of Frenchness and Catholicism would enable the former to survive: *L'enseignement français au Canada* [1934–5]; and *Histoire du Canada français depuis la découverte* (4 parts, 1950–2) of which a definitive edition in two volumes was published in 1962. His articles, essays, and addresses are collected in *Notre maître le passé* (3 vols, 1924–44) in which he takes up the thesis that the French are an apostolic race whose mission in North America is the preservation of Latin Christian culture; *Dix ans d'Action française* (1926); *Orientations* (1935); *Directives* (1937); and *Pour bâtir* (1953). *Mes mémoires: Tome I, 1878–1920* (1970) and *Tome II, 1920–1928* (1971), based on part of the volumes bequeathed by Groulx, is a major contribution to French-Canadian social and intellectual history and gives an insight into the formation of Groulx's nationalism. *Roland-Michel Barrin de La Galissonière, 1693–1756* (1970), in the Canadian Biographical Series, was completed only a few months before Groulx's death at the age of 89. It describes the work of a governor of New France who sought to expand and consolidate the French Empire in America.

Under the pseudonym 'Alonié de Lestres', Groulx wrote two novels: *L'appel de la race* (1922), which points out the conflicts that can arise from intermarriage between French- and English-speaking Canadians and uses as an example the hostility aroused by Regulation 17 of the Ontario government, which limited the hours of teaching French in Ontario schools (1912); and *Au cap Blomidon* (1932), the story of a descendant of an Acadian family who worked on his ancestral farm and finally acquired it from the English-speaking owners.

An appreciation of Groulx's work is found in *L'oeuvre de l'abbé Groulx* (1923) by Olivar Asselin. *L'abbé Lionel Groulx* (1937) by André Laurendeau is a eulogy of the abbé's progress as a student. *Le nationalisme de Lionel Groulx* (1970) by Jean-Pierre Gaboury is one of the latest attempts to interpret Groulx's thought. *L'abbé Groulx: variations on a nationalistic theme* (1973) edited by Susan Trokimenkoff is an anthology of documents for history students. NS/DF

Grove, Frederick Philip (1879–1948). There is considerable disagreement between the account of Grove's life before he came to

Canada given in his *In search of myself* (1946)—which for many years was considered to be autobiographical—and the findings of Professor Douglas Spettigue of Queen's University, who has investigated Grove's origins in Europe. Grove tells us that he was born in Russia in 1871 while his parents were visiting there. His wealthy father, the son of an Englishman, owned Castle Thurow in Sweden, where Grove lived until he was fourteen. He says he spent the next two years in Europe, chiefly travelling with his mother until she died in 1887. He was educated by tutors, then at schools in Berlin and Hamburg. He describes accompanying an uncle on a research expedition across Siberia; studying archaeology at the Sorbonne and in Rome; travelling widely on his own, going as far away as New Zealand; visiting North America in 1892 and learning (in Toronto) that his father had died in bankruptcy; and becoming an itinerant farm labourer in the west until he started teaching in 1912.

In the spring 1972 issue of *Queen's Quarterly* Professor Spettigue reveals that Grove was a German, Felix Paul Greve, born at Radomno on the Polish-Prussian border on February 14, 1879. He grew up in Hamburg, attended the University of Bonn, and also studied in Rome and Munich. He was a free-lance writer and translator from 1902 to 1909 and came to Canada in 1909 or early in 1910. The years between 1910 and 1912 when he started to teach are still a blank.

Grove was engaged as the teacher of a rural school in Hesketh, Man., in 1912, the year he married. In 1915 he was made principal of Gladstone High School in northern Manitoba. His wife took a teaching position at Falmouth, some thirty miles north, and Grove visited her on weekends. Feeling isolated, he began to write: his journeys by bicycle and horse and sleigh in winter inspired his first published books, *Over prairie trails* (1922) and *The turn of the year* (1923). In 1917 he moved to a school near Falmouth where he suffered a back injury that eventually brought on intermittent paralysis of the legs for the rest of his life; in 1922 he was teaching in Rapid City. In 1925 he published his first and probably his best novel, *Settlers of the marsh* (which had the neighbourhood of Falmouth, called Plymouth, as its setting). *A search for America,* based on travels in North America, appeared in 1927, and another novel, *Our daily bread,* in 1928. In 1929 the Groves moved to Ottawa where he was editor of the Graphic Press. After a year they bought a farm north of Simcoe, Ont., where he lived until he died. He suffered a paralytic stroke in 1944 and thereafter was supported by a pension from the Canadian Writers' Foundation. He was awarded the Lorne Pierce Medal of the Royal Society of Canada for distinguished service to Canadian literature in 1934 and was elected a Fellow of that society in 1941. *In search of myself* won a Governor General's Award.

Over prairie trails (1922)—vivid descriptions in essay form of seven winter drives from Gladstone to Falmouth—and *The turn of the year* (1923)—evocations of prairie scenery—portray a northern climate that is both beautiful and treacherously harsh and elicits from man a superhuman struggle for survival. *Settlers of the marsh, Our daily bread* (1928), *The yoke of life* (1930), and *Fruits of the earth* (1933) are laboriously conceived but realistic novels of prairie life that occasionally rise to a certain power and offer subtle insights into character. They deal with man's struggle against nature and with the clash between generations. Tragedy in these books is caused by the revolt of young people against the stern qualities required by their fathers during the pioneering era. By placing *Settlers of the marsh* and *The yoke of life* in a barren, stony district of northern Manitoba, where the distance from markets placed the pioneer at the mercy of the merchant, Grove gives an air of inevitability to the sacrifices made by the women and children. The outcome of one such sacrifice is conveyed in *Settlers of the marsh* in which Ellen rejects an offer of marriage because of a promise she made to her mother, who had been destroyed by child-bearing, miscarriages, and backbreaking work. (Canadians were not prepared for so frank a discussion of sex; there was an outcry on the publication of this novel and it did not sell.) *Our daily bread* deals with the bewilderment and total defeat of John Elliot, a 'prairie Lear' who had alienated his wife and children by his absorption in building the material prosperity through which he hoped to bind them to prairie life. With the exception of one daughter, all his children are mismated because they seized the first chance to escape from home or because they were attracted by characteristics opposite to those of their father. Elliot dies in a state of desolation and complete isolation. In *Fruits of the earth* another intelligent and strong-willed pioneer, Abe Spalding, builds up a prosperous farm in Manitoba and, by his resourcefulness, becomes the benevolent despot of the district in which he lives. When the pioneer battle has been won, Spalding is repudiated, first by his only surviving son who abandons farming, then by the people of his district when he himself is defeated as a candidate for local office. In this book, however, Grove hints at a reconciliation between father and son and a return of Abe Spalding to the domain of public affairs.

In these prairie novels there is always a minor character who maintains a good relationship with his son, and it is on the possibility of reconciling the generations that Grove concentrates in *Two generations: a story of present-day Ontario* (1939). The setting of this story is a well-established dairy farm after the First World War, when women's rights had become recognized. Ralph Patterson's wife intervenes successfully between her authoritarian husband and his children, and so Grove reaches a tripartite reconciliation between stern pioneer qualities, the rights of individuals, and the mutual respect and esteem on which family ties are built. In *The master of the mill* (1944) Grove uses a flashback technique to follow the progress of a family industry from the tyranny of the pioneer builder to the tyranny of the machine age, by which employer and employee alike are bound and dehumanized.

Many of Grove's short stories, unlike his novels, stress the beauty and joy of prairie life, and they show a tolerance of human folly and weakness that also has little part in his novels. Harsh climate, blizzards, thin soil, poor harvests, depression conditions, and hard work still dominate the scene, but work can be personally rewarding, and even tragedy is lightened by acts of neighbourliness. Grove's stories first appeared in the *Winnipeg Tribune Magazine*, the *Canadian Forum*, and *Queen's Quarterly*. A collection was accepted by the Ryerson Press in 1948 but was not published. Desmond PACEY made a selection from them, and from manuscripts in the Grove papers, and published them with an introduction under the title originally chosen by Grove, *Tales from the margin* (1971).

Grove was also the author of *It needs to be said* (1929), a book of essays based on speeches, and *Consider her ways* (1947), a fantasy about ants that satirizes human society.

The most recent study of Grove is by Margaret R. Stobie in the Twayne World Authors series (1973). She deals with his life after 1912 and examines his books critically. (Professor Spettigue has written a book on Grove's life up to 1913 that will be published in the fall of 1973.) See also *Frederick Philip Grove* (1969) by Douglas O. Spettigue in the Studies in Canadian Literature series, which describes the first stage of the author's researches into Grove's origins, and a book of representative criticism with the same title edited by Desmond Pacey (1970) in the Critical Views on Canadian Writers series. (Professor Pacey, who published a study of Grove in 1945, has come to different conclusions about Grove's early years than Professor Spettigue. He has done some research of his own in Sweden and describes it in the *Journal of Canadian Fiction*, winter 1972, vol. 1, no. 1.)

Over prairie trails, *Settlers of the marsh*, *A search for America*, *Fruits of the earth*, and *The master of the mill* are all available in paperback in the New Canadian Library, in which a critical study on Grove by Ronald Sutherland also appears in the Canadian Writers Series (1971). NS/WET

Gullett, D. W. See HISTORY STUDIES IN ENGLISH 13.

Gundy, H. Pearson. See HISTORY STUDIES IN ENGLISH 15.

Gunther, Erna. See INDIANS 4.

Gurd, C. See ANTHOLOGIES IN ENGLISH 1.

Gurik, Robert (1932–). Born in France of Hungarian parents, he came to Canada in 1951, studied at the Polytechnical Institute of Montreal, and became a graduate engineer. He is one of Québec's most prominent contemporary playwrights and one of the least classifiable. His plays are rarely set in a recognizable social milieu, yet he has emerged as a politically committed writer. While his early plays deal in general with the situation of modern man, from 1968 he took an open stand in favour of independence. But his method is allegory rather than the direct transposition of social reality.

It has been possible to follow Gurik's development as a dramatist, as he is an extremely public writer. Many of his plays have been reworked for new productions. He has also submitted them for criticism to public readings at the Centre d'Essai des Auteurs dramatiques. We have therefore a number of works that vary greatly in quality, but that all form part of an organic whole. For instance, his first play, *Api*, was presented at the Dominion Drama Festival in 1966, but was considered too slow-moving and was also handicapped by technical failures. It was published as *Api or not Api* in the same year. Gurik reworked the text and it was produced as *Api 2967* (1971) in 1967. In 1969 a new production was staged in Venice. The play takes place in the future. Man leads a devitalized existence, the aim of which is to live as long as possible. He no longer knows happiness and pain, good and evil. His whole life is rationalized: the pills he eats for his meals, the length of his conversations, even the number of movements he needs to make. While men and women still differ physically, reproduction is brought about by pills, and the number of births per day is statistically predetermined. Into this impersonal world comes an unidentified object called Api. A professor is told to carry out laboratory tests on Api, and engages a female assistant, E 3253. Although neither of them knows this, Api is an apple. So the professor and his assistant are about to relive the history of mankind: for them the apple represents what it represented for Adam and Eve—mystery, adventure, and knowledge (in this case, knowledge of the past). By setting his play in the future, Gurik is focusing his attention on man in the twentieth century, torn between the past and the future. The two scientists try to discover the reality behind words that man no longer uses, such as love, kiss, God, and peace. The implication is that, if the words are no longer used in the future, it is because present-day man is in danger of making them meaningless. The protagonists rediscover the act of love, supposedly obsolete—for, Gurik argues, man's life should be devoted to the search for personal happiness.

Le pendu (1967) takes up the theme of words and their underlying reality. Gurik shows that words like 'happiness' and 'freedom' have no abstract meaning but represent different things for different people, and particularly for different social classes. This play won the Dominion Drama Festival award in 1967 and has been translated as *The hanged man* (1972) by Philip London and Laurence Bérard. Yonel, the hero, sees himself as a modern-day Christ but fails to win any disciples for his plan to make everyone in the world equally rich. Instead, the village poor hang him. Yonel is not a positive hero: 'He wants to reform, improve a given world, borrowing its laws, the rules of its game . . . But Yonel is out of time; he expresses a truth which belongs to yesterday, or again to tomorrow, a truth which is in contradiction with reality.' More than the previous play, *Le pendu* is a political metaphor. It was, however, performed as a metaphysical tragedy, a fate reserved for many of Gurik's plays. It would seem that many (though not all) of the professional actors and directors who have worked on them are unable to grasp the political consciousness that underlies them. This reveals the basic contradiction in Gurik's dramaturgy: he is a politically committed writer yet is quite content to have his plays become a commodity and be produced within the traditional theatrical system. Further, his two subsequent plays lack the dramatic strength of *Le pendu*. *Hamlet, Prince du Québec* (1968), based on Shakespeare's play, is a piece of propaganda for Québec independence. But even here the political message was blunted by self-indulgent performances. Further, the parallels Gurik finds between Denmark and present-day Québec come too pat and, finally, falsify history. *À coeur ouvert* (1969), too, is a mechanical transposition: the Heart Bank is the U.S.A., its directors the U.S. government, the coalmen represent the Blacks, the laundrymen the Chinese, and so on. The strings show, the formula is too obvious. *Les tas de sièges* (1971), a program of three plays inspired by the October Crisis of 1970, is more spontaneous. *D'un séant à l'autre* shows the meeting of two people brought together by a marriage bureau. The only thing they have in common is an ability to withdraw into interior monologue. When they finally embrace, they strangle each other to the strains of 'O Canada'. The other two plays are less symbolical. In *J'écoute*, Louise and Jean-Guy are celebrating their first wedding anniversary. They are being employed as phone-tappers during the crisis. The moral implications of what they are doing lead to their break-up as Louise betrays her husband to the authorities for his mild nationalist sentiments. In *Face à face*, Pierre Edouard is a shy soldier, brought into the town, he believes, to protect the population from 'revolution and sedition'. He meets a prostitute who leads him to question momentarily his preconceptions about law and order and the role of the English language in Québec. After they hurriedly make love, the woman is shot by a second soldier. These two plays show the effect of a specific political situation on the behaviour of ordinary people and are far more eloquent than Gurik's overtly 'political' pieces. He is at his best when his political beliefs guide his writing instead of dictating it. This is also the case in his latest play, *Le procès de Jean-Baptiste M* (1972), which retells the life of an office worker who has just shot three of his employers, directors of a large chemical company. For Gurik, the company is a microcosm of modern society, and office workers are the new proletariat: 'They leave work more exhausted, even if there are no physical marks; it is a new form of alienation and suffering.' The strength of the play is that Jean-Baptiste is not an extremist but a modern-day Everyman. The point of crisis comes about because of the conflict between the individual's aspirations to a better quality of life and the capitalist system's insistence on greater productivity. Are we not, Gurik suggests, all potential murderers in such an intolerable situation? Which of us can condemn Jean-Baptiste for his act?

Gurik's other plays are *Les louis d'or* (1966), *Le kangourou* (1967), and *La palissade* (1971—with *Api 2967*). He has also written a novel, *Spirales* (1966), an experimental work in the style of a *roman-fleuve*. It traces the breakdown of the narrator, who feels that his self is totally cut off from the world. Where Louise's betrayal of her husband and Jean-Baptiste's shooting of his bosses can be seen as despairing attempts at self-expression, the character in *Spirales* is incapable of even such a gesture. In this sense the work can be seen as an early sketch for the themes that now preoccupy Gurik in his plays. JC

Gustafson, Ralph (1909–). Born near Sherbrooke, Qué., Ralph Barker Gustafson was educated at Bishop's College in Lennoxville and at Oxford. He lived in New York for many years before returning to Lennoxville where he joined the staff of the English department at Bishop's University.

Gustafson's first book of poems, *The golden chalice* (1935), won the Prix David of the Province of Québec. The collection consists of finely polished sonnets, a narrative poem, and lyrics in traditional forms; it also includes a denunciation of modern poets. *Alfred the Great* (1937), a play in blank verse written while he was a student at Oxford, was inspired by admiration for the character, courage, and achievements of that king. In *Epithalamium in time of war* (1941) and *Lyrics unromantic* (1942) Gustafson began to adopt the stanza forms and ellipses of the moderns whose works he had earlier deplored. *Flight into darkness* (1944) is a collection of the poems in these two works to which some new lyrics were added. In 1960 Gustafson published *Rocky Mountain poems*, which conveys a sense of height and space, and *Rivers among rocks* in which the rocks are symbols of features in modern life. In both collections the ellipses and neologisms are carried to a point at which the poems sometimes become cryptic. His wide range of subject-matter is especially evident in *Sift in an hourglass* (1966).

Gustafson's craggy and dense verse is somewhat tempered by a colloquial voice that emerges every now and again in the poems in *Ixion's wheel* (1969), in which he deals principally with his responses to his travels in Europe; there are also meditations on death in poems arising from the demise of some famous literary figures. For his *Selected poems* (1972) he chose a representation from all phases of his writing career. He has also published *Theme and variations for sounding brass* (1972): a collection of five poetic sequences on political themes (the Québec crisis of October 1970, the Russian invasion of Czechoslovakia, the shootings at Kent State University).

As an editor Gustafson has compiled three anthologies for Penguin—*Anthology of Canadian poetry (English)* (1942); *Canadian accent* (1944), a collection of stories and poems by contemporary Canadian authors; and *The Penguin book of Canadian verse* (1958; rev. 1967)—as well as the anthologies *Voices* (1943) and *A little anthology of Canadian poets* (1943).

While living in New York Gustafson contributed critical articles and short stories to literary magazines. His short stories have appeared in *Best American stories* (1948 and 1950) and *Canadian short stories* (1960), which contains 'The pigeon'. A collection of them was compiled under the title *Summer storm*, which is not yet published. NS/PS

Gutteridge, Don. See POETRY IN ENGLISH 2.

Gwyn, Richard. See HISTORY STUDIES IN ENGLISH 12.

H

Haggart, Ron. See HISTORY STUDIES IN ENGLISH 12 and POLITICAL WRITINGS IN ENGLISH 1.

Haggerty, Joan. See FICTION IN ENGLISH 6.

Hall, G. K. See HISTORY STUDIES IN ENGLISH 17.

Hall, Henry F. See HISTORY STUDIES IN ENGLISH 15.

Halpert, Herbert. See FOLKLORE: BIBLIOGRAPHY and HISTORY STUDIES IN ENGLISH 16.

Hamelin, Jean. See FICTION IN FRENCH 2; HISTORY STUDIES IN ENGLISH 1; HISTORY STUDIES IN FRENCH 1 and 7; and POLITICAL WRITINGS IN FRENCH 1.

Hamelin, Marcel. See HISTORY STUDIES IN ENGLISH 1; HISTORY STUDIES IN FRENCH 11; and POLITICAL WRITINGS IN FRENCH 4.

Hamilton, N. Raphael. See HISTORY STUDIES IN ENGLISH 2.

Hamilton, W. D. See LITERARY STUDIES IN ENGLISH 4.

Hannon, Leslie. See HISTORY STUDIES IN ENGLISH 2.

Harbron, John. See POLITICAL WRITINGS IN ENGLISH 5.

Hardin, Herschel. See DRAMA IN ENGLISH 2.

Hare, John. See ANTHOLOGIES IN FRENCH; FICTION IN FRENCH: SHORT STORIES; and HISTORY STUDIES IN FRENCH 1 and 4.

Harker, Herbert. See FICTION IN ENGLISH 2.

Harkin, Thomas. See POLITICAL WRITINGS IN ENGLISH 5.

Harlow, Robert. See FICTION IN ENGLISH 2.

Harper, J. Russell. See HISTORY STUDIES IN ENGLISH 7 and 16; INDIANS 4.

Harrington, Lyn. See CHILDREN'S BOOKS IN ENGLISH 1 and 6.

Harris, Bess. See HISTORY STUDIES IN ENGLISH 16.

Harris, Christie. See CHILDREN'S BOOKS IN ENGLISH 1, 2, 3, and 6.

Harris, Robin S. See HISTORY STUDIES IN ENGLISH 15 and 17.

Harris, Tom. See CHILDREN'S BOOKS IN ENGLISH 6.

Harris, W. Eric. See POLITICAL WRITINGS IN ENGLISH 2.

Harron, Donald. See BELLES LETTRES IN ENGLISH.

Hartweg, Raoul. See ESKIMOS: BOOKS IN FRENCH.

Harvison, C. W. See HISTORY STUDIES IN ENGLISH 12.

Harwood, Elizabeth. See HISTORY STUDIES IN ENGLISH 16.

Hawkins, John. See HISTORY STUDIES IN ENGLISH 11.

Hawkins, William. See POETRY IN ENGLISH 2.

Hawthorn, Audrey. See INDIAN LEGENDS AND ART.

Hawthorn, Harry Bertram. See INDIANS 1.

Haycock, Ronald G. See INDIANS 3.

Hayes, John. See INDIANS 5.

Hayne, David. See HISTORY STUDIES IN ENGLISH 2; HISTORY STUDIES IN FRENCH 11; and LITERARY STUDIES IN FRENCH 5.

Heaps, Leo. See HISTORY STUDIES IN ENGLISH 8.

Hébert, Anne (1916–) is a cousin of Hector de Saint-Denys GARNEAU, whom she saw frequently during summers spent at Sainte - Catherine - de - Fossambault, Qué., where she was born and where both families had summer homes. An invalid for many years, she was educated by her parents. In 1953–4 she worked as a script-writer for the National Film Board and since then has divided her time between Canada and France. She was awarded the Molson Prize in 1967.

Like that of her cousin, Anne Hébert's poetry contains the symbols of solitude and death, but she uses her imagination and powers of expression to weave them into patterns representing fulfilment and release. Her collections are *Les songes en équilibre* (1942), *Le tombeau des rois* (1953), and *Poèmes* (1960), an augmented edition of *Le tombeau des rois* that won a Governor General's Award. She has carried her mastery of symbolism and fantasy into a collection of surrealist short stories, *Le torrent* (1950). One of them, 'L'ange de Dominique', links death with complete liberation through the free movements of the dance, and the title story portrays a spirit tormented by repression. (*Le torrent* was re-issued with four new stories in 1967.) The struggle to escape also provides the theme of her symbolic novel *Les chambres de bois* (1958), winner of the Prix Duvernay. A young couple have shut themselves away from the world. Into the stifling atmosphere of their apartment comes an intruder who settles herself in; the wife escapes to a new life. In *Kamouraska* (1970), which is based on a Québec murder-case of the nineteenth century, a woman watching over the deathbed of her husband thinks back over her life: her earlier marriage to a man of sadistic cruelty, her flight to a lover who is obliged to leave her after killing her husband, her own trial and acquittal, and her eventual 'safe' marriage to the man who now lies dying. The style is staccato, almost abrupt, and Anne Hébert's poetic vision and method are here more closely attuned to her subject matter than in her earlier fiction. *Kamouraska*, which won the Prix des Libraires de France, has been made into a film by Claude Jutra, Anne Hébert herself collaborating on the script. It has been translated under the original title by Norman Shapiro (1973). Three of Hébert's plays—*Le temps sauvage*, *La mercière assassinée*, and *Les invités au procès*—were published in a single volume in 1967.

Some of her poems have been translated by F. R. SCOTT and published in *St-Denys Garneau and Anne Hébert: translations/traductions* (1962). There is also a group of translations in John GLASSCO's *The poetry of French Canada in translation* (1970). Anne Hébert's poetry and early fiction are discussed in *An outline of contemporary French-Canadian literature* by J. Raymond Brazeau (1972), and Pierre Pagé and René Lacôte have published studies of her writing in the Écrivains canadiens d'aujourd'hui (1965) and the Poètes d'aujourd'hui (1969) series respectively. *Dialogue sur la traduction à propos du 'Tombeau des rois'* (1970)—with a preface by Northrop FRYE—is an exchange of letters between Anne Hébert and F. R. Scott that appeared previously in *The Tamarack Review;* if offers interesting insights into the process of translation. A translation of Anne Hébert's 'La maison de l'Esplanade' (from *Le torrent*)—'The house on the Esplanade'—is in *Canadian short stories* (1960) edited by Robert Weaver. NS/JM

Hébert, Jacques. See ANTHOLOGIES IN FRENCH.

Heeney, Arnold. See HISTORY STUDIES IN ENGLISH 12.

Heeney, Brian. See HISTORY STUDIES IN ENGLISH 12.

Heizer, Robert F. See INDIANS 5.

Hellyer, Paul. See POLITICAL WRITINGS IN ENGLISH 4.

Helwig, David (1938–). Born in Toronto, he spent part of his boyhood in Niagara-on-the-Lake, returning to Toronto to attend the University of Toronto. He did graduate work in English at the University of Liverpool. He now teaches at Queen's University.

His first book was *Figures in a landscape* (1968) which contained poems and two plays. It was later revised: the plays and some poems were removed and an extra group of poems was added under the title that was also used for the whole book, *The sign of the gunman* (1969). A third book of poems, *The best name of silence*, appeared in 1972.

Much of Helwig's poetry recalls events from his past as well as incidents from the life of his family, but he manages to lift them from the purely private because he sets them not only in the firm context of his own personal responses but also in a wide external context as he recounts how outside events constantly impinge on the securities of family life. The poems increasingly meditate on the passing of time and the inevitable journey to rot and dissolution. Even the very act of poetry is paradoxical for him: like other things in the world it may have only a transient existence, 'is only for now', but still 'Only/the pages of books/endure'. The language of the poems is not excessively figurative and his poetry shows a wide variety of form with some use of traditional metres and rhymes as well as an inventive use of rhythmic patterns.

Helwig has published two works of fiction: a collection of short stories, *The streets of summer* (1969), and a novel, *The day before tomorrow* (1971). His fiction shows some of the same concerns as his poetry. The short stories often deal with people who feel themselves trapped, placing their present state against memories of the past or against an imagined ideal. The characters are interested in gaining some freedom in their personal lives, but in most cases their dreams of independence remain unfulfilled. *The day before tomorrow* deals with the relationship of two brothers whose ideals about society take different roads: one becomes a spy, the other re-examines his role as a participant in radical action. Helwig works out these relations in a narrative that unfolds the different viewpoints.

Helwig was associated with the editorial board of the literary magazine *Quarry* and has collaborated in the editing of two volumes of short stories: *Fourteen stories high* (1971) with Tom Marshall and *Stories 72* (1972) with Joan Harcourt. He has worked as a teacher of creative writing at Kingston Penitentiary and edits a magazine of writing by prison inmates across Canada, *Words from Inside*. He is co-author with 'Billie Miller' of *A book about Billie* (1972), created from tape-recorded interviews with a habitual criminal who was on parole from Collins Bay Penitentiary. PS

Hembroff-Schleicher, Edythe. See HISTORY STUDIES IN ENGLISH 16.

Hénault, Gilles (1920–). Born at St Majoric, Qué., and educated in Montreal, he is a poet, a journalist, and a critic of art and theatre. He was a newspaperman with *Le Jour* (1939), *Le Canada* (1940–2), *La Presse* (1942–4), and worked with the Canadian Broadcasting Corporation (1944–6) and radio station CKAC in Montreal (1946–8). From 1949 to 1956 he was a union organizer and publicist for trade unions in Montreal and Sudbury, and from 1957 to 1959 a free-lance writer for Radio-Canada (the French-language network of the CBC). In 1959 he was one of the founders of the literary review *Liberté*. He was director of the arts section at *Le Devoir* in 1960–1 and commentator on international affairs with *Le Nouveau Journal* and Radio-Canada in 1962. He was a writer for the Royal Commission on Bilingualism and Biculturalism during 1963 and was an interviewer for Radio-Canada in 1965. From 1966 to 1971 he was director of the Museum of Contemporary Art in Montreal, and has also held the position of professor in the École Nationale de Théâtre. He is at present a free-lance writer.

Hénault has published five collections of poetry: *Théâtre en plein air* (1946), *Totems* (1953), *Voyages au pays de mémoire* (1959), *Sémaphore* (1962), awarded the Prix du Grand Jury des Lettres, and *Signaux pour les voyants* (1972), which won a Governor General's Award. One of the seminal poets of modern French-Canadian poetry, he is distinguished from his two major contemporaries, Paul-Marie LAPOINTE and Roland GIGUÈRE, by his resistance to the influence of surrealism; by the clarity, warmth, and intellectual control of his verse; and by his notion that the poetic process is from the irrational to the rational, which he has described as being 'at once from the inside and the outside'. He has also written plays for radio and scripts for documentary films. In 1946 he was the co-founder with Eloi de GRANDMONT of 'Les Cahiers de la File Indienne', a series of brochures illustrating the work of prominent Québec artists. Representative English translations of Hénault's work appear in *The poetry of French Canada in translation* (1970) edited by John GLASSCO. Poems by him have also been translated into Italian, Spanish, Ukrainian, and Serbo-Croatian. JG

Henderson, J. L. H. See HISTORY STUDIES IN ENGLISH 5.

Hendrick, George. See LITERARY STUDIES IN ENGLISH 4.

Hendry, C. E. See INDIANS 6.

Hendry, Tom. See DRAMA IN ENGLISH 3.

Henry, Ann. See DRAMA IN ENGLISH 3.

Herbert, John. See DRAMA IN ENGLISH 2.

Héroux, Denis. See HISTORY STUDIES IN FRENCH 3.

Hertel, François (1905–) is the pseudonym of Rodolphe Dubé, who was born in Rivière-Ouelle, Qué., and educated at Sainte-Anne-de-la-Pocatière and at the Seminary of Trois-Rivières. He entered the Jesuit Order but left it in 1947, spent the next two years as editor of the review *Franco-américaine*, and then went to live in Paris, where he has published some of his writings under the imprint Éditions de la Diaspora.

Possessor of a quick intelligence that seizes on new ideas and philosophies as they are first expounded but seldom explores them in depth, Hertel has written poetry, novels, and reflective and philosophical essays. His first collection of poems, *Les voix de mon rêve* (1934), was traditional romantic verse, but he broke new ground and influenced young poets in *Axe et parallaxes* (1941) in which he gave poetic expression to abstract ideas. His other collections of poems are *Strophes et catastrophes* (1943), *Cosmos* (1945), *Quatorze* (1948), *Mes naufrages* (1950), *Poèmes européens* (1961), *Anthologie 1934–1964* (1964), and *Poèmes perdus et retrouvés, anciens et nouveaux, revus et corrigés* (1966). He made a selection of his poetry and added some new verse for *Poèmes d'hier et d'aujourd'hui: 1927–1967* (1967).

In Hertel's short novel, *Le beau risque* (1939), a rebellious schoolboy is led to devote himself to the unremunerative study of pure science in the hope of benefiting future generations. Very different are the experimental novels *Mondes chimériques* (1940), *Anatole Laplante, curieux homme* (1944), and *Journal d'Anatole Laplante* (1945), in all of which Anatole Laplante, the rational man, becomes engaged in endless intellectual excursions with the perverse and mocking Charles Lepic, whose long monologues raise disturbing metaphysical questions. *Six femmes, un homme* (1950) and *Jérémie et Barabbas* (1959) are two collections of short stories that reveal his gift for sardonic humour. *Louis Préfontaine, apostat: autobiographie approximative* (1967) is a confusing, unsuccessful autobiographical novel that he began in 1949.

Hertel's first two essays, *Leur inquiétude* (1936), written for and about adolescents, and *Pour un ordre personnaliste* (1942), express the idea that French Canadians should devote themselves to working for the betterment of their province. *Nous ferons l'avenir* (1945) is a commentary on the position of Québec within confederation. In this essay Hertel expresses his opinion that increasing demands for autonomy will lead to decentralization of the federal government and that the Franco-American communities will join Québec. *O Canada, mon pays, mes amours* (1959) explains French Canada to French readers and gives a good deal of attention to *vieux parler*, the survival of words and expressions brought to New France by colonists of the seventeenth and early eighteenth centuries. Hertel's journal, *Un Canadien errant* (1953), expresses the sense of exile that followed his break with his friends and with the traditions of his province. *Journal philosophique et littéraire* (1961) is an account of the stages by which he came to accept the existentialist view that death, a state of non-being, is also the end of the human spirit. Québec in the late sixties inspired *Cent ans d'injustice? Un beau rêve: le Canada* (1967) and *Divigations sur le langage*

(1969), which contains fulminations on the decay of the French language, particularly as it is used in the literature of Québec; it includes a two-act play, 'L'assassin'.

In 1972 Hertel published *Souvenirs, historiettes, réflexions* and *Tout en faisant le tour du monde*, two collections of personal sketches about his life and travels. NS

Hertzman, Lewis. See HISTORY STUDIES IN ENGLISH 12 and POLITICAL WRITINGS IN ENGLISH 7.

Hickerson, Harold. See INDIANS 5.

Hiebert, Paul G. See FICTION IN ENGLISH 2.

Higginbotham, C. H. See HISTORY STUDIES IN ENGLISH 8.

Hill, Douglas. See HISTORY STUDIES IN ENGLISH 8.

Hill, Kay. See CHILDREN'S BOOKS IN ENGLISH 1, 2, and 4.

Hine, Daryl (1936–). Born in Burnaby, B.C., he studied classics and philosophy at McGill University. He left Canada in 1959, living for the most part in France where he served on the staff of the Canadian Legation in Paris. He returned to this continent to do postgraduate work in comparative literature at the University of Chicago, where he has taught since 1967. He was appointed editor of the magazine *Poetry* in October 1969.

Hine's poetry appeared in magazines when he was fifteen, and a slim pamphlet, *Five poems*, was published in 1954. Since then he has published *The carnal and the crane* (1957), *Heroics* (1961), *The devil's picture book* (1961), *The wooden horse* (1965), and *Minutes* (1968).

Much of Hine's poetry is drawn from his reading in classical literature and expresses a constant theme of the duality of existence as experienced in the polarities of art and life. The poems are full of references to mirrors, dreams, surfaces, and depths to emphasize dualities. They sometimes reveal a search for reconciliation, even though the discoveries may be of horrifying worlds or of a deeper isolated existence, leading to states of desolation and incomprehension, expressed in images of bleak landscapes and ruins. At times myth, legend, and art offer some consolation. In *Minutes* there is a new emphasis on personal relationship as a stable focus for a world in disorder in which an individual's existence may be transitory and meaningless. Hine has a masterly control of form, often using traditional techniques, although in his recent work he has shown an interest in a freer form and a more conversational tone. As a result his poetry, which sometimes seemed too detached and rarefied because of its use of strict structures and classical subject matter, has become more lively.

This emphasis on the classics is evident in Hine's plays, including a verse translation of Euripides' *Alcestis*, which has been broadcast by the CBC and the BBC. A lighter tone emerges in some of *The Homeric hymns* (1972), in which Hine's use of classical metres in translating these Greek poems is technically adroit.

Hine's wide interest in mythology is the basis for his novel *The prince of darkness & co.* (1961), a satire on a British author who lives on a Mediterranean island where he writes popularizations of the more sinister features of myths. *Polish subtitles: impressions from a journey* (1963) is a dryly humorous account of a month spent in Warsaw where Hine was engaged to edit English subtitles for a Polish film. PS/NS

History studies in English. The most impressive feature of historical writing in Canada in the last six years is its quantity. Over five hundred books have appeared: one has the impression that no worthwhile manuscripts have remained unpublished. Approximately half the books considered here were written by professional historians attached to universities, archives, or such institutions as the Historical Section of the Canadian Armed Services. Forty-three were originally produced as Ph.D. theses. The volume of publication is partly a reflection of the increasing number of professional historians who staffed the expanding university departments in the 1960s, and was facilitated by the unprecedented scale of generous research and publication grants made available by the Canada Council. But the upsurge of interest in the Canadian past was also stimulated by the celebration of the centennial of confederation and sustained by the current wave of nationalist introspection. There is also an element of uncritical nostalgia in some of the literature, particularly that portion of it—almost half the titles—produced by professional writers, journalists, and amateur historians.

These books of course vary greatly in quality. The following commentary is descriptive rather than rigorously critical and is intended to illustrate the scope and range of the literature. It includes works by journalists on contemporary politics and studies by art historians that contain substantial historical information. Also included are previously published books that have become available in English translations and others that have been substantially revised or updated. Reprints have been excluded, along with most collections of documents and previously published essays intended primarily for use in schools and universities. Regrettably, local histories have been for the most part omitted. A large number of these have appeared and anyone interested might be directed to recent numbers of the following provincial historical periodicals that sometimes list and review them: *BC Studies*, *Alberta Historical Review*, *Saskatchewan History*, *Ontario History*, *Revue d'histoire de l'Amérique française*, *Acadiensis*, *Nova Scotia Historical Quarterly*, and *Newfoundland Quarterly*.

There are obvious difficulties in classifying these historical studies in mutually exclusive categories, but the areas in which they group themselves might be suggested in a general way. In spite of its bulk, the literature is quite uneven in its coverage of the nation's past. About four-fifths of these books deal with Canadian history after 1867. In regional terms there are approximately twenty-five books on the Maritime provinces, about half on the period before 1800; seventy on Québec and French Canada, almost half on the years before 1783; around seventy on Upper Canada and Ontario; about one hundred on the prairie provinces and British Columbia; and twenty or so on the north and the arctic. Books of a biographical nature, including memoirs and collections of personal papers and journals, comprise slightly less than one quarter of the total. Approximate totals for various fields and themes are: military history, including biographies of military figures and studies of defence policies, 50; economic history, including the lives of businessmen and histories of labour organizations, 55; religious history, 20; education, 30; ethnic groups, 25. About one third of the total includes works devoted exclusively to political history.

1. *Surveys and essays.* Kenneth McNaught's *The Pelican history of Canada* (1969) concentrates on the central themes of economic expansion, the divisions between French and English, and the persistent continental attraction—and rejection—of the United States. The point of view is sympathetic to the left and the emphasis is generally political. *The Canadians, 1867–1967* (1967), edited by J. M. S. CARELESS and R. Craig Brown, is a collection of essays arranged in two parts: in the first, eleven historians survey each decade since 1860; in the second, various experts describe developments in the arts, sciences, education, religion, and economic growth since confederation. The first section has been published separately as *Part one of The Canadians, 1867–1967* (1967). In *Colonists and Canadiens, 1760–1867* (1971), edited by J. M. S. Careless, eleven historians survey the period decade by decade. *Baneful domination: the idea of Canada in the Atlantic world, 1581–1971* (1971) by Glen Frankfurter is an amateurish summary underlining the threats to Canada's survival and independence from Britain and the United States, with a heavy emphasis on the eighteenth and nineteenth centuries. *A concise history of Canada* (1968) by Gerald S. Graham and *Canada's five centuries: from discovery to present day* (1971) by W. Kaye Lamb are reliable, well-illustrated condensed accounts.

Canada's first century, 1867–1967 (1970) by Donald G. CREIGHTON is a readable but gloomy survey of the gradual breakdown or betrayal of the great nineteenth-century institutions and patterns of life upon which Canada depended for her existence in the past and can no longer rely for her survival in the future. Creighton's *Towards the discovery of Canada: selected essays* (1972) contains both previously published studies on such subjects as the role of the merchant class in early nineteenth-century Canadian politics, confederation and the west, and Sir John A. Macdonald, as well as new essays on the perils to Canadian survival in the present and on history as a literary art.

Canada: a geographical interpretation (1968) edited by John Warkentin is an indispensable collection of essays on the theme of the geographical changes in the country since 1867. A more personal approach is contained in George WOODCOCK's *Canada and the Canadians* (1970), a travel book that explains the contemporary scene in historical terms. It is notable for its appraisals of recent cultural developments and for its feeling for localities, particularly the north. A historian's interpretation of the character of Canadian nationality, William L. MORTON's *The Canadian identity* (2nd ed., 1972), has been reissued with a new chapter containing his reflections on the 1960s. The second edition of Morton's textbook survey *The kingdom of Canada* (1969) contains a chapter on the 1960–8 period. Substantial additions have also been made to Edgar McInnis's *Canada: a political and social history* (3rd rev. ed., 1969), and to *Canada: a modern study* (rev. 1971) by Ramsay G. COOK, with John Ricker and John Saywell.

Three textbooks that incorporate some of the conclusions of more recent scholarship on certain episodes and themes are *Canada: unity in diversity* (1967) by Paul G. Cornell, Jean Hamelin, Fernand OUELLET, and Marcel TRUDEL; *Northern destiny: a history of Canada* (1969) by John S. Moir and Robert E. Saunders; and *The Canadian experience* (1968) by D. M. L. Farr and John S. Moir.

An attempt to present Indian history on its own terms and not merely as a subordinate sub-theme in Canadian history is *The Canadian Indian: a history since 1500* (1972) by E. Palmer Patterson II. The point of view is revisionist but the historical content, almost completely derived from secondary sources, is disappointing. *The image of the Indian* (1971) by Ronald G. Haycock analyses the changing attitudes to Indians as they are represented in the popular magazines from 1900 to 1970. (Though additional historical works on Indians are mentioned below, see INDIANS for a more complete listing.)

A number of books of essays that reflect the current interests and research of professional historians have been compiled in honour of historians of the past generation. All these books contain valuable full bibliographies of the scholars to whom they are dedicated. *Character and circumstance: essays in honour of Donald Grant Creighton* (1970) edited by John S. Moir consists of fourteen essays on such divergent topics as the American Revolution and Indian history; Sir Robert Borden and Anglo-Canadian relations during the First World War; the social criticism of Stephen Leacock; violence in Canadian history; Laurier, King, and foreign policy; and charisma and Canadian politics. A less substantial collection, *On Canada: essays in honour of Frank H. Underhill* (1971), edited by Norman Penlington, contains four notable essays: on the element of determinism in the thought of Harold Innis, Northrop FRYE and Marshall MCLUHAN; on F. H. Underhill and the *Canadian Forum* in the 1930s; on Lord Durham and the French Canadians; and on the Canadian Radio League and the movement for a publicly owned national broadcasting system. In another book in the same genre, *Empire and nations: essays in honour of Frederic H. Soward* (1969) edited by Harvey L. Dyck and H. Peter Krosby, fourteen contributors focus on Commonwealth relations and Canada's foreign policy. *Policy by other means: essays in honour of C. P. Stacey* (1972) edited by Michael S. Cross and Robert Bothwell contains various studies of episodes in Canadian military and political history. Some of the subjects treated are the defence of Canada in the Seven Years' War; Colonel Otter and the Boer War; Liberal Party finance from 1935 to 1945; and the separate-school taxation issue in the Ontario election of 1937.

In *Regionalism in the Canadian community, 1867–1967* (1969) edited by Mason Wade, sixteen essayists dwell upon the subject mainly in relation to French Canada and the Maritimes. Ramsay Cook's *The Maple Leaf forever: essays on nationalism and politics in Canada* (1971) concentrates on the current debate about the Canadian nationality and seeks to view it in terms of the distinction between a nationalist-state and the nation-state. *Idées politiques des premiers ministres du Canada/The political ideas of the prime ministers of Canada* (1969) edited by Marcel Hamelin is an uneven collection of papers: some are genuine studies of political thought and attitudes while others are merely anecdotal accounts or summaries of political episodes.

2. *Early exploration: New France and the Maritimes to 1763.* A brilliant narrative and a vast store house of information, *The European discovery of America: the northern voyages*, A.D. *500–1600* (1971) by Samuel Elliot Morison, ranges from the supposed pre-Columbian voyages to Cartier, Frobisher, Davis, and Gilbert. *Sixteenth-century North America: the land and the people as seen by Europeans* (1971) by Carl O. Sauer attempts to show what the

continent looked like before repeated contacts and settlement changed everything; it is based upon Spanish, French, and English explorers' accounts of the landscape and of Indian societies. *Samuel de Champlain* (1972) by Samuel Elliot Morison is an expert reassessment of the founder of New France with a special emphasis on his work as an explorer. Marquette, the Jesuit missionary and co-discoverer of the Mississippi River, has been capably treated in *Jacques Marquette, S.J., 1637–1675* (1968) by Joseph P. Donnelly; the records of his travels are critically evaluated in *Marquette's explorations: the narratives re-examined* (1970) by N. Raphael Hamilton. Two biographies of another explorer/trader, whose efforts also focused on the Mississippi, are *La Salle: the life and times of an explorer* (1968) by John Upton Terrell and *La Salle* (1967) by E. B. Osler. The Terrell is a superior study of a personality, with very effective descriptions of native and Indian life. The Osler is derivative and at times uncertain of the historical context. Leslie F. Hannon's *The discoverers: an illustrated history* (1971) and *Forts of Canada: the conflicts, sieges and battles that forged a great nation* (1969) are picture-book surveys.

France in America (1972) by W. J. ECCLES authoritatively chronicles the rise and fall of the French empire in North America and the West Indies from early fishing expeditions around 1500 to 1783. Eccles' *The Canadian frontier, 1534–1760* (1969) deals with the expansion of commercial, military, and religious enterprise in Acadia, Louisiana and the west and with the impact of the 'frontier' upon the colony and the mother country. It is a shrewd and realistic survey, especially effective in analysing the independent role of the Indians and in drawing comparisons between the frontier of New France and that of the English seaboard colonies. In two lectures—*Canadian society during the French regime/La société canadienne sous le régime français* (1968)—Eccles assesses the aristocratic and paternalistic ethos of the colony and reveals some little-known aspects of the day-to-day life of its people. *Daily life in early Canada* by Raymond Douville and J. D. Casanova (1968) presents a more traditional and familiar picture of social life. *The beginnings of New France: 1524–1663* (1973) by Marcel Trudel offers a comprehensive narrative of the colony's history from the early contacts to the assumption of direct royal administration. It goes into much detail on the role of the fur-trade companies and their failure to promote settlement. *Introduction to New France* (1968) by the same author is a synopsis of the development of the colony and its chief institutions. *The administration of New France/L'administration de la Nouvelle France, 1627–1760* (1970) by André Vachon, is a succinct analysis of its governmental institutions. The *Dictionary of Canadian biography: Volume II, 1701–1740* (1969) edited by David Hayne and André Vachon contains entries on governors, merchants, artisans, religious figures, and Indian leaders who died between 1701 and 1740.

Word from New France: the selected letters of Marie de l'Incarnation (1967), edited and translated with an introduction by Joyce MARSHALL, provides rich detail about life in the colony between 1639 and 1672 and is especially effective in conveying the religious enthusiasm of that period. Montreal was founded on a wave of religious idealism and its early difficulties are described in *Montreal under Maisonneuve, 1642–1665* by Gustave LANCTOT (translated by Alta Lind Cook, 1969). Bruce G. Trigger's *The Hurons: farmers of the north* (1969) is an investigation by an anthropologist of their culture as a functioning social system on the eve of its disruption in the mid-seventeenth century. Though not a historical study, the book is extremely important for understanding this Indian culture on its own terms and for appreciating its function within the French trading system.

Anglo-French imperial rivalry and the military collapse of the colony have been re-examined in several works. Guy FRÉGAULT's *Canada: the war of the conquest* (translated by Margaret M. Cameron, 1969) was originally published in 1955. Though it deals almost exclusively with military events, it was one of the first books to advance—without demonstrating in detail—the contention that the conquest smashed a functioning society and left behind a 'nation' without a state. *New France: the last phase, 1744–1760* (1968) by G. F. G. STANLEY also stresses that the conquest smothered an emergent national community, though for the most part the book is a straightforward history of military campaigns. *With Wolfe to Quebec: the path to glory*

(1972) by Oliver Warner dwells on the British leader and the battle on the Plains of Abraham. *Guerillas and grenadiers: the struggle for Canada: 1689–1760* (1969) by Ian K. Steele is a short summary covering a broader period. In *The battle for James Bay, 1686* (1971) by W. A. Kenyon and J. R. Turnbull the French capture of three Hudson's Bay Company posts is presented through the accounts of participants on both sides. *Yankees at Louisbourg* (1967) by George A. Rawlyk narrates the New Englanders' capture of the French fortress in 1745. *Roland-Michel Barrin de la Galissonnière, 1693–1756* (1970) by Lionel GROULX is a slight and ineffectual biography of the interim-governor of New France from 1747 to 1749 and a champion of French expansion. *Seventeenth-century Canada: source studies* (1970) edited by Cary F. Goulson and *The French tradition in America* (1969) edited by Yves F. Zoltvany are two useful collections of documents illustrating various features of the colony, the latter extending down to 1810.

English enterprise in Newfoundland, 1577–1660 (1969) by Gillian T. Cell describes the persistent and tangled conflict between the fishery and settlement on the Island. The poetical record of an early visitor has been assembled in *The new found land of Stephen Parmenius: the life and writings of a Hungarian poet, drowned on a voyage from Newfoundland, 1583* (1972) edited by David B. Quinn and Neil M. Cheshire. *Joseph Banks in Newfoundland and Labrador, 1766: his diary, manuscripts and collections* (1971) edited by A. M. Lysaght contains the illustrated catalogues of flora and fauna as well as other related papers by the naturalist who was to provide leadership for the scientific group that sailed with Cook in 1768–71. *Acadia: the geography of early Nova Scotia to 1760* (1968) by Andrew Hill Clark is a historical geographer's interpretation of early maritime history.

3. *The fur trade and exploration.* E. E. Rich has given a lucid and balanced narrative account of the fur trade from the French period, through the rivalry between the Hudson's Bay Company and the North West Company, down to the disintegration of HBC control in the mid-nineteenth century in *The fur trade and the northwest to 1857* (1967). *The Hudson's Bay Company* (1971), a brief history by George Woodcock, is popular and colourful. (*The great fur opera: annals of the Hudson's Bay Company 1670–1970*) (1970) by Kildare DOBBS and the British illustrator Ronald Searle is a witty entertainment based on the Company's history.) The Hudson's Bay Record Society, which began publishing material from the Company's archives in 1938, has issued three more volumes. *Saskatchewan journals and correspondence: Edmonton House, 1795–1800; Chesterfield House, 1800–1802* (1967), edited with an introduction by Alice Johnson, illuminates both the Company's difficulties in recruitment and in procuring adequate trade goods during the war with France and the extension of the trade into the Saskatchewan country on the eve of the violent conflict with the North West Company. *Andrew Graham's observations on Hudson's Bay, 1767–91* (1969), edited by Glyndwr Williams with an introduction by Richard Glover, includes fascinating detail on natural history and Indian culture as well as information on the daily routine of the trade. *Peter Skene Ogden's Shake Country journals, 1827–28 and 1828–29* (1971), edited by Glyndwr Williams with an introduction by David E. Miller and David H. Miller, contains much useful information on the fur trade on the Pacific slope. (A number of earlier volumes in this series have been reprinted recently.) The life of a Company servant who worked at Fort Albany and James Bay and retired to Red River is chronicled in *A Londoner in Rupert's Land: Thomas Bunn of the Hudson's Bay Company* (1969) by Denis Bayley.

Less restricted in scope than its title implies, *Firearms, traps and tools of the mountain men* (1967) by Carl P. Russell includes an excellent discussion of the equipment and implements of the fur traders. Collections of rather specialized essays on various facets of the trade are: *Aspects of the fur trade: selected papers of the 1965 North American Fur Trade Conference* (1967) issued by the Minnesota Historical Society and *People and pelts: selected papers of the Second North American Fur Trade Conference* (1972) edited by Malvina Bolus. *Beyond the river and the bay* (1970) by Eric Ross reports on what the west was like in 1811 as seen through the eyes of an imaginary contemporary author of a guide book for prospective settlers. It draws with scrupulous accuracy an authentic picture of the landscape, communications, and supply problems of the fur trade, the trade routes and posts, and relations with the Indians.

The journals and letters of Sir Alexander Mackenzie (1970), edited with an introduction by W. Kaye Lamb, is the definitive documentary record of the explorer's voyages to the Arctic Ocean in 1789 and to the Pacific in 1793. A readable short assessment of the explorer's character and achievement is provided by Roy Daniells in *Alexander Mackenzie and the north west* (1969, 1971). The exploits of explorer-surveyor David Thompson have been presented in a collection of his own writings in *David Thompson: travels in western North America, 1784–1812* (1971) edited by Victor G. Hopwood, and in a brief life, *David Thompson: fur trader, explorer, geographer* (1971) by James K. Smith. The records of two explorers of the Pacific coast have been made available in *Journal of a voyage on the north west coast of North America during the years 1811, 1812, 1813, and 1814* (1969) by Gabriel Franchère (translated by Wessie T. Lamb and edited with an introduction by W. Kaye Lamb) and in *The journals of Captain James Cook: Volume* III, *The voyages of the 'Resolution' and 'Discovery', 1776–80* (1967), edited by J. C. Beaglehole, which chronicles Cook's visit to Nootka and his failure to enter the Northwest Passage by way of Bering Strait.

4. *British North America: 1763–1812.* The position of the British North American colonies in the wider imperial setting on the eve of the disruption of the old colonial system is set out in *The British Empire before the American Revolution: Volume* XIII, *The triumphant empire* (1967) by Lawrence Henry Gipson. Gustave Lanctot's *Canada & the American Revolution, 1774–1783* (translated by Margaret M. Cameron, 1967) presents a detailed and judicious examination of the responses of various groups within Canada to the revolution and makes clear why the colony remained outside it. Though the clergy in general stood against the opposition to Britain, *Pierre Gibault, missionary, 1737–1802* (1971), a biography by Joseph P. Donnelly, shows how one priest supported American independence in spite of the orders of his superior, the Bishop of Québec. The ill-fated and fumbling military campaign to coerce Canada into the resistance against Britain is recounted by Harrison Bird in *Attack on Quebec: the American invasion of Canada, 1775* (1968); and the assault is described by a British officer in *Canada preserved: the journal of Captain Thomas Ainslie* (1968) edited by Sheldon Cohen. *The loyal Whig: William Smith of New York and Quebec* (1969) by L. F. S. Upton is a biography of one supporter of the British connection who, while in New York, advocated a constitutional solution to the imperial problem and later, as councillor and chief justice of Quebec, played a crucial part in shaping the institutions of that colony. *The Iroquois in the American Revolution* (1972) by Barbara Graymont contains an excellent discussion of the reasons for the migration of some of these Indians to Canada.

Nova Scotia in the revolutionary period has been studied in two works of religious history. *Henry Alline, 1748–1784* (1971) by J. M. Bumsted is a short biography of the leader of the religious revival that swept Nova Scotia during the revolutionary war. In contrast to its focus on spiritual reform, *A people highly favoured of God: the Nova Scotia Yankees and the American Revolution* (1972) by Gordon Stewart and George Rawlyk looks at the religious movement in terms of the insecurities and confusion of loyalties of those New Englanders who had earlier migrated to Nova Scotia and who found in Alline's preaching a resolution to their inner conflicts of allegiance. The American and then the French Revolutions generated a conservative reaction in attitudes towards colonies, and *The Anglican design in Loyalist Nova Scotia, 1783–1816* (1972) by Judith Fingard analyses the efforts made to strengthen the Anglican Church as a buttress to the social order and the British connection.

One of the major sources for the social and economic history of Nova Scotia in the period is the diary kept by the merchant Simeon Perkins between 1780 and 1812. The fourth volume, *The diary of Simeon Perkins, 1797–1803* (1967), edited with an introduction by G. Bruce Fergusson, contains an interesting account of daily life in the town of Liverpool. *Clarkson's mission to America, 1791–1792* (1971), also edited by G. Bruce Fergusson, chronicles an early effort to assist the Negroes in Nova Scotia and New Brunswick. *Uncommon obdurate: the several public careers of J. F. W. Des Barres* (1969) by G. N. D. Evans is a life of the British military engineer, cartographer, and artist who prepared *The Atlantic Neptune* (a remarkable series of charts and aquatint views of the east coast made between 1763 and 1773) and later became the governor of Cape Breton and Prince Edward Island. *The Newfoundland journal of Aaron Thomas, able seaman in* H.M.S. *Boston* (1968) edited by Jean M. Murray has a record of a voyage from England to Newfoundland and back in 1794 and 1795 that includes a résumé of Newfoundland history. *Newfoundland journeys* (1971) edited by Addison Brown is an anthology of travel writings covering the last two hundred years. *Halifax: warden of the north* (1965; 1971) by Thomas H. RADDALL has been reissued in a revised edition. An episode in the naval war of 1812, the capture of the U.S.S. *Chesapeake* by the H.M.S. *Shannon* in 1813, is graphically described in *The Shannon and the Chesapeake* (1970) by H. F. Pullen.

5. *Upper Canada, 1791–1841.* Much of the writing on this period is in the form of slim, popular biographies. *Governor Simcoe and his lady* (1968) by Marcus Van Steen stresses the more positive achievements of that enthusiastic soldier who sought to mould the colony in the image of British society. *William Berczy, co-founder of Toronto* (1967) by John Andre traces the career of a pioneer who brought a group of German settlers from New York State to Markham, north of York, and later became a painter in Montreal. The Anglican clergyman who was one of the pillars of the 'family compact' has been the subject of three short, sympathetic studies: *John Toronto: a biography of Bishop Strachan* (1969) by Sylvia Boorman, which is overly romantic; *John Strachan: pastor and politician* (1971) by David Flint, a lively portrait of the personality and his times; and *John Strachan, 1778–1867* (1969) by J. L. H. Henderson, a solid contribution to an understanding of his ideas. Henderson edited *John Strachan: documents and opinions* (1969), an excellent selection from his letters and pamphlets. *William Lyon Mackenzie: rebel against authority* (1971) by David Flint is a succinct and fair appraisal of that excitable protestor. One of Mackenzie's predecessors is depicted in *Robert Gourlay, gadfly: forerunner of the Rebellion of Upper Canada, 1837* (1971) by Lois D. Milani, a rather amateurish political biography written from within the traditional Whig framework of interpretation, though some new material has been used. *Soldier of fortune: the story of a nineteenth-century adventurer* by Ella Pipping (translated from the Swedish by Naomi Walford, 1971) is an account of the life and times of Mils Gustaf Von Schoultz, the Polish-born soldier who led the American assault on Prescott Mill in 1838. *Ryerson of Upper Canada* (1969) by Clara THOMAS focuses on the activities of this leader of Methodism in the years before 1844 when he became superintendent of education. Professor Thomas's *Love and work enough: the life of Anna Jameson* (1967) is a thorough but somewhat undigested treatment of the Victorian author—disappointing on the eight months she spent in Upper Canada in the mid-1830s. *Laura Secord: the legend and the lady* (1971) by Ruth McKenzie is a short, argumentative essay that attempts to put Laura back on her pedestal as heroine of the War of 1812. *The journals of Mary O'Brien 1828–1838* (1968) edited by Audrey Saunders Miller presents an interesting view of settlement at Thornhill, Vaughan Township, and Shanty Bay from 1828 to 1838. *Gentle pioneers: five nineteenth-century Canadians* (1968) by Audrey Y. Morris details the experiences of the Strickland and Moodie families in the Peterborough area. In *Look to the north star: a life of William King* (1969) Victor Ullman traces the work of an anti-slavery advocate who founded the Negro community of Elgin, near Chatham.

One of the chief issues raised by the early reform movement—the land question—has been treated exhaustively in two monographs. In *The clergy reserves of Upper Canada: a Canadian mortmain* (1968) Alan Wilson convincingly argues that much of the criticism of the system was misplaced and that in fact after 1827, when the holdings were put up for sale, these lands were a positive stimulus to economic growth. In *Land policies of Upper Canada* (1968) Lillian F. Gates carefully traces the management of land from the founding of the colony to the 1850s in the broad context of British policy, local interests, and comparisons with American experience.

An informative and informal social history of the town of York—its buildings, daily life, and business activities—is *Toronto in 1810* (1970) by Eric W. Hounsom. *Rural Ontario* (1969) is a pictorial record of existing early buildings, beautifully photographed by Ralph Greenhill with an introduction on architectural styles and techniques of construction by Verschoyle B. Blake. Ralph Greenhill collaborated with Thomas D. Mahoney in *Niagara* (1969), portraying the history and development of the falls and the Niagara frontier in the early nineteenth century through historical illustrations and a descriptive text. Illuminating for the background of immigration into Upper Canada is H. J. M. Johnston's *British emigration policy, 1815–1830: 'shovelling out paupers'* (1972), a study of the national system of emigration advocated by Wilmot Horton to remedy pauperism and overpopulation in Britain. It analyses the attitudes of officials, cabinet ministers, and economists towards various plans for assisted colonization. Charles M. Godfrey offers a glimpse into an unusual aspect of social history in his short *The cholera epidemics in Upper Canada, 1832–1866* (1968).

The journal of Major John Norton, 1809–1816 (1971), edited by Carl F. KLINCK and James J. Talman for the Champlain Society, contains the observations of a confidant of Joseph Brant on the Six Nations Confederacy and Indian culture. The Indian leader is the subject of a romanticized biography by John W. Jakes: *Mohawk: the life of Joseph Brant* (1969). Harrison Bird's *War for the west: 1790–1813* (1972) is a narrative of the Indian wars up to the War of 1812.

Salvation! O the joyful sound: the selected writings of John Carroll (1967) contains vivid excerpts from the books of a pioneer Methodist minister on growing up in York, the experiences of a circuit rider, impressions of fellow preachers, and the vicissitudes of the Canadian Methodist Conference. It is edited, with an informative introduction on Canadian Methodism, by John Webster Grant. *The church in the British era* (1972) by John S. Moir deals with the development of the various denominations in British North America from the conquest to confederation.

A number of histories of localities have appeared: two of the more successful are *History of Perth County to 1867* (1967) by W. Spafford and H. J. M. Johnston and *Brant County: a history 1784–1945* (1967) by C. M. Johnston. A substantial number of local and county histories, travellers' books, and county atlases have been reprinted.

6. *The Canadas: 1841–1867.* Historians writing in English have been more interested in the reconciliation of the French and English tensions under the union of 1841 than in the upheavals in Lower Canada in 1837. One account of that episode, *Rebellion: the rising in French Canada, 1837* (1971) by Joseph SCHULL, is a popular narrative of events centred on personalities and skirts any examination of the basic social and economic causes. *The union of the Canadas: the growth of Canadian institutions, 1841–1857* (1967) by J. M. S. Careless is a full-scale survey of this crucial period when colonial self-government was achieved and major institutions consolidated. It is particularly effective in weaving together the complex themes of the development of a crypto-federal system, economic growth and the building of canals and railways, and the gradual breakdown of the 'party system' in the early 1850s. The conventional theme of responsible government has been examined again from a fresh perspective by William Ormsby in *The emergence of the federal concept in Canada, 1839–1845* (1969), which re-emphasizes the fact that the chief condition for the success of self-government was the prior rejection of the assimilation of French Canada. *The last cannon shot: a study of French-Canadian nationalism, 1837–1850* (1969) by Jacques Monet analyses in considerable detail the debate within French Canada concerning the most effective means by which her national survival could be ensured. It shows how moderate leaders accepted the union, which was originally intended as an agency of assimilation, and used British institutions for their own purposes. In *The Baldwins and the great experiment* (1969) R. M. and J. Baldwin follow the story of three generations of this Irish family, which came to Upper Canada in 1799, and stress the roles of Dr William Warren Baldwin, who was credited with popularizing the idea of responsible government, and his son Robert who helped to carry it into effect.

The Canadian crisis and British colonial policy, 1838–1841 (1972) by Peter Burroughs deals with the background to the revolts of 1837 in terms of British policy, stresses the problem of accommodating French-Canadian nationalism within the Empire, and illuminates the genesis of the Durham report. The historical importance usually attached to that document is questioned in *The Durham Report and British policy* (1972) by Ged Martin. The attitudes of English radicals are presented in *The colonial reformers and Canada, 1830–1849: selections from documents and publications* (1969) edited by Peter Burroughs.

Elizabeth Nish has reconstructed from newspaper accounts the debates of the early years of the union in *Debates of the Legislative Assembly of United Canada, 1841–1867* in three volumes: *1841* (1969), *1842* (1971), and *1843* (1972).

John Garner's *The franchise and politics in British North America, 1755–1867* (1969) is an able investigation of the pre-confederation franchise. It examines the qualifications necessary to vote in each colony; the disqualifications of Catholics, Jews, Quakers, minors, Indians, and women; and the case is made that agitations for broadening the franchise and improving the electoral system were not based on any convictions about the rights of man but simply on shifting political interests and advantage. The deeply held belief in the inferiority of American political institutions and other aspects of 'anti-Americanism' are analysed in *Canada views the United States: nineteenth-century political attitudes* (1967) by S. F. Wise and R. Craig Brown.

MacNab of Dundurn (1971) by Marion MacRae is both a biography of Sir Alan MacNab and a history of his home, Dundurn Castle, Hamilton. The *Dictionary of Canadian biography: Volume* x, *1871 to 1880* (1972), edited by Marc La Terreur, contains a wealth of information on major and minor figures active in the period who died between 1871 and 1880.

Despite its rather misleading sub-title, *The education of Canadians, 1800–1867: the roots of separatism* (1968) by Howard Adams is concerned with the development of Catholic and Protestant education and should be used with caution. *Unequal union: confederation and the roots of conflict in the Canadas, 1815–1873* (1968) by Stanley B. Ryerson suggests the potential usefulness of the Marxian approach but suffers from an overly rigid and simple application of the categories.

7. *Canada: confederation to the 1920s.* William L. Morton has attempted to convey the flavour of mid-Victorian Canada in *The shield of Achilles: aspects of Canada in the Victorian age/Le bouclier d'Achille: regards sur le Canada de l'ère victorienne* (1968), a collection of essays mainly by younger historians ranging over such themes as the idea of mission in early Upper Canada, the idea of progress, the struggle between liberalism and ultramontanism in Québec, Canadian attitudes to the Crimean War, viceregal influences on Canadian society, and the creation of a model Indian community in British Columbia. *The elegant Canadians* (1967) by Luella Creighton is a delightful evocation of the manners and customs of the upper classes in the confederation era. *Portrait of a period: a collection of Notman photographs, 1865 to 1915* (1967) edited by J. Russell Harper and Stanley Triggs contains many fine photographs of people and places as well as a sketch of the Montreal-based Notman firm of photographers.

Other helpful sources of information on the social history and material culture of Victorian Canada are *Building with wood and other aspects of nineteenth-century building in Ontario* (1967) by John I. Rempel, a rather technical account, and *Canada builds: 1867–1967* (1967) by T. Ritchie, which contains capsule descriptions of the succession of architectural styles and buildings. *The barn: a vanishing landmark* (1972) by Eric Arthur and Dudley Witney discusses five major types of barns found in the northeastern United States, Ontario, and Québec, and is illustrated with over four hundred photographs. Other facets of social history are examined in *A heritage of light* (1968) by Loris Russell, which describes lamps and lighting in the early Canadian home; *Clean and decent: the fascinating history of the bathroom and water closet* (1967) by Lawrence Wright; and *'Keep me warm one night': early handweaving in eastern Canada* (1972) by Dorothy K. Burnham and Harold B. Burnham. These three books discuss their subjects within the spacious context of Britain and the United States as well as Canada. *Sports and games in Canadian life: 1700 to the present* (1969) by Nancy Howell and Maxwell L. Howell is an informal and episodic study of the sporting scene since 1700. *A shopper's view of Canada's past: pages from Eaton's catalogues, 1886–1930* (1969) edited by George P. de T. GLAZEBROOK, Katharine B. Brett, and Judith McErval presents fascinating sidelights on fashions and tastes. Though intended mainly as guides to collectors of artifacts, there is much useful information for the social historian in *Nineteenth-century pottery and porcelain in Canada* (1967) by Elizabeth Collard; *A guide to the pre-confederation furniture of English Canada* (1967) by Don R. Stewart; and *Canadian silversmiths, 1700–1900* (1966) by John E. Langdon.

With the exception of Joseph Schull's *The*

nation makers (1967), a slight though pleasingly told story of the making of confederation, this subject has not attracted much attention in the last six years. The views of one opponent of the scheme—the premier of Ontario from 1862 to 1864—are carefully assessed in *John Sandfield Macdonald: 1812–1872* (1971) by Bruce W. Hodgins. *The assassination of D'Arcy McGee* (1968) by T. P. Slattery is a meandering biography of the Irish-Canadian politician. The same author's '*They got to find me guilty yet*' (1972) centres on the trial of McGee's murderer and raises some doubts about whether the right man was punished. Though it is mainly a collection of previously published essays, *Culture and nationality* (1972) by A. G. Bailey includes two new papers on the young nationalist intellectuals of Canada First. *Fenians and Anglo-American relations during reconstruction* (1969) by Brian Jenkins, while primarily a study in Anglo-American diplomacy, provides useful background on the impact of the Fenian movement on Canada. *Orangeism: the Canadian phase* (1972) by Hereward Senior surveys the organization from the 1830s to the 1890s. *Monck letters and journals, 1863–1868: Canada from Government House to confederation* (1970) edited by William L. Morton recaptures personal detail, the atmosphere, and the feelings of Canadians in the period. Another compilation, *Documents on the confederation of British North America* (1969) edited by G. P. Browne, contains official dispatches and papers relating to British North American union in the years 1858 to 1867.

In *Canada 1874–1896: arduous destiny* (1971), Peter B. Waite wrote a sound though rather conventional political history stressing the difficulties of maintaining national unity. Interesting for its fresh anecdotes, this work is weak on labour, social, cultural, and intellectual developments. *The national dream: the great railway, 1871–1881* (1970) and *The last spike: the great railway, 1881–1885* (1971) by Pierre BERTON provide an engrossing and fast-moving narrative of the building of the Canadian Pacific Railway, which is viewed as the focal point of Canadian national effort in the post-confederation generation. Readable, sparkling with character sketches, and especially impressive in describing construction difficulties, this work has been correctly criticized for assuming that there was no feasible alternative to the expensive line and for identifying Canadian national interest with the interests of central Canada. (*The impossible railway* (1972) is a single-volume edition published for the American market.) Berton's *The great railway illustrated* (1972) contains 277 excellent photographs along with an abridgement of the original text. *Canadian Pacific: a brief history* (1968) by J. Lorne McDougall is a short, able summary of the railway's entire history. The life of the engineer who surveyed the passes through the Rocky Mountains has been briefly told for general readers in *Man of steel: the story of Sir Sandford Fleming* (1969) by Hugh MacLean. H. V. Nelles has edited and written a splendid introduction to T. C. Keefer's *Philosophy of railroads and other essays* (1972), which mirrors the faith in railway technology in mid-nineteenth-century Canada.

The career of the dominating political figure of the period is recapitulated in a brief biography, *John A. Macdonald: the man and the politician* (1971) by Donald Swainson, and selections from Macdonald's correspondence have been made available in three books: *The papers of the prime ministers: Volume* I, *The letters of Sir John A. Macdonald, 1836–1857* (1968) edited by J. K. Johnson; *The letters of Sir John A. Macdonald, 1858–1861* (1969) edited by J. K. Johnson and C. B. Stelmack; and *Affectionately yours: the letters of Sir John A. Macdonald and his family* (1969) edited by J. K. Johnson. The first two contain interesting material relating to Macdonald's business interests and his political affairs; the third contains two hundred family letters from 1842 to 1891 that reveal much about his domestic tragedies.

Macdonald's rival in Ontario is the subject of *Oliver Mowat's Ontario* (1972) edited by Donald Swainson, though the best of the eleven essays deal with dominion-provincial relations and facets of the social and economic development of Ontario in the later nineteenth century. The twenty-five articles in *Profiles of a province: studies in the history of Ontario* (1967) edited by Edith G. Firth range from the Loyalist migration to contemporary trends in tourism. *Life in Ontario: a social history* (1968) by George P. de T. Glazebrook is a general survey, especially informative on nineteenth-century life. *Your loving Anna: letters from the Ontario frontier* (1972) edited by Louis Tivy is a collection of letters written by

Anna Leveridge, a settler in Hastings County, to her relatives in England from 1883 to 1891. *John Ramsay of Kildaton: being an account of his life in Islay and including the diary of his trip to Canada in 1870* (1969) by Freda Ramsay and John Ramsay contains the observations of an improving landlord who assisted Scots settlement in the Lake Simcoe and Georgian Bay districts and visited the settlers in 1870. His comments about the state of the country are not especially significant, however. A 1973 publication, Loris Russell's *Everyday life in colonial Canada* is a short book of social history that centres mainly on the colonists' occupations, social activities, and sports.

The antecedents of one of the most bitter issues in French-English relations in the later 1880s is explored exhaustively by Roy C. Dalton in *The Jesuits' estates question, 1760–1888: a study of the background for the agitation of 1889* (1968). Ramsay Cook's *Provincial autonomy: minority rights and the compact theory, 1867–1921* (1969) is an extended essay on the origins, development, and uses of the idea that confederation represented a compact of provinces or cultures. The beliefs of the French-Canadian nationalist Henri Bourassa are delineated in two studies: *Henri Bourassa and French-Canadian nationalism: opposition to empire* (1968) by Casey Murrow, an undergraduate essay; and *Henri Bourassa and the golden calf: the social program of the nationalists of Quebec (1900–1914)* (1969) by Joseph Levitt, a more original work that deals with the ways in which these intellectuals accommodated industrialism and urbanism into their corporatist social philosophy. In *French-Canadian nationalism: an anthology* (1969) Ramsay Cook has collected twenty-five essays ranging over a hundred years by both the interpreters and the exponents of *la survivance*.

Wilfrid Laurier: the great conciliator (1971), a brief biography by Barbara Robertson, is a fair but rather conventional assessment. The life of one of Nova Scotia's major political figures—premier of the province from 1884 to 1896 and then Laurier's minister of finance—is described by Bruce Fergusson in *Hon. W. S. Fielding: Volume* I, *The mantle of Howe* (1970) and *Volume* II, *Mr minister of finance* (1971). *Letters to limbo by the Right Honourable Sir Robert Laird Borden* (1971) edited by Henry Borden contains the former prime minister's reflections on men and things in early twentieth-century Canada as seen from the mid-1930s.

The problem of Canada's relations with the British Empire in the nineteenth century was a complex one and has recently been examined from the perspective of defence and military affairs. *Britain and the balance of power in North America: 1815–1908* (1967) by Kenneth Bourne is a review of British strategic and military planning from the time when an American attack on Canada was seen as a realistic eventuality to the time when American predominance on the continent was accepted as permanent. *Safeguarding Canada: 1763–1871* (1968) by J. Mackay Hitsman examines the plans produced on both sides of the Atlantic for the defence of Canada, the strategists who made them, and the limited extent to which actual preparations were effected. In *Canada and 'Imperial defense': a study of the origins of the British Commonwealth's defense organization, 1867–1919* (1967) Richard Arthur Preston traces the failure of Great Britain to control and commit the military and naval forces of the autonomous dominion to automatic participation in imperial wars. The problems of military and naval cooperation are seen from the point of view of the dominions, especially Canada, as well as from the centre of the Empire. *Ministers and generals: politics and the Canadian militia, 1868–1904* (1970) by Desmond Morton analyses the conflicts between the British General Officers commanding the Canadian militia and their political superiors. It not only explains the gradual acceptance by Canadians of the responsibility for framing their own military policies but also describes the militia as a social institution and the place of patronage in it. A study in intellectual history, Carl Berger's *The sense of power: studies in the ideas of Canadian imperialism, 1867–1914* (1970), attempts to explain the attraction of the British connection to some Canadians and to suggest why they believed Canada could best attain national status within a transformed empire. *The Alaska boundary dispute: a critical reappraisal* (1972) by Norman Penlington is a résumé of the background of this issue since 1825, the diplomacy leading to the settlement of 1903, and the effects upon Canadian opinion.

A notable contribution to the sparse literature on religious and intellectual history is Charles F. O'Brien's *Sir William Dawson: a life in science and religion* (1971), which lucidly examines the involvement of Dawson, a McGill University scientist, in the debate over the religious implications of the theory of evolution in the late nineteenth century. *The social passion: religion and social reform in Canada, 1914–1928* (1971) by Richard Allen is a detailed study of the impact of the Protestant social gospel on the early-twentieth-century progressive movement. The ramifications of this reform impulse are related to the Winnipeg General Strike and the Progressive Party, labour churches and church union, prohibition, social work, and the peace movement. *The church in the Canadian era* (1972) by John Webster Grant is an able survey of religion since confederation that is mainly institutional and denominational in focus.

The military operations involving Canadian troops in the First World War are described in a masterpiece of condensation: *The road past Vimy: the Canadian Corps, 1914–1918* (1969) by D. J. Goodspeed. He is also the author of a centennial survey: *The armed forces of Canada, 1867–1967: a century of achievement* (1967). *Canada and the First World War* (1969) by John Swettenham is a short illustrated history that touches on the domestic scene. *Vimy!* (1967) by Herbert F. Woods is a full critical treatment of that battle. *The gunners of Canada: the history of the Royal Regiment of Canadian Artillery: Volume* I, *1534–1919* (1967) by G. W. L. Nicholson ranges over the role of artillery since the French régime and the battles for Louisbourg; there is a substantial section on the First World War. Three personal accounts of this war are: *Fighting men* (1967) by Leslie M. Frost, nostalgic recollections of the men he served with from Orillia; *Canada at Vimy* (1967) by D. E. Macintyre, a narrative based on letters to his wife; and *Ghosts have warm hands* (1968) by Will R. BIRD, an evocative picture of life in the trenches, the patrols, and hand-to-hand fighting by a veteran of the 42nd Royal Highlanders of Canada who served in France and Flanders.

A useful though sketchy summary of the activities of the four thousand Canadians recruited for the Siberian Expeditionary Force after the armistice is given in *Allied intervention in Russia, 1918–1919, and the part played by Canada* (1967) by John Swettenham. Three of the twelve essays in *War and society in North America* (1971) edited by J. L. Granatstein and R. D. Cuff deal with the impact of the First World War on Canada. These are on a Canadian businessman's views of the war and reconstruction; an explanation of the conscription crisis in terms of the relations of French and English to the Canadian militia since 1868; and Canadian wartime leadership.

Canadian diplomatic activities for this period have been copiously documented in four volumes of sources published by the Department of External Affairs: *Documents on Canadian external relations: Volume* I, *1909–1918* (1967); *Documents on Canadian external relations: Volume* II, *The Paris Peace Conference of 1919* (1969) edited by R. A. MacKay; *Documents relatifs aux relations extérieures du Canada/Documents on Canadian external relations: Volume* III, *1919–1925* (1971) edited by Lovell C. Clark; and *Documents relatifs aux relations extérieures du Canada/Documents on Canadian external relations: Volume* IV, *1926–1930* (1971) edited by Alex I. Inglis. *Historical documents of Canada: Volume* V, *The arts of war and peace, 1914–1945* (1972) edited by C. P. STACEY concentrates on the great issues of national policy. *The Dafoe-Sifton correspondence, 1919–1927* (1966), edited by Ramsay Cook for the Manitoba Record Society, is useful for presenting the opinions of two influential Liberal nationalists on Canada's national status and her relations with other states as well as their attitudes towards the farmers' political revolt.

8. *The prairie west.* Douglas Hill's *The opening of the Canadian west* (1967) is a popular narrative history of the west from the fur trade to the creation of Saskatchewan and Alberta in 1905. It is based entirely on secondary sources and it breaks no new ground, but it is effective in describing the problems of pioneering on the prairies and the settlement of diverse ethnic groups. Both *The taming of the Canadian west* (1967) by Frank Rasky and *An illustrated history of western Canada* (1971) by Tony Cashman are more noteworthy for their illustrations than for the reliability of their narrative. *The centennial history of Manitoba* (1970) by James A. Jackson, a reliable summary, does not attain the literary power of *Manitoba: a history* (2nd ed., 1967) by William L. Morton, which has been reissued with a chapter on development in the province since 1955. *A*

history of Alberta (1972) by James G. MacGregor is an enthusiastic and uncritical survey of that province.

Four recorders of Rupert's Land: a brief survey of the Hudson's Bay Company courts in Rupert's Land (1967) by Roy St. George Stubbs deals with the characters and careers of four judges and provides both a lucid account of the administration of justice and an effective description of the social climate of the Red River colony in the generation before 1870 as it was reflected in court proceedings. The development of law and legal institutions in Manitoba over a longer period is traced in *Substantial justice: law and lawyers in Manitoba, 1670–1970* (1972) by Dale and Lee Gibson. *The valley comes of age* (1967) by Stanley N. Murray chronicles the changes in agriculture in the Red River area from 1812 to 1920.

Irene M. Spry has edited for the Champlain Society and written an excellent introduction to *The papers of the Palliser expedition, 1857–1860* (1969), which contains the classic report as well as the journals and related correspondence of the British exploring party that described the geography and assessed the agricultural potentialities of the prairies. *The John Wickes Taylor correspondence, 1859–1870* (1968), edited by Hartwell Bowsfield for the Manitoba Record Society, presents an illuminating picture of American interests at Red River at the time of its transfer to Canada as seen from the perspective of an energetic advocate of American expansionism.

Some of the most interesting recent literature on western settlement is in the form of biographies and memoirs. John McDougall's *Parsons on the plains* (1971) edited by Thomas Bredin contains selections from the autobiographical books of that pioneer Methodist missionary. *Remember Butler: the story of Sir William Butler* (1967) by Edward MCCOURT is a readable biography of an imperial soldier who is now recalled chiefly for his accounts of the great lone land published in the early 1870s. In his eminently fair vignette, *Louis Riel: the rebel and the hero* (1971), Hartwell Bowsfield describes and assesses the intriguing personality and career of the Métis leader. *The last war drum* (1972) by Desmond Morton re-examines the military history of the campaigns of 1885 in a broad setting; the book's many unfamiliar illustrations are of particular interest. *Crowfoot: chief of the Blackfeet* (1972) by Hugh Dempsey is a scholarly and meticulously researched biography of an Indian leader who stood aloof from the rebellion and whose life mirrors the decline of the Blackfeet people. *In Rupert's Land: memoirs of Walter Traill* (1970) by Mae Atwood records the experiences of a Hudson's Bay Company clerk in various western posts in the 1860s, while in *Prairie storekeeper* (1970) D. E. Macintyre describes his life as a general storekeeper at Tuxford, Sask., and his later career as a real estate agent in the years before the First World War. Helen Evans Reid attempts valiantly but not without excessive special pleading to restore the reputation of a controversial leader of a group of British colonists in *All silent, all damned/the search for Isaac Barr* (1969). John H. Blackburn's *Land of promise* (1970) edited by John Archer is a rich memoir of an American settler's farming experiences in the Edmonton area from 1911 to the 1930s. In *The American farmer and the Canadian west, 1896–1914* (1968) Karel D. Bicha is mainly concerned with estimating the numbers of these immigrants. *Only farmers need apply: official Canadian government encouragement of immigration from the United States, 1896–1911* (1972) by Harold M. Troper surveys official activities and finds them to have been moderately successful. A nostalgic and at times hilarious account of homesteading in southern Saskatchewan from 1912 to the early 1920s is presented in *Homesteader: a prairie boyhood recalled* (1972) by James M. Minifie. One of the best records of homesteading in Alberta, partly based on a journal kept in 1906–7, is presented in *Of us and the oxen* (1968) by Sarah Ellen Roberts. (An American edition was published as *Alberta homestead: chronicle of a prairie family* (1971).) In the same genre, *Raisins and almonds* (1972) by Fredelle B. Maynard is a beautifully written and evocative account of growing up in a Jewish family in several small prairie towns. Martin Nordegg's '*The possibilities of Canada are truly great*': *memoirs, 1906–1924* (1971) edited by T. D. Regehr is the saga of a German immigrant who developed the Alberta coal fields and became a partner of the railway builders, Mackenzie and Mann. These memoirs, which are peppered with arresting comments about Canada, contain a chapter on the social life of a coal-mining community and reveal a good deal about the mentality of the swashbuckling business developers in a period of hectic expansion.

James H. Gray has written four colourful and popular books on the social life of the prairie west: *Men against the desert* (1967), a survey of the efforts made since the drought of the 1930s to rehabilitate the short-grass country in the Palliser triangle; *The boy from Winnipeg* (1970), a sensitive and poignant autobiographical memoir of growing up in the metropolis of the prairies in the era of the First World War; *Red lights on the prairies* (1971), an account of prostitution, and efforts to stamp it out, in prairie cities and towns from the early years of the century to the 1920s when, ironically, the professionals fell victim to a looser moral code and the competition of amateurs; and *Booze: the impact of whisky on the prairie west* (1972), which mordantly examines abuses of alcohol on the frontier, the temperance movement, and prohibition. James G. MacGregor tells a more sedate story of the rise of a major city in *Edmonton: a history* (1967) and describes its role as a back door to the Yukon gold fields in *The Klondike rush through Edmonton, 1897–1898* (1970). A useful companion volume is *Gold rush: a pictorial look at the part Edmonton played in the great gold era of the 1890s* (1971) by James Blower. *Maintain the right* (1972) by Ronald Atkin deals with the early years of the RCMP.

The prairie political tradition continues to attract attention. A useful and succinct synthesis of the existing literature is *Democracy and discontent: progressivism, socialism and Social Credit in the Canadian west* (1969) by Walter Young. A biography of one of the leaders of the Winnipeg General Strike and a reforming M.P. from 1926 to 1939, *The rebel in the House: the life and times of A. A. Heaps, M.P.* (1970) by Leo Heaps is disappointingly thin and uncritical. *Agrarian socialism: the Cooperative Commonwealth Federation in Saskatchewan: a study in political sociology* by S. M. Lipset was reissued in 1968 with additional material by others on the evolution of the party. *Off the record: the C.C.F. in Saskatchewan* (1968) by C. H. Higginbotham is an impression of that party's achievement by a sympathetic journalist. *Social Credit: the English origins* (1972) by John Finlay provides a useful basis for comparing the Alberta movement with the original doctrine. *Politics in Saskatchewan* (1968) edited by Norman Ward and Duff Spafford is an excellent collection of fourteen essays on political history that develops such diverse themes as the conservatism of the electorate, female suffrage, the role of the Ku Klux Klan in the election of 1929, the ethnic vote and radicalism in the 1930s, and the dispute over the introduction of medicare. *Doctors' strike: medical care and conflict in Saskatchewan* (1967) by Robin F. Badgley and Samuel Wolfe is a broad treatment of the issue. A less substantial but no less important collection, *Prairie perspectives* (1970) edited by David P. Gagan, contains papers on Liberal and Conservative Party support on the prairies from 1917 to 1968, a study of prairie agriculture, reflections on the assimilation of 'foreigners' to the British-Canadian mode of life, and an especially forceful and provocative warning against recent changes in Indian policy.

Though not a strictly historical account, *Northern plainsmen: adaptive strategies and agrarian life* (1969) by John W. Bennett is an illuminating investigation of the patterns of life, organization, and inter-relationships of four groups—native peoples, ranchers, farmers, and Hutterians—in a southwestern Saskatchewan community.

A large number of local and community histories of particular localities in the west have been published in recent years. Typical of the best of these efforts is *The prairie W.A.S.P.: a history of the rural municipality of Oakland, Manitoba* (1969) by J. A. D. Stuart.

9. *British Columbia.* During the nineteenth century British Columbia developed behind the shield of British sea-power, which maintained sovereignty in the region against the expanding empires of both the United States and Russia. This theme is analysed in depth in *The Royal Navy and the northwest coast of North America, 1810 to 1914: a study in British maritime ascendancy* (1971) by Barry M. Gough. A large part of the early history of the province has been retold in two popular biographies of the Hudson's Bay Company official who served as governor of Vancouver Island from 1851 to 1863 and governor of British Columbia from 1858 to 1864: *James Douglas: servant of two empires* (1969) by Derek Pethick and *James Douglas: Father of British Columbia* (1971) by Dorothy Blakey Smith. *Charles Wilson's diary of the survey of the 49th parallel, 1858–1862, while secretary of the British Commission* (1970) edited by George F. G. STANLEY offers a reliable report of the

experiences of the British part of the survey of the Canadian-American boundary through the mountains. The adventures of mainly nineteenth-century travellers in the mountains is the subject of *The Canadian Rockies: early travels and explorations* (1969) by Esther Fraser.

British Columbia and confederation (1967) edited by George W. Shelton contains eight solid articles on the colony's entry into the Canadian union in 1871, including appraisals of the social and economic state of the colony at that time, the debate over the merits of confederation, and assessments of the political figures involved. In *Kootenai Brown: his life and times* (1969), William Rodney has skilfully sifted fact from legend to tell the story of a colourful character who was chief scout with the Rocky Mountain Rangers during the rebellion of 1885, a guide for the North West Mounted Police, and a game warden at Kootenay Lakes Forest Reserve.

In his *Portraits of the premiers: an informal history of British Columbia* (1969) and *The men at Cary Castle: a series of portrait sketches of the lieutenant-governors of British Columbia, 1871 to 1971* (1972) Sydney W. Jackman has written vignettes of major government figures. *Politicians of a pioneering province* (1969) by Russell R. Walker is the anecdotal recollection of a newspaperman about provincial politics since the 1920s. The first of a projected two-volume study, *The rush for spoils: the company province, 1871–1933* (1972) by Martin Robin is a tough and realistic analysis of the province's political tradition in terms of class conflict and business domination that at times becomes a philippic. Recent political life has been quite differently presented in two journalistic accounts: Ronald B. Worley's *The wonderful world of W. A. C. Bennett* (1971), an exercise in hagiography by a close associate, and Pat McGree's *Politics in paradise* (1972), an indictment of the Social Credit régime.

The development of the province's chief urban centres has been chronicled in *A history of Victoria, 1842–1970* (1970) by Harry Gregson; in *Victoria: the fort* (1968) by Derek Pethick, on the fur-trade period up to the 1860s; and in *Vancouver* (1970) by Eric Nicol, which is more of a sensitive dévoté's response to the place than a rigorous analysis of its past. An example of effective local history is *The Queen Charlotte Islands, 1774–1966* (1968) by Kathleen E. Datzell.

10. *The north and the arctic.* The history of the north and arctic continues to be told largely in terms of human endurance and heroic adventure. *The polar passion: the quest for the north pole* (1967) by Farley MOWAT contains selections from the annals of polar exploration since the Norse voyages, interspersed with enthusiastic introductions. In *Arctic fever: the search for the Northwest Passage* (1971) Doug Wilkinson gives a brief survey—adding nothing new—of the exploits of Frobisher, Hearne, Parry, and Franklin. The fate of the latter is the subject of *Arctic breakthrough: Franklin's expeditions, 1819–1847* (1970) by Paul Nanton and *In search for Franklin* (1970) by Leslie H. Neatby, who edited a graphic and moving record of hardship, *Frozen ships: the arctic diary of Johann Miertsching, 1850–1854* (1967). It contains the personal diary of a young German member of the Moravian Brotherhood who was engaged as an interpreter in the search for Franklin and whose ship was lost in ice for three years. In *Campbell of the Yukon* (1970), edited by Clifford P. Wilson, the experiences of a Hudson's Bay Company servant who explored the headwaters of the Laird and Yukon Rivers and in 1852 made an epic march over three thousand miles is told through his own records. *Death on ice* (1972) by Cassie Brown with Harold Horwood narrates the disastrous seal hunt off Newfoundland in 1914 in which seventy-eight sealers perished.

The opening of the Canadian north: 1870–1914 (1971) by Morris Zaslow traces Canadian expansion into the prairie west, the Pacific slope, the Yukon, the northern portions of Québec, Ontario, and the prairie provinces, and into the arctic. Especially informative on policies towards the native peoples and resource development, the book connects the history of the north to the history of southern Canada for the first time in a systematic fashion. *The politics of the Yukon territory, 1898–1909* (1968) by David R. Morrison analyses the agitation for a government more responsive to local needs than the territorial administration that was created and controlled by Ottawa after the gold rush. *Klondike: the last great gold rush: 1896–1899* (2nd ed., 1972) by Pierre Berton is an expanded version of an earlier classic, with additional material comparing Canadian and American institutions on the frontier.

The biography of a physician and surgeon who worked in the eastern arctic and at Aklavik near the mouth of the Mackenzie has been told by Dudley Copland in *Livingstone of the arctic* (1967), while in *Judge of the far north* (1968) Jack Sissons has committed to print some characteristically testy opinions about his work as a judge of the Territorial Court of the Northwest Territories at Yellowknife, his defence of Indians, and his regular feuds with distant officialdom. In *Yellowknife* (1968) Roy Price laments the passing of that frontier town and its decline into respectability. *The big ship: an autobiography of Henry A. Larsen* (1967) has much useful material on the RCMP and on law enforcement in the north as well as a description of the 1940 voyage of the *St Roch*, the first ship to traverse the Northwest Passage from west to east. *Nunaga: my land, my country* (1971) by Duncan Pryde is the autobiographical story of a fur trader who worked among the Eskimo people from 1955 to 1971.

Canada's north (1967) by R. A. J. Phillips and *The political economy of the Canadian north* (1968) by Kenneth J. Rea deal chiefly with the contemporary scene, though both contain some historical material.

11. *Canada in the depression.* A short and lucid introduction to Canadian political life in the depression era can be found in *The politics of chaos: Canada in the thirties* (1972) by Blair Neatby. *The dirty thirties: Canadians in the great depression* (1972) edited by Michiel Horn and *The wretched of Canada: letters to R. B. Bennett, 1930–1935* (1971) edited by L. M. Grayson and Michael Bliss are documentary collections, the latter devoted entirely to pleas for help from those who suffered most. *The great depression: essays and memoirs from Canada and the United States* (1969) compiled by Victor Hoar has a paper on Canadian monetary policy, reflections on the socialist League for Social Reconstruction, and a fine piece by Hugh MACLENNAN on what it was like to be in your twenties in the thirties. *The Mackenzie-Papineau Battalion: Canadian participation in the Spanish Civil War* (1969) by Victor Hoar is an account of the 1,250 men recruited in Canada who fought in the XV International Brigade against Franco. Largely based on interviews with the survivors and some memoirs, it emphasizes the activities at the front rather than Canadian attitudes to the conflict.

The anatomy of a party: the national CCF, 1932–1961 (1969) by Walter Young is a cogent analysis of the origins and evolution of the CCF in terms of the dichotomy between the regenerative, missionary, and educational movement and the party committed to electoral success. *Mitch Hepburn* (1967) by Neil McKenty is a sprightly profile of the rambunctious Liberal premier of Ontario from 1934 to 1942; there are especially informative accounts of Hepburn's stance in the Oshawa Strike, his bitter feud with Mackenzie King, and his association with the mining magnates from northern Ontario. A rather wooden biography, *The life and times of Angus L.* (1969) by John Hawkins, tells the story of Angus L. Macdonald, who was Liberal premier of Nova Scotia from 1933 to 1940 and from 1945 to 1954 and minister of national defence for naval services in King's wartime government. *The man from Margaree: selections from the writings of M. M. Coady* (1971) edited by Alexander F. Laidlaw provides an introduction to the work and ideas of the leader of the Antigonish cooperative movement in the 1930s and 1940s. *The Canadian social inheritance* (1972) by J. A. Blyth is a rambling and disjointed survey of the impact of industrialism on Canada with an emphasis on movements for social reform.

Two monographs on the diplomatic history of the period are Richard N. Kottman's *Reciprocity and the North Atlantic triangle, 1932–1938* (1968), on the Canadian-American trade accords of 1935 and 1938 and the Anglo-American pact of 1938, and Aloysius Balawyder's *Canadian-Soviet relations between the world wars* (1972), a chronicle of both important and inconsequential contacts. *Soldiers of the international: a history of the Communist Party of Canada, 1919–1929* (1968) by William Rodney is a rather arid survey of the party. In the author's view it suffered from an overly zealous adherence to Marxist doctrine and total subordination to Moscow, which customarily misinterpreted Canadian developments. This view is inadvertently illustrated in *Canada and the Russian Revolution: the impact of the world's first socialist revolution on labor and politics in Canada* (1967) by Tim Buck. *Memoirs* (1967) by Dana Wilgress is a slim volume of recollections by a Canadian diplomat who saw extensive service in Russia.

A woman in a man's world (translated by

Joyce Marshall, 1972), the autobiography of Thérèse F. Casgrain, is concerned chiefly with her public life from the 1920s to the 1960s as one of the leaders in Québec of the women's rights movement and the CCF and a founder of the Voice of Women. It is an invaluable addition to the literature of Canadian feminism. Two of the three essays prepared for the Royal Commission on the Status of Women in Canada and published under its auspices as *Cultural tradition and political history of women in Canada* (1971) are rather thin, but the one on the history and status of women in the province of Québec is an able survey and an informative treatment.

12. *Canada, 1939–1972: war, politics, external policy*. C. P. Stacey's *Arms, men and governments: the war policies of Canada, 1939–1945* (1971) is an authoritative examination of Canadian war policies. Based on an exhaustive use of all the available sources, it illuminates nearly every aspect of wartime-Canada's relationship to the allied war organizations, Canadian-American cooperation, supply and development, and the Canadian government's policies on atomic energy and manpower and conscription. It concludes that these policies were not effectively coordinated and that Canada had little influence on major strategic decisions. The publication of those parts of Mackenzie King's voluminous diary dealing with public affairs has been completed with the appearance of *The Mackenzie King record: Volume* II, *1944–1945* (1968); *Volume* III, *1945–1946* (1970) and *Volume* IV, *1947–1948* (1970) edited by J. W. Pickersgill and D. F. Forster. These volumes are indispensable sources for all aspects of Canadian politics and policies in the period. In *The politics of survival: the Conservative Party of Canada, 1939–1945* (1967) J. L. Granatstein has effectively analysed and explained the sorry fate of the Tory party. Divided over the issues of conscription and social welfare, the party in his view was reduced to an ineffectual role in the war years. The same author's *Conscription and the Second World War, 1939–1945: a study in political management* (1968) is a useful short introduction to wartime manpower policies. *McNaughton: Volume* I, *1887–1939*; *Volume* II, *1939–1943*; *Volume* III, *1944–1966* (1969) by John Swettenham is a monumental biography of A. G. L. McNaughton whose career touched many varied fields. He was general officer in the First World War; chief of staff of the army in the inter-war years; inventor of the cathode-ray direction finder; general officer commanding the Canadian forces from 1939 to 1943; minister of national defence; chairman of the Canada-United States Permanent Joint Board on Defence; president of the Atomic Energy Control Board of Canada; and permanent Canadian delegate to the United Nations and chairman of the International Joint Commission. The work is informative on all these activities and is particularly good on the military side of the conscription crisis during the Second World War. Another soldier, E. L. M. Burns, who served as a signal officer and staff captain in the First World War at the Somme and Vimy Ridge and as Commander of the 1st Canadian Corps in Italy in the Second World War, tells his own story in *General Mud: memoirs from two world wars* (1970).

The Reader's Digest Association has compiled a profusely illustrated two-volume study, *The Canadians at war: 1939–45* (1969), which provides a generally satisfactory impressionistic account of events through extracts from books, condensed articles, and specially written essays. An additional volume, *The tools of war: 1939–45* (1969), describes arms and armour and is a useful reference work. Most of the recent literature on the military history of the Second World War, however, is on individual units or branches of the service. In *The gunners of Canada: the history of the Royal Regiment of Canadian Artillery: Volume* II, *1919–1967* (1972), G. W. L. Nicholson concludes his survey of that corps, and in *More fighting Newfoundlanders: a history of Newfoundland's fighting forces in the Second World War* (1970) he completes his survey of the Island's contribution to the allied cause. *The Seaforth Highlanders of Canada, 1919–1965* (1969) by Reginald H. Roy traces the evolving tradition of that regiment and contains striking descriptions of the campaigns before Ortona and the Po Valley. Surveys of particular branches of the services are: *A history of Canadian naval aviation 1918–1962* (1967) by J. D. F. Kealy and E. C. Russell; *Canadian military aircraft* (1970), a picturebook by J. A. Griffin; *Usque ad mare: a history of the Canadian coast guard and marine service* (1968) by Thomas E. Appleton; and *The navy chaplain and his parish* (1967) by Waldo E. L. Smith. *The mouth of the wolf* (1967) by John B. Windsor is the story of George Patterson, a Canadian escaped prisoner-or-war in Italy who learned Italian and became a secret agent in enemy territory.

Mackenzie King's successor is the subject of a sympathetic and sometimes uncritical biography, *Louis St Laurent, Canadian* (1967) by Dale C. Thomson. Though a valuable source of information about national policies from 1941 to 1957, the book emphasizes the chief events of St Laurent's career rather than an assessment of his personality, and it fails to take up a sufficiently detached perspective on either the man or the party he headed. *Pipeline: Trans-Canada and the great debate: a history of business and politics* (1970) by William KILBOURN is a crisp and fast-moving account of the interests and personalities in the great pipeline debate that led to the rejection of the Liberal Party in 1957; it is especially revealing on the outlook of C. D. Howe and his business associates.

Search for identity: Canada, 1945–1967 (1967) by the late Blair Fraser is a topical survey by a veteran press-gallery journalist that concentrates on the personalities and issues in national politics. '*Blair Fraser reports*': *selections, 1944–1968* (1969) edited by John Fraser and Graham Fraser is a collection of Fraser's best news stories and political analyses. In *The horsemen* (1967) C. W. Harvison recalls his years of service with the RCMP from 1919 to 1963. He is especially interesting on national security just before and during the Second World War and on the Igor Gouzenko case.

The politician who carried Newfoundland into union with Canada in 1949 has been assessed in a lively biography, *Smallwood: the unlikely revolutionary* (1968) by Richard Gwyn, which is also an excellent history of the province since confederation. A second edition (1972) brings the story down to Smallwood's resignation. *Newfoundland: island into province* (1967) by St John Chadwick is mainly a constitutional study, informative on international diplomacy and the fisheries disputes but deficient on the period of commission government and confederation. *Politics in Newfoundland* (1971) by S. J. R. Noel is a brilliant examination of the political culture of the Island in the twentieth century and suggests not only the ways in which confederation has changed Newfoundland but also how early and entrenched patterns of political life persist.

The Canadian annual review of public affairs edited by John T. Saywell and Donald F. Forster, published annually since 1961, is a reliable factual guide, especially thorough in its coverage of the political scene. *Vision and indecision* (1968) by Patrick Nicholson is a useful survey of the Diefenbaker-Pearson period, 1956 to 1967. *The distemper of our times: Canadian politics in transition, 1963–1968* (1968) by Peter C. Newman is an episodic and sometimes overtly clever journalistic effort that reports on the political scene during Lester Pearson's primeministership. In *Gentlemen, players, and politicians* (1970) Dalton Camp relates his fortunes in politics from the later 1940s in Nova Scotia to 1957. The first volume of Lester Pearson's autobiography appeared a few months before he died in December 1972. In *Mike: the memoirs of the Right Honourable Lester B. Pearson: Volume* I, *1897–1948* (1972) he recounts his career up to the time he became secretary of state for external affairs. Anecdotal and enlivened by a sense of the incongruous and the ridiculous, the best parts of the book relate to Pearson's work in the foreign service at Geneva, London, and Washington. A favourable and at times adulatory assessment of John Diefenbaker is presented in *The chief* (1968) by Thomas Van Dusen. *The party's over* (1971) by James Johnston and *Night of the knives* (1970) by Robert Coates are two defences of Diefenbaker by staunch loyalists. In her lively and gossipy *Memoirs of a bird in a gilded cage* (1968) Judy LaMarsh recalls her years in national politics from 1960 to 1968 and unburdens herself of confidences large and small. In *Vanier: soldier, diplomat and governor general* (1970) Robert Speaight wrote a warm and sympathetic if not very penetrating portrait of the late governor general.

The historical origins and dimensions of the resurgence of French-Canadian nationalism in the 1960s have been described in *Quebec confronts Canada* (1967) by Edward M. Corbett and *Community in crisis: French-Canadian nationalism in perspective* (1967) by Richard Jones, a perceptive introductory treatment. *The French-Canadians, 1760–1967* (rev. ed., 1968) by Mason Wade contains a new chapter on the period 1945 to 1966. The nature of French-Canadian representation in the cabinets of 1867, 1878, 1896, 1911, 1921,

1935, and 1948 is assessed by different experts in *Cabinet formation and bicultural relations* (1970) edited by F. W. Gibson. A Paris journalist's appraisal of the resurgence of French-Canadian nationalism and its implications for Canadian cooperation with Europe, *Canada: Europe's last chance* (translated by Penny Williams, 1968) by Claude Julien, is flawed by a less-than-thorough grasp of Canadian history. In *The rise of a third party: a study in crisis politics* (1971) Maurice Pinard explains the eruption of the Social Credit movement in Québec in the early 1960s. Pierre Vallières's *White niggers of America: the precocious autobiography of a Quebec 'terrorist'* (translated by Joan Pinkham, 1971) is an indispensable document for understanding the mentality and ideology of one of the founders of the Front de Libération du Québec and for its descriptions of growing up poor in Québec. An equally interesting manifesto indicating how separatists look back upon the history of French Canada is *A history of Quebec: a patriot's handbook* (translated by Baila Markus, 1971) by Léandre Bergeron. *Terror in Québec: case studies of the FLQ* (1970) by Gustave Morf is a psychiatrist's commentary on the personalities of the terrorists.

The emergence of Pierre Elliott Trudeau is reported by Donald Peacock in *Journey to power* (1968) and the election of 1968 is competently described by Martin Sullivan in *Mandate '68* (1968). Anthony Westell's *Paradox: Trudeau as prime minister* (1972) is a description of political events since 1968 and contains few surprises. *Shrug: Trudeau in power* (1971) by Walter Stewart is a more critical treatment.

The crisis of October 1970 has become the subject of several instant histories: *Rumours of war* (1971) by Ron Haggart and Aubrey E. Golden; *Quebec '70: a documentary narrative* (1971) by John T. Saywell, a well-rounded selection of material; and Gérard Pelletier's *The October crisis* (translated by Joyce Marshall, 1971), a defence of the federal government's role. Denis Smith's *Bleeding hearts . . . bleeding country: Canada and the Québec crisis* (1971) and Marcel Rioux's *Quebec in question* (translated by James Boake, 1971) both seek to place the episode in a larger historical and moral perspective.

Canadian provincial politics: the party systems of the ten provinces (1972) edited by Martin Robin consists of ten essays by different scholars elucidating political cultures and traditions. The general emphasis is historical. *Pendulum of power: Canada's federal elections* (1968) by James Murray Beck is a useful source of information on campaigns, issues, and results since 1867. In *Canadian party platforms, 1867–1967* (1968) D. Owen Carrigan has compiled the party manifestos and in *The Canadian dictionary of parliament* (1968) J. K. Johnson presents factual biographies of every member of parliament and senator since confederation. *Fifteen men: Canada's prime ministers from Macdonald to Trudeau* (1969) by Gordon Donaldson is a collection of brief sketches. In *Responsible government in Ontario* (1969) Fred F. Schindeler investigates the working relationships between the executive and the legislature and documents the shift of initiative and influence to the former. *People vs politics* (1969) by Jean A. Laponce is a study of the opinions and attitudes of voters in a British Columbia constituency during the elections of 1963 and 1965. Two works on policy formation are: *Apex of power: the prime minister, the cabinet, and political leadership in Canada* (1971) by Thomas A. Hockin and *Federal-provincial diplomacy: the making of recent policy in Canada* (1972) by Richard Simeon, which centres on recent dominion-provincial conferences on pensions, revenue sharing, and the revision of the constitution.

The evolution of the constitution has been the subject of three studies: *A short history of the Canadian constitution* (1969) by George F. G. Stanley, a routine survey with a strong defence of provincial rights; *Confederation at the crossroads: the Canadian constitution* (1968) by E. Russell Hopkins, over half of which is devoted to the period before the British North America Act; and *The Judicial Committee and the British North America Act: an analysis of the interpretative scheme for the distribution of legislative powers* (1967) by G. P. Browne, a rigorous legal study. *The British tradition in Canadian law* (1969) by Bora Laskin contains four lectures on the transference of the English common law to the provinces, the history and structure of superior courts, the independence of the judiciary, the development of trial by jury, legal education and scholarship, and federalism.

The biography of an institution: the civil service of Canada, 1908–1967 (1972) by J. E.

Hodgetts, William McCloskey, Reginald Whitaker, and V. Seymour Wilson is a full-scale examination of the Civil Service Commission of Canada.

In defence of Canada: peacekeeping and deterrence (1972) by James EAYRS is the third volume of his analysis of Canadian defence and external policy since the First World War. The book deals with the problems of demobilization, Canada's policy towards the United Nations, the Commonwealth, the control of atomic energy, and continental defence in the years 1943 to 1949. The memoirs of Arnold Heeney, *The things that are Caesar's: memoirs of a public servant* (1972) edited by Brian Heeney, are most valuable for what he tells of his years as Canadian ambassador to Washington, though the work is rather weakened by an excess of diplomatic circumspection. Canadian foreign policy since the Second World War has been dominated by the country's inevitable decline in importance on the international stage. This is the underlying theme in *Canada in world affairs: Volume* X, *1957–1959* (1968) by Trevor Lloyd and *Canada in world affairs: Volume* XII, *1961–1963* (1968) by Peyton V. Lyon, which contends that this tendency was also reinforced by Diefenbaker's indecisiveness regarding the acquisition of nuclear warheads and his aggravation of Canadian-American relations. *Canada's changing defence policy, 1957–1963: the problem of a middle power in alliance* (1968) by John B. McLin is an expert assessment of the problems of military cooperation with the United States from the formation of NORAD to the decision of the Pearson government to accept nuclear warheads for Canadian weapons. In *Canada and three crises* (1968) Robert W. Reford examines the role of a middle power in three international crises—over China's off-shore islands, Suez, and Cuba—and stresses the relatively substantial margin for freedom of manoeuvre. The leader of the Canadian delegation to international disarmament conferences between 1960 and 1968, Lt Gen. E. L. M. Burns, reviews his experiences in *A seat at the table: the struggle for disarmament* (1972). A vigorous critique of Canadian policy since the onset of the Cold War from the perspective of the 'new left' is offered in *Partner to Behemoth: the military policy of satellite Canada* (1970) by John W. Warnock. *Peacekeeping: international challenge and Canadian response* (1968) edited by Alastair Taylor, David Cox, and J. L. Granatstein includes essays on the support of Canadian decision-makers for peacekeeping operations under the auspices of the United Nations, the military requirements for such activities, and a survey of Canada's involvement. A rather ineffectual collection, *The Canadian military: a profile* (1972) edited by Hector Massey, contains nine essays, mainly on recent policy, but two are of a historical character: an assessment of the Canadian military tradition and an examination of the influence of the military in shaping the country. In *Canadian foreign policy, 1945–1955: selected speeches and documents* (1971) R. A. MacKay has edited a useful selection of material and in a pamphlet, *Canadian-West Indian union: a forty-year minuet* (1968), Robin W. Winks has explored an obscure strand of Canada's external policy.

The recent review and restatement of Canadian foreign-policy objectives has stimulated a number of critiques and studies. Two of the best are *Trudeau and foreign policy: a study in decision-making* (1972) by Bruce Thordarson, a reliable analysis of the influence of the prime minister in shaping the recent changes, and *Canada's search for new roles: foreign policy in the Trudeau era* (1972) by Peter C. Dobell, which is exceptionally good in assessing the environment in which Canadian policy-makers work. Other contributions to the debate that contain detailed information as well as general insights of historical interest are: *An independent foreign policy for Canada?* (1968) edited by Stephen Clarkson; *Canada in NATO* (1970) by John Gellner; *Half a loaf: Canada's semi-role among developing countries* (1969) by Clyde Sanger; *Alliances and illusions: Canada and the NATO-NORAD question* by Lewis Hertzman, John W. Warnock, and Thomas A. Hockin; *Canadian foreign policy: options and perspectives* (1971) by Dale C. Thomson and Roger F. Swanson; *The Canadian condominium: domestic issues and foreign policy* (1972) by Thomas A. Hockin *et al.*; and *Canada and the Biafran tragedy* (1970) by Andrew Brewin and David Macdonald.

An outline of Canadian diplomatic relations with the United States since 1939 can be found in *The United States and Canada* (1968) by J. R. Mitchell. *The United States and Canada* (1968) by G. M. Craig is a balanced and judicious survey, intended for American readers, concentrating on the historical background of contemporary issues. Aimed at the same audience, but with less effect, is *Canada and the U.S.A.: a background book about internal conflict and the new nationalism* (1972) by Richard J. Walton. *Canadian-American relations: the politics and economics of interdependence* (1967) edited by David A. Baldwin and Frank Smallwood is an informative survey, especially of the economic side of the relationship. *The influence of the United States on Canadian development: eleven case studies* (1972) edited by R. A. Preston is a disparate series of papers ranging from a disquisition on the American impact on Canadian political science to two fine studies on labour history. *Close the 49th parallel etc: the Americanization of Canada* (1970) edited by Ian Lumsden is more polemical than historical, though it is significant for the perspective in which past developments are placed.

13. *Economic history: business, labour, cities.* A collection of sixteen essays, with a major emphasis on the period from the mid-nineteenth century, has been compiled by David S. MacMillan in *Canadian business history: selected studies, 1497–1971* (1972). These develop such topics as the Newfoundland fishery in the seventeenth century; commerce in New France; Scottish mercantile and shipping operations in the North American Colonies, 1760–1825; the business community in Victoria, B.C., and the Montreal business community, 1837–1853; social origins of the business élite, 1870–1885; the views that Canadian businessmen had of their enemies; the entrepreneurial activities of George Stephen and Peter Buchanan, London agent for the Great Western Railway; and the lobbying activities of the B.C. Electric Railway. Two further essays contain valuable bibliographies of the field and a guide to source material. *Westcountrymen in Prince Edward's Isle: a fragment of the great migration* (1967) by Basil J. Greenhill and Ann Giffard studies the ventures, especially ship-building, of Devon merchants in Prince Edward Island in the half-century after Waterloo. In *Canada's first bank: a history of the Bank of Montreal* (1967), Volume II, Merrill Denison completes his officially sponsored study of that institution. In contrast to Volume I (1966), which covered the first twenty-four years in some depth, this volume treats the remaining 126 years rather lightly and fails to continue the study of the intimate association of the bank and the Montreal business community that was a marked feature of the earlier volume. Another officially commissioned history, also based on business records but shorter and more lively, is *The century of the sun: the first hundred years of Sun Life Assurance Company of Canada* (1971) by Joseph Schull. In *A global corporation: a history of the international development of Massey-Ferguson Limited* (1969) E. P. Neufeld deals mainly with the firm's successes and failures in adjusting to the international business environment in the years after 1945. The same author's monumental *The financial system of Canada* (1972), though centred on the recent past, contains a wealth of historical information on the subject.

In a pioneer work, *Ideas in exile: a history of Canadian invention* (1967), J. J. Brown chronicles an impressive list of the products of Canadian ingenuity and invention from Saunders' Marquis wheat, Bell's telephone, and the first diesel locomotive, to Bovril beef-extract, Pablum baby cereal, and the paint roller. He raises the general question of why a country with an impressive record in the field of invention should not have been able to create home industries based on this fact, and concludes that the failure was due to an ingrained conservatism. *Renewing nature's wealth: a centennial history of the public management of lands, forests and wildlife in Ontario, 1763–1867* (1967) by Richard S. Lambert and Paul Pross is a comprehensive study of resource policy in that province. *Canadian parks in perspective* (1970) edited by J. G. Nelson contains an informative essay on national park policy from 1887 to 1914. The first volume of *A history of agriculture in Ontario* (1969) by G. Elmore Reaman covers all aspects of farming from the Huron Indians to the end of the nineteenth century; the second chronicles developments in the twentieth century. *Men and meridians: the history of surveying and mapping in Canada: Volume I, Prior to 1867; Volume II, 1867–1927* (1967) by Don W. Thompson is a densely detailed examination of the subject ranging from Old World conceptions of cartography to the mapping involved in Canada's assertion of sovereignty in the arctic in the 1920s. *The development of Canada's staples, 1867–1939: a documentary collection* (1971) edited by Kevin H. Burley illustrates the problems and evolution of the economics of wheat, energy resources, pulp and paper, and mining.

The biographies of businessmen have dwelt upon the colourful and the adventurous. *Honest Ed's story: the crazy rags to riches story of Ed Mirvish* (1972) by Jack Batten is a fragmentary journalistic impression of the Toronto merchant. *Bush pilot with a briefcase* (1972) by Ronald Keith is a life of Grant McConachie, who became president of Canadian Pacific Airlines. It reads like a boy's adventure story and is uninformative on his presidency and on such subjects as the competition with Trans Canada Airlines. More rewarding for its material on business life is *O'Brien: from waterboy to one million a year* (1967) by Scott Young and Astrid Young, a biography of Michael John O'Brien who made a fortune in mining claims and railway construction and was one of the founders of the Montreal Canadiens hockey club. A businessman who worked for Massey-Ferguson in Europe and South America, James S. Duncan, sketches his own portrait in *Not a one-way street* (1971). *Beaverbrook* (1972) by A. J. P. Taylor is rather sketchy on Max Aitken's career in Canadian business life before the First World War. *The book and life of a little man: reminiscences of Frederick Mendel* (1972) by Frederick S. Mendel is the autobiography of the founder of Intercontinental Packers and a well-known art collector.

Two sound treatments of professional groups are provided by D. W. Gullett in *A history of dentistry in Canada* (1971) and by H. E. MacDermot in *One hundred years of medicine in Canada (1867–1967)* (1967). In *Before the age of miracles* (1972) W. V. Johnston relates the experiences of a country doctor in rural Ontario in the 1920s and 1930s. T. F. Rose's *From shaman to modern medicine: a century of the healing arts in British Columbia* (1972) is a short informative chronicle.

Canadian labour history has been written largely in terms of trade-union development and political struggles rather than as the social history of a class. In *The trade union movement of Canada, 1827–1959* (1967) Charles Lipton chronicles the evolution of the movement from a Marxist point of view and in terms of strikes, organizing campaigns, legislation, and political battles. In *Times of trouble: labour unrest and industrial conflict in Canada, 1900–66* (1971) Stuart Jamieson outlines and accounts for the pattern of industrial unrest in relation to both permanent and temporary forces at work. Based almost entirely on secondary sources, the study is nevertheless a first-rate synthesis and reliable guide to the topic. *No power greater: a century of labour in British Columbia* (1967) by Paul A. Phillips presents a detailed survey of labour in a province with a long tradition of radicalism and unstable industrial relations. *International unionism: a study in Canadian-American relations* (1967) by John H. G. Crispo includes a substantial historical section on the background of American and international unions in Canada that is based on the debatable contention that such unions introduced labour organization into the country earlier than would have been the case without this American assistance, and that the American unions strengthened the Canadian movement generally. Two major works attempt to describe and explain the complex relationship between labour and the Canadian political tradition: *Radical politics and Canadian labour, 1880–1939* (1968) by Martin Robin surveys the relations between the trade unions and socialist movements, and *Canadian labour in politics* (1968) by Gad Horowitz analyses the relations between labour and the CCF from 1932 to 1961. This straightforward historical analysis has a lengthy introductory discussion on the reasons for the persistence of a fringe of tory radicalism in Canada in contrast to the United States. *The Brandon packers' strike: a tragedy of errors* (1971) by G. W. MacDowell is an analysis of labour relations and labour legislation arising from a recent strike with an account of the inquiry into the dispute. In *Canadian labour in transition* (1971) edited by Richard U. Miller and Fraser Isbester, eight experts assess the evolution of the Canadian industrial relations system.

By far the best book to appear on urban history is *Montreal: a brief history* (1969) by John Irwin Cooper, an all-too-short account, which deals with the internal texture of the city, the relations of French and English, social classes, reform movements, and the city's commercial power. *Victorian Toronto, 1850–1900: pattern and process of growth* (1970) by Peter G. Goheen is a specialized study by an urban geographer of the patterns of growth within the city in a period of rapid industrialization and population increase; it is particularly effective in showing how social classes and occupational groups were spacially segregated. The pattern of industrialism in the same period is examined by another study in historical geography, *Spacial evolution of manufacturing: southern Ontario, 1851–1890* (1972) by James M. Gilmour. *Nineteenth-century cities: essays on the new urban history* (1969) edited by S. Thernstrom and Richard Sennett contains an essay on the social structure of Hamilton, Ont., in the mid-nineteenth century based on a computerized study of assessment roles and census reports.

More conventional in approach but still rewarding for the local atmosphere they evoke are: *Montreal: from mission colony to world city* (1969) by Leslie Roberts; *Toronto* (1967) by Bruce West; and *The story of Toronto* (1971) by George P. de T. Glazebrook. *Fighting back: urban renewal in Trefann Court* (1972) by Graham Fraser is a journalist's detailed account of the conflicts between urban planners and residents over the future of a Toronto neighbourhood in a five-year period.

14. *Ethnic groups.* The history of immigrants and ethnic groups other than French or English is becoming a topic of growing interest, partly because of their increasing consciousness of ethnicity and also because of the claims put forward by some spokesmen for greater recognition of these groups in a country officially defined as bilingual. The *Report of the Royal Commission on bilingualism and biculturalism: Book* IV, *The cultural contribution of the other ethnic groups* (1969) is a comprehensive survey of patterns of immigration; social, political, and economic adjustment; the preservation of original language and culture; education; and contributions to arts, letters, and crafts.

Historical accounts of various groups in specific areas are: *Ethnic groups in Upper Canada* (1972) by Jean Burnet; *Strangers entertained: a history of ethnic groups in British Columbia* (1971) by John Norris; and *Land of the second chance: a history of ethnic groups in southern Alberta* (1972) by Howard Palmer, based on previously published newspaper articles.

There are several good recent histories of individual groups. *The Doukhobors* (1968) by George Woodcock and Ivan Avakumovic is readable, comprehensive, and sensitive to the larger questions that the experience of this minority in Canada raises about Canadian tolerance of different peoples. *The Blacks in Canada* (1971) by Robin W. Winks is a massive, densely detailed, and exhaustively documented work on a people who have always lived on the margin of Canadian life. *Vilni zemli (free lands): the Ukrainian settlement of Alberta* (1969) by J. G. MacGregor is an imaginative narrative of immigration and settlement from 1891 to the 1920s, excellent on the divisions, especially the religious differences, within the Ukrainian community. *Hutterian Brethren* (1967) by John W. Bennett is a cultural anthropologist's analysis of the values, social controls, and economic and social organization of that group in both Canada and the United States.

Not in the same class, but still useful both for factual information and in some cases as reflections of the ways in which representatives of ethnic groups look back on their own histories, are: *The Ukrainians in Canada* (1967) by Ol'ha Woycenko; *Slovaks in Canada* (1967) by Joseph M. Kirschbaum; *Lithuanians in Canada* (1967) by Pr. Gaida, *et al.*; *The Poles in Canada* (1968) by Ludwik Kos-Rabcewicz-Zubowski; *The Czechs and Slovaks in Canada* (1968) by John Gellner and John Smerek; *The Icelanders in Canada* (1967) by W. J. Lindal; *The Jewish community in Canada: Vol.* I, *A history* (1970) by Stuart E. Rosenberg; *The Poles in Manitoba* (1967) by V. Turek; *History and integration of Poles in Canada* (1967) by William B. Makowski; *A pictorial history of the Doukhobors* (1969) by Koozma J. Tarasoff; and *Vancouver's Svenskar: a history of the Swedish community in Vancouver* (1970) by Irene Howard.

Slavs in Canada: Volume II, *Proceedings of the second national conference on Canadian Slavs* (1968) and *Slavs in Canada: Volume* III, *Proceedings of the third national conference on Canadian Slavs* (1971), edited by Cornelius J. Jaenen, contain highly specialized research papers, some on historical subjects.

The old colony Mennonites: dilemmas of ethnic minority life (1969) by Calvin Wall Redekop is a sociologist's comparison of the conservative groups in Mexico and Canada. *Lost fatherland: the story of the Mennonite emigration from Soviet Russia (1921–1927)* (1967) by John B. Toews is on the background of the migration from Russia, especially the Ukraine, after the First World War.

15. *Education; intellectual life; journalism.* A comprehensive textbook survey by nine contributors, *Canadian education: a history* (1970)—edited by D. Wilson, R. M. Stamp, and Philippe Audet—attempts to treat educational history as a facet of social history. At times it succeeds, as in its coverage of the 1870–1914 period and its treatment of the conflicts over religion and language, but sometimes this aim is submerged in a dreary chronicle of legislative enactments. More restricted thematic surveys are *A brief history of Canadian education* (1968) by F. Henry Johnson, which emphasizes public elementary and secondary schooling, and *Industry and education: a century of Canadian development* (1969) by O. J. Firestone. *Quiet evolution: a study of the educational system in Ontario* (1967) by Robin S. Harris is a lucid survey of developments over the past century, with some modest proposals for reform. Of unprecedented monumentality, W. G. Fleming's *Ontario's educative society* (1971–2), in eight volumes, covers the expansion during the 1960s.

Studies of particular universities, generally chronological and heavily factual, are: *Of mud and dreams: the University of Waterloo, 1957–1967* (1967) by James Scott; *Queen's University at Kingston* (1967) by H. Pearson Gundy; *The University of Saskatchewan: a personal history* (1970) by W. P. Thompson; *Brandon College: a history, 1899–1967* (1969) by C. G. Stone and F. V. Garrett; *The Georgian spirit: the story of Sir George Williams University* (1967) by Henry F. Hall; and *Behind the hill: a book about UNB* (1967) by Scott Wade. The backgrounds of three components of the University of Toronto are related in *The first forty years, 1914–55: Connaught Medical Research Laboratories, University of Toronto* (1969) by R. D. Defries; *An uncommon fellowship: the story of Hart House* (1969) by Ian Montagnes; and *Henry Carr—revolutionary* (1969) by Father Edmund J. M. McCorkell, a biography of the educator who brought St Michael's College into full federation with the university and played a major role in founding the Pontifical Institute of Medieval Studies. *Catholic post-secondary education in English-speaking Canada: a history* (1971) by Lawrence K. Shook is exhaustive.

The social history of public education in one western Canadian province has been examined in *Schools of the foothills province: the story of public education in Alberta* (1967) by John W. Chalmers and in *The little white schoolhouse* (1968) and *Pulse of the community* (1970) John C. Charyk studies the rise and fall of the one-room rural school. *John Jessop: gold seeker and educator* (1971) by F. Henry Johnson is a biography of the founder of the British Columbia school system. *A family writ large* (1971) by Cedric W. Sowby is the memoir of the headmaster of the élite school, Upper Canada College, in the period 1949–65. *Canada's RMC: a history of the Royal Military College* (1969) by Richard Arthur Preston relates the development of this officer-training institution.

Teachers' rise to professional status has been described in two officially sponsored books: *High button bootstraps* (1968) by Doris French, an account of the Womens' Teachers Federation of Ontario, and *Teachers of the foothills province: the story of the Alberta Teachers' Association* (1968) by John W. Chalmers.

Two autobiographies that reveal a good deal about the world of the university scholar and teacher are *A slice of Canada: memoirs* (1967) by Watson KIRKCONNELL and *My first seventy-five years* (1967) by A. R. M. LOWER. In *A new theory of value: the Canadian economics of H. A. Innis* (1972) Robin Neill gives an erudite analysis of the ideas of this influential economic historian and his interpretation of the peculiar characteristics of the country's economic development. Recent literature in the humanities and social sciences is evaluated by several contributors to *Scholarship in Canada, 1967: achievement and outlook* (1968) edited by R. H. Hubbard. The history of an institution that is indispensable to historical writing has been briefly told in *Archives: mirror of Canada's past* (1972) compiled by the staff of the Public Archives of Canada and illustrated by reproductions of documents, pictures, and maps from its collection. *Forum: Canadian life and letters, 1920–1970: selections from 'The Canadian Forum'* (1972) edited by J. L. Granatstein and Peter Stevens reprints two hundred and fifty poems, short stories, and articles on politics, society, and literature from the past fifty years of that journal. The Province of Ontario *Royal Commission on Book Publishing: background papers* (1972) contains nineteen studies with a historical focus, including one on the development of trade-book publishing in

Canada and another on the authorization of textbooks for Ontario schools since 1846.

Though W. H. Kesterton provides a factual summary of the history of Canadian newspapers in *A history of journalism in Canada* (1967), most of the recent literature on the subject concentrates on individual newspapermen: *The paper tyrant: John Ross Robertson of the 'Toronto Telegram'* (1971) by Ron Poulton; *Ottawa editor* (1967), the experiences and opinions of Charles A. Bowman, who was in charge of the Ottawa *Citizen* from 1914 to 1945; *A gentleman of the press* (1969) by Floyd S. Chalmers, the life of Col. J. B. Maclean who founded the Maclean-Hunter Publishing Company; *While I still remember* (1968) by Wilfrid Eggleston, the autobiography of a newspaperman, writer, and broadcaster who was on the secretariat of the Rowell-Sirois Commission and chief press censor during the Second World War; and *Dafoe of the 'Free Press'* (1968) by Murray Donnelly, an assessment of a personality more than a systematic treatment of John W. Dafoe's stand on public issues. In *News and the Southams* (1968) Charles BRUCE set out to establish whether common ownership of various papers imposed editorial unanimity and found, by examining the coverage of such events as the rise of Aberhart in Alberta, that it did not. In *Those were the days: the days of Benny Nicholas and the lotus eaters* (1969) Peter Stursberg describes life with the editor of the Victoria *Times* and also reveals a good deal about the city and its society in the 1930s.

The politics of Canadian broadcasting, 1920–1951 (1969) by Frank W. Peers is a thorough analysis of the evolution of broadcasting policy and the conflicts between the groups that were opposed and those that were committed to the idea of broadcasting as an instrument of national purpose. In *Mister Broadcasting: the Ernie Bushnell story* (1971) Peter Stursberg sketches the career of a veteran executive with the CBC.

16. *The arts.* One of the major movements in Canadian painting has been appraised in *The Group of Seven* (1970) by Peter Mellen and in *The Group of Seven* (1970) by Dennis Reid. The former, which is skeptical of the claims of originality made by members of the group and its nationalistic interpreters, concentrates on a discussion of the pictures, which are superbly reproduced. The latter is a catalogue with an extensive introduction closely based on manuscript sources. *There is no finality: a story of the Group of Seven* (1972) by Harry Hunkin is apparently intended for juvenile readers and repeats most of the myths recent critics have dispelled. *Tom Thomson: the Algonquin years* (1969) by Ottelyn Addison and Elizabeth Harwood is yet another look at the mystery of the painter's death. *The nude in Canadian painting* (1972) by Jerrold Morris is introduced by an essay that tries to explain the unfavourable response that Canadians generally have accorded pictures of nudes in spite of the fact that Canadian artists have created some excellent ones: there are eight colour plates and sixty-four black-and-white reproductions. *Four decades: the Canadian Group of Painters and their contemporaries, 1930–1970* (1972) by Paul Duval, a factual survey of the art scene since the disbanding of the Group of Seven, is a useful antidote to the convention that Canadian painting ended with that school. *Contemporary Canadian painting* (1972) by William Withrow is an introductory reference guide to twenty-four painters active since 1945. It contains biographical information about them, statements by the individual artists of their purposes, and reproductions of their most representative work.

A number of assessments and biographies of individual artists have appeared. *Thomas Davies* (1972), edited with an introduction by R. H. Hubbard, is the catalogue of an exhibition organized by the National Gallery of Canada. It includes an interesting essay by C. P. Stacey on the life of this military artist who made several tours of duty in Canada in the second half of the eighteenth century and executed some fine water colours of the domestic life of the Indians and settlers as well as of natural scenery. R. H. Hubbard is also the editor of *Thomas Davies in early Canada* (1972), which reproduces twenty-nine of these pictures in colour. *The artist was a young man: the life story of Peter Rindisbacher* (1970) by Alvin M. Josephy Jr is a study of the first competent artist to depict the people and environment of Red River in the early nineteenth century. The Prince Edward Island painter who did the famous group portrait of the Fathers of Confederation and who was intimately involved in Canadian artistic circles at the turn of the century is the subject of a full-scale biography by Moncrieff Williamson, *Robert Harris, 1849–1919: an unconventional biography* (1971). J. Russell Harper, who wrote the valuable and handsome *Painting in Canada: a history* (1966), is the author of *Paul Kane's frontier, including 'Wanderings of an artist among the Indians of North America' by Paul Kane* (1972), a lavishly illustrated book containing a scholarly introduction on the artist as well as a carefully annotated edition of his own account of his travels in the west in the mid-nineteenth century. Harper's *Early painters and engravers in Canada* (1970) contains over four thousand biographical entries on artists who worked in Canada before 1867. In *M.E. a portrayal of Emily Carr* (1969) by Edythe Hembroff-Schleicher the author reminisces about her friendship with the British Columbia artist in the early 1930s and includes an exchange of correspondence between them. *The art of Alex Colville* (1972) by Helen J. Dow is the first large-scale survey of the work of this 'magic realist', but the text is unnecessarily allusive and confusing. *Lawren Harris* (1969), edited by R. G. P. Colgrove and Bess Harris, includes selections from the artist's own writings and full-colour reproductions of his pictures but is singularly lacking in interpretation and biographical information.

Nineteenth-century plays, actors, and travelling troups are chronicled in *A stage in our past: English-language theatre in eastern Canada from the 1790s to 1914* (1968) by Murray D. Edwards, a survey most suggestive of shifting popular tastes and fashions. *Canada's National Ballet* (1967) by Herbert Whittaker is uncritical and wooden. *Lawrence Doyle, the farmer poet of Prince Edward Island: a study in local songmaking* (1971) by Edward Ives is a notable contribution to folk culture. *Christmas mumming in Newfoundland: essays in anthropology, folklore and history* (1969) edited by Herbert Halpert and G. M. Story contains various essays of this folk custom in a broad social and historical setting. *Creative Canada: a biographical dictionary of 20th-century creative and performing artists* in two volumes (1971 and 1972)—compiled by the Reference Division, McPherson Library, University of Victoria—is an informative reference work that is to be followed by a third volume.

17. *Some bibliographies and reference works published between 1967 and 1972.* Designed for the general reader, *Read Canadian* (1972) edited by Robert Fulford, Dave GODFREY, and Abraham Rotstein contains articles on Canadian books about many aspects of Canadian life and letters. However, the section on recommended history books—and, one suspects, on other subject areas as well—is rather eccentric. *The Oxford companion to Canadian history and literature* (1967) by Norah Story contains over two thousand entries, conveniently cross-referenced, on all subjects and figures with useful bibliographical commentaries.

Two up-to-date guides to both general and specialized readings are *Bibliography of Canadian bibliographies* (2nd ed., 1972) compiled by Douglas Lochhead and *Reference aids in Canadian history in the University of Toronto Library* (1972) compiled by Jane Clark.

The inventories of two libraries that are good general bibliographies of books and periodicals are Harvard University Library's *Canadian history and literature* (1972) and the Royal Commonwealth Society Library's *Subject catalogue: Volume* v, *The Americans* (G. K. Hall, 1971).

Recently published listings on particular localities include the series *Canadian local histories to 1950: a bibliography*, of which two volumes have appeared: *The Atlantic provinces: Newfoundland, Nova Scotia, New Brunswick, Prince Edward Island* (1967) by William F. E. Morley and *La province de Québec* (1971) by André Beaulieu. These carry full bibliographical descriptions and many analytical notes and give selected locations of the material. *Northern Ontario, a bibliography* (1968) compiled by Loraine Spencer and Susan Holland contains a section on historical literature. *Local histories of Ontario municipalities published in the years 1958–1969* (1969) by Barbara B. Aitkin mainly lists city and county histories. The 4-volume *Catalogue of the Library of the Arctic Institute of North America, Montreal, Canada* (1968) contains some 70,000 entries in many languages relating to the arctic and sub-arctic. The *Catalogue of the library: Volume* II, *Voyages and travels* (1968) of the National Maritime Museum (London) lists over 1,200 books on the subject from the Vikings to the present. Valuable guides to the history of the prairie provinces are *Bibliography of Manitoba, from holdings in the Legislative Library of Manitoba* (1970) compiled by Marjorie Morley and the projected *Catalogue of the Glenbow Historical*

Library by G. K. Hall, to be published in four volumes. Two chronological and annotated lists of published material on the Pacific coast are *Navigations, traffiques & discoveries, 1774–1848: a guide to publications relating to the area now British Columbia* (1970) compiled by Gloria M. Strathern and Margaret H. Edwards and *A bibliography of British Columbia: laying the foundations, 1849–1899* (1968) by Barbara J. Lowther.

The following are useful guides to particular subjects and themes: *Canadian urban history: a selected bibliography* (1972) by Gilbert A. Stelter; *A reading guide to Canada in world affairs, 1945–1971* (1972) compiled by Laurence Motiuk and Madeline Grant; *A bibliography of Iroquoian literature* (1969) compiled by Paul L. Weinman; *Canadian ethnic groups: a selected bibliography of ethno-cultural groups in Canada and in the province of Ontario* (1972) by Andrew Gregorovich; *A bibliography of the Group of Seven* (1971) by Dennis Reid; *The Brock bibliography of Canadian plays: 1900–1972* (1972) by Richard Cummings, *et al.*, which lists no less than nine hundred items; and *A bibliography of higher education in Canada: supplement, 1971* (1971) by Robin S. Harris. *A check list of Canadian literature and background materials, 1628–1960* (1972) by R. E. Watters has been revised and includes previously overlooked and other additional material. The Lexicographical Centre for Canadian English at the University of Victoria, B.C., has published *Dictionary of Canadianisms on historical principles* (1967), which has historical notes on distinctive Canadian names and expressions. CB

History studies in French. Six years is a short period of time in the history of a people, even if they have been filled with events of various kinds that have demanded moments of reflection, a new departure, another way of doing and living the same thing. It is amazing how little influence contemporary events and happenings have had on what historians, professional and otherwise, write about. For instance in 1967 Canadians of all sorts celebrated the hundredth anniversary of the birth of their country in the midst of one of the most expensive international extravaganzas ever experienced. One would have expected that many historians would seize upon the occasion, but they did not. The same may be said for the historical aspects of terrorism in the Québec calamity of October 1970 or the radicalization of the labour movement in 1971–2. It would be interesting to launch a study on what moves historians to choose the subject matter they do.

In the period studied for this survey, some 200 books were classified and analysed. Many were not worth the exercise, since they constituted accumulations of notes and impressions that had been gathered over the years and passed on to countless generations of students. Many of the works under review reflected limited research: too often the newspaper was the most important source of information. This may be owing to the lack of sources; the apparently unsurmountable difficulties in setting up proper archival procedures; the reluctance of French Canadians to part with their family papers, possessions, and heirlooms; and the constant jurisdictional battles between La Bibliothèque nationale and Les Archives nationales. Surely if the study of history is to proceed in Québec, some settlement of this dispute and the development of effective working instruments will have to be achieved soon.

Another evident weakness in the books examined is the inadequate editorial attention many of them received. Too often one had the impression that the publisher presented the text more or less as it was submitted without making any editorial improvements. When an author fails to give a manuscript unity, to enrich it with adequate footnotes and bibliographies, or to give it an overall plan and direction, he is in need of good editorial assistance. Many of these books are mere drafts of what they might have been if they had received some editorial polish. Perhaps too many books are being published in Québec: quality has given way to quantity.

The narrowness of scholarly interests is also a matter of grave concern. There is an overwhelming preoccupation with political and constitutional history, with biography in a traditional mould, and with historical polemics. This may be because the period under review coincides with the end of La Révolution tranquille and the beginning of the era of *laissez-faire* federalism and liberalism. Consequently French-Canadian intellectuals have assumed the responsibility of *une politique de combat*, which keeps in the foreground the on-going struggles of their people. It is sad that they have not noticed that the struggle has shifted and that the 1960s gave rise to the americanization and internationalization of Québec—a difficult process of adaptation to which historians could have contributed. Instead they left it to television.

What is well done, however, is extremely well done. This can be seen in the many new editions of the works of distinguished scholars: Michel BRUNET's *Canadians et Canadiens* (1972); Guy FRÉGAULT's and Marcel TRUDEL's *Histoire du Canada par les textes, Tome I* (1971), and Michel Brunet's second volume in the same series; Robert RUMILLY's monumental *Histoire de la Province de Québec*; and Guy Fregault's various works on diverse aspects of the history of New France. Excellence comes shining through as well in the publications of younger historians whose works are noted below.

However, this writer is convinced that the best history written in Québec during this period, and today, is the result of team work. Here and there in Québec, historians in the universities, in the pre-university educational system, and even in the civil service have been coming together to write history. The result is often breathtaking. The most notable example of this process of historical writing is 'L'équipe du Boréal Express', a group that includes scholars from various universities, civil servants, and teachers from CEGEPS (Collège d'enseignement général et professionel) and high schools who conduct and publish historical projects. Their contribution to historical writing in Québec has been not only spectacular but also interesting, engrossing, and enriching in its imaginative search for subject matter and its capacity to relate their work to the interests of young people. Another such group is at the Université du Québec.

For the purposes of this entry the following general categories have been established: 1. Textbooks, surveys, and bibliographies; 2. Essays, collections, and proceedings; 3. New France; 4. Québec and Canada, 1760–1867; 5. Québec and Canada, 1867–1945; 6. Modern Québec and Canada. In addition specialized works have been grouped together in the following sections: 7. Social and economic history, urban studies; 8. Institutions; 9. The professions; 10. The arts, literature, sports, and leisure; 11. Biographies, autobiographies, memoirs, and speeches.

1. *Textbooks, surveys, and bibliographies.* Fifteen important textbooks and surveys were published in Québec between 1967 and 1972. Some of the most interesting are noted below.

General de Gaulle, the 'chansonniers québécois', and some films seem to have rekindled the spark of interest that France has always kept alive about Québec, even if it is somewhat bruised in its collective soul. In the 1960s many French intellectuals paid visits of various lengths to Québec and proceeded to explain French Canadians to themselves and to the world. As a result French publishers have reprinted Marcel Giraud's four-volume *Histoire du Canada* (4th ed., 1967), while Les Éditions du Seuil issued *Canada* (1967) by Robert Hollier. These general histories of French Canada are certainly adequate introductions but, like all Canadian histories emanating from France, they tend to emphasize the French dimension of Canadian life and history as opposed to its American dimension.

Charles-Marie Boissonnault emphasized the military elements in French-Canadian life—a new approach—in his *Histoire politico-militaire des Canadiens français: 1763–1945* (1968). Jean-Jacques Lefebvre's *Le Canada, l'Amérique: géographique, historique, biographique, littéraire* was reissued in 1969. In 1845–8 F.-X. Garneau published his monumental *Histoire du Canada depuis sa découverte jusqu'à nos jours*, written in answer to Durham's claim that French Canadians did not have any history and documenting the continuous development of the French-Canadian people. It was republished in six volumes under the title *Histoire du Canada français* (1969). Another famous work was reissued by Les Éditions du Boréal Express: Sir Thomas Chapais's *Cours d'histoire du Canada: 1760–1867* in eight volumes, first published in 1919–33.

The three best modern surveys were two titles produced by the talented young scholars of Boréal Express: *Histoire: 1534–1968* (1969) and *Canada-Québec: synthèse historique* (1970), which combine historical documents with a flowing narrative; they are amply and attractively illustrated and unburdened by unnecessary footnotes. The same excellence and concern with the relationship of Québec's past with its ever-changing present are also apparent in *Histoire des Canadas* by Rosario Bilodeau, Robert

Comeau, Denise Julien, and André Gosselin.

Jean Hamelin, a historian at Laval in the post-New France period and in modern history, has published an excellent survey, *Le Canada français: son évolution historique* (1972).

The most important bibliographical source published in this period is *Guide d'histoire du Canada* (1969) by André Beaulieu, Jean Hamelin, and Benoît Bernier. Extremely well organized and easy even for the uninitiated to use, it is indispensable to the proper development of any knowledge of Québec and Canada. Philippe Garigue, writing in 1956 for an English-speaking audience, presented his *Bibliographical introduction to the study of French Canada* (1956). In 1967 he published the useful *Bibliographie du Québec (1955–1965)*, to which he added articles in periodicals and reviews dealing with such subjects as population, social institutions, historical evolution of ideologies, and general culture. Of special interest, and dealing specifically with the period 1867 to 1970, is *Histoire du Québec: bibliographie sélective* (1970) by R. Durocher and P. A. Linteau. Le Conseil du Livre, which is the official organization for all book publishers in Québec, published in 1968 *Catalogue de l'édition canadienne au Canada français*. A new edition grouping some 10,000 titles was made available in April 1973. Of more limited scope and for specialized interests are: *Les imprimés dans le Bas-Canada, 1801–1810* (1967) by John Hare and Jean-Pierre Wallot; *Bibliographie de la péninsule du Québec-Labrador* (1968) prepared by the Centre d'études nordiques de l'Université Laval; and *Bibliographie sommaire sur la confédération* by Cameron Nish (1967).

2. *Essays, collections, and proceedings.* Countless pamphlets, collections of essays, and papers read at various seminars and conferences descend upon the Québec public yearly in a never-ending stream. For the most part the titles included in this entry deal with the perpetual themes of French-Canadian concern: Where are we going and how are we going to get there? Some are angry books; others tend to be more philosophical; while still others point in various directions that unfortunately seem to lead nowhere. The past tends to be used to account for anger rather than to demonstrate human courses of action. An exception to this trend, however, is Maurice Séguin's *L'idée d'indépendance au Québec* (1968). He demonstrates that the essential element of the French-Canadian community has been the driving force to complete its history; its essential weakness, this incomplete development. Lionel GROULX had the same preoccupation in his various writings but found the solution at another level, the spiritual—a fact that is aptly demonstrated by Benoît Lacroix in his *Lionel Groulx: textes choisis* (1967).

Gérard Bergeron, with his usual clarity, analyses the historical evolution of the political/social crisis of French Canada in the 1960s in *Les Canadiens français après deux siècles de patience* (1967) and traces the continuity of the French-Canadian dilemma. The almost insurmountable difficulties in two peoples' occupying the same space and country are etched very well by Michel Brunet in his *Québec-Canada anglais: deux itinéraires, un affrontement* (1968). For Jean-Louis Roy, the brilliant young director of McGill University's French Canada Studies Programme, the need to be masters in their own house is a recurring theme of Québec history and he analyses it well in his *Maîtres chez nous: dix années d'Action française* (1968). More polemical is Léo Tremblay's *La liberté ou la déchéance et la mort* (1969). The most impressive book on the evolutionary theme—and the most maddening—is without any doubt Léandre Bergeron's *Petit manuel d'histoire du Québec* (1970). A well-known radical and an excellent writer, Bergeron has created a salutary popular history that condemns the previous historical emphasis on church-state relations, on political squabbles among the French-Canadian bourgeoisie, and on other élites of French-Canadian society to the neglect of the intrinsic dynamism of the people. No book has been more influential with all Québécois regardless of age or class since the publication of *Les insolences du Frère Untel*. This is a 'document de combat' and as such has played a great part in making Québécois aware of their essential weaknesses, which are caused as much by themselves as by others.

The sixtieth anniversary of the founding of *Le Devoir*, Québec's most distinguished newspaper, provided the occasion for a score of Québec pundits (Fernand DUMONT, Claude Morin, Léon Dion *et al.*) to think about their society and its relation to others. That the event occurred in the midst of the terror of the October crisis of 1970 makes of *Le Québec qui se fait* (1971) edited by Claude Ryan another important book in the period under review—the only book that dealt seriously with the decade 1960–70. The first part discusses the October crisis and the second deals with the instruments—constitutional, social, cultural, etc.—needed to forge a new destiny as Canada transforms itself from 'two races' to 'two nations', in the words of Claude Ryan. Pierre Vallières's *Nègres blancs d'Amérique* (1968) has also had a profound influence on the Québec of today. In its autobiographical parts it vividly portrays a deprived life and society in Québec that all too many have been familiar with. Its honesty, vitality, and sad despair are matched only by Gabrielle ROY's *Bonheur d'occasion*. Of lesser importance—because of the narrow range of the authors' experience—are Solange Chaput-Rolland's *Regards 1967: Québec, année zéro* (1968)—which appeared in an English translation by Gretta Chambers under the title *Reflections: Quebec, year one* (1968)—and Claude Julien's *Le Canada, dernière chance de l'Europe* (1968).

3. *New France*. In the period 1967–72 the chief concern of historians was New France. Some twenty-three titles appear to be worth mentioning. The following are interesting introductions to the period: *La Nouvelle France* (1967) by Denis Héroux *et al.* and *Inititations à la Nouvelle France* (1967) by Marcel Trudel. As for the day-to-day living of the *habitants* and the scope of their utensils and the like, the reader can find an excellent account in Robert-Lionel SÉGUIN's *La civilisation traditionnelle de 'L'habitant' aux XVIIe et XVIIIe siècles* (1967). See also his *Le costume civil en Nouvelle-France* (1968), *Divertissements en Nouvelle-France* (1968), and his interesting study of moral attitudes and behaviour, *La vie libertine en Nouvelle-France* (2 vols, 1972). However, the most important and complete social history remains Émile Salone's *La colonisation de la Nouvelle-France: étude sur les origines de la nation canadienne-française*, first published in Paris in 1905 and reissued in 1970. See also Lucien Campeau's *Monumenta Novae Franciae I: la première mission d'Acadie 1602–1616* (1967) and G. E. Baillargeon's *La survivance du régime seigneuriale à Montréal: un régime qui ne veut pas mourir* (1968). André Vachon provides a wide panorama in his excellent *L'administration de la Nouvelle France, 1627–1760* (1971), to which theme and concern Gustave LANCTOT lends his expertise and talent in *L'administration de la Nouvelle France* (1971). André Lachance has presented good documents in his *Textes et documents pour servir à l'étude de l'histoire économique et sociale de la Nouvelle France* (1969). Among the many monographs dealing with the Indians, the best work was done in France by Raymond Douville and J. D. Casanova: *Vie quotidienne des Indiens du Canada à l'époque de la colonisation française* (1967).

In his thorough study, *Les Juifs de la Nouvelle France* (1968), Denis Vaugeois concludes that Jews greatly assisted the British conquest by serving as suppliers to the British. Another group is studied by Cameron Nish in *Les Bourgeois Gentilhommes* (1969), which adds some new fuel to the longlasting controversy about the presence of a 'dynamic' bourgeoisie in New France. Explorers have not been neglected and the most interesting of the works published on them are Antoine Champagne's *Les La Vérendrye et le poste de l'ouest* (1969) and his further study in 1971 on the same subject (*Nouvelles études sur . . .*); *Nouveaux documents sur Champlain et son époque, 1560–1622* by Robert Le Blant and René Beaudry; Marcel Trudel's *Jacques Cartier: textes choisis et présentés . . .* (1968); and René Beaudry's *Marc Lescarbot* (1968). In the same series of short studies, Classiques Canadiens, Marcel Trudel offered *Samuel de Champlain* (1968) and Guy and Lilianne Frégault *Frontenac* (1967).

Most biographical writing on various personages of new France appeared in biographical collections. However there are four book-length biographies of special merit: Jean Claude Dubé's *Claude-Thomas Dupuy: intendant de la Nouvelle France, 1678–1738* (1969); Léo-Paul Desrosiers's *Paul de Chomedey, sieur de Maisonneuve* (1967); and Guy Frégault's *Pierre LeMoyne d'Iberville* (2nd ed. 1968).

The eighteenth century is of course Guy Frégault's main preoccupation. In his *Le 18e siècle canadien* (1968) he demonstrates his encyclopedic knowledge of sources and his great capacity to give texture and life to the events and moments and developments about which he writes. These same characteristics can be observed in *La civilisation de la Nouvelle-France (1713–1744)*, first published in 1944, which was reissued in 1969.

4. *Québec and Canada: 1760–1867*. French-Canadian scholars did not attach much

importance to this period between 1967 and 1972. Only some thirteen works are worth mentioning. The first ones deal with series of documents: *L'Acte de Québec et la Révolution américaine* (1970) and *Les troubles de 1837–38* (1969) edited by Jacques Lacoursière and Denis Vaugeois and the two excellent 'journals' of Boréal Express: *Journal d'histoire du Canada: 1760–1810* and *1810–1841*. These 'journals' are not strictly documents but treatments of major events of the times, reported as though in a newspaper—a fascinating method of study. The large format is fresh and lively.

The only reprint of importance dealing with this period is Michel Brunet's *Les Canadiens après la conquête, 1758–1775: de la révolution canadienne à la révolution américaine* (1969).

Only one survey history appears to be worth remembering: *L'Amérique du Nord britannique: la colonisation et la formation du Canada continental* (1970) by R. Lehaise and Noël Vallerand.

The period of the troubles in Lower Canada, beginning with 1818 and ending with the Durham Report, has been treated in the following significant works: *Précis des événements publics qui se rattachent à l'histoire du Canada depuis 1818 à 1842* (1968), first published in 1842, and *Le rapport Durham* (1969) by Denis Bertrand and Albert Desbiens. With great historical skill Jean Charles Bonenfant eliminates a considerable number of clichés about French Canadians and confederation in his fine treatment, *La naissance de la confédération* (1969).

Intellectual history of the period is well presented in Claude Galarneau's *La France devant l'opinion canadienne, 1760–1815* (1970) and in André Lefebvre's *La Montréal Gazette et le nationalisme canadien: 1835–1842* (1971).

Jean Pierre Wallot and John Hare continue their monumental task of putting some order into the socio-economic history of the early nineteenth century with their *Confrontations: choix de textes sur les problèmes politiques, économiques et sociaux du Bas-Canada 1806–1810* (1972). The Marxist tradition, which has been too absent from French-Canadian historiography, makes its appearance with Gilles Bourque's *Question nationale et classes sociales au Québec: 1760–1840* (1970). The Reciprocity Treaty is the subject of an excellent essay by Pierre Trudel, *Le Traité de Réciprocité: 1854* (1968).

The above-mentioned books are of genuine merit, but the best historical treatise on the period is Jean Paul Bernard's *Les Rouges, libéralisme, nationalisme, et anticléricalisme au milieu du XIXe siècle* (1971). It is a most thorough study and a truly modern one.

5. *Québec and Canada, 1865–1945*. In 1967, during the celebrations for the centennial of confederation, there were many compilations relating to Canada's first century, but none of them originated in Québec. One can conclude that Québec (or Canadian) history dealing with the process of establishing, and living in, Canada up to the Second World War has not interested Québec scholars. Much of what they have written can be found in articles, in unpublished theses, in papers read at symposiums of various kinds, and in television and radio talks. One book stands out, however: Jean Provencher's *Québec sous la loi des mesures de guerre, 1918* (1971). It studies a dimension of the conscription crisis in the First World War that for some reason had been forgotten. Its interest and significance were increased by the fact that it could be related to the October crisis of 1970 when governments again saw fit to apply restrictive measures. There was of course no war but what has been called 'an apprehended insurrection'.

6. *Modern Québec and Canada*. Robert Rumilly dominates this period with the continuation of his monumental *Histoire de la Province de Québec*. In 1967 he published the 36th volume: *L'autonomie provinciale*. In 1968 Volumes 37 and 38 appeared: *Premier gouvernement Duplessis*, on Duplessis's first tenure of office, and the first of four volumes on French Canadians and the Second World War: *La guerre de 1939–1945: Ernest Lapointe*. The following three volumes of the series appeared in 1969: Volume 39—*La guerre de 1939–1945: le plébiscite*; Volume 40—*La guerre de 1939–1945: le Bloc populaire;* and Volume 41—*La guerre de 1939–1945: Duplessis reprend les rênes*. De Gaulle's famous visit to Québec was captured in *De Gaulle au Québec: le dossier des quatre journées* (1967) edited by Jean Tainturier.

Beyond these titles, French-Canadian historians do not appear to have had much interest in the modern period.

7. *Social and economic history; urban studies*. These are comparatively new fields of study as far as French-Canadian scholars are

concerned. Work in social history particularly is advancing, however. Teams of researchers are being established and emphasis is now being placed on this field. At Université Laval they are studying the history of various trades, while at the Université de Québec (Montreal) they are studying the social politicalization of the labour force. Much work is also being done in the field of ethnology by L.-R. Séguin of the Université de Montréal and G. P. Bernard of the Université de Québec (Montreal) is supervising the development of research in urban history, beginning with Montreal. Jean-Louis Roy of McGill is studying all aspects related to the book's history in French-Canadian society. There are some excellent books, even though many of them are simply collections of articles and papers. The best of these are Albert Faucher's *Histoire économique et unité canadienne* (1970) and Fernand OUELLET's *Éléments d'histoire sociale du Bas-Canada* (1972).

Two excellent economic histories appeared between 1967 and 1972. Fernand Ouellet published his long-awaited *Histoire économique et sociale du Québec, 1760–1850: structures et conjoncture* (1968) and the period from 1851 to 1896 was superbly covered by Jean Hamelin and Yves Roby in their *Histoire économique du Québec 1851–1896* (1971), which won a Governor General's Award. Still in the realm of economic history but dealing with a more particular subject is Maurice Séguin's *La nation canadienne et l'agriculture 1760–1850: essai d'histoire économique* (1970).

Much has been written on French-Canadian immigration to the United States, but few studies excel Yolande Lavoie's *L'émigration des Canadiens aux États-Unis avant 1930* (1972). Immigration into French Canada is just beginning to interest scholars and it is hoped that forthcoming studies will be as good as René Bélanger's *Les Basques dans l'estuaire du St Laurent* (1971). Of more specialized interest, but fascinating as social history nevertheless, is Norman Lafleur's *La drave en Mauricie: histoire et tradition* (1969), on the economic and social conditions of logging and the loggers themselves.

Robert Rumilly dominates urban history with his three-volume *Histoire de Montréal* (1970); when it was completed he turned his attention to the history of a region: *Histoire du Saint Laurent* (1970). The histories of particular parishes were relatively popular in the period under review. The parish of Sainte Marie in the Beauce district became the subject of a fine monograph by H. Provost: *Sainte Marie de la Nouvelle-Beauce* (1967).

8. *Institutions.* Much attention was paid to one of the traditional institutions of French Canada, the Church. The Catholic Action movement, which played a significant role in the formation of present French-Canadian political leaders working in the federal and provincial scenes, was treated by Gabriel Clément in *Histoire de l'Action catholique au Canada français* (1972). A rather uncritical study of the Church and its role in Canada is given by Herman Plante in *L'église catholique au Canada* (1970). Lucien Lemieux wrote of Québec as the first ecclesiastical province in Canada in *L'établissement de la première province ecclésiastique du Canada: 1783–1844* (1968).

Education and social institutions were also well treated, particularly by Marc Lebel, Pierre Savard, and Raymond Vézina in *Aspects de l'enseignement 1765–1945 au Petit Séminaire de Québec* (1968), by Oliver Maurault in *Le collège de Montréal, 1767–1967* (1967), by M. D'Allaire in *L'Hôpital-général de Québec: 1692–1764* (1971), and by Robert Rumilly in *Cent ans d'éducation 1869–1969: le collège de Montréal* (1969) and *Histoire de l'École des Hautes Études commerciales* (1967).

9. *The professions.* The history of nursing in Québec was studied by Édouard Desjardins, Suzanne Giroux, and Eileen C. Flanagan in *Histoire de la profession infirmière au Québec* (1970). Jean-Louis Roy dealt with one of the most influential professions in Québec in *Histoire de la Corporation des Agronomes de la Province de Québec* (1971).

10. *The arts, literature, sports, and leisure.* It was interesting to discover many titles dealing with these subjects, which are all very important aspects of French-Canadian life. A general historical work dealt with the role of folklore in Québec life and society: *La chanson folklorique dans le milieu canadien-français traditionnel* (1969) by Mary Ann Griggs. The history of French-Canadian theatre was seen through the development of the Théâtre du Nouveau Monde in Louis-Martin Tard's *Vingt ans de théâtre au nouveau-monde—histoire d'une compagnie théâtrale canadienne* (1971). Art was given two fine treatments, one general and one particular, in Jean-René Ostiguy's *Un siècle de peinture canadienne 1870–1970* (1971) and Jean Trudel's

Un chef-d'oeuvre de l'art ancien du Québec: la chapelle des Ursulines (1972).

Two fine studies of French-Canadian literature appeared in this period. Pierre de Grandpré directed a series of studies published under the title *Histoire de la littérature française du Québec* (4 vols, 1967). Brunet Berthelot published his *Histoire de la littérature canadienne-française* (1971), which contains not only a survey of the historical development of French-Canadian literature but also a series of analytical essays on particular authors. Since the period under review was also a revolutionary one, it was inevitable that a historian should attempt to study for the first time the theme of revolution in French-Canadian literature. This Joseph Costisella did very well in *Esprit révolutionnaire dans la littérature canadienne-française* (1968).

The only history of a particular sport was Pierre Luc's *L'histoire du sport automobile au Québec* (1971). It is hoped that in years to come, more historians will devote time to this particular aspect of popular culture.

11. *Biographies, autobiographies, memoirs, and speeches.* 1969 saw the publication of *Biographies canadiennes-françaises*, a collaborative effort that is a Who's Who of professional Québécois. In addition there appeared regularly the invaluable *Dictionnaire biographique du Canada* (co-published with an English-language edition). Volume I (1967)—edited by André Vachon, Marcel Trudel, and George W. Brown—deals with Canadian figures who died between 1600 and 1700. Volume II (1969)—edited by David M. Hayne and André Vachon—covers the period 1701 to 1740. Marc La Terreur edited Volume X (1972), dealing with the period 1871–1880.

Between 1967 and 1972 some seventy biographies of diverse value were published in Québec. The vast majority of them were very short studies of political, literary, and artistic figures—they were in no way major critical works. (Biographical writing in French Canada has not reached the same depth and range as in English-speaking Canada: French-Canadian historians have always been interested in synthesizing their history, and the biographical method does not lend itself to this.) Unfortunately it is not possible to list more that a few of them. The laicization of education has been for some time a source of conflict in Québec. When the process was finally achieved in the 1960s it was fitting that a historian should recall one of the precursors of the struggle: *Joseph-François Perrault, 1753–1844, et les origines de l'enseignement laïque au Bas-Canada* (1969) by J.-J. Lolois is a valuable and interesting study. Estelle Mitchell wrote *Messire Pierre Boucher* (1967), an extensive biography of an official of France who had much influence on Louis XIV's revocation of the Charter of the Hundred Associates that made New France a crown colony. The surgeon and physician Joseph-Charles Taché (1820–94) is the subject of a fine biography by E. Bossé: *Joseph-Charles Taché: un grand représentant de l'élite canadienne-française* (1971).

Les Ré-éditions Québec reprints many long-forgotten but still useful works. They collected passages from the voluminous writings of Denis Benjamin Viger (1774–1861), who participated in the upheavals of the first half of the nineteenth century and was a politician of considerable influence, in *Oeuvres politiques, extraits* (1970).

Gaston Carrière's *L'apôtre des prairies* (1967), on Joseph Hugonward, and D. Fremont's *Mgr Provencher et son temps* (1968) are biographies of two missionaries of the west.

It is difficult to know where to place Lionel Groulx (1878–1967). As priest, educator, nationalist leader, defender of French-Canadian *survivance*, and leader and prophet, he somewhat defies categorization. As scholars begin to assess the body of his work they will be much aided by the publication of *Mes mémoires*, two volumes of which have now appeared: *1878–1920* (1970) and *1920–1928* (1971). They are a major contribution to the social and intellectual history of French Canada.

One of the Fathers of Confederation was the subject of a long-awaited biography: *Hector-Louis Langevin: un père de la confédération canadienne, 1826–1906* (1969) by André Désilets. Raoul Dandurand, who wanted to become a senator more than anything else, left an unpublished manuscript that Marcel Hamelin edited: *Les mémoires du Sénateur Raoul Dandurand 1861–1942* (1967). Maurice Duplessis (1890–1959) is enjoying a revival in Québec at the present time, even though Robert Rumilly and Conrad Black have yet to publish their biography of him. However, many who had encounters with him have set down their experiences, notably the journalist-lawyer Rémi Chalout, who wrote *Mémoires politiques* (1969), and

Georges Émile Lapalme, who served as liberal leader during most of Duplessis's tenure of office and published his memoirs in two volumes in 1969 and 1970: Volume I—*Le bruit des choses réveillées* and Volume II—*Le vent de l'oubli*. Both books are well written and documented and are important instruments for the study of the modern period.

With all the concern about French-Canadian nationalism it was inevitable that Henri Bourassa (1868–1952) should be the subject of publication. Since many difficulties prevent the writing of a modern biography, Robert Rumilly's *Henri Bourassa: la vie publique d'un grand Canadien*, originally published in 1953, was re-issued in 1969. Dale Thomson's fine biography, *Louis Saint-Laurent*, was translated into French and published in 1968. The same year also saw a translation of Joseph SCHULL's popular biography, *Laurier*. Gérard Bergeron continued to satirize Canadian politicians in his witty if sometimes painful *Ne bougez plus: portraits de quarante politiciens* (1968).

1971 saw the publication of the enchanting journal of a vivacious young lady from St Hyacinthe: *Fadette: le journal d'Henriette Dessaules, 1874–1880*. Thérèse Casgrain wrote in *Une femme chez les hommes* (1971) of all the struggles she undertook to make women the equal of men, and it is to her credit that her autobiography is written without malice or bitterness. It was published in an English translation by Joyce MARSHALL (*A woman in a man's world*) in 1972. LLP

Hitsman, J. Mackay. See HISTORY STUDIES IN ENGLISH 7.

Hoar, Victor. See HISTORY STUDIES IN ENGLISH 11 and LITERARY STUDIES IN ENGLISH 4.

Hockin, Thomas A. See HISTORY STUDIES IN ENGLISH 12 and POLITICAL WRITINGS IN ENGLISH 7.

Hodgetts, J. E. See HISTORY STUDIES IN ENGLISH 12.

Hodgins, Bruce W. See HISTORY STUDIES IN ENGLISH 7.

Holder, P. See INDIANS 5.

Holland, Susan. See HISTORY STUDIES IN ENGLISH 17.

Hollier, Robert. See HISTORY STUDIES IN FRENCH 1.

Holmes, John. Pseudonym used by Raymond SOUSTER.

Hood, Hugh (1928–). Born in Toronto and educated at the University of Toronto, he taught English at St Joseph's College, Hartford, Conn., until 1961, when he joined the English department of the Université de Montréal. Completely bilingual, he has become thoroughly familiar with the cities of Toronto and Montreal, which provide settings for his fiction along with the decaying towns of Nova Scotia. He uses clear and precise prose to convey the motivation and skills of the artist, the film maker, the sportsman, and treats individuals in the context of their families, friends, and associates. Underlying his work is a firm but unobtrusive Christian attitude and a belief that each person requires a purpose in life. He moves easily from the serious to comedy and satire.

A prolific and skilful short-story writer, Hood portrays urban life, chiefly in Toronto and Montreal. The stories in *Flying a red kite* (1962), in which individual and family situations gain much from the locale, cover a wide range. The title story, set in Montreal, about a few hours at the end of the working day of an overwrought businessman ends as a charming domestic idyll. A humorous story, 'Recollections of the Works Department', is based on an actual job experience in Toronto. Another story, a tragedy, takes place in 'Stoverville', a small Ontario town that turns up frequently in his writing, and yet another deals with a nuclear attack in the vicinity of New York. In *Around the mountain: scenes from Montreal life* (1967) most of the stories are centred either on a group of people or on some aspect of urban development. The subjects include sport; the local custom that all leases terminate on 30 April; and the intensity of Québec politics. The sophisticated stories in *The fruit man, the meat man, and the manager* (1971) include the tragic 'Cura pastoralis'; the fantasy 'Places I've never been'; and 'Going down to Williamstown', the nostalgic memories of a man whose avaricious relatives surround him on his deathbed, already quarrelling over the spoils.

In Hood's first novel, *White figure, white*

ground (1964), an artist's need for time to develop his talent and style are sacrificed to the cruel demands made on him by agents and dealers. The inner struggle is intensified by his need to understand the failure that brought about the slow death of his father, who had been forced into a career for which he had no calling. Hood's second novel, *The camera always lies* (1967), contrasts the American sex-oriented, ruthless film industry with the artistic integrity of French producers. *A game of touch* (1970) is a satire on both politics and the big company as well as an exposition of man's need for companionship at his own emotional level. By using a brash young man as his chief protagonist, Hood shows how a group of amateur football players gradually breaks up as the members become aware of their respective social responsibilities. The scene is Montreal, but the characters represent the world in microcosm. *You can't get there from here* (1972) satirizes the devious motivations of the Great Powers in their dealings with emerging African nations. The novel also parallels some features of the Canadian situation. Hood's 'Leofrica' is a federation of two tribes that differ in language, customs, and economic development, in which the more developed area arrogates to itself most of the political plums. While the novel is essentially tragic, it is lightened with many comic scenes.

Hood is the author of a sports biography, *Strength down centre: the Jean Béliveau story* (1970), which was also published in French (*Puissance au centre: Jean Béliveau*). NS

Hopkins, E. Russell. See HISTORY STUDIES IN ENGLISH 12.

Hopwood, Victor G. See HISTORY STUDIES IN ENGLISH 3.

Horn, Michiel. See HISTORY STUDIES IN ENGLISH 11.

Hornsey, Richard. See POETRY IN ENGLISH 2.

Horowitz, Gad. See HISTORY STUDIES IN ENGLISH 13 and POLITICAL WRITINGS IN ENGLISH 4 and 9.

Horwood, Harold. See FICTION IN ENGLISH 3.

Hounsom, Eric W. See HISTORY STUDIES IN ENGLISH 5.

Houston, James. See CHILDREN'S BOOKS IN ENGLISH 1, 5, and 6; ESKIMOS: BOOKS IN ENGLISH; and FICTION IN ENGLISH 2 and 3.

Howard, Blanche. See FICTION IN ENGLISH 5.

Howard, Irene. See HISTORY STUDIES IN ENGLISH 14.

Howell, Maxwell. See HISTORY STUDIES IN ENGLISH 7.

Howell, Nancy. See HISTORY STUDIES IN ENGLISH 7.

Howith, Harry. See POETRY IN ENGLISH 2.

Hubbard, R. H. See HISTORY STUDIES IN ENGLISH 15 and 16.

Hunkin, Harry. See HISTORY STUDIES IN ENGLISH 16.

Hunter, Martin. See DRAMA IN ENGLISH 3.

Hunter, Robert. See FICTION IN ENGLISH 7.

Hutchison, Bruce (1901–). Born in Prescott, Ont., and raised and educated in British Columbia, he began his journalistic career as a sports writer but shortly, with his appointment to the parliamentary press gallery in 1925, made commentary on national life his lifework. Since 1944 he has been editor successively of the Winnipeg *Free Press*, the Victoria *Times*, and the Vancouver *Sun*. He has also written for the *Financial Post* and *Maclean's*. His books are patriotic, emotional in their gusto, and often romantic in their optimism. In *The unknown country* (1942; rev. 1948), which won a Governor General's Award, he optimistically claimed that French- and English-speaking Canadians were growing together in understanding but that they were only beginning to know the true substance and possibilities of the nation. Fifteen years later in *Canada: tomorrow's giant* (1957) he described the character of communities in diverse regions across the country and alleged that he could perceive a new self-understanding among Canadians. *The Fraser* (1950), in the Rivers of America series, praised the manner in which the people of British Columbia had been able to make the most of their physical environment. Hutchison's concern for Canadian-American relations was expressed in *Canada's lonely neighbour* (1954), written at the height of McCarthyism, wherein he asserted that Canada must interpret Americans to Europe and the world. *The struggle for the border* (1955) shows that however much the peoples of Canada and the United States differ, their cooperation and peaceful relationships should serve as an international model. In the political novel *The hollow men* (1944) he drew on his experience as a parliamentary reporter. He used the same experience for *The incredible Canadian: a candid portrait of Mackenzie King, his times, and his nation* (1953), for which he won a Governor General's Award. Writing before the King papers became available for historical research, he explained that the man and the nation were inseparable: they were both mysteries. *Mr Prime Minister, 1867–1964* (1964), a collection of engaging sketches of Canada's leading statesmen, is an evaluation of their careers and accomplishments. In 1967 Hutchison wrote the text for *Canada: A year of the land*, which was published by the National Film Board and is mainly of interest for its splendid photographs. His *Western windows* (1967) is a collection of short essays on life-styles and his past career. DF

I

Ianora, Claudio. See FICTION IN ENGLISH 4.

Immarigeon, Henrietta. See POLITICAL WRITINGS IN FRENCH 3.

Indians (see also INDIAN LEGENDS AND ART). Centennial year witnessed the publication of the first major survey of the Canadian Indian (the Hawthorn and Tremblay below), signalling one of the many new directions in the literature. Traditionally it tended to treat Indian cultures within a framework of the major culture areas (Northwest Coast, Subarctic, Plains, and Eastern Woodlands), and to focus on the ethnographies of single tribes. The new direction in publishing cut across tribal- and culture-area boundaries and focused on patterns of behaviour—in such spheres as education and economic development—common to most Indians as an ethnic category in Canadian society. Significantly some of this literature was written by Indians themselves. Second, while standard ethnographic monographs continue to be published, and are clearly needed, in some culture areas such as the Subarctic and the Eastern seaboard, more attention has been devoted to reconstructing aboriginal cultures not on the basis of the aging informant, as was common at the turn of the century, but by the critical use of archival and historical documents of explorers, missionaries, and traders. Third, a growing realization of the social consequences of a culture's adaptation to its physical-natural environment led to many ecological studies of band-level societies in the Subarctic and to new arguments concerning the functions of the potlatch in Northwest Coast societies. Finally, the literature has been broadened by the input of historians and legal scholars who are now examining the history of Indian-white relations from contact time (the 1500s in the east) to the present. This historical interest has led to the reprinting of a major reference, *Indian treaties and surrenders from 1860 to 1902* (3 vols, Coles; 1971 facsimile edition of the 1891–1912 printing), along with other older out-of-print treatises on the Canadian Indian.

1. The first major examination of the present condition of Canadian Indians was *A survey of the contemporary Indians of Canada* edited by Harry Bertram Hawthorn (2 vols, Queen's Printer, 1966–7), the product of a

federally commissioned study. From a sample of reserves across Canada, materials on economic development, education, voluntary associations, political development, and legal status were synthesized and then combined with recommendations on Indian policy and administration to the federal government. This report emphasizes the recognition of special status for Indians and recommends that self-determination should replace traditional federal paternalism. It was only partly heeded by the government in *The statement of the government of Canada on Indian policy* (1969), a 'White Paper' proposing that the Indian Act, which provides Canada's 240,000 Indians with special legal status, be abrogated and that the Indian administration be phased out as a special clientele department and its responsibilities allocated to the provinces. This policy announcement led to the growth of provincial Indian associations that began to act as pressure groups opposing the policy. The consequence of this policy rejection was the valuable addition to the literature of many works by Indians themselves. Harold Cardinal's *The unjust society: the tragedy of Canada's Indians* (1969) was an immediate response to the policy, as were *The only good Indian: essays by Canadian Indians* (1970), a collection edited by Waubageshig; *Bulletin 201* (1970) edited and published by the Anglican Church of Canada; and *For every North American Indian who begins to disappear, I also begin to disappear* (Neewin Publishing Co., 1971), a collection of essays about the relations between North American Indians and whites edited by W. Pelletier *et al.* Providing an alternative response to the White Paper was William Wuttunee's *Ruffled feathers: Indians in Canadian society* (Bell Books, Calgary, 1971), which argued for Indian integration into Canadian life and criticized the red-power movement for its negativism.

2. Indian authors like Wuttunee and Cardinal clearly reveal in their publications a search for a personal and group identity. This has also been expressed in the form of biographies—for example in *Red on white: the biography of Duke Redbird* (1971), edited by Marty Dunn; Alan Morley's *Roar of the breakers: a biography of Peter Kelly* (1967); and *Guests never leave hungry: the autobiography of James Sewid: a Kwakiutl Indian* (1969) edited by James P. Spradley. *Tatanga Mani* (1969) by J. W. Grant MacEwan is the biography of Chief Walking Buffalo of the Stonies and MacEwan's *Portraits from the Plains* (1971) is a series of brief sketches of thirty-three western Indians. Norma Sluman's *Poundmaker* (1967) imaginatively reconstructs the life of the Cree Chief who sided with Riel in 1885 and commanded the Indians at the skirmishes at Cut Knife Hill and Batoche. Deriving data from archival materials and interviews with present-day tribesmen, Hugh A. Dempsey has written *Crowfoot: chief of the Blackfeet* (1972), a very readable biography of one of Canada's outstanding Indian leaders. *Recollections of an Assiniboine Chief* (1972) by Ochankugahe (Dan Kennedy) edited by James R. Stevens contains legends and stories relating to the Indian way of life on the northern plains in the late-nineteenth and early-twentieth centuries. Stevens also edited James Redsky's *First leader of the Ojibway: Misquona-queb* (1972), a similar miscellany that has little concrete information on its subject. *An Indian remembers: my life as a trapper in northern Manitoba* (1971) by Tom Boulanger presents his memoirs of seventy years as a trapper, fisherman, trader, and freighter. In *Touch the earth: a self-portrait of Indian existence* (1972) by T. C. McLuhan, Indians discuss their fate.

3. The reassessment of Indian policy led some scholars to re-examine the history of the Indian administration and the legal status of Indians in Canada. Robert Surtees' *The original people* (1971) and E. Palmer Patterson's *The Canadian Indian: a history since 1500* (1972) attempt to cover the vast historical span of administrative events that remain in need of much more research attention. *The image of the Indian* (Waterloo Lutheran University Monograph Series, 1971) by Ronald G. Haycock interestingly documents changing attitudes to Indians as they have been reflected in popular Canadian magazines from 1900 to 1970. Legal causes for the current condition of Indians and a better understanding of the history of judicial treatment were explored in the Indian-Eskimo Association's *Native rights in Canada* (2nd ed., 1972) edited by Peter A. Cumming and N. H. Mickenberg.

4. The history of Indian-white contact and its effects on the tribes have received greater attention from scholars. *North American Indians in historical perspective* (1971) edited by Eleanor B. Leacock and Nancy O. Lurie

provides an excellent summary of the process of change in tribes from all the aboriginal culture areas of Canada. Fraser Symington's *The Canadian Indian: the illustrated history of the great tribes of Canada* (1969) presents a more general overview enhanced by the use of drawings, paintings, and photographs. Desmond Morton's *The last war drum* (Canadian War Museum Historical Publications No. 5, 1972), presents an illustrated description of the last military conflict between Métis and Plains Indians and the federal government. Plains tribal culture is graphically depicted in *Paul Kane's frontier: including 'Wanderings of an artist among the Indians of North America' by Paul Kane* by J. Russell Harper (1971) through a biographical introduction and the reproduction of Kane's classic text and particularly his paintings, which describe western Indian life in the 1840s. *Portraits from North American Indian life* (1972) by Edward S. Curtis is an impressive and valuable album of period photographs. It is a selection based on Curtis's twenty-volume photographic record of Indians in the American and Canadian West covering a period of some thirty years, beginning in 1896.

A reconstruction of Indian cultures at the time of contact has been undertaken by many ethnohistorians from archival materials. The Northern Science Research Group of the Department of Indian Affairs and Northern Development has published two very scholarly and useful works along these lines. *Les Amérindiens du Nord-Ouest canadien au 19e siècle selon Émile Petitot* by Donat Savoie (2 vols, 1971) is an account of the Loucheux and the Eskimo-Tlingit of the Mackenzie Delta area derived from the writings of the Rev. Émile Petitot of the Oblate Order. The second, a reference work, *Fur trade posts of the Northwest Territories 1870–1970* (1971) by Peter J. Usher, is a compendium of the locations, history, and dates of operations of the posts throughout the arctic and subarctic. On the west-coast area Erna Gunther published *Indian life on the northwest coast of North America as seen by the early explorers and fur traders during the last decades of the eighteenth century* (1972). On the Eastern Woodlands area, James Pendergast and Bruce Trigger brought together their combined specialties of archaeology and ethnohistory to deal with the question of whether the Dawson archaeological site is the village of Hochelaga visited by Cartier in *Cartier's Hochelaga and the Dawson site* (1972). Eastern-seaboard contact has been documented by A. G. Bailey in *The conflict of European and eastern Algonkian cultures: a study in Canadian civilization* of which the second edition (1969) contains new materials on the Laurentian Iroquois.

5. By 1967 the Indian was in a vastly different social and economic position than he had been at contact. In the expansive Subarctic, ecological adaptation to the environment had shifted from hunting to trapping and a growing dependency on trading posts, and with this came a major change in band structure, as indicated in *Band societies* (1965) and *Ecological essays* (1966), Bulletins of the National Museums of Canada edited by David Damas. Cornelius Osgood's *The Han Indians: a compilation of ethnographic and historical data on the Alaska-Yukon boundary area* (Yale University Publications in Anthropology, No. 74, 1971) provides a thorough examination of one specific tribe of the western Subarctic. *The changing cultures of the Snowdrift Chipewyan* by James VanStone (National Museums of Canada, 1965) still presents the most accessible and current study of a tribal group that has lost its trapping base and has found a new dependence on a welfare economy in the absence of any opportunities for employment.

On the Northwest Coast, dependence on salmon and the mammal life of the sea remained, but trade goods from Europeans and new trading networks led to the florescence of the potlatching culture. Franz Boas's *Kwakiutl ethnography* (1966) edited by Helen Codere provides a classic source of traditional west-coast culture. Phillip Drucker and Robert F. Heizer reassess the function of the potlatch—the reciprocal exchange rituals that validated the assumption of hereditary titles within the social hierarchy of west-coast culture—in their *To make my name good: a reexamination of the southern Kwakiutl potlatch* (1967), as do Abraham Rosman and Paula G. Rubel in their *Feasting with mine enemy: rank and exchange among Northwest Coast societies* (1971). Ronald and Evelyn Rohner in *The Kwakiutl: Indians of British Columbia* (1970) provide a clear and useful picture of contemporary reserve life.

By adopting the horse, the Plains Indians and to a lesser extent those of the Plateau rendered their nomadic hunting practices more efficient, developed warfare and coup-counting to a greater degree than was aboriginally practised, and established larger trading networks. These overall changes are documented in *Flathead and Kootenay: the rivers, the tribes and the region's traders* (1969) by O. W. Johnson; *The hoe and the horse on the Plains: a study of cultural development among North American Indians* (1970) by P. Holder; and *Indian life on the Upper Missouri* (1968) by John Ewers. A collection of articles edited by Ethel Nurge, *The modern Sioux: social systems and reservation culture* (1970), provides an excellent picture of the contemporary life style of the Sioux.

The traditional culture patterns of the semi-sedentary hunting and hoeing cultures of the Eastern Woodlands Indians are described in *The Woodland Indians of the Western Great Lakes* (1970), a useful overview by Robert and Pat Ritzenthaller; with a tribal focus in *The Chippewa and their neighbours: a case study in ethnohistorical method* (1970) by Harold Hickerson; and in *The Huron: farmers of the north* (1969) by Bruce Trigger. Mission life among the Iroquoian-speaking Hurons is described by John Hayes in *Wilderness mission: the story of Sainte Marie among the Hurons* (1969), generously illustrated with photographs of the reconstruction. Iroquois participation in the American War of Independence has been documented in detail by Barbara Graymont in *The Iroquois in the American Revolution* (1972), and in a less scholarly fashion by G. Elmore Reaman, who follows Iroquois history from the Revolution to the present day at Grand River Reserve in *The trail of the Iroquois Indians* (1967). Politically active progressive Iroquois provide the subject matter of Sally Weaver's *Medicine and politics among the Grand River Iroquois* (National Museums of Canada, 1972). Leadership development, defined politically and economically, has been treated by several authors in Norman A. Chance's collection of papers entitled *Conflict in culture: problems of developmental change among the Cree* (Canadian Research Centre for Anthropology, Saint Paul University, Ottawa, 1968). Here the Cree of northern Québec are the subject of action-oriented research designed to formulate ways of introducing change that will minimize conflict.

6. Much of the current literature dealing with culture change reflects a seeking of causes for various 'failures'. The poverty among Indian groups and the demoralization that accompanies it, along with economic marginality, have been treated by both layman and scholar. Heather Robertson's *Reservations are for Indians* (1970) is a journalistic account of the devastation of poverty in the Subarctic. Not too dissimilar is Alan Fry's fictionalized account of his dealings with Indian poverty in British Columbia while he was acting as Indian Agent. His *How a people die* (1970), while poorly written, gives some indication of the complexities if not the impossibilities of making the Indian administration on reserves operate for the betterment of Indians. *The proceedings of the Special Senate Committee on Poverty Number 14* (January 20, 1970) provides the government's facts-and-figures assessment of the poverty profile.

More scholarly treatments of this economic marginality are presented in *The economic status of the Canadian Indian: a re-examination* (1969) by Paul Deprez and G. Sigurdson and in *Welfare: hidden backlash* (1971) by Morris C. Shumiatcher. New material of good quality on economic underdevelopment in the Maritimes and the Plains reserves appears in *Native peoples*, Volume 1 of *Minority Canadians* (1971) edited by Jean L. Elliott.

The search for causes of failure in treating the Indian has extended to the established churches, as evidenced by C. E. Hendry's *Beyond traplines* (Anglican Church of Canada, Toronto, 1969) in which the traditional role of the church is examined and a new course of action is proposed.

Some of the most formidable scholarly indictments of failure have come from researchers on Indian education, who have demonstrated the futility of, and the harm caused by, applying the unmodified middle-class school system to Indian children who understand little English and can look forward to few occupational opportunities for which formal or vocational training would prepare them. Harry F. Wolcott's *A Kwakiutl village and school* (1967) and A. R. King's *The school at Mopass: a problem of identity* (1967) are excellent analyses of this order. More psychologically oriented are *Culture change and education: a study of Indian and non-Indian views in southern Alberta* (1969) by L. C. Lyon and J. W. Friesen and *Intelligence and cultural environment* (1969) by P. E. Vernon. Both books look to perceptual and attitudinal factors in the drop-out patterns and learning abilities of Indians.

Since the Second World War, Indians, like many other Canadians, have begun to migrate from rural areas to the cities. Consequently modes of adaptation to urban styles of life have assumed a good deal of interest. Mark Nagler's *Indians in the city: a study of urbanization of Indians in Toronto* (1970) explores various patterns of adaptation and concludes that occupational factors play a major role in success or failure. H. Brody's *Indians on Skid Row: the role of alcohol and community in the adaptive process of Indian urban migrants* (Northern Science Research Group, Ottawa, 1970) offers a closer look at one of the causes and consequences of destitution/adaptation.

Although studies on Indian crime patterns are becoming more numerous, *Indians and the law*, published by the Canadian Corrections Association (Ottawa, 1967), is still the best overview. It describes the difficulties of translating concepts of law and order cross-culturally and applying them to the Indian people with a sense of justice.

To overcome the problem of generally inaccessible scholarly materials, several edited readers have appeared that are devoted to a general review of the current status of the Canadian Indian. Those most relevant to the Canadian scene are Mark Nagler's *Perspectives on the North American Indians* (1972), Norman Sheffe's *Issues for the seventies: Canada's Indians* (1970), and Gerald Walsh's *Indians in transition: an inquiry approach* (1971). To locate further material on the Indian, attention should be directed to two journals: *Anthropologica*, published by the Canadian Research Centre for Anthropology, Saint Paul University, Ottawa; and *Recherches amérindiennes au Québec*, published in Montreal by the Société des Recherches amérindiennes au Québec. The National Museums of Canada, Ottawa, continues to publish several series of monographs dealing with the prehistory, physical anthropology, linguistics, and ethnology of the Canadian Indian, and has recently begun to reissue some of its out-of-print classics. For the most comprehensive map coverage of Indian reserves in Canada the reader should consult *Atlas of Indian reserves and settlements in Canada* (1971), published by the Department of Indian Affairs and Northern Development, Ottawa. For a mapping of the tribes and culture areas, Robert F. Spencer's and Eldon Johnson's *Atlas for anthropology* (Wm. C. Brown Company, Dubuque, Iowa, 1960) should be consulted. SMW

Indian legends and art (see also INDIANS). While legends and folk tales among Canadian Indians are both rich and varied, they have been less the subject of extended booklength treatment by scholars recently than in the early decades of the century. Myths and legends can take a variety of forms within a culture. They may combine obscure historical facts with fictionalized embellishments, as does the Dekanawidah myth that recounts the formation of the formidable League of the Iroquois (see *Parker on the Iroquois* (1968), edited by W. N. Fenton), or they can tell dramatic stories of purely mythical creatures, as in *The girl who married the bear* (National Museums of Canada, 1970), a common folktale among the tribes of the southern Yukon, which Catharine McClellan analyses to discern the theme of disharmony between man and animals.

Religion, art, folklore, and material culture are collectively a natural unit of discourse because they share the function of representing and restating significant values and ideals of a culture, whether the medium of conveyance is the verbal statement, the carving in wood, or the acting out of a complex ritual such as the midewiwin, described by Ruth Landes in her *Ojibwa religions and the midewiwin* (1968). The literature consequently reflects this interrelationship by combining two or more of these facets of culture in a single presentation.

The Northwest Coast Indians, with their elaborate rituals of the potlatch and associated dramas, complete with extensive costuming, provide a popular source of data for authors to draw upon in writing on art, material culture, and folklore. The potlatch has been the subject of much study. George Clutesi's *Potlatch* (Gray's Publishing Ltd, Sydney, 1969), one of the most interesting accounts, relates the stories of the potlatches he has attended and combines them with the oral tradition of his tribe, the Tse-shaht of British Columbia. His discussion of oral tradition is even more extensive and unusual in *Son of raven, son of deer: fables of the Tse-shaht people* (Gray's Publishing Ltd, Sydney, 1967), in which he recounts the legends of the raven and deer as they were told to him by his parents and contrasts these with European nursery rhymes to indicate how the Indian admonish their children to behave well.

In the field of material culture, museum catalogues are often superior sources because they usually contain careful documentation and useful photographs and diagrams. Erna Siebert's *North American Indian art: masks, amulets, wood carvings, and ceremonial dress from the Northwest Coast* (1967) provides such documentation and illustration of the material-culture collections from the Northwest Coast maintained in two Soviet museums. *L'art des Indiens d'Amérique* by Erna Siebert and Werner Forman (Paris, Éditions Cercle d'Art, 1967) provides further documentation on west-coast material culture collected by Russian explorers in the eighteenth and nineteenth centuries. Audrey Hawthorn's well-illustrated and well-researched *Art of the Kwakiutl Indians and other Northwest Coast tribes* (1967) documents a wide range of artifacts. The National Museums of Canada's recent Gitksan exhibition is extremely well illustrated in a catalogue entitled *'Ksan: breath of our grandfathers: an exhibition of 'Ksan art* (1972). The tragedy of decaying material culture on the west coast—particularly well depicted for the mortuary poles, totem poles, and old longhouses on the Queen Charlotte Islands—is graphically presented by Anthony L. Carter in *This is Haida* (Anthony Carter, Vancouver, 1968) through the use of photographs. Paul Wingert's *Primitive art: its traditions and styles* (1962) is still a major source for commentary on art among pre-literate peoples; it contains valuable chapters on the development of art traditions in all the aboriginal culture areas of Canada. More superficial in coverage is Joseph H. Wherry's *Indian masks and myths of the west* (1969), which contains only scattered references and is a less concentrated treatment than his *The totem pole people* (1964) with its useful plates.

Hugh W. McKervill's *The salmon people: the story of Canada's west coast salmon fishing industry* (Gray's Publishing Ltd, Sydney, 1967) combines both legend and history to describe the development of the fishing economy from aboriginal practices involving salmon rites that were sacred ceremonies to modern-day commercial enterprises. Traditional medical practices are compared with those of European medicine by R. Geddes Large in *Drums and scalpel: from native healers to physicians of the North Pacific Coast* (Mitchell Press Ltd, Vancouver, 1968), based on the memoirs of his physician-father who worked among the Bella Bella in the early twentieth century. The folk history of the Bella Coola from contact to the present has been recorded by Cliff Kopas in *Bella Coola* (Mitchell Press Ltd, Vancouver, 1970) and Norman H. Lerman and Helen S. Clark have reported folk tales obtained from Indian women in the interior of British Columbia in *Once upon an Indian tale: authentic folk tales* (1968). *Légendes indiennes du Canada* by Claude Melançon (1967) provides some thirty-three legends from the Northwest Coast, the Eastern Woodlands, and the Atlantic regions.

While Ruth Underhill's *Red man's religion* (1965) is still one of the most useful general sources on the American Indian, two more recent publications on ritual and ideology should be noted. *Pre-Columbian American religions* (1968), edited by Walter Krickberg and Herman Trimborn, contains a useful article on North America by Werner Muller in which he discusses the acquiring of a guardian spirit by the Algonkians and Athapaskans of the Subarctic, and the Iroquois dream quest. The ghost dance, while recorded in its spread throughout the American plains and among the Indians in the 1880s, did diffuse to Canada; its development is concisely analysed by Alice B. Kehoe in her article 'Ghost dance legend in Saskatchewan, Canada' in the journal *Plains Anthropologist* (1968, Part I, pp. 296–304).

Additional material on the Plains Indians is presented by William K. Powers in his well-illustrated study *Indians of the northern plains* (1969). He discusses material culture, ritual, and dances among the Plains Ojibwa and the Sarsi. Plains Cree and Blackfoot legends are described in Frances Fraser's *The wind along the river* (1968).

The outstanding example of scholarly work on dance and song in the Eastern Woodlands is Gertrude P. Kurath's *Dance and song rituals of Six Nations Reserve, Ontario* (National Museums of Canada, 1968). In this finely illustrated and diagrammed monograph she presents a choreographic and musical survey of the longhouse rituals maintained by the conservative Iroquois who adhere to the religion of Handsome Lake. The historical background of this religion, and its consequences for the Iroquois, have received extensively detailed treatment by Anthony F. C. Wallace in *The death and rebirth of the Seneca* (1970). At a more personalized level of legend-telling, Alma Greene recounts in *Forbidden voice* (1971) the folklore of the Six Nations through her autobiographical account of reserve life at Grand River.

From the Eastern Algonkian area Philip K. Bock's *The Micmac Indians of Restigouche: history and contemporary description* (National Museums of Canada, 1966) provides a section on folklore, religion, and dances set in a well-documented background of the historical development of the reserve and its current cultural patterns.

The contemporary Indian search for identity is reflected in a collection of poems, writings, and chants edited by Kent Gooderham entitled *I am an Indian* (1969). SMW

Inglis, Alex I. See HISTORY STUDIES IN ENGLISH 7.

Isbester, Fraser. See HISTORY STUDIES IN ENGLISH 13.

Ives, Edward D. See FOLKLORE: BIBLIOGRAPHY and HISTORY STUDIES IN ENGLISH 16.

J

Jack, Donald. See DRAMA IN ENGLISH 4.

Jackman, Sydney W. See HISTORY STUDIES IN ENGLISH 9.

Jackson, James A. See HISTORY STUDIES IN ENGLISH 8.

Jacob, Michelle. See CHILDREN'S BOOKS IN FRENCH.

Jaenen, Cornelius J. See HISTORY STUDIES IN ENGLISH 14.

Jaffary, Karl. See POLITICAL WRITINGS IN ENGLISH 8.

Jakes, John W. See HISTORY STUDIES IN ENGLISH 5.

James, L. W. See FOLKLORE: BIBLIOGRAPHY.

Jamieson, Stuart. See HISTORY STUDIES IN ENGLISH 13.

Jasmin, Claude (1930–). Born in Montreal, he studied at the Collège Grasset and graduated from the École des Arts appliqués. He has been a ceramist, actor, art teacher and critic, television designer at Radio-Canada, and latterly director of the literary and art pages of the *Journal de Montréal*.

Jasmin has published five novels, two plays, a collection of short stories, three *récits*, and a short book about his reactions to criticism of his work, *Jasminuịɯsɐſ* (1970). His first novel was *Et puis tout est silence . . .*, written in 1959 and published in book form in 1965. Based on his experiences as an *animateur de théâtre* for the city's parks department, it also has childhood reminiscences of the multi-ethnic working-class area of north-east Montreal where he grew up and that reappears in nearly every novel. *La corde au cou* (1960), which won him a Prix du Cercle du Livre de France, is a violent novel about a schizophrenic who kills in order to achieve temporary liberation from a life of cultural and economic alienation. *Délivrez-nous du mal* (1961) deals with homosexuality in the tenuous relationship between the wealthy André Dastous and Georges Langis, a translator of modest origins. *Ethel et le terroriste* (1964) is based on a transposition of the first fatal FLQ incident in April 1963, when a night-watchman was accidentally killed by a bomb placed at a Montreal armoury. (It was published in an English translation by David Walker, 1965.)

Pleure pas Germaine! (1965) also deals in part with the terrorist phenomenon. It is a *joual* novel in which the narrator and his family try to retrace their identity by a long auto trip through Québec to the mother's native Gaspé. Jasmin's novels (the second, third, and fourth have been the most successful) are full of social hatred for the well-to-do and reflect shame for the heroes' low social rank. There is also a strong degree of disgust for shallow intellectualism and pretension. Revolt and violence, some of it politically motivated, and revulsion against the absence or weakness of the father or father-figure, are other recurring features. Also the defeat of the 1837 Rebellion haunts some of the characters, several of whom are translators—symbolic figures of French-Canadian alienation. All Jasmin's novels are narrated in the first person. The style is nervous and often rough-hewn, achieving moments of catching poetry in *Ethel et le terroriste*. The characters are usually in flight, and withdraw from reality through play-acting.

Blues pour un homme averti (1965) and *Tuez le veau gras* (1970) are the only two plays by Jasmin, of the dozen or so he has written, to be published. The first is the story of an alcoholic abandoned by his father in childhood. Caught up in a web of crime, he mistakes a pursuing police inspector for his ever-awaited father. The second play deals with the moral conflict faced by an intellectual of working-class origin who gives up his dream of organizing a union among the woodworkers of his home town because of threats against the livelihood of members of his family.

Les coeurs empaillés (1967) is a story collection dealing mainly with women who unrealistically hope for affection, happiness, and gratitude and then are cruelly and sadly disappointed, often dying senselessly. *Rimbaud mon beau salaud!* (1969) is an imaginary 'dialogue' between Jasmin and the famous French poet—that other *provincial* and *écrivain maudit*. It is one of Jasmin's most convincing pieces of writing, with striking childhood reminiscences and evocations of the past, present, and future of Québec and its people. *L'Outaragasipi* (1971), described as a saga about the settlers of the Portage-Assomption area of Québec, is a thin work that does not achieve the aim of linking history and actuality. On the other hand *La petite patrie* (1972), a *récit* in which the author again returns to childhood recollections, is engaging and often moving. Several critics urged Jasmin to use the material therein more amply in the novel form, which he has not utilized since 1965. For a critical evaluation of Jasmin's novels see Gilles MARCOTTE's 'L'aventure romanesque de Claude Jasmin' in *Littérature canadienne-française* (1969). B-ZS

Jenkins, Brian. See HISTORY STUDIES IN ENGLISH 7.

Jennings, Fabian. See DRAMA IN ENGLISH 3.

Johnson, Alice. See HISTORY STUDIES IN ENGLISH 3.

Johnson, Elden. See INDIANS 6.

Johnson, F. Henry. See HISTORY STUDIES IN ENGLISH 15.

Johnson, J. K. See HISTORY STUDIES IN ENGLISH 7 and 12.

Johnson, O. W. See INDIANS 5.

Johnston, George (1913–). Born in Hamilton, Ont., George Benson Johnston was educated at the University of Toronto. He served in the air force during the Second World War, taught English at Mount Allison University from 1947 to 1949, then joined the staff of Carleton University, Ottawa where he is Professor of English. His well-known first collection of verse, *The cruising auk* (1959), a graceful series of short and witty poems that express or make fun of middle-class mores, can also be read as a three-part poem in which a pool is used as a symbol of life and as an element in which life must be lived. It is unified by a similarity of structure in the individual poems, which are characterized by subtle irony and an air of detachment. Johnston's second collection, *Home free* (1966), includes two long poems: 'Under the tree' and 'Love in high places'. The poems in these two books have been reprinted, together with some new poems, in *Happy enough: poems 1935–1970* (1972). Johnston's new poems retain his graceful style and careful structures, but they are more personally oriented as he meditates with calm acceptance on the passing of time and the approach of death. These poems express a stoic contentment and a quiet embracing of mortality that does not surrender the feelings of pleasure in what life has to offer.

A translator from the Norse, Johnston published in 1963 *The saga of Gisli*, with an introduction and notes by Peter Foote. NS/PS

Johnston, H. J. M. See HISTORY STUDIES IN ENGLISH 5.

Johnston, James. See HISTORY STUDIES IN ENGLISH 12.

Johnston, W. V. See HISTORY STUDIES IN ENGLISH 13.

Johnstone, John. See POLITICAL WRITINGS IN ENGLISH 5.

Jolicoeur, Catherine. See FOLKLORE: BIBLIOGRAPHY.

Jolliffe, Edward B. See FICTION IN ENGLISH 2.

Jonas, George (1935–). Born in Budapest, he came to Canada in 1956 and has worked since then for the Canadian Broadcasting Corporation in Toronto, first as a radio-drama script editor and then as a television producer. In his poetry Jonas pictures modern man as wandering in a vacuum, surrounded by violence and sudden death, lacking permanent values to fortify his existence, his emotional life often as obsolescent as the artifacts he produces. In *The absolute smile* (1967), poems of alienation and loss in which the protagonist leads an unheroic and empty life, the style is declarative and undecorative. This plainness works against the sense of meaninglessness to produce a tone of ironic wit. This same undecorated style recurs in *The happy hungry man* (1970) in which a lyric and more positive note appears occasionally, only to be undercut by a rejection of any attempt at amelioration of man's predicament. Although the poems are written in the first person, the pervasive cynical tone effectively distances the reader from the generally bleak details; but at times this tone seems too non-committal and militates against involvement in the desperate situation of modern man. PS

Jones, D. G. (1929–). Douglas Gordon Jones was born in Bancroft, Ont., and educated at the Grove School in Lakefield, at McGill University, from which he graduated in 1952, and at Queen's University, where he received his M.A. in 1954. He taught at the Royal Military College in Kingston, at the Ontario Agricultural College in Guelph, and at Bishop's University, before he became Professeur Agrégé in the Department of English at the University of Sherbrooke. He is founder and editor of *Ellipse*, the only bilingual journal in Canada where English- and French-Canadian writings are reciprocally translated.

Jones first became known as a poet of unusual and rather unfashionable lyrical clarity and philosophic intensity. His first volume, *Frost on the sun* (1957), was followed by *The sun is axeman* (1961) and *Phrases from Orpheus* (1967). As the title of this most recent book of verse suggests, Jones tends to see his larger, embracing forms in mythological terms, though he has been saved from the amorphous vagueness of much mythopoeic poetry by an aesthetic precision and economy of language and by a neo-imagistic sharpness of outline.

A concern for the guiding myths of literature is also evident in Jones' single but important work of criticism, *Butterfly on rock* (1970), in which he seeks out the dominant themes and images in the literature of Canada. He sees them as emanations of the mythical and moral structure of our society at a critical changing point when it ceases to be the garrison world described by Northrop FRYE and enters into a dialogue with the natural world it had formerly rejected in fear. GW

Jones, Joseph. See LITERARY STUDIES IN ENGLISH 4.

Jones, Richard. See HISTORY STUDIES IN ENGLISH 12 and POLITICAL WRITINGS IN ENGLISH 1.

Josephy, Alvin M., Jr. See HISTORY STUDIES IN ENGLISH 16.

Juhász, Ferenc. See POETRY IN ENGLISH 4.

Julien, Claude. See HISTORY STUDIES IN ENGLISH 12 and HISTORY STUDIES IN FRENCH 2.

Julien, Denise. See HISTORY STUDIES IN FRENCH 1.

K

Kalman, Rolf. See DRAMA IN ENGLISH 4.

Karpeles, Maud. See FOLKLORE: BIBLIOGRAPHY.

Kattan, Naim. See BELLES LETTRES IN ENGLISH and BELLES LETTRES IN FRENCH.

Kealy, J. D. F. See HISTORY STUDIES IN ENGLISH 12.

Kearns, Lionel. See POETRY IN ENGLISH 2.

Keefer, T. C. See HISTORY STUDIES IN ENGLISH 7.

Kehoe, Alice B. See INDIAN LEGENDS AND ART.

Keith, Ronald. See HISTORY STUDIES IN ENGLISH 13.

Keith, W. J. See LITERARY STUDIES IN ENGLISH 4.

Kent, Cromwell. Pseudonym used by Francis SPARSHOTT.

Kenyon, W. A. See HISTORY STUDIES IN ENGLISH 2.

Kesterton, W. H. See HISTORY STUDIES IN ENGLISH 15.

Kilbourn, William (1926–). William Morley Kilbourn was born in Toronto and educated at the University of Toronto and at Oxford and Harvard Universities. In 1951 he was appointed to the history department of McMaster University and in 1962 became the first chairman of the Humanities Division at York University, Toronto. He was for several years on the editorial boards of the *Canadian Forum* and *The Tamarack Review*, a drama critic for CBC radio, and a member of the Isaacs Gallery Ensemble, a mixed-media group in the performing arts. In 1969 he was first elected as a Toronto alderman and has gained a respected reputation as a radical on City Council. In 1973 he was elected to the executive committees of the City and of Metropolitan Toronto.

Kilbourn brings to all his writings a rare combination of accomplishments and interests: a graceful and witty literary style, a sound training as a historian, and active involvement in several facets of Canadian life, notably politics, religion, and the arts. His first book, *The firebrand: William Lyon Mackenzie and the rebellion in Upper Canada* (1956), is a memorable and convincing study of one of colonial Canada's most interesting characters. In *The elements combined: a history of the Steel Company of Canada* (1960) he lifts company history beyond the panegyric and examines the evolution of 150 years of a steel corporation and its predecessors in relation to the vicissitudes of technological change and of Canadian political, economic, and social life. Another company, Trans-Canada Pipe Lines, is the subject of *Pipeline* (1970) in which Kilbourn is able to intertwine and explain the complex political and economic problems facing the Canadian government and the natural gas industry in the 1950s. He is also the author of *The making of a nation: a century of challenge* (1965; rev. 1973), a brief illustrated history of Canada since 1867.

Kilbourn edited *Canada: a guide to the peaceable kingdom* (1970), a collection of topical essays on various aspects of the Canadian identity; *The restless church: a response to 'The Comfortable Pew'* (1966); and *Religion in Canada: the spiritual development of a nation* (1969). He has contributed essays to *The Canadians*; *The new Romans*; *The literary history of Canada*; *John Toronto: new poems by Dr Strachan*; *Inside City Hall: the year of the opposition*; *The open gate: Toronto's Union Station*; and several other books. DF

Kilgallin, Tony. See ANTHOLOGIES IN ENGLISH 2.

King, A. R. See INDIANS 6.

Kirby, William. See LITERARY STUDIES IN FRENCH 2.

Kirkconnell, Watson (1895–). Born in Port Hope, Ont., he was educated at Queen's University, served in the First World War, studied music in Toronto from 1920 to 1922, and then completed his education at Oxford University. He joined the staff of Wesley College, Winnipeg, where he taught first English and then classics. He was head of the English department of McMaster University from 1940 to 1948 when he became president of Acadia University. He retired in 1963. He was elected to the Royal Society of Canada in 1936 and was awarded the Lorne Pierce Medal for outstanding service to Canadian literature.

A distinguished scholar, Kirkconnell has made numerous contributions to several literary fields. His mastery of languages is shown in his compilation *The celestial cycle: the theme of Paradise Lost in world literature, with translations of the major analogues* (1952); he supplemented it in *That invincible Samson: the theme of Samson Agonistes in world literature with translations of the major analogues* (1964) and *Awake the courteous echo: the themes of Comus, Lycidas, and Paradise Regained in world literature with translations of the major analogues* (1973). Other works in this field are *An outline of European literature* (1927) and *The European heritage: a synopsis of European cultural achievement* (1930). His metrical translations are *European elegies: one hundred poems chosen and translated from European literature in fifty languages* (1928); *The North American book of Icelandic verse* (1930); *The Magyar muse: an anthology of Hungarian poetry, 1400–1932* (1933); *Canadian overtones: an anthology of Canadian poetry written originally in Icelandic, Swedish, Hungarian, Italian, Greek, and Ukrainian* (1935); *A golden treasury of Polish lyrics* (1936); *A little treasury of Hungarian verse* (1947); the Polish epic *Pan Tadeusz; or The last foray in Lithuania* (1962); and *The Ukrainian poets, 1189–1962* (1963), which he translated with C. H. Andrusyshen, who also collaborated with him in translating *The poetical works of Taras Shevchenko* (1964).

Kirkconnell's own verse was collected in *The tide of life* (1930); *The eternal quest* (1934); *The flying bull and other tales* (1940), 'tall tales' told by a representative assortment of travellers who are snowbound at a prairie hotel; and in three small pamphlets, *Manitoba symphony* [1937?], *Lyra sacra: four occasional hymns* (1939), and *Western idyll* (1940). *Titus the toad* (1939) is a book for children. His *Centennial tales and selected poems* was published in 1965. In the field of social studies Kirkconnell wrote *Canadians all: a primer of national unity* (1940). He collaborated with Séraphin Marion in compiling an anthology of prose and verse, *Tradition du Québec/The Quebec tradition* (1946), for which he provided translations of the French selections, and with A. S. P. Woodhouse in the survey *The humanities in Canada* (1947). For many years he contributed the section 'Publications in other languages' to the annual survey 'Letters in Canada' in the University of Toronto *Quarterly*; his first review included publications of 1935–7 and his last those of 1965. There is a selective list of Kirkconnell's work in the *Acadia Bulletin* (January 1961).

Kirkconnell's *A slice of Canada: memoirs* (1967) is particularly interesting for its descriptions of the development of his scholarly projects. NS

Kirschbaum, Joseph M. See HISTORY STUDIES IN ENGLISH 14.

Kiyooka, Roy. See POETRY IN ENGLISH 2.

Klein, A. M. (1909–72). Abraham Moses Klein was born in Montreal and educated at McGill University and at the Université de Montréal; he was called to the bar in 1933 and practised law until 1954. He was editor of *The Canadian Jewish Chronicle* from 1939 to 1954 and was active in the Labour Zionist movement and as a socialist: he was an unsuccessful CCF candidate in the 1948 election. In the mid-1940s he was associated with the Montreal poets who were publishing the magazine *Preview* and from 1945 to 1947 was visiting lecturer in poetry at McGill University. In 1957 the Royal Society of Canada awarded him the Lorne Pierce Medal for distinguished service to Canadian literature.

Klein's first three collections of poetry—*Hath not a Jew . . .* (1940), *Poems* (1944), and *The Hitleriad* (1944), a satire on the Nazis—have as their most prominent themes anti-semitism and mankind's responsibility for the Nazi holocaust. They reflect Klein's learning in Jewish law, philosophy, culture, and history; his warm feeling for Jewish folk-ways and parable; and the influence of James Joyce in his use of language. The only book of Klein's that is specifically Canadian is *The rocking chair and other poems* (1941), which won a Governor General's Award. As Miriam WADDINGTON has pointed out, Klein was a poet of the minorities—the Jew, the French Canadian, the Indian, and the poet—and this is nowhere more evident than in *The rocking chair*, which contains poems on all these groups. It is a book that is very much rooted in Klein's Canadian self, and the portraits, love poems, and poems of social criticism contained in this collection are enduring images of the Canadian experience.

For *The second scroll* (1951) Klein turned once again to the Jewish heritage for his subject matter. It is a complex parable about a spiritual pilgrimage to the Promised Land (Israel), consisting of a short novel and a series of glosses made up of dramatic fragments, poems, and prayers. It has been reprinted in the New Canadian Library with an introduction by M. W. Steinberg.

Klein began a book about James Joyce, and three chapters appeared in literary magazines in Canada and the United States, but in the mid-1950s he suffered a breakdown, retired from all his activities, and was inactive until his death.

In *A. M. Klein* (1970) Miriam Waddington has written an informed and illuminating study that is of particular interest for its discussion of Klein's three-dozen Marxist radical poems, written in the 1930s, which were never collected in his lifetime. *The rocking chair* is the only collection of Klein's poetry in print, but a selection of his poems can be found in *Poets between the wars* (1967) edited by Milton Wilson. An edition of Klein's collected poems is in preparation, with an introduction by Mrs Waddington. WET

Klinck, Carl F. (1908–). Carl Frederick Klinck was born at Elmira, Ont., and educated at Waterloo College, the University of Western Ontario, and at Columbia University. He taught English at Waterloo College and then at the University of Western Ontario where he was head of the English department from 1948 to 1955 and Senior Professor from 1955 to 1973, when he retired. His ability to make a scholarly appraisal of the background influences of a writer adds substance to his literary studies. These include *Wilfred Campbell: a study in late provincial Victorianism* (1942) and the biographical section of *Edwin J. Pratt: the man and his poetry* (1947), written in collaboration with Henry W. Wells. He edited with R. E. Watters the well-known college text *Canadian anthology* (1955; rev. 1966). He wrote prefaces to the New Canadian Library reprints of Frances Brooke's *The history of Emily Montague*; Susanna Moodie's *Roughing it in the bush*; John Richardson's *Wacousta*; *'Tiger' Dunlop's Upper Canada;* and Rosanna Leprohon's *Antoinette de Mirecourt*. He edited *William 'Tiger' Dunlop, 'Blackwoodian Backwoodsman': essays by and about Dunlop* (1958); collaborated with Brandon Conron and Guy Sylvestre in the biographical dictionary *Canadian writers/Écrivains canadiens* (1964); and was general editor of the *Literary history of Canada* (1965), for which he wrote two chapters on literary activities in the Canadas (Ontario and Quebec) from 1812 to 1880. He wrote the introduction to Abraham S. Holmes' *Belinda; or The rivals*, published by the Alcuin Society in 1970, and in collaboration with James J. Talman edited the Champlain Society edition of *The journal of Major John Norton 1816* (1970). NS

Klymasz, Robert B. See FOLKLORE: BIBLIOGRAPHY.

Koch, Eric. See FICTION IN ENGLISH 1.

Kopas, Cliff. See INDIAN LEGENDS AND ART.

Kos-Rabcewicz-Zubowski, Ludwik. See HISTORY STUDIES IN ENGLISH 14.

Kottman, Richard N. See HISTORY STUDIES IN ENGLISH 11.

Krickberg, Walter. See INDIAN LEGENDS AND ART.

Kroetsch, Robert (1927–). Born in Heisler, Alta, he was educated at the University of Alberta. He worked for two years as a labourer on the Fort Smith Portage and sailed for two seasons on the Mackenzie River before continuing his studies at McGill University. He has studied and taught at various universities and now teaches English at the State University of New York, Binghamton, N.Y.

The western and northern landscapes are integral to the themes of Kroetsch's fiction and exert their influence on the varied characters he depicts. His exceptional versatility has made him a master of several styles. The direct narrative style of the adventure tale is used in his first novel, *But we are exiles* (1965), in which the theme of exile is worked out at four levels. Delayed in getting out of the Mackenzie River, a boat struggles in an alien and hostile world with blinding snow, ice, fog, and shifting sandbars; the sense of exile is felt by the crew as they think of their homes; and this is heightened by the presence of a corpse, the cause of the delay and the symbol of exile from life itself. Central to the novel is the conflict between Mike Hornyak and Peter Guy, each of whom is exiled by his double role of betrayer and betrayed. *The words of my roaring* (1966) is a comic novel about the Alberta election of 1935 in which Bible-thumping William Aberhart, parodied as Applecart, promises salvation from depression, drought, and eastern parasites who batten on debt-ridden farmers. Kroetsch restrains his exuberance, however, as he depicts the fundamental decency and subtle relations between two candidates in a rural community and portrays the desperate condition of the farmers.

Kroetsch's skill as a novelist made a further advance in *The studhorse man* (1969) in which he adopted the approach of a pseudo-academic biography. The narrator, the inmate of a mental hospital, makes of Hazard Lepage a mythological figure of the West as he describes his at times uproarious—and in the end fatal—search across Alberta for a mare for his blue stallion. A complex novel that employs parody, burlesque, and word-play with technical ingenuity, it reveals both the biographer and the studhorse man as it explodes the myth of frontier opportunity. It won a Governor General's Award. A fourth novel, *Gone Indian*, appeared in 1973.

Kroetsch's anthology *Creation* (1970) includes (along with work by James BACQUE and Pierre Gravel) his excellent story 'The yellow prairie sky', about the hazards of farming; some of his poetry; and a recorded conversation between himself and Margaret LAURENCE in which they discuss his ideas on writing.

Kroetsch is also the author of *Alberta* (1968), a volume in the Traveller's Canada series. His description of the land and urban development is combined with relevant stories about the various types of people who have been associated with the province since pioneer days. His collected poems, *The stone hammer poems*, will be published in 1973. NS

Krosby, H. Peter. See HISTORY STUDIES IN ENGLISH 1.

Kurath, Gertrude P. See INDIAN LEGENDS AND ART.

Kushner, Eva. See LITERARY STUDIES IN FRENCH 4.

Kwavnick, David. See POLITICAL WRITINGS IN ENGLISH 5.

L

Laberge, Marie. See POETRY IN FRENCH.

Lacerte, Rolande. See CHILDREN'S BOOKS IN FRENCH.

Lachance, André. See HISTORY STUDIES IN FRENCH 3.

Lachance, Bernard. See POETRY IN ENGLISH 3.

Lacôte, René. See LITERARY STUDIES IN FRENCH 4.

Lacoursière, Jacques. See HISTORY STUDIES IN FRENCH 4 and POLITICAL WRITINGS IN FRENCH 7.

Lacroix, Benoît. See BELLES LETTRES IN FRENCH; HISTORY STUDIES IN FRENCH 2; and LITERARY STUDIES IN FRENCH 4.

Ladoo, Harold Sonny. See FICTION IN ENGLISH 4.

Lafleur, Norman. See HISTORY STUDIES IN FRENCH 7.

La Follette, James E. See FOLKLORE: BIBLIOGRAPHY.

La Forest, Gérard V. See POLITICAL WRITINGS IN FRENCH 3.

Laforte, Denis. See POLITICAL WRITINGS IN FRENCH 5.

Laidlaw, Alexander F. See HISTORY STUDIES IN ENGLISH 11.

Lalande, Gilles. See POLITICAL WRITINGS IN ENGLISH 6 and POLITICAL WRITINGS IN FRENCH 3.

Lalonde, Michèle (1937–). Born and educated in Montreal, she holds a Ph.L. from the Université de Montréal. She was acclaimed at an early age as one of Québec's outstanding lyric poets, but she has published only two collections of verse, *Songe de la fiancée détruite* (1958) and *Geôles* (1959), both of which demonstrate her gift for rendering a personal anguish with consummate skill and passion. The early themes of solitude and imprisonment in these collections are sharply opposed in her *Terre des hommes* (1967), an important poem as well as a *pièce de circonstance* that was written for public recitation—with musical counterpoint for massed choir and full orchestra by the Montreal composer André Prévost—and presented at the inauguration of Expo 67. In this long lyric poem, which expresses the collective alienation of modern man, her abilities found wider scope. In recent years the subject of her poetry has been the more specific alienation of the French-speaking people of Québec and she has reached the public mainly by way of recitals and readings and participation in poetry 'happenings', recordings, films, etc. Michèle Lalonde's much-discussed poem 'Speak white', an eloquent and impassioned plea for French culture against an invading and inevitably English-speaking North American culture, was delivered by her as part of a program of 'Poems and songs of the resistance' that toured Québec with great success in 1968–9, and was published in *Socialisme '68* (No. 15). Translations of this and other poems by Michèle Lalonde were featured in *Ellipse* No. 3 (Spring 1970); others are in *The poetry of French Canada in translation* (1970) edited by John GLASSCO and *Contemporary Literature in Translation*, No. 12 (Winter 1971–2). JG

LaMarsh, Judy. See HISTORY STUDIES IN ENGLISH 12.

Lamb, W. Kaye. See HISTORY STUDIES IN ENGLISH 1 and 3.

Lambert, Richard S. See HISTORY STUDIES IN ENGLISH 13.

Lanctot, Gustave (1883–). Born at Saint-Constant, Qué., he was educated at the Université de Montréal, and at Oxford and the Sorbonne. Appointed to the staff of the Public Archives of Canada in 1912, he became deputy minister in 1937 and retired in 1948. His most important historical works are *L'administration de la Nouvelle-France* (1929), a specialized study of the constitutional framework of the French colony; *Le Canada d'hier et d'aujourd'hui* (1934), a general survey of Canada's development first as a colony and then as a nation; *L'oeuvre de la France en Amérique du Nord: bibliographie sélective et critique* (1951); and the first three volumes of his *Histoire du Canada* (1960–3) which covers the period to 1763 (vol. 1, translated by Josephine Hambleton, 1963; vols 2 and 3, translated by Margaret Cameron, 1964 and 1965). More recently, Gustave Lanctot has published *Le Canada et la révolution américaine* (1965) and *Montréal sous Maisonneuve* (1966), which was published in an English translation by Alta Lind Cook as *Montreal under Maisonneuve: 1642–1665* (1969).

Lanctot has delighted in investigating historical questions around which some cherished legend has grown, demolishing some of these legends and adding his weight to others. In the first volume of his *Histoire du Canada*, he supports the theory that a colony of Irish monks found a home on the St Lawrence River at the end of the ninth century. In *Filles de joie ou filles du roi; étude sur l'émigration féminine en Nouvelle-France* (1952) he attacks the view that the King's Girls were women of low character and brings evidence to show that they were carefully selected as suitable brides for the settlers of New France. *Faussaires et faussetés en histoire canadienne* (1948) is a collection of short articles on common historical errors, and in *Réalisations françaises de Cartier à Montcalm* (1951) and *Une Nouvelle France inconnue* (1955) Lanctot deals with the lesser-known historical facts. In *Jacques Cartier devant l'histoire* (1947) he develops his thesis that Cartier visited the American coast prior to the voyage of 1534 and corrects views expressed by earlier writers. *François-Xavier Garneau* (1926; Eng. ed. 1927) contains a short biography, a critical appreciation, and an anthology. It was reprinted under the title *Garneau: historien national* (1946). Lanctot edited the symposium *Les Canadiens français et leurs voisins du sud* (1941) and wrote some of the articles. This volume, in the Carnegie series on 'Relations of Canada and the United States', won the Prix David. He also edited *The Oakes Collection: new documents by Lahontan concerning Canada and Newfoundland* (1940) and collaborated with A. G. Doughty in editing *Cheadle's journal of trip across Canada: 1862–1863* (1931). *The royal tour of King George VI and Queen Elizabeth in Canada: 1939* (1964) by Barbara Urquhart is a condensation of Lanctot's official report of that tour. NS/J-LR

Landes, Ruth. See INDIAN LEGENDS AND ART.

Landry, Louis. See POLITICAL WRITINGS IN FRENCH 3.

Lane, Patrick. See POETRY IN ENGLISH 2.

Lane, Red. See POETRY IN ENGLISH 2.

Lane, Travis. See POETRY IN ENGLISH 2.

Langdon, Eustella. See FOLKLORE: BIBLIOGRAPHY.

Langdon, John E. See HISTORY STUDIES IN ENGLISH 7.

Langevin, André (1927–). Born in Montreal, he was orphaned very young, having lost both his father and his mother by the time he was seven. During the next five years he received his schooling in an institution that he later referred to as 'asylum-like'—a 'locked-in world' that was especially cruel to children, where the conditions were worse that those inflicted on the prisoners in the Saint-Vincent-de-Paul penitentiary: the child was dehumanized and reduced to a mere number. From there he passed directly into a classical college where he made his first contact with the sons of the French-Canadian bourgeoisie. His first job was as a messenger for the Montreal newspaper *Le Devoir*. After six months he suddenly became responsible for the paper's literary section and remained in this position for three years, reading voraciously and 're-educating' himself. During this period he was influenced by the writings of Sartre and Camus and particularly by Gabrielle ROY's first novel *Bonheur d'occasion*. He subsequently accepted employment with the French network of the Canadian Broadcasting Corporation, where at the end of the 1940s and in the early 1950s he discovered 'a fine group with open minds, people who had become educated on their own'. At present a producer for Radio-Canada, Langevin has also frequently contributed articles to publications such as *Le Magazine Maclean* and *Le Nouveau Journal* on subjects of current political or social interest. He married the daughter of one of the longest-established doctors of Thetford Mines, the town that served as the setting for his second novel, *Poussière sur la ville*. He lives in Frelighsburg in the Eastern Townships.

Langevin is the author of four novels that have securely established his reputation as one of the most significant contemporary Québec writers. His first novel, *Évadé de la nuit* (1951), won him his first Prix du Cercle du Livre de France and revealed his powerful talent. A work of youth, lacking in unity, forced in tone, flawed by various excesses, it is nonetheless one to which the reader cannot remain indifferent. It is the drama of human incommunicability that prevents the characters from meeting other than in death. Jean Cherteffe, abandoned as a child by his alcoholic father and raised in an orphanage, struggles in vain to free himself from his obsession with his dead father's memory by attempting to rehabilitate Roger Benoît, a drunken poet. The first two sections of the book end with Jean's total defeat in his efforts to 'reclaim the soul' of the abject Benoît, who commits suicide. The last two parts of the novel relate the growing love between Jean and Micheline, the daughter of Judge Giraud, their slow and painful search for happiness, the death of Micheline in childbirth, and the suicide of Jean in the snow.

In *Poussière sur la ville* (1953), one of the best French-Canadian novels, Langevin relates the tragedy of Alain Dubois, a young medical doctor in the mining town of Macklin, and his wife Madeleine, who publicly flaunts her unfaithfulness to him with a lover, Richard Hétu, under her husband's own roof. The influence of Camus is evident, and metaphysical and existential considerations form the core of the book. The plight of Alain Dubois is that he is desperately searching for happiness for himself and his wife in a brutal and absurd universe where there is no escape from suffering and no answers except in pity and a sense of human solidarity. This short novel, which was translated by John Latrobe and Robert Gottlieb as *Dust over the city* (1955), has all the earmarks of a classical tragedy and is written in a beautifully simple style. The tone of pessimism is less profound than in *Évadé de la nuit*. It won for Langevin his second Prix du Cercle du Livre de France; it was later made into a movie filmed in Thetford Mines by Arthur Lamothe.

The attitude of pity for his fellow men is one of the fundamental attitudes adopted by Pierre Dupas in Langevin's third novel *Le temps des hommes* (1956). Less successful than *Poussière*, this work traces the unhappy fate of a man who had lost his faith ten years earlier when he was obliged to watch helplessly as a twelve-year-old boy suffered and died of cerebrospinal meningitis.

The characters in Langevin's world belong among the outcasts and down-trodden of the earth, who are swallowed up by despair because of their inability to communicate, or to escape from their eternal solitude. His first three novels are a sort of severe and bitter tribute to them, inspired by a feeling of profound pity and compassion in the face of their unhappiness.

In the sixteen years following *Le temps des hommes* Langevin published no further novels and for twelve years refused to give press interviews. The appearance in 1972 of his fourth novel, *L'élan d'Amérique*, was heralded as a significant literary event and in March 1973 it was awarded the Grand Prix littéraire of the city of Montreal. It is infinitely complex and full of symbolic imagery; it is also a poem that constantly shifts back and forth between dream and reality. In the course of the long beginning of the novel, Langevin presents Claire Smith, who is married to Stephen Peabody, the rich vice-president of the United States Pulp and Paper Company who may in fact be her real father. Claire is an American, although on her mother's side her roots are in Québec. Amoral, liberated, but spiritually lost and empty, she is constantly searching in vain for the male who will dominate her. Among her countless unsuccessful adventures, two leave a lasting imprint on her. David teaches her tenderness, but the inconstancy of Claire drives him to suicide. From Antoine, a guide working for an American logging company, she learns dignity and force. Antoine has left his wife and children to live in the forest. (The pages devoted to his marriage are frightening.) A tremendous moose appears in the forest—'l'élan d'Amérique'. Weighing a ton, it symbolizes the perfection of creation and of man, the male, the master of the universe. The first instinctive reaction of Claire Peabody is to slaughter him, that of Antoine to protect him. But in the end the moose is killed and Antoine brings back to Claire its head and antlers. He then flees from a world full of ugliness and disorder, seeking refuge in the woods, and Claire, after shoving the moosehead out of the Cessna that was flying her back to civilization, commits suicide by jumping after it. Allegorically Antoine represents Québec—dispossessed, caught in a trap, despoiled of everything. Claire offers a desolating spectacle of existential solitude in contact with a French Canada constantly reduced to defending its frontiers forever menaced by outsiders. In this book Langevin has written pages full of rare violence denouncing some of the conditions that enslave the people of Québec: existential alienation, exploitation, dispossession, assimilation by the North American whole.

Langevin is also the author of two stage plays and three television dramas that have met with only limited success. His first dramatic work, *Une nuit d'amour*, was produced by the Théâtre du Nouveau Monde in 1954. The action takes place in Acadia after the conquest. *L'oeuil du peuple*, a three-act satire on municipal political corruption and leagues for moral decency, was written in

1957 and staged in November of that year by the Théâtre du Nouveau Monde.

Langevin's first television drama, *La neige en octobre*, was presented in 1968. His second, broadcast by Radio-Canada on November 5, 1972, on the program 'Les Beaux Dimanches', presented a couple in their forties who, having dug up the hatchet, interminably settle old scores. His third, *Jouer au cerceau sur un pont*, was completed in 1972 and is scheduled for production. LWK

Langevin, Gilbert. See POETRY IN FRENCH.

Langford, Cameron. See CHILDREN'S BOOKS IN ENGLISH 5.

Languirand, Jacques (1930–). Born in Montreal, he was educated at the Collège Saint-Laurent and in Paris. In 1950 he joined the staff of the French network of the Canadian Broadcasting Corporation and has since worked for radio and television. He was briefly secretary-general of the Théâtre du Nouveau Monde and now lectures at McGill University and the National Theatre School.

A playwright, Languirand takes as his subject the tragi-comic perplexity of the individual who, lacking serious purpose, makes weak and misunderstood efforts to free himself from the pressures of a society in which he feels stifled and before which he feels guilty. In Paris Languirand came under the influence of Sartre and Camus, although the style of his dramaturgy has been likened to that of Ionesco and Beckett. *Les insolites* (1962) won the first Dominion Drama Festival award in 1956 and, in the year of its publication, the Governor General's Award. It is a remarkably well-constructed first play, outstanding for the author's sense of dialogue, which may be explained by the fact that Languirand already had several years' theatrical experience as an actor and director. This play demonstrates Languirand's ability to exploit a totally ludicrous situation: the characters are mere puppets, the play says nothing and consists largely of verbal byplay for its own sake. For the author it was an exercise in automatic writing, the lines succeeding one another up to a totally arbitrary ending after two acts. *Les grands départs* (1958), perhaps his best play, develops the theme of aimlessness. Each of the characters is trapped in his own solitude, incapable of communicating with the others. In endless monologues they look back on their frustrated dreams and desires. In fact there is no 'grand departure': the family wait, their cases ready, but the movers never arrive. On the contrary two members of the family return, their earlier departure having proved unsuccessful. In the end it is the grandfather who leaves—suddenly, arbitrarily, and with no explanation. *Le gibet* (1960) shows us Perplex perched on top of a pole throughout the play. He is making an attempt on the world-endurance record. Beneath the surface, however, his gesture is meant to reaffirm the supremacy of the individual will in a society that seeks to make people conform and pursue materialistic ends. Perplex momentarily relieves the monotony in the lives of his friends and neighbours, but his gesture is misunderstood and he is abandoned by them. Although in the fifties Languirand was considered one of the three leading Québec dramatists, his work did not export well: *Les violons de l'automne* (1962, with *Les insolites*) was a resounding failure in Paris. His vision of modern society bringing out all that is sordid and ugly in mankind, the theme of *Le gibet*, is here concentrated in the actions and words of three old people. No doubt plays about the old are never very popular, and a tragic and crude ending would also be more than many audiences could stomach. With this play Languirand seemed to reach the limits of his exploration of his early themes. These first four plays were produced between 1956 and 1960 and may be considered Languirand's major works for the theatre.

Languirand has written eight plays since 1960, of which three have been published. *Klondyke* (1971), a historical musical comedy, was a successful attempt at popular theatre and was taken to England by the TNM for the Commonwealth Arts Festival in 1965. It is the best of his later works, reflecting his ability to manipulate modern theatrical techniques, and foreshadowing the 'shows' of Michel TREMBLAY and Jean BARBEAU. The play chronicles the ups and downs of the pioneers who took part in the celebrated Yukon 'gold rush' in 1898. The other published plays are *Diogène* (1965) and *Les cloisons* (1966). In 1966, after two years with the TNM, Languirand expressed his total disgust with the theatre. He thereupon proposed to continue his experiments in 'collective creation', begun with

Klondyke, in a popular theatre setting away from the centre of Montreal. Unfortunately his plans for the Centre culturel du Vieux-Montréal never reached fruition because of a lack of subsidies. His multi-media show, *L'âge de pierre*, received its only performance, in Toronto, as *Man, Inc.* Since 1967 Languirand has abandoned the theatre, concentrating on his radio program for the French network of the CBC and on writing a thousand-page book, *Communication*, the first volume of which, *De McLuhan à Pythagore*, appeared in 1972.

In 1963 Languirand published a psychological novel, *Tout compte fait; ou, l'Eugène*, which takes up the themes of the earlier plays, with Eugène looking back on his mediocre life and regretting his youthful ambitions. Languirand's other works are the humorous *Dictionnaire insolite* (1961) and a travel-book, *J'ai découvert le Tahiti* (1961). JC

Lapalme, Georges Émile. See HISTORY STUDIES IN FRENCH 11.

LaPierre, Laurier. See POLITICAL WRITINGS IN ENGLISH 4.

Lapointe, Gatien (1931–). Born in Sainte-Justine, Qué., he was educated at the Université de Montréal. He lived for several years in Europe and wrote a doctoral thesis on Paul Eluard for the University of Paris. He teaches at the Université du Québec in Trois-Rivières, where he is also director of the Éditions des Forges. Lapointe has published five volumes of poetry: *Jour malaisé* (1953); *Otages de la joie* (1955); *Le temps premier, suivi de Lumière du monde* (1962), which won the Prix du Club des Poètes; *Ode au Saint-Laurent, précédée de J'appartiens à la terre* (1963), which won a Governor General's Award as well as the Troisième Prix de la Province and the Prix du Maurier; and *Le premier mot, précédé de Le pari de ne pas mourir* (1967).

After some early verse that spoke of the solitude of the poet and the pain of living in an imperfect world, Gatien Lapointe has written consistently in a style that perfectly expresses the poet's infectious mood of courage, hope, and purposefulness. Verbs predominate—verbs of action in the active voice, generally in the present or future tenses and the first person singular or in the imperative. Sentences are short and vigorous and negations are almost totally absent. The old painful dualism of flesh and spirit is forgotten or perhaps deliberately silenced. The poet demands a kind of knowing and remembering that is simple and unintellectual. In *Ode au Saint-Laurent* Lapointe attempts a physical identification with the great river that is the life-blood of his land. His style precludes the possibility of narration or even of much development, but it powerfully and nobly proclaims the poet's faith in his role and in the power of the word to create a sense of reality and being that can keep the hideous fact of death at bay. There are tears and pain, doubts and questionings, but they pale beside the profusion of dynamic assertions that make up Lapointe's poetic discourse. This enthusiasm is founded on a wager, an act of blind faith in words. 'Je donne parole à tout ce qui vit . . ./ J'ouvre à l'homme un champ d'être.' Excerpts from *Ode au Saint-Laurent* appear in *Contemporary Literature in Translation*, No. 12 (Winter 1971–2). Translations of four other poems are in *The poetry of French Canada in translation* edited by John GLASSCO. CRPM

Lapointe, Paul-Marie (1929–). Born at Saint-Félicien, Qué., he was educated at the Collège de Saint-Laurent and at the École des Beaux-Arts, Montreal. He has been engaged in television, was editor-in-chief of *Le Magazine Maclean*, and is at present a public-affairs supervisor for the television network of Radio-Canada.

Lapointe is a surrealist poet who expresses anger and disgust with the modern world. His first collection of poems, *Le vierge incendié* (1948), was criticized for lack of discipline; the book nevertheless became one of the seminal works in the modern poetry of Québec and a major surrealist influence. In his later collections, *Choix de poèmes: arbres* (1960) and *Pour les âmes: poèmes* (1965), there is an increased organization of thought and selectivity of language in the poems concerned with human brutality and man's despair, and a constant suggestion that mankind itself is a species doomed to extinction by its pursuit of materiality. His *Le réel absolu* (1971), a selection from his previous volumes, was the outstanding collection of the year, winning the Prix David and a Governor General's Award. *Six poèmes* (1965) is a selection from his earlier work, with naive English translations by Jean Beaupré and Gael

Turnbull; other English versions of his work have appeared in *The poetry of French Canada in translation* (1970) edited by John GLASSCO and were featured in the review *Ellipse*, No. 11 (1972). NS/JG

Laponce, Jean A. See HISTORY STUDIES IN ENGLISH 12 and POLITICAL WRITINGS IN ENGLISH 5.

Large, R. Geddes. See INDIAN LEGENDS AND ART.

Laroche, Maximilien. See LITERARY STUDIES IN FRENCH 4.

Larocque, André. See POLITICAL WRITINGS IN FRENCH 4.

La Rocque, Gilbert. See FICTION IN FRENCH 3.

Larue-Langlois, Jacques. See POETRY IN FRENCH.

Laskin, Bora. See HISTORY STUDIES IN ENGLISH 12.

Lasnier, Rina (1915–). Born at Saint-Grégoire, Qué., she was educated partly in Montreal and partly in England before attending the Université de Montréal. She has been employed as a librarian, journalist, and secretary.

Rina Lasnier won the Prix David in 1943 and the Prix Duvernay in 1957 for her poetry and plays. Both are inspired by religious feeling. While showing an awareness of the spirit of revolt and the changing attitudes brought about by the quiet revolution of Québec, she has retained her veneration of the past. Her first collection, *Images et proses* (1941), is largely religious in inspiration. Her talent was hobbled in *Madones canadiennes* (1944) in which each lyric was written as a text for one of a series of pictures used by Marius Barbeau to illustrate the art of Québec as exemplified in statues of the madonna. Her full lyric powers were brought out in *Le chant de la montée* (1947), a series of chants inspired by the story of Jacob and Rachel. In *Escales* (1950), *Présence de l'absence* (1956), *Mémoire sans jours: poèmes* (1960), *Les gisants* (1963), and *L'arbre blanc* (1966) she reached the height of her poetic stature, establishing herself as one of the most important poets of her generation. Her mastery of the lyric was fully sustained in *La salle des rêves* (1971) for which she received the first A. J. M. SMITH Prize awarded annually to the most distinguished collection of poems published in Canada in either French or English. Although written in prose, the tales and sketches of *Miroirs: proses* (1960) are so impressionistic that they may well be classed with her poetry.

Rina Lasnier's plays were inspired by the religious history of Québec. *Féerie indienne: Kateri Tekakwitha* (1939) is based on the life of the celebrated Mohawk girl (1656–1680?), an Indian convert and recent candidate for beatification; *Le jeu de la voyagère* (1941) on the career of Marguerite Bourgeoys; and *Les fiançailles d'Anne de Noüe* (1943) on the work of a Jesuit missionary. *Notre-Dame du pain* (1947) was written for the Eucharistic Congress held in Ottawa. Rina Lasnier has also written *La mère de nos mères* (1943), a biographical essay on Marguerite Bourgeoys. A bibliography and representative selections from her verse and prose are in *Rina Lasnier: textes choisis* (1964) by Jean Marcel; a further anthology of her poetry, *La part du feu* (1970), carries a critical introduction by Guy ROBERT. The essay *Rina Lasnier* (1964) by Eva Kushner belongs more to the field of apologetics than to literary criticism.

Rina Lasnier was awarded the Québec Provincial Prize in 1967, and in 1971 the Molson Prize for outstanding achievements in the arts, the humanities, and the social sciences. She has been a member of the Académie canadienne-française since its founding in 1944. Her poems have been translated into English, Spanish, Italian, and Ukrainian. NS/JG

La Terreur, Marc. See HISTORY STUDIES IN ENGLISH 6 and HISTORY STUDIES IN FRENCH 11.

Laurence, Margaret (1926–), *née* Wemys. Jean Margaret Laurence was born in Neepawa, Man., and educated at United College, Winnipeg, an affiliate of the University of Manitoba. Married in 1948, she lived in England until 1949, and then in Somaliland for two years and in the Gold Coast (Ghana) until 1957. She spent five years in Vancouver before making her home in Buckinghamshire, Eng. She has retained her link with Canada, spending her summers near Peterborough, Ont. She was writer-in-residence at the University of Toronto in 1969–70.

Margaret Laurence's writing is distinguished by penetrating and wise characterizations that grow out of her admiration for the vitality of the human spirit, by a sturdy attitude towards the problems of life and compassion that can find expression in humour, and by technical skill that can weave the inner and outer lives of people into fiction that is significant and true. Neepawa, transmogrified into the small prairie town of Manawaka, links her novels of the Canadian west: *The stone angel* (1964), *A jest of God* (1966), *The fire-dwellers* (1969), and *A bird in the house* (1970). Ninety-year-old Hagar Shipley in *The stone angel* is one of the great characters of modern literature. Formidable and cantankerous, painfully aware of her lapses of memory, she struggles to maintain her independence of a son and a daughter-in-law she distrusts. During periods of lucidity she reflects on her life, discovering that her difficulties were brought on by her own headstrong acts and her inability to be kind or to rejoice when life was full and she was vigorous.

Hagar had the character to triumph over the sordid situation into which a foolish marriage had led her. Rachel Cameron, the protagonist of *A jest of God*, is a sex-starved virgin of thirty-four who is on the verge of nervous collapse as she copes with a neurotic mother. Rachel must be jolted by the traumatic but ludicrous sequel to a summer's folly before she summons enough courage to break with her narrow existence as a school teacher and establish herself and her mother in Vancouver where her sister Stacey lives. This novel won a Governor General's Award and was made into the film *Rachel, Rachel*.

Rachel's sister Stacey, who had left Manawaka for Vancouver when she was seventeen, is the more complex central character of *The fire-dwellers*. Emotionally immature at thirty-nine, with four children whom she loves, Stacey rages against her limited life, advancing middle age, and her own inadequacies until she is shocked out of her self-pity, first by hearing of the deprivations of a halfbreed family she had known as a child and then by the near blindness of her father-in-law, a situation that calls forth the best in her nature. Mrs Laurence finds plenty of scope for wit in Stacey's acts and reflections and in following the misadventures and ultimate success of Stacey's husband, Clifford MacAindra, a salesman.

A bird in the house, in which each chapter is a short story, follows the development of a child growing up in a household of strong, sometimes eccentric adults who must bow to the whims of a tyrannical grandfather. Vanessa MacLeod flits among her elders with the bewilderment, curiosity, and secret reservations of a highly observant child. She develops into a young woman who becomes capable of viewing the eccentricities of her relatives humorously.

Working from her knowledge of Africa, Mrs Laurence wrote *This side Jordan* (1960) in which she laid bare the conflicting attitudes with which Africans and European residents faced the approaching independence of Ghana. *The tomorrow-tamer* (1963) is a collection of short stories on an African theme. *The prophet's camel bell* (1963) is an account of two years spent in Somaliland; it was published in the United States under the title *New wind in a dry land* (1964).

Mrs Laurence is also the author of *Jason's quest* (1970), a story for children, and of *Long drums and cannons* (1971), a study of contemporary Nigerian literature. An appreciation of her work will be found in *Margaret Laurence* (1969) by Clara THOMAS, a volume in the Canadian Writers Series of the New Canadian Library, which also includes *The stone angel*, *The tomorrow-tamer*, and *The fire-dwellers*. NS

Laurendeau, André. See BELLES LETTRES IN FRENCH; DRAMA IN FRENCH intro. and 1; and POLITICAL WRITINGS IN FRENCH 4.

Laurin, Camille. See POLITICAL WRITINGS IN FRENCH 4.

Lavoie, Yolande. See HISTORY STUDIES IN FRENCH 7.

Lax, Jerry. See POLITICAL WRITINGS IN ENGLISH 2.

Laxer, James. See POLITICAL WRITINGS IN ENGLISH 2.

Layton, Irving (1912–). Born in Romania, he came to Montreal with his parents

(Lazarovitch) at the age of one, and was educated at Baron Byng High School and Macdonald College where he earned a B.Sc. in agriculture. After brief service in the Canadian Army (1942–3), he did post-graduate work in economics and political science at McGill University, obtaining an M.A. in 1946. For some years he taught English at a parochial school in Montreal, while teaching part-time at Sir George Williams College. He was appointed writer-in-residence at Sir George in 1965, and to a similar post at the University of Guelph in the winter of 1969. He was awarded a Doctor of Civil Laws by Bishop's University in 1970. Since 1969 he has been professor of English at York University, Toronto.

Layton was a member of the active group of young poets in Montreal who contributed to the poetry magazine *First Statement*, founded by John Sutherland in 1942. With Louis DUDEK in 1943, he joined Sutherland in editing the magazine and remained an editor until after it merged with *Preview* in 1945 to become *Northern Review*. He resigned in the 1950s when a change in editorial policy was adopted by Sutherland. In 1952 he was associated with Dudek and Raymond SOUSTER in founding Contact Press, a cooperative venture to publish the work of Canadian poets. Together with Robert Currie, he was instrumental in shaping the editorial policy of Aileen Collins' magazine *CIV/n* (1953–54). In 1955 he was invited by Charles Olson to join the faculty of Black Mountain College in North Carolina and the editorial board of the *Black Mountain Review*, but declined the invitation. However, he was in close contact with the American poets Robert Creeley, Cid Corman, and Jonathan Williams throughout the 1950s, and in 1956 edited a Canadian issue of Corman's magazine *Origin*.

Layton's poetry has dazzled, puzzled, angered, and astonished its readers since its first publication. From his earliest books he has vigorously opposed the aestheticist concept of the poem as a paradigm of the beautiful. To Layton the poem must convey truth, and truth can reside in the most ignoble and 'unpoetic' subjects and be expressed in blatantly non-poetic forms. The craft of poetry lies in finding the words, however unconventional, by which the vision of truth can be made manifest. Layton can see no unpoetic subjects, no non-literary words, no boundaries on the possible form of poetic utterance. The poet must simultaneously be as resourceful as a master criminal and as imaginative as the universe.

Most of Layton's collections of poetry are prefaced by attacks on those who would allegedly restrict the freedom of the poet's imagination—professors, critics, clergymen, rationalist poets, puritan editors; these people are abetted by the female in attempting to confine the poet's Apollonian spirit to a world of comfort, convention, and predictability. Layton here defiantly breaks what is to him a puritan embargo on image, magic, and sexuality; in doing so he makes the irrational an accepted part of Canadian poetry for the first time since Lampman and Carman. His vitality and ironic vulgarity, moreover, create an irrational that is vivid and brutal where before it had been sentimental and vague. Perhaps the most important aspect of his rehabilitation of the irrational is his invariably including himself among the liars, hypocrites, Yahoos, and philistines of whom he writes. His voice thus comes from inside the primal energy and vileness of our world, as an honest testimony to its dangers and powers.

Layton began serious publishing in *First Statement* magazine in 1943; between 1943 and 1952 he wrote relatively little, publishing three books, two of which reprint significant portions of the first, and contributing a small number of poems to *Cerberus* (1952), a collection he shared with Dudek and Souster. From 1953 onward he has been extraordinarily prolific, publishing an average of one book a year. The first two decades of Layton's career—*Here and now* (1945), *Now is the place* (1948), *The black huntsmen* (1951), *Love the conqueror worm* (1953), *In the midst of my fever* (1954), *The long pea-shooter* (1954), *The cold green element* (1955), *The blue propeller* (1955), *The bull calf and other poems* (1956), *The improved binoculars* (1956), *Music on a kazoo* (1956), *A laughter in the mind* (1958), and *A red carpet for the sun* (Governor General's Award)—establish the underlying dichotomies of Layton's vision: poet *v.* society, poetry *v.* literature, the individual *v.* the state, passion *v.* reason, creativity *v.* order, sacrifice *v.* rationalization, rudeness *v.* decorum, imperfection *v.* perfection, life *v.* art. The later poems continually expand the amount of the ostensibly horrific, trivial, or crude that this life-affirming vision must necessarily and paradoxically include. His later collections—*The swinging flesh* (1961), *Balls for a one-armed juggler* (1963), *The laughing rooster* (1964), *Collected poems* (1965), *Periods of the moon* (1967), *The shattered plinths* (1968), *The whole bloody bird: obs, alphs, and pomes* (1969), *Nail polish* (1971), and *Lovers and lesser men* (1973)—get increasingly angry and strident in tone, possibly because the poet sees his growing critical acceptance as ever more likely to 'emasculate' his poems with the stamp of literary respectability. His poetry can be examined in depth in *Selected poems* (1969) and *The collected poems of Irving Layton* (1971).

Layton edited *Pa-nic: a selection of contemporary Canadian poems* (1958) and *Love where the nights are long: Canadian love poems* (1962). He collaborated with Louis Dudek in editing *Canadian poems: 1805–1952* (1952). In 1972 he published *Engagements: the prose of Irving Layton*, a collection of ten stories, articles, prefaces, and reviews.

Eli MANDEL has written a critical study of Layton's poetry for the series Canadian Writers and Their Work (1969). FD

Lazure, Jacques. See POLITICAL WRITINGS IN FRENCH 2.

Leacock, Eleanor B. See INDIANS 4.

Lebel, Marc. See HISTORY STUDIES IN FRENCH 8.

Leblanc, Jacques. See ESKIMOS: BOOKS IN FRENCH.

Le Blant, Robert. See HISTORY STUDIES IN FRENCH 3.

Leclerc, Félix (1914–). Born at La Tuque, Qué., he was educated there, at a secondary school in Ottawa and at the University of Ottawa, which he attended for two years. From 1934 to 1942 he was employed as a radio announcer in Quebec City and Trois-Rivières and by Radio-Canada. He became a popular performer, reading his stories and poems and singing his own songs on the radio and from 1942 to 1945 acting with the Compagnons de Saint-Laurent. A precursor of the French-Canadian chansonniers who have become internationally popular, from 1951 to 1953 he lived in Paris, where he had a large following as a singer; he toured Europe and the Near East and was known as 'le Canadien'. He received the Prix du Disque français in 1951 and 1958. In 1966 he went back to Europe where he has remained popular—he recently had a highly successful tour with Robert Charlebois. He lives on the Île d'Orléans.

Leclerc is a troubador whose 'songs are on all lips', a writer who is simple without being naive. His books of stories, fables, songs, poems, plays, and reminiscences reflect his love of nature and folklore, his lighthearted attitude to life, his humour, and a fresh and spontaneous style of writing. His personal popularity in Québec is revealed by the fact that all his books have been reissued several times, and by the cover blurb of his latest publication, a novel—*Carcajou: ou le diable des bois* (1973)—which says merely: 'Félix Leclerc n'a pas besoin d'être présenté. Il est *lui*. Beaucoup plus qu'un célèbre, un grand Québécois.' His first publications were *Adagio* (1943), stories; *Allegro* (1944), fables; and *Andante* (1944), poems. (*Le hamac dans les voiles* (1952) is a selection from these three books.) He has written two memoirs: *Pieds nus dans l'aube* (1946), about his happy childhood in La Tuque, and *Moi, mes souliers: journal d'un lièvre à deux pattes* (Paris, 1955), about his careers as writer, actor, playwright, singer etc. Other books are *Dialogues d'hommes et de bêtes* (1949), *Le fou de l'Île* (Paris, 1958), and *Le calepin d'un flâneur* (1961). His plays are *Théâtre de village* (1951), *L'auberge des morts subites* (1964), *Sonnez les matines* (1964), and *Le p'tit bonheur* (1966). *Les chansons de Félix, le Canadien* was published in Paris in 1950; *Chansons pour tes yeux* in 1968; and *Cent chansons*—with an interview by Jean Dufour and a study of Leclerc by Marie-José Chauvin—in 1970.

See *Félix Leclerc* (Paris, 1964) edited by Luc Berimont, an essay with selections from Leclerc's writings; *L'univers poétique de Félix Leclerc* by Jean-Claude le Pennec (1967), which includes Leclerc's poems written between 1934 and 1966; and the portfolio on him in Dossiers de documentation sur la littérature canadienne-française (1967). WET

Lee, Alvin. See LITERARY STUDIES IN ENGLISH 4.

Lee, Dennis (1939–). Born in Toronto, he attended the University of Toronto and taught for four years at Victoria College there.

He was one of the founders of Rochdale College and co-founded with Dave GODFREY the House of Anansi Press. He teaches in the Division of Humanities at York University, Toronto. His poetry collections are *Kingdom of absence* (1967) and *Civil elegies* (1968), which was expanded from seven to nine poems and republished as *Civil elegies and other poems* (1972). It won a Governor General's Award. *Wiggle to the laundromat*, a collection of poems for children illustrated by Charles Pachter, appeared in 1970. Lee also co-edited with Roberta Charlesworth the textbooks *An anthology of verse* (1964) and *The second century anthologies of verse: book 2* (1967).

Lee's poetry is deeply informed by the pessimism of George GRANT's *Lament for a nation*. In his cultural concerns he is a sort of Canadian Matthew Arnold, unbearably conscious of our discontinuity with the past, of our loss of faith in God and in human values and institutions. In *Kingdom of absence* Lee sees a 'cosmos gone askew'; he deplores the emptiness of life along the razor's edge of unmeaning. These poems—in which images of alienation, absence, loss, and disinheritance abound—have some of the ratiocination and anger of John Donne's sonnets, which they resemble in a number of ways. Lee struggles to discover a language that will capture the peculiar intersection of his private and public selves: the suffering spirit and the troubled but concerned citizen. And to a certain extent he is successful in *Civil elegies* (1968) where, from the vantage point of Toronto's Nathan Phillips Square, he documents his country's 'failure of nerve' and his own complicity. The elegies extend beyond themselves to encompass the history of material interests, imperialism, and war. Lee is a deeply concerned poet; at times his manner and matter remind one of Pound's *Cantos*. There is too much abstraction in the elegies; ideas often dominate the poetry at the expense of image and sound. However, these poems are more concrete, more visceral than Lee's early work; they have more of the 'grunt of prose' for which he has been seeking, more of the 'grainy sense of life' that, in the world beyond the poem, is fast disappearing. GG

Lee, Ronald. See FICTION IN ENGLISH 1.

Lefebvre, André. See HISTORY STUDIES IN FRENCH 4.

Lefebvre, Jean-Jacques. See HISTORY STUDIES IN FRENCH 1.

Lefebvre, Jean-Paul. See POLITICAL WRITINGS IN FRENCH 2.

Lefrançois, Alexis. See POETRY IN FRENCH.

Légaré, Romain. See LITERARY STUDIES IN FRENCH 4.

Lehaise, R. See HISTORY STUDIES IN FRENCH 4.

Leitch, Adelaide. See CHILDREN'S BOOKS IN ENGLISH 5.

Lemelin, Roger. See ANTHOLOGIES IN FRENCH and BELLES LETTRES IN FRENCH.

Lemieux, Germain. See FOLKLORE: BIBLIOGRAPHY.

Lemieux, Lucien. See HISTORY STUDIES IN FRENCH 8.

Lemieux, Vincent. See POLITICAL WRITINGS IN FRENCH 4.

Lemire, Maurice. See LITERARY STUDIES IN FRENCH 2.

Le Moine, Roger. See LITERARY STUDIES IN FRENCH 4.

Le Moyne, Jean (1914–). Born in Montreal, he was educated at the Collège Sainte-Marie. In 1934 he was one of the founders of the magazine *La Relève*, which published his first essays. He travelled frequently to Europe and became acquainted with the French philosopher Jacques Maritain. In 1938 he attended the Congrès des Études carmélites. On his return to Montreal he worked at *La Presse* as translator and journalist. He later became an editorial writer for *Le Canada*, where he established the first weekly book page. Between 1953 and 1959 he was editor-in-chief of *La Revue moderne* and contributed to *La Revue dominicaine* and *Cité libre*. With Robert Élie he edited the *Poésies complètes* (1949) and the *Journal* (1954) of Saint-Denys GARNEAU, one of his most intimate friends. In 1961 he studied American philosophy in Chicago and San Francisco on a fellowship from the Canada Council. For many years a writer and producer at the National Film Board, he is now a member of the staff of the prime minister in Ottawa.

In *Convergences* (1961) Le Moyne gathered together essays he had written over the past twenty years on the most diverse subjects, notably the religious atmosphere of French Canada, the role of women in French-Canadian society and literature, and music. They were written at a time when the Church still dominated the structure of French-Canadian society, and Le Moyne—in common with Saint-Denys Garneau, Robert Charbonneau, and Robert Élie—felt this dominance as a restriction. He opposed not only the power of the clergy but a form of religious life based on Jansenist dualism that inhibited the blossoming of a true spiritual life and, in fact, of life itself. Le Moyne expressed these sentiments in essays that are at once passionate and reflective, lyrical and concise. A landmark in the intellectual and cultural life of French Canada, in which the winds of change were already being felt, *Convergences* won a Governor General's Award and the Prix France-Canada. An English translation by Philip Stratford, *Convergence*, appeared in 1968. Le Moyne received the Molson Prize in 1969. NK

LePan, Douglas (1914–). Douglas Valentine LePan was born in Toronto. He was educated at the University of Toronto, at Oxford, and taught at Harvard. During the Second World War he served in the artillery in the Italian campaign. He then joined the department of external affairs, where he rose to the rank of assistant under-secretary of state. In 1959 he left the federal service to become professor of English at Queen's University. He was principal of University College, Toronto, from 1964 to 1970, when he was appointed University Professor. In 1972 he won the Blumenthal Prize, awarded by *Poetry*, for four poems.

LePan's distinctive style as a poet comes from the smoothness with which his mature reflections follow the images to which they are linked. His admiration goes to the man of action, the *coureur de bois* of the seventeenth and eighteenth centuries and their modern counterparts who have the courage to travel beyond the regulations with which modern man is hemmed about. However, his understanding is not withheld from the desperate and heartsick man who does not dare even dream of better things than are provided in the closely packed urban quarters to which he has become accustomed. LePan's poetry has been collected in *The wounded prince and other poems* (1948) and in *The net and the sword* (1953), a volume based on his experiences during the Italian campaign that received a Governor General's Award. Selections from his poetry have been included by A. J. M. SMITH in *The Oxford book of Canadian verse* (1960) and *Modern Canadian verse* (1966). LePan is also the author of a novel, *The deserter* (1964), in which a soldier, who has never shirked danger, deserts after the armistice is signed. He lives the life of the hunted while he searches for the meaning of life and for an understanding of the relationship of human beings to each other. The search leads him to the conclusion that man is responsible for his acts and for the consequences of those acts on himself and on others. This novel, which won a Governor General's Award, is available in paperback in the New Canadian Library. NS

Lerman, Norman H. See INDIAN LEGENDS AND ART.

Leroi-Gourhan, André. See ESKIMOS: BOOKS IN FRENCH.

Leslie, Kenneth. See POETRY IN ENGLISH 1.

Levac, Claude. See DRAMA IN FRENCH 2.

Levenson, Christopher. See POETRY IN ENGLISH 1.

Lévesque, Raymond. See POETRY IN FRENCH.

Lévesque, René. See POLITICAL WRITINGS IN ENGLISH 1 and POLITICAL WRITINGS IN FRENCH 3.

Levine, Norman (1924–). Born in Ottawa and educated at the High School of Commerce there, he served in the Second World War. He lives in Cornwall, Eng. In 1965–6 he was poet in residence at the University of New Brunswick.

The poverty in which Levine's childhood was spent, the experiences of war, and the revulsion against commercialism and vulgarity that led him to leave Canada are influences that underlie his competent lyrics in *The tightrope walker* (1950) and his short semi-autobiographical novel *The angled road* (1953). They are expressed with great force in his autobiography *Canada made me* (1958). His collection of short stories, *One way ticket* (1961), set in England and Canada, deals with people who lack a purpose in life.

While Levine has continued to use both Canadian and English characters, his choice of language and situation has come closer to the English than to the Canadian idiom, and there is an increasing tendency to rework the same themes. Offsetting this defect is his development of the polished style of the miniaturist; this is particularly effective in his later short stories. In the novel *From a seaside town* (1970), the protagonist, Joseph Le Grand, a travel writer, combines gentle nostalgia for his Canadian Jewish origins with happiness arising out of his life in England, his marriage to a gentile, and his relations with his children. His struggles against poverty and his dealings with a mixed assortment of friends and acquaintances evoke both grief and humour. The polished writing in Levine's second collection of short stories, *I don't want to know anyone too well* (1971), set in both Canada and England, is sometimes cynical, sometimes amusing; it can rise to pathos, as in one of the Canadian stories, 'By the Richelieu'.

Levine edited the anthology *Canadian winter's tales* (1968). NS

Levitt, Joseph. See HISTORY STUDIES IN ENGLISH 7.

Levitt, Kari. See POLITICAL WRITINGS IN ENGLISH 2.

Lewis, Richard. See ESKIMOS: BOOKS IN ENGLISH.

Liberté. See LITERARY MAGAZINES IN FRENCH 2.

Lighthall, W. D. See ANTHOLOGIES IN ENGLISH 1.

Lillard, Charles. See POETRY IN ENGLISH 4.

Lindal, W. J. See HISTORY STUDIES IN ENGLISH 14.

Linteau, P. A. See HISTORY STUDIES IN FRENCH 1.

Lipset, S. M. See HISTORY STUDIES IN ENGLISH 8.

Lipton, Charles. See HISTORY STUDIES IN ENGLISH 13.

Literary magazines in English. By the end of 1972 readers with literary interests could choose their fare from nearly a hundred magazines being published in Canada. The choice ranges from a few academic university quarterlies, through numerous small magazines of a more or less independent status, to a proliferation of little magazines from almost every region in the country. In addition several commercial magazines have increased their literary offerings considerably since 1966.

Those magazines firmly subsidized by universities tend to be the most stable, and the most staid. *The University of Toronto Quarterly* (1931–) easily maintains its position as the most academically prestigious of these journals. Aside from donning a more attractive cover in recent years and modernizing its production, *UTQ* has not varied its policy of offering scholarly articles on the humanities with a special emphasis on English studies. It accepts no original creative work and is not concerned to reflect current national or international movements. It does continue to serve contemporary Canadian literature, however, with its valuable annual review supplement 'Letters in Canada'. *UTQ* is currently edited by William F. Blissett. *The Queen's Quarterly* (1893–) also appeals to a learned audience with articles written by experts on politics, foreign affairs, science, arts and letters. However, since 1920 QQ has published original verse and prose and continues to reserve several pages for reviews of contemporary literature. In 1972 Kerry McSweeney succeeded H. Pearson Gundy as editor. *Dalhousie Review* (1920–) celebrated its fiftieth year in 1970 with a lengthy editorial by C. L. Bennett in the spring issue recounting the history of the review. *DR* offers a broad range of scholarly articles for the general reader. It also publishes original short stories and poems and devotes as many as forty pages to reviews, paying generous attention to books by Canadians. In 1971 Alan Bevan became editor.

Literary magazines in English

Until 1959 no other university-sponsored literary quarterlies existed to challenge the supremacy of *UTQ*, *QQ*, and *DR*. Since that date several new journals of considerable stature have emerged. *Canadian Literature* (1959–), emanating from the University of British Columbia, will be fourteen years old in 1973. Exclusively devoted to criticism and reviews of letters in Canada, *CL* continues to provide a stimulating forum for scholars, students, and general readers of Canadian literature. The consistent, urbane policy of founding editor George WOODCOCK, combined with felicitous design, printing, and format, have made *CL* one of the most dependable, informative, and readable of university journals. *CL* publishes articles in French as well as English and until recently has published an annual checklist of Canadian books in both languages. One must agree with the suggestion in the tenth-anniversary issue (No. 41, Summer 1969) that *CL* has been a mirror of the sixties in Canada, reflecting and chronicling an extraordinarily vigorous growth of interest and activity in our literature 'without getting caught in the trap of a narrow nationalism'.

West Coast Review was established at Simon Fraser University in 1966. The title page quotes Whitman: 'The theme is creative and has vista.' Editor Frederick Candelaria invites submissions, in French or English, of poetry, fiction, drama, essays and reviews. The emphasis is on contemporary North American writing, but drawings, photography, and music are included. A special feature is a continuing bibliography of avant-garde writing. Begun as a tri-annual, *WCR* became a quarterly in 1970.

The Malahat Review, an 'International Quarterly of Life and Letters', first published by the University of Victoria in 1967, is the most elegant of the new magazines. Its founding editors were John Peter and Robin SKELTON, with Frank Kermode as British advisory editor. Malahat is a mountain that overlooks Victoria and the name was chosen to avoid any indication of a limitation in the journal's content. *MR* is devoted to international culture and was launched as a centennial project to emphasize 'the coming of age of our country'. From the beginning it has offered a wide spectrum of established international writers, including many Britons and a few Canadians. It publishes short fiction, plays, poetry, critical articles, literary memoirs, and previously unpublished literary documents such as the letters, journals, and manuscripts of distinguished authors. No. 1 included an article, accompanied by several superb photographs, on the sculpture of Henry Moore. With No. 21, Robin Skelton became editor-in-chief and began a series of short editorial 'Comments'. Issues are sometimes organized around a theme, a recent example being No. 23 (1972) devoted to Nietszche, which includes a transcript of a tape by Eli MANDEL and Irving LAYTON on the philosopher. *MR*, now in its seventh year, maintains its initial sophistication and high professional standards.

Centennial year also witnessed the publication of *Mosaic* from the University of Manitoba, under the editorship of Kenneth McRobbie. A quarterly for 'the comparative study of literature and ideas', *Mosaic* devotes each issue to a sober, scholarly theme. No. 1 (1967) dealt with literature and history. Vol. 6, No. 2 (1972) explores the 'Eastern European Imagination in Literature'. Though it does not publish or review current creative writing, *Mosaic* does review scholarly books and accepts pertinent critical articles in either French or English. R. G. Collins has replaced R. P. Hoople as associate editor.

In 1970 the first issue of *Ariel* appeared, founded by editor A. Norman Jeffares at the invitation of the University of Calgary. 'A Quarterly Review of International English Literature', *Ariel* succeeds *A Review of English Literature*, which had been restricted to work by Commonwealth writers. *Ariel* publishes critical articles and reviews but also poems and English translations of poems from all over the world. Reacting against 'too much dull academic criticism', editor Jeffares calls for criticism that 'should be literature in itself . . . enjoyable to read, pleasurable for specialist and general reader alike'. Mr Jeffares agreed to edit *Ariel* for three years and will be succeeded by George Wing.

Editor Alwyn Berland of *Wascana Review* (1966–) also has an antipathy to academic criticism. *WR* aims to publish poetry, fiction, art work, and 'impure criticism written by men (not technicians) who aim to reach other men (not bibliographies)'. Established as a semi-annual in 1966, *WR* addresses itself to 'whatever general audience our particular human voice will reach'. Begun independently, *WR* now acknowledges a partial subsidy from the University of Saskatchewan.

The University of Windsor Review is also a bi-annual. Founded in 1965, edited by Eugene McNamara and including among its early associate editors the prolific and talented Joyce Carol Oates, *UWR* publishes scholarly articles 'in the arts, sciences, politics and social sciences'. In addition each issue includes a limited amount of short fiction, poetry, and reviews.

The Journal of Canadian Studies, founded in 1968 when the University of Trent came into existence, is not primarily a literary journal. It does, however, occasionally publish articles on the work of Canadian writers, and it provides studies of the context—society and history—out of which Canadian writers emerge. Another more sharply literary scholarly tool is *Canadian Notes and Queries* (1968), subsidized by booksellers Bernard Antmann, Inc., in Montreal and edited by W. F. E. Morley from Queen's University. *CNQ* appears two or three times a year. It is bilingual and is 'devoted to the concerns of anyone working in Canadian Studies in the Humanities'.

The British Columbia Library Quarterly (1938–) is a source of both bibliographical and literary material. *BCLQ* has always carried book reviews and articles relating to regional literary developments. Since 1967, however, the journal has adopted colourful covers and a sprightly tone. It has increased its literary coverage: it now accepts original creative work and in 1971 added a fiction section. The present editor is Bryan Bacon. The *BCLQ* is not sponsored by a university but has obviously close connections with the academic circuit in British Columbia.

Developments in recent years indicate that the old distinction or stigma of university journals as 'academic' is less and less meaningful. Most university quarterlies in Canada now include creative work and take some account of contemporary movements in literature and related arts. Furthermore, many universities lend their names and/or some degree of financial assistance to otherwise independent ventures by individuals or groups of faculty and students. Thus a considerable number of recently founded magazines are attached in some way to universities, though the editors maintain a freedom and flexibility of policy not characteristic of the older university quarterlies. These newer 'university' magazines are more creatively oriented. They are generally less stable but not necessarily shorter-lived, since the patronage of the university and, frequently, additional support from the Canada Council and other sources assure them of a measure of security not enjoyed by the truly 'independent' magazines.

The oldest magazine to be associated in its readers' minds with a university is *The Fiddlehead.* In this case it was members of the English Department of the University of New Brunswick who founded the magazine in 1945 and have kept it afloat financially. Editor Fred COGSWELL, long known for his dedication, piloted the magazine through the crucial sixties. In 1967 *The Fiddlehead* received a substantial grant from the Canada Council, whereupon it donned a glossy cover, increased its number of pages, and began to pay its contributors. Under Kent Thompson (1967–71) the magazine stiffened its policy, added critical commentary, and wavered towards monthly publication. In 1970 *The Fiddlehead* celebrated its twenty-fifth anniversary—a remarkable achievement for any small literary magazine. Robert Gibbs became editor in 1971. *The Fiddlehead* has since resumed its quarterly schedule, its eclecticism, and its emphasis on the work of new young poets.

Prism International, a quarterly that began as an independent magazine (*Prism*) in 1959, sought the financial assistance of the University of British Columbia in 1964. *PI* was one of the first Canadian magazines in Canada, apart from *Delta* (1957–66), to profess an interest in contemporary literature from other continents. Its early issues featured original poems in Chinese, Yiddish, Hungarian, and other languages, side by side with English translations, as well as new poems and fiction in English and French. Since then *PI* has moved closer to the concerns of the Creative Writing Department to which its editors are attached. Now a tri-quarterly, *PI* still publishes some translation but this task is now more exclusively the function of another tri-quarterly, *Contemporary Literature in Translation (1968–)*. *CLT* was for a time partially subsidized by UBC, but with the aid of the Canada Council it has become an independent magazine owned and edited by Andreas Schroeder and Michael Yates.

Literary magazines in English

Founded at the University of Manitoba in 1968, *The Far Point* is a semi-annual under the editorship of Myron Turner and George Amabile. *FP* is devoted to poetry and articles on poetry of the 'post World War II' era and is North American in orientation. It offers annual poetry prizes of $100, $75, and $50. No. 6 (Winter 1971) reported budgetary difficulties and announced that in future *FP* would appear in smaller special issues. Regular periodical publication has apparently been suspended.

Ellipse from the Université de Sherbrooke has attracted several external sponsors. Founded in 1969 as a quarterly designed to present the work of French and English writers in translation, *Ellipse* is edited by a board of writers and translators, including D. G. JONES. Dedicated to narrowing the gap between cultures, *Ellipse* has so far concentrated on poetry. Each issue is devoted to a pair of poets who comment on each other's work in translation and who are commented upon in bilingual critical articles. For example, in No. 8/9 (Fall 1971), translations of poems of Paul CHAMBERLAND and Allan Ginsberg appeared and the commentaries included an article on Ginsberg by George BOWERING translated into French.

The English Department of St Francis Xavier University spawned a quarterly in the spring of 1970 that achieved independent status by the fall of 1971. *The Antigonish Review* is edited by R. J. MacSween and publishes poetry, stories, criticism, and short reviews as well as art work. It is a colourful, sprightly journal with a pronounced interest in Ezra Pound dominating its early issues.

In 1971 three other magazines with university connections were launched. *Event*, a tri-quarterly published by Douglas College, New Westminster, B.C., appeared in the spring under the editorship of David Evanier. *Event* has the advantage, shared by several British Columbia magazines, of being printed by the Morriss Printing Company, thus ensuring an impressive physical appearance. *Event* No. 1 contained many poems and some stories, mostly by Americans, and no reviews or criticism. In the fall of 1971 *Impulse* appeared, edited by writer-in-residence Peter Such, from Erindale College, Ont. Planned as a tri-quarterly, *Impulse* moved to independent quarterly status with issue no. 3, thanks to assistance from the Canada Council and the Ontario Council for the Arts. *Impulse* publishes poems and short fiction by many established Canadians, but reserves some space for new young writers. The winter of 1971 saw the first issue of *White Pelican* from writers associated with the University of Edmonton. A quarterly review of the arts, *WP* is interested in contemporary music, theatre, and painting, and publishes poetry, fiction, articles, and short reviews. So far each issue has been supervised by a different editor and has focused on a theme. One issue was devoted to concrete poetry. No. 4 was edited by Dorothy LIVESAY and featured Canada's north. Other editors are Sheila Watson, Stephen Scobie, Douglas Barbour, John Orrell, and Norman Yates.

In the spring of 1972 the students and faculty of Capilano College in West Vancouver published the *Capilano Review* edited by Pierre Coupey. The attractive first issue of this proposed tri-quarterly included the work of many established west-coast Canadian poets and two Russians, Voznesensky and Evtushenko. Ten pages were used to introduce visual poetry to Canadian readers. As of January 1973, Issue 2 has yet to appear.

Also in 1972 Atkinson College, Toronto, launched *Exile*. This quarterly will contain no scholarly or academic criticism; it is to be a haven, says editor Barry Callaghan, for imaginative writers from all over the world. The first two issues included work by John Montague of Ireland, Samar Attar of Syria, Yehudi Amichai of Israel, Yehia Hakki of Egypt; and Morley CALLAGHAN, Margaret ATWOOD, Marie Claire BLAIS, and Joe ROSENBLATT 'of Canada'.

The name of the University of New Brunswick is temporarily associated with another recent magazine. In 1972 the first issue of the *Journal of Canadian Fiction* appeared, published by the English department. *JCF* was founded by David Arnason and John G. Moss as a quarterly devoted to new fiction, critical studies of Canadian fiction, review articles, and interviews. An attractive $8\frac{1}{2} \times 11$ format with good paper, clear type, and a stiff spine, *JCF* lends itself to easy handling and readability. Special features include checklists of Canadian theses in both English and French and a bibliography of Canadian literary criticism. (Such features will partially make up for the discontinuation of the bibliographical Annual Supplement of *Canadian Literature*.) Signifying the need for a national magazine devoted to fiction, *JCF* reached over 1,000 subscribers by its fourth issue (Fall 1972). Now, having attracted Canada Council assistance, it is planning larger issues and more special features, as well as a payment of $100.00 per printed story. The magazine is now independently published and will be relocated in the near future. *JCF*'s success to date has overshadowed the existence of another magazine of fiction out of western Canada. No. 1 of the *Canadian Fiction Magazine* appeared in the winter of 1971. *CFM* is a quarterly edited by Jane Kennon and R. W. Stedingh in North Vancouver. It accepts the work of Canadians whether they live in or out of Canada. The first issue contains a manifesto by Andreas Schroeder calling for the 'new' short story and an essay by Michael Bullock noting the death of naturalism and the growth of super-realism in fiction. Contributors include Michael Yates and other west-coast writers. *The Canadian Fiction Magazine* has the same format as *JCF* but suffers in comparison from inferior techniques of reproduction, a disadvantage that may be overcome if the magazine can obtain financial aid.

In addition to these two, a third magazine devoted to fiction is planned for 1973. *The International Fiction Review*, a scholarly bi-annual, will emanate from the German department of the University of New Brunswick and will publish (in English) reviews of current fiction from Europe, Latin America, the Orient etc. According to editor S. Elkhaden, *IFR* will also include critical essays, bibliographical material, bio-graphical information, and interviews with fiction writers.

A bilingual review, *Le Chien d'Or/The Golden Dog*, moved quietly into small book-stores in Montreal in January 1972. Founded as a biannual by Michael Gnarowski of Sir George Williams University's English department and Carlo Fonda of Loyola's modern languages department, *The Golden Dog* No. 1 contained critical assessments of Leo Kennedy and Desmond PACEY, poems by Louis DUDEK, a prose poem in French by Louis Geoffroy, an interview with Irving Layton, and an article by Neil Compton on language. This first issue seemed to have its back turned to anything west of Montreal: it appears that the bilingual *GD* was intended to help balance the scales against the plethora of magazines that now reflect west-coast, American, and inter-national interests. Regrettably No. 2 of this promising biannual has not appeared as of January 1973. *The Golden Dog* does not acknowledge any financial assistance. Its future may well depend on the grace of granting agencies.

Quarry is a magazine that began as a students' publication at Queen's University in 1951. In 1965 it became a quarterly under the editorship of Tom Eadie and Tom Marshall, both of Queen's. *Quarry* has maintained an eclectic policy and over the years has introduced many new poets as well as publishing the established Canadians. Volume 19, published with the aid of Canada Council and other grants, announced a new tri-quarterly schedule and extended a welcome to French contributors. *Quarry* is now an independent magazine currently published by Oberon Press, Ottawa, and edited by W. J. Barnes.

Among the few stable quarterlies that served Canadians faithfully throughout the sixties, *The Tamarack Review* has from its beginning (1956) been independent of university patronage. Subsisting on private aid and considerable support from 'the Canada Council, the hard core among Toronto publishers, and the Hudson's Bay Company', *TR* has always paid its contri-butors, maintained high standards of produc-tion and content and, until recently, appeared on schedule. For more than a decade *TR* has serenely pursued its intention of printing the best in belles lettres, verse, short fiction, and ur-bane reviews by established writers; sometimes writers from other countries were featured and occasionally pages were opened to new young writers. *TR*'s stability seemed ensured when, on the strength of a sizeable Canada Council grant, it hired a managing editor in 1966. Recently, however, *TR* has begun to appear irregularly and in its fourteenth year (1971) it temporarily suspended publication with No. 59. Robert Weaver's remark in his tenth-anniversary editorial was apparently prophetic: 'In the next ten years I hope that other editors with different commitments will be publishing their own magazines (if they do, they will undoubtedly give us a hard time).'

The Canadian Forum, the oldest independent journal of its kind in Canada, celebrated its fiftieth anniversary in 1970. Under the editorship of Milton Wilson, and then Abraham Rotstein, *CF* continued throughout the sixties to make a significant contribution to the development of literature in this country. Especially under Milton Wilson, who followed Northrop FRYE as poetry editor, *CF* maintained an exceptionally high quality of literary fare, including new poetry, fiction, and reviews. Since 1968 *CF* has undergone several face-lifts, modernized its layout, and improved its quality of paper and printing. New policies accompanied the new look, involving feature issues devoted to journalistic coups and numbers planned around specific themes. Many lesser-known, new, and even experimental poets have begun to appear recently under the policy of the new poetry editor, Peter Stevens. However, the practice of allowing young poets to write carping reviews of each other's work has lowered the quality of the review section. At the end of 1972 *CF* announced its need to increase its advertising revenue, a sign that may indicate that this journal is heading into financial straits or, more hopefully, that it anticipates fuller expansion.

The Canadian Author and Bookman was fifty-one years old in 1972. The organ of the Canadian Authors' Association, *CA&B* is a quarterly publication combining the functions of trade journal, house organ, and creative outlet for its members. In recent years it has carried an increased number of literary offerings, as well as notices, technical advice, and marketing information. In 1968 *CA&B* absorbed the CAA's other main publication, *Canadian Poetry*, and now features a poetry supplement edited by James Fritch. Mary E. Dawe is general editor. *CA&B* is now published in Edmonton.

Among independent magazines that flourished and died in the sixties, we have already noted the demise of *Evidence*. Founded in Toronto in 1960, this quarterly had some of the flair of *Evergreen Review*. It failed in the competition for grants, however, and could not maintain its quarterly schedule. The last issue, No. 10, appeared in 1967. *Edge*, a bi-annual founded in 1963 by Henry Beissel at Edmonton, saw itself 'as a rallying point for the forces of dissent and protest across the country'. The first issue drew adverse attention from Alberta government officials—and thereby attracted a large number of subscribers. *Edge* was thereafter billed as 'the most controversial publication in Canada' and was sustained, completely independent of university support or other grants, through to No. 9 in 1969. Every issue of *Edge* was 'a gauntlet thrown in the face of the establishment', featuring articles decrying various abuses, attacking censorship, giving space in the last two issues, for example, to Québec separatist Léandre Bergeron and to Canada's aficionado of pornography, John GLASSCO. The radical challenge of such articles, however, was balanced by more sober critical analyses of world events, censorship, and educational reform. *Edge* published original fiction, poetry, and the drawings of Norman Yates among others. A notable occasional feature was the lengthy 'Poetry Chronicle' by Edward A. Lacey (pseud.)—an incisive review article on Canadian poetry written in delightfully witty, urbane prose. *Edge* did not fold for financial reasons alone; Henry Beissel chose to end it, feeling it had served its purpose. Had his repeated requests for grants been well received, however, Canada might not have lost this provocative, fearless periodical quite so soon.

Culture is another deceased independent magazine. A thoroughly bilingual review devoted to cultural activities in the field of the humanities, this quarterly frequently published articles of literary interest. It also provided bibliographical information and periodical indices for both French and English literature. *Culture*, published in Quebec City under the editorship of Edmond Gaudron, reached its twenty-fifth year of regular publication in 1965 and survived beyond that to its last issue, Volume 31, in 1971.

A phoenix among independent magazines, *Open Letter* has recently (Winter 1971–2) been revived by Coach House Press. The original *OL*, founded in 1965 by Frank DAVEY out of Royal Roads College in Victoria, B.C., was distributed free in stapled, typescript mimeograph. Devoted to debate, controversy, and experiment, it was mostly given over to in-group correspondence between alumni of *Tish* magazine. The new series is more impressive in every way. Roughly 5″× 8″, with a stiff spine and an attractive design, and averaging 100 pages of solid prose, *OL* is now in its fourth issue of a tri-quarterly schedule.

It is devoted to avant-garde literary theory, criticism, and reviews, and intends to provide coverage of small-press productions from Canada, the United States, and England. Some of the in-group flavour remains, but on the whole *OL* offers stimulating competition to established reviews with its serious commitment to a new aesthetic and its aggressive challenge to conservative criticism in Canada. *OL* retains a link with its Vancouver origins by way of contributing editor Stan Persky. Frank Davey, now a resident of Toronto, remains at the helm. Other contributing editors are George Bowering, Victor COLEMAN, and Fred Wah. David Dawson and Ted Whittaker have recently been replaced by bp NICHOL and Steve McCaffery.

Open Letter is a small-press publication that, despite its professional appearance, has much in common with the little magazines that constitute the literary underground. Of such magazines Canada boasted about thirty in 1966. Since then the number has been at least tripled. However, it is the nature of little magazines to be ephemeral. Many last only a few issues and of these the details must be recorded elsewhere. Those that survive beyond ten issues sometimes aspire to the rank of small independent journals, but the typical little magazine is stubbornly attached to its small élite audience and the freedoms of its underground status. Of little magazines born in the sixties that survived until recently, *Alphabet* (1960–71) will be most sorely missed. '*ABC*' was a stimulating semi-annual that articulated Canadian experience in documentary, mythic, and imaginative terms. Born of editor James REANEY's interest in archetypal criticism and dependent for 'orchestration' on Reaney's extraordinary talents, *Alphabet* was unique and is irreplaceable. *Yes* is another little magazine that folded recently. Founded in 1956 and edited by Michael Gnarowski and Glen Siebrasse, *Yes* appeared irregularly, in varying size and format. Partial towards Montreal writers in the tradition of *First Statement*, *Yes* absorbed Dudek's *Delta* in 1966 and expired, after a relatively long life, in 1970.

Among the 'littles' of the sixties that have survived are *Imago* (1964–), founded and edited by George Bowering and dedicated to the long or serial poem. Issue 18 appeared at the end of 1972. Bowering envisages two more issues, which will complete his planned series. The original function has been fulfilled to the extent that other publications are now willing to give space to long poems. *Intercourse* (1966–), 'Canada's only eighthly magazine', was founded by Raymond Fraser. It has persistently indulged in humour of slapstick variety mixed with its serious intents. It has published new poets who display kinship with the values of the *First Statement* tradition and with the work of Alden NOWLAN, Milton ACORN, Al PURDY. Fraser gave up the editorship to Louis Cormier in 1970. Since then *Intercourse* has appeared only twice, the last double issue, 15/16, displaying a pronounced seriousness and a Buddhist orientation. Cormier is now a resident monk at the Zen Centre in Montreal.

Blew Ointment (1963–) continues to be the biggest, most erratic and baffling of little magazines. Editor Bill BISSETT continues his prolific and fascinating experiments in typography and graphics and his tangential but unrelenting attack on the book culture and all its bourgeois assumptions about literature.

The newcomers in the little-magazine field are too numerous even to list here. Suffice it to say that almost every region of this country is now represented—even Seven Persons, Alta, which boasts its own *Repository* (1972–). Over sixty such magazines have emerged in Canada since 1967. About half of these survived their first year of publication and several new ones spring up for every one that dies.

At the opposite end of the literary spectrum from the little magazines are the 'popular' magazines designed for national distribution. Few of these commercially based periodicals offer more than an occasional poem and a few token book reviews; but several do deserve mention for their literary offerings. *Saturday Night* remains the oldest and best-known of Canada's commercial magazines of opinions and ideas. Founded in 1887, *SN* has survived many vicissitudes—changes in ownership and editorship, shifts in political direction and editorial policy, transformations of appearance and uneven quality of content. It had some illustrious years under the gifted man of letters B. K. Sandwell, after which it floundered through several financial near-disasters and brave new starts. In 1962 it died as a fortnightly and was reborn as a monthly.

It ran into severe editorial and financial problems again in the mid-sixties but was revived by the resourceful enterprise of Arnold Edinborough and redeemed by the witty and brilliant journalism of Kildare DOBBS, George Woodcock, and others. In 1968 Robert Fulford became editor and since that time the magazine has moved steadily towards financial security and editorial stability. Since Fulford took over, the literary content of *SN* has been increased considerably in both quality and quantity. Poems are now given prime space, book reviews are ample, and occasional issues feature new and young writers. Now governed by a new board and published by Second Century Canada Publications, *SN* celebrated its eighty-fifth birthday in December 1972.

Canadian Dimension, founded in 1963 by editor Cy Gonick as a bimonthly, is now published eight times a year. Primarily a journal of the political left, *CD* has recently shown some signs of a more than token interest in Canadian literature. In addition to the occasional story or poem and the regular few pages of book reviews, *CD* is on the verge of offering a series of articles devoted to Canadian letters. So far only one such article has appeared. Since *CD* directs itself to Canadian intellectuals, it would seem appropriate for literature to be considered as one of its more serious concerns.

The Atlantic Advocate (1956–) is a monthly 'consumer magazine' with a broad circulation and a regional bias. Published in Fredericton, *AA* serves the Atlantic provinces well as an additional outlet for short fiction, poetry, book reviews, and articles on regional literary history.

Jewish Dialogue is a quarterly magazine that is hoping to make it commercially. Founded in Toronto in 1970 by editors David Cohen and Joe Rosenblatt, *JD* was 'started in the belief that Canada needed a high-quality magazine devoted to contemporary Jewish arts and letters [cf. *Commentary* in the U.S.] . . . and that the business community would be willing to support it.' *JD* seems well pleased with the support of its advertisers so far; and it manages to keep its scores of small ads shored up on left-hand pages throughout the magazine so that its literary and art work remain immaculate. *JD* publishes many established poets and other poems and graphics 'by Canadian artists who deserve attention'. In addition there are articles of current interest especially slanted towards a Jewish audience. Non-Jewish readers, however, will find much of *JD* appealing: it is colourful, entertaining, and informative.

It remains to note, among commercially based magazines, the brave birth and death of *Parallel*. This represents the second courageous effort of Montrealers in the sixties to establish a quality magazine devoted to literature, politics, and the arts. (The first, *Exchange*, planned as a monthly and edited by Stephen Vicinczcy, lasted for three issues in the winter of 1961. It was absorbed by *The Commentator*, a magazine devoted to political, social, and economic issues and almost devoid of literary interest.) *Parallel* (1966–7), edited by Peter Desbarats, was designed as a bi-monthly for Canadians with a sense of style—'the first magazine ever published in this country which could conceivably interest a non-Canadian', claimed the editorial in No. 1. Robert Weaver, commenting in *Tamarack* on the imminent demise of *Parallel*, noted the impracticality of a bi-monthly schedule for advertisers and distributors and the poor quality of the magazine's literary offerings. In the context of commercial magazines, however, *Parallel* was unusual in its openness to creative work. Said Weaver in 1967: '*Maclean's* calls itself Canada's National Magazine and couldn't care less about the country's novelists, poets and short-story writers . . . *Weekend*, and *The Canadian*, with their huge captive audiences, do even less for the country's best writers. *Parallel* at least had good intentions.'

Finally two trade journals deserve notice for the degree to which they serve the literary interests of this country. *Quill and Quire*, in small newspaper format, 'published since 1935 for the Canadian Book Trade', appears monthly and is devoted to news and information about publishing and literary events. It also publishes numerous book reviews and features full-page articles, such as 'The State of Canadian Poetry' by Peter Stevens (December 1972). *Books in Canada*, established in 1971, is a book-review magazine in stapled tabloid format on newsprint. It carries scores of publishers' advertisements and gives extensive review coverage of books produced by commercial publishers. This magazine emerged after the Clery report, commissioned by the Canadian

Book Publishers Council in 1971, concerning the promotion of books in Canada. The establishment of *Books in Canada*, under the editorship of Val Clery, came as a shock and a death blow to the editors of a remarkably similar publication that had been emanating from Montreal since 1968. Peter Lebensold's *The Five Cent Review* had much the same format and intentions as *B in C*. *FCR* offered the reader a great deal for his nickel. Though it came out only four times in 1969, it was planned as a 'monthly review of the arts in Canada'. Barry Lord was editor; George Bowering, Clive Denton, and Peter Smith were among the associates. *FCR* hoped for, and asked for, the support of the book trade; instead that support went to *Books in Canada*, Toronto based. So Montreal has once again tried and failed to establish a commercial literary magazine. Publisher Peter Lebensold can take consolation in the fact that his other enterprise, *Take One*, the film magazine, has been and still is a huge success, financially and otherwise. Needless to say, though both *Quill and Quire* and *Books in Canada* do provide useful service to Canadian publishers and readers, they by no means satisfy our need for a journal of the calibre of the *New York Review of Books*. Hopefully the best is yet to come in this range of the literary spectrum.

WF

Literary magazines in French. The recent sharp increase in national awareness, with its corresponding development of interest in French-Canadian studies, has resulted in a sudden expansion in the number of periodicals concerned either wholly or partly with literature and, in particular, with Canadian literature in French. For the period in question (January 1967 – December 1972), and not including those of a bilingual character, over eighty periodicals have to be taken into consideration, although not all of them will be treated in this article. Perhaps one of the most important aspects of this phenomenon is the decentralization or scattering that is taking place, a small but steadily rising proportion of magazines being published outside such established centres as Montreal or Quebec City, indeed even outside the province. Within Québec this can of course be explained in part by the desire of more and more French Canadians to learn about their past and to participate in the shaping of their future, a tendency that has been stimulated by such factors as the establishment of local *Centres culturels*; the financing of special projects through local-improvement grants, etc.; and the implantation in even fairly remote areas of CEGEPs (Collèges d'Enseignement général et professionnel) and *constituantes* of the Université du Québec. Outside the province one can attribute this development to a growing self-awareness on the part of French-speaking communities who fear increased assimilation as well as to a new interest among English-speaking Canadians in *le fait français* or *québécois*. Nor should the role of universities, government agencies, and other public organizations in the publishing field be neglected, as more of them produce their own journals. Their particular advantage over private and independent periodicals lies in a certain element of continuity and financial security.

One should also note the growing, if not universal, tendency to replace the term French Canadian or French Canada, even in semi-official organs, either by the more nationalist Québécois or Acadien or by supranational expressions like *la francophonie*. Although these two terminologies reflect different orientations on the part of those who use them, they both appear to be symptomatic of a search for an identity that is not purely Canadian. In some cases, of course, the idea of *la francophonie* is a reaction to the concept of Québec as a separate nation and may even reveal a certain insecurity among French-speaking minorities outside the province who feel threatened by the present polarization of attitudes.

A quick historic glance will show that some periodicals of an earlier date have either lost their importance or disappeared (e.g. PARTI PRIS); that others have survived, although not necessarily without having undergone some sea-change; and that many new periodicals have made an appearance, not always of a lasting nature. Here again, socio-political circumstances as well as economics play an important role.

1. Among earlier publications that have disappeared, one may list *Les Cahiers de l'A.C.T.A.*, published in Montreal by the now-defunct Canadian Amateur Theatre Association, and *La Scène au Canada*, which owed its existence and recent demise to the Toronto-based Canadian Theatre Centre, a

federally subsidized organization dedicated to the encouragement of professional theatre in Canada. *Théâtre vivant*, first published in 1966 by Holt, Rinehart and Winston Ltd of Montreal, resulted from the activities of the Centre d'Essai des Auteurs dramatiques de Montréal. Although not necessarily responsible for, it certainly coincided with, the upsurge of French-Canadian theatre and included in its issues, of which the last appeared in 1969, plays by such now well-established figures as Antonine MAILLET, Robert GURIK, and Michel TREMBLAY. *Digeste-Éclair*, a popular magazine extremely general in nature but containing a few literary articles, was published monthly in Ville d'Anjou from 1964 to 1969. A bold attempt to renew both the form and the content was made early in 1969 under the title *Dimensions*, when the novelist Victor-Lévy BEAULIEU became the editor. Much greater attention was paid to the literary production of Québec, but in the new format the magazine lasted for only three issues. *Jeunesses littéraires du Canada*, which changed its name to *J.L. du Québec* in 1968, was the organ of a youth association and published from 1963 to 1970 a series of bulletins containing articles of literary criticism tending to be based on religious and moral values, as well as works by young poets. *Les Cahiers bibliographiques*, an analytical index of French-Canadian writing, disappeared in 1969 (after three years of existence) when its director, Réginald Hamel, resigned and the Centre for French-Canadian Studies that produced it was absorbed into the main library of the Université de Montréal. A short-lived political periodical that also tried to exert some influence on the literary production of Québec was *Révolution québécoise* (1964–5), published by Pierre Vallières. *Cité libre* figured largely on the Québec scene for sixteen years (1950–66), although not without undergoing periodic transformation. It is probably best remembered for such well-known members of its editorial board as Gérard Pelletier, Pierre Elliott Trudeau, and Pierre Vallières. Although far from being entirely literary in its interests, it was extremely influential in its early years in the cultural and social reawakening of Québec and its contribution in this field must be recognized. However, after the beginning of the Quiet Revolution its moderate reformist tendencies and pro-Ottawa orientation, reflecting as they did an earlier stage in the evolution of Québec, prevented it from having the impact of *parti pris*, which represents a turning-point in the history of the province and possibly of Canada. *Cité libre* did not entirely cease to function in 1966 when the periodical disappeared: from 1967 to 1971 it published a series of *Cahiers* of a socio-economic nature, each one treating a separate theme and bearing on such diverse topics as celibacy in the Catholic Church and the student revolt of May 1968 in France.

The most important and influential Québec film magazine was *Objectif* (1960–7), almost the only publication to devote serious critical attention to Québec films. Several of its editors have become directors and are vital contributors to the development of Québec cinema: e.g. Jean-Pierre Lefebvre, Jacques Leduc, and Robert Daudelin, the current president of the Cinémathèque québécoise.

Other periodicals that disappeared, only to reappear under different titles, will be discussed at the same time as their replacements.

2. Among the many reviews that have survived to the present day there are several that, while playing an important role in the cultural life of French-speaking Canadians, are not totally literary. The oldest of these is *Action nationale*, published monthly in Montreal since 1931. The present director is F.-A. Angers, president of the Société Saint-Jean Baptiste of Montreal. The revue is dedicated to preserving traditional values and is therefore rather conservative and nationalist in its orientation, as well as in its appreciation of French and French-Canadian literature. *La Revue de l'Université d'Ottawa*, which also dates back to 1931, publishes articles in both English and French and is mainly theological in its orientation. It does, however, occasionally devote some space to articles on writers like Émile Nelligan and François-Xavier Garneau.

Les Cahiers des Dix, a publication of La Société des Dix since 1940, reflects the interests of its authors in the history, sociology, and ethnology of Québec, and its literary pages tend to concentrate on the productions of the nineteenth and early twentieth centuries. *Relations* was created in Montreal in 1941 by the École sociale populaire as an expression of Catholic culture in Québec. It continues to devote many of its pages to literary criticism, remaining in close contact with the contemporary scene, and its recent issues reflect the broader ecumenical approach of the Church. Another periodical of a conservative nature is *La Vie française*, first published at Laval in 1946 by Le Comité de la survivance française en Amérique to act as a link between the various French-speaking groups in all of North America. In 1952 the title of the organization changed to Le Conseil de la vie française, but the review retains its historical and documentary approach, in which a certain form of French patriotism plays an important part.

Vie des Arts, a quarterly magazine that has been in existence since January 1956, is, as its title suggests, mainly concerned with the visual and plastic arts, although it has included some articles on literature. *Recherches sociographiques* dates back to 1960 and is a publication of the Department of Social Sciences of Université Laval. Although the contents are mainly of a sociological nature, they frequently include substantial reviews of French-Canadian literature and newspapers and learned articles on various aspects, past and present, of the cultural life of the province.

Québec and *Culture vivante* are publications of the Québec Ministère des Affaires culturelles. The former, which has been in existence since 1964, is essentially aimed at presenting to a European public the political, social, and cultural aspects of Québec and is issued three times a year in Paris. Such well-known figures as Jean ETHIER-BLAIS, Alain Pontaut, Monique BOSCO, and Jean BASILE contribute reviews on important French-Canadian writers. *Culture vivante*, a quarterly magazine, presented in a very elegant format and extremely interesting on a visual level, is concerned with all aspects of the various arts and crafts of the province and includes articles on individual writers; special issues have been devoted to different movements and genres and to language in Québec.

The annual *Livres et auteurs canadiens*, which changed its title in 1969 to *Livres et auteurs québécois*, continues to provide, under the editorship of Adrien Thério, a useful bibliographic tool and includes a survey of all the publications of the year and essays on various writers. The growing importance of this volume is reflected by its increasing size. *Vient de paraître*, created in 1966, is a monthly bulletin devoted to news and information about publishing and literary events and also contains synopses of numerous publications.

Of the surviving periodicals that are entirely literary in their orientation, some tend to combine research or scholarly articles with the publication of original creations. The oldest of these is *Écrits du Canada français*, which was first published in 1954 and is subsidized by the Canada Council. The managing editor is Claude Hurtubise of Les Éditions H.M.H. of Montreal. Although this periodical publishes many hitherto unknown or little-known writers as well as works that have appeared separately, its particular appeal perhaps lies in the fact that it makes available to the public earlier texts that have been long out of print or texts that for diverse reasons would not easily find a publisher. *Liberté* continues to play an important role in the literary and artistic life of French Canada. Originally published in 1959 as a bi-monthly publication of Les Éditions de l'Hexagone—involving some of Québec's best-known names such as Jean-Guy PILON and Jacques GODBOUT—it has undergone several changes over the years. For a time Hubert AQUIN was its editor. It sponsors the annual Rencontre des Écrivains, a conference of poets and writers, and presents such diverse writers as Yves PRÉFONTAINE and Claude JASMIN. After the first few issues it gradually became more nationalist and socialist in character. It has been instrumental in making known in Québec a certain number of foreign writers, but lately, under the editorship of Pilon, it has tended to devote more and more of its space to new and unknown Québec writers, particularly students.

La Barre du Jour, whose list of contributors includes some of the most exciting names in present-day Québec, has been publishing constantly if irregularly since 1965. After a somewhat neutral beginning, it has become more and more overtly political and is committed to the cause of unilingualism, a specific Québec identity, and the democratization of literature and other arts. It has published a number of significant studies of the literature of the province and its special issues on Roland GIGUÈRE, Gaston MIRON, the Automatistes, and *parti pris* are impressive documents. This review has also offered hitherto unpublished works of an important nature by writers like Claude Gauvreau and

Albert Laberge, etc. Furthermore the role of this periodical as a creative workshop for the most important of the younger writers, and of poets in particular, makes it one of the most interesting in the history of the province.

Lettres et Écritures, which dates back to December 1963 (although not without interruption), is published by the students of the arts faculty of the Université de Montréal. Over the past few years it has undergone a political transformation and is committed to the emergence of a culture that is specifically québécois, seeing the act of creation as an affirmation, if not a revolt, in itself. *Études françaises*, published quarterly since 1965 by Les Presses de l'Université de Montréal, is a scholarly journal containing learned articles by well-known Canadian and international figures in various areas of literature, although naturally reflecting the present increased interest in French-Canadian studies by the considerable number of articles it publishes in this domain.

The only significant purely creative periodical of this period is *Poésie*, published every three months in Quebec City. It first appeared in the winter of 1966 under the aegis of La Société des Poètes canadiens-français, which was founded in 1923 (and still holds its annual convention at the Maison Montmorency outside Quebec). The aim of the Society has always been to encourage the development of French-Canadian poetry and to this end it organizes competitions, publishing the best entries in its review. From 1970 onwards a clear shift in its editorial policy became evident, leaving more room for aesthetic and thematic exploration.

3. As for the new periodicals that have proliferated since the winter of 1966, some form of relatively arbitrary grouping is probably necessary. The most important of the underground magazines is *Mainmise*, edited by 'Pppenelope' (Jean BASILE), the first issue of which appeared in October 1970. Although it cannot and would not wish to be termed a literary magazine—rejecting as it does literary criticism as an ego-trip and devoting its pages to the counter-culture of drugs, pornography, violence and rock-music—it has nevertheless contributed to the art of the comic strip and given rise to some remarkable underground poetry.

L'Envers du Décor, entirely sponsored by Air Canada, has been the official periodical of *Le Théâtre du Nouveau Monde* since 1968 and offers biographies, bibliographies, and other useful information concerning the authors of the plays to be produced. *Théâtre-Québec* issued three numbers in 1970 but was soon replaced by *Jeune-Théâtre*, which owed its creation in April 1971 to a decision made at the thirteenth annual congress of A.C.T.A. to found a regular theatre journal devoted to breaking down the traditional barriers between professionals and amateurs. After two issues containing general information and critical articles it became extremely political and, since October 1972, has been the organ of l'Association québécoise du Jeune Théâtre under the direction of Jean Fleury of La Cité des Jeunes in Vaudreuil. It encourages theatre as an expression of national identity and is particularly favourable to attempts like *Le Théâtre . . . Euh!* in Quebec City to demystify theatre.

Three film magazines are published in Québec at present. *Séquences*, the oldest, is sent only to subscribers and is the organ of the Catholic colleges' film societies. *Cinéma-Québec*, founded in May 1971, with sixteen numbers to date, gives special attention to Québec cinema—its production, problems, future prospects; the N.F.B. etc.—and attempts to review all the films shown in Montreal. It is also interested in the cinema of developing countries. Because it is the only film magazine that is published regularly, it has no rigid editorial policy and appears to be rather eclectic. *Champ libre*, on the contrary, which has published three numbers in two years, attempts to elaborate a Marxist-Leninist method of interpretation and criticism. Its editors are not so much concerned with bringing out a magazine regularly as with using film as a means of political education and intervention; they organize projections and discussions of political films in Montreal and outside and they have written several of the monographs on Québec film makers published by Le Conseil québécois pour la Diffusion du Cinéma.

Since *parti pris* ceased publication in 1968, several efforts have been made to renew or parallel its particular contribution to the artistic, intellectual, and political life of Québec. Examples are *Point de Mire* (1969–72); *Maintenant*, which was originally founded as a Dominican periodical in 1962 but radically changed its socio-political orientation in 1971 after the departure of Father Bradet; *Le Digeste québécois*, created in the spring of 1972 and whose editorial board includes such well-known names as Léandre Bergeron, Robert Burns, Georges Dor, and Andrée Bertrand-Ferretti; and *Noir et Rouge*, of which only three issues appeared from 1968 to 1969. Declaring itself to be the review of the Québec New Left, the latter was affiliated with *Our Generation*, the international New Left Quarterly of Radical Scholarship and Movement Analysis. Such attempts have been largely unsuccessful in spite of the frequently high quality of the magazines—partly because the fundamental problems raised by *parti pris* in such fields as social reorganization, national identity, and language remain basically unchanged and therefore lend themselves to repetitiveness; partly because none of the periodicals have quite the same broad scope as *parti pris*; and partly because they all suffer from the same financial difficulties that prevent them from undertaking longterm exhaustive enquiries into the fields they wish to examine. Certainly the most significant of *parti pris*'s successors is *Presqu'Amérique*. Founded in Quebec City in October 1971 under the direction of René Beaudin, it ceased publication in 1973 for financial reasons. Its title was inspired by one of Robert Charlebois' songs. In spite of its rather 'pop' appearance, it was a serious, highly political periodical, specifically designed to encourage the development of what is called the *Québecanthrope man*—the inhabitant of that still nonexistent America of our aspirations. Like *parti pris* it presupposed the necessity for an independent Québec; indeed it assumed the inevitability of independence. Also like *parti pris* it neglected no aspect of the socio-economic and cultural life of the province, nor of the rest of the world, and although each issue had a lead article on a specific theme, chronicles on all the arts were always included and one whole issue was concerned with the literature of Québec.

Two other periodicals of a socio-political nature but that devote some attention to literature are *Rive gauche* and *L'Acayen*. The former has been published at Drummondville, Québec, since March 1972 and relies on a local initiative grant from Canada Manpower as well as on aid from local enterprises. Its declared aim is to encourage regional development and awareness and it has close links with the Drummondville Centre culturel. *L'Acayen*, also published for the first time in 1972, is particularly interesting in that it is an Acadian periodical addressing itself to French-speaking Acadians. Aggressively political, it is intended to affirm *le fait français* in the only area outside Québec where it seems to the editors to be viable.

Forces is the organ of the public-relations department of Hydro-Québec. No expense has been spared on its presentation. Although its main interest lies in economics, industry, and science, it occasionally publishes interesting articles on French-Canadian writers and in particular on theatre.

In the bibliographical area *Lectures*, a monthly bibliographical and documentary review of Les Éditions Fides in Montreal—one of Québec's oldest and most traditional publishing houses, particularly known for its educational texts intended for Catholic schools—rendered excellent service to teachers, librarians, and other students of literature from 1946 until 1966, when it ceased publication mainly for financial reasons. However, Fides has continued to publish in this field, first of all with its *Fiches bibliographiques* (1967–70), which were replaced by *Le Livre canadien*, a loose-leaf publication containing synopses, criticism, and moral evaluations of all French-Canadian publications or translations into French that are done in Canada. Fides also publishes an annual index.

A number of universities have begun or resumed publishing periodicals of a scholarly nature. *La Revue de l'Université de Moncton* was founded in 1967 at the request of the faculty association of that university; it is published quarterly under the direction of Serge Morin. Whereas the faculty members are responsible for the contents, the administration has agreed to help with the financing and distribution. The contents cover all disciplines, not just literary studies, and even include some articles written in English. However, one issue is of particular interest to students of literature in French from outside Québec. A youth grant in 1971 furnished the opportunity to collect an impressive number of poems by young Acadian writers, many of whom were extremely promising, and the January 1972 issue not only published the most interesting of these productions but also serious articles on the evolution of Acadian poetry over the last twenty years as well as on individual well-established writers. Université Laval, after publishing *La Revue de l'Université Laval* from 1946 to 1966, now publishes under the aegis of its arts faculty *Études littéraires*, a quarterly that first appeared in April 1968. Its purpose is to provide a link between the three continents of *la francophonie*: America, Europe, and Africa. Its pages are open to all conceptions of literature and are particularly attentive to new research in the field of literary criticism. Each issue focuses on one subject, be it a writer, a theme, or a genre, etc. Volume 1, number 3, published the text of the major papers and discussions of the La Rencontre mondiale de la poésie—on the theme 'Le Poète et la Terre des Hommes'—which took place on the Expo site in September 1967. *La Revue de l'Université Laurentienne*, also first published in 1968, is a bilingual publication, reflecting the bilingual nature of this Sudbury university. It appears three times a year and is intended to provide a meeting-ground for the various disciplines, although *Les Cahiers laurentiens*, an integral part of the review, is particularly concerned with the propagation of *la francophonie* as an international humanistic phenomenon. The particular interest of this periodical lies in its multi-disciplinary and supranational vocation. Le Centre de Recherche en Civilisation canadienne-française of the Université d'Ottawa, which came into official existence in 1969, not only publishes its own biennial bulletin of information but also sponsors seven different collections providing bibliographies, scholarly studies, reprintings of earlier works, as well as original creations. The best-known of these is no doubt *Archives de la littérature canadienne-française*, edited by Paul WYCZYNSKI, which first appeared in 1960 as a publication of Le Centre de Recherche en Littérature canadienne-française (since absorbed into the new more broadly-based centre). It is an annual collection of scholarly essays and documents on a single subject and it offers an overview of the year's publications. *Critère* has been published in Montreal since 1970 by the faculty of the Ahuntsic CEGEP. Each issue revolves around a specific theme and so far only one has been specifically literary. However, excellent articles of literary criticism are sometimes included. *Nord* is a quarterly published at Sillery since the fall of 1971. Specifically literary in character, each issue is devoted either to a specific writer or to a genre. So far the subjects covered are Michel TREMBLAY, Jacques POULIN, Pierre Morency, and contemporary theatre in Québec. Although the articles are not all of the same high standard, this periodical constitutes an excellent research tool. *Protée*, a quarterly that first started in 1972, is the product of the department of the humanities at the Université du Québec at Chicoutimi and includes studies in the various human and social sciences. Literature is not, of course, neglected: in particular one significant article on Marie-Claire BLAIS has been published.

Other university periodicals that have appeared or risen again like phoenixes lay greater emphasis on creativity. The oldest and youngest of these is *Co-incidences*, which has had a chequered career. It was originally established in 1961 under the title *Tel Quel* as a graduate-student review subsidized by the arts faculty of the University of Ottawa. After only two issues the existence of the important French structuralist review *Tel Quel* obliged the editors to change the title to *Incidences* and this magazine appeared at irregular intervals from November 1962 to April 1969, to be replaced in March 1971 by *Co-incidences*, a quarterly. The present editor is Adrien Thério. The original intention was to encourage students to express themselves in the way they found best and most interesting. In fact the contributors have not always been students and include names like Jacques BRAULT, Cécile CLOUTIER, and Gaston Miron. The magazine is essentially literary in orientation, and although some space is devoted to critical articles (usually of French-Canadian writers and written by graduate students), most of the entries are original creations, showing no single tendency either towards classical or experimental forms, towards international or *québécois* French. *Les Cahiers de Sainte-Marie* resulted from a decision made in 1967 by the faculty of Le Collège Sainte-Marie to create its own series of publications in order to provide a forum for their research activities. The articles are mainly concerned with contemporary Québec literature and are varied both in quality and critical approach. Some original creations were included, such as texts of television plays by Françoise LORANGER and Hubert Aquin, as well as earlier unobtainable texts of historical interest. These *Cahiers* were succeeded in 1969, after the setting up of the Université du Québec, by *Les Cahiers de l'Université du Québec*, which publishes a variety of series in different disciplines. One of these, entitled *Recherches en symbolique*, has so far offered two numbers on symbolism in literature, with interesting articles on writers like Hubert Aquin. Another series, *Voix et Images du Pays*, issued five numbers between 1969 and 1972 under the direction of R. Bérubé. They contain reviews, particularly in the field of French-Canadian literature, along with original works and out-of-print texts. *Voix et Images* is one of the most important periodicals in Québec and is indispensable to researchers. *Présence francophone* is a voluminous production, born in 1970, of Le Centre d'Études de Littérature d'Expression française at the University of Sherbrooke. The list of contributors is long and impressive and the periodical is one of several intended to form a link between the various elements of world-wide *francophonie*. The contents are very diverse and extremely important. They include reports and texts on international conferences, fairly exhaustive bio-bibliographies on different writers and their works, reviews and articles on literature in French, and many original writings.

Of the most useful non-university publications one should mention *Le Supplément littéraire*, occasionally published by *Le Devoir* and whose contribution is by no means negligible. *Stratégies*, a new periodical published quarterly in Longueuil, appeared in the bookstores in the fall of 1972. Although not attached to any particular university, it is highly academic in nature and promises to be a significant step forward in the history of literary criticism in Québec. It is young in approach as well as in age and brings to the analysis of literary production the semiological and structuralist methods associated with *Tel Quel* and *Semiotike* etc.

A great many 'little magazines' of a creative bent have also come into existence over the past years. Not all have flourished but some have survived the stresses and strains involved in such enterprises. The list is long and not all can be mentioned here. It is interesting, however, to note that many are the work of students in various institutions across the province. *Passe-partout*, published by the editions of the same name in St Constant, issued twelve slim brochures in 1965 containing works by young poets who have since become well known. After a silence of five years a new series, entitled *Poèmes* with the same format, picked up the task of making known to the public new young writers—poets in particular. A more attractive effort was made in 1967 with *Quoi*, an elegant and visually appealing magazine focusing on aesthetics and coordinated by the poet Raoul DUGUAY. However it survived for only two issues. *Les Herbes rouges*, which borrowed its title from a book of poems by Jean-Paul Filion (*Demain les herbes rouges*, 1962), has issued seven numbers since its inception in October 1968. Although some of its contributors publish in its pages for the first time, many of them, as the title would indicate, are associated with the literary explosion that took place in Québec after the publication in 1948 of Émile Borduas's *Le Refus global* and with the ensuing liberation of French-Canadian writing. They include such names as Jacques FERRON and Marcel Hébert. The contents—plays, poems, and prose—are eclectic; one issue is sometimes devoted to a single writer. In spite of its irregularity, this periodical should be seen as a reflection of the significant changes that have taken place on the Québec literary scene. *Ether* is due to the initiative of the Collège Edouard-Montpetit in Longueuil and, starting in 1969, has published several issues containing writings, mainly poetry, of an experimental nature tending to reflect the youth culture. One of the most significant writers to appear in its pages is Nicole Brossard, who is also a member of the editorial board of *La Barre du Jour*. *Poèmes inédits* is a series of small fascicules published in Quebec City since 1970 by Jean Royer, the director of the literary pages of *Le Soleil*. *L'Illettré*, which has a newspaper format, lasted about one year (1970–1). The editors were Victor-Lévy Beaulieu, Jean-Claude Germain, Jean-Marie Poupart, and Pierre Turgeon. Without belonging in any real sense to a counter-culture, it was subversive in its approach to literature. The title itself was a gauntlet and reflected the editors' desire to affirm *le québécois* as the language of the province. One of the interesting small periodicals to enter the scene in 1972 was *Geste et Parole*, published jointly by the arts and literature department of the Collège Marie-Victorin and its information service. The first preface indicated that it was intended to be an act of reflection, criticism, and creation in the field of Québec dramatic writing. It would appear, however, that future numbers will not be confined to this area.

The prospects—whether in the field of creative writing, research, or literary criticism and critical methods—are extremely bright and bear witness to the ever-increasing vigour of French Canada. MV/AM-T

Literary studies in English. 1. The temper of an awakening nationalism and an ever-increasing public funding of the arts have brought about a burst of Canadian publishing, which has included an unprecedented number of literary studies. It is interesting to note that for the period 1967–72 the number of book-length studies by individual critics who have addressed themselves to general problems, as opposed to collections of essays or monographs on a single writer, has been surprisingly small. (Another observation: of the fifty-four books published in this field, only six were written by women—Margaret ATWOOD, Elspeth Buitenhuis, Phyllis Grosskurth, Patricia Morley, Clara THOMAS, and Miriam WADDINGTON.) There were only three full-length books of this kind: *The long journey* by Jack Warwick, *Butterfly on rock* by D. G. JONES, and *Survival* by Margaret Atwood. Perhaps we are still in the pioneer state described by E. K. Brown in *On Canadian poetry* (1943), where the concern for securing the basic necessities leaves no time for sustained reflection on literary problems. Or else Canadian society, which has begun to recognize itself in the novels, poems, and plays of its artists, may not yet have had time to develop enough to encourage the equally important function of criticism. Another answer may be that the material of Canadian literature is not thought to be rich or varied enough to deserve the study of serious scholars. Northrop FRYE, the most remarkable and original critic that Canada has so far produced, prefaces *The bush garden*, his collection of writings on Canadian literature, with the comment that these essays are 'episodes in a writing career which has been mainly concerned with world literature and has addressed an international reading public, and yet has always been rooted in Canada and has drawn its essential characteristics from there.'

What have been episodes in Frye's writing career have been decisive documents in their effect on the development of literary criticism in Canada. Most critics have agreed, with varying emphases and interpretations, that the geography, the bicultural nature of the population, and the colonial origins of Canada have shaped the literature. The interpretation of these major facts has varied widely, and some critics, like George WOODCOCK and A. J. M. SMITH, have welcomed the variety of interpretations as the mark of a mature eclecticism. But there is a catch to the concept of eclecticism. It is a term that screens the fear, the vagueness, and the inconclusiveness that only too often conceal a lack of real theoretical conviction, and it results in a soft-minded descriptive impressionism in lieu of firm critical theory. An eclecticism that attempts to reconcile conflicting values without ever allowing these values to be declared, or the concealed conflicts to be opened up for discussion, can never reconcile them. The only genuine eclectic, who assimilates, interprets and reconciles everything, is not likely to be a critic at all but, as Coleridge pointed out, an artist.

Another problem common to all the critics discussed below is that none of them states his underlying critical assumptions, and few of them even trouble to define their critical terms. The assumptions and critical terms have therefore to be laboriously puzzled out by the reader.

2. Northrop Frye, the critic who has dominated Canadian literary thought, is a writer who has a genius for perceiving unusual details and making original connections between them. His retrospective collection of articles on Canadian literature in *The bush garden: essays on the Canadian imagination* (1971)—which includes his important and still-relevant 'Letters in Canada' poetry reviews (1950–9), written for the *University of Toronto Quarterly*, and his well-known Conclusion to the *Literary history of Canada*—makes it clear that he is so much a critic of particulars that even his generalizations are particular. When the latter are borrowed by other critics and lifted out of the context of Frye's own marvellously spun web,

they always result in a crude distortion of his theories. Every specific detail in Frye's criticism supports his general edifice, and every single one of them is necessary to sustain it. His theories are actually built up from the relations between the particulars and not, as with other critics, from a mere putting together of them. To understand Frye you have to be able to encompass all the myriad details of his argument, and then it turns out to be not one argument but a many-faceted spiralling series of them. It is impossible to paraphrase or summarize Frye's writings and beliefs, for what he says is contained in a structure that is both self-creating and self-renewing.

One may take issue with Frye's contention that criticism must avoid evaluation and the making of judgements while a literature—like Canada's—is still in the process of being created. And one must be aware when reading Frye that he speaks from what is basically a philosophically idealist position. Furthermore his emphasis on pattern in literature has had the effect of dividing form from content, at least in the minds of his students and followers, and thus his influence perpetuates a dichotomy that he deplores elsewhere in his own writings.

Within Frye's unique idealist system, however, all elements unite to create a brilliant, witty, and generous enchantment. His style is light, clear, lucid, almost angelic. It is only his sudden bursts into colloquial expressions that remind us that he is human and Canadian. The brilliance that emanates from his work is so integral a part of it that it lights up only the relation between the ideas contained in his own world. When carried over into other lesser minds, this light often has by its very power the effect of producing blindness and confusion. Frye's genius is as untransferable as it is abundant, and so it has inadvertently had the effect of limiting the scope of Canadian criticism to his own interests, and of confining it to an implicit idealistic position.

D. G. Jones' *Butterfly on rock: a study of themes and images in Canadian literature* (1970) is an ambitious but unsystematized commentary on Canadian literature from its beginnings to the present. Jones sets out to find a 'general way of looking at Canadian literature which will allow us to acknowledge the many negative characteristics and yet maintain that the literature has a basically positive character.' On the whole he denies that the negative image in Canadian literature dominates, and asserts that the Canadian identity and a central myth have always been present in the literature, but that up to now the critics have failed to recognize and describe it correctly.

While Jones is interesting in his discussion of the older writers—Carman, Lampman, Scott, and Charles D. G. Roberts—and his book is full of critical flashes, they are not always elaborated sufficiently. Its greatest weakness is that it does not follow up its opening argument to the end. Like so many other Canadian critics, Jones discusses his literary ideas in shifting metaphoric terms and this does much to mar and obscure an otherwise fine and sensitive prose style.

He starts off by using the ideas of Frye and Jung and ends up with those of Eiseley and the existentialists. His attempt to accommodate Canadian literature to existentialist philosophy is a failure, partly because no literature can be encompassed by a mere philosophic system, even one as varied and flexible as the existential. Because Jones' interests are philosophical and psychological as well as literary, he tends to leave out of account political and economic considerations.

His attitude is implicitly historical, but his approach is mythopoeic and relies on an elaborate tracing of archetypes. He uses the Old Testament symbols of Adam, the fall from Eden, the Ark and rebirth to pose his questions, but he answers them from a New Testament point of view in the Christian terms of grace and resurrection. He is thereby led to emphasize the work of those writers that can be translated into their mythical equivalences, so that a literal—as opposed to a symbolic—Old Testament poet like A. M. KLEIN, and an important socially prophetic poet like Dorothy LIVESAY, are hardly mentioned. He concludes that our poets all affirm life despite the cultural pressures within Canadian society to deny and suppress the irrational and passionate sides of it.

Jones is aware that the conflict between man and nature manifests itself in all cultures, not just the Canadian, and that the degrees of intensity of the conflict vary in each culture. He suggests that in Canada the conflict engendered by man's encounter with the wilderness has not resulted in more alienation but in less. For Canadian writers, nature remains the source where they can find renewal for their sense of community and validation for their collective dream of the future.

Survival: a thematic guide to Canadian literature (1972), by the poet and novelist Margaret Atwood, reads like a book-length gloss on the author's novel *Surfacing* rather than a work of literary criticism. It has many of the features of a novel, such as inventiveness and political urgency, and makes verbal claims to causal connections that are not supported by the evidence of argument or research. Poems and novels have their own logic, different from that found in critical discourse. Instead of proceeding by argument the novel offers a logic of style and emotion that is conveyed by means of symbols, images, and metaphors. Since it is never possible to argue with images, and since *Survival* consists almost entirely of metaphors and images, all critical discussion of the problems it considers is ruled out.

Atwood sees literature as 'the mirror of a nation's psyche' and declares that her book will mirror and describe, but in no way attempt to judge or evaluate, the works she examines. She does not state the criteria for her selection of examples, which is heavily weighted with works from the recent past. (Selection itself is always an evaluative act.) The thesis in *Survival* is similar to the one in *Butterfly on rock*; every country has a core symbol, or as Jones puts it, a central myth. Atwood believes that survival is the core symbol of the Canadian spirit and proposes a model of the four basic positions of survival, the adoption of one or all of which she considers essential if Canadians are to survive in a difficult, grudging, and often unfriendly world. The four 'victim positions' that she describes are really only new names for the familiar stages of individual psychological growth; in her attempts to simplify language Atwood ends up with a confusing mixture of sexual and political terminology. Translated into ordinary words, her four steps in individual growth and development start with the denial of reality, go on to the displacement of it and the subsequent rationalization, then to resistance. Finally, when the fourth stage is reached—the overcoming of the negative aspects of resistance—a new equilibrium can be achieved that offers a high degree of consciousness.

Survival is an imaginative and politically outspoken *tour de force*, inspired by the positive impulse to popularize Canadian literature, but it is not a literary study. Neither can it be considered a reliable critical tool, for it offers too frail a metaphysical structure to deal with the vast array of historical and empirical facts that must be dealt with in any consideration of the present situation in Canadian literature. It has an excellent and useful bibliography.

Desmond PACEY is one Canadian critic who has attempted to deal with empirical realities, but in a simplistic way. One of the first scholars to take the study of Canadian literature seriously, he boldly asserted the existence of such a literature as early as 1938 in 'At Last a Canadian Literature', an article that was originally published in the *Cambridge Review* and is now reprinted in his *Essays in Canadian Criticism: 1938–1968* (1969). Although at that time Pacey defended the idea of a national literature, he also deprecated its derivativeness, which he ascribed to the pretension and hypocrisy of Canada's colonial politics. By 1950, in a later essay called 'Literary Criticism in Canada'—the best of his four essays on literary criticism—Pacey noted that the absence of a body of criticism informed by literary theory was the most serious hindrance to the development of the country's literature. According to him, Canadian criticism was deficient in the evaluative function, and relied too heavily on the kind of academic skills employed in categorizing and classifying. The three obstacles that a developing literature encountered in Canada were the absence of a single dominating figure, the small size of the literary community, and the failure of Canadian universities to offer courses in Canadian literature at either graduate or undergraduate levels.

By 1965 Pacey seems to have changed his mind about history, and his vocabulary about literature. In 'The Canadian Imagination' (1965) he adopted the romantic, idealistically coloured view of earlier critics like Lionel Stevenson and later ones like Frye and theorized that the Canadian imagination was 'mainly a function of landscape and climate and only secondarily of a society'. He also postulated a psychology of paradox against a background of grandeur into which he placed 'the image of man dwarfed but spiritually indomitable amid a wilderness that . . . frightens and fascinates.'

Since no equivalent existed in politics to balance the dramatic landscape, the Canadian writer could only deal with social themes indirectly and ironically through satire, or else romantically through historical novels. The only other alternative open to him, according to Pacey, was to avoid human conflict altogether and write about animals. In spite of this, Pacey looked rosily to a future that he hoped would develop out of new and hitherto undreamed of combinations of the English and French traditions. In his final essay on the subject, 'The Outlook for Canadian Literature' (1968), Pacey takes a retrospective look at his own career and the accompanying changes in the literary climate in Canada and abroad.

A more detailed picture of the literary flavour of the forties, together with an intimate account of the intellectual atmosphere of those days, may be gleaned from the newly collected writings of John Sutherland (1919–56)—the editor of *First Statement* and *Northern Review* between 1943 and 1954—in *John Sutherland: essays, controversies, and poems* (1972), edited with an introductory memoir by Miriam Waddington. Through these editorial pieces and essays Sutherland emerges as a critic who tried to define national literature not through political means or core symbols but through the psychological, textual, and historical analysis of contemporary Canadian writing. He worked indefatigably and against heavy financial odds to launch, handprint, and publish almost single-handedly a magazine of high literary quality, *Northern Review*. He was a prolific writer and commentator who was especially interested in poetry, and the only critic of his time—or ours—ever to challenge A. J. M. Smith's division of Canadian literature into native and cosmopolitan traditions. His essays on Earle BIRNEY, A. M. Klein, P. K. PAGE, E. J. PRATT, and James REANEY remain as fresh and relevant as on the day they were written and serve as a reminder that Canada lost one of its most brilliant young critics when he died.

Addressing himself to similar problems of national literature in *Second image: comparative studies in Quebec/Canadian literature* (1971), almost twenty-five years later, Ronald Sutherland chooses the focus of a comparative approach to French-English literature for the six essays he has gathered together in this study. In his philosophical point of view he is closer to John Sutherland than to the majority of other Canadian critics. Unlike them, he rarely resorts to the use of the familiar rhetoric of myth, mask, and persona. Instead Ronald Sutherland draws on the historical and sociological fact and on moral values as they emerge in the literature. He traces similar themes and parallel developments in the two cultures to prove his thesis that a country's literature defines its nationality. According to him, literatures have always provided such definitions for the peoples of older cultures; in Canada our literature has performed the same function but the process has not been as readily understood or interpreted. He views Canadian French and English literature as two parts of a single whole, and his study, by choosing the language of traditional argument instead of mystical apocalyptic pronouncement, opens up new and much-needed fields of critical inquiry.

Another English-language publication on French-Canadian literature is Jack Warwick's *The long journey: literary themes of French Canada* (1968), a synthesis that shows how the North—the *pays d'en haut*—has provided a basic source of symbolic and metaphoric imagery through three centuries of writing, from Gabriel Sagard to THÉRIAULT, LANGEVIN, and ROY *et al.* (Published in translation as *L'appel du nord dans la littérature canadienne-française* (1972), it is discussed in more detail in LITERARY STUDIES IN FRENCH.)

Odysseus ever returning: essays on Canadian writers and writing (1970) by George Woodcock, with a preface by William H. New, is a collection of critical essays written between 1954 and 1970. Most of them are on individual writers (MACLENNAN, Moore, CALLAGHAN, LAYTON, COHEN, Birney, and Smith). There are two general essays on literary criticism. In the first, 'Away from lost worlds' (1955), Woodcock stresses regionalism, the importance of geographic factors and the sense of place, at the same time as he asserts the existence of a unifying factor in all English-language literatures. After deploring the influence of institutional settings such as universities and the CBC on the writers of the nineteen forties and fifties, he goes on to divide the novelists into representative groupings—immigrant, Jewish, and regional. He notes the regional richness from which the poets draw their sustenance and hypothesizes a basis of social realism for the Montreal poets that he contrasts with the metaphysical mystic underpinnings of the Toronto ones.

The second essay on criticism is in two parts: the first half, written in 1955, states his own critical credo as being that of defining, interpreting, and elucidating the Canadian literary tradition. He finds that a Canadian literature exists, that it is strongly regional in character but must be understood comparatively—i.e. regionally and locally within a larger cosmopolitan tradition rather than the merely national. In 1955 he noted that Canadian criticism had not kept pace with Canadian novels and poems, but by 1966 the situation had changed and he welcomed the kind of critical dialogue that related Canadian writing to the Canadian experience. Woodcock sees the existence of a Canadian criticism as one aspect of the whole literature, and pictures the critic of the future as a wide-ranging and eclectic diarist for the philosophical, sociological, and mythological voices of Canadian writers.

The title *Articulating West: essays on purpose and form in modern Canadian literature* (1972) by William H. New is somewhat misleading. New teaches in the West, at the University of British Columbia, but this group of twenty-two essays and reviews is a gathering of work published in various journals during the past five years and is not necessarily on western subjects. 'West' is not used descriptively but in its metaphoric sense of exploration and discovery. The groupings of the essays under subtitles such as 'Developing a Language of Myth', 'Problems of Ordering Reality', 'Ending the Liberal Pageant', 'Developing the Texture of Language', and 'Voices for the Soundless Fugue' indicate New's ambitions and interests but do not always live up to their titular promises by making a contribution to the problems of form either as they exist generally, or, more specifically, in Canadian literature.

The organizing principle underlying the essays (which include pieces on Pratt, W. O. Mitchell, WILSON, MacLennan, RICHLER, LAURENCE, AVISON, and Birney) is stated in the introduction: 'To speak the language of "West" is not to be merely regional in bias, therefore, but to articulate the tension between order and disorder, myth and reality, that underlies Canadian writing.' Taking landscape to be the central inspiration of the language and art of Canadian writers, he elaborates: 'What the rhetoric [or landscape] in a sense displays, therefore, is the elusiveness of its subject and the ambivalence necessary to convey such Protean vitality.' This kind of academic language almost justifies some of the attacks levelled against it by Irving Layton in the book below.

Not strictly speaking a conventional literary study, *Engagements: the prose of Irving Layton* (1972) edited by Seymour Mayne brings together in the first of its four sections a number of flamboyant and extravagant, but very acute, critical interpretations of the Canadian literary scene. Some, such as the review of Klein's *The Hitleriad*, go back as far as 1944, and others, like 'Forever Honeyless: Canadian Criticism', are a severe indictment of the contemporary critics Frye, Louis DUDEK, and Tallman, and especially of their academic terminology and theories. The rest of the book consists of forewards and prefaces to his own books of poetry and includes the introduction to the anthology *Canadian poems: 1850–1952*, which Layton edited with Dudek in 1952. Mayne has reprinted ten of Layton's short stories as well as an entertaining assortment of brief and vituperative letters to editors and others.

Contexts of Canadian criticism: a collection of critical essays (1971), edited with an introduction by Eli MANDEL, brings together a group of thirteen important essays written between 1943 and 1969 by such diverse writers as H. A. Innes, George GRANT, and Dorothy Livesay. By avoiding all historical sequence, and omitting any discussion of economic factors, the editor seeks to frame a series of ideas about the context of Canadian criticism—the social and historical (E. K. Brown, W. L. MORTON, Innis, Underhill *et al.*), the theoretical (Frye, MCLUHAN, SPARSHOTT), and 'Patterns of Criticism' (Milton Wilson, Robert McDougall, Livesay *et al.*). The approaches Mandel selects as being representative are varied and, as he says himself, 'oblique'; but they are not nearly as oblique as his own discussion of them in his introduction. His insistence on understanding the frontier as something symbolic and mystical, instead of as something that is and has been also pragmatic and real, leads him to misunderstand E. K. Brown and to misinterpret him as a nineteenth-century evolutionist. He declares that for Frye, society is really 'a series of conventions, a form of art', and following on from this view Mandel gives the notion a theological twist by suggesting that 'To see it [society] as art is to see it theatrically, as the possibility of ritual and therefore of grace.' The essays that follow are all important and not so perplexing. Many of them have long been out of print so that it is an enriching experience to reread them in the light of present developments.

The making of modern poetry in Canada: essential articles on contemporary Canadian poetry in English (1967), edited by Louis Dudek and Michael Gnarowski, was the first comprehensive collection—from 1910 to the early sixties—to bring together some of the most useful Canadian literary articles and background materials that had long been inaccessible. The editors have grouped the material into eight sections, the first four of which are linked historically and the second four thematically; there are also three essays (by Smith, Bonenfant, and F. R. SCOTT) on relations with French-Canadian writing. This is a valuable introduction to the vast amount of material that still awaits retrieval and fuller documentation.

3. Of the remaining book-length literary studies on individual writers, Donald Theall's *The medium is the rear-view mirror: understanding McLuhan* (1971) is the most comprehensive and learned. Theall is the first critic to relate McLuhan's theories to their rich traditional sources in English literature and Catholic culture. In tracing the development of McLuhan's thought, verbal surfaces, style, and method from *The Gutenberg Galaxy* to *Through the vanishing point*, he shows how McLuhan's literary training gave him a thorough knowledge of ancient rhetoric (the art of persuasion) and how he adapted Pope's methods of juxtaposition and defeated expectancy to Freud's theory of wit, to Joyce's ideas about language, and to A. N. Whitehead's insights into chance. According to Theall, McLuhan invented a new form, the 'essai concret', which uses various kinds and sizes of print and type to convey meaning through shape, scale, and tone, as well as through words. Theall likens McLuhan's social role to Addison's in the eighteenth century, which was essentially the role of a popularizer who offered the newly emerging mercantile class the assurance that what seemed unfamiliar was really familiar, and therefore to be neither feared nor avoided.

Three younger critics have written an individual study and two comparative studies: *The novels of Hugh MacLennan* (1969) by Robert H. Cockburn, *The immoral moralists: Hugh MacLennan and Leonard Cohen* (1972) by Patricia A. Morley, and *The style of innocence: a study of Hemingway and Callaghan* (1972) by Fraser Sutherland.

4. By far the greater number of literary studies published in our period have been commissioned books on individual writers in a series (i.e. uniform) format—although each series has its own general editor(s) and inner *gestalt*. No less than four series of studies of individual Canadian writers were launched between 1967 and 1972, while the same period saw the inclusion for the first time of studies of some Canadian writers in an American series, Twayne's World Authors Series.

Most of these books keep clear of judgements and content themselves with offering biographical information about the author and a thematic analysis and/or a description of his work. Occasionally, as in W. J. Keith's *Charles G. D. Roberts* (1969) and Ernest Redekop's *Margaret Avison* (1970), we get scholarly studies, or elegant and humane critical ones as in Robertson DAVIES' *Stephen Leacock* (1970) and George Hendrick's *Mazo De La Roche* (1971); while the original research by Douglas O. Spettigue for *Frederick Philip Grove* (1969) and by Miriam Waddington for *A. M. Klein* (1970) has unearthed unpublished documents that form the basis of new linguistic approaches and textual readings. Other books that show individual critical acumen are *James Reaney* by Alvin Lee and *Hugh MacLennan* (1969) by George Woodcock. In the series Critical Views on Canadian Writers, two books have introductions of real merit: *E. J. Pratt* (1969) edited by David G. Pitt and *Mordecai Richler* (1971) edited by David Sheps. On the whole, however, the drawbacks of casual editing and writing and an air of anonymous scholarship pervade most of these series books. To judge by them, an uninspired kind of thematic analysis remains the most prevalent general tool in Canadian literary criticism. Critical terms are seldom defined, limits are hardly ever located, and the problems of how theme and pattern are related and become reunited in the work of individual writers is rarely faced and much less are answers ever attempted. The series are listed below:

CANADIAN WRITERS (in the New Canadian Library)
General editor: Dave GODFREY

Earle Birney (1971) by Richard H. Robillard
Leonard Cohen (1970) by Michael ONDAATJE
Northrop Frye (1971) by Ronald Bates
Frederick Philip Grove (1969) by Ronald Sutherland
Margaret Laurence (1969) by Clara Thomas
Stephen Leacock (1970) by Robertson Davies
Malcolm Lowry (1971) by William H. New
Hugh MacLennan (1970) by Alec Lucas
Marshall McLuhan (1969) by Dennis Duffy
E. J. Pratt (1969) by Milton Wilson
James Reaney (1971) by Ross G. Woodman
Mordecai Richler (1970) by George Woodcock

CANADIAN WRITERS AND THEIR WORK
General editor: William French

Marie-Claire Blais (1970) by Philip Stratford
Hugh Garner (1972) by Doug Fetherling
Irving Layton (1969) by Eli Mandel
Hugh MacLennan (1969) by Peter Buitenhuis
Gabrielle Roy (1969) by Phyllis Grosskurth
Robertson Davies (1972) by Elspeth Buitenhuis

STUDIES IN CANADIAN LITERATURE
General editors: Hugo McPherson & Gary Geddes

Margaret Avison (1970) by Ernest Redekop
Earle Birney (1971) by Frank DAVEY
Morley Callaghan (1969) by Victor Hoar
Frederick Philip Grove (1969) by Douglas Spettigue
A. M. Klein (1970) by Miriam Waddington
Hugh MacLennan (1969) by George Woodcock
Brian Moore (1969) by Hallvard Dahlie
E. J. Pratt (1971) by Sandra Djwa
Al Purdy (1970) by George BOWERING
Charles G. D. Roberts (1969) by W. J. Keith

WORLD AUTHORS SERIES
General editor: Joseph Jones

Morley Callaghan (1966) by Brandon Conron
Bliss Carman (1966) by Donald Stephens
James Reaney (1969) by Alvin A. Lee
Ethel Wilson (1968) by Desmond Pacey
Mazo de la Roche (1971) by George Hendrick
Charles Sangster (1971) by W. D. Hamilton

CRITICAL VIEWS ON CANADIAN WRITERS
General editor: Michael Gnarowski

A. M. Klein (1970) edited by Tom Marshall
Archibald Lampman (1970) edited by Michael Gnarowski
The McGill Movement: A. J. M. Smith, F. R. Scott and Leo Kennedy (1969) edited by Peter Stevens
E. J. Pratt (1969) edited by David G. Pitt
Mordecai Richler (1971) edited by David Sheps
Ernest Buckler (1972) edited by George M. Cook

CANADIAN LITERATURE
General editor: George Woodcock

Dramatists in Canada: selected essays (1972) edited by William H. New
Wyndham Lewis in Canada (1970) edited by George Woodcock
Malcolm Lowry: the man and his work (1971) by George Woodcock
The sixties: Canadian writers and writing of the decade (1969) edited by George Woodcock

MIRIAM WADDINGTON

Literary studies in French. 1. Among the recent surveys of French writing in Canada, the most encyclopedic is the four-volume *Histoire de la littérature française du Québec* (1967, 1968, 1969), published under the general editorship of Pierre de Grandpré. It attempts to combine all methods, ranging from the illustrated manual to the collection of individual articles on themes, influences, and genres. Gérard Tougas's *Histoire de la littérature canadienne-française* (1960), which was revised and extended in 1967, uses the single method of grouping notes on authors under period and genre headings; a new chapter surveys in rather general terms the history of the literary interaction between Québec and France. Other surveys vary from the frankly panoramic—Paul Gay's *Notre littérature: guide littéraire du Canada français* (1969), Guy Sylvestre's *Panorama des lettres canadiennes-françaises* (1969)—to specialization by genre, as in *La poésie canadienne-française: perspectives historiques et thématiques, profils de poètes* (1969) edited by Paul WYCZYNSKI, Bernard Julien, Jean Ménard, and Réjean Robidoux, or by decade, as in Pierre de Grandpré's *Dix ans de vie littéraire au Canada français 1955–1965* (1966). The influence of growing pedagogical needs is evident in most of these manuals and surveys, a fact that renews a very important bias in literary criticism. The survey, by its nature, stresses the notion of cultural collectivity, and much of this writing is in fact closer to cultural synthesis than literary analysis.

This gives rise to some striking resemblances with the older nationalist school of literary criticism associated with the name of Camille Roy. Guy ROBERT, in *Aspects de la littérature québécoise* (1970), starts to argue anew the old question of 'a literature or some writers' and states almost in Roy's very words that 'it is a question of being ourselves'. *Aspects de la littérature québécoise* is a collection of Robert's articles and papers. The inquiry is not sustained throughout the book, but some main ideas are. In the first place he characterizes Québec culture as being alienated by identification with a minority language and by its colonial history and reflexes, which include the obsession with the masterpiece as a writer's goal. In the end he rejects the name 'French Canadian', as other writers have done before him, in favour of a 'homo-quebecoisis', whose poetry is to be a liberation from the fatigue of cultural survivalism. Clément Moisan's *L'age de la littérature canadienne* (1968) repeats the old argument about the difficulties of a young literature in a society that had the problems of a pioneering existence as well as an uncertain political future; the new twist is that he finds the same is true of early English writers in Canada, and from there he makes a general parallel. His proximity to historical determinism is about the same as Guy Robert's though it is without the historical pessimism of Robert that is so characteristic of Michel BRUNET's disciples.

2. Jean-Charles Falardeau is a sociologist with an interest in literature, which reverses the more common combination of the *littérateur* who makes pronouncements on society. *Notre sociéte et son roman* (1967) includes a series of previously published articles, and a new examination of the works of Roger Lemelin and Robert Charbonneau, but the attempt to find a valid way of relating literature to society gives the book its unity. One method employed is the straightforward assessment of the intentional socio-economic thesis, which is then compared to the related problem as it existed in the author's own time. The main result of this method is to show that didactic novelists are no better as prophets than they are as artists; Gérin-Lajoie was preaching rural settlement when it had just ceased to be a serious solution to French-Canadian survival problems, and P.-J.-O. Chauvau and Errol Bouchette were similarly behind the real developments of their own time. The ideal French-Canadian societies imagined by these writers are, however, a positive indication of a common ideological feature: a strong tendency to carry a localized economic crisis into questions of language and nationality, and to seek a strong social structure capable of solving everything at once.

Another of Falardeau's critical methods is the discovery and interpretation of the key symbol. Lemelin's 'pente douce', for instance, is not merely a background physical feature in novels describing Québec; it is the symbol of the desire for social ascension. In many cases, however, the meaning of the symbol is not so obvious. The desire for departure, so frequent in nineteenth-century narratives, is plausibly rationalized by the various heroes. It is in the total of such departures that we are to perceive a collective problem, the feeling of being trapped in a dead-end society. Falardeau makes no attempt to relate this to departure themes outside Canada. Nor does he mention Jacques LANGUIRAND's play, *Les grands départs*, which is the major Canadian work on this theme. Other themes treated by Falardeau are time and space perceived in fiction, and the concentration by Charbonneau and Lemelin on adolescence. While Falardeau's study is very revealing, and is a serious attempt to interpret Canadian works in terms of their own world, its capacity to reveal literary values appears limited. However, it provides strong support for further inquiry.

Falardeau's most fruitful method has been more strictly sociological. By analysing the world of fiction as if it were a real society, he is able to make confident comparisons between the two. Applying this either to selected authors, or to census-type surveys of masses of imagined characters, he makes some startling revelations. Imagined proletarian families are incomplete, usually by the absence of a father. Middle-class families are rare but father-dominated. These results raise some hard questions about social realism, which becomes more interesting for the key symbols it creates than for its erratic documentary value.

Literary studies in French 2

L'esprit révolutionnaire dans la littérature canadienne-française (1968) is a frankly ideological work by Joseph Costisella, originally a thesis at Bordeaux University. Costisella has shown great devotion to collecting everything from 1837 to 1900 that could come within his rather broad definition of 'revolutionary'. He does not attempt to place it in a wider context, either political or literary. His own comments amount to an angry denunciation of all other literary historians, and of all shades of political conservatism, which he usually equates with absolute monarchy. The technique of quotation out of context is frequently abused. But in spite of all this, there are two important features to be noted. One is that a compendium of inflammatory remarks made during a relatively calm period of history is a useful tool to correct our perspectives. The other is that the thesis in itself constitutes the best example of an imported ideological interpretation acting on Québec culture. As literary methodologies go, it is far from revolutionary, working on the simple assertion that a literature is the reflection of its nation.

Les grands thèmes nationalistes du roman historique canadien-français (1970) by Maurice Lemire is a full and factual account of nationalist themes in historical novels. It is at first sight a truncated subject: neither the themes nor the genre are treated in full. However, the advantage of this method is its exactness. Each of the themes, such as the deportation of the Acadians, is followed through all the novels in which it has been used to display nationalist sentiment. Lemire argues, at the end of all this evidence, that the double constraint of Victorian respectability and clerical domination kept French-Canadian writers from expressing the kind of open restlessness that we see now. They found indirect ways, such as dwelling on glorification of the past and on historic grievances. The evidence shows, among novelists, a most convincing preference for the themes that make French Canadians feel uncomfortable. The positive themes—heroic stories of missionaries, pioneers, and soldiers—occupy a smaller place. This raises a serious question of method: if non-historical novels about pioneers etc. were counted, would the balance not be reversed? What does it signify to show that certain themes have been found more suitable for historical novels? Lemire does not attempt to answer this question, but there remains the obvious argument that, since history has been such a focal point in French-Canadian thinking, it is interesting to be exactly informed about its projections into fantasy. Lemire makes no claims for great artistic achievements in the genre; indeed, he perhaps rather underplays some of the best writers.

François Bigot is shown to occupy a special place in French-Canadian fiction: he is the scapegoat for the Conquest, which is otherwise scarcely treated at all. His betrayal, and in some cases that of the whole French administration, is used to show that the *Canadiens* were not conquered. This face-saving device was first published by Mrs Leprohon in 'The manor house of Villerai' and received a more artistic expression by William Kirby in *The golden dog*. It is not clear how far French-Canadian writers are indebted to these English-Canadian authors, but as Lemire says, the betrayal myth is a rare case of a pan-Canadian nationalist theme.

An equivalent exchange within pan-French influences is the 1837 rebellion. The two novels that raise this event to a bitter anti-English story are Régis de Trobriand's *Le rebelle* (1842), the first to use it as historical fiction, and Jules Verne's *Famille sans nom* (c. 1889). The long series of French Canadians who adopted the device from 1859 to 1928 indicate, however, that the invention of these two Europeans did not fall on deaf ears. Here again it seems necessary to go beyond the strict limits of genre maintained by Lemire in order to get a proper understanding. Within the genre Canadian writers are found to be less indignant than their European models and are even inclined to show armed conflict as the unfortunate result of blundering misunderstanding rather than as a heroic encounter. Lemire ascribes this sometimes to the desire for *bonne entente*, sometimes to timidity. The theme seems to have died down until Jacques FERRON revived it in 1959 with his play *Les grands soleils*.

A different way of treating literature in relation to the collective imagination is Jack Warwick's *The long journey: literary themes of French Canada* (1968), which was published in French as *L'appel du nord dans la littérature canadienne-française* (1972). The method here is basically like the Jungian explanation of recurrent patterns, although this theory is not discussed. Instead the continuity, in writing, of an imaginative appeal of the *pays d'en haut* is explored. From 1632 to 1962 there are gaps, but these are partly filled by showing through historical documents that feelings about the bush and the *coureurs de bois* persisted even if they were not being made into literature. Indeed, the whole question of initial European contact with American nature is regarded as essential to the formation of a set of imaginative patterns that continue to be characteristic of French-Canadian writing. Comparison with Frederick Jackson Turner's frontier thesis or George GRANT's notion of the 'primal' is invited, not made. On the other hand the myth does not remain constant. The French-Canadian imaginative perception of geographical space has been modified by historical developments and has produced a region that is here called the pseudo-North, more compelling than Arctic wastes. Finally, the local colour of these regions can dwindle, leaving a polyvalent myth as their special legacy.

The main movements found in this configuration are empire (the desire to impose a cultural presence on the continent), quest (the journey for an illumination of self and cosmos), regeneration (modifications of the Frenchman's *bon sauvage* in French-Canadian heroes), and revolt, in which it is found that an imaginative capacity to challenge established canons has always existed along with the better-known submissiveness of the Québec rural tradition. Although these themes have their counterparts elsewhere, their combination and interaction in French-Canadian writers are regarded as a distinctive literary creation—a culturally characteristic variant of what might be a universal myth.

A thorough detailed study of similar thematic content in both English- and French-language novels is to be found in Antoine Sirois's *Montréal dans le roman canadien* (1968). This introductory survey of French-Canadian social history reaches the conclusion that the sequence of agriculturalism and urbanization created a double set of values, while the conclusion of the whole study is that novelists writing about Montreal are unanimous in deploring the cultural, moral, and intellectual emptiness of their North American city. The book establishes in abundant detail how Montreal has been described physically, how the three major ethnic groups (French, English, and Jewish) describe themselves and each other, how the different socio-economic classes are shown in novels of the two languages, how families within the three ethnic groups appear in both languages, and what notions of religion are to be found in these fictional accounts of Montreal life. It emerges that heroes of novels in both languages tend to be less interested in the proletarian sectors of the city than in establishment Westmount, which they find to be a colossal disappointment. It might be argued that the discrepancy between the hero's goal or lost ideal and the author's dissatisfaction with the highest values of Westmount indicate a common pattern in the Montreal novel that is fully compatible with the structural theories of Georg Lukacs. But there is no room for such speculation in Sirois's very full documentation of content. Montrealers' views of each other abound in platitude and stereotype. It is no coincidence that there is only one comprehensive Montreal novel: MACLENNAN's *Two solitudes*.

Montréal dans le roman canadien is so far the most thorough close comparison of French- and English-Canadian literature. It is based on the very reasonable assumption that unity of place and other material should give rise to meaningful similarities and differences. Ronald Sutherland's *Second image: comparative studies in Quebec/Canadian literature* (1971) offers another type of comparison. In this collection of articles, Sutherland brings together various themes that he has found identical or comparable in the two bodies of writing, such as racism, the loss of traditional morality, and Calvinism-Jansenism. He too easily assumes that French and English cultural developments in Canada have been parallel. His failure to relate Jansenism to its historical definition, for instance, seriously limits what he has to say on that subject in Canada, and thus on any comparison. (See also LITERARY STUDIES IN ENGLISH 2 and 4.)

3. Pure literary studies published in the 1967–72 period are fewer in number than these cultural syntheses, though there are numerous volumes of *mélanges* and other collections of articles on diverse subjects. Drama and poetry have been the main items of recent interest. Poetry has always been regarded as the privileged genre, both because of its predominance in French-Canadian

publishing and because of its traditional claim to give direct expression to the quintessence of individual and collective problems.

The theatre in Québec has quite recently shown a rapid growth and its new place is being evaluated. Jean-Cléo Godin and Laurent Mailhot, in the first two chapters of *Le théâtre québécois* (1970), raise two major questions: Is Québec's theatrical tradition twenty-five or three hundred years old and what is the relation of theatre to literature? Their answers are marked by a commendable prudence as well as by valuable information and an awareness of the theoretical scope of their questions. The remaining ten chapters discuss one playwright each and emphasize the use of poetic language and symbol. A brief general conclusion discusses the rapid experimentation with dramatic structure of the last few years and concludes that the modern Québec theatre is a genuine mediation between the emotions and the daily realities of its public.

Gilles MARCOTTE in *Le temps des poètes: description critique de la poésie actuelle au Canada français* (1969) makes a very comprehensive synthesis of the poetic life of Québec from the beginning of Les Éditions de l'Hexagone in 1953 to the present. With some fifty poets to discuss and categorize Marcotte is inevitably reduced in many cases to brief and almost independent statements. Nevertheless there is a sustained thesis. Hexagone is found in retrospect to have been the revolution in Québec poetry that it superficially appeared to be. It found the way from the isolation of the individual poet to a revitalization of his role in the community. This, Marcotte insists, does not mean political didacticism, although some poets like Paul CHAMBERLAND may have been spokesmen for specific political movements. The great precursors, particularly Saint-Denys GARNEAU and Alain GRANDBOIS, made the rupture with traditional forms, which Marcotte regards as immobile, to admit the drama of language and existence. It led them to isolation, which in turn pointed to the need for community. Subsequent poets, but especially Gaston MIRON, explore the arduous roads of québécois self-discovery. Miron himself easily identifies with the language of the people, but finds painful the need to experiment with language that will give him the poetic power to say what he means. Chamberland's alienation is opposite (but perhaps complementary): poetic facility is a barrier to his political consummation and he has to resist it with a determined anti-poetry. But in either case the essential modernity is there: poetry is used to transcend individual space and seeks not merely to express but to become the dream of a whole generation.

Such arguments raise many difficulties. The reader at times feels adrift in a sea of clichés without definition: *prise de conscience*, *volonté d'action*, and so on. 'The absence of doctrine' is a term of high praise rather than a step towards some new understanding. The alienation of the poet by his solitude is neither clearly distinguished from nor cogently equated with other forms of alienation. Above all, the step forward from the personal to the collective on the one hand is presented as a definitive turning-point associated with the founding of Hexagone and on the other appears to be a constantly renewed aim. However, *Le temps des poètes* is an accurate and at times illuminating account of the poetic scene from 1953 to the present and offers a convincing way of bringing the facts of the 1930s into the same perspective.

The language continues to be a prime question. Since the invention of the derogatory name *joual*, attitudes have been rapidly diversified and complicated. Descriptions, dictionaries, and glossaries have appeared. Authors have exploited this vein of Québec originality, often while denouncing it as the living symbol of their alienation. Jean Marcel, typically, takes advantage of the popularity of the word in his title *Le joual de Troie* (1973). Less typical is his discussion of the linguistic and ideological phenomena around it. He fustigates the bourgeois intellectuals who affect a cult of lower-class speech and diminishes the exaggerated place they have given to lexical peculiarities in their simplistic attitude to language. Syntax and morphology are invoked to remind us that there is one French language, as Mario Pei and Henry Alexander are invoked to assert that there is one English language. Most of the book is a violent attack on Henri Bélanger's use of local words to postulate distinct thought patterns in *Place à l'homme* (1971).

4. Studies of individual authors commonly have a biographical orientation, and one might conveniently take the collection Écrivains d'aujourd'hui as a rough equivalent

of the 'l'homme et l'oeuvre' formula well known in France. Recent titles in this series are *Ringuet* (1970) by Jean Panneton, *Marcel Dubé* (1970) by Maximilien Laroche, and *Félix-Antoine Savard* (1970) by André MAJOR. Lignes québécoises, a series published by Les Presses de l'Université de Montréal in which the orientation is much more exegetic, offered studies of Desrosiers, Saint-Denys Garneau, and Germaine Guèvremont in 1973. Classiques canadiens, which has increased both its list of titles and the content of critical material, has added *Pamphile Le May* (1969) by Romain Légaré, *Jules-Paul Tardivel* (1970) by Pierre Savard, *Joseph Marmette* (1969) by Roger Le Moine, *Octave Crémazie: 1827–1879* (1970) by Michel Dassonville, and *Louis Dantin* (1968) by Yves Garon. Éditions Seghers (Paris) published *Anne Hébert* (1969) by René Lacôte and *Gilles Vigneault* (1969) by Lucien Rioux in their Poètes d'aujourd'hui and Chansonniers d'aujourd'hui series. In the realm of non-series literary studies, Saint-Denys Garneau continues to be a preferred subject, partly because of the release of new documentation and partly because an ideological reaction against him has provoked a reassessment. See *Saint-Denys Garneau et ses lectures européennes* (1969) by Roland Bourneuf, *Saint-Denys Garneau: 1912–1943* (1969) by Benoît Lacroix, and *Saint-Denys Garneau* (1969) by Eva Kushner. Other studies on various authors are: *Ducharme l'inquiétant* (1967) by Michel Van Schendel, *Jacques Ferron malgré lui* (1970) by Jean Marcel, *Jacques Ferron* (1971) by Jacques de Roussan, *Jean-Charles Harvey et son oeuvre romanesque* (1969) by Guildo Rousseau, *Jean-Charles Harvey, précurseur de la révolution tranquille* (1970) by Marcel-Aimé Gagon, *Jasmin par Jasmin* (1970) by Claude JASMIN, *Xavier Marmier et le Canada avec des documents inédits* (1967) by Jean Ménard, *Nelligan, poésie rêvée poésie vécue* (1969) edited by Jean ETHIER-BLAIS, *'La Terre' de Zola et 'Trente arpents' de Ringuet* (1970) by Jacques Viens, and *Gilles Vigneault* (1968) by Aline Robitaille.

The growth of individual author-studies must be set against our earlier remarks on the preponderance, in the general sector, of cultural syntheses. If we also take periodicals into account, it must be said that the ideological applications of literature have acted both as a rival and as a catalyst to deliberations on the nature of literary texts.

5. *Bibliographie critique du roman canadien-français, 1837–1900* (1968) edited by David Hayne and the late Marcel Tirol contains substantial listings around its subject, amounting to an inventory of bibliographies on the whole area. Its critical notes vary from the laconic to the non-existent, according to the nature of each item. Its special feature is its near-exhaustive documentation of the contemporaneous reception of the novels; and it is also generously selective on modern criticism. It may be complemented by *Guide bibliographique des thèses littéraires canadiennes de 1921 à 1969* (1970) by Antoine Naaman, which includes a section on French-Canadian literature. JW

Little, Jean. See CHILDREN'S BOOKS IN ENGLISH 2, 4, and 5.

Littlejohn, Bruce. See ANTHOLOGIES IN ENGLISH 3.

Livesay, Dorothy (1909–). Born in Winnipeg, she came with her family to Ontario as a child. She was educated at the University of Toronto and at the Sorbonne. On her return to Canada she studied at the School of Social Science, University of Toronto, and did welfare work in Montreal, New Jersey, and Vancouver. In 1937 she married Duncan Macnair. From 1960 to 1963 she taught English for UNESCO in Northern Rhodesia (Zambia). She has also taught at the Universities of Alberta, British Columbia, and Victoria and been writer-in-residence at the University of New Brunswick. In 1947 the Royal Society of Canada awarded her the Lorne Pierce Medal for distinguished service to Canadian literature. She lives in Victoria.

Green pitcher (1928), Dorothy Livesay's first book of poems, is a small collection of brief lyrics that show the influence of imagist techniques and are written in the manner of the American poet Elinor Wylie. The poems are gnomic fragments of description with some attempts to embody within the images statements about personal relationships. This subject-matter and technique are used more elaborately and successfully in *Signpost* (1932), a series of lyrics that detail the varying moods of elation, disappointment, and loss in human love. It also contains a longer poem, 'The City Wife', that foreshadows the poet's later interest in longer forms. During the worst years of the depression her poetry developed a revolutionary turn, particularly in the title poem of her volume *Day and night* (1944), which won a Governor General's Award. Dorothy Livesay remained sensitive to the problems of the age in the more prosperous years that followed the Second World War. She won a Governor General's Award a second time for *Poems for people* (1947). Her long poem *Call my people home* (1950) was written as commentary for a radio broadcast (1947) on the evacuation of Japanese Canadians from the British Columbia coast during the Second World War. *New poems* appeared in 1956 and her *Selected poems: 1926–1956*, with an introduction by Desmond PACEY, in 1957. In 1964 the Unitarian Service Committee published *The colour of God's face*, a short sequence of poems inspired by her African experience. Revised and retitled 'Zambia', it was included in *The unquiet bed* (1967). This book showed a new freedom for Dorothy Livesay both as a poet and as a woman, particularly in a series of confessional love poems expressed in a more open lyrical style that evolved in part from the linguistic studies she pursued in writing her thesis for her M.Ed. This new personal poetry was also evident in *Plainsongs* (1969), which was extended and reissued in 1971.

Dorothy Livesay has also published *The documentaries* (1968), a selection of some of her longer poems, particularly those associated with social protest, to which she has written prose introductions giving autobiographical information and setting the poems in a personal and social context. The full range of her poetry can be seen in *Collected poems: the two seasons* (1972), which includes her long poem, 'Disasters of the Sun', originally issued as a folder in 1971.

She has also edited an anthology, *Forty women poets of Canada* (1972). PS

Lloyd, Trevor. See HISTORY STUDIES IN ENGLISH 12 and POLITICAL WRITINGS IN ENGLISH 4.

Lochhead, Douglas. See ANTHOLOGIES IN ENGLISH 1; HISTORY STUDIES IN ENGLISH 17; and POETRY IN ENGLISH intro. and 2.

Lolois, J.-J. See HISTORY STUDIES IN FRENCH 11.

Loranger, Françoise (1913–). Born in Montreal, she lives in Quebec City. Her literary career began with a novel, *Mathieu* (1949), and continued with a number of plays and series for television, until she wrote her first play for live theatre, *Une maison . . . un jour* (1965), performed by the Théâtre du Rideau Vert in Montreal. *Encore 5 minutes* (1967) was the second and last play she wrote for the traditional live theatre, and since *Le chemin du roy* (1969) Mme Loranger has turned her attention to 'participatory theatre', at the same time taking an openly political stance.

The theme of her early work is the individual's quest to discover his identity and gain control of his destiny. In the later plays the individual is replaced by the collectivity, in particular the Québec people. *Une maison . . . un jour* is about the generation gap. The son has sold the ancestral home for demolition, but the father refuses to leave and clings to the furniture inside as if his life depended on it. The home is a social microcosm inhabited by the family: its threatened demolition symbolizes the break-up of family life in our modern society. The young are opposed to tradition, which they consider strangles any possibility of self-fulfilment. For the older generation the home, the fixed social structure they are used to, represents security. In *Encore 5 minutes*, which won a Governor General's Award, this conflict is concentrated in one person, Gertrude, and the play is therefore much more effective as theatre. We are once again in a bourgeois household—in this case a 'white, empty room' where Gertrude, in her dressing-gown, paces to and fro. The room is, symbolically, Gertrude's cell: she has given up her individual freedom to live a semblance of life centred only on the comforts of her possessions and her family. The crisis occurs when her husband makes her see that their son, Renaud, is no longer a small child and has been living his own life for several years. It is further intensified by the unexpected return of their daughter. Gertrude realizes that the members of the family are autonomous and refuse the identities she has tried to attribute to them. Her choice is clear: she can either go on pretending or leave the home and live for herself at last. She leaves, though not before the family has tried to trap her into staying. The ending is therefore optimistic: Loranger believes that each of us is capable of determining his own life.

This play was a critical and box-office success. But instead of resting on her laurels, Loranger abandoned the bourgeois theatre and wrote *Le chemin du roy* in collaboration with Claude Levac. This is a sort of 'happening' based on General de Gaulle's visit to Quebec in 1967, brilliantly staged by Paul Buissonneau as a hockey match. Québec beats Ottawa 4 to 2 and the show ends with the winning team singing 'We shall be ourselves. Québec must be made and we are making it.' Even in its printed form the show retains its spontaneity. The wealth of creative talent involved explains the show's success and its importance for Québec theatre. But Loranger's subsequent work is disappointing. *Double jeu* (1969) takes place during an adult-education class. The lecturer describes a plot to his group and they are required to enact it. A young girl sees a stranger on the other side of the river and sets off in search of him, as she believes this will be her only chance of happiness in life. But she must pass through a forest and cross a river and a marsh to reach him. She is ferried across the river on condition that she pose in the nude for the boatman. She is guided across the marsh but must make love to the man who takes her. When she reaches the young stranger, he refuses her because she has already given herself to another man. The teacher believes that improvising on this story-line will enable the individuals in his class to come to know themselves. What follows, then, is a kind of 'collective creation'. At the beginning of the second act the audience too is invited to join in. In fact, as usually happens in this 'participatory theatre' *à la* Living Theatre, the audience is manipulated. The script is so structured that no-one who joins in has any opportunity of altering the course of the play. *Médium saignant* (1970) describes the situation in Québec at the time of the notorious 'Bill 63': medium rare. Loranger has said, 'The real subject of the play isn't unilingualism, it's collective fear. . . . But collective fear experienced individually by everyone who is afraid of the reactions of his *milieu*, afraid of what people will say. Who is afraid of asserting himself.' So *Médium saignant* continues the themes of the other plays. In it there is much discussion of the language problem by the town councillors, mostly representing the French-Canadian establishment, and by a number of cultural *animateurs* representing the newly awakened and militant Québécois. Unfortunately the latter are just as stereotyped as the former, and the play consists much of the time of a string of slogans; it is too simplistic to make good political theatre. It is a pity if Mme Loranger has abandoned her fine gift for observation that distinguished *Encore 5 minutes*, as her attempts to renew her techniques of expression and to create a form of theatre firmly based in Québec's social and cultural reality should place her in the forefront of the province's new artistic movement. Her other published plays—*Georges . . . oh! Georges* (1965), *Un cri qui vient de loin* (1967, with *Encore 5 minutes*), *Jour après jour* (an early version of *Georges . . . oh! Georges*), and *Un si bel automne* (1971)—were written for television.

The same themes are evident in Mme Loranger's novel, *Mathieu*. The problems of her solitary young hero, hiding his anguish under a mask of cynicism, can be seen as both personal and collective. JC

Loranger, Jean-Aubert. See POETRY IN FRENCH.

Lorrimer, James. See POLITICAL WRITINGS IN ENGLISH 8.

Lower, A. R. M. (1889–). Born in Barrie, Ont., Arthur Reginald Marsden Lower was educated at the University of Toronto and served with the Royal Naval Volunteer Reserve during the First World War. After completing his studies at Harvard, he taught history at Tufts College, Mass., at Harvard, and at United College, Winnipeg, where he was head of the department for eighteen years. He became professor of history at Queen's University in 1944, Douglas professor of history in 1952, and McLaughlin professor of history in 1955; he is now professor of history, emeritus. Elected to the Royal Society of Canada in 1941 (president, 1962–3), he was awarded the Tyrrell Medal for historical research in 1947. He has contributed many articles to scholarly publications and current periodicals and was instrumental in originating the *International Journal*.

Lower has been noted for his provocative

university lectures and for the candid, witty, charming nature of his writing. Environmentalism, nationalism, and the historian's responsibility to help develop a national consciousness have been three recurring themes in much of his writing. Early in his career he worked for a short time on the staff of the Public Archives of Canada and with Harold Innis prepared the second volume of *Documents illustrative of Canadian economic history: 1783–1885* (1933). He shared Innis's interest in the staple industries and wrote *The North American assault on the Canadian forest: a history of the lumber trade between Canada and the United States; with studies by W. A. Carrothers on the forest industries of British Columbia and of the forest industries of the maritime provinces by S. A. Saunders* (1938), a volume in the Carnegie series on the Relations Between Canada and the United States. This book examines the lumber trade with the United States and the importance of the industry in Canadian development. His *Settlement and the forest frontier in eastern Canada* (1936) was published along with a study by Innis on *Settlement and the mining frontier* as volume I in the Canadian Frontiers of Settlement series. While he concluded that the influence of nature on frontiersmen was relatively good and produced initiative, adaptability, a hospitable spirit, and optimism, he was also concerned with the effects of a harsh environment in Ontario's northland. With *Great Britain's woodyard: British America and the timber trade, 1763–1867* (1973) he completed his study of the trade and industries based on the forests of eastern Canada and embodied his belief that Canada should not be 'a source of good things that others come and take away'.

Lower's survey of foreign policy, *Canada and the Far East* (1940), prepared for the Canadian Institute of Pacific Relations, is somewhat prophetic in that he foresaw that a Japanese-American war was almost certain to occur, to be followed by the antagonism of Russia and the United States. *Colony to nation: a history of Canada* (1946; rev. 1964), among other matters, traces Canadian internal problems—so evident during the war—in part to the contrary pull of British and American traditions, but in larger part to the historic differences between the two peoples, English and French. Lower stresses that there are two Canadas, two ways of life—the French and the English—and that Canadian unity has yet to be attained. The historian as an artist can perceive the true potentialities of Canada and should therefore seek to promote loyalty of the citizen to the country, not to any particular race. The colonial mentality must be surmounted if the barrier between French and English is to be removed. Yet abandoning the effort to become a nation would not bring internationalism but merely make Canadians into Americans.

In 1940 Lower became president of the Winnipeg Civil Liberties Association and increasingly turned his thoughts to the importance of preserving liberty in the world. He stated his case most forcibly in *This most famous stream: the liberal democratic way of life* (1954), a historical and philosophical analysis of the development of liberalism in western society. He appealed to the universal love of freedom—the external spirit of man—to react against modern moral relativism that appeared to denigrate liberal values and the democratic political system. Lower rejected deterministic views of man and opted for free will and individual self-determination. In *Canada: nation and neighbour* (1952) he examined the geographical and historical determinants of Canadian foreign policy—especially as they related to the United States. *Canadians in the making: a social history of Canada* (1958) studies the complex interrelationships between economic change and social behaviour. In this book Lower claimed that Canada had moved towards nationhood through four stages of economic and cultural development: trading post to pioneer settlement to colony to provincial status. Lower also contributed 'Theories of Canadian federalism—yesterday and today' to *Evolving Canadian federalism* (1958) in the Duke University Commonwealth Studies series. Here he stressed that a flexible federalism, open to compromise and change, had well served the vast country with its divergent and separate communities.

Lower co-authored the high-school text *Canada—a nation: and how it came to be* (1948). It emphasized two themes: Canada's persistent struggle to overcome geography and the process by which two incompatible and stubborn cultures attempted to learn to live together. *Unconventional voyages* (1953) is a recollection of north-country experiences and naval days. *My first seventy-five years* (1968) is

Lower's autobiography. In the course of these lively and outspoken reminiscences the progression of his liberal nationalism is revealed, along with the formation of his environmentalism and his philosophy of the historian's craft. DF

Lower, Thelma R. See CHILDREN'S BOOKS IN ENGLISH 2.

Lowry, Malcolm (1909–57). Clarence Malcolm Lowry, who also went by the name of Malcolm Boden Lowry, and published as Malcolm Lowry, was born in Birkenhead, a Cheshire dormitory town to Liverpool, where his father was a wealthy cotton broker with Methodist affiliations. Educated in upper-middle-class schools, Lowry early displayed—especially in an enthusiasm for jazz that led him in his teens to attempt a career as a song-writer—an inclination to break away from the business life his family assumed he would follow. This inclination was first expressed in an active way when, in 1928, he signed on as cabin boy in a freighter bound for the China coast, an experience whose more harrowing aspects found a place in his first novel, *Ultramarine*; however, it did not prevent his sailing two years later as deckhand on a ship bound for Oslo where he went in search of the Norwegian novelist Nordahl Grieg. Already Lowry's growing enthusiasm for literature had led him into a correspondence with the American poet and novelist Conrad Aiken, who took him as a paying guest in the summer of 1929 and was a perceptible influence on his writing. In the autumn of 1929 Lowry entered St Catharine's College, Cambridge, graduating in 1932; but his encounters with Aiken, Grieg, and with younger writers he met at Cambridge, and his maritime experiences during these formative years, contributed far more to his literary persona than the terms of academic study.

At Cambridge Lowry began seriously to write. *Ultramarine* was completed by 1932; rewritten after the manuscript was stolen from the car of a publisher's reader, it finally appeared in 1933. This was the strange beginning of a strange career, marked by intense industry and little apparent production. Lowry published only two books during his lifetime, *Ultramarine* (which he later rejected as immature) and *Under the volcano* (1947). Another of his novels, *In ballast to the white*, was lost, this time irretrievably—burnt in 1945 when a fire destroyed a shack he inhabited at Dollarton, B.C. But his scanty publication was due mainly to an obsessional inability to complete to his own satisfaction any work longer than a short story. During the years following the completion of *Under the volcano* in 1945 he worked on a whole cycle of novels of which it would form part, to be entitled eventually *The voyage that never ends*.

Two of the novels to be included in the cycle, *Dark as the grave wherein my friend is laid* and *October ferry to Gabriola*, were published posthumously, in 1968 and 1970 respectively. So also were *Lunar caustic* (1963), a novella; *Hear us O Lord from heaven Thy dwelling place* (1961), a short-story collection; *Selected poems* (1962); and *Selected letters* (1965).

In these works one can trace Lowry's physical journey through life, shadowed by alcoholism and paranoia, and his inner journey, marked by spiritual hopes and terrors. His life between leaving Cambridge and his death twenty-five years later can be divided into three periods. First was the time of wandering, in Spain and France, Mexico and the United States. During this period he married his first wife, Jan Gabrial, in 1933; went to Hollywood in 1935; and in 1936 proceeded to Mexico, which made a profound and morbid impression on him and inspired *Under the volcano*, the first version of which he completed in 1937. In 1938 he left Mexico for the United States and in 1939 reached Canada where he married Margerie Bonner in 1940 and where he lived until 1954, mainly in a beach shack at Dollarton. The profound impression his Canadian years made on him is shown not only in the stories contained in *Hear us O Lord* but also in *October ferry to Gabriola*. There were interludes—at Oakville, Niagra-on-the-Lake, again in Mexico (a disastrous journey during which Lowry found his way into prison), and in Haiti. In 1954 he left Canada to wander in Europe and to die—choking in his sleep—at Ripe in Sussex in the summer of 1957.

Under the volcano has often been treated as Lowry's only successful work; it is clearly his best. In this story of the murder of an alcoholic British consul, the human drama is integrated in a closely knit formal and metaphorical structure, and the sinister aspects of Mexico are admirably used to symbolize the metaphysical overtones; the strong autobiographical element is exemplarily subsumed in the fictional. In none of the other novels is the structural integration so complete. The facts and preoccupations of Lowry's life are insistently obvious in all, though *October ferry to Gabriola* presents a deeply moving if imperfect counterpart to *Under the volcano*—Lowry's Paradiso as compared with his Inferno. His short stories remain, next to *Under the volcano*, his most complete and self-consistent works.

Four studies of Lowry have recently appeared: by Daniel B. Dodson in the Columbia Essays on Modern Writers series (1970), by William H. New in the Canadian Writers Series (1971), by Richard Hauer Costa (1972), and by Douglas Day (1973). In *The private labyrinth of Malcolm Lowry* (1969) Perle Epstein examines *Under the volcano*'s cabbalistic symbolism. *Malcolm Lowry: the man and his work* (1971) is a collection, edited by George WOODCOCK, of critical essays on Lowry's writing, reminiscences of the man, and items by Lowry unpublished elsewhere.

GW

Lowther, Barbara J. See HISTORY STUDIES IN ENGLISH 17.

Lowther, Pat. See POETRY IN ENGLISH 2.

Luc, Pierre. See HISTORY STUDIES IN FRENCH 10.

Lucas, Alec. See ANTHOLOGIES IN ENGLISH 2 and LITERARY STUDIES IN ENGLISH 4.

Ludwig, Jack. See ANTHOLOGIES IN ENGLISH 1.

Lumsden, Ian. See HISTORY STUDIES IN ENGLISH 12 and POLITICAL WRITINGS IN ENGLISH 2.

Lunn, Janet. See CHILDREN'S BOOKS IN ENGLISH 2.

Lurie, Nancy O. See INDIANS 4.

Lyon, L. C. See INDIANS 6.

Lyon, Peyton. See HISTORY STUDIES IN ENGLISH 12 and POLITICAL WRITINGS IN ENGLISH 7.

Lyon, William. See POLITICAL WRITINGS IN ENGLISH 5.

Lysaght, A. M. See HISTORY STUDIES IN ENGLISH 2.

M

MacArthur, F. H. See FOLKLORE: BIBLIOGRAPHY.

McClellan, Catharine. See INDIAN LEGENDS AND ART.

McClelland, Hugh. See CHILDREN'S BOOKS IN ENGLISH 2.

McCloskey, William. See HISTORY STUDIES IN ENGLISH 12.

McCorkell, Edmund J. M. See HISTORY STUDIES IN ENGLISH 15.

McCourt, Edward (1907–72). Edward Alexander McCourt was born in Ireland and came to Canada with his family in 1909. Educated at the University of Alberta, he won a Rhodes Scholarship and spent the next five years at Oxford. He returned to Canada in 1937 and taught English in several colleges and universities. He was professor of English at the University of Saskatchewan from 1944 until his retirement. His literary study, *The Canadian west in fiction* (1949), which is confined to the prairie provinces, discusses the achievements of Ralph Connor (Charles

Gordon), Frederick Niven, Frederick Philip GROVE, and other novelists who have written of prairie life; but large areas of prairie fiction, as he points out himself, are not touched. An enlarged and revised edition was published in 1970.

In his first novel, *Music at the close* (1947), McCourt described the vicissitudes of rural development during the twentieth century. It was reprinted in the New Canadian Library (1966) with an introduction by Allan Bevan. In *Home is the stranger* (1950) he dealt with the reaction of an Irish war-bride to prairie conditions in the post-war years. The scenery of the Cypress Hills area plays a significant part in *Walk through the valley* (1958), but this novel is primarily a study of the reaction of a sensitive boy to his Irish-born father whose conversation inspires him with romantic dreams but whose whisky-running operation involves him in sordid realities. McCourt used a university setting for *The wooden sword* (1956), in which a professor forces himself to cure a war neurosis by remembering his dreams, and for *Fasting friar* (1963), an unflattering portrait of administrative officers and faculty who face a debatable issue over academic liberty and security of tenure. *The road across Canada* (1965) is a motor travelogue along the Trans-Canada Highway, interspersed with informal bits of local history.

For young readers McCourt wrote three stories about the North West Rebellion: *The flaming hour* (1947), in which he dealt with the attitudes of the Indian tribes; *Buckskin brigadier* (1955), based on the activities of the Alberta field force during the suppression of the uprising; and *Revolt in the west: the story of the Riel rebellion* (1958). The last two are volumes in the Great Stories of Canada series.

McCourt's narrative skill shows to advantage in *Remember Butler* (1967), a biography of Sir William Butler who served in Canada, except for periods of leave, from 1868 to 1873. (Butler's *The great lone land* (1872) and *The wild north land* (1873) are classics in the literature of the northwest.) McCourt also gave new insights into the history and life of the west in *Saskatchewan* (1968) and *The Yukon and Northwest* (1969), two books in the Traveller's Canada series. NS

MacDermot, H. E. See HISTORY STUDIES IN ENGLISH 13.

Macdonald, David. See HISTORY STUDIES IN ENGLISH 12.

MacDonald, Jack. See POLITICAL WRITINGS IN ENGLISH 5.

MacDonald, Jim. See POLITICAL WRITINGS IN ENGLISH 5.

McDonough, John T. See DRAMA IN ENGLISH 2.

McDougall, J. Lorne. See HISTORY STUDIES IN ENGLISH 7.

McDougall, John. See HISTORY STUDIES IN ENGLISH 8.

MacDowell, G. W. See HISTORY STUDIES IN ENGLISH 13.

McErval, J. See HISTORY STUDIES IN ENGLISH 7.

MacEwan, J. W. Grant. See INDIANS 2.

MacEwen, Gwendolyn (1941–). Born in Toronto, Gwendolyn MacEwen attended primary and secondary schools in that city and in Winnipeg, but received no higher academic education. Her career, as she describes it, has been 'mainly literary', including the writing of plays—so far unpublished—for CBC radio as well as the fiction and poetry for which she is known to readers rather than listeners. In 1971 she married the Greek singer Nikos Tsingos, and with him she operated the Greek Horse, a Toronto coffee house.

Gwendolyn MacEwen has published two novels, *Julian the magician* (1963) and *King of Egypt, king of dreams* (1971), as well as a collection of short stories: *Noman* (1972). In verse she is represented by two early privately published pamphlets, *Selah* (1961) and *The drunken clock* (1961), and by four larger volumes, *The rising fire* (1963), *A breakfast for barbarians* (1966), *The shadowmaker* (1969)—which won a Governor General's Award—and *The armies of the moon* (1972).

In MacEwen's verse and prose alike the reader is tempted, as Margaret ATWOOD has said, 'to become preoccupied with the brilliant and original verbal surfaces she creates'. But this bright enamel of words and images, which woos one's initial pleasure on reading her work, overlies profundities of thought and feeling. Gwendolyn MacEwen is preoccupied with time and its multiple meanings, with the ambivalences of existence, with the archetypal patterns that emerge and re-emerge from ancient times to now. These concerns recur throughout her poetry; they take on personified form in her fantasy-novels —in *Julian the magician*, with its early renaissance preoccupation with hermetic philosophies and their ambiguous relationship to Christianity, and in *King of Egypt, king of dreams* and its imaginative reconstruction of the gallant, futile life of the heterodox pharoah Akhnaton. *Noman* is united by the central enigmatic character who names the book, and here the protean quality of MacEwen's talent takes full flight in her vision of Kanada (*sic*), taken up in the mythological sweep that unites us with every temporal past and every spatial present.

Gwendolyn MacEwen reads some of her poetry on the CBC recording *Open Secret*. GW

McFadden, David. See POETRY IN ENGLISH 2.

McGhee, Robert. See ESKIMOS: BOOKS IN ENGLISH.

McGreer, Pat. See HISTORY STUDIES IN ENGLISH 9.

MacGregor, James G. See HISTORY STUDIES IN ENGLISH 8 and 14.

McInnis, Edgar. See HISTORY STUDIES IN ENGLISH 1.

Macintyre, D. E. See HISTORY STUDIES IN ENGLISH 7 and 8.

MacKay, R. A. See HISTORY STUDIES IN ENGLISH 7 and 12.

McKechnie, Anne. See CHILDREN'S BOOKS IN ENGLISH 6.

McKenty, Neil. See HISTORY STUDIES IN ENGLISH 11.

MacKenzie, Jean. See CHILDREN'S BOOKS IN ENGLISH 5.

McKenzie, Ruth. See HISTORY STUDIES IN ENGLISH 5.

McKervill, Hugh W. See INDIAN LEGENDS AND ART.

McKim, Audrey. See CHILDREN'S BOOKS IN ENGLISH 6.

McKinnon, Barry. See POETRY IN ENGLISH 2.

MacKinnon, Stuart. See POETRY IN ENGLISH 2.

McLaughlin, Laurie. See CHILDREN'S BOOKS IN ENGLISH 4.

MacLean, Hugh. See HISTORY STUDIES IN ENGLISH 7.

MacLennan, Hugh (1907–). Born at Glace Bay, Cape Breton, N.S., he was educated at Dalhousie University, won a Rhodes Scholarship to Oxford, and completed his classical studies at Princeton University. His thesis on a Roman religious and cultural centre in Egypt, *Oxyrhynchus: an economic and social study*, was published in 1935. He taught Latin and history at Lower Canada College, Montreal, from 1935 to 1945. (He was awarded a Guggenheim Fellowship in 1943 and studied in New York for a year.) After 1945 he worked at journalism and broadcasting until 1951, when he accepted a part-time teaching appointment at McGill University. He joined the English staff full time in 1964 and is now a professor. He was awarded the Lorne Pierce Medal for Canadian literature in 1952 and was elected to the Royal Society of Canada in 1953.

MacLennan's achievement as a novelist has been to use the Canadian social environment for the first time in fiction as an important influence on the lives of his characters; in so doing he gave the reader an early and memorable expression of the nature of the country's character. His novels (except for *Each man's son*) are therefore social novels in which great importance is given to national preoccupations, including the emergence of a Canadian identity, the reconciliation of French and English Canada, Canadian relations with the U.S., and life in the Depression years. MacLennan's Scots-Presbyterian background gave him another theme in the damaging effects of puritanisn, and of its consequent guilt feelings, on the human spirit; and his classical education provided his fiction, perhaps unconsciously, with elements of the

Odyssian myth, which George WOODCOCK first noted (and discusses in an essay in *Odysseus ever returning*). The six novels MacLennan has so far written have been criticized for their didactic qualities, revealed most obtrusively in authorial reflections and in a certain over-explicitness about what he intends his characters to mean; for the contrivances of the plots; and for the hollow and rhetorical treatment of human feeling, especially of sexual relationships. Yet MacLennan's descriptions of Canadian places, the Canadian atmosphere, and certain aspects of the Canadian character are written with great sensitivity and insight and can speak to readers today, in some cases decades after they were written. He has produced at least two memorable characters—Athanase Tallard in the first part of *Two solitudes* and George Stewart in *The watch that ends the night*. Above all his novels are the product of literary craftsmanship, which frequently arouses admiration in scenes of action and in the powerful delineation of the characters' inner lives.

MacLennan's first novel is one of the best. *Barometer rising* (1941) is set in Halifax immediately before and after the explosion that destroyed the north end of the city on 5 Dec. 1917. (His description of this disaster is one of the great set-pieces in Canadian fiction.) The evidence that vindicates Neil Macrae, a young Canadian officer who had been accused of refusing to obey an order during his service overseas, is revealed simultaneously with the death of his accuser in that explosion. The characters in this novel express various attitudes towards the Canadian identity, and the catastrophe itself symbolizes a break with the past and, in the mind of the idealistic and visionary Neil, the possibility of a great destiny for his country. *Two solitudes* (1945) was the most widely read novel of its time for its then unusual revelations of French-English conflicts in Quebec; it confirmed MacLennan's reputation as an important writer. Athanase Tallard, a French Canadian, cooperates with English-speaking capitalists to develop the natural resources of the province and is denounced by his nationalist compatriots who regard such cooperation as a treason. When his persistence brings him into conflict with the parish priest, Tallard loses his influences and is promptly dropped by his English-speaking colleagues. In the second part of the novel, Tallard's son Paul—half French and half Irish and educated in English schools—rather unconvincingly personifies the union of the two races.

The inhibiting power of puritanism is one of the themes in *The precipice* (1948) and *Each man's son* (1951). The former, MacLennan's least successful novel, also reflects the ambivalent attitudes of Canadians towards the United States, for Lucy Cameron flees to New York to escape the dullness and Puritan standards of a small Ontario town (expertly conveyed), only to reject the merciless competition and false values she finds there. The structure of *Each man's son* is more complicated, for it treats different attitudes towards love held by the destiny-ridden inhabitants of a Cape Breton mining town. The most clearly defined of these attitudes are those of Dr Daniel Ainslie, who vainly tries to solve his conflicts by the cold light of reason, and of the pugilist Archie MacNeil, whose only outlet is in violence that culminates in the murder of his wife, the intruder into the home that he had deserted, and in his own death. His young son Alan, who has witnessed the murders, becomes a terrified orphan who is adopted by Ainslie. *Return of the sphinx* (1967) bears a relationship to both *Each man's son* and *Two solitudes*. Alan Ainslie, who had married a French Canadian, makes his home in Montreal but as he has become a cabinet minister he spends most of his time in Ottawa. There he tries to reconcile the just demands of Québec, the impatience of the separatists, and the national interest. At the same time his efforts are being undermined by his nationalist son Daniel, whose vanity and sense of isolation make him a pawn to an unscrupulous separatist. Daniel turns to violence and is arrested; his father resigns. Though the motivation of the characters is not very clear, alienation of one kind or another plays an important part: among the many situations that portray this are the liaison between Daniel and an older woman and that of his sister Chantal with her father's elderly friend.

MacLennan's most highly praised novel, *The watch that ends the night* (1959), is a study of moral courage in the face of psychological disaster, exemplified by George Stewart, a university professor, whose precarious peace is based on acceptance of the knowledge that his wife Catherine is slowly dying. This peace is shattered: first by the return of Catherine's former husband, Jerome Martell, who had been reported dead ten years earlier, and then by the manner in which Martell walks away from the destructive situation his return has created. MacLennan explains in his essay 'The story of a novel' in *Masks of fiction* (1961) that this book deals with what he terms 'spirit-in-action' rather than 'character-in-action'. Encompassing some fifty years, it skilfully accommodates many shifts in time in vignettes that include a climactic event in Martell's boyhood in the New Brunswick woods (another fine set-piece), the intellectual climate of the Depression years in English Montreal, and that city in the fifties.

Both *Two solitudes* and *The watch that ends the night* won a Governor General's Award.

A distinguished essayist, MacLennan also won a Governor General's Award for the first and second collections of his essays, *Cross-country* (1949) and *Thirty and three* (1954). These, with his third collection, *Scotchman's return and other essays* (1960), are lucid and attractive presentations of his observations on Canadian character and the Canadian scene (his essays on Montreal and Halifax are outstanding) and of nostalgic visits to Scotland and Oxford, written in a polished conversational style. The essays in *Seven rivers of Canada* (1961) constitute a travel book in which description is heightened by a continuous commentary on geography and history. MacLennan's knowledge and love of the country are summed up in the text he wrote for *The colour of Canada* (1968) in the Canadian Illustrated Library.

MacLennan's writings have been widely discussed by critics. See *Hugh MacLennan* (1969) by George Woodcock in the Studies in Canadian Literature series; *Hugh MacLennan* (1969) by Peter Buitenhuis in the Canadian Writers and Their Work series; *The novels of Hugh MacLennan* (1970) by Robert Cockburn; and *Hugh MacLennan* (1970) by Alex Lucas in the Canadian Writers Series of the New Canadian Library. A book of essays on his work, *Hugh MacLennan* (1973), has been edited by Paul Goetsch.

Two solitudes, *Each man's son*, and *Return of the sphinx* are in the Laurentian Library; *Barometer rising* is in the New Canadian Library; and *The watch that ends the night* is a Signet novel. WET/NS

McLeod, Jack. See POLITICAL WRITINGS IN ENGLISH 4.

McLin, John B. See HISTORY STUDIES IN ENGLISH 12.

McLuhan, Marshall (1911–). Herbert Marshall McLuhan was born in Edmonton, Alta, and educated at the University of Manitoba and at Cambridge. He taught in several American colleges from 1936 to 1944 when he accepted a post at Assumption College, Windsor, Ont. In 1946 he went to St Michael's College, Toronto, where he is Professor of English. He was made director of the University of Toronto Centre for Culture and Technology in 1963. (He left Toronto for one year, 1967–8, to be Albert Schweitzer Professor of Humanities at Fordham University, New York.) He was elected to the Royal Society of Canada in 1964.

Adapting the New Criticism to the rhetorics of mass communication, McLuhan's *The mechanical bride: folklore of industrial man* (1951) is a sardonic commentary on popular culture and its mechanization of the human personality, presented in the form of witty discussions of magazine and newspaper advertisements. In the *Gutenberg galaxy: the making of typographical man* (1962), which won a Governor General's Award, *Understanding Media: the extensions of man* (1964), and *The medium is the message* (1967), McLuhan forsook overt moral bias to speculate on the nature and effects of mass communications, developing ideas from Harold Innis, Walter Ong, and others in a highly personal system. *Counterblast* (1969) attests to the important influence of Wyndham Lewis and *Culture is our business* (1970) is among other things a reminder that McLuhan is still above all a literary man. McLuhan's all-inclusive theories, expressed in brilliant paradoxes, have excited world-wide controversy and established their author as one of the best-known international celebrities of the sixties.

McLuhan has always been a genial collaborator. A selection from the periodical *Explorations* (1953–9), in which he collaborated with Edmund S. Carpenter, was published as *Explorations in communication* (1960). With Quentin Fiore in *War & peace in the Global Village* (1968) he explored the topics of pain and violence; with Harley Parker he speculated on art in *Through the vanishing point: space in poetry and painting* (1968). He co-authored *From cliché to archetype* (1970) with Wilfred Watson and *Take today: the executive as dropout* (1972) with Barrington Nevitt. His literary essays were brought together in *Interior landscape: the literary criticism of Marshall McLuhan, 1943–62* (1969) edited by Eugene McNamara.

From an extensive literature, succinct critical studies by Jonathan Miller (*McLuhan*, 1971) and Dennis Duffy (*Marshall McLuhan*, Canadian Writers Series, 1969) possess some interest. *The medium is the rear view mirror: understanding McLuhan* (1971) is a more elaborate explication by a former McLuhan disciple, Donald F. Theall. Often more difficult than its original, it has impressed many students of McLuhan, though not the man himself. KD

McLuhan, T. C. See INDIANS 2.

MacMillan, David S. See HISTORY STUDIES IN ENGLISH 13.

McNamara, Eugene. See POETRY IN ENGLISH 2.

McNeil, Florence. See POETRY IN ENGLISH 2.

MacNeill, James A. See ANTHOLOGIES IN ENGLISH 2.

McPherson, Hugo. See LITERARY STUDIES IN ENGLISH 4.

Macpherson, Jay (1931–). Born in England, she came to Newfoundland as a child and then to Ottawa. She was educated at Carleton College, Ottawa, and at Victoria College, University of Toronto. She is now Associate Professor of English at Victoria College. A sophisticated poet and a master of intricate styles, she draws upon a fund of biblical and mythological knowledge to create the symbols that have given her work distinction. Her small books, *Nineteen poems* (1952) and *O earth return* (1954), were followed in 1957 by *The boatman* (in which 'O earth return' forms a sequence). It is a series of intricately related short poems—in which there are echoes of ballads, carols, nursery rhymes, hymns etc.—through which she traces the progress of the awakened soul ('poor child') from the earthbound state to its redemption by Christ ('the fisherman'). Noah ('the boatman') symbolizes the role of the artist in saving the world ('the sleepers') from drowning. *The boatman*, which won a Governor General's Award, was republished with additional poems as *The boatman and other poems* (1968). She is also the author of the prose work *Four ages of man* (1962), a book of classical myths for young readers. NS

MacRae, Marion. See HISTORY STUDIES IN ENGLISH 6.

MacSkimming, Roy. See FICTION IN ENGLISH 7.

McWhirter, George. See POETRY IN ENGLISH 2.

Magazines. See LITERARY MAGAZINES IN ENGLISH and LITERARY MAGAZINES IN FRENCH.

Maheu, Robert. See POLITICAL WRITINGS IN FRENCH 3.

Maheux-Forcier, Louise. See FICTION IN FRENCH 2.

Mahoney, Thomas D. See HISTORY STUDIES IN ENGLISH 5.

Mailhot, Laurent. See LITERARY STUDIES IN FRENCH 3.

Mailhot, Michèle. See FICTION IN FRENCH 3.

Maillet, Andrée. Born in Montreal, she is a distinguished journalist and lecturer as well as the author of poetry, novels, short stories, and plays for theatre, television, and radio. Her writing first appeared in *Le Petit Journal*, *Photo-Journal*, *Le Jour*, *La Nouvelle Relève*, *La Revue populaire*, *Jovette*, and *Amérique française*. After several years' residence in France, she became a member of L'association de presse anglo-américaine in Paris following publication of her series of articles written with the Russian army of occupation in Germany. From 1952 to 1960 Andrée Maillet was editor of *Amerique francaise*. She was the founder of the P.E.N. Club canadien-français and is president of the P.E.N. in Québec as well as a member of the Association canadienne des journalistes et écrivains de tourisme. In 1972 she was elected to the Académie canadienne française.

Andrée Maillet has published three collections of verse: *Élémentaires* (1964), *Le paradigme de l'idole* (1964), and *Le chant de l'Iroquoise* (1967); four novels: *Profil de l'orignal* (1953), *Les remparts de Québec* (1965), *Le bois-pourri* (1971), and *Le doux mal* (1972); and four collections of short stories: *Les Montréalais* (1963), *Le lendemain n'est pas sans amour* (1963), *Le chêne des tempêtes* (1965), which was awarded the Prix littéraire de la Province de Québec (it was published in an English translation by F. C. L. Muller as *Storm oak* (1972)), and *Nouvelles montréalaises* (1966). She is also the author of two plays: *Le meurtre d'Igouille: tragédie burlesque* (1965) and *La Montréalaise* (1967); of two plays for television: *Souvenirs en accords brisés* (1966) and *La perdrière* (1971); and of a play for radio, *Belle Gersende et l'habitant* (1972).

Andrée Maillet's novels show great insight into feminine psychology. Her most popular novel, *Les remparts de Québec*, presents a firm and penetrating portrait of a young girl, rendered in a prose style of great pathos and beauty. Her poetry deals with the renaissance of her country and is marked by an extraordinary richness and daring in the use of language, even while it avoids all the excesses of contemporary lyricism. It speaks with directness, strength, and truth of the seasons, of love and death, and above all records her feelings of hope as they are derived from sensuous experience; it testifies to her ability to transform such experience into a poetry couched in the language of everyday. JG

Maillet, Antonine (1929–). Born at Bouctouche, N.B., she was educated at schools in Memramcook and Moncton and at the Université de Montréal and Laval, where she received a Doctorat ès Lettres in 1970. She teaches literature and folklore at Laval.

Antonine Maillet is the leading writer of Acadia. She has revealed to a large public, through her books and particularly through many performances by Viola Leger of *La Sagouine*—on stage and, soon, on film—the striking character of Acadian oral culture and language, which is a version of the sixteenth-century French of her ancestors, somewhat 'distorted by the climate and sharpened by the sea; by the salty air in the larynx and the obsessive beating of the waves in the ears.' The success of *La Sagouine* aroused interest in all her novels. *Pointe-aux-Coques* (1972), a village chronicle, was unnoticed when it first appeared in 1958 but has been reissued by the publisher Leméac, which has inaugurated two new series with two of her books: 'Répertoire acadien' (*La Sagouine*) and 'Roman acadien' (*Don l'Orignal*). *On a mangé la dune* (1962), tales about children, and *Par derrière chez mon père* (1972), a collection of picturesque, boisterous sketches and lively portraits (e.g. 'Soldat Bidoche') are in the same humorous, touching, folkloric vein. Maillet's *L'Acadie pour quasiment rien* (1973) is a very personal travel guide. Her thesis *Rabelais et les traditions populaires en Acadie* (1972) collects for the first time more than five hundred archaisms (from Touraine and Berry) still used in the francophone ghettos of the Atlantic provinces.

Maillet learned her craft from her pioneer relatives, from rural folklore, village entertainers, and at election meetings and social gatherings. Her inspiration comes from the observant storytelling child she was. At once direct, spicy, and learned, Maillet's writings are meant to be narrated, performed. Her language is not *chiac* (from Shediac, the small fishing port near Moncton)—the equivalent of the most anglicized urban *joual*—but an old domestic French, coloured (and somewhat gratingly roughened, coarsened) by her personal touch and a special local intonation and accent. *La Sagouine* (freely translated as The Slattern) is a series of sixteen monologues that offer the reminiscences, grievances, anecdotes, and homilies of a seventy-two-year-old charlady, a former prostitute, the wife of an Acadian fisherman. Anticlerical and philosophical, anarchistic and naively revolutionary, a folk-prophet, the old scrubwoman is a striking contrast to the colourless heroine of Longfellow—an anti-Evangeline. As she talks it is Acadia speaking—to others and for itself. *Les Crasseux* (1968), a dialectical drama, and the fantasy *Don l'Orignal* (1972)—which won a Governor General's Award—treat similar themes and have recurring types. The 'gens d'En-bas' (those who live on the other side of the tracks) fight with the big shots, the powerful, who are named for their occupations—the Mayoress, the Barber, the Milliner, the Playboy—while Noume, Citrouille, General Michel-Archange, La Sainte, La Cruche, and other 'Sagouins' are given surnames. These actor-storytellers appear in one work after another—indestructible, welcomed, having echoes of Homer, Rabelais, Balzac, and of characters in a picaresque novel, while remaining Acadians, that minority within a minority. LM

Major, André (1942–). Born in Montreal, he early became interested in separatist politics and was expelled from the Collège des Eudistes for his writings in leftist student publications. He was a contributor to PARTI PRIS but broke with the group in 1965 after an ideological quarrel to become editor of the literary section of *L'action nationale*, the organ of the older Catholic nationalists of the right. He has been arts editor of the weekly tabloid, *Le Petit Journal*, a publisher's reader, and a theatre and book critic for *Le Devoir*. He works for a Montreal publisher.

A precocious poet, his first collection, *Le froid se meurt*, was published in 1961. This was followed by *Holocauste à 2 voix* (1962) and *Poèmes pour durer* (1969), his own selection from his earlier work with new poetry. He writes of winter and coldness, usually as metaphors for Québec and its people, of the everyday life of city streets, and of love and the flight of time. Some of his poems are personal, others political. All are marked by great energy and simplicity, hard clear images, and a very sure use of language.

Major's short stories, most of which deal with Montreal slum life, have been published, along with those of Jacques BRAULT and André BROCHU, in *Nouvelles* (1963) and in his own collection, *La chair de poule* (1965). A story from the latter group, 'La semaine dernière pas loin du pont', was made into a short film. Another, 'Mental test pour tout le gang', is a thinly disguised, rather scathing account of the arrest of Hubert AQUIN. His novel, *Le cabochon* (1964), written, like the stories, while he was a member of the *parti pris* group, is the ideological and personal history of a young Montreal slum-dweller's progress towards revolutionary politics. *Le vent du diable* (1968), a somewhat romanticized love-triangle with a rural setting, may be read simply as such or more symbolically, the two young women involved representing two aspects of the hero's love for his 'native land' of Québec. Major is also the author of *Félix-Antoine Savard* (1968) in the collection Écrivains canadiens d'aujourd'hui, a critical biography of the older nationalist writer to whom he feels deeply indebted. He was one of the six young French-Canadian poets included by Jacques GODBOUT and John Robert COLOMBO in the bilingual anthology *Poésie/Poetry* (1964).

An account of Major's ideological shift, with translations of extracts from his poetry and prose, can be found in *The shouting signpainters* (1972), Malcolm Reid's study of the *parti pris* writers. Translations of some of Major's poems have been published in *The poetry of French Canada in translation* (1970) edited by John GLASSCO. JM

Major, Henriette. See CHILDREN'S BOOKS IN FRENCH.

Makowski, William B. See HISTORY STUDIES IN ENGLISH 14.

Malaurie, Jean. See ESKIMOS: BOOKS IN FRENCH.

Malouin, Reine. See ANTHOLOGIES IN FRENCH.

Mandel, Eli (1922–). Elias Wolf Mandel was born in Estevan, Sask.—'a small town', he tells us, that 'bears the mark of Cain'. He left the University of Saskatchewan to serve in the Army Medical Corps during the Second World War. He then studied at the Universities of Saskatchewan and Toronto, and taught English at the Collège Militaire Royal de St Jean and the University of Alberta. In 1963 he was appointed to Glendon College, Toronto, but returned to Edmonton a year later. In 1967 he moved from Alberta to an appointment at York University, Toronto, where he is professor of English and humanities. Since then he has lived in Toronto, but has spent summers in Vancouver and Portugal and one sabbatical (1971–2) travelling in Europe, principally in Spain.

Mandel began publishing poetry in the early 1950s in magazines such as *CIV/n* and *Contact*; his first significant collection, 'Minotaur poems', appeared together with poems by Phyllis WEBB and Gael Turnbull, in the Contact Press anthology, *Trio* (1954). His first book was *Fuseli poems* (1960); this was followed by *Black and secret man* (1964), *An idiot joy* (Governor General's Award), *Stony plain* (1973), and *Crusoe* (1973), a selected poems. Throughout this time Mandel has also been extremely active as an editor and critic. In 1966 he published *Criticism: the silent-speaking words,* eight essays calling for an emotionally engaged criticism that recognizes that poetry is 'beyond system'; they had been previously presented as radio talks on the CBC. In 1969 he published a monograph on his fellow poet and colleague at York, Irving LAYTON. Mandel's editing has been instrumental in shaping the direction of Canadian poetry and in advancing the careers of many Canadian poets. His first anthology, *Poetry 62/ Poésie 62* (1961, co-edited with Jean-Guy PILON), brought to public attention a number of the neglected newcomers of the 1950s—Al PURDY, Milton ACORN, D. G. JONES, Alden NOWLAN, Leonard COHEN, and John Robert COLOMBO. A later anthology, *Poets of contemporary Canada: 1960–1970* (1972), in the New Canadian Library, gave Joe ROSENBLATT and Bill BISSETT their first significant publication in a textbook format. Mandel's other anthologies include *Five modern Canadian poets* (1970), *Eight more Canadian poets* (1972), *Contexts of Canadian criticism* (1971), and *English poems of the twentieth century* (1971), co-edited with D. E. S. Maxwell.

The Second World War, and the horrors of the Jewish concentration camps in particular, appear to have had a profound effect on most of Mandel's poetry. Although specific references to the war do not occur until his most recent volume *Stony plain,* all of his work is characterized by macabre images of suffering and destruction, and by a pervasive pessimism. The 'Minotaur poems' of *Trio* concern themselves with the brutality of the western Canadian landscape, a land of 'sharp rocks . . . /cold air where birds fell like rocks/ and screams, hawks, kites and cranes.' *Fuseli poems* is titled in honour of the eighteenth-century Swiss-born English painter Henry Fuseli, whose work frequently depicted tragic subjects fantastically contorted by desperation and isolated in wildly Gothic backgrounds. The poems here speak of horrifying violence, despair, self-accusation, 'fables of indifferent rape/and children slain indifferently/and daily blood.' The succeeding volumes, as their titles indicate—*Black and secret man, An idiot joy, Stony plain*—suggest little change in this bleak outlook. For Mandel the world is static—an arena of eternal and meaningless persecution. In Germany there is Auschwitz; in Estevan, Sask., a sun that kills 'cattle and rabbis . . . in the poisoned slow air.'

In style, Mandel is intellectual and meditative—an ironic poet rather than an angry one. A central feature of his work is a deliberate lack of emotion, a lack that Mandel uses to amplify the stark hopelessness of his outlook. His early work is exceedingly complex in its syntax, formal in its prosody, and literary in its references. It appears written for a scholarly rather than a public audience. Here, as in most of his work, Mandel sees ancient myths and literary stories alive in contemporary actuality, but in this poetry the mythic often obscures the actual and personal. Because the poems thus lack a strong sense of the actual events that brought the particular myths to the poet's attention, many of the myths seem arbitrarily applied. However, beginning with the poetry of *Black and secret man,* Mandel enriches his work through the introduction of open verse-forms, spare but colloquial language, simplified syntax, and reportorial detail. While the meditative style remains, a tone of resourcefulness and wit replaces the earlier sombreness. Mandel's recent poetry has been increasingly experimental: prose poems, concrete poems, and found poems can be seen in both *An idiot joy* and *Stony plain.* Mandel's black and mythological vision of the present is still maintained, but the mythology is now effectively rooted in anecdotal actuality. FD

Manning, E. C. See POLITICAL WRITINGS IN ENGLISH 4.

Manny, Louise. See FOLKLORE: BIBLIOGRAPHY.

Marcel, Jean. See LITERARY STUDIES IN FRENCH 3 and 4.

Marchand, Olivier. See POETRY IN FRENCH.

Marcotte, Gilles (1925–). Born in Sherbrooke, Qué., he was educated there and at the Université de Montréal. He was literary critic for *Le Devoir* before becoming literary editor of *La Presse.* His perceptive observations on the work of modern French-Canadian authors are made with clarity and force in *Une littérature qui se fait: essais critiques sur la littérature canadienne-française*

(1962, 1971) and in the essay 'L'expérience du vertige dans le roman canadien-français' in *Les écrits du Canada français* (XVI, 1963). He is also the author of the novel *Le poids de Dieu* (1962), the story of Claude Savoie, a young priest from a middle-class family who, having been sent directly from the seminary to a working-class parish, passes through a mental crisis to arrive at a new understanding of the purposes of the priesthood. The book is both an examination of spiritual values and a work of social criticism, for Claude Savoie's difficulties have their roots in the educational system through which he has passed. The novel has been translated into English by Elizabeth Abbott under the title *The burden of God* (1964). In *Retour à Coolbrook* (1965), another novel, the protagonist Marcel Parenteau insulates himself by emotional detachment, which destroys him.

Marcotte's stature as a critic has risen constantly. *Le temps des poètes: description critique de la poésie actuelle au Canada français* (1970), a profound, witty, and acute survey of modern French-Canadian poetry, won the Grand Prize for Literature of the City of Montreal. His criticism is notable for taste, erudition, and an up-to-date recognition of all literary trends and movements, further displayed in *Présence de la critique* (1968) and *Les bonnes rencontres: chroniques littéraires* (1971). *Au milieu de la course de notre vie . . .*, a dramatic trilogy, was produced on television by the Canadian Broadcasting Corporation in 1966. *Le son et l'image: textes pour le radio et la télévision*, appeared in *Les écrits du Canada français* (XXX, 1970). NS/JG

Marie-Ursule, Soeur. See FOLKLORE: BIBLIOGRAPHY.

Marlatt, Daphne. See POETRY IN ENGLISH 2.

Marois, Russell. See FICTION IN ENGLISH 7.

Marshall, Joyce (1913–). Born in Montreal, she was educated at McGill University. She lives in Toronto where she is a free-lance writer, editor, and translator. She is the author of two psychologically interesting novels: *Presently tomorrow* (1946), set in the Eastern Townships of Québec, about four schoolgirls at a religious retreat, one of whom has a sexual encounter with an Anglican clergyman; and *Lovers and strangers* (1957), about an unsuccessful marriage. Many of her short stories have been read on the CBC program 'Anthology'. Her best-known story is 'The old woman', which was included in *Canadian short stories* (1960) edited by Robert Weaver; a recent story, 'A private place' appears in *Stories 73* (1973) edited by David HELWIG and Joan Harcourt. A sensitive translator from the French, she has translated Gabrielle ROY's *La route d'Altamont* (*The road past Altamont*, 1966) and the title story from *La rivière sans repos* (*Windflower*, 1970); an abridgement of Eugène CLOUTIER's *Le Canada sans passeport* (*No passport: a discovery of Canada*, 1968); Gérard Pelletier's *La crise d'Octobre* (*The October crisis*, 1971); and Thérèse Casgrain's *Une femme chez les hommes* (*A woman in a man's world*, 1972). She also edited and translated a selection of the letters of Marie de l'Incarnation in *Word from New France* (1967), for which she provided valuable scholarly background material in the form of a long introduction and copious historical notes.

WET

Marshall, Tom. See LITERARY STUDIES IN ENGLISH 4 and POETRY IN ENGLISH 2.

Martin, Claire (1914–). Born in Quebec City, she was educated by the Ursulines and by the Soeurs de la Congrégation de Notre-Dame. An unhappy childhood and adolescence led to her later preoccupation with the social condition of women. In 1945, after a career as broadcaster, first in Quebec and later with Radio-Canada in Montreal, she married the chemist Rolland Faucher. She lived in Ottawa until her husband's retirement in 1972 and now makes her home in France.

Claire Martin came rather late to writing, her first book, *Avec ou sans amour* (1958), a collection of short stories, being published when she was forty-four. Awarded the Prix du Circle du Livre de France, it was followed by two novels, *Doux amer* (1960) and *Quand j'aurai payé ton visage* (1962), and two memoirs of her childhood, *Dans un gant de fer* (1965) and *La joue droite* (1966), which won a Governor General's Award. They were translated by Philip Stratford and published in one volume as *In an iron glove* (1968). In 1971 her third novel appeared, *Les morts*, her dramatization of which was performed by the Théâtre du Rideau vert in Montreal.

In her novels ands tories, as well as in her

autobiographical books, Claire Martin conceals her sensitivity behind a mask of sarcasm, but even the least-attentive reader can discern her lyricism, delicacy, and tenderness. Her style is incisive and employs witticisms, humour, paradox, and even aphorisms. In her two books of reminiscences she reveals an unhappy childhood—a father of almost monstrous cruelty and a society whose weight she felt as a real oppression. As well as works of literature, these books are a testimony and a document. Her tone in the novels is free and lyrical; the characters are clearly delineated, both in the roles they play and the emotions they are trying to conceal. NK

Martin, Yves. See POLITICAL WRITINGS IN FRENCH 1.

Mary-Rousselière, Guy. See ESKIMOS: BOOKS IN FRENCH.

Massey, Hector. See HISTORY STUDIES IN ENGLISH 12.

Masson, Jack. See POLITICAL WRITINGS IN ENGLISH 8.

Masters, D. C. (1908–). Donald Campbell Masters was born in Shelburne, Ont., and educated at the University of Toronto and at Oxford. He was on the staff of Queen's University, 1938–9, and then of United College, Winnipeg, until 1944 when he went to Bishop's University, Lennoxville, Qué. Since 1966 he has been on the staff of the University of Guelph, where he is professor of history. He was elected to the Royal Society of Canada in 1953.

Masters' writings reveal a wide social concern and range from economic to church history. In *The reciprocity treaty of 1854: its history, its relation to British colonial and foreign policy and to the development of Canadian fiscal autonomy* (1937) he places the treaty within the context of Canada's inexorable progress towards independence from Great Britain. In his preface to the edition of 1963, however, he explains that the treaty can be seen as a swing of the pendulum—Canada alternately favouring the United States and then Britain. *The rise of Toronto: 1850–1890* (1947) examines the chronological and progressive development of the city and points out those geographic and human characteristics that enabled Toronto to reach 'metropolitan' status in competition with its rivals. In *The Winnipeg General Strike; a study in western labour radicalism* (1950)—in the Social Credit in Alberta series—he concludes that the strike was not seditious conspiracy but, as its supporters publicized, a struggle to gain collective bargaining rights. *Bishop's University: the first hundred years* (1950) is a history of that institution. *A short history of Canada* (1958), with documents, briefly surveys the country's development. *Canada in world affairs: 1953–55* (1959), a volume in the biennial series sponsored by the Canadian Institute of International Affairs, examines Canadian attempts to maintain a distinctive and nationally acceptable foreign policy—its components being cooperation with Great Britain and the United States, wariness of the USSR, conscientious response to the UN and to NATO, and limited commitment to Korea and South-East Asia. *The Christian idea of history* (1962), first given as a lecture at Waterloo Lutheran University, proclaims that the Christian historian should achieve a synthesis between objective historical facts and his beliefs; Christian standards must be applied in the evaluation of conduct in the search for truth, scientific or otherwise. *Protestant church colleges in Canada: a history* (1966), volume 4 of the Studies in the History of Higher Education in Canada series, explains that, while colleges before 1870 presented the definite point of the church they represented, the process of liberalization and secularization has proceeded to the extent that college faculties today are an intellectual hodgepodge—a replica of the university world at large. Masters has also written *Reciprocity: 1846–1911* (1961), a booklet in the Canadian Historical Association series, and *The coming of age: the modern era: 1914 to 1967* (1967), thirteen radio talks published by the CBC. He wrote the final chapter of John Bartlet Brebner's *Canada: a modern history* (1960) and revised it in 1970. DF

Mathews, Robin. See POLITICAL WRITINGS IN ENGLISH 2.

Mathias, Philip. See POLITICAL WRITINGS IN ENGLISH 2.

Mathieu, Pierre. See POETRY IN FRENCH.

Maugey, Axel. See POETRY IN FRENCH.

Mauraült, Oliver. See HISTORY STUDIES IN FRENCH 8.

Maynard, Fredelle B. See BELLES LETTRES IN ENGLISH and HISTORY STUDIES IN ENGLISH 8.

Mayne, Seymour. See LITERARY STUDIES IN ENGLISH 2 and POETRY IN ENGLISH 2.

Meisel, John. See POLITICAL WRITINGS IN ENGLISH 5.

Melançon, Claude. See INDIAN LEGENDS AND ART.

Meldgaard, Jorgen. See ESKIMOS: BOOKS IN ENGLISH.

Mellen, Peter. See HISTORY STUDIES IN ENGLISH 16.

Melzack, Ronald. See CHILDREN'S BOOKS IN ENGLISH 1 and 4.

Ménard, Jean. See LITERARY STUDIES IN FRENCH 1 and 4.

Métayer, Maurice. See CHILDREN'S BOOKS IN ENGLISH 6.

Metcalf, John (1938–). Born in Carlisle, Eng., he was educated at the University of Bristol. He came to Canada a year after graduation and has taught in various high schools in and near Montreal. He has lectured in English at Loyala College, Montreal, and is now writer-in-residence at the University of New Brunswick.

Metcalf's fine craftsmanship shows in the texture of his prose and in his handling of the simple incidents round which his stories are built. Short poetic descriptions of nature, an understanding of childhood innocence and experience and the contrasting perception of adult resentments, give colour and vitality to his work, which is lightened by whimsical humour or satire.

The lady who sold furniture (1970) is a novella to which short stories have been appended. The novella deals with a female confidence trickster who uses her lover's affection for her child to make him the object of suspicion while she disappears. The accompanying short stories show a sympathetic understanding of childhood experiences and of the tragedy of approaching senility. His short novel, *Going down slow* (1972), contrasts the defiant and scornful attitude of a young Englishman teaching in Montreal with the way in which another young Englishman turns the educational system to his advantage. A touching scene with a neglected child lightens this tale of bitterness and folly.

Metcalf's short stories have appeared in various literary magazines and anthologies. He has edited three anthologies of stories by recent Canadian writers—*Sixteen by twelve* (1970), *Kaleidescope* (1972), and *The narrative voice: short stories and reflections by Canadian authors* (1972). All three anthologies are arranged to provide distinctive differences of style and incident, and each contains one or two of his own stories, the most striking of which are 'Robert standing' and 'The children green and golden', both in *The narrative voice* and both covering a wide range of emotions. Another powerful Metcalf story is 'The estuary' in which hidden conflicts and tensions are slowly revealed; it is in *Sixteen by twelve.*

Metcalf has also edited with Gordon Callaghan two poetry anthologies for high schools: *Rhyme and reason* (1968) and *Salutation* (1971). NS

Metcalfe, John. See FICTION IN ENGLISH 6.

Michaud, Rollande. See ESKIMOS: BOOKS IN FRENCH.

Michaud, Yves. See POLITICAL WRITINGS IN FRENCH 4.

Mickenberg, N. H. See INDIANS 3.

Mickleburgh, Brita. See ANTHOLOGIES IN ENGLISH 3.

Migué, Jean-Luc. See POLITICAL WRITINGS IN FRENCH 1.

Milani, Lois D. See HISTORY STUDIES IN ENGLISH 5.

Miller, Audrey Saunders. See HISTORY STUDIES IN ENGLISH 5.

Miller, Richard U. See HISTORY STUDIES IN ENGLISH 13.

Mills, John. See FICTION IN ENGLISH 4.

Minhinnick, Jeanne. See FOLKLORE: BIBLIOGRAPHY.

Minifie, James M. See HISTORY STUDIES IN ENGLISH 8.

Miron, Gaston (1928–). Born in Sainte-Agathe-des-Monts, Qué., he began to write when he was about fourteen. In 1947 he went to Montreal where he worked at various jobs and published his first poems in *Le Devoir* and *Amérique française*. In 1953 he was one of the founders of Les Éditions de l'Hexagone and, with Olivier Marchand, published a joint book of poems, *Deux Sangs*. At about this time he began to write the three great verse cycles—'La batèche', 'La marche à l'amour', and 'La vie agonique'—that form the core of his work and gave birth to two secondary sequences, 'L'amour et le militant' and 'Poèmes de l'amour en sursis'. They appeared in fragments, along with other pieces, in newspapers, magazines (*Liberté*, PARTI PRIS), and anthologies from 1962 onwards. From time to time Miron gave up writing temporarily in order to devote himself to political and social action. In 1957 and 1958 he ran unsuccessfully as a candidate for the NDP; and in the 1960s he became a militant separatist and something of a legend among the revolutionary-minded young of Montreal, whom he roused with his enthusiasm and his poems. He was active in the Rassemblement pour l'indépendance nationale (RIN) and was detained during the crisis of October 1970. Miron is now the director of Les Éditions de l'Hexagone.

In 1970 Miron published *L'homme rapaillé*, a selection of fifty-seven poems and some prose articles. Poetry that had been intentionally neglected by the poet—freely delivered in public readings and private recitations and scattered about in newspapers and magazines—was at last granted its importance. The book had tremendous critical and popular success: it was awarded the Prix de la revue *Études françaises* and the Prix France-Canada in 1970, the literary prize of the city of Montreal in 1971, and the Prix littéraire Belgique-Canada in 1972.

Claude Ryan considers Miron to be 'in the forefront of those who have revealed the new universe of Québec values in which the intellectual and creative activity of our society is gradually evolving.' Miron has rediscovered and used in his poetry an oral French-Canadian tradition; at the same time he is acquainted with all the poetic refinements of the francophone world. Uniting common speech with the most modern and creative inventions of contemporary French poetry, he writes poems of sadness, longing, hope, and joy—nature and love poems and some emotion-filled separatist lyrics. According to André Vachon (in an essay in *L'homme rapaillé*), he is among the great contemporary poets of the French language. Issue 5 of *Ellipse* is partly devoted to Miron and contains Vachon's essay on him in an English translation. Jacques BRAULT wrote a celebrated essay on him, 'Miron le magnifique', which was published by Les Presses de l'Université de Montréal. NK

Mitchell, Estelle. See HISTORY STUDIES IN FRENCH 11.

Mitchell, J. R. See HISTORY STUDIES IN ENGLISH 12.

Mitchell, Ken. See FICTION IN ENGLISH 2.

Mitiarjuk. See ESKIMOS: BOOKS IN FRENCH.

Moir, John S. See HISTORY STUDIES IN ENGLISH 1 and 5.

Moisan, Clément. See LITERARY STUDIES IN FRENCH 1.

Monet, Jacques. See HISTORY STUDIES IN ENGLISH 6.

Montagnes, Ian. See HISTORY STUDIES IN ENGLISH 15.

Montminy, Jean-Paul. See POLITICAL WRITINGS IN FRENCH 1.

Moore, Brian. See FICTION IN ENGLISH 1.

Morency, Pierre. See POETRY IN FRENCH.

Morf, Gustave. See HISTORY STUDIES IN ENGLISH 12; POLITICAL WRITINGS IN ENGLISH 1; and POLITICAL WRITINGS IN FRENCH 7.

Morin, Claude. See POLITICAL WRITINGS IN FRENCH 3.

Morin, Rosaire. See POLITICAL WRITINGS IN FRENCH 3.

Morison, Samuel Elliot. See HISTORY STUDIES IN ENGLISH 2.

Morley, Alan. See INDIANS 2.

Morley, Marjorie. See HISTORY STUDIES IN ENGLISH 17.

Morley, Patricia A. See LITERARY STUDIES IN ENGLISH 3.

Morley, William F. E. See HISTORY STUDIES IN ENGLISH 17.

Morris, Audrey Y. See HISTORY STUDIES IN ENGLISH 5.

Morris, Jerrold. See HISTORY STUDIES IN ENGLISH 16.

Morrison, David R. See HISTORY STUDIES IN ENGLISH 10.

Morton, Desmond. See HISTORY STUDIES IN ENGLISH 7 and 8; INDIANS 4.

Morton, W. L. (1908–). Born in Gladstone, Man., William Lewis Morton was educated at the University of Manitoba and, as a Rhodes scholar, at Oxford. He was the head of the history department of the University of Manitoba from 1950 to 1963, and Provost of its University College from 1963 to 1965. He then became master of Champlain College and Vanier Professor of Canadian history at Trent University. He was awarded the Tyrrell Medal of the Royal Society of Canada in 1958 and the Medal of Service, Order of Canada, in 1969.

As a historian of prairie society, Morton is without a peer. As a national historian his thought has evolved through several stages and he continually shows an uncommon willingness to investigate new horizons in the Canadian experience. His early distaste for the Metropolitan (or Laurentian) thesis was presented in 'Clio in Canada: the interpretation of Canadian history' in the *University of Toronto Quarterly* (1946), where he maintained that Canada is a regional as well as a multicultural community and that too little attention has been paid by historians and politicians to the aspirations of the west. This thought is developed in *The progressive party in Canada* (1950; rev. 1967), in the Social Credit in Alberta series, which won a Governor General's Award. Here he traces the fortunes and misfortunes of the farmers' protest movements in the 1920s and illustrates not only the control of the east over western sectionalism but also the need for more equitable economic and political opportunities across the nation than Canadians as yet have been able to devise. *Manitoba: a history* (1957; rev. 1967) shows that the province could become the epitome of the political binational and bicultural identity of Canada and is instead becoming a unilingual mosaic community. Morton perceives a gradual change in Manitoba's outlook under Ontario's influence and worries that, in the 1960s, a conformist, egalitarian-thinking, somewhat reactionary clique in Winnipeg seemed to be gaining ascendancy. *One university: a history of the University of Manitoba, 1877–1952* (1957) is a study of the development of curricula and the beginnings of research as well as an examination of organizational and administrative expansion. Although denominational colleges were accepted in the corporate life of the early university in an attempt to blend differing traditions and to reconcile conflicting values and cultures, the university lost its opportunity to be the leading institution of the prairies when, in 1917, these colleges did not gain more than affiliate status. This study was re-issued in 1972 with an added chapter on the 1960s.

Morton's evolving historical perspective can be seen in *The Canadian identity* (1961) where his interests begin to shift to continental problems. Here he emphasizes the harshness of the Canadian environment and the psychological impact on Canadians of endurance and survival. Pluralism is now recognized in the context of a national history that is determined by geographical realities. *The kingdom of Canada: a general history from the earliest time* (1964) stresses the importance of the monarchy and parliamentary institutions in Canada's struggle and the survival of Canada despite intense competition from the United States. *The critical years: the union of British North America, 1857–1873* (1964) raises confederation to the level of 'moral purpose'; it is treated not simply as practical politics but as an expression of the desire of cultural and regional groups to have a dominant central government to guarantee the well-being of the country. This book is a volume in the Canadian Centenary series of which Morton is the executive editor. *The shield of Achilles: aspects of Canada in the Victorian age/Le bouclier d'Achilles: regards sur le Canada de l'ère victorienne* (1968), of which Morton is the editor and for which he wrote a concluding essay, is a bilingual collection of social and cultural studies showing the tastes, prejudices, and interests of the mid-Victorians through the eyes of its preachers, soldiers, missionaries, teachers, and politicians. It reveals that ideas of providence and progress and the 'rural' myth of respectability and manliness were shared by both the French and the English of the period. The common environmental problems helped them to overcome the conflict of their external ties—the English to the Empire, the French to the papacy—and a new, ordered, peaceful free society came into being with confederation. Morton's essay, 'Lord Monck, his friends, and the revitalizing of the British Empire' in John S. Moir's *Character and circumstance* (1970), reveals the character of his continuing work on confederation.

Morton edited for the Champlain Society *Alexander Begg's Red River journal and other papers relative to the Red River resistance of 1869–70* (1956), in which he analyses the events of the period. The introduction he wrote for *The London correspondence inward from Eden Colvile 1849–1852* (1956), published for the Hudson's Bay Record Society, interestingly outlines the events and sketches the character of the Red River society at mid-century. He is also editor of *Manitoba: the birth of a province, volume 1* (1965), a collection of nine documents and two appendices relating to the transfer of Rupert's Land to Canada in 1869, published for the Manitoba Record Society. His introduction gives a balanced explanation of Louis Riel's resistance to the Canadian government and of the events leading to the rapprochement. Morton collaborated with Margaret Morton Fahrni on *Third crossing: a history of the town and district of Gladstone in the province of Manitoba* (1946) and with Margaret Arnett MacLeod on *Cuthbert Grant of Grantown: warden of the plains of Red River* (1963; rev. 1973). In contrast to previous historical pictures, Grant is depicted as a constructive leader—the Métis who brought his people to accept the Red River settlement and to become a colony within it.

Morton has contributed essays to *The Canadians, 1867–1967* (1967) edited by J. M. CARELESS and R. Craig Brown and to *Historical essays on the Prairie provinces* (1970) edited by Donald Swainson. DF

Motiuk, Laurence. See HISTORY STUDIES IN ENGLISH 17.

Mowat, Farley (1921–). Born in Belleville, Ont., he was educated at the University of Toronto, but his education was interrupted by service in the Second World War, after which he spent the years 1947 and 1948 in the arctic before taking his degree in 1949. He is a free-lance writer.

A man of strong opinions, Mowat has been accused of jumping to conclusions without a careful examination of the background of his subject, particularly in his first book, *People of the Deer* (1952), in which he castigated officials and missionaries, blaming them for the plight of the caribou-hunting aborigines of the Barren Lands. After further study of the Indians and Eskimos of that area he wrote a more moderate book, *The desperate people* (1959). Despite the obvious prejudices of the author, these books are sincere expressions of indignation at the plight of a people whose way of life was disrupted by contact with white civilization. In *The regiment* (1955) Mowat gives a history of the Hastings and Prince Edward Regiment in the Second World War. Having spent a great deal of his time sailing off the coast of Newfoundland, he has written vividly about the sea: *The grey seas under* (1958), a history of the rescue work done by the Foundation Company's salvage tug that had once assisted him and his father when they were in difficulties during a gale; *The serpent's coil* (1961), the story of a daring rescue during a North Atlantic hurricane in 1948; and *The boat who wouldn't float* (1969), a humorous account of sailing on his schooner. In *Westviking: the ancient Norse in Greenland and North America* (1965) he gives his views on the findings of anthropologists and archaeologists who have studied traces of Viking settlements in North America. Believing that the narratives of explorers should be presented in a form that will hold the attention of the general reader, he has edited *Coppermine journey* (1958), the narrative of Samuel Hearne, and *Ordeal by ice* (1960), selections from the narratives of arctic explorers. He presents another selection of explorers' writings, with his own commentary, in *The polar passion: the quest for the North Pole: with selections from arctic journals* (1967), a lavishly produced book with many contemporary drawings and photographs.

Mowat's books for children include *Lost in the Barrens* (1956), which won the Governor General's Award; *The Black Joke* (1962), a story about rum-running from St Pierre and Miquelon; and *The curse of the Viking grave* (1966). Books about animals are *Owls in the family* (1961), about his household pets; the very popular *The dog who wouldn't be* (1957); *Never cry wolf* (1963) in which he contends that the wolf is not dangerous to man; and *A whale for the killing* (1972), the gripping account of Mowat's vain effort to save a whale that was trapped in a Newfoundland cove and killed by the local inhabitants.

Sibir: my discovery of Siberia (1970) is an account of trips made there by Mowat in 1966 and 1969 as the guest of the Union of Soviet Writers. Mowat also wrote the text for two illustrated books, *Canada north* (1967) and *This rock within the sea* (1968), a photographic essay by John de Visser on Newfoundland.

NS

Munro, Alice (1931–). Born in Wingham, Ont., and educated at the University of Western Ontario, she has lived for many years in British Columbia—in Vancouver and then Victoria, where her husband operates a bookstore.

Alice Munro is a highly gifted writer of fiction that grows out of memories of her childhood in southern Ontario. Unlike most writers who draw on their small-town upbringing, she depicts 'Jubilee' as a place to be remembered with warmth; its foibles and people, brought to life with countless revealing details, are subjects for gentle mockery. Most of her stories are told by a child or adolescent, but 'The office' and 'The Peace of Utrecht' show her ability to see life through the eyes of older women. Both stories are included in her collection *Dance of the happy shades* (1968), which won a Governor General's Award. The title story shows some snobbish women, anxious to parade the musical training they are giving their daughters, being confronted by a display of talent—the only one at the recital—from a retarded child.

The linked short stories that make up *Lives of girls and women: a novel* (1971) trace the development of a refreshingly secure child, Del Jordan, through childhood and adolescence in Jubilee. Del faces life with all the bewilderment, little humiliations, secret curiosity, and mockery of an intelligent well-mannered girl. The differences between her eccentric mother, her gentle fox-farming father, who teaches her not to be afraid of an unusual character who is slightly mad, and her mildly malicious spinster aunts, give her experience in judging her elders and selecting friends. Del's adolescent curiosity about sex leads her into escapades from which she is lucky to escape unharmed. No great trials come her way, but from small-town gossip and the small-town characters, which are part of daily life, she learns to sense grief, developing understanding with maturity. NS

Murphy, Arthur L. See DRAMA IN ENGLISH 2 and 3.

Murray, Jean M. See HISTORY STUDIES IN ENGLISH 4.

Murray, Stanley N. See HISTORY STUDIES IN ENGLISH 8.

Murrow, Casey. See HISTORY STUDIES IN ENGLISH 7.

Musgrave, Susan. See POETRY IN ENGLISH 2.

Myers, Martin. See FICTION IN ENGLISH 4.

N

Naaman, Antoine. See LITERARY STUDIES IN FRENCH 5.

Nagler, Mark. See INDIANS 6.

Nanogak, Agnes. See CHILDREN'S BOOKS IN ENGLISH 6.

Nanton, Paul. See HISTORY STUDIES IN ENGLISH 10.

Naubert, Yvette. See FICTION IN FRENCH 3 and SHORT STORIES.

Neatby, Blair. See HISTORY STUDIES IN ENGLISH 11.

Neatby, Leslie H. See HISTORY STUDIES IN ENGLISH 10.

Neill, Robin. See HISTORY STUDIES IN ENGLISH 15.

Nelles, H. V. See HISTORY STUDIES IN ENGLISH 7.

Nelson, J. G. See HISTORY STUDIES IN ENGLISH 13.

Neufeld, E. P. See HISTORY STUDIES IN ENGLISH 13.

New, William H. See LITERARY STUDIES IN ENGLISH 2 and 4.

Newlove, John (1938–). Born in Regina, he lived in Verigin among Indians, Doukhobors, and other ethnic groups, and studied at the University of Saskatchewan. Since then he has been often on the road, down-and-out in Vancouver and Terrace; he is now employed as an editor in a Toronto publishing house. His poetry projects two dominant personas: the hurt animal and the detached analyst of emotions. The sense of hurt that grips the poems in his early books—*Grave sirs* (1962), *Elephants, mothers & others* (1963), *Moving in alone* (1965), *Notebook pages* (1965), and *What they say* (1967)—the hurt of alienation and loss, has persisted, but the focus has shifted somewhat from the individual ego to the world at large and from description to analysis. Newlove's most recent books—*Black night window* (1968), *The cave* (1970), and *Lies* (1972), which won a Governor General's Award—are more interesting because they are more penetrating, more historical. He has written that we are busy acquiring 'the knowledge of our/origins, and where,/we are in truth,/whose land this is and is to be.' Newlove has produced a number of fine poems—such as 'The Pride', 'Crazy Riel', and 'Ride off any horizon'—that hold a steady mirror up to our society; and the images reflected therein are far from complimentary. He has a mean eye for the phony and hypocritical in himself and others; he is a meticulous cartographer of the landscapes of conscience, charting the failure, betrayal, and guilt of private or collective man. His characteristic poetic voice is personal, almost confessional, but it is a voice that is restrained and modulated by degrees of irony in a manner reminiscent of post-war British poetry. Newlove's irony lies in the distance between what is said in a poem and the manner of the saying: treating a serious subject in a light, mocking manner. His poems have at their best a tense lyricism or grim humour; at their worst an air of exhaustion or self-indulgence. GG

Newman, Peter C. See HISTORY STUDIES IN ENGLISH 12 and POLITICAL WRITINGS IN ENGLISH 5.

nichol, bp (1944–). Born in Vancouver, barrie nichol has lived in several Canadian cities and now lives in Toronto. He has worked as a teacher and librarian and at present is associated with a psychotherapy clinic. He is Canada's leading exponent of concrete and sound poetry, which frees language from accumulated layers of meaning in an attempt to return to a purely emotional response. In the short sequences called *Scraptures*, published through the 1960s, and in *Dada Lama* (1968) nichol used the page as a field on which he broke words into their component syllables in order to examine their existence as separate sounds. In giving these syllables independent life, he could then reconstitute the language by injecting this individually new but basic life within the words he had chosen to break apart. In *ABC: the aleph beth book* (1971) nichol focuses on the single letters of the alphabet, creating graphic designs to free the form of each letter in order to show how letter-forms can reveal other forms and emphasize the inner spirit and mystery of language. The various sides of nichol's poetry were brought together in *Journeying and the returns* (1967) containing a book of poetry, some poem-objects (cards, fold-out papers, small notebooks, graphics), and a recording of the poet reading some of his own sound poetry. He was awarded a Governor General's Award for *Still water* (1970), a series of boxed cards printed with short, imagistic, haiku-like fragments of scenes and moods. *The martyrology* (1972) is a long poem in two volumes based on the lives of imaginary saints. The poet laments the decay of language and tries to reach beyond the limits of ordinary words to find the true spirit of speech, just as his imaginary saints constantly seek beyond ordinary life for a spiritual vision. In this poem nichol sets the search in a framework of his personal life.

nichol has written some books of lyric poetry—short-lined meditations on his search for a real source of spiritual life, his despairs, his relations with friends and lovers, his memories of his own past, and his travels. The best of these lyrical sequences are *Monotones* (1971) and *The other side of the room* (1971). He has also written some experimental prose in *Two novels* (*Andy* and *For lunatik Jesus*) (1969) and *The true eventual story of Billy the Kid* (1970), his comic undercutting of a legend.

An unceasing entrepreneur of concrete poetry, nichol was the editor of *The cosmic chef* (1970), the first anthology of Canadian concrete poetry. He has also edited several mimeographed magazines devoted to it, the best known being *Ganglia* and *Gronk*. He is a member of a quartet of sound poets called The Four Horsemen, who appear briefly in a movie about nichol, *Sons of Captain Poetry*, made by Michael ONDAATJE. PS

Nichol, James. See DRAMA IN ENGLISH 3.

Nichols, Ruth. See CHILDREN'S BOOKS IN ENGLISH 3 and 6; FICTION IN ENGLISH 5.

Nicholson, G. W. L. See HISTORY STUDIES IN ENGLISH 7 and 12.

Nicholson, Patrick. See HISTORY STUDIES IN ENGLISH 12.

Nicol, Eric. See CHILDREN'S BOOKS IN ENGLISH 6 and HISTORY STUDIES IN ENGLISH 9.

Nish, Cameron. See HISTORY STUDIES IN FRENCH 1 and 3.

Nish, Elizabeth. See HISTORY STUDIES IN ENGLISH 6.

Nixon, Robert F. See POLITICAL WRITINGS IN ENGLISH 8.

Noel, Sid J. R. See HISTORY STUDIES IN ENGLISH 12.

Nordegg, Martin. See HISTORY STUDIES IN ENGLISH 8.

Norris, John. See HISTORY STUDIES IN ENGLISH 14.

Norris, Len. See HISTORY STUDIES IN ENGLISH 6.

Nowlan, Alden (1933–). Born in Windsor, N.S., Nowlan began working at fifteen, taking various jobs in lumbermills and on farms. Completing his formal education at eighteen, he left Nova Scotia for New Brunswick, where he has been editor of the Hartland *Observer* and night-news editor of the Saint John *Telegraph-Journal*. In recent years he has been honoured with a Guggenheim Fellowship, a Governor General's Award (for *Bread, wine and salt*, 1967), and a Doctor of Letters from the University of New Brunswick. Since 1969 he has been writer-in-residence at the University of New Brunswick.

Nowlan began publishing poetry and short stories in the mid-1950s: his first collection of verse, *The rose and the puritan*, appeared in 1958. Throughout his career his poetry has been consistent in style and theme. The bulk of his poems are short anecdotal lyrics, conversational in tone and frequently directed toward some moral perception. He writes chiefly about small-town New Brunswick, the constricted lives of its inhabitants, and the complexity of his own role as its compassionately observing poet. The latter subject is indicated by the title of his selected poems, *Playing the Jesus game* (1970); like Christ, Nowlan finds that he must not only pity and forgive his fellow man but share personally his limitations and tragedies. Nowlan's emphasis of the essential innocence and helplessness of his variously benighted characters—escapist, credulous, treacherous, adulterous, murderous, insane—gives to many of his poems a suggestion of sentimentality that the poet, through realistic imagery and colloquial dialogue, must work to dispel. His other collections of poetry are *A darkness in the earth* (1959), *Under the ice* (1960), *Wind in a rocky country* (1961), *Things which are* (1962), *The mysterious naked man* (1969), and *Between tears and laughter* (1971). His work is also available on a record, *Alden Nowlan's Maritimes*.

Nowlan's collection of short stories, *Miracle at Indian River* (1968), echoes his poems both in centring on small-town New Brunswick characters and in presenting the naive dreams and stupid failures of these characters as largely accountable to the brutality of the circumstances in which fate has forced them to live. Nowlan's first novel, *Various persons named Kevin O'Brien*, appeared in 1973. FD

Nowlan, David. See POLITICAL WRITINGS IN ENGLISH 8.

Nowlan, Nadine. See POLITICAL WRITINGS IN ENGLISH 8.

Nugilak. See ESKIMOS: BOOKS IN ENGLISH.

Nurge, Ethel. See INDIANS 5.

O

O'Brien, Charles F. See HISTORY STUDIES IN ENGLISH 7.

O'Broin, Padraig. See POETRY IN ENGLISH 1.

Ochankugahe (Dan Kennedy). See INDIANS 2.

Ondaatje, Michael (1943-). Born in Ceylon, he attended school in England and came to Canada in 1962. He attended Bishop's University, the University of Toronto, and Queen's University, where he received an M.A. He has taught at the University of Western Ontario and is now assistant professor of English at Glendon College, York University, Toronto. He is married to the painter Kim Ondaatje. He has published four books of poetry: *The dainty monsters* (1967), *The man with seven toes* (1969), *The collected works of Billy the Kid* (1970), which won a Governor General's Award, and *Rat jelly* (1973). He has also written a critical study, *Leonard Cohen* (1967), in the Canadian Writers Series of the New Canadian Library; edited an anthology of animal poems by Canadians, *The broken arc: a book of beasts* (1971); and made a film about bp NICHOL called *Sons of Captain Poetry*.

Ondaatje's poetry shows the signs of this collision of three cultures in its energy, its personal flavour, and its formal beauty. *The dainty monsters* contains personal lyrics, often humorous and self-mocking, that belong to his North American heritage; it also contains more formal, objective pieces—like 'Peter' and 'Elizabeth'—that have their roots in the English narrative tradition. But whether a poem takes the route of personal experience or imagined life, its images will suggest a brush with the unknown, the unnatural: 'nature breeds the unnatural', the poet says. Many of his poems contain an element of the gothic: macabre and highly detailed scenes whose exotic coloration brings to mind the canvases of his favourite painter, Henri Rousseau.

Ondaatje is a talented narrative poet. His *Man with seven toes*, a disturbing tale of the

Australian outback, is remarkable for its dramatic intensity and economy of language. His capacity to render thought and feeling through the use of unusual, striking images accounts for much of the success of this book and also of *The collected works of Billy the Kid*, a novelistic sequence of poems and prose that explores the psychic and physical life of the American folk-hero. Both books abound in surreal, nightmarish imagery, often connected with dismemberment or death. GG

Orban, Edmond. See POLITICAL WRITINGS IN FRENCH 5.

Ormsby, William. See HISTORY STUDIES IN ENGLISH 6.

Osgood, Cornelius. See INDIANS 5.

Osler, E. B. See HISTORY STUDIES IN ENGLISH 2.

Ostiguy, Jean-René. See HISTORY STUDIES IN FRENCH 10.

Ouellet, Fernand (1926–). Born in Lac-Bouchette, Lac St-Jean, Qué., he was educated at Université Laval, where he obtained a Doctorat ès Lettres (histoire) in 1965. In the course of his studies in Paris and Washington, he received diplomas from Stage international d'Archives in 1953; the Institute on Archival Administration, American University, in 1956; and the Institute on Records Management, American University, in 1957. After five years as assistant archivist at the national archives in Quebec City and as a professor at the faculty of commerce of Université Laval, he was appointed professor in the history department of Carleton University, Ottawa, in 1965. Since 1967 Ouellet has been a member of the Royal Society of Canada, from which he received the Tyrrell Medal in 1970. He was president of the Canadian Historical Association in 1969. He has been awarded the Grand Prix littéraire de la Ville de Montréal and the Prix David, the most important literary distinction conferred by the Québec government.

Ouellet's thorough studies have made him one of the leading historians of nineteenth-century French Canada. His first publication, *Histoire de la Chambre de Commerce de Québec* (1959), was devoted to socio-economic history, a field in which Ouellet has become outstanding. He followed *Papineau: textes choisis* (1958) with two studies of this controversial family: *Papineau: un être divisé* (1960) and *Julie Papineau: un cas de mélancolie et d'éducation janséniste* (1961). Ouellet reinterpreted his subjects socio-psychologically, in the light of original documents, trying to understand their nature and behaviour.

From his *Histoire économique et sociale du Québec, 1760–1850: structures et conjoncture* (1968) there emerged a profound re-evaluation of the socio-economic foundation of French-Canadian society. Using the quantitative approach to account for its commercial progress, Ouellet gave much importance to the changing social stratifications of Québec society and the mental universe on which the merchants and the clergy founded their beliefs and their actions. Because of the global and sectorial perspectives of Ouellet's research, this book was soon considered to be a classic.

With Paul G. Cornell and Jean Hamelin, Ouellet contributed to *Canada, unity in diversity* (1967), published in French as *Canada: unité et diversité* (1968)—one of the rare occasions where English- and French-Canadian historians have tried to define the Canadian experience with a consensus attitude.

In 1972 a collection of Ouellet's most important articles was published, called *Eléments d'histoire sociale du Bas-Canada*. J-LR

Ouellette, Fernand (1930–). Born in Montreal, he was educated at the Collège Séraphique and the Université de Montréal. He worked as a bookseller before joining Radio-Canada, where he is now a producer of cultural programs. He has published five collections of poems: *Ces anges de sang* (1955), *Séquences de l'aile* (1958), *Le soleil sous le mort* (1965), *Dans le sombre* (1967), and *Poésie* (1971), his collected poems, which was awarded the Prix France-Canada. His collection of essays on various literary subjects, *Les actes retrouvés* (1970), won a Governor General's Award, but Ouellette declined it. A man of very wide cultural interests, he was a friend of Edgar Varèse, the French musician, about whom he wrote the first work in the French language, *Edgar Varèse* (1966). He has had a long correspondence with Henry Miller and knows Anaïs Nin and the poet Pierre-Jean Jouve, who has had a great influence on his writing.

Ouellette's poetry is an experience of

liberation and a quest for wholeness. It traces a spiritual adventure that begins in *Ces anges de sang* with the birth 'of a soul new-born from the womb of night and still unwashed, opening his greedy lungs for a first breath of light and air. [These poems] speak of a French Canadian at grips with the age-old tribal dualism he had injected into his soul.' In *Séquence de l'aile* he glories in 'the infinite spaciousness of life and of man' and discovers woman. In *Soleil sous la mort* his acceptance of the self passes into a celebration of life through an acceptance of the 'two poles of existence': the daily presence of death in life and the reconciliation of opposites—darkness and light, pain and joy, flesh and spirit—that leads him in *Dans le sombre* to explore love through eroticism. His poems are made exciting by their passionate energy and the sometimes surreal and obsessive use of blood, the sun, space, lightning, sexuality, and death to express his spiritual growth and liberation. Issue 10 of *Ellipse* is partly devoted to Ouellette and contains translations of some of his poems and of two essays by him, one of which is quoted from above. NK

Ouvrard, Hélène. See FICTION IN FRENCH 3.

P

Pacey, Desmond (1917–). William Cyril Desmond Pacey was born in Dunedin, N.Z., and educated in England, in Caledonia, Ont., at the University of Toronto, and at Cambridge University. He taught English at Brandon College, Winnipeg, from 1940 to 1944 when he became head of the English department at the University of New Brunswick, where he is now professor of English and vice-president. Known chiefly as a critic, he is the author of *Creative writing in Canada: a short history of English Canadian literature* (1952; rev. 1968), a useful critical survey of the main works of Canadian literature from 1750; *Ten Canadian poets: a group of biographical and critical essays* (1958) on Charles Sangster, Sir Charles G. D. Roberts, Bliss Carman, Archibald Lampman, Duncan Campbell Scott, E. J. PRATT, A. J. M. SMITH, F. R. SCOTT, A. M. KLEIN, and Earle BIRNEY; and the chapters on 'The writer and his public' and 'Fiction 1920–1940' in the *Literary history of Canada* (1965). An early supporter and interpreter of GROVE, he wrote *Frederick Philip Grove* (1945) and more recently edited an anthology of critical essays on him in the Critical Views of Canadian Writers series (1970) and a selection of Grove's short stories, *Tales from the margin* (1971). Pacey's *Essays in Canadian criticism: 1938–1968* appeared in 1969. (See LITERARY STUDIES IN ENGLISH 2.) He edited *The selected poems of Charles G. D. Roberts* (1956) and *A book of Canadian stories* (1947; 4th ed. 1962). A collection of his own short stories, *The picnic and other stories*, was published in 1958. He is also the author of three books for children: *The cow with the musical moo and other verse for children* (1952), *Hippity Hobo and the bee* (1952), and *The cat, the cow and the kangaroo* (1968). In 1966 he edited *Our literary heritage*, for use as a textbook. NS

Packard, Pearl. See FICTION IN ENGLISH 3.

Page, P. K. (1916–). Patricia Kathleen Page was born at Swanage in the south of England and came to Canada in 1919 when her parents settled in Red Deer, Alta. She was educated at St Hilda's School in Calgary and later studied art in Brazil and New York. During the late thirties she worked as a shop assistant and radio actress in Saint John, and later as a filing clerk and historical research worker in Montreal. She associated with the poetry movement that flourished there in the early forties, and in 1942 became one of the editors of *Preview*. Her poetry was first published—other than in periodicals—as part of *Unit of five* (1944), a collection in which Ronald Hambleton first substantially introduced to the reading public not only his own poetry and P. K. Page's, but also that of Louis DUDEK, Raymond SOUSTER, and James Wreford. P. K. Page's first individual book of verse was *As ten as twenty* (1946); her second, *The metal and the flower* (1954), won a Governor General's Award. In the interval she had worked for several years as a scriptwriter at the National Film Board. In 1950 she married William Arthur Irwin, and it is under the name of P. K. Irwin that she has gained a notable second reputation as a visual artist since her first exhibition in 1960.

From 1953 to 1964 P. K. Page lived mainly abroad—in Australia, Mexico, Brazil, Guatemala, and the United States. Her travels considerably influenced her later poems, which were published—along with the earlier works she wished to preserve—in *Cry Ararat!* (1967).

P. K. Page has published, under the nom-de-plume of Judith Cape, a romantic novel, *The sun and the moon* (1944); she has also written radio plays, short stories, and some personal essays on her writing and painting that have appeared in *Canadian Literature* (Issues 41 and 46). But her poems remain her most significant writings, and in spite of their comparatively small number (she found only fifty-seven that she wished to preserve from thirty years of work when she made the selections for *Cry Ararat!*), their quality has been so exceptional and so consistent that they have won her a leading position in the modern tradition of poetry in Canada.

Her early verse was largely dominated by themes of social protest and technically influenced by the English poets of the thirties. By the end of the forties she became more concerned with isolated human situations, the plight of the solitary or of those whom circumstances had condemned to appear contemptible, and some of her poems of this period—minute imaginary biographies—come as near as any writer can to the meeting of satire and compassion.

From the inner landscape of these middle poems P. K. Page has moved towards a mystical concern for the view out from the mind towards images that suggest the way of liberation from the alienated, prisoned self. Technically her poetry has moved towards an ever-greater purification of the line. It is characterized by accuracy of rhythm, period, and internal echo; it is also dense with a metaphysical intent beyond its great immediate attractiveness. GW

Palmer, Howard. See HISTORY STUDIES IN ENGLISH 14.

Palmer, John. See DRAMA IN ENGLISH 3.

Paltiel, K. Z. See POLITICAL WRITINGS IN ENGLISH 5.

Panneton, Jean. See LITERARY STUDIES IN FRENCH 4.

Paradis, Suzanne (1936–). Born in Beaumont, Qué., she graduated from the École normale in Quebec City. She was for a time in charge of the Centre d'art at Val-Menaud in the Lake St John region. She married the poet Louis-Paul Hamel in 1961.

The poetry of Suzanne Paradis—which is rhythmic and usually set in conventional rhymed hexameters—is notable for its abundance of metaphors and for a wealth of imagery that is sometimes barely under control but always evocative. She writes with great verve and passion of the quest for individual freedom, of the celebration of life and nature in all their aspects, and of love and personal fulfilment. Her collections are *Les enfants continuels* (1959); *À temps, le bonheur* (1960); *La chasse aux autres* (1961); *La malebête* (1963); *Pour les enfants des morts* (1964), which was awarded the Prix France-Canada; *Le visage offensé* (1966); *L'oeuvre de pierre* (1968), winner of the Prix Du Maurier; and *Pour voir les plectrophanes naître* (1970). She has also published a book of short stories, *François-les-Oiseaux* (1967), and four novels: *Les hauts cris* (1960), *Il ne faut pas sauver les hommes* (1961), *Les cormorans* (1968), and *Emmanuelle en noir* (1971). The fluid style of her poetry becomes too studied in her fiction. Her gifts for metaphor and image-making overpower her novels and stories and make them unduly pretentious and obscure. The subject-matter is melodramatic. *Emmanuelle en noir* is a study of incest, madness, and violence, told through interior monologue and letters. In *Les cormorans* the inhabitants of a lonely island are destroyed gradually by murder, suicide, and natural disaster, leaving only a boy and girl to set off together in a skiff in search of a new life.

Suzanne Paradis is also the author of *Femme*

fictive, femme réelle (1966), a study of the female characters in the novels of French-Canadian women writers. An English translation of one of her poems, which fails to capture the rhythmic and compelling quality of the original, has been published in *The poetry of French Canada in translation* (1970) edited by John GLASSCO. JM

Parent, Charles. See ANTHOLOGIES IN FRENCH.

parti pris—founded by Pierre Maheu, André MAJOR, and Paul CHAMBERLAND, *et al.*—was a political and cultural review published in Montreal from 1963 to 1968 by a group of young Québec intellectuals. Its founders reacted against the generation of intellectuals that preceded them, and specially those around the review *Cité libre*. They reproached them for denouncing, on the one hand, the political corruption of the Duplessis régime and particular cases of injustice without attacking the fundamental injustices they considered to be rooted in the economic and social structure of Québec society. They also criticized their analytical approach: where the older generation tried to analyse Québec society impartially and 'objectively', *parti pris* proposed a partisan and radical perspective. Their political ideology was polarized, in the beginning, by the ideas of alienation and liberation. They saw Quebeckers as alienated because they were colonized and exploited. At the political level the provincial government, devoid of power and revenue, depended on the federal government. At the economic level the resources and corporations were controlled by foreigners—Anglo-Canadians and Americans. The 'clerico-bourgeois élite', by maintaining humanist and religious 'myths' encouraging submission, supported the power of the 'colonizers'. According to *parti pris*, Québec society had entered a revolutionary phase. The struggle for political and economic independence, and against the traditional élites, would lead to a secular, independent, and socialist state. This initial ideology, mainly centred on the idea of decolonization, later developed into a certain radicalization. The leaders of the review defined the situation in a Marxist perspective: the struggle for political independence appeared only as the first step towards social revolution. After independence they foresaw a class struggle between the 'capitalist bourgeoisie' (Québécois as well as Anglo-Canadian and American) and the working class allied with the revolutionary left. During the first stage of the revolution, however, the revolutionary forces would have to form a temporary tactical alliance with the French-Canadian bourgeoisie in order to achieve political independence.

The review soon became the rallying point of the young French-Canadian left in Québec, and tried to develop into a movement. Some of its members founded the short-lived Mouvement de libération populaire (MLP). In 1968, when René Lévesque launched the Mouvement souveraineté-association (MSA, which later became the Parti Québécois), a split occurred in *parti pris*. Some of its spokesmen were ready to support the MSA tactically as a first stage toward a social revolution. Others called for the founding of a radical party. This conflict, plus the view by the editors that the main aims of *parti pris* (independence, secularism, and socialism) had become widely popularized, led them to cease publication.

Five years after its disappearance, *parti pris* still exercises its influence. Its criticism of the new élites emerging from the Quiet Revolution, and of the mainstream independence movement, is still at the centre of debate in leftist circles. Its ideas also contributed to the radicalization of trade unions, to student activism, to the emergence of citizens' committees, and to the founding of FRAP (Front d'action populaire) in Montreal at the end of the sixties. CT

The magazine *parti pris* and the publishing house Les Éditions parti pris (founded in 1964), which is still active, have played an important role in the literary and artistic development of Québec. Among the creative writers whose works were published under the auspices of the review are novelists Jacques RENAUD, André MAJOR, and Laurent Girouard, and poets Paul CHAMBERLAND and Gérald GODIN. Contributing to the review were poet Raoul DUGUAY and film-makers Denys Arcand and Pierre Maheu. Although older than the founders and editors of *parti pris*, Claude JASMIN and Jacques FERRON also had some of their prose works published by Les Éditions parti pris. The publishing house has lately specialized in poetry, and in essays on political, economic, and social topics, including translations of books by radical authors like

Stanley B. Ryerson and James Laxer. The literary theories of *parti pris* were outlined by many of its above-mentioned collaborators in the January 1965 issue entitled 'Pour une littérature québécoise'. There it was proposed that the vehicle for a new orientation in creative writing should be *joual*—the deformed, truncated, and highly anglicized speech of the uneducated masses of Québec, and especially Montreal. The use of international French, it was felt, would be a travesty and would not allow Québécois to recognize their colonized status. Although this controversial approach has had many detractors, its durability is seen in the plays of Michel TREMBLAY and Jean BARBEAU and in the novels of V.-L. BEAULIEU, the monologues of Yvon Deschamps, and the songs of Robert Charlebois.

For more information on the political and literary importance of *parti pris*, see Malcolm Reid's *The shouting signpainters: a literary and political account of Quebec revolutionary nationalism* (1972). See also issue 31–2 of *La Barre du jour* (Winter 1972), which is devoted entirely to *parti pris*. B-ZS

Pasquale, Dominique de. See DRAMA IN FRENCH 2.

Patenaude, Luce. See POLITICAL WRITINGS IN FRENCH 3.

Patry, André. See POLITICAL WRITINGS IN FRENCH 3.

Patterson, E. Palmer. See INDIANS 3.

Patterson, Pat. See CHILDREN'S BOOKS IN ENGLISH 6.

Peacock, Donald. See HISTORY STUDIES IN ENGLISH 12 and POLITICAL WRITINGS IN ENGLISH 5.

Peacock, Kenneth. See FOLKLORE: BIBLIOGRAPHY.

Pearce, Jon. See ANTHOLOGIES IN ENGLISH 3.

Pearson, Lester B. See HISTORY STUDIES IN ENGLISH 12.

Peers, Frank W. See HISTORY STUDIES IN ENGLISH 15.

Pellerin, Jean. See POLITICAL WRITINGS IN FRENCH 3.

Pelletier, Gérard. See HISTORY STUDIES IN ENGLISH 12; POLITICAL WRITINGS IN ENGLISH 1; and POLITICAL WRITINGS IN FRENCH 7.

Pelletier, W. See INDIANS 1.

Péloquin, Claude (1940–). Born in Montreal, he refuses to reveal anything about his childhood except that he began to write at a very early age. His life since 1960 has been entirely devoted to a wide variety of artistic media including films, multidimensional shows, readings, songwriting, and the publication—often at his own expense and with limited circulation—of at least ten books of poetry. He has worked with such well-known sculptors and painters as Armand Vaillancourt, Jean-Paul Mousseau, and Jordi Bonet, exploring new forms of expression in the language and plastic arts. In 1965 he founded 'le Zirmate', a group that performed collective creations in the Montreal area and later at Expo 67. In 1969, as well as doing research with Robert Moog, inventor of the Moog Synthesizor, Péloquin wrote the script for the National Film Board movie *Le Nouvel Homme*. He has also worked with pop singer Robert Charlebois, for whom he has written a number of very well-known songs.

Péloquin is difficult to classify as a writer, standing rather alone in the literary landscape of Québec. His first books—including *Jéricho* (1963), *Les essais rouges* (1964), and *Les mondes assujétis* (1965)—are fairly traditional in form but show clearly the obsession that will become the main theme of all his later poetry: man's fight against death. Here as always his style oscillates between philosophical abstractions and the most concrete elements of modern life. *Manifeste subsiste* (1965) and *Calorifère* (1966) reveal the growing influence of surrealism on his work, particularly in the use of 'automatic writing'. Péloquin's philosophy and poetics are given their clearest expression in *Manifeste infra suivi des Émissions parallèles* (1967), which is a strong attack on romanticism and academism and a plea for poetry that would use the full powers of the imagination to explore the unconscious, the unknown, and the 'hidden reality': in short, poetry must become the new science. Following *Pyrotechnies* (1968), *Pour la grandeur de l'homme*—published in 1969 and reprinted in 1971—denounces all the death forces oppressing modern man and proposes, in its visionary thrust, the systematic development of the powers of the mind for the conquest of the 'unlimited'. *Le repas est servi* (1970) and the 'trip novel' *Mets tes raquettes* (1972) continue the poet's reflections in a series of sometimes very short aphorisms that celebrate the greatness of man striving towards eternity amid the hypocrisy and lies of the modern world. Péloquin has also contributed to various publications and journals in Québec, France, Argentina, and California. PN

Pendergast, James. See INDIANS 4.

Penlington, Norman. See HISTORY STUDIES IN ENGLISH 1 and 7.

Pépin, Marcel. See POLITICAL WRITINGS IN FRENCH 6.

Perez, Nora. See CHILDREN'S BOOKS IN ENGLISH 2.

Perreault, E. G. See FICTION IN ENGLISH 3.

Peter, John. See FICTION IN ENGLISH 6.

Peterson, Len. See DRAMA IN ENGLISH 2 and 3.

Pethick, Derek. See HISTORY STUDIES IN ENGLISH 9.

Petitot, Emile. See ESKIMOS: BOOKS IN FRENCH.

Pfeifer, Lillian. See CHILDREN'S BOOKS IN ENGLISH 1.

Phelan, Josephine. See CHILDREN'S BOOKS IN ENGLISH 1.

Phillips, David. See POETRY IN ENGLISH 3.

Phillips, Paul A. See HISTORY STUDIES IN ENGLISH 13.

Phillips, R. A. J. See HISTORY STUDIES IN ENGLISH 10.

Pickersgill, J. W. See HISTORY STUDIES IN ENGLISH 12.

Pilon, Jean-Guy (1930–). Born at Saint-Polycarpe, Qué., he graduated in law from the Université de Montréal in 1954. He has been a producer for Radio-Canada, founder-director of the review *Liberté*, animator of many literary *rencontres* and a representative of *sociétés d'écrivains* (work that has taken him to many countries and kept him constantly on the move), director of Les Éditions de l'Hexagone, poetry critic for *Le Devoir*, and director of Éditions l'Actuelle. In all these roles and as a poet in his own right he has worked patiently to give reality to his conviction that literature has a key role to play in the emergence of the nation to which he belongs. He is a member of the Royal Society of Canada and the Quebec Arts Council. He received a Governor General's Award for his collected verse, *Comme eau retenue: poèmes 1954–1963* (1970), which contains all the poems in his earlier collections: *Les cloîtres de l'été* (1954), *L'homme et le jour* (1957), *La mouette et le large* (1960), *Recours au pays* (1961), and *Pour saluer une ville* (1963). He has published two other volumes of verse, *La fiancée du matin* (1953) and *Saison pour la continuelle* (Paris, 1969); a novel, *Solange* (1966); and has edited two anthologies of Canadian poetry, *Poetry 62/Poésie 62* (1961) with Eli MANDEL and *Poèmes 70* (1970).

Pilon's debt to Alain GRANDBOIS is very apparent in *Les cloîtres de l'été*, which is full of a sense of the absurd contradiction between the impatient desires of youthful life and the shadow of death. The older poet taught Pilon to break free from Québec's destructive narcissism and to respond to the appeal of the world. But the author of *Recours au pays* is aware that he is one of the 'fils blessés de pères humiliés'. His real sense of hope, expressed in the clarity and tenacity of his poetry and in his belief in the precious presence of the 'femme-patrie' is tempered by a painful awareness that the land of Québec is not yet justified or even recognized and that this ideal remains elusive, clouded as it is with a heritage of false horizons and taunting phantasms. Is the 'eau retenue' in the title of his collected poems a furtive tear shed over the passage of time, as has been suggested, or rather the fluid power of the word, pent up behind a retaining wall, ready to bring light and strength to our lives? CRMP

Pinard, Maurice. See HISTORY STUDIES IN ENGLISH 12.

Pipping, Ella. See HISTORY STUDIES IN ENGLISH 5.

Pitseolak. See CHILDREN'S BOOKS IN ENGLISH 5 and ESKIMOS: BOOKS IN ENGLISH.

Pitt, David G. See LITERARY STUDIES IN ENGLISH 4.

Plante, Herman. See HISTORY STUDIES IN FRENCH 8.

Plante, Marie. See CHILDREN'S BOOKS IN FRENCH.

Plunkett, Thomas J. See POLITICAL WRITINGS IN ENGLISH 8.

Poetry in English (see also ANTHOLOGIES IN ENGLISH). The rate of publication of poetry books gained momentum in the 1960s, increasing to such an extent in the late sixties and early seventies that it is not possible to mention in this survey all the books that were published in our period. There was a strong emphasis on the work of new poets, but there was also a fair representation of books by established poets; they, along with anthologies, provide us with an unequalled opportunity to examine the development of modern poetry in Canada.

Two well-known anthologies were revised: *The Penguin book of Canadian verse* (2nd ed., 1967) edited by Ralph GUSTAFSON and *The blasted pine: an anthology of satire, invective and disrespectful verse chiefly by Canadian writers* (2nd ed., 1967) edited by A. J. M. SMITH and F. R. SCOTT. Intending to revise his well-known *Oxford book of Canadian verse* (1960), A. J. M. Smith instead produced an entirely new anthology, *Modern Canadian verse: in English and French* (1967). Other good modern anthologies are Milton Wilson's *Poets between the wars* (1967), devoted to PRATT, Scott, LIVESAY, Smith, and KLEIN; three anthologies edited by Eli MANDEL: *Poets of contemporary Canada 1960–1970* (1972), *Five modern Canadian poets* (1970), and *Eight more Canadian poets* (1972); *Fifteen Canadian poets* (1970) edited by Gary Geddes and Phyllis Bruce; and *Made in Canada: new poems of the seventies* (1970) edited by Douglas Lochhead and Raymond SOUSTER. John Robert COLOMBO edited three anthologies that contain interesting background material on the work of our poets: *How do I love thee?: sixty poets of Canada (and Quebec) select and introduce their own work* (1970); *Rhymes and reasons: nine Canadian poets discuss their work* (1971); and *New directions in Canadian poetry* (1971).

1. *Established poets.* The work of some poets who are no longer living was revived in new editions. E. J. Pratt's *Selected poems* (1968) was issued in paperback with a critical introduction by Peter Buitenhuis. A. J. M. Smith edited and wrote an introduction to *The collected poems of Anne Wilkinson* (1968), which includes a prose memoir by this very fine poet (q.v.), 'Four corners of my world'. The poems of Bertram Warr, killed in the Second World War, were collected by Len Gasparini and published with a short introduction by Earle BIRNEY as *Acknowledgement to life* (1970). The poetry of W. W. E. Ross, one of the first modern poets in Canada, was selected by Raymond Souster and John Robert Colombo and published with a memoir by Barry Callaghan in *Shapes and sounds* (1968).

Two poets who were prominent in the modern-poetry movement of the 1940s published with distinction in our period. Dorothy Livesay was caught up in the new movement that was burgeoning on the west coast when she returned to Vancouver after living in Africa. Her interest in the oral dimensions of language was renewed and gave rise to some remarkable new poems, particularly ones concerned with human love, in *The unquiet bed* (1967) and *Plainsongs* (1969; revised and extended 1971). She revised and republished some of her earlier political poems and included them with a new and previously unpublished long poem in *The documentaries* (1968). The work of her whole poetic career, including previously unpublished poems both old and new, was gathered together in *Collected poems: the two seasons* (1972). P. K. PAGE, who has devoted her creative energies mainly to painting in recent years, included some new poems based on her travels in South America and Australia in a selection of poems from her work of the 1940s and 1950s, *Cry Ararat!* (1967), which was illustrated with her own drawings.

Many other established poets published representative collections of their work during this period. John GLASSCO's *Selected poems* (1971) shows the calmly meditative and wittily civilized work of a poet who has pursued his own individual course through the years.

Poetry in English I

George JOHNSTON's collected poems, *Happy enough: poems 1935–1972* (1972), show in the recent poems quiet contentment with life, even as it moves towards old age and death. Miriam WADDINGTON's *Driving Home: poems new and selected* (1972) offers a guarded affirmation in the search for identity she began in *Say yes* (1969). Her short-lined poems employ a language that successfully combines the colloquial with her own special heritage of Slavic Jewishness. Robin SKELTON, who had published poetry for many years in England before immigrating to Canada in 1962, wrote some modern versions of Greek epigrams in his *200 poems from the Greek anthology* (1970). His *Selected poems* (1968), which contains recollections of English incidents, concludes with some poems of Canadian scenes. His personal poems of reminiscence become more confessional in tone in *The hunting dark* (1970) and *Private speech* (1971).

Fred COGSWELL has been very active on the Canadian poetry scene. Besides running the Fiddlehead Press, he has written four volumes of his own poetry: *Star-people* (1968), *Immortal plowman* (1969), *In praise of chastity* (1970), and *The chains of Lilliput* (1971). His poems can be sardonic and sensitive by turn, showing a reconciliation of the foibles of mankind and sometimes turning in mockery on himself in forms both traditional and modern. He published *From the inside* (1972) by Heather Spears, whose earlier book, *The Danish portraits* (1967), cleverly welds her concern with painting to personal statements about love and the artistic process. Another poet Cogswell has published over the years is Dorothy Roberts whose *Extended* (1967) is concerned with landscape, placing specific locales in larger terms in language sometimes craggily dense, sometimes indirect, but generally successful. Fiddlehead Press brought out a fine collection, *Waiting for the barbarians* (1971), by Christopher Wiseman, who emigrated from England during our period. It closes with a sequence centring on the figure of the Barbarian, a persona operating both as modern man in a technological age and as the poet himself. Christopher Levenson, another poet who came from England via the United States, published *Cairns* (1969) and *Stills* (1972). His poetry is carefully wrought, ranging over personal themes and meditations on history and place; its humour is sometimes savage, sometimes good-naturedly mocking.

Gael Turnbull, who returned to England, issued *A trampoline: poems 1952–1964* (1969). Kenneth Leslie, who had published books of poetry through the 1930s but who had never really joined in the crusade for new poetry, writing principally in traditional metres and forms, included a few new poems in *The poems of Kenneth Leslie* (1971), published by a new publisher in Québec, the Ladysmith Press. George WOODCOCK, a prolific man of letters who turned his attention from poetry to verse drama when he came to Canada in 1949, published his *Selected poems* in 1967. Padraig O'Broin's *No casual trespass* (1967), a collected poems, was the last book of this Celtic-oriented poet who died in the late sixties. Other poets who published collected or selected poems were Milton ACORN in 1967; Earle Birney, Alden NOWLAN (under an American imprint), and Leonard COHEN in 1968; Elizabeth BREWSTER in 1969; R. G. EVERSON in 1970; Louis DUDEK, Eldon GRIER, Irving LAYTON, and Phyllis WEBB in 1971; Ralph GUSTAFSON, Al PURDY, James REANEY, and Raymond Souster in 1972.

Some of these poets also published volumes of new verse. Acorn's poetry retained its political slant and its obsessive focus on public figures in relation to the common people in *More poems for people* (1972). The same interest occurs in Gustafson's five poetic sequences about political violence in *Theme for sounding brass* (1972), but the poems in his earlier *Ixion's wheel* (1969) arise out of his travels and his responses to mortality in thoughts on dead poets, old buildings, and public figures. Birney's experimentation with form and sound runs through *Rag and bone shop* (1970), which also has poems in his loosely narrative vein. In *The energy of slaves* (1972) Cohen turned away from the emphasis on song in his previous volumes to produce a new stripped-down directness, reflecting an almost wilful anti-poetic and anti-romantic stance that gives these poems a confessional substance. Nowlan published three new volumes: *Bread, wine and salt* (1967), *The mysterious naked man* (1969), and *Between tears and laughter* (1971). His poetry retained its focus on the Maritimes and its people but it has also become much more personal as it details his experiences both at home—particularly in a moving series about a stay in hospital—and abroad. He has developed an idiosyncratic verse that moves conversationally yet is capable of shifting into dense textures. Dudek returned to his interest in the long poem with *Atlantis* (1968), recounting his travels in Europe in search of the fundamental reality underlying the surface of life and finding it in the continuing flux of existence; his ideas are expressed in long paragraphs cataloguing detail and rising to sustained passages of noble utterance. Some of the section titles in Brewster's selected poems, *Passages of summer* (1969)—'Past as presest', 'On considering objects', 'Elegies', 'Explorations', 'Devotions'—could well serve as a summary of her poetic interests in her next volume, *Sunrise north* (1972). Grier's poetry was presented with graphic accompaniments in *Pictures under the skin* (1967), an assemblage of poems, drawings, photographs, and collages.

Probably the three most prolific of our established poets were Al Purdy, Raymond Souster, and Irving Layton. Both Purdy and Layton travel extensively, their journeys forming the basis of many poems: Purdy's Arctic expedition in *North of summer* (1967), his visits to Newfoundland and Cuba in *Wild grape wine* (1968), and to Japan in *The Hiroshima poems* (1972); Layton's Greece, Israel, and Nepal visits, particularly in *The whole bloody bird* (1969)—a book that is split into three sections labelled obs (observations), aphs (aphorisms), and pomes (poetry). In 1968 Purdy published a revised version of the book that saw the beginning of his present style, *Poems for all the Annettes*. Another Purdy book that focused primarily on previously published poems was his *Love in a burning building* (1970). Layton's style has remained fairly constant over the years, although critics felt that it had become somewhat arrogantly dogmatic in *Periods of the moon* (1967) and *The shattered plinths* (1968). In *Nail polish* (1971) he reworked his recurrent themes about man's ambiguous nature, duplicity, imbecility, and capacity for both love and evil, but in most of these poems there is a new mellowness, a tone of acceptance, even though anger and ridicule do break out occasionally. In a way the volumes of Raymond Souster published during this period are addenda to his collected poems, for they contain many previously unpublished poems from his poetic past—in *Lost and found: uncollected poems 1945–1965* (1968) and *The years* (1970), a retrospective collection from the 1940s through the 1960s. There is new verse in *As is* (1967) and *So far so good* (1969), both of which contain some poems that are longer than is usual with Souster.

Two poets who emerged in the fifties published important single volumes in our period. In some of the poems of D. G. JONES' *Phrases from Orpheus* (1967), the poet assumes the Orphic tone, in contrast to short imagist pieces and deeply felt confessional poems. Eli Mandel's *An idiot joy* (1967) is a startlingly original departure for this poet, away from the mythopoeic strain into irrationality and poetry that is deeply and seriously ironic.

Phyllis GOTLIEB's *Ordinary, moving* (1969), a volume devoted to examining her Jewishness from a personal standpoint, closes with a splendid mosaic of children's rhymes and songs intertwined with personal reminiscences. Daryl HINE's interest in classical studies, which is apparent in the mythic and literary references in his earlier poetry, still looms large in *Minutes* (1968) and in his translations, *The Homeric hymns* (1972). *The boatman*, the well-known book of poems by Jay MACPHERSON, who has written little new poetry since it was first published in 1957, was re-issued in 1968 as *The boatman and other poems*. In *A cardboard garage* (1969) Francis SPARSHOTT divides his poetry into two sections: 'brittle bodies'—poems written in regular and traditional metres—and 'soft engines', poems of looser structure. He writes mostly philosophic meditations on history and place that are enlivened by sharp irony and humour. His ironic wit is well in evidence in *A book* (1972), published under the pseudonym Cromwell Kent. Michael Collie's *The house* (1967) is a series of interconnected poems with some oblique narrative interest centring on a house on Fundy Bay but covering a wide range of place and time in loose verse paragraphs. Ronald Bates in *Changes* (1968) writes a carefully contrived poetry of meditative calm, variations on philosophic ideas and landscapes. R. A. D. FORD, whose work with the diplomatic service has taken him to many countries, published some new poems arising from his responses to life in South America and the Middle East in *The solitary city* (1969). His skill with language is evident in the second half of this book, which consists of translations from Russian, Serbo-Croat, Portuguese, and French poetry.

2. *The younger poets*. The west coast has exercised a dominant influence on Canadian

poetry through the 1960s, mainly through the group who first started the magazine *Tish*: George BOWERING, Lionel Kearns, and Frank DAVEY. Bowering is the most prolific of these poets and in 1971 published *Touch*, a selection culled from the several volumes he published in the 1960s and including one of his long poems, *Baseball*, which was issued separately in 1968. He also published two long sequences: *Rocky mountain foot* (1969), responses to the province of Alberta at historical, political, and personal levels, and *Genève* (1972), a series of poems based on the random dealing of a pack of Tarot cards, the poet allowing his writing to follow his associations with each card. (He has said that he believes in letting poetry flow to make a 'graph of the mind moving'.) For several years Bowering also edited the magazine *Imago*, which was devoted solely to the long poem and poetic sequence—the form he gave to his own *Sitting in Mexico* (1969). *Imago* published long poems by the other two principal poets associated with the Tish movement: Kearns and Davey. Kearns' *Pointing* (1967) is a collection of short lyrics that are at times wittily epigrammatic. His wit and humour were given full rein in *By the light of the silvery McLune* (1969) in which the poems are on the whole humorous in content and the form is looser, with longer lines and a generally colloquial tone; they sometimes have the characteristics of prose-poems. Davey also used this form in *Weeds* (1970), which, together with the short lyrics in *King of swords* (1972), documents his responses to a crisis in his private life. His *Four myths for Sam Perry* (1970) is a series of poems based on his reactions to the death of a friend. Davey has been the most polemical of this group in his concern with its poetic principles. He has written several critical defences of the poets associated with the American school—generally referred to as the Black Mountain poets—and is the editor of a magazine devoted to critical debate, *Open Letter*.

Other poets now resident in Vancouver started presses. Seymour Mayne began the Very Stone House Press and more recently Ingluvin Press. Patrick Lane, who has been associated with these presses, brought out *The sun has begun to eat the mountain* (1972), a selection of his poems taken from previously published books. Lane has been a constant traveller and his poems record his experiences on the road, his casual acquaintances and meetings, memories of his past, his occasional jobs, all expressed directly in verse that is undecorated yet evocative with detail. It is a personal poetry that transcends the self-pitying confession, yet it is candid, probing into the poet's inner being. This book is illustrated with the author's own intricately grotesque drawings. Lane collected the poetry of his brother (who died in 1964): *The collected poems of Red Lane* (1968). Although Red Lane was associated with the west-coast movement, he was essentially a maverick poet and this volume is a testimony to his unique contribution to Canadian poetry: it avoids the theoretic eclecticism of his contemporaries on the west coast by using a direct colloquial style. Seymour Mayne has published a series of broadsheets containing his punning experiments with words, but his poetry became less whimsical and more resilient and tough in *Mouth* (1970). Mayne's press also brought out Marya Fiamengo's *Silt of iron* (1972), which shows a wide range of form and language that is both exuberant and austere. This book is most successful when the author examines her own Serbo-Croat background and past. Her work was also included in another Ingluvin book, an anthology edited by Dorothy Livesay, *Forty women poets of Canada* (1972). Another of the poets included in this anthology is Pat Lowther, who published an impressive first volume, *This difficult flowring* (1968).

Talonbooks operates out of Vancouver and has shown a catholicity of selection. It published the *Selected poems* of Phyllis Webb, but it tends to concentrate its energies on publishing newer poets who have been influenced in their general trends by the Tish movement. One of its founders, Jim Brown, has published several of his own books. In *If there are any Noahs* (1967), through *Forgetting* (1969), to *Towards a chemistry of real people* (1971), he has moved towards a specifically oral poetry and plays with themes relevant to the counter-culture. Other poets associated with Talonbooks are David Phillips, Pierre Coupey, Jamie Reid, John Hulcoop, Helene Rosenthal, among others, as well as some poets who respond openly to the landscape of the prairies, the interior, or of northern and coastal British Columbia. I am thinking here of Barry McKinnon's *The carcasses of spring* (1971), Ken Belford's *Fireweed* (1968) and *The post electric cave man* (1970), and Gary Geddes'

Rivers inlet (1972), a lyric sequence of personal recollection in which the poet tries to see a pattern in his past that connects with his present.

Another small British Columbia publisher is Sono Nis Press, directed by J. Michael Yates, a poet who is deeply influenced by modern European literature. He grafted a kind of nightmarish surrealism onto his experience of the Canadian north to produce a sequence of powerful prose-poems about bleak minimal existence in *The Great Bear Lake meditations* (1970), published by Oberon Press. The same sense of void, both inner and outer, where beyond the poet's 'last sense of wilderness, the first wilderness begins', occurs in Yates's *Parallax* (1971). His press has published some other surrealistic poetry, notably *The ozone minotaur* (1969) and *File of uncertainties* (1971) by Andreas Schroeder. Another poet associated with this press is Florence McNeil, whose *The rim of the park* (1972) succeeds in looking at childhood, the past, and ordinary events without floundering in nostalgia and sentimentality, mainly because the lines are uncluttered and the figurative language is sharply defined. She also wrote *A silent green sky* (1967), which is more specifically related to the natural scene, and a narrative sequence, *Walhachin* (1972), concerning the attempt by a group of English settlers before the First World War to plant orchards in the dry interior of British Columbia. Susan Musgrave's *Songs of a sea-witch* (1970) are densely textured poems; outer landscape is used as a mirror of her inner tensions, which are expressed in nervy lines and dislocated images. She has sloughed off some of this obscurity in *Entrance of the celebrant* (1972) in which she looks at the world that underlies surface reality, touching on the primitive and the magical. Yates, George McWhirter, and Andreas Schroeder edited the anthology *Contemporary poetry of British Columbia* (1970).

To move to Toronto, Gwendolyn MACEWEN's poetry continued its examination of the mythic implications of the psyche in *The shadow-maker* (1969). The language, imagery, and structure of this book are more formal and less exotic than in her previous work, but she returned to exuberance in *The armies of the moon* (1972), a fascinating attempt to connect cosmic exploration with the discoveries of the poet's own psychic continent. John NEWLOVE progressed from *Black night window* (1968), a collection that extended his previous work in its use of his prairie background and suggested the direction of his later work in poems devoted to an obsessive examination of personal motive and mood. *The cave* (1970) is a series of elusive and cryptic poems, mostly fragmentary, about private guilts and neuroses associated with alienation in modern society and in human relationships. This vein continues in *Lies* (1972), which contains a harder poetry of fierce irony and mercilessly naked revelations that is nonetheless held firmly in control by the poet's objective tone, even in the most personal lyrics. Margaret ATWOOD's second volume, *The animals in that country* (1968), was followed by a recreation of the experience of an English gentlewoman in the backwoods of Upper Canada, *The journals of Susanna Moodie* (1970)—one of the most popular recent books of poetry—and a book of poems dealing generally with ambiguities of the self and the environment, *Procedures for underground* (1970). Her tough images, broken lining, and sharply turned wording focus with uncompromising relentlessness on the man-woman relationship in *Power politics* (1971). Margaret Atwood is associated with the House of Anansi Press (originally founded by Dennis LEE and Dave GODFREY), which issued a series of anthologies in an attempt to give a continuing picture of Canadian poetry through the work of new and developing poets: *T.O. now: the young Toronto poets* (1968), *Canada first* (1969), *Soundings* (1970), and *Mindscapes* (1971). This press also introduced some new poets in individual volumes: Barry Charles, David Knight, Janis Rapaport, Ian Young, and Doug Fetherling, an expatriate American who developed a cryptic, allusive style in a collection of short lyrics, *Our man in Utopia* (1972). Another Anansi poet is Robert Flanagan, who writes a stripped-down poetry in *Body* (1970) and pursues this style to its bare bones in *Incisions* (1972).

Dave Godfrey left Anansi to start New Press, which printed first volumes by Andy Wainwright and Grant Johnston as well as a collection of poems by Ottawa poet William Hawkins, *The gift of space* (1971), and the more formally organized poetry of Henry Beissel, *Face on the dark* (1970). An offshoot of New Press, Press Porcépic, brought out work by two new poets, Eldon Garnet and Tim Inskter.

Poetry in English 2

Stan Bevington's Coach House Press, Toronto, introduced some new and on the whole attractive ideas of typography and design into Canadian poetry publishing. They published the books of Michael ONDAATJE, whose *The dainty monsters* (1967) was an impressive debut, moving between personal statement and historic and mythic narrative. He developed the narrative strain in *The man with seven toes* (1969), using a mixture of flamboyant descriptive material, dramatic devices, and realistic detail to tell the story of the journey of an escaped convict and a stranded woman through the interior of Australia. He adapted and extended this narrative technique in *The collected works of Billy the Kid* (1970), a highly personal look at the American outlaw that is a mélange of poetry and prose. Relying on dramatic monologue and a clever manipulation of the narrative, he steers it between adventure and reminiscence, realism and invention. Coach House publishes verse that tends to stem from an interest in oral poetry, and the layout and design of the books often attempt to embody this interest in the manner of a musical score to indicate the specific manner in which the writer means his work to be read aloud. Such poetry can be found in Daphne Marlatt's *Vancouver poems* (1971). She had previously published *Frames* (1968), a narrative sequence of prose and poetry based on Hans Christian Andersen's 'The snow queen', and *Leaf leaf/s* (1969). Other books arising from these particular linguistic and poetic concerns are Mike Doyle's *Earth meditations: one to five* (1971), David Cull's *Cancer rising* (1970), and David McFadden's *Letters from the earth to the earth* (1969) and *Poems worth knowing* (1972). McFadden, a poet who writes of domesticity in matter-of-fact colloquial language, also published *Instant pleasure* (1972). Roy Kiyooka, a painter who also writes poetry, shows these same influences, but his own artistic concerns come into the poems along with his Japanese background. *Nevertheless these eyes* (1967) contains short lyrics, many of which arise from the poet's admiration for the English painter Stanley Spencer. *StoneD gloves* (1971) includes photographs by the author to expand these poems about the gloves of workers abandoned at the Expo site in Montreal.

The energetic Weed/Flower Press, operated by Nelson Ball in Toronto, published some interesting small chapbooks, including the work of Ball himself as well as collections by better-known poets: John Newlove's *What they say* (1967), Doug Fetherling's *My experience in the war* (1970), and David McFadden's *The poem poem* (1967). This press also brought out *Old friends' ghosts* (1971) by Victor COLEMAN, whose *Light verse* (1969) is made up of lyrics fashioned after the method of American poets Williams, Creeley, and Olson. At times Coleman's lyrical sequences turn into political areas, as in *Parking lots* (1972), a series of longer poems, and *America* (1972). (Coleman is associated with Coach House Press, referred to above.)

George JONAS writes with a European sensibility in his two books, *The absolute smile* (1967) and *The happy hungry man* (1970), which express an existential bleakness in undecorated, declarative stanzas and a mood of cynical, ironic wit. This mood appears also in Harry Howith's *Fragments of the dance* (1969). Although his irony is used against human love, it is sometimes undercut by love poems that are both playful and serious. Playfulness and comedy are a part of Joe ROSENBLATT's poetry in *Bumblebee dithyramb* (1972), which includes a selection from his two previous volumes, *The L.S.D. Leacock* (1968) and *Winter of the lunar moth* (1968). His animal poems show an exuberant delight in life, and this zest also comes through in his poems about people. He includes in *Bumblebee* some sharply directed political poems. The politics of nationalism and independence are present in Dennis Lee's two volumes, *The kingdom of absence* (1967) and *Civil elegies* (1968; rev. 1972). The first of these books talks of spiritual crisis and despair in somewhat personal terms, while the second extends into aspects of the Canadian national crisis. These poems, written in long-lined paragraphs, are filled with allusions to historical and cultural talismen as Lee meditates on loss of identity.

Delta, based in Montreal, published the work of some new poets in an interesting series of small pamphlets called *Quarterbacks*, as well as in more substantial collections such as *In the silence of the year* (1971) by Stephen Scobie and *Landfall* (1971) by Douglas Barbour, who also published a series of connected lyrics, *White* (1972), and an interesting personal narrative poem, *Poem as long as the highway* (1971). Glen Siebrasse, the moving spirit behind Delta, published his own *Man: unman* (1969) and *Jerusalem* (1971)—

philosophical poems that are carefully organized and sometimes thickly, even opaquely, textured.

Oberon Press, Ottawa, issued an interestingly catholic selection of poetry books, including Souster's *The years* and *So far so good* (see above); bp NICHOL's *ABC: the aleph beth book* (1971); *Catalan poems* (1971), a first volume by George McWhirter; *Skydeck* (1972) by Stuart MacKinnon, who had previously published *The welder's arc* (1969); and *Cannibals* (1972), the zestful and surrealistic poems of Stanley Cooperman whose work had already appeared in *The owl behind the door* (1968) and *The day of the parrot* (1969). The very personal poetry of David HELWIG is contained in three volumes, *Figures in a landscape* (1968), *The sign of the gunman* (1969), and *The best name of silence* (1972). Oberon also published the anthology *Made in Canada: new poems of the seventies* (1970), assembled under the auspices of the League of Canadian Poets and edited by Douglas Lochhead and Raymond Souster.

Under Fred Cogswell's direction Fiddlehead Poetry Books published an impressive list of poets and was particularly receptive to new poets. His list includes Al Pittman, Bernell MacDonald, Terry Crawford, Don Bailey, Joy Kogawa, Lloyd Abbey, Louis Cormier, Brenda Fleet, and Marc Plourde, among others. M. Lakshmi Gill in *Mind walls* (1971) shows a delicacy of phrasing in witty social poems and brief haiku-like poems. She followed this with some experiments with form in *First clearing* (1972), which also contains the sparse lyricism of her earlier book; the subtitle of this volume, 'An immigrant's tour of life', summarizes the thematic material. Cogswell was responsible for publishing long poetic sequences by Don Gutteridge concerned with re-creations of Canadian historical events and personages—*Riel* (1968) and *Death at Quebec* (1971)—as well as a series of autobiographical poems, *The village within* (1970).

Fiddlehead Press and Fred Cogswell have been associated with Fredericton for many years, and this Maritime city has long been a poetic centre. During our period it was active poetically with writers both established and new. Many of them have been mentioned as poets published by the Fiddlehead Press; others include Robert Cockburn, author of *Friday night Fredericton* (1968); Ken Thompson, who wrote *Hard explanations* (1968); and Travis Lane, who brought out *An inch or so of garden* (1970). William Bauer contributed original poems of hard-edged wit in *Cornet music for Plupy Shute* (1969) and *Everett Coogler* (1971). Robert Gibbs' poetry in *The road from here* (1968), *Earth charms heard so rarely* (1970), and *A dog in a dream* (1971) concentrated generally on personal memories in loosely structured verse that occasionally shows a sharp dramatic flair.

Besides Toronto and Vancouver, there were other cities as well as Fredericton that could be classed as centres for poetry. Kingston, the home of David Helwig and Stuart MacKinnon whose work has already been mentioned, is also the residence of Tom Marshall, whose *Silence of fire* (1969) contains a range of poems dealing with both public and private themes and showing a sensitive response to place, especially in the long sequence 'Macdonald Park' based on his reaction to the city of Kingston and its history. He continued this theme in the title sequence of his next volume *Magic water* (1971), which includes a long poem for several voices as well as some highly personal but rather fragmentary and private poems. Gail Fox dealt with personal themes in the sensitive and probing poems of *The dangerous season* (1970) as well as in a sequence of a somewhat analytic nature, *The royal collector of dreams* (1970). Joan FINNIGAN is another poet who has had some association with Kingston. Her poetry during this period covered a range of interests in structure and form. *Entrance to the greenhouse* (1968) is a sequence of small imagist lyrics about the cycle of time but with an emphasis on growth and life. The largest and most representative collection of her highly personal poetry is *It was warm and sunny when we set out* (1970). She also published a long sequence, *In the brown cottage at Loughborough Lake* (1970), that moves through moods of depression to a reconciliation with her present life.

Windsor, Ont., has emerged as a poetic centre. Nine poets were represented in *Contraverse* (Concorde Press, 1971), an anthology of Windsor poetry edited by Dorothy Farmiloe. An earlier anthology, *21x3* (1968), contains the work of three Windsor poets who have all published separate volumes. Dorothy Farmiloe in *The lost island* (1968), *Poems for apartment dwellers* (1971), and *Winter orange mood* (1972) expresses subjective responses to a wide variety of topics, with the poet firmly at the centre of poems generally written in a loose paragraph form. Eugene McNamara's *Outerings* (1971) and *Hard words* (1972) are both melancholic in tone, often focusing on the passing of time, enlivened by toughness of language and by humour. He has attempted two longer poetic sequences, *Love scenes* (1970) and *The Dillinger poems* (1971). His fullest and most representative collection to date is *Passages and other poems* (1972). Len Gasparini's poetry is contained in *Cutty Sark* (1970), *Tunnel to Detroit* (1971), and *The somniloquist* (1972). He organizes his poetry in neat, concise lyrics and employs sensitive and directly honest diction. Many of his poems derive their effective tone of ironic realism from the interplay of a commonplace toughness and offhand diction with stanzas that are almost traditional in form. He has also published *Pelee Island suite* (1972), a short sequence. Others associated with the Windsor poetry scene are Don Polson, whose *Wakening* (1971) and *Brief evening in a Catholic hospital* (1972) contain poems of direct response to his own life and family in a vein stemming from Raymond Souster; Richard Hornsey, whose *Going in* (1972) reveals a rich delight in family life in poems of brief lyrical insights; and C. H. Gervais, who has published many small volumes of personal lyrics, sometimes too privately personal, in short-lined notations. Some of his books are *St Anne* (1968), *Other marriage vows* (1969), *Something* (1969), and *A sympathy orchestra* (1970). His fullest collection is *Bittersweet* (1972), published by a new press in Guelph, Ont., Alive Press. Peter Stevens lived on the prairies for several years and his response to western Canada, together with his expressions of family life and marriage, are contained in *Nothing but spoons* (1969) and *A few myths* (1971). His most representative collection, which includes some longer poems and sequences, is *Bread crusts and glass* (1972).

Other poets whose work has not yet appeared in separate volumes but only in anthologies have tried to express their reactions to the plains of western Canada and to life in the settlements. Among the most notable of these new poets are Dale Zieroth, Sid Marty, and Andrew Suknaski. The last named has also been involved in experimental writing and graphic design in poetry. All three of these poets appear in *Storm warning* (1971) edited by Al Purdy, an anthology of the work of younger writers who might very well be the next generation of Canadian poets. Some of them, together with better-known Canadian writers, are represented in an anthology published in the United States, *New Canadian and American poetry* (1971).

3. *Experimental poetry*. John Robert Colombo, the chief practitioner in Canada of 'found' poetry in which he relines prose as poetry, published *John Toronto* (1969), *The great wall of China* (1970), and *The great San Francisco earthquake and fire* (1971). In this period Colombo also published *Neo poems* (1970), aphoristic writing in an original style of prose-poem. F. R. Scott's *Trouvailles* (1968) is another example of 'found' poetry.

This was simply one form of experimentation. Probably the most original and innovative poet of this period was bp nichol, whose output included a recording and loose leaves of poetry in the package *Journeying and the return* (1967). He also produced various slim pamphlets focusing on meaning and syllabic sound in a sequence of what the poet calls 'scraptures' that can also be written as prose—as in *Nights on prose mountain* (1970), a series of cards printed with single poems of Japanese simplicity, almost calligraphic in effect; *Still water* (1970); and graphic designs of the alphabet, *ABC: the aleph beth book* (1971). Nichol also wrote some small books of meditative lyrics; his most extensive writing in this mode was *The martyrology* (1972), a double-volume long poem linking aspects of his own life with the lives of imaginary saints. He edited an anthology of Canadian concrete poetry, *The cosmic chef* (1970). Bill BISSETT is another mainly experimental poet. He wrote a mixture of religious chants, reflecting on his concern for the ecological state of the world, that show something of an oriental influence. He has also written some vituperatively radical protest poems. Both sides of Bissett's poetic character exist in a selection of his poetry, *Nobody owns th earth* (1971) edited by Margaret Atwood and Dennis Lee. He has published several volumes of his work through the Blew Ointment Press, which he operates. It issued the writing of other poets who are loosely associated with Bissett and share many of the same concerns. Among them were Maxine Gadd, Bernard Lachance, Kent West, and Judith Copithorne, whose

Release (1969), *Rain* (1969), *Runes* (1970), and *Miss Tree's pillow book* (1971) were presented in her own calligraphy, with pen designs and illustrations interwoven with the words. Many examples of this experimental, orally oriented, and typographically adventurous poetry were collected in *West coast seen* (1969), edited by two poets who have also published volumes of their own, David Phillips and Jim Brown.

4. *Translations.* Translation has been a part of the Canadian poetry scene during these years. Nicholas Catanoy, a Romanian poet living in Fredericton, was instrumental in having Romanian poems translated by Canadian poets; some of these translations—by such diverse Canadian poets as Irving Layton, John Newlove, and Alden Nowlan—can be found in magazines and in their books. (Catanoy was also responsible for the translation of Canadian poems appearing in Romanian magazines.) Within Canada, *Volvox* (1971), edited by Charles Lillard and J. Michael Yates, is a collection of poems written in the unofficial languages and translated into English by the authors themselves or with the help of other Canadian poets. Kenneth McRobbie and Ilona Duczynska translated some of the brilliant verse of Ferenc Juhász in *The boy changed into a stag: selected poems 1949–1967* (1970). These difficult and impressive poems of family, elevated to the cosmic scale of the family of man, transcend moods of despair and the inevitability of death; they appear here in English versions that exist as poems in their own right.

Two new magazines devoted to translation have appeared: *Ellipse*, which gives translations of both English- and French-Canadian poetry, and *Contemporary poetry in translation*, which includes English versions of poems drawn from a wide variety of languages. John Glassco edited *The poetry of French Canada in translation* (1970), a useful anthology of French-Canadian poems translated by English-Canadian poets, including the editor himself. Fred Cogswell, who is also represented in the Glassco book, published two volumes of his versions of French-Canadian poetry: *One hundred poems of modern Quebec* (1970) and *A second hundred poems of modern Quebec* (1971). Walter Bauer's poetry, written in German while he was living in Canada, was translated by Henry Beissel and published in *The price of morning* (1969). PS

Poetry in French. The late sixties and early seventies have seen a strengthening of the sense of a tradition in French-Canadian poetry and the beginnings of a genuine diversification. The previous decade, with the publication in Luc Lacourcière's 'Collection du Nénuphar' of the works of poets such as Émile Nelligan, Paul Morin, Robert CHOQUETTE, and Hector de Saint-Denys GARNEAU, had marked the founding of a tradition: the poet need no longer be obsessed with his solitude, need no longer feel, as the poets of the first forty years of the century felt, that their poetry was 'un rêve charmant et inutile'. The collected verse appearing in the sixties and early seventies was published mainly by the house that since 1953 had done most to foster the cause of Québec poetry, Les Éditions de l'Hexagone, operated by a group of poets. They have followed their elegant edition of the *Poèmes* (1963) of Alain GRANDBOIS with equally elegant editions of the work of poets most of whom were in their forties and whose reputations were made: Roland GIGUÈRE's *L'âge de la parole* (1965); Jean-Guy PILON's *Comme eau retenue* (1968); Olivier Marchand's *Par détresse et tendresse* (1971); Paul-Marie LAPOINTE's *Le réel absolu* (1971); and Fernand OUELLETTE's *Poésie* (1972).

The consolidation of a tradition has been carried further by the critical assessment of the part played by Les Éditions de l'Hexagone in the fifties and sixties. The important reference work *La poésie canadienne-française* (1969)—volume IV of the Archives des lettres canadiennes—contains, in addition to a bibliography of French-Canadian poetry from its origins to 1967, a useful chapter on Hexagone by J.-L. Major. Gilles MARCOTTE's excellent study *Le temps des poètes* (1969) is largely devoted to the role of Hexagone and the poets of the group. Axel Maugey's *Poésie et société au Québec* (1972), though with a broader aim and a different approach, covers much of the same ground.

Elsewhere, François HERTEL offered an enlarged edition of his collected poems, *Poémes d'hier et d'aujourd'hui (1927–1967)* (1967). Other poets of an older generation to provide a sense of continuity in the ephemeral world of modern poetry have been Alfred DESROCHERS with *Elégies pour l'épouse en-allée* (1967), Félix-Antoine SAVARD with *Symphonie du Misereor* (1968) and *Le bouscueil* (1972), Rina LASNIER with *La salle des rêves* (1971), and Anne HÉBERT whose passionate and dreamlike evocation of love and violence in the prying, superstitious world of mid-nineteenth-century Québec in her novel *Kamouraska* (1970) reminds us of the intimate links between her prose and her poetry.

New editions, too, and critical editions of the poetry of the past are helping to make more real the sense of a tradition in Québec poetry. A facsimile edition of the first book of verse published in French in Canada, Michel Bibaud's *Épîtres, satires, chansons, épigrammes et autres pièces de vers* (1830, 1969), is now available. The University of Ottawa's centre for the study of French-Canadian civilization, in addition to its projected edition of the works of François-Xavier Garneau, has published the complete poetry of Octave Crémazie presented by Odette Condemine under the title *Oeuvres I: Poésies* (1972). A new edition of the poems of Jean-Aubert Loranger, *Les atmosphères suivi de poèmes* (1970), has introduced this little-known poet of the twenties to his 'true contemporaries', in the words of his editor Gilles Marcotte. 1971 saw the publication in a single volume (1320 pages), prepared with scrupulous care by Jacques BRAULT and Benoît Lacroix, of the *Oeuvres* of Hector de Saint-Denys Garneau.

One other volume of collected poems, whose appearance had been long awaited, also set its seal on the period in its own rather different way. In April 1970 the well-known though virtually unpublished poet Gaston MIRON was awarded the Prix de la revue *Études françaises* for that year and the prize was accompanied by the publication of *L'homme rapaillé*, a collection of his verse and prose. This book has since been awarded three further literary prizes: the Prix France-Canada (1970), the Grand Prix littéraire de la ville de Montréal (1971), and the Prix Belgique-Canada (1972). More than any other poet of his generation, Miron has inspired the young poets now writing in Québec by his encouragement and example. Poetry for him is the struggle with words against the non-poem, against the sense of dispossession he sees as the lot of the Québécois and that is the denial of the sense of identification with self in a specific time and place that makes poetry possible. In the public square, where he feels his place is rather than in the ivory tower of esoteric verse, Miron proclaims the refusal of that death in life that he calls 'la vie agonique'.

In the spirit of Miron's verse and of his stance as an artist, poetry met its public in the 'Nuit de la poésie' held in Montreal on 27–28 March 1970. The whole spectrum of Québec poetry was represented, from Claude Gauvreau to Claude PÉLOQUIN, in a range of moods from discreet confidences to wild vaticinations. A similar spectacle in early 1971 brought the poets into the public forum, this time to express in their 'poèmes et chants de la résistance' their feelings about the climate produced in Québec by the War Measures Act. (A number of poets were among the detainees—among others Gaston Miron; Jacques Larue-Langlois, whose *Plein cap sur la liberté: poèmes de prison* appeared in 1971; and Michel Garneau, author of *Language 1, 2, 3* (1972).) Some of the poems of Larue-Langlois were read; Georges Dor, Gilles VIGNEAULT, and Pauline Julien sang; there was a lot of instant theatre; and the accent was on satire provided by Michèle LALONDE, Yvon Deschamps, and Raoul DUGUAY. In 1972 Duguay, Péloquin, and Claude Saint-Germain took their 'Show de la parole' on the road. Gaston Miron's patient stand had paid off: poetry had become a public act.

The singer-poets have continued to enjoy enormous success and in some cases have further enhanced their reputations by publishing collections of songs, poems, and monologues. Gilles Vigneault has added four titles in recent years to an already lengthy list: *Les gens de mon pays* (1967), *Tam-ti-delam* (1967), *Ce que je dis c'est en passant* (1970), and *Les dicts du voyageur sédentaire* (1970). It has been estimated that Vigneault's published songs and poems have sold over 100,000 copies. Georges Dor has enjoyed a similar popularity and published two recent volumes: *Poèmes et chansons—1* (1968) and *Je chantepleure encore* (1969). Clémence Desrochers with *Sur un radeau d'enfant* (1969) and Félix LECLERC with *Cent chansons* (1970), Raymond Lévesque with *Quand les hommes vivront d'amour* (1968) and *Au fond du chaos* (1972) are other 'poètes de la chanson' to put their work into print.

Gilles Vigneault is one of the French-Canadian poets introduced to the French in Pierre Seghers' prestigious collection 'Poètes d'aujourd'hui', the others being Hector de Saint-Denys Garneau, Alain Grandbois, Rina Lasnier, Anne Hébert, and Félix Leclerc. Special numbers of several French reviews surveying contemporary literature in Canada have given pride of place to the poets—*Lettres nouvelles* (1967), *Europe* (1969), *Revue d'histoire littéraire de la France* (1969), and *Revue d'esthétique* (1969)—serving further to bring international recognition for French-Canadian literature.

The sixties has also been a period of reflection on the nature of the developments in function and theme undergone by the French-Canadian poetic tradition. Gaston Miron offers a theory of the changing role of poetry, seeing three stages since the Second World War. From the surrealist manifesto *Refus global* in 1948 to 1956, isolated poets were discovering the power of an imagination set free. From 1956, when the experience of Hexagone was beginning to give a group of poets the feeling of sharing a common national adventure, Québec poetry gradually gained its independence. With the appearance of literary reviews such as *La Barre du jour* and *Quoi* in 1965–7, the phase of definition for the collective ideology, stated by poets and in poetic terms, was over. From that point Québec poets were free to select individual styles and objectives. The poetry of the late sixties and early seventies is marked by this new-found freedom to explore, experiment, and create. This evolution is illustrated perfectly by the literary career of Paul CHAMBERLAND. In *Genèse* (1963) the individual consciousness stirs to life. *Terre Québec* (1964), *L'afficheur hurle* (1965), and *L'inavouable* (1968) declare the poet's involvement in Québec's self-determination in every sense. In his most recent work, *Éclats de la pierre noire d'où rejaillit ma vie* (1972), Chamberland no longer sees the need to contribute to what Jacques GODBOUT calls 'le texte national', the realization through literature of the spiritual emancipation of the people of Québec, and feels free to explore a private mystical world.

One view of the evolution of the thematic content of French-Canadian poetry has been provided by Pierre Châtillon, the poet and teacher whose long silence after the publication of *Les cris* (1957) was broken by a revised edition of the same text in 1968, followed by *Soleil de bivouac* (1969) and *Le journal d'automne de Placide Martel* (1971). In volume IV of the *Archives des lettres canadiennes* he studies the theme of fire in Québec poetry, which has replaced gradually the still waters of silence, despair, loneliness, and alienation; the pools of the forest; the islands of the night; the frozen fixity and barrenness of the cold north. Fire, the Promethean revolt against the inevitable, with its triple symbols, each implying both life and destruction—the sun, blood, and woman seen as the object of sexual desire—has erupted into this still cold world like 'un geyser de feu' (Grandbois). This theme and its importance for the poets of the fifties and sixties is beautifully illustrated in Fernand OUELLETTE's commentaries on his own poetry in *Les actes retrouvés* (1970). This 'marche au soleil' (Ouellette), this 'marche à l'amour' (Miron), explains the presence in recent Québec poetry of the poetry of the north, a poetry of revolt that Ouellette elsewhere calls 'une voix en naissance qui hurle' and 'le délire de l'explosion du sang dans la chair', and of poetry that finds in an eroticism freely expressed the celebration of the reconciliation of Québec man with himself. Examples of the latter may be found in Ouellette's own *Dans le sombre* (1967) and Chamberland's *L'inavouable* (1968). Other poets of the fifties and sixties whose work receives fuller comment elsewhere in this *Supplement* and who have been active in the period 1967–72 are Jacques Brault, Cécile CLOUTIER, Fernand DUMONT, Michèle LALONDE, Gatien LAPOINTE, Andrée MAILLET, Suzanne PARADIS, Claude Péloquin, Jean-Guy Pilon, Yves PRÉFONTAINE, and Pierre TROTTIER.

Other poets who have continued to add to their work during these years are a number of women writers. Monique BOSCO, poet of elegant melancholy punctuated with racy flashes of pique, published *Jéricho* (1971). Marie Laberge in *L'hiver à brûler* (1968), *Soleil d'otage* (1970), and *Reprendre souffle* (1972) introduced into her poetry of tender nostalgia discordant allusions to an importunate, ugly reality. Gemma Tremblay, author of nine collections of verse in twelve years, has added *Les feux intermittents* (Paris, 1968), *Les seins gorgés* (1969), and *Souffles du midi* (1972), writing most of this poetry, as the last title suggests, in the south of France. Leaving behind the stifling sense of outrage Montreal sometimes gave her, she can give unrestrained expression to the torrent of images she feels in her veins.

Among the men, Gilbert Langevin is founder and director of the Éditions Atys and a poet and songwriter. He has published nine collections of poems since 1959, the most recent being *Un peu plus d'ombre au dos de la falaise* (1966), *Noctuaire* (1967), *Pour une aube*

(1967), *Ouvrir le feu* (1971), and *Stress* (1971). He means his rancorous poetry to be 'agressive, délivrante, prémonitoire', a nagging provocation, a call to vigilance in a world where fantasy, disgust, apathy, and death constantly invite despair. Neologisms, shock-words, and fractured rhythms keep him from the clutches of 'la Yesmanie'. Guy ROBERT—teacher, art critic, literary critic, poet, and publisher at the Éditions du Songe—has added to his already impressive output *Une mémoire déjà* (1968) and *Québec se meurt*, *Trans-apparence*, *Ailleurs se tisse*, and *Intrême-Orient* (1969). The love poems in André MAJOR's collection *Poèmes pour durer* (1969) are often suffused with restrained bitterness and a grating edge that echo the persistent 'difficulté d'être' of the Québécois.

Québec poetry continues to evolve through the activities of poets connected with publishing houses like Hexagone or Déom or with literary magazines. PARTI PRIS (1963–8), a literary and political review, continued the themes and attitudes of the Hexagone group through the writings of a large number of poets of whom the best known were Paul Chamberland, Gaston Miron, André Major, and André BROCHU. Malcolm Reid in his *The shouting signpainters* (1972), taking his title from that of a long poem of Paul Chamberland, tells the fascinating story of *parti pris*, and a special number of *La Barre du jour*, No. 31–2 (1972), contains reflections by the members of that group on the adventure they shared. The publishers of *La Barre du jour* and *Liberté* and their contributors continue to fulfil the role played in the past by *parti pris*—that of serving as a focal point for poetic creation and experiment. Sometimes in recent years this experimentation has taken extreme forms—Claude Gauvreau's thunder of syllables; Raoul Duguay's jazz poetry accompanied by manifestos on 'le stéréo-poème audio-visuel'; Luc Racine's poetry inspired by serial composition in music; Marie-Francine Hébert's typographical experiments; Guy Robert's concrete poetry; Roger Soublière's poetry in a tin can for the supermarket age; as well as the poem-collage, the poem-gag, and even the poem-trip. The suicide of one of these experimenters, Claude Gauvreau, in 1971 was an event in the world of Québec poetry commented on with great sympathy and frankness in the press and followed by the production of his controversial play *Les oranges sont vertes*, the promise of the imminent publication of his complete works, and discussions of his role in the group of signatories of the surrealist manifesto of 1948, *Refus global*. (See *Culture vivante* 22, 1971; *Le Devoir*, 24 July 1971 and 2 September 1972.)

A number of young poets, among them several gifted and prolific writers, have continued to explore the central theme described by Pierre Châtillon—finding expression in the tension between the atavistic cold, from which they burst out in a fury of desire, and what Fernand Ouellette calls 'la démence charnelle'. Among these, Juan Garcia, Moroccan born and now living in Spain, was awarded the Prix de la revue *Études françaises* 1971 for his *Corps de gloire*, which includes his earlier *Alchimie du corps* (1967) and other poems. Pierre Morency, too, exploits this theme in terms almost identical with those in which we have just defined it, as his titles suggest: *Poèmes de la froide merveille de vivre* (1967), *Poèmes de la vie déliée* (1968), and *Au nord constamment de l'amour* (1970). The last volume contains his *Poèmes de la froide merveille de vivre*, which won the Prix Du Maurier in 1968. Others are continuing in the wake of Paul-Marie Lapointe, Ouellette, and Préfontaine. Michel Beaulieu, one-time director of Éditions Estérel, is the epitome of the dedicated writer and one of the most industrious of the younger poets. For him writing is 'un travail acharné' and some of this patient persistency and conscious determination is apparent in *Erosions* (1967), *0:00* (1969), *Charmes de la fureur* (1970), and *Paysage* (1971). In 1972 he won the Prix de la revue *Études françaises* for *Variables* (1973), which contains a study of the poet by G.-A. Vachon. Marcel Bélanger, with *Prélude à la parole* (1967) and *Plein-vent* (1971), affirms his faith in anxiety—the exemplary anxiety of the artist aware of his situation as a stranger in the modern world—as an antidote to the threat of annihilation. This revolt expresses itself in the nervous energy and muscularity of his verse. Pierre Mathieu—author of *Ressac* (1969), *Interlune* (1970), and *Mots dits québécois* (1971)—is one of those who have benefited from the sense of identification with Québec that earlier poets had discovered and affirmed; in the confidence this has given him he can begin to lay claim to a certain happiness. Alexis Lefrançois, whose early poems appeared in *Liberté* (no. 61, 1969) and *Études françaises* (vol. 5, no. 4, 1969), has published *Calcaires* (1971) and

36 petites choses pour la 51 (1972). Particularly in the second work—a collection of monologues printed on pages shaped like the back of a bus, the 51—he shows himself to be a poet of assurance and originality. Beneath a superficial playfulness he offers a world-worn wisdom and a plea for simplicity in an age of complexity that strike a new note in French Canada.

More promising for the future are the efforts of those young poets who, impatient with the uniformity, complaisance, and lack of radical ideas in recent French-Canadian poetry, have attempted to renew poetic language by smashing the shackles of the conventional logic of grammar and creating surprise effects through unusual clashes of vocabulary. Guy Robert has described some of the qualities of this 'langage éclaté' in the following terms in a review of Germain Beauchamp's *La messe ovale* (1969): 'a supple and thoughtful vocabulary, an articulate and inventive syntax, an evident system of symbolic reference, a "literary" distancing displaying a certain irony with regard to literal language and an intelligent, playful attitude towards the conventions implied by the network of passive emotional responses between reader and writer.' The poetry of Nicole Brossard, one of the editors of *La Barre du jour*, in *L'écho bouge beau* (1968), *Suite logique* (1970), and *Le centre blanc* (1970), may well serve to characterize this new sensitivity to the deceptive efficacy of the act of writing and to the need to remain constantly alert to the hidden snares inherent in literary conventions, conscious of the finality and inflexibility of the printed page. Some of the poetry of Luc Racine in *Opus I* (1969), *Villes* (1970), and *Les jours de mai* (1971) has this same slightly awkward grace and sharp awareness, as does that of the young Sherbrooke poet Gaston Gouin, who died in a road accident in the summer of 1970. He wrote *Temps obus* (1969) and *J'il de noir* (1971).

Gradually, in displaying a greater diversity, the poetry of Québec is finding a new maturity, the medium is becoming the message, and the poem is beginning to speak in its own right. CRPM

Political writings in English. Not many years ago one could easily pack one's entire library of recent additions to Canadian political writings in a small briefcase. For a variety of reasons—the rapid development of the teaching of the social sciences in Canada, the more aggressive publishing policy of Canadian-owned and Canadian-based companies, and the conclusion of a lengthy period of introspection on the part of many concerned with Canada's internal, continental, and international condition—the situation has changed dramatically. There are now many books on Canadian politics of two main types: solid scholarly monographs that elaborate features of the political system hitherto often merely sketched by the authors of general texts; and commentaries on current problems, often in the form of edited collections when academics are involved, but usually representing a rich variety of reactions to events.

1. *Québec.* There was surely no more spirited exchange of views than arose over the FLQ's kidnapping of Cross and Laporte and the federal government's use of regulations under the War Measures Act to deal with the crisis. Marcel Rioux's *Quebec in question* (1971) brought the analysis of the growing independentist mood of Québécois up to date in its English edition (translated by James Boake) by including an account of the events of late 1970, complete with lengthy extracts of the FLQ communiqués. Although he did not commend the FLQ for its action, it was clear that for the author Ottawa's 'over-reaction' helped to carry the separatist movement one step further down the road to independence. Interestingly enough, no book appeared from English Canada to defend the Trudeau government's action. Indeed, both Denis Smith's *Bleeding hearts . . . bleeding country* (1971) and Ron Haggart's and Aubrey Golden's *Rumours of war* (1971) ran counter to the heavily supportive trend of opinion in the country as a whole (especially in the early months), either in seriously questioning the appropriateness of the government's response to genuine bargaining with the FLQ over the terms of Cross's release, or by expressing concern for the damaging longrun effect on the quality of democracy in Canada as well as for the prospects of Québec's continuation within confederation. Abraham Rotstein's collection of articles from the January 1971 *Canadian Forum*, published as *Power corrupted: the October crisis and the repression of Quebec* (1971), told all in the title. John Saywell's *Quebec '70* (1971)—an attempt to look at

events in Québec 'without the benefit of hindsight or the danger of speculation'—succeeds in presenting an interpretation favourable to the governments' actions, though this stance is implicit. Not at all subtle in its defense of the War Measures Act was Gérard Pelletier's *The October crisis* (1971). For him, critics of firm action were naive or mistaken: the danger in the turbulent situation was not the threat of the FLQ as such but the potential damage of right-wing totalitarianism, brought on by a weakening of support for the current régime by great numbers of people consciously or unconsciously sympathetic to the FLQ.

There were other books on more general aspects of Québec politics. Prime Minister Trudeau himself contributed three works—*Federalism and the French Canadians* (1968), *Approaches to politics* (1970), and *Conversations with Canadians* (1972). The latter is a slight piece, being collections of remarks on diverse subjects, including his favourite theme of the 'just society'. However, the earlier books are an important contribution to the contemporary debate, for they set out the basic political philosophy of a man who not only wrote very lucidly but enjoyed the decidedly rare distinction of being able to implement his views as public policy.

The views of another politician, René Lévesque, as yet somewhat removed from political power, provided the chief opposition to Trudeau's Québec position. *Option Quebec*, which appeared in both English and French in 1968, set out the main electoral planks for the Parti Québécois and developed the arguments for the desirability of an economic union between an independent Québec and the remaining Canadian state. A. Brichant's *Option Canada: the economic implications of separatism for the province of Quebec* (1968), published by the Canada Committee—a Québec-based group organized to counter the separatists' message—summoned up an impressive list of economic consequences designed to give pause to potential converts.

In addition there were several attempts to interpret political events in Québec: Richard Jones's *Community in crisis: French-Canadian nationalism in perspective* (1967; rev. 1972) presented the most thorough analysis of developments within Québec. E. M. Corbett's *Quebec confronts Canada* (1967) attempted to do the same but with less success. The Glendon College Forum's *Quebec year eight* (1968) recorded the presentations of several speakers at a weekend conference at which the seeming inevitability of Québec's separation emerged as the *leit-motif*. Marcel Faribault offered his 'thoughts on the mounting crisis' in *Unfinished business* (1967); Ramsay COOK drew together an anthology of nationalist writings in *French Canadian nationalism* (1969), many of which were made available in translation for the first time. Robert Chodos and Nick Auf der Maur edited *Quebec: a chronicle 1968–1972* (1972), which reviewed the period from a leftist perspective. R. M. Burns' collection of essays in *One country or two?* (1971) looked boldly at the consequences of Québec's separation for Canada and for relations between the new states that would result.

Pierre Vallières's autobiography appeared in a translation by Joan Pinkham as *White niggers of America* (1971) and exposed unilingual readers to the confused but brilliant mind of a Québec separatist revolutionary. Later Gustave Morf's study of the case histories of several young terrorist prisoners in Québec emerged in English, with an additional chapter written after the FLQ crisis, as *Terror in Quebec: case studies of the FLQ* (1970). Vallières's *Choose!* (1972) outlined the basis of his 'tactical realignment' and, in revealing his support for the Parti Québécois, affirmed his belief in the inevitability of gradualness. *The shouting signpainters: a literary and political account of Quebec revolutionary nationalism* (1972)—which discusses Vallières, the PARTI PRIS writers, and other creative nationalists—is a vivid discursive account of the lively intellectual climate of French Montreal in the late 1960s.

2. *Foreign domination*. Consciousness of the disadvantages of extensive American ownership of the Canadian economy—raised in a still muted form by the report of a government task force under the chairmanship of Melville Watkins, *Foreign ownership and the structure of Canadian industry* (1968)—led to a minor renaissance of political economy and to a considerable outpouring of critical comment on Canada's 'colonial relationship' with the United States. It was the type of reaction that—as it was broadened in Ian Lumsden's collection, *Close the 49th parallel* (1970), to include concern for American cultural and political influences—made the continentalist themes of Stanley R. Tupper's and Douglas

Bailey's *One continent—two voices* (1967) decidedly unfashionable. The Lumsden book, edited for the University League for Social Reform and sub-titled 'The americanization of Canada', must have contributed simultaneously to the heightening of awareness of the problems and to some despair that anything would be done about them. If the ULSR book suffered from a certain unevenness as a result of many voices, Kari Levitt's *Silent surrender* (1970) did not escape the defects of a single author's overly zealous effort to force the entire analysis of the multinational corporation in Canada into the suggestive conceptual framework of Harold Innis's metropolitan-hinterland model. Still, this study was impressive, the more so for representing an economic analysis that was integrated into a socio-political context. The left-wing critique of Canada's colonial position in Lumsden's and Levitt's books was further developed in *Capitalism and the national question in Canada* (1972) edited by Gary Teeple. George GRANT's *Technology and empire* (1969) offered a sharp contrast to the political economist's concerns; here Professor Grant continued the reflections he began in his earlier book, *Lament for a nation* (1965), on Canada's place in North America. Ramsay Cook's *The maple leaf forever* (1972) focused on the political thought of Grant and Trudeau and questioned the wisdom of the emerging nationalism in Canada.

Robin Mathews and James Steele brought together a collection of articles and documents that drew attention to the extent of the involvement of American citizens in higher education in Canada in *The struggle for Canadian universities* (1969). Dave GODFREY and Melville Watkins also put together an interesting set of readings, *Gordon to Watkins to you: a documentary of the battle for control of our economy* (1970), which was especially valuable for its listing of Canadian firms that were subject to take-over from 1963 to 1969. As Watkins moved to the radical fringe on the Americanization issue, Abraham Rotstein moved to the centre of prominence, first as the contributor of a forward to an otherwise somewhat obscure book by Gunnar Adler-Karlson on the subject of 'Functional socialism' but published in Canada under the title *Reclaiming the Canadian economy* (1970)—presumably because of its practical suggestions for exercising social control over foreign ownership without public ownership; then as general editor of the *Canadian Forum*'s dramatically leaked version of the long-expected government report on American ownership and control of the Canadian economy, published as *A citizen's guide to the Herb Gray report* (1971); and later as co-editor with Jerry Lax of a collection of readings, *Independence: the Canadian challenge* (1972). Others had joined the cause. W. Eric Harris's *Canada's last chance!* (1970) argued that Canada should apply for economic but not political membership in the Common Market and thereby offset its dependence on U.S. investment. W. H. Pope in *Elephant and the mouse* (1971) presented a perspective on the problem aptly summarized by the title. A government review of the issue finally emerged in 1972 as a publication of the Government of Canada (*Foreign direct investment in Canada*) with no specific authorship and with the claim that it was 'not a statement of government policy nor should it be assumed that the government endorses all aspects of the analysis'. It was left to later official proposals for policy implementation to reveal how accurate the disclaimer was.

Closely related to the American ownership theme, but singled out for particular attention by a few authors, was the problem of Canadian natural resource policy. James Laxer was first off the mark with *The energy poker game* (1970), which rejected Walter Gordon's 'buy-back' approach to resource industries and favoured outright nationalization. In *Forced growth* (1971) Philip Mathias ably documented several of the major problems associated with government-subsidized natural-resource exploitation projects as part of a general program of economic development designed to offset regional disparities, and warned against expecting substantial employment benefits from the investment. The concerns of the environmentalist were added to those of the economic nationalist in *Natural resource policy in Canada* (1972) by Thomas Burton. The author hoped that a long-term change in values (chiefly away from the belief that bigger is necessarily better) would provide the framework within which a more rational policy would be worked out; in the meantime he favoured greater social control of individuals and groups, in line with the theme of functional socialism developed by Alder-Karlson.

3. *Indian policy*. The Liberal government's *White paper on Indian policy* (1969)—which revealed the government's intention to reverse past policies and at the same time not recognize claims to aboriginal rights—drew a variety of protests, the most articulate of which were Harold Cardinal's *The unjust society* (1969), Edgar Dosman's *Indians: the urban dilemma* (1972), and Heather Robertson's *Reservations are for Indians* (1970). Dosman's book was more than a critique of the government's past policy and of the proposed amendments of the White Paper: it was a careful analysis of the plight of the Indian who had left the reserve for the city—a concern hitherto rather neglected in favour of the slightly more obvious difficulties of the Indian on the reservation.

4. *Political ideas*. Generally speaking, critical comment on Canadian politics was from the left, but there were a number of important exceptions. E. C. Manning in *Political realignment* (1967) appealed for an exploration of the political possibilities of a Progressive Conservative/Social Credit alliance, and Paul Hellyer's *Agenda: a plan for action* (1971) presented the ideas along which the author hoped a new political party composed of disgruntled Liberals and Conservatives might be formed. John Diefenbaker's *These things we treasure* (1972) criticized the alleged decline of Parliament since his stewardship, particularly because of Mr Trudeau's attitudes and behaviour. Donald Smiley's *Canadian political nationality* (1967) combined a political scientist's overview of developments in Canadian federalism with a moderate partisan's prescription. After rejecting the particularism of the regional approach to Canadian politics, Smiley argues the need for a sense of political nationality in Canada strong enough to draw everything together and concluded that the post-Diefenbaker Conservatives offered the nation the best hope in this respect.

Charles Taylor's *The pattern of politics* (1970) was the most important critical statement from a single author on the left. Taking up some of the themes arising from John Porter's analysis of Canadian society (*The vertical mosaic*) and Gad Horowitz's exploration of the centrist nature of the Liberal party in Canada (*Canadian labour in politics*), Taylor made explicit the different stands on current issues that follow from adopting the alternative stances of the politics of concensus or the politics of polarization. Taylor was an important contributor to a book of essays that he edited along with Laurier LaPierre, Jack McLeod, and Walter Young entitled *Essays on the left* (1971) and compiled as a tribute to T. C. Douglas, then retiring leader of the New Democratic Party. The diversity of viewpoint and preoccupation of the professoriate in Canada was as well revealed by this *Festschrift* as it was in two other collections of the period under review: *Agenda '70* (1970), edited by Trevor Lloyd and Jack McLeod, and *Visions 2020* (1970) edited by Stephen Clarkson. D. I. Roussopoulos' collection of essays, *The new left in Canada* (1970), indicated the concerns of younger critics on the further extreme of the political spectrum in Canada. The essays reflect one of the significant radical themes of the period: the link between the need for a greater participation by students in university government and the need for participating in the system as a whole.

5. *Leadership and elections*. The emergence of Trudeau as Liberal leader and the parliamentary majority secured for his party in the 1968 election excited considerable comment. John Harbron's *This is Trudeau* (1968) and Douglas Stuebing's *Trudeau: a man for tomorrow* (1968) concentrated on the biographical details of the colourful prime minister, whereas Martin Sullivan in *Mandate '68* (1968) detailed both the leadership convention and the subsequent election campaign. Although the subtitle to Donald Peacock's *Journey to power: the story of a Canadian election* (1968) suggested that it was concerned with the general election, this event was hardly the book's major focus. More valuable was his story of Trudeau before the leadership convention, told from the vantage point of a special assistant to the then prime minister, Lester Pearson.

Interest in the 1972 election was considerable, but the preoccupation with personality had waned a little. Three books are noteworthy. Jim McDonald and Jack MacDonald put together a number of contributions written by their fellow Parliamentary Interns as the *Canadian voter's guide book* (1972). If this collection underplayed the socio-economic bases of Canadian politics in favour of the issues of the campaign and an analysis of their impact in various regions, John Meisel's *Working papers on Canadian politics* (1972) offered a useful balance. Based on extensive post-election surveys of public opinion in 1965 and 1968, Professor Meisel's discussion of party images and of the relationship between language use and political behaviour offered an intriguing background to the eventual election outcome. W. A. Wilson's *The Trudeau question* (1972) provided the general reader with an attractively written and illustrated overview of the interplay of issues and personalities that preceded the campaign, as well as some 'hard data' on the electoral record of the political parties since 1953.

Elections in general attracted more attention than ever before from academics. James Murray Beck took on the enormously difficult task of assessing every federal election up to and including the 'Trudeaumania' election of 1968 in *Pendulum of power* (1968). Owen Carrigan's compilation, *Canadian party platforms 1867–1968* (1968), served as a good companion to it. Professor Terrence Qualter's *The election process in Canada* (1970) was descriptive in another sense: it provided detailed summaries of the legal and behavioural differences in Canadian electoral practices, not only over time but, especially useful, among provinces. William Lyons' *One man—one vote* (1970) was by contrast a more narrowly focused study of the politics of redistribution, in particular of the redistribution of seats in the House of Commons prior to the 1968 election—the first independent redistribution in Canadian history. Jean Laponce's *People vs politics* (1969)—a study of political opinions of the constituents of one federal riding, Vancouver-Burrard, in the mid-1960s—revealed how much understanding of the Canadian political process could be extracted from subjecting the complex interrelationships of social and attitudinal characteristics to intensive and sophisticated analysis. Another angle on Canadian elections was provided by K. Z. Paltiel's *Political party financing in Canada* (1970), which drew heavily from the 1966 *Report of the Committee on Election Expenses* of which Paltiel was the research director. The pattern of continuously spiraling election expenditures is documented with information on the activities of the parties in the 1968 general election.

Public opinion in Canada had not received much attention until Mildred Schwartz published the results of her analysis of Canadian Institute of Public Opinion data since the Second World War in *Public opinion and Canadian identity* (1968). This analysis provided concrete evidence for the generalization that Canada is a polity lacking many widely shared values and beliefs. John Johnstone's analysis of the opinions of young Canadians thirteen to twenty years of age, *Young people's images of Canadian society* (1969), provided further evidence of cultural diversity.

Interest groups—or pressure groups, as they are also called—had been virtually ignored in Canada since S. D. CLARK's study of the Canadian Manufacturers Association in the pre-Second World War period. David Kwavnick's *Organized labour and pressure politics* (1972), which analyses the impact of the Canadian Labour Congress on the federal government in the period 1956 to 1968, was therefore an important addition to the literature on the Canadian political process. *Citizen participation* (1971), edited by James Draper, presented a variety of views on this hitherto neglected topic.

In many ways the most significant political writings centred on the question of where political power lay in the Canadian system. Journalist commentators made a great deal of the impact of Prime Minister Trudeau's personality and preferences on the conduct of politics in Ottawa. The 'presidentialization' of Canadian politics, reflected allegedly in the growth of the Prime Minister's Office and the increasing significance of the Privy Council Office staff in the policy-planning process, was the concern of Walter Stewart's *Shrug: Trudeau in power* (1971), Lubor J. Zink's *Trudeaucracy* (1972), and, to a lesser extent, Anthony Westell's *Paradox: Trudeau as prime minister* (1972). Thomas Hockin's *Apex of power* (1971) brought together the views—many previously published—of academics on the same subject, but with rather less agreement on the ultimate interpretation. Peter Newman's *Distemper of our times* (1968) had as its manifest subject a retrospective account of the political battle both inside and outside the House of Commons between Mr Pearson and Mr Diefenbaker, the fading leaders of the two major parties. At another level, however, it provided—because of the author's proximity to so many valuable sources of information in the nation's capital—an intriguing insight into the subtleties of the exercise of power at the top. It therefore represented one of the most substantial political books of the period under review.

6. *The bureaucracy and policy formation.* Even more important, however, were the studies of the role of the bureaucracy in policy-making and—in the case of one of the few major studies of the political process of Canadian federalism—of the interaction of bureaucrat and politician at the federal and provincial levels. A major exponent of the second theme was Donald Smiley, first in his study for the Laurendeau-Dunton Commission, *Constitutional adaptation and Canadian federalism since 1945* (1970), and later in his more wide-ranging book, *Canada in question: federalism in the '70's* (1972). To the notion of 'executive federalism' —the type of federal-provincial relations Canadians have become accustomed to in which the legislatures in the provinces and at the federal level appear to have little or nothing to contribute—was added a broader framework in which differences in party organization and financing and varying concentrations of foreign ownership of the Canadian economy are linked in a dynamic conception of Canadian federalism. It was in this context that Richard Simeon's extremely able case studies of federal-level policy-making, *Federal-provincial diplomacy* (1972), appeared. In this book the Canada Pension Plan, the Victoria Conference's unsuccessful attempt at constitutional reform, and the work of the Tax Structure Committee are each the subject of extremely careful analysis based not only on the published record, but—crucially for the type of decision-making study in question—on interviews with scores of civil servants and politicians. Political scientists will need more case studies of a similar type before the general synthesis can be written, but the trail is now well and truly broken.

Bruce Doern and Peter Aucoin threw further light on the role of the non-politician decision-makers in Ottawa in *The structure of policy-making in Canada* (1971). In addition to their treatment of the inter-relationship of the Prime Minister's Office, the Privy Council Office, the Treasury Board, and the Finance Department, they contributed valuable pieces on the place of advisory committees in the policy-making process as well as a critique of the changing function of government White Papers. Bruce Doern's *Science and politics in Canada* (1972) explored the long-neglected question of the inter-relationship between organized science and government in Canada. Finally we may notice three further books on various aspects of the federal bureaucracy, all resulting from studies commissioned in one way or another by the government: Kathleen Archibald's report for the Public Service Commission on job discrimination and employment opportunities, *Sex and the public service* (1970); Gilles Lalande's report for the Royal Commission on Bilingualism and Biculturalism, *The Department of External Affairs and biculturalism* (1969); and a further study for the latter commission by Michel Chevalier and James R. Taylor, *Dynamics of adaptation in the federal civil service* (1971).

7. *Foreign policy.* Canada's foreign policy, and particularly the question of Canada's position in NATO, attracted a good deal of attention. Typical of the discussion from within the universities was Stephen Clarkson's selection of essays, *An independent foreign policy for Canada* (1969). Written almost exclusively from the point of view of critics who condemned prevailing Canadian foreign policy, it examined the possibilities of non-alignment with NATO, withdrawal from NORAD, and the desirability of adopting new peace-keeping initiatives. The essential message was that 'quiet diplomacy' was obsolete and that if it ever was effective it now meant tacit endorsement of U.S. foreign policy. These were also the themes of *Alliances and illusions* (1969) by Lewis Hertzman, Thomas Hockin, and John Warnock, and of John Warnock in *Partner to behemoth* (1970). John Gellner in *Canada in NATO* (1970) and Peyton Lyon in *NATO as a diplomatic instrument* (1971) presented the more orthodox and ultimately prevailing view that Canada's ties with NATO offered valuable entrées to international councils that Canada could ill afford to give up; besides, the defense of Europe was said to require Canada's continued contribution. *Canada and three crises* (1968) by Robert W. Reford examined Canada's role in the offshore-islands crisis of 1954–5, Suez in 1956, and Cuba in 1962, and discovered a useful role for Canada in all three. *Peacekeeping: international challenge and Canadian response* (1968) by Alastair Taylor, David Cox, and J. L. Granatstein offered a further collection of views on a possible role for the Canadian Armed Forces if the NATO obligations were reduced or abandoned altogether, and Harald Von Riekhoff's *NATO: issues and prospects* (1967) added yet another interpretation of the controversy.

The Trudeau government invited broader participation than had been customary in Canadian foreign-policy formulation when it issued as a kind of White Paper six separate booklets under the general title *Foreign policy for Canadians* (1970). The process that Barry Farrell correctly described in *The making of Canadian foreign policy* (1969) certainly did not leave much room for initiatives from the public or even from the legislature. Bruce Thordarson's case study of the policy review, *Trudeau and foreign policy: a study in decision-making* (1972), was therefore less significant for its confirmation of the importance of the prime minister in the total picture than it was for the suggestion of some impact through caucus of the Liberal backbenchers who participated in the Standing Committee on External Affairs and National Defence. Although this case study does not fully pin down the ambiguous role of Mitchell Sharp as minister of external affairs, the analysis constitutes an important addition to the study of the Canadian political process begun by other young Canadian political scientists, with the concentration on the pattern of decision-making at the top. Peter Dobell, director of the Parliamentary Centre for Foreign Affairs and Foreign Trade, which assisted MPs with their attempt to comprehend the issues involved in the review, explained the changes in *Canada's search for new roles* (1972), a book meant for British readers but that is very useful to Canadians both as a commentary on the process and as the product of policy formulation. It is well complemented by Dale C. Thomson's and Roger Swanson's *Canadian foreign policy: options and perspectives* (1972), since the latter deliberately aims at filling the gaps for the non-specialist left by the White Paper.

Defensive alignments were not the sole preoccupation of students of Canada's role in international relations. Clyde Sanger examined the effectiveness of Canada's external-aid programs in *Half a loaf* (1970) and found Canada's 'semi-role' a great deal better than nothing, and Donald Waterfield in *Continental water boy* (1970) scrutinized the effects of the Columbia River Treaty on Canada and discovered a great many long-term disadvantages, despite the apparent short-term cash benefits for British Columbia. Finally, Thomas Hockin compiled a collection of papers, *The Canadian condominium* (1972), which, in bringing together both domestic issues and external policy, confirmed the trend implicit in the analysis of the Canadian condition begun by political economists concerned with Canada's economic relationship with its dominant continental co-tenant, the United States.

8. *Provincial and local politics.* Most of the books on politics in Canada in our six-year period dealt with national questions or processes at the federal level. However, several were concerned with municipal and provincial or regional politics and as such they added substantially to a rather underdeveloped literature. Sid Noel's *Politics in Newfoundland* (1971) and Fred Schindeler's *Responsible government in Ontario* (1969) are both solid scholarly works, the former completing the monographic treatment of the Atlantic provinces in the Canadian Government Series, the latter—with its critical assessment of executive-legislative relations in the most populous province—turning the spotlight of academic inquiry on a too-long neglected aspect of the Canadian political system. The Toronto *Telegram*'s 'Canada's '70 Team' reported on the situation in the regions in several books: *British Columbia: the great divide* (1969); *The prairies: alienation and anger* (1969); *Ontario: the linch pin* (1969); *Quebec: the threat of separatism* (1969); *The Atlantic provinces: struggle for survival* (1969); and the overview, *A summary coast to coast* (1969). The series added up to an invaluable record of the diversity of viewpoint and preoccupation in Canada at the end of the decade. This diversity was explored in a different manner through a set of ten separate analyses of the party systems in each of the provinces in Martin Robin's collection *Canadian provincial politics* (1972), with equally interesting results. Current western discontent generally received attention from John Barr and Owen Anderson in *The unfinished revolt* (1971) and in *Prairie perspectives* (1970) edited by David T. Gagnon. Issues in Ontario politics were examined by Robert F. Nixon in *The Guelph papers* (1970), a collection of papers read at a conference of provincial Liberals. Saskatchewan warranted a book on its own: *Politics in Saskatchewan* (1968) by Norman Ward and Duff Spafford drew together a set of historical essays and analyses of the contemporary situation to add substantially to the literature on a province that has received a great deal of scholarly examination in the last few years.

Apart from the work of the academic specialists in local government—*Politics and government of urban Canada* (1972), a collection by Michael Goldrick and Lionel Feldman, *The Canadian municipal system* (1969) by Donald C. Rowat, *Emerging party politics in Canada* (1972) by Jack Masson and James D. Anderson, and *Urban Canada and its government* (1968) by Thomas J. Plunkett—most books on municipal politics were about Toronto. James Lorrimer's *The real world of city politics* (1970) was a series of case studies of citizens' groups in conflict with Toronto politicians and officials. His second book, *Citizen's guide to city politics* (1972), examines the links between the 'property industry' and local government, but despite the title it is avowedly not a manual on how to fight City Hall. The radical-conservative critique on Toronto politics, typical of the early 1970s, was well summarized in *Inside City Hall* (1971), edited by John Sewell and his regular colleague-contributors to the periodical *City Hall*, William KILBOURN and Karl Jaffary. That critique received effective expression in David and Nadine Nowlan's *The bad trip* (1970), an analysis of the disadvantages of the Spadina Expressway that became the bible of the movement aimed at stopping further expressway construction in Toronto—and contributed to the decision of the provincial government to halt construction. Less successful was the attempt by Toronto Liberals in 1970 to capture power at City Hall by dint of concerted party effort. *City Lib* (1972) by Stephen Clarkson, who ran as the Liberal mayoralty candidate, analysed the effort from the vantage point of both a political scientist and the centrally involved participant.

9. *Political parties.* Finally, several important books on political parties emerged. There is still no single major book on Canadian political parties as a whole—indeed there is still no monographic study of the Liberal party—but the fascination for the parties of the left continued. Martin Robin's *Radical politics and Canadian labour, 1880–1930* (1968) filled a gap in our understanding of the development of labour and left-wing politics in Canada, a story that Gad Horowitz brought up to the foundation of the New Democratic Party with his *Canadian labour in politics* (1968). It was in the latter book, incidentally, that Horowitz developed his belief that the 'Tory touch' in English-Canadian political culture helped to prepare the ground for viable socialist parties in the country. Walter Young contributed two books on party politics: *Democracy and discontent* (1969), a general overview of political developments in the 1920s and 1930s, aimed at the general reader, and *Anatomy of a party: the national CCF: 1932–61* (1969), a major and perhaps definitive monograph that argued the case for seeing the success of the national CCF as a movement though not as a party. Young carefully examines the tension between these two tendencies in relation to party organization and structure, electoral support and tactics, and the behaviour of the parliamentary caucus. William Rodney examined the history of the Canadian Communist party between 1919 and 1929 in *Soldiers of the International* (1968).

The Conservative party came in for attention in a major way from only one author. *The politics of survival* (1970) by J. L. Granatstein—a valuable book on a limited period that stimulates one's curiosity to read a more wide-ranging study of the party by the author—revealed the torments of the Conservative party in its efforts to recover from the defeat of the 1935 election. DH

Political writings in French. Between 1967 and the end of 1972 French-Canadian scholars wrote well over 225 books on various aspects of Québec's political life. In addition there were countless tracts and pamphlets, some written by well-known politicians and scholars while others had little to arouse interest in them. The same weaknesses found in the books examined for HISTORY STUDIES IN FRENCH can also be discerned in the political writings. However it must be admitted that political science is a new field of research in Québec and the best material by far is scattered in various periodicals and journals and in papers delivered at seminars and conferences. It is to be hoped that some efforts will be made to gather this material together in books of readings so that it can be more widely used. The same wish for book publication may be expressed for some excellent PH.D. theses that are buried in the archives of universities.

For the purposes of this entry the materials published between 1967 and 1972 that may be said to be scholarly have been grouped in the following categories: 1. Bibliographies, surveys, and collections; 2. Essays and political economy; 3. Constitutional developments and federal-provincial relations; 4. Politics and political parties; 5. Administrations; 6. Labour; and 7. The October crisis of 1970.

1. *Bibliographies, surveys, and collections.* This category groups reference works and books that will introduce the general reader to the various points of view and problems expressed by political scientists. No thorough bibliography along the lines of the *Guide d'histoire du Canada* (1969) by André Beaulieu, Jean Hamelin, and Benoît Bernier has been published as far as political science is concerned. Most of the works examined, however, contain bibliographies of diverse lengths, and the *Catalogue de l'édition au Canada français: 1970–1,* which lists its titles under subject headings, promises to become a useful tool. No bibliography has been published in our period dealing with specific subjects such as constitutional problems, labour, confrontation, etc. The reader must therefore be grateful to Robert Boily for his remarkable *Bibliographie—le système politique québécois et son environnement* (1971), which is well conceived in every respect.

The only survey published in this period is Louis Sabourin's *Le système politique du Canada: institutions fédérales et québécoises* (1969) in which a vast range of experience is brought to a multitude of subjects concerning political science. Unfortunately in this collection of essays by learned scholars no provision has been made for the study of the phenomenon of para-political groups.

Among the other essay collections that tend to link all the disciplines in the social sciences concerned with Québec's life and society, five are of particular interest: *Le Québec: rétrospective et temps présent* (1967) by Olivier Durocher: *La société canadienne-française* (1971) edited by Marcel Rioux and Yves Martin—available in English in the Carleton Library as *French-Canadian society: volume 1*—which contains the most important articles of social scientists who wrote in the 1940s and 1950s and sought to give a new interpretation of Québec's economic and social life; *Le Québec d'aujourd'hui—regards d'universitaires* (1971) edited by Jean-Luc Migué; *La fin d'un règne* by Gérald Fortin (1971), which deals with the end of rural Québec and the beginning of a new urbanized and industrialized society (it won a Governor General's Award); and *Idéologies au Canada français: 1850–1900* (1971) edited by Fernand DUMONT, Jean-Paul Montminy, and Jean Hamelin.

2. *Essays and political economy.* Jacques Grand'Maison, the eminent parish priest and scholar of St Jérome, has been confronting traditional power and values for some time now, with the purpose of preparing French Canadians to face new challenges and discover new perspectives. His desire for new democratic centres of power is revealed in his *Vers un nouveau pouvoir* (1969). His *Nationalisme et religion* (1970) is an exploration of the relationship of these constant themes in French-Canadian life. In his *Stratégies sociales et nouvelles idéologies* (1971) he attempts to make a bridge between the baggage of our past and the instruments of the future. He favours more democratic structures, less centralization at all levels. Furthermore he accepts the argument that a lack in the development of an effective political conscience among French Canadians has not been due to our craving for *patronage* and our alleged fascistic tendencies, but to the fact that relevant information has historically been kept away from the people by administrators and clergy and other élitist groups. (It is interesting to note that every time information was not controlled, radicalization and 'revolution' resulted.)

Some of the best political writing in Québec has taken the form of subjective expressions of rage (as in Vallières's book below) or of a sense of futility in the face of the presumed incapacities of the Québécois. See for instance Pierre Vallières's *Nègres blancs d'Amérique* (translated by Joan Pinkham and published in 1971 as *White niggers of America*), which contains a memorable account of the life of the Montreal poor, understandable anger, and a good deal of philosophical nonsense; *La jeunesse du Québec en révolution* (1970) by Jacques Lazure; *Manifeste pour la liberté de l'information* (1971) by C. J. Devirieux; *Participation et contestation: l'homme face aux pouvoirs* (1972) by Martin Blais; and *Lettres et colères* (1969) by Pierre Vadeboncoeur. Vallières's *L'urgence de choisir* (1971)—translated by Penny Williams as *Choose!* (1972)—is a moving statement describing his discovery of other forms of action than the terrorist-revolutionary one he adopted in *Nègres blancs.*

More sober and detached in outlook were Pierre Elliott Trudeau's twenty essays on Québec politics in the fifties, *Les cheminements de la politique* (1970), which was translated by

Ivon Owen and published in English as *Approaches to politics* (1970), and *L'impossible Québec! Essai d'une sociologie de la culture* (1968) by Jacques Brillant. The latter, however, is a somewhat superficial discussion of the economy, the language, and of constitutional and governmental interference and liberty. Brillant comes to the conclusion that democracy in Québec is sick.

Sweden and democratic socialism have almost mesmerized French-Canadian thinkers, particularly independentist ones. This concern led no doubt to Jean-Paul Lefebvre's *Réflexion d'un citoyen sur l'avenir du Québec et sur quelques aspects de l'expérience suédoise* (1968). Since political independence was much talked about and planned during the sixties and early seventies, some economic frameworks and optimism had to be provided. Roma Dauphin in *Les options économiques du Québec* (1971) and a group of scholars and Québec thinkers (Jean-Louis Gagnon *et al.*) in *Le Canada au seuil de l'abondance* (1969) attempted to link the development of the possible common market between Québec and the U.S. with a historical analysis of Québec's economic development since 1815. The second book attempts to look at traditional social values in the presence of affluence.

3. *Constitutional developments and federal-provincial relations.* The complex question of Québec's possible options has been brilliantly explored in Richard Arès's *Nos grandes options politiques et constitutionnelles* (1972), which recommends that either independence or some form of associate status is the only acceptable alternative to Québec's inclusion in Canada's present confused federal structure. See also his *Dossier sur le pacte fédératif de 1867: la confédération, pacte ou loi?* (2nd ed., 1967). Also of interest is *Les relations intergouvernementales au Canada 1867–1967* (1971) by Gérard Veilleux, which is a historical analysis demonstrating how little the principles of coordination and collaboration have been used in the exercise of power in Canada.

Some scholars have turned their attention to the collective results of what may be described as constitutional uncertainty. The best works on this subject are *Le Canada français après deux siècles de patience* (1967) by Gérard Bergeron; *La question du Québec* (1969) by Marcel Rioux, intended for French readers and coming out in favour of independence; *La pyramide de Babel* (1967) by Maurice Giroux; and *Le pouvoir québécois . . . en négociation* (1972) by Claude Morin, a deputy minister of intergovernmental affairs spanning four provincial governments who chronicles the development of his frustration over the negotiation of Québec power.

Many solutions have of course been given. Federalism under its many aspects has been brilliantly studied by Pierre Elliott Trudeau in *Le fédéralisme et la société canadienne-française* (1967)—published in English as *Federalism and the French Canadians* (1968)—and *La constitution canadienne et le citoyen* (1969). Gilles Lalande in his *Pourquoi le fédéralisme: contribution d'un Québécois à l'intelligence du fédéralisme canadien: essai* (1972) combines theory and practice in a particularly interesting way. After a thorough theoretical appraisal of federalism, he proceeds to demolish ten arguments that are most often made against the federalist formula.

Of lesser importance, but still of some influence in the overall debate on Québec's life within the Canadian union, are *. . . et l'assimilation, pourquoi pas?* (1969) by Louis Landry; *Lettres aux nationalistes québécois* (1969) by Jean Pellerin; and *Le rêve séparatiste* (1967) by Louis Rochette.

Before his untimely death in 1972 Marcel Faribault dealt with the problem of constitutional review and revision. In both *Vers une nouvelle constitution* (1967) and *La révision constitutionnelle* (1970) his thesis seems to have been that of the Union Nationale of the middle sixties—the kind of constitutional revision that would destroy the minority status of French Canadians within confederation: unless equality was adopted, independence was inevitable. Those who had accepted a form of particular status for Québec were demolished in *Le statut particulier, une illusion* (1967) by Rosaire Morin. Morin went on to explain his vision of the Québec of tomorrow in his *Demain, que sera le Québec* (1969), which tends to describe Québec along traditional nationalistic lines.

The Parti Québécois under René Lévesque continued the slow process of convincing French Canadians of the value of independence and of drafting suitable economic and social programs that would deal with the perplexing problems in these areas. In Lévesque's *Option Québec* (1968) the entire philosophical, national, and emotional thesis of independence was laid bare (it was published in English as *An option for Quebec* in the same year), while in his *Quand nous serons vraiment chez nous* (1972) a Scandinavian-style economic and social program was drafted. The leadership contest that followed the death of Daniel Johnson led to the examination of a union with the United States. Much ridiculed at the time of its publication, *Indépendance et marché commun Québec-États-Unis* (1970) by Rodrigue Tremblay is now considered to be a valuable contribution to the on-going search for a solution.

The themes of federal-provincial affairs with reference to immigration, foreign affairs, the role of the supreme court, and Québec's control over her own territory were exceptionally well explored in the following books by Jacques Brossard: *L'immigration: les droits et pouvoirs du Canada et du Québec* (1967); *Les pouvoirs extérieurs du Québec* (1967), written with André Patry and Elisabeth Weiser; *La cour suprême et la constitution: le forum constitutionel au Canada* (1968); and *Le territoire québécois* (1970), written with Henrietta Immarigeon, Gérard V. La Forest, and Luce Patenaude. The question of territorial integrity is also studied in *L'affaire du Labrador: anatomie d'une fraude* (1968) by Roger J. Bédard.

The presence of French Canadians at various levels of Canadian federal life were studied *en profondeur* by scholars attached to the Royal Commission on Bilingualism and Biculturalism. Various volumes—some in French, others translated—were published in this period. The interested reader should consult Information Canada.

Language rights were debated but not as much as the overall question of the constitutional relationship between French- and English-speaking Canadians—by Robert Maheu in *Les francophones du Canada 1941–1991* (1970) and by F. A. Angers in *Les droits du français au Canada* (1971) and *Pour orienter nos libertés* (1969). No doubt the results of the Gendron Commission on the language of Québec and the determination of the Bourassa government to make French the working language of Québec and to achieve what is called full cultural autonomy will provide subjects for many books in the forthcoming six years.

4. *Politics and political parties.* In the general field of politics, the following may serve as a useful introduction: *Ces choses qui nous arrivent: chronique des années 1961–1966* (1970) by André Laurendeau, a collection of his editorials in *Le Devoir; Les programmes électoraux du Québec: un siècle des programmes politiques québécois* (1970) by Jean-Louis Roy; *Les idées politiques des premiers ministres du Canada* (1969) by Marcel Hamelin; and *Quatre élections provinciales au Québec 1956–1966* (1968), a superb political analysis by Vincent Lemieux.

In spite of all the interest in, and the clichés about, civic government, only one book dealt with civic politics. Naturally it was about Jean Drapeau, the mayor of Montreal. *La démocratie à Montréal ou Le vaisseau dort* (1972) by Marcel Adam (with its title pun on the name of Drapeau's ill-fated restaurant) is the result of a close scrutiny of the subject by a good journalist, but its quality is uneven.

The provincial elections of April 1970, with all the conflicts they brought to Québec society, were well analysed in *Une élection de réalignement: l'élection générale du 29 avril 1970 au Québec* (1970) by Vincent Lemieux, Marcel Gilbert, and André Blais; *Ma campagne électorale avec la pègre, la jeunesse, les séparatistes, les Anglo-Canadiens, les profiteurs, le peuple* (1970) by 'Clamars' (Raymond Bériault); *La victoire du Québec* (1970) by Mario Beaulieu; and *Le coup d'état du 29 avril 1970* (1970) by Bernard Smith.

The federal and liberal ideology was treated in his usual lucid way by Pierre Elliott Trudeau in his *Réformes de P. E. Trudeau* (1968). French-Canadian participation in Ottawa was dealt with by two flamboyant politicians. Réal Caouette introduced the public to his correspondence in his *Réal Caouette vous répond . . . 24 importants extraits de la correspondance du chef du R.C.* (1971) and Gilles Grégoire, who began his political career as a Créditiste and ended it as an Indépendantiste, related his Ottawa experience in *Aventure à Ottawa* (1969), in which he reveals his capacity for enjoying his role along with his disillusionment about French-Canadian power in Ottawa.

Some politicians wrote about Québec politics to express personal anguish, participation, criticism, or their platforms. For the Liberals: *Bourassa, Québec!* (1970) by Robert Bourassa and *Je conteste! chronique de la politique québécoise* (1969) by Yves Michaud. For the Union nationale: *L'union vraiment nationale* (1969) by J. C. Cardinal; *Le panier des crabes: un témoignage vécu par l'Union nationale sous Daniel Johnson* (1970) by Jérôme Proulx;

and *L'Union nationale—son histoire, ses chefs, sa doctrine* (1969). For the Créditistes: *Camil Samson et le défi créditiste: le parti et l'équipe* (1970) by Camil Samson. For the Parti Québécois: *Ma traversée du Québec* (1970) by Camille Laurin; *Défis au Parti Québécois* (1972) and *Le Parti Québécois en bref* (1971) by André Larocque.

5. *Administration*. Little publishing was done in this field. It is hoped, however, that the Université du Québec—with its research facilities, its presence over a large territory, and its Institute of Civil Administration—will establish research teams to study the many and varied aspects of both administration and institutions. A fine and scholarly beginning has been made, however, with the most scholarly political-science research.

The whole process of electoral reform, from constituency to governmental organization and options, was dealt with by Robert Boily in *La réforme électorale au Québec* (1971). A year earlier the entire field of electoral laws was studied by a team of young researchers headed by André Bernard and Denis Laforte in *La législation électorale au Québec, 1790–1967* (1970). In the same year Henri Brun analysed the formation of Québec's political institutions in their historical perspective in *La formation des institutions parlementaires québécoises 1791–1831* (1970).

Several attempts have been made to rationalize the role of the member of any legislative assembly—whether it be in Ottawa, Québec, or elsewhere. André Gélinas, in his fine *Les parlementaires et l'administration au Québec* (1969), looked at the administrative role that more and more members of the National Assembly must assume. Unfortunately the only political institution that was analysed was a defunct one: the Legislative Council in *Le Conseil législatif de Québec* (1967) by Edmond Orban.

6. *Labour*. The late 1960s and the early 1970s have seen the profound radicalization of the labour movement in Québec, and most of the literature was 'une littérature de combat'. In this context it was fitting that Les Éditions du Jour should reissue what is now a classic: *La grève de l'amiante* (1970), Pierre Elliott Trudeau's brilliant analysis of the socio-economic structure of Québec at the time of the Asbestos strike in 1949. Both the CSN (Confédération des Syndicats nationaux) and the FTQ (Fédération des Travailleurs du Québec) published important documents that indicated the direction to come. Three collections of reports published by the CSN (written by the president, Marcel Pépin, in collaboration) are worth mentioning: *Le deuxième front* (1968), *Le camp de la liberté* (1970), and *Pour vaincre* (1972), all reflecting a militant socialist stance. The FTQ published a similar series. For example in 1967: *La sécurité sociale*, *Reconnaissance politique sur la liberté d'association*, and *Administration de la justice au Québec*. In 1968: *Commission d'enquête sur la santé et le bien-être social*, *Situation de la femme au Canada*, and *Chômage*. In 1969: *Documents de travail de la FTQ*. And in 1971: *L'état rouage de notre exploitation*, *Documents sur la syndicalisation sectoriale*, and *Documents sur la politique salariale*. The manifestos of the CSN, the FTQ, and the Fédération des Enseignants du Québec have been translated in *Quebec: only the beginning* (1972), edited and introduced by Daniel Drache.

The radicalization process was foreshadowed by the formation of FRAP—the Front d'action politique—which regrouped all the community groups in Montreal in order to fight the Montreal civic elections of 1970. See *Les salariés au pouvoir* (1970), the political manifesto of the Front d'action politique.

Two historical works of some importance were published in this period: *Les syndicats catholiques* (1969) by J. P. Archambault and *Dans le sommeil de nos os: quelques grèves au Québec de 1934 à 1944* (1971) by Evelyn Dumas. The most exhaustive study of Québec syndicalism was written by the distinguished scholar Louis-Marie Tremblay: *Le syndicalisme québécois* (1972).

7. *The October crisis of 1970*. This may have been the most important moment in the twentieth century of French-Canadian evolution and life in Québec. It is, of course, still too much in our minds and hearts for us to be detached and 'scholarly' about it: it was a terrifying experience, the results of which are only beginning to be felt. Perhaps the three best philosophical treatments of the crisis were those by Fernand Dumont, Pierre Vadeboncoeur, and Gérard Pelletier. Dumont's *La vigile du Québec: Octobre 1970: l'impasse?* (1971) captured the condition of paralysis in which all Québécois found themselves. By adding to his book various articles and studies that he had published previously in various journals, Dumont demonstrated with intel-

lectual and literary brilliance that being caught in an impasse is the normal condition of Québécois. In *La dernière heure et la première* (1970) Pierre Vadeboncoeur poetically assessed the end of the old régime and the beginning of a new one in which the citizens had to be in control. Gérard Pelletier's *La crise d'octobre* (1971)—translated by Joyce MARSHALL and published in English as *The October crisis* (1971)—presented the liberal apologia. *Le terrorisme québécois* (1970) by Gustave Morf attempted to explain the psychological mentality of the members of the FLQ—an irrelevant and stupid book. Three 'instant books' dealt with the evolution of the crisis: Jacques Lacoursière's *Alarme citoyens!* (1970), Jean-Claude Trait's *FLQ 1970: offensive d'automne* (1970), and Maurice Champagne's *La violence au pouvoir* (1971). The most effective and useful of these books is Lacoursière's. In *L'opinion publique et la crise d'octobre* (1971) two young scholars, Michel Bellavance and Marcel Gilbert, attempted to study the role of public opinion. It is a learned and effective treatise. LLP

Polson, Don. See POETRY IN ENGLISH 2.

Pommingille, Louis. See CHILDREN'S BOOKS IN FRENCH.

Pontaut, Alain. See DRAMA IN FRENCH 5.

Pool, Beckman H. See ESKIMOS: BOOKS IN ENGLISH.

Pope, W. H. See POLITICAL WRITINGS IN ENGLISH 2.

Porter, John. See POLITICAL WRITINGS IN ENGLISH 4.

Poulin, Jacques (1937–). Born in Saint-Gédéon, in the Beauce region of Québec, he was educated at Université Laval, where he took a bilingual Arts degree that enabled him to earn his living for a number of years as a commercial translator. He lives outside Quebec City.

Poulin has written three novels: *Mon cheval pour un royaume* (1967), *Jimmy* (1969), and *Le coeur de la baleine bleue* (1970). A fourth will be published in 1974. Poulin writes with ease and grace and humour; he seems to share none of the usual preoccupations of Québec novelists of his generation—the Church, the land (escaping from it or rediscovering it), Québec's political affairs. One of the chief influences in his writing is J. D. Salinger: the debt is obvious, but the novels, particularly *Jimmy*, are more an *hommage* than an imitation.

The setting for Poulin's novels is largely the old part of Quebec City, which he makes contemporary and North American, filled with light and childish delight. But one of the pervading themes is destruction—of an older order, old buildings, old styles of life. New life springs from the old, however, and one is struck particularly by the humanity of the attitudes and characters in the novels of this very important, unjustly neglected young writer. SF

Poulton, Ron. See HISTORY STUDIES IN ENGLISH 15.

Powers, William K. See INDIAN LEGENDS AND ART.

Pratt, E. J. (1882–1964). Born in Western Bay, Nfld, Edwin John Pratt was educated at St John's Methodist College. After a tour of preaching and teaching at island outports, he enrolled at Victoria College, University of Toronto, where he graduated in philosophy in 1911. He received his M.A. in 1912, his B.D. in 1913, and his PH.D. in theology in 1917. He was a demonstrator in psychology at University College until 1920 when he joined the department of English at Victoria College, where he remained until his retirement in 1953. He was editor of the *Canadian poetry magazine* from 1936 to 1942. He was elected to the Royal Society of Canada in 1930 and was awarded the Lorne Pierce Medal for distinguished service to Canadian literature. He was made CMG in 1946.

His first book of poetry was *Rachel* (privately printed, 1917), the portrait of a mother waiting for news of her seaman son who has been drowned in a wreck. This and about two thirds of the lyrics in *Newfoundland verse* (1923) he chose to omit from his *Collected poems* (1944). Pratt is regarded as a major narrative poet. His first two books of narrative verse are fantasies of the sea, of which he had an encyclopedic knowledge. (All his narratives draw heavily on concrete detail and actual facts, which Pratt was able to turn into poetry with great skill and originality.) *The witches' brew* (1925), published two years before Ontario abandoned prohibition, was a timely and zestful extravaganza about the effects of alcohol on fish and on their natural enemy, a giant cat. The cold-blooded fish, who have had no moral training, drink and remain sinless but are destroyed by the warm-blooded cat in an intoxicated frenzy that finally leads him to swim towards that mecca of early twentieth-century bellicosity, the Irish Sea. *Titans* (1926) contains Pratt's epic tale of the whale fishery, 'The cachalot' (first published in the *Canadian Forum* in 1925), and 'The great feud', an allegory on the mutual destructiveness of war; from this mammoth carnage in the animal world, only a female anthropoid ape escapes. There was a change of pace in *The iron door: an ode* (1927), a symbolic treatment of the mystery of death that ends in an affirmation of immortality. *The Roosevelt and the Antinoë* (1930) is the story of a rescue during a storm at sea and a celebration of the courage and endurance of seamen. Pratt's shorter poems were gathered together in *Verses of the sea* (1930) and *Many moods* (1932). His powerful dramatic narrative *The Titanic* (1935) reflects the pride and overconfidence with which that 'unsinkable' ship was launched, the shock and tragedy of her loss, and the strength and weaknesses of men in the face of death.

Pratt's concern at the rising tide of fascism can be seen in *The fable of the goats and other poems* (1937) for which he received a Governor General's Award; the title poem ends on a weak note, however, and was excluded from the second edition of the *Collected poems* (1958). The Second World War provided many themes for *Still life and other verse* (1943) and for three other works: *Dunkirk* (1941), a vivid picture of a nation at war; *They are returning* (1945), Pratt's reflections on the end of the war; and *Behind the log* (1947), which catches the significance of the laconic reports of submarine attacks on convoys that had lost all meaning through sheer repetition.

Pratt turned inland and to Canadian history for two major works. *Brébeuf and his brethren* (1940) is a twelve-part epic of the early Jesuit missions to the Indians. It was read over the radio in 1943 and was set to music by Healey Willan and sung in Toronto in 1944. *Towards the last spike* (1952) is a tribute to the Scotsmen whose vision, resourcefulness, and determination bound the country with the steel line of the Canadian Pacific Railway. The central figure is Sir John A. Macdonald who, planning the attempt, was disgraced in the Pacific Scandal of 1873, rose again in 1880 and, with the help of two other Scots, George Stephen and Donald A. Smith (Lord Strathcona), and of William Van Horne, conquered the 'sea of mountains' by 1885. Pratt received Governor General's Awards for both books.

In the lecture 'E. J. Pratt and his critics' (*Our living tradition*, 2nd ser. 1959), Earle BIRNEY reviews the long period in which Pratt's work was neglected or underestimated and deprecates more recent attempts, such as that of John Sutherland, in *The poetry of E. J. Pratt: a new interpretation* (1956), to invest it with deep mystical significance. Birney comes to the conclusion that Pratt was a master of language and of narrative verse who had a democratic vision and a zest for the heroic in man as he faces fate, the elements, and brute force. He recognizes Pratt's 'profession of faith' as that found in 'The truant' (*Still life and other verse*), a poem in which man refuses to bow to the meaningless and mechanical force that orders the universe. This appreciation of the directness and simplicity of Pratt's work is shared by Northrop FRYE in his discerning introduction to the second edition of the *Collected poems* (1958).

Pratt's *Selected poems* (1968) edited by Peter Buitenhuis is available in paperback. For further critical study of Pratt's works, see *Edwin J. Pratt: the man and his poetry* (1947) by Henry W. Wells and Carl F. KLINCK; *E. J. Pratt* (1969) by Milton Wilson in the Canadian Writers Series; *E. J. Pratt* (1971) by Sandra Djwa in the Studies in Canadian Literature series; and *E. J. Pratt* (1969), edited with an excellent introduction by David G. Pitt, in the Critical Views on Canadian Writers series. NS

Préfontaine, Yves (1937–). Born in Montreal, Préfontaine studied there and in Paris before taking up a post at McGill University. For ten years he was on the editorial board of *Liberté* and briefly, in 1962, was editor of that review. From the outset his poetry attracted appreciative attention by its creative power and stylish assurance. In 1968 *Pays sans parole* (1967) was awarded both the Prix France-Canada and the Prix des Concours littéraires du Québec.

In the late fifties and early sixties Préfontaine was the poet who most insistently explored the myth of the vast inhospitable north as the symbol of the spiritual paralysis and aphasia threatening the emerging poetry of Québec. His development from the tumultuous images and desperate cries of *Boréal* (1957; reissued 1967), to the more sober stoicism and the sense of belonging of *Débâcle* (1970) and *À l'orée des travaux* (1970), reflects the thematic evolution of French-Canadian poetry from the theme of the difficulty of living, of death in life, to that of the land rediscovered and repossessed. His words are a violent challenge to an unwelcoming world, conceived in terms of the American continent, or, in the manner of Alain GRANDBOIS, in cosmic terms. Préfontaine's poetry has none of the specific reference of CHAMBERLAND's, though the city, the 'heavy city wreathed in fog and weighing oppressively on our words', is his native Montreal, which he would wish less foreign and inhospitable to him. The disturbing violence of his language, the apparent facility, the luxuriant vocabulary bordering on preciousness—with its neologisms (*ouraganer*, *nuaisons*) and its archaisms (*épousailles*)—the wild imbalance and the lurid richness of the outpourings of his creative imagination, are the measure and the signs of this man's courageous protest against Québec's congenital mutism. 'Et je m'acharne à parler', he says defiantly. However, the elegance of his verse and the use of epithets that can at times be hollow ones dilute the poet's anger, and it is surprisingly with a positive feeling of hope that we leave this poetry on the threshold of the task that Québec has set herself: 'à l'orée des travaux'.

CRPM

Preston, Richard Arthur. See HISTORY STUDIES IN ENGLISH 7, 12, and 15.

Price, Roy. See HISTORY STUDIES IN ENGLISH 10.

Pross, Paul. See HISTORY STUDIES IN ENGLISH 13.

Proulx, Jérôme. See POLITICAL WRITINGS IN FRENCH 4.

Provencher, Jean. See HISTORY STUDIES IN FRENCH 5.

Provost, H. See HISTORY STUDIES IN FRENCH 7.

Pryde, Duncan. See ESKIMOS: BOOKS IN ENGLISH and HISTORY STUDIES IN ENGLISH 10.

Pullen, H. F. See HISTORY STUDIES IN ENGLISH 4.

Purdy, Al (1918–). Alfred Wellington Purdy, who writes as Al Purdy and A. W. Purdy, was born at Wooller, Ont.—'of degenerate Loyalist stock', as he has claimed; spent most of his childhood at Trenton; and was educated at Albert College, Belleville. During the thirties he rode freight trains to Vancouver, where he worked for several years; during the Second World War he served in the Royal Air Force, mostly at the remote air base of Woodcock, B.C. Having no university training and few academic inclinations, he worked at many jobs, mainly casual and manual. In recent years he has worked as a free-lance writer and at related tasks, such as lecturing and poetry reading. He has travelled far: through most of Canada from Newfoundland to the west coast of Vancouver Island and north to Baffin Island; abroad to Cuba and Mexico, to Greece, Italy and France, and to Japan and Africa. He is a poet 'for whom the visible world exists' palpably and directly, and the experiences of travel have always played an immediately recognizable part in shaping both the content and the mood of his work. But the heart of his world, the place that gives a name to so many of his poems and appears as the symbolic omphalos of his imaginative world, is Roblin Lake, in deep Loyalist country near Ameliasburgh, Ont., where he built his house by the waterside with his own hands and to which he returns as to an oasis from all his travels.

Like most writers who seek to live by their craft, Purdy has practised in a variety of genres, from radio and television plays—of which he has written more than a dozen, all unpublished—to criticism, and from book reviews to travel essays. He has even edited a polemical anthology in criticism of the United States and by implication in support of Canadian nationalism, *The New Romans* (1969), as well as anthologies of recent Canadian poetry such as *Fifteen winds* (1969) and *Storm warning* (1971).

But poetry remains his essential mode. He has written verse restlessly, copiously, since he was thirteen. His first volume, *The enchanted echo* (1944), was a collection of conservatively traditional lyrics. There is an appropriateness in the title of the book he published fifteen years after, *The crafte so longe to lerne* (1959)—which followed on *Emu, remember!* (1957)—for this was the volume in which his special character as a poet first became obvious both in the opening of forms and the thematic evolution of a type of poetry that is really a philosophic continuum where the here-and-now, immediately perceived, becomes the Blakean grain wherein—if not the world—at least universal values are reflected.

Purdy might be described by a superficial reader as a versifying journalist. He goes on a journey and out of its experiences a book of verse emerges. A great part of *The Cariboo horses* (1965), which won him a Governor General's Award, and the whole of *North of summer* (1967) and *Hiroshima poems* (1972), emerged from such travels, and many of the poems they contain were written during the actual trips. The interval between conception and creation is often surprisingly short; the poems sometimes seem to serve Purdy as a diary might serve another man. This leads to unevenness in tone, though one suspects Purdy controls this to an extent by weeding out much of a voluminous production. At his least successful, the result is a harsh flatness, though this rarely happens, since an engaging conversational fluency is almost always present. At his best, there emerges a transfiguration of place and its inhabitants. But Purdy is more than a versifying geographer; his great, undisciplined, autodidactic learning has given him a historical sense rare among Canadian poets after PRATT, and his poems of Ontario, particularly in *Wild grape wine* (1968), evoke—as few other writers have done so vividly—the sense of Canada as an old country resonant with echoes.

Essentially what characterizes Purdy's poetry—shown in greatest variety in the *Selected poems* (1971)—is the apparent spontaneity with which the rovings of a speculative and originally erudite mind have been trapped into compelling forms. With humour and anger he has liberated from an early dependence on moribund romantic models a talent perhaps more idiosyncratic than those of any of his Canadian contemporaries. Notable among Purdy's other books of verse are the two considerably differing collections entitled *Poems for all the Annettes* (1962 and 1968) and *Love in a burning building* (1970).

George BOWERING has published a study of Purdy in the Studies in Canadian Literature series (1970). Purdy introduces and reads some of his poems on the CBC recording *Al Purdy's Ontario*. GW

Q

Qualter, Terrence. See POLITICAL WRITINGS IN ENGLISH 5.

Quinn, David B. See HISTORY STUDIES IN ENGLISH 2.

Quinton, Leslie. Pseudonym of Madeline A. Freeman, Lyn Harrington, and Audrey McKim. See CHILDREN'S BOOKS IN ENGLISH 6 and FOLKLORE: BIBLIOGRAPHY.

R

Racine, Luc. See POETRY IN FRENCH.

Raddall, Thomas (1903–). Thomas Head Raddall was borne in Hythe, Eng., and came to Halifax in 1913. He enlisted as a wireless operator when he was fifteen and served on ships and at coastguard stations in Nova Scotia. In 1922 he became a bookkeeper for a Nova Scotia paper mill, was promoted to accountant in 1925, and retired in 1938 to devote himself to writing. His first short stories appeared in *Blackwood's Magazine* and later in Canadian and American magazines. He was elected to the Royal Society of Canada in 1949 and was presented with the Lorne Pierce Medal for literature in 1956.

Raddall's strong historical sense and his understanding of the manners, customs, and speech patterns of Nova Scotia communities contribute to the success of his fiction, whether it is set in the past or the present. His short stories are collected in *The pied piper of Dipper Creek* (1939), which has an introduction by John Buchan and won a Governor General's Award; *Tambour and other stories* (1945); *The wedding gift and other stories* (1947); *A muster of arms and other stories* (1959), tales of the Second World War; and *At the tide's turn and other stories* (1959), a selection from his earlier collections made for the New Canadian Library. *Footsteps on old floors* (1968) is a collection of short sketches, each commemorating local history or legend. They include an account of Grey Owl and the yarn of the mystery ship 'Mary Celeste', a derelict.

Raddall's historical romances show careful research into the early history of Nova Scotia and are vigorously written. In these, as in his other fiction, he makes effective use of local colour. *His Majesty's Yankees* (1942) is set during the American Revolution and stresses the desire of the early colonists in Nova Scotia to remain neutral. For this book Raddall made good use of *The neutral Yankees of Nova Scotia* by J. B. Brebner and of the diary of Simeon Perkins. *Roger Sudden* (1944) is a story of the Seven Years' War and the capture of Louisbourg in 1758. *Pride's fancy* (1946) is the swashbuckling tale of a privateer in the West Indies during the fight for the independence of Haiti. *The governor's lady* (1960) centres on the ambitious wife of Sir John Wentworth and begins with an account of the Wentworth family before the American Revolution; the story terminates with Wentworth's appointment as lieutenant-governor of Nova Scotia. In *Hangman's beach* (1966) Raddall gives a shocking exposé of the cruelty to seamen stationed on board British vessels at Halifax (1803–12), a crucial period in the Napoleonic war during which hundreds of French prisoners of war were held on Melville Island. He also draws a picture of Peter McNab and his family that reveals the rapid development of Nova Scotia trade during those years. Novels with a contemporary setting are *The nymph and the lamp* (1950), in which Raddall drew on his experience as a wireless operator at Cape Sable to depict the isolation and depressing consequences of living on sand dunes; *Tidefall* (1953), the story of a scoundrel who made a fortune through crimes at sea but lost it later in a shipping enterprise; and *Wings of the night* (1956), in which an appreciation of the beauty of the forests is combined with an awareness of the economic difficulties of Nova Scotia. *The nymph and the lamp* was translated into French in 1952 and reprinted in the New Canadian Library in 1963. Raddall is also the author of *Halifax: warden of the north* (1948), a local history that won a Governor General's Award. An enlarged and revised edition was published in 1965. NS

Ramsay, Freda. See HISTORY STUDIES IN ENGLISH 7.

Ramsay, John. See HISTORY STUDIES IN ENGLISH 7.

Rasky, Frank. See HISTORY STUDIES IN ENGLISH 8.

Rawlyk, George A. See HISTORY STUDIES IN ENGLISH 2 and 4.

Raymond, Louis-Marcel. See BELLES LETTRES IN FRENCH.

Rea, Kenneth J. See HISTORY STUDIES IN ENGLISH 10.

Reader, H. J. See FOLKLORE: BIBLIOGRAPHY.

Reaman, G. Elmore. See HISTORY STUDIES IN ENGLISH 13 and INDIANS 5.

Reaney, James (1926–). Born on a farm near Stratford, Ont., he was educated at the University of Toronto, where he received an M.A. in 1949. He taught English at the University of Manitoba until 1956 and then returned to Toronto to work on a doctorate under Northrop FRYE; he received his PH.D. in 1958. He taught for two more years at Manitoba and then went to the University of Western Ontario, where he is professor of English. From 1961 to 1971 he edited and for a time typeset *Alphabet: a semi-annual devoted to the iconography of the imagination.*

Reaney is perhaps Canada's most imaginative literary artist—a highly inventive poet and playwright whose genius is to see 'the whole world in a local grain of sand' and to communicate this vision to reader and audience by letting symbol and myth illuminate and make intelligible everyday life and human experience—particularly childhood. He began writing when he was in his teens; he published poetry while he was in university and a book in 1949. *The red heart,* which won a Governor General's Award, attracted interest for its imaginative evocation of the part of southwestern Ontario where he grew up and for the very personal vision the poems revealed, one that accommodated both sophistication and naiveté, the real and the fantastic (or macabre). This award was also given to Reaney for *A suit of nettles* (1958) and in 1962 for *Twelve letters to a small town* and *The killdeer and other plays. A suit of nettles,* modelled on Spenser's *Shepherd's Calendar,* is a series of poetic dialogues, one for each month of the year, among geese on an Ontario farm. It is a difficult, witty, metrically ingenious satire on Canadian life that has a didactic purpose: 'to beat fertility into a sterile land'. *Twelve letters* is an idyllic tribute to Stratford and *The dance of death at London, Ontario* (1963), published by his own Alphabet Press with drawings by Jack Chambers, is comic/grim satire. Reaney's *Poems* (1972), edited with an introduction by Germaine Warkentin, contains all the poetry in these books as well as some previously unpublished verse and the poems from his plays.

Reaney turned to dramatic writing after he had become established as a poet. His first work for the theatre was the libretto for the chamber opera *Night-blooming Cereus* by John Beckwith, which was completed in 1953 (though not produced until 1960). It was published in 1962 in *The killdeer and other plays,* which included *The sun and the moon* and *One-man masque.* This was followed by *Colours in the dark* (1969), *Listen to the wind* (1972), and *Masks of childhood* (1972), which contains three plays: *The easter egg, Three desks,* and a revised version of *The killdeer.* Reaney has also written several children's plays, of which *Names and nicknames* (1969) has been published. An ambitious play, *Donnelly,* on which he has been working since 1968, has not yet been published; it is to be produced in Halifax in 1973.

These plays have established Reaney as the leading dramatist in English Canada. Some of them are written mainly or partly in verse and treat themes also found in his poetry: the contrasting worlds of innocence and experience, the evil forces that lie beneath the surface of every man, the power of love to redeem men, the process of growth from childhood to adolescence to maturity. He is more at home writing a non-linear, kaleidoscopic type of drama than one based on the assumptions of the realistic theatre. Indeed, the complexity and abundance of events in his plays often make them confusing and unsatisfying for those who read them with the preconceptions of realistic drama. The plays are rich in symbolism and patterns of imagery and often present a fanciful, surrealistic world. Little attempt is made to develop plot or character; the lack of concern for character development sometimes deprives the plays of emotional depth and hinders our involvement in them.

The libretto for the chamber opera *Night-blooming Cereus* has to do with the themes of loneliness and reconciliation. It was performed at Hart House Theatre in 1960, along with *One-man masque* (with Reaney himself as the performer), a short poetic fantasy on birth, death, and other stages of human life, and *The sun and the moon,* which includes elements of farce (as do most of Reaney's plays) in showing the evil influences that lie beneath a small Ontario community. The introduction of melodrama (another convention Reaney is fond of) brings these influences to the surface when an abortionist falsely accuses the local parson of fathering her child. The comic and redemptive dimension of the play is heightened when her wilfulness is thwarted by her own miscalculations, and peace is restored to the chastened community.

Masks of childhood, the title of one of Reaney's collections of plays, suggests the central place the world of the child has in Reaney's work—as a symbol of unspoiled innocence, as a mask to hide a deeper world of evil, and as a shield used by those who cannot enter the adult world of risk and responsibility. *The killdeer*, shortened and made more compact in its 1972 version, emphasizes the hold of a violent or inhibiting past upon the lives of children from different families; they are able to break free from it only through their mutual love and forgiveness. *Three desks* is a macabre and farcical treatment of the childishness and hostility that can affect the life of an academic community, in this case a small liberal-arts college on the prairies. *The easter egg* is a symbolic exploration of the Christian themes of redemption and resurrection. They are developed through the experiences of Kenneth, who has been considered retarded by his stepmother but is finally brought out of his arrested state by the patient and understanding Polly. *Colours in the dark*, which was first produced at Stratford, Ont., in 1967 under the direction of John Hirsch, is Reaney's most successful play to date. It shows him to be in surer command of the free dramatic form towards which all his plays have tended. Of its forty-two scenes, which give impressions of growing up in southwestern Ontario, Reaney says: 'This one has a new play before you every two minutes.' *Listen to the wind* adds a sombre note to the optimism of some of the earlier plays. Centred on the efforts of a sick boy to reunite his parents by having them take part in a play he has adapted—*The saga of Caresfoot Court*—it shows that the child's design is not successful, though he goes to bed believing it has been. The play-within-a-play technique contrasts the worlds of imagination and reality in which we all live. Reaney's ability to come to grips with more realistic situations while developing new forms of dramatic structure has been carried even further in an as yet unpublished trilogy on the events surrounding the massacre of the Donnelly family near London, Ont. One part, called *Sticks and stones*, will be produced in the fall of 1973. Reaney's increasing awareness of the potentialities and limitations of the stage and his productive imagination suggest that he has still much to contribute to Canadian drama.

Reaney has also written a novel for children, *The boy with an R in his hand* (1965), about York (Toronto) in the 1820s. He is the subject of two interesting critical studies: by Alvin Lee in the Twayne World Authors Series (1969)—this book is particularly valuable for its discussion and explanation of *A suit of nettles*—and by Ross G. Woodman in the Canadian Writers Series of the New Canadian Library (1971). WET/JN

Redekop, Calvin Wall. See HISTORY STUDIES IN ENGLISH 14.

Redekop, Ernest. See LITERARY STUDIES IN ENGLISH 4.

Redsky, James. See INDIANS 2.

Reford, Robert W. See HISTORY STUDIES IN ENGLISH 12 and POLITICAL WRITINGS IN ENGLISH 7.

Regehr, T. D. See HISTORY STUDIES IN ENGLISH 8.

Reid, Dennis. See HISTORY STUDIES IN ENGLISH 16.

Reid, Dorothy. See CHILDREN'S BOOKS IN ENGLISH 1.

Reid, Helen Evans. See HISTORY STUDIES IN ENGLISH 8.

Reid, John. See FICTION IN ENGLISH 6.

Reid, Malcolm. See PARTI PRIS; POETRY IN FRENCH; and POLITICAL WRITINGS IN ENGLISH 1.

Rempel, John I. See HISTORY STUDIES IN ENGLISH 7.

Renaud, André. See ANTHOLOGIES IN FRENCH.

Renaud, Jacques (1943-). Born and brought up in the Montreal working-class area of Rosemont, he attended a public secondary school. After failing his Grade XI examinations he began a series of manual jobs, then became a clerk in the municipal film library. He has also worked in advertising, as a journalist, and as a researcher for a CBC French-network television program. He became associated with the separatist/Marxist magazine PARTI PRIS soon after it was founded in 1963. Renaud is best known for his powerful and shocking short novel, *Le cassé* (1964), which was the first in the series *Paroles*, put out by that magazine's publishing house. Written when the author was just twenty-one and living in the squalid area of 'Centre-Ville', this novel is the first creative prose work in Québec in which the truncated, highly Anglicized *joual* of the most deprived sections of the Francophone poor of Montreal is used both for dialogue *and* narration. The title itself is a *joual* word based on the English slang expression 'broke' (penniless). It also conjures up images of a central figure who is beaten, crippled, disoriented. Indeed the hero, Tit-Jean, is probably the most totally alienated character in Québec literature, and the novel has been called 'le chant ultime de la dépossession'. Tit-Jean conceives and perpetrates a brutal murder of a 'goofball' peddlar whom he wrongfully takes to be a secret lover of his mistress and mother of his child. The murder takes on an escapist and ritualistic character, giving temporary feelings of liberation to the frustrated hero. In spite of some weakness in characterization and an occasional maladroitness in the narrator's interjections, *Le cassé* contains striking lower-depths poetry and skilful cinematic techniques. It is the best prose work of the *parti pris* group of writers. It was translated into English as *Flat broke and beat* (1968) by Gérald Robitaille.

Renaud had already published a short poetry collection, *Electrodes* (1962), at the age of nineteen. His poems are full of anguish, hatred, solitude, and cold. Some show the influence of the cosmic and geological themes of Alain GRANDBOIS. Dominant are the theme of unrequited love and a hallucinatory sense of guilt. Although there is originality in the vocabulary and some of the images, and a brief anticipation, near the end, of the social milieu of *Le cassé*, the poems suffer from *préciosité* and an unconvincing, overworked pathos.

Renaud returned to the novel form with *En d'autres paysages* (1970), an unsuccessful attempt to wed cosmogony and fantasy with social realism. The hero, Luc Richard, has fled to a rural village after having killed his wife (and some of his children?). A guilt-ridden fugitive, he tries to find a *raison d'être* through teaching in the village school and making love to his landlord's young daughter, Marie. The attempt fails and at the novel's end Marie is dead and flames destroy her father's property. The style is frequently gauche—the realistic framework is unstably mixed with phantasms and mystical passages, and shifts in the narrative voice lead only to confusion. Yet the text contains some fine prose poetry; an engaging portrait of the farmer, Paillette, and his daughter; and a potentially successful though thinly developed character, Jean-Guy ('le Bâtard'), who is reminiscent of his spiritual brother, Tit-Jean.

For an interesting discussion of *Le cassé* and Jacques Renaud, see Malcolm Reid's *The shouting signpainters: a literary and political account of Quebec revolutionary nationalism* (1972). B-ZS

Rich, E. E. See HISTORY STUDIES IN ENGLISH 3.

Richard, Jean-Jules (1911–). Born in St-Raphaël, in the Beauce region of Québec, of farm parents (his mother was illiterate), he first left home at fourteen and started to write poetry and even novels at an early age. At fifteen he attended a classical college but was expelled after two years for protesting against a teacher's mistreatment of a fellow pupil. From that time on he has been an independent man, employed successively as bookseller, freelance journalist, and construction worker in Québec and as far away as British Columbia. During the Depression, Richard rode the rods with thousands of other young unemployed from one end of Canada to the other and took part in the 'Hunger March' of 1937. He was in a delegation that met Prime Minister R. B. Bennett to demand better pay for youth in the relief work camps.

Richard was in the Canadian army and took part in the Normandy invasion of 1944, in which he was wounded. A short-term pension allowed him to write his first novel, *Neuf jours de haine* (1948). Dedicated to two friends, one Francophone the other Anglophone (both killed in that action), and to a comrade-in-arms of Ukrainian origin, it is a grisly account of war and its dehumanization.

In an ironic style marked by breathless short sentences and sense impressions, the 'hatred' of its title lashes out against Naziism and oppression, but also against venal politicians and militarism and its system of social caste, no matter of what ethnic origin ('Le colonel est un marchand de sacrifices'). The book suffers, though, from uncreative repetition and lack of economy. Richard's second book *Ville rouge* (1949) is a collection of short stories—the last of which carries the title, an image for the endless blood-red brick walls of the poor areas of Montreal and Quebec City. Written before and at the beginning of the Second World War, the stories are full of popular speech and present vignettes of the seamier side of life, with alcoholics, prostitutes, perverts, and other marginal beings or characters who rebel against the accepted canons of religious and social respectability. This book—and Richard's second novel, *Le feu dans l'amiante* (1956; 2nd ed. 1971)—had a recognized influence on the young group of writers around PARTI PRIS. It was published by the bookseller Henri Tranquille, for whom Richard has worked off and on, and in whose store—a rare meeting-place in Montreal where one could discuss advanced social and artistic ideas in the 1940s and 1950s—he became friends with the painter Jean-Paul Mousseau, writer-critic Claude Gauvreau, and poet Gaston MIRON. *Le feu dans l'amiante* is a largely journalistic novel about the 1949 Asbestos strike, considered a turning-point in Québec's social history. Published at the author's expense in Toronto, because it was highly critical of Premier Maurice Duplessis and the Québec police, it has moments of great power in its rendering of the dynamite blasts that regulate life in Asbestos, the all-pervading dust and silicosis, and the collective attempts at social reform. Again, monotonous, unsubtle repetition, weak characterization, and faulty grammar weaken a book that one critic has said, 'eût pu être bien autre chose: notre premier grand roman social'. *Le feu dans l'amiante* was published when the author was being hounded in Québec because of his participation in the left-oriented Canadian Peace Congress and found it almost impossible to earn a living.

Because of his difficult personal situation, Richard became depressed during the 1950s and burned a number of manuscripts. After a decade of obscurity, he re-emerged in 1965 with his third novel, *Journal d'un hobo*, a too-long extension of an excellent story, 'Prélude en si mineur', from his *Ville rouge*. The book is the diary of a hermaphrodite rod-runner who travels from 'his' native Acadia all the way to B.C. and is involved in both sexual and social adventures with other unemployed youth during the Depression. The *Journal* contains poetic flashes of the rail-way yards and hobo camps and its author revolts against the social system that caused so much human grief in the Depression years. Yet the sexual and social threads do not intertwine and boredom sets in.

Richard has recently become very active as a novelist and published three novels in a row at the beginning of the 1970s: *Faites-leur boire le fleuve* (1970), *Carré Saint-Louis* (1971), and *Exovide Louis Riel* (1972); he is expected to bring out several titles in 1973. The first, winner of the Prix Jean-Béraud and probably the author's best work, is a drama of the Montreal waterfront, with its conflicts between longshoremen and their Anglophone bosses as well as between rival groups of dockers and underworld characters who wield influence in the union. The second is based on the author's observations of 'hippies' and young drug-cultists who gathered in the square of the title, near Richard's home, in the summer of 1970. The novel on Riel deals with the Saskatchewan rebellion led by the legendary Métis chief and his eventual hanging. All three books suffer in varying degrees from outdated narrative techniques and a tendency towards melodrama and caricature. Yet Jean-Jules Richard is a natural writer who has made his mark and would undoubtedly have produced work of higher quality had he benefited from more formal education and enjoyed material and social conditions more conducive to artistic creation. For an illuminating interview with Richard on his formative years and world outlook, see 'Jean-Jules Richard au présent' by Réginald Martel in *Liberté*, 81 (1972), pp. 40–52.

B-ZS

Richards, Jack. See CHILDREN'S BOOKS IN ENGLISH 6.

Richler, Mordecai (1931–). Born in Montreal, he was educated at Sir George Williams University and spent two years abroad before returning in 1952 to Canada, where he joined the staff of the Canadian Broadcasting Corporation. In 1959 he went to England on a Canada Junior Arts Fellowship and made his home there, supplementing his income by scriptwriting. In 1966 he was in the United States on a Guggenheim Fellowship and in 1967–8 he was writer-in-residence at Sir George Williams University. He returned to Canada in 1972. He lives in Montreal and teaches twice a week at Carleton University, Ottawa.

Richler's early European novels were not entirely successful satires on the purposeless, sometimes vicious lives of expatriates, radicals, and revolutionaries, and on committed and uncommitted refugees. *The acrobats* (1954), set in Spain, is a sometimes confused first novel, but this defect is overcome in *A choice of enemies* (1957). Set in London, it moves to a confrontation between Norman Price, a Canadian who loses his teaching post in an American university during a loyalty purge, and Ernest Haupt, a German who has killed Norman's brother in a brawl.

Richler's later satirical novels, with their multiplicity of well-differentiated characters, owe much to the fertility of his imagination, to a brilliant sense of comedy, to his role as a social critic, and to his experiences while growing up on St Urbain St, Montreal, then a Jewish quarter—experiences that he has fictionalized in 'The writer's world (1): The war, chaverim and after' in *Canadian Literature* (1963, no. 18) and in *The street* (1969), a collection of stories pulsing with characters and associations from his boyhood. He has also written two sardonic novels about the Jewish community in Montreal: *Son of a smaller hero* (1955) and *The apprenticeship of Duddy Kravitz* (1959), an entertaining story of an ambitious and amoral youth who develops into a ruthless manipulator of business deals. Two farcical satires portray worlds of grotesque fantasy inhabited by monsters and scapegoats. *The incomparable Atuk* (1963)—satirizing Canadian television and publishing etc.—centres on the visit to Toronto of a cannibalistic Eskimo. The more ambitious *Cocksure* (1968), set in London, fantasizes ruthless commercialism of the arts and the relationship of Christian and Jew. Some of its destructive humour depends on an essentially adolescent scatology and it was a controversial winner of a Governor General's Award; it was coupled with Richler's *Hunting tigers under glass* (1968), a collection of essays. In the highly acclaimed *St Urbain's horseman* (1971), which also won a Governor General's Award, the scene shifts from London to Israel to Montreal as Richler penetrates the dissatisfactions, guilt, and fears of middle-aged Jake Hersch, a frustrated television and film director, happy in his marriage to a gentile but jealous of his gentile friend. Hersch seeks relief for his inner turmoil in a fantasy that his scoundrely cousin, Joey, a fine horseman—the central symbol of the novel, St Urbain's Horseman—will avenge the Jews by killing a Nazi war criminal who had escaped to Paraguay. Satire of the English, of Canadians, of many Jews *et al.*; a comic main plot; recurring reminders of the extremes of human evil represented by the black deeds committed in the Nazi gas chambers—all these elements are richly combined in this complex examination of modern society.

Richler's *Shovelling trouble* (1972), a collection of essays and reviews, reveals his considerable aptitude for comedy and satire on other than Jewish themes—though some of these pieces show an obsession with Jewish-gentile relations. His Penguin anthology, *Canadian writing today* (1970), contains selections of fiction and non-fiction.

See *Mordecai Richler* (1971) by George WOODCOCK, a volume in the Canadian Writers Series, and *Mordecai Richler* (1971) edited by G. David Sheps in the Critical Views on Canadian Writers series.

All Richler's books except for his first two novels are available in paperback—*Son of a smaller hero*, *The apprenticeship of Duddy Kravitz*, and *The incomparable Atuk* in the New Canadian Library. NS

Ricker, John. See HISTORY STUDIES IN ENGLISH 1.

Rioux, Lucien. See LITERARY STUDIES IN FRENCH 4.

Rioux, Marcel. See HISTORY STUDIES IN ENGLISH 12; POLITICAL WRITINGS IN ENGLISH 1; and POLITICAL WRITINGS IN FRENCH 1 and 3.

Ritchie, T. See HISTORY STUDIES IN ENGLISH 7.

Ritzenthaller, Pat. See INDIANS 5.

Ritzenthaller, Robert. See INDIANS 5.

Robb, Dodi. See CHILDREN'S BOOKS IN ENGLISH 6.

Robert, Guy (1933–). Born at Sainte-Agathe-des-Monts, Qué., and educated at the Université de Montréal, he has taught there, at the École des Beaux-Arts, and at the Université du Québec in Montreal where he is literary director for the University Press. He edits poetry at his own publishing house, the Éditions du Songe, and as director of the important collection 'Poésie canadienne' for the Librairie Déom. He is the art critic for *Le Maclean* and has written regularly for the periodical *Maintenant*. In the mid-sixties he was the founder and controversial director of the Musée de l'art contemporain, which he left in order to mount the much-admired international exhibition of contemporary sculpture at Expo 67 for which he wrote the catalogue, prefaced with a lengthy introduction to modern sculpture, *Sculpture* (1967).

Guy Robert has played an active part over the last fifteen years in the cultural revolution in Québec, which he considers more important than the social and political revolution it has accompanied, and has dedicated himself to the two strategic weapons in this revolution: poetry and publishing. He began writing with two ambitious essays, *Vers un humanisme contemporain* (1958) and *Connaissance nouvelle de l'art* (1963), a work that attempts to explain in psychological terms man's creative activity in every branch of art—poetry, fiction, music, and the visual and plastic arts. He has written impressive and attractively produced essays on Québec's major post-war artists—*Pellan, sa vie et son oeuvre* (1963), *Robert Roussil* (1965), *Jean-Paul Lemieux* (1968), *Riopelle* (1970), and *Borduas* (1972). Lemieux and Riopelle co-operated with Robert in producing these studies of them, which firmly emphasize their works or art—avoiding what Lemieux calls 'les indiscrétions biographiques, détestables et inutiles'. They display Robert's poetic skill with words as he evokes Lemieux's unique portrayal of a time, space, and solitude specifically of Québec, or describes the technique by which Riopelle produced his luminous mosaics in paint. We learn, incidentally, of Riopelle's life-long admiration for Grey Owl, which helps to explain the painter's fascination with nature and the 'avalanche' of works depicting owls that Riopelle produced in the late 1960s. Robert has also written *L'école de Montréal* (1964), *Jérôme, un frère jazzé* (1969), *Le Su et le tu: récit symbolique* (1969), *Yves Trudeau, sculpteur* (1971), and *Le grand théâtre de Québec* (1971). As a literary critic he published a thesis, *La poétique du songe: essai sur la poésie d'Anne Hébert* (1962), in which he presented under twenty-two headings examples illustrating the thematic content of Anne HÉBERT's poetry, and a critical edition of Sylvain Garneau's *Objets retrouvés* (1965). An original anthology containing poetry and personal comment by the poets represented, *Littérature du Québec: tome I—témoignages de 17 poètes* (1964), included Robert's own sequence of poems, *Neige de mai*, in which by celebrating his love for a woman, he finds his land and his voice as a poet. He republished this anthology in an enlarged form in 1970 under the title *Littérature du Québec: poésie actuelle*, replacing *Neige de mai* by some of the poems he published in 1969 in *Québec se meurt*—poems demonstrating that his commitment is inspired by some bitterness at the constant threat to the survival of Québec's French culture. *Aspects de la littérature québécoise* (1970) collects a number of Robert's essays, broadcast talks, and public lectures, including a splendid mock-serious psychoanalytical study of the 'sacre' (the blasphemous oath) in Québec speech.

Robert's considerable output of over twenty-five books in fifteen years includes seven volumes of verse. Starting with the theme of spiritual regeneration in *Broussailles givrées* (1958) and the myths of sea and sun, memory and desire, in *Et le soleil a chaviré* (1963) and *Une mémoire déjà (1959–1967)* (1968), he progresses through the celebration of the land, woman, and the power of the word in *Neige de mai* (1964) to the more esoteric universe of *Ailleurs se tisse* (1969), *Intrême-Orient* (1969) and *Trans-apparence* (1969)—a universe that the second of these works defines as 'orient extrême pays d'intérieur'. The two last-mentioned books and *Syntaxe pour Lardera* (1969)—a study of the work of the Parisian engraver who also illustrated *Trans-apparence*—are deluxe productions from Robert's own Éditions du Songe. *Intrême-Orient*—the result of the combined efforts of the poet, the artist Monique Charbonneau, the master-binder Pierre Ouvrard, and the engraver Albert

Dumouchel, on whose work Robert published a monograph, *Albert Dumouchel* (1971)—appeared in a limited edition of only 45 copies. Robert's latest book, however, a study of Paul-Émile Borduas, provides reassuring evidence that he is not forsaking his public for the secluded world of a private vision. *Borduas* (1972) is characteristic of Robert's prolific work, produced often in the face of bitter criticism, which can be seen as an act of faith in the reforming power of art—in art as social therapy. CRPM

Roberts, Dorothy. See POETRY IN ENGLISH 1.

Roberts, Leslie. See HISTORY STUDIES IN ENGLISH 13.

Roberts, Sara Ellen. See HISTORY STUDIES IN ENGLISH 8.

Robertson, Barbara. See CHILDREN'S BOOKS IN ENGLISH 2 and 5; HISTORY STUDIES IN ENGLISH 7.

Robertson, Heather. See INDIANS 6 and POLITICAL WRITINGS IN ENGLISH 3.

Robidoux, Réjean. See LITERARY STUDIES IN FRENCH 1.

Robillard, Richard H. See LITERARY STUDIES IN ENGLISH 4.

Robin, Martin. See HISTORY STUDIES IN ENGLISH 9, 12, and 13; POLITICAL WRITINGS IN ENGLISH 8 and 9.

Robitaille, Aline. See LITERARY STUDIES IN FRENCH 4.

Robitaille, Claude. See FICTION IN FRENCH: SHORT STORIES.

Robitaille, Gérald. See BELLES LETTRES IN FRENCH.

Rochette, Louis. See POLITICAL WRITINGS IN FRENCH 3.

Rodney, William. See HISTORY STUDIES IN ENGLISH 9 and 11; POLITICAL WRITINGS IN ENGLISH 9.

Rohner, Evelyn. See INDIANS 5.

Rohner, Ronald. See INDIANS 5.

Rose, T. F. See HISTORY STUDIES IN ENGLISH 13.

Rosen, Sheldon. See DRAMA IN ENGLISH 4.

Rosenberg, Stuart E. See HISTORY STUDIES IN ENGLISH 14.

Rosenblatt, Joe (1933–). Born in Toronto, he attended Central Technical School to grade ten and since then has worked at a variety of trades, including plumbing and welding. He was one of the poets who held public readings in Allan Gardens, Toronto, in the 1960s. He lived for two years in British Columbia before returning to Toronto where he now edits the magazine *Dialog*.

Some of the poems in his first small collection, *The voyage of the mood* (1964), were reprinted in *The LSD Leacock* (1966). This was followed by *Winter of the luna moth* (1968) and *Bumblebee dithyramb* (1972), a selected poems that also includes some new poems as well as drawings by the author. A further selection of his drawings, *Greenbaum*, was published in 1972.

Many of Rosenblatt's poems are about animals and insects and take a zestful look at these creatures, their teeming life as well as their predatory instincts. In some poems the preying and devouring that go on in animal life act as a parallel to the rapacious life within a consumer society. Rosenblatt also deals with political exploitation, the profit-and-loss theme, and the boss-worker relation. He has written poems based on characters derived from comic strips. This vein of fantasy is particularly apparent in a sequence about bees, insects, and flowers in which his usual exuberance of language, together with some humorous excess and typographical experiment, create a world of zany rhythms and vigorous and affirmative life. PS

Rosman, Abraham. See INDIANS 5.

Ross, Eric. See HISTORY STUDIES IN ENGLISH 3.

Ross, Sinclair (1908–). Born near Prince Albert, Sask., he joined the staff of the Royal Bank of Canada and served in many prairie communities before moving to Montreal. In realistic stories of prairie life, published originally in *Queen's Quarterly*, and in the powerful novel *As for me and my house* (1941), he has vividly recreated the harshest features of the prairie environment during the 1930s: the desolate communities; the isolation of the farms cut off by winter blizzards and snow drifts; the constant and violent winds; periods of drought and the catastrophic rain and hail storms that could devastate a farm in a few minutes. The prosperity of some farmers with richer land and more protected areas increases the bitterness of those stricken by the elements. It is not surprising that men rendered speechless by such catastrophe should seek comfort from the horses that have shared their wasted labour, and that the women, finding no comfort from their silent men, should crack under the strains of isolation. Ross's stories have been republished in the New Canadian Library under the title *The lamp at noon and other stories* (1968) with an introduction by Magaret LAURENCE.

As for me and my house, also in the New Canadian Library, is set in a bleak, windswept, impoverished prairie community where the environment intensifies the lack of communication between husband and wife. The story is told in a diary kept by the wife of Philip Bentley, a frustrated artist who entered the ministry without a vocation and who has been shunted from one poor community to another, always a failure. While presenting a single point of view, that of Mrs Bentley, Ross has impressively created a complex portrait of her that has many ironies and ambiguities. The reader is able to judge her objectively, to perceive both reality and her misjudgements of it. This aspect of the novel is discussed by William H. New in an essay in his *Articulating west: essays on purpose and form in modern Canadian literature* (1972).

Ross has given happier pictures of the prairies in *The well* (1958) and *Whir of gold* (1970). In the former, a young delinquent who has fled from Montreal and found summer employment on a prairie farm is softened by the beneficent effects of the open landscape and the freedom of the life. *Whir of gold* begins with the joyful experience of a young boy as he rides a magnificent horse that has the reputation of being a killer; his ego is bolstered further by his skill with the clarinet and by his successful defiance of his parents. These qualities develop into arrogance that fails him when he goes to seek his fortune in the urban environment of Montreal and accounts for his intolerable treatment of the girl to whom he owes his life, an escape from a possible prison sentence, and an opportunity to make a new beginning. NS

Ross, W. W. E. See POETRY IN ENGLISH 2.

Rotstein, Abraham. See HISTORY STUDIES IN ENGLISH 17 and POLITICAL WRITINGS IN ENGLISH 1 and 2.

Roussan, Jacques de. See LITERARY STUDIES IN FRENCH 4.

Rousseau, Guildo. See ANTHOLOGIES IN FRENCH and LITERARY STUDIES IN FRENCH 4.

Rousseau, Jacques. See ESKIMOS: BOOKS IN FRENCH.

Rousseau, Jérôme. See ESKIMOS: BOOKS IN FRENCH.

Roussel, Paul. See FICTION IN FRENCH: SHORT STORIES.

Roussopoulos, D. I. See POLITICAL WRITINGS IN ENGLISH 4.

Routier-Drouin, Simone (1901–). A grand-niece of the historian François-Xavier Garneau, she was born and educated in Quebec City and has made a career in journalism and the Canadian diplomatic service. After newspaper experience and residence in Paris, where she worked in the Archives of Canada from 1930 to 1940, she was press attaché at the Canadian embassy in Brussels from 1950 to 1954 and became Canadian vice-consul in Boston, Mass., in 1954, leaving this position on her marriage to Fortunat Drouin in 1958.

Simone Routier was early recognized as a fresh and vibrant Canadian poet, winning the Prix David in 1928 for her first collection of poems, *L'immortel adolescent*, which was typical of the clarity, fluidity, and mastery of technique that have characterized all her work. Leaving Canada for Paris in 1930, she wrote *Ceux qui seront aimés* (1931), *Paris-Amour-Deauville* (1932), and *Les tentations* (1934). She returned to Canada on the outbreak of war and later entered the Dominican convent at Berthier, Qué., but left after eighteen months, convinced that she had no vocation for the religious life. Nevertheless this experience had widened her horizon and she moved from romantic themes toward the religious symbolism of the three collections of poems that were published in 1947: *Je te fiancerai*, *Le long voyage*, and *Les psaumes du jardin clos*. In this year she was elected to the Académie canadienne-française. In 1962, after fifteen years of silence, she returned to poetry, publishing mainly in periodicals.

Her prose is also marked by clarity, conciseness, and grace. *Adieu Paris* (1940) is an expression of regret on leaving Paris. *Réponse à désespoir de vieille fille* (1943) is a traditional statement of faith in the ability of the spirit to find satisfaction in the world as it is, but it opposes rather than answers Thérèse Tardif's impassioned prose poem, *Désespoir de vieille fille* (1943), a protest against the fear of sensual satisfaction inculcated in young people by Jansenist teachings. Representative examples of Simone Routier's poetry are found in *The Oxford book of Canadian verse* (1960) and *Modern Canadian verse* (1967) edited by A. J. M. SMITH and in *Anthologie de la poésie canadienne-française* (4th ed. 1963) edited by Guy Sylvestre. A translation of her poem 'Psalm' by John GLASSCO appears in *The poetry of French Canada in translation* (1970).

JG

Roux, Jean-Louis. See BELLES LETTRES IN FRENCH and DRAMA IN FRENCH 2.

Rowat, Donald C. See POLITICAL WRITINGS IN ENGLISH 8.

Roy, Carmen. See FOLKLORE: BIBLIOGRAPHY.

Roy, Gabrielle (1909–). Born in Saint-Boniface, Man., she was educated there and at the Winnipeg Normal School. After teaching for some years in rural Manitoba, she travelled in England and France where she studied drama and began to write. When war forced her return to Canada, she continued to write stories and articles in Montreal, meanwhile observing the people of Saint-Henri who were to provide the material for *Bonheur d'occasion* (1945), her immensely successful first novel. She was elected to the Royal Society of Canada in 1947 and the same year married Dr Marcel Carbotte. In 1971 she was awarded the Prix David by the Québec government for her entire body of work. She lives in Quebec City.

Gabrielle Roy's prairie background and passion for the Canadian arctic have given her writing a breadth and an absence of regional pettiness not common among French-Canadian writers. Fully bilingual, she hesitated at first about whether to write in English rather than her native French. She is a fine craftsman with a style that is at once simple, strong, and delicately poetic. Her characters are usually rather humble people whom she handles without falsity or over-emotion so that they become symbols of man's quest for a joy that is often ephemeral, his persistent courage, and his striving for an understanding with his fellows that is seldom more than fleeting and many times too late. She is particularly adept in the portrayal of strong women characters like the mothers in *Bonheur d'occasion* and *La petite poule d'eau*. There is occasional sexual violence in her novels and stories, but usually love is shown as tenderness between old and young, or between family members, rather than as passion. *Bonheur d'occasion* is the compassionate study of a large Montreal slum family whose desperate poverty is relieved, ironically and doubtless only temporarily, by the outbreak of war and opportunity for military service. Even the pregnant daughter who has been deserted by her lover finds a solution to her dilemma by marriage to a soldier. The novel was awarded the Prix Femina, the first Canadian work to win a major French literary prize. The English version, translated by Hannah Josephson as *The tin flute* (1947), won a Governor General's Award and has been re-issued in the New Canadian Library (1958) with an introduction by Hugo MacPherson. The central figure of *Alexandre Chenevert* (1955), Gabrielle Roy's other Montreal novel, is a middle-aged, emotionally inhibited bank teller who is tormented by his inability to express love in his own life and by his uselessness in face of the miseries of which he is informed daily by radio and newspapers. He dies a slow death from cancer but learns finally that love exists, even for him, and that his life has not been as valueless as he believed. The book was translated by Harry Binsse as *The cashier* (1955). The New Canadian Library edition (1963) has an introduction by W. C. Lougheed.

Three Manitoba books, all linked short

stories rather than novels, make imaginative use of material from Gabrielle Roy's own past. *La petite poule d'eau* (1950), a poetic and moving account of life in a remote settlement in northern Manitoba, has been published in a deluxe edition (1971) with twenty-four original woodcuts by Jean-Paul Lemieux. The English version, translated by Harry Binsse as *Where nests the water hen* (1950), has been reissued in the New Canadian Library (1961) with an introduction by Gordon Roper. The lively and varied stories in *Rue Deschambault* (1955) cover a girl's growing from childhood to adolescence in Saint-Boniface amidst people of every nation, pioneers of the west. The book was translated by Harry Binsse as *Street of riches* (1957) and won the Prix Duvernay and a Governor General's Award. Brandon Conron contributed the introduction to the New Canadian Library edition (1967). *La route d'Altamont* (1966), translated the same year by Joyce MARSHALL as *The road past Altamont*, provides new and more intense insight into the same period in this girl's life, focusing upon the girl, her mother, and grandmother in four connected stories that describe a sort of circle of time in which the generations succeed and pass one another, meeting in only rare flashes of understanding, and journeys lead always back to their beginnings.

In *La montagne secrète* (1961), a young painter's arctic journey and the mountain that he finds, loses, and ultimately finds again frame a parable of the artist's lifelong quest for his subject and his efforts to express it. The novel was translated by Harry Binsse as *The hidden mountain* (1962). The four stories of *La rivière sans repos* (1970) use the arctic background more explicitly to depict Eskimos in a state of transition, drawn without choice into the white man's world and still uneasy with his gifts: his medicine that uselessly prolongs life, a wheelchair, the telephone. In the long title story, which was published separately in translation by Joyce Marshall with the title of *Windflower* (1970), the gift is an illegitimate child born of a brief brutal meeting between an American soldier and a young Eskimo girl. In her efforts to bring up and keep her son, the mother shifts desperately between white and Eskimo ways, not quite at home with either, and loses the boy finally to the white man and his wars. Gabrielle Roy has also published *Cet été qui chantait* (1972), a collection of nineteen stories and sketches, many very brief, each adding a dab of light or intensity to the picture of a summer in Charlevoix County in Québec.

J. Raymond Brazeau discusses Gabrielle Roy's fiction in *An outline of French-Canadian literature* (1972) with particular attention to *The road past Altamont*. Full-scale studies have been published by Monique Genuist (*La création romanesque chez Gabrielle Roy*, 1966) and by Phyllis Grosskurth in the Canadian Writers and Their Work series (1969). Biographical and critical material, with a complete bibliography, is available in the Dossiers de documentation sur la littérature canadienne-française. JM

Roy, Jean-Louis. See HISTORY STUDIES IN FRENCH 2 and 9; POLITICAL WRITINGS IN FRENCH 4.

Roy, Raoul. See FOLKLORE: BIBLIOGRAPHY.

Roy, Reginald H. See HISTORY STUDIES IN ENGLISH 12.

Roy, Yves. See HISTORY STUDIES IN FRENCH 7.

Rubel, Paula G. See INDIANS 5.

Rule, Jane (1931–). Born in Plainfield, N.J., and educated at Mills College, Oakland, Calif., she did some postgraduate work at University College, London, Eng., and at Stanford University. She has travelled extensively in the United States and southern Europe, living for a time in Greece. She works intermittently at all sorts of jobs, but chiefly at teaching. She came to Canada in 1956 and is now a Canadian citizen. She teaches creative writing at the University of British Columbia.

Jane Rule's conversational style and tightly knit sentences skilfully convey the outward normalcy and hidden grief of her characters. Occasional deliberate inversions of word order or phrase cause the reader to pause long enough to become painfully aware of the loneliness, deprivation, and, in some cases, sense of guilt of women who realize that their love must be barren because they are so overwhelmingly attracted to their own sex that they cannot endure a normal sexual relationship.

In *The desert of the heart* (1964) Evelyn Hall

waits out her six weeks in Reno to get a divorce after sixteen years of marriage during which her frigidity and revulsion have wrecked her husband. Her remorse and guilt are so deep-seated that only after a long struggle can she bring herself to become the lover of a young lesbian whose link with another girl has been broken. In *This is not for you* (1970) Katherine George, a lesbian from Vancouver, pours out her grief in an unposted letter that reveals how she strove to protect her friend Esther from developing her latent lesbianism, which to Katherine's dismay is developed by a more aggressive fellow student. A summer holiday spent in Europe brings Katherine and Esther into contact with various sexual relationships, and tragedy is brought home by suicide. Esther, after failing to consummate a marriage, secures an annulment and enters a religious order.

Comedy and tragedy are well blended in *Against the season* (1971) in which every character is vital to the life of a decaying American seaport where the old, awaiting death, stave off loneliness; the middle-aged resort to marriage or lesbianism; and an awkward adolescent boy gets the brusque introduction to sex that he needs. The most striking characters are old Miss Amelia Lawson, a cripple from birth who harbours pregnant girls and sees them through their delivery, and the irrepressible Agate, Amelia Lawson's protegé. Amelia, reading the diaries of her dead sister, Beatrice, is shattered by their malicious and incestuous observations. Amelia's own bitter suffering is revealed only in her death throes. NS

Rumilly, Robert (1897–). Born at Fort-de-France, Martinique, he was educated in France and served in the French army during the First World War. Disgusted with the leftist politics of France, he immigrated to Canada where he has taken a keen interest in survivals of the spirit of the old French culture in the province of Québec. His strong aversion to socialist ideas is expressed in the polemical essay *L'infiltration gauchiste au Canada* (1956).

Rumilly is a prolific writer. His chronicles, whether presented as history or biography, are always interesting and forcefully presented; however they show his ingenuity in skirting difficult and ambiguous points and should therefore be read cautiously. His major work, still incomplete, is his *Histoire de la province de Québec* (41 vols, 1940–63), based on an omnivorous and well-digested reading of books, pamphlets, and newspapers, supplemented by occasional glances at manuscript sources. It begins at confederation and has so far reached the 1940s. Some volumes are arranged as biographical studies. Other historical chronicles by Rumilly are: *Histoire des Acadiens* (2 vols, 1955), *Histoire du Canada* (1951), *Histoire des Franco-Américains* (1958), *Histoire de l'École des Hautes Études commerciales* (1967), and *Cent ans d'éducation* (Collège Notre-Dame, 1969). His biographical works are *Sir Wilfrid Laurier, Canadien* (1931), a short sketch; *Mgr Laflèche et son temps* (1938); *Papineau* (1944); *Le Frère Marie-Victorin et son temps* (1949); *Henri Bourassa: la vie publique d'un grand Canadien* (1953); and two series of sketches based on interviews: *Chefs de file* (1934) and *Artisans du miracle canadien* (1936). Rumilly is also the author of *Littérature française moderne (panorama)* (1931), a short critical essay on modern French writers; *La plus riche aumône: histoire de la société de Saint-Vincent-de-Paul* (1946); and *L'autonomie provinciale* (1948).

More recently Rumilly has taken up the study of the French-Canadian urban experience. The results of his work in this area have appeared in *Histoire de St-Laurent* (1970) and *Histoire de Montréal* (3 vols, 1970–2). His long-awaited biography of Duplessis appeared in 1973: *Maurice Duplessis et son temps: I, 1890–1944; II, 1944–1959*. NS/J-LR

Russell, Carl P. See HISTORY STUDIES IN ENGLISH 3.

Russell, E. C. See HISTORY STUDIES IN ENGLISH 12.

Russell, Loris. See HISTORY STUDIES IN ENGLISH 7.

Ryan, Claude. See HISTORY STUDIES IN FRENCH 2.

Ryerson, Stanley B. See HISTORY STUDIES IN ENGLISH 6.

Ryga, George (1932–). Born in Deep Creek, a small town in northern Alberta, he was raised in a Ukrainian farming community there. His formal education consisted of seven years in a one-room schoolhouse. His occupations after that included farm labour, construction jobs, and radio work at a station in Edmonton. Since 1962 he has made his living as a professional writer and now lives in Summerland, in the Okanagan valley of British Columbia. His writing has included poetry, radio, television and stage plays, film scripts, short stories, and novels.

Four of his stage plays have been published, three of them in *The ecstasy of Rita Joe and other plays* (1971) edited by Brian Parker. All four plays contain heroes who are rebelling against their society or are trapped in a social situation that is almost unbearable. His one-act play *Indian*, a vivid portrayal of an Indian labourer harassed by a heartless employer and an impersonal government official, was first presented on CBC television in 1962 and then on stage in 1964. Of this play Ryga writes: 'Within it I won a freedom in form and content which I felt at the time to be unique in Canadian theatrical and television literature.' The play is remarkable for the way in which it dramatizes the spare, elliptical English spoken by the Canadian Indian to emphasize the elemental situation of a man and a people who have lost the sense of their own worth. *The ecstasy of Rita Joe* is a much fuller and grimmer presentation of the plight of the Canadian Indian. The heroine is unable to live by the old ways of her people or to adapt to the white man's ways in the city. This play was commissioned by the Vancouver Playhouse for Canada's centennial year. It was the first play to be presented in the new theatre of the National Arts Centre, Ottawa, in 1969; in 1971 the Royal Winnipeg Ballet presented a ballet version of the work in the Centre's Opera House. *Grass and wild strawberries*, Ryga's least effective play, dramatizes the conflicts between the hippie culture and middle-class society. Its opening production in Vancouver proved highly popular among the young, but nevertheless lost the Playhouse many of its patrons.

Captives of the faceless drummer (1971), commissioned by the Vancouver Playhouse for production in February 1971, is centred on the kidnapping of a Canadian diplomat by a group of young revolutionaries. While its setting is Canada 'tomorrow', the play has many parallels with the October crisis of 1970. When the board of directors of the Vancouver Playhouse reversed its decision to produce the play, there was a bitter controversy during which the artistic director, David Gardner, was dismissed. (The play was subsequently produced in April 1971 at the Vancouver Art Gallery and in 1972 at the St Lawrence Centre in Toronto and at Festival Lennoxville, Qué.) Possibly Ryga's best play to date, it does not take sides between the diplomat and the 'Commander' of the revolutionaries but shows the agonies and sympathies that are common to both of them and to men generally when they come to doubt their own way of life. Ryga's dramatic technique is often a blend of realism, poetry, dance, song, and a juxtaposition of past and present. While his most effective dialogue catches the colloquial speech of his oppressed characters, the poetry in his plays is not always successful.

Ryga's two published novels, *Hungry hills* (1963) and *Ballad of a stone-picker* (1966), both relatively short, are set in rugged rural communities in Alberta. The first is the story of an unloved youth who makes his way as best he can, honestly and dishonestly. The second depicts the struggles, physical and psychological, of a sensitive man who has sacrificed much of his life by staying with his parents on the family farm so that his younger brother can pursue studies that lead to a Rhodes scholarship. Both novels contain a variety of characters ranging from simple country folk to deeply disillusioned and quite mad individuals. Ryga's descriptive passages and vignettes of rural life are sometimes written in highly poetic language and are often marked by a compassionate sense of humour. The novels show an evocative power and an intensity of narration that make one wish Ryga would publish more in this form. He has reportedly written seven other novels that are unpublished to date. JN

S

Sabourin, Louis. See POLITICAL WRITINGS IN FRENCH 1.

Sach, Marilyn. See CHILDREN'S BOOKS IN ENGLISH 3.

Saladin d'Anglure, Bernard. See ESKIMOS: BOOKS IN FRENCH.

Salone, Emile. See HISTORY STUDIES IN FRENCH 3.

Samson, Camil. See POLITICAL WRITINGS IN FRENCH 4.

Sanger, Clyde. See HISTORY STUDIES IN ENGLISH 12 and POLITICAL WRITINGS IN ENGLISH 7.

Sauer, Carl O. See HISTORY STUDIES IN ENGLISH 2.

Saunders, Robert E. See HISTORY STUDIES IN ENGLISH 1.

Sauvageau, Yves. See DRAMA IN FRENCH 4.

Savard, Félix-Antoine (1896–). Born in Quebec City, he grew up and was educated at Chicoutimi, spending his summers in the woods and travelling on the Saguenay River. Ordained a priest in 1922, he taught at the Chicoutimi Seminary until 1927 and then served in various parishes in Charlevoix County before founding the parish of Saint-Philippe de Clermont there in 1931. In 1934 he gathered a group of unemployed and their families and, in line with Québec policy of the time, assisted them in the founding of two new farm-settlements in Abitibi. He was appointed to the arts faculty of Université Laval in 1945 and became dean of arts in 1950. Elected to the Royal Society of Canada in 1945, he resigned in 1954 and became a member of the French-Canadian Academy in 1955. Now retired from Laval, he lives in Saint-Joseph-de-la-Rive in Charlevoix. In 1968 he was awarded the Prix David as a tribute to his entire body of work.

Savard's experiences and knowledge of the lumbering and pioneering areas have provided a vivid and authentic background for his books, which are rather more prose-poems than novels and charged with a strong nationalistic bias. He is an excellent stylist, notable for his richness of imagery and his blending of lively Canadian regionalisms with classical French. *Menaud, maître-draveur* (1937) is the story of a veteran of the log drive whose obsession with the 'invaders' reflects his bitterness over the exploitation of the natural resources of Québec by 'foreign' capital. When his son is drowned and his daughter seems about to marry a man who has 'sold out' to the English, he becomes enraged and eventually loses his mind. His daughter meanwhile refuses to marry a traitor to her people. The book was honoured by the French Academy and awarded the Prix David of the Québec government (which was then given for single works). Savard rewrote the book in 1944 and again in 1960. It was translated by Alan Sullivan as *Boss of the river* (1947). *L'abatis* (1943) is an account of Savard's experiences with the new farm-settlements in Abitibi. *La minuit* (1948), which was awarded the Prix Duvernay, is a romance set in the parish of La Basque, near Tadoussac, and a strong plea for the preservation of religious traditions. In 1957 Savard received a Guggenheim Fellowship and in 1959 he published *Le barachois* (winner of a Governor General's Award)—a tribute to the Acadians and their folklore—and *Martin et le pauvre*, a retelling of the legend of Saint Martin of Tours who gave his cloak to a beggar. *La folle* (1960) is a play in free verse in which the heartbroken cry of an Acadian woman whose child has been stolen by an unfaithful husband is heard against the background of a chorus representing conscience and the natural law. A second play, *La dalle-des-morts* (1965), set in 1830, dramatizes man's need to explore and woman's fate to lament. It was performed in 1965 by the Théâtre du Nouveau Monde under the direction of Jean Gascon.

Savard is also the author of two books of poetry, *Symphonie du Misereor* (1968) and *Le Bouscueil* (1972), and of *Journal et Souvenirs: I, 1961–1962* (1973).

A study of Savard's work by André MAJOR in the Écrivains canadiens d'aujourd'hui series (1968) speaks of his excellence as a stylist, the epic qualities of his writing, and the relevance of his themes and attitude to the young nationalist writers of today. Biographical and critical material, with a complete bibliography, is available in the Dossiers de documentation sur la littérature canadienne-française. JM/NS

Savard, Pierre. See HISTORY STUDIES IN FRENCH 8 and LITERARY STUDIES IN FRENCH 4.

Savoie, Donat. See ESKIMOS: BOOKS IN FRENCH and INDIANS 4.

Saywell, John T. See HISTORY STUDIES IN ENGLISH 1 and 12; POLITICAL WRITINGS IN ENGLISH 1.

Scalabrini, Rita. See CHILDREN'S BOOKS IN FRENCH.

Schindeler, Fred F. See HISTORY STUDIES IN ENGLISH 12 and POLITICAL WRITINGS IN ENGLISH 8.

Schmitz, Nancy. See FOLKLORE: BIBLIOGRAPHY.

Schneider, Lucien. See ESKIMOS: BOOKS IN FRENCH.

Schroeder, Andreas. See POETRY IN ENGLISH 2.

Schull, Joseph (1910–). John Joseph Schull was born in South Dakota but came with his parents to Moose Jaw, Sask., in 1913. He was educated at the University of Saskatchewan and at Queen's University. During the war he served as an intelligence officer with the Royal Canadian Navy and after demobilization he became a free-lance writer. Since then he has written hundreds of dramas and documentaries for radio and television. He is the author of two long poems, *The legend of Ghost Lagoon* (1938), a swashbuckling tale of the sea, and *I, Jones: private soldier* (1945), an expression of the disillusionment and indignation of a soldier caught up in the brutality of the Second World War. He was commissioned by the navy to write *The far distant ships: an official account of Canadian naval operations in the Second World War* (1950). His *100 years of banking in Canada: a history of the Toronto-Dominion Bank* (1958) is a clearly written account of the growth of the banking institution set against the background of Canada's economic development, 1856–1956. *Laurier: the first Canadian* (1965)—French translation, 1968—is an excellent popular biography that portrays the Liberal prime minister as courageous, charming, and dignified—a man of sparse yet pragmatic political ideas. Laurier is presented as the natural successor to John A. Macdonald; he takes hold of the confederation movement and by reconciling French and English purposes makes Canada into a nation. This biography won a special award from the Québec department of cultural affairs and the University of British Columbia Medal for Popular Biography. *The nation makers* (1967) is an account of confederation. A novel set in the 1890s, *The jinker* (1968), narrates the conflicts of two captains of sealing ships off the coast of Newfoundland. *The century of the Sun: the first hundred years of the Sun Life Assurance Company of Canada / Un Astre centenaire: les cents premières années de Sun Life du Canada, compagnie d'assurance-vie* (1971) is a traditional company history. *Rebellion: rising in French Canada, 1837* (1971) reconstructs in a lively and colourful manner the events and circumstances surrounding the Lower Canadian rebellion and suggests that failure to solve problems of that era are still causing difficulties in Canada today.

For young readers Schull has written three volumes in the Great Stories of Canada series: *The salt-water men: Canada's deep-sea sailors* (1957), about sailing ships off the Atlantic provinces; *Battle for the rock: the story of Wolfe and Montcalm* (1960); and *Ships of the great days: Canada's navy in the Second World War* (1962). DF

Schwartz, Mildred. See POLITICAL WRITINGS IN ENGLISH 5.

Scobie, Stephen. See POETRY IN ENGLISH 2.

Scott, Chris. See FICTION IN ENGLISH 4.

Scott, F. R. (1899–). The son of Frederick George Scott, Francis Reginald Scott was born in Quebec City and educated at Bishop's

College, Lennoxville, and at Oxford University where he held a Rhodes scholarship. On his return to Canada he studied law at McGill University, was called to the bar in 1927, and in 1928 joined the faculty of law at McGill where he was dean of law from 1961 until his retirement in 1964. He was elected to the Royal Society of Canada in 1947 and awarded the Lorne Pierce Medal for distinguished service to Canadian literature in 1962. He was technical-aid representative for the United Nations in Burma in 1952 and was a member of the Royal Commission on Bilingualism and Biculturalism. In 1965 he was awarded the Molson Prize given by the Canada Council for outstanding achievements in the arts, the humanities, and the social sciences.

A distinguished authority on constitutional law, Scott contributed to the important symposium *Evolving Canadian federalism* (1958). He has been active in left-wing political movements, having been an organizer of the League for Social Reconstruction (1932) and a contributor to its publication, *Social planning for Canada* (1935). He was president of the league in 1935–6 and national chairman of the Co-operative Commonwealth Federation from 1942 to 1950. He wrote the studies *Canada today: a study of her national interests and national policy* (1938) and was co-author with David Lewis of *Make this your Canada: a review of* CCF *history and policy* (1943). *Canada and the United States* (1941) was prepared after a year spent at Harvard on a Guggenheim Fellowship. With Michael Oliver he co-edited *Quebec states her case* (1964), translations of excerpts from articles and speeches by French Canadians on aspects of the 'quiet revolution' in that province.

Scott began publishing poetry in 1925 when, as a law student, he collaborated with A. J. M. SMITH in founding the *McGill fortnightly review*, an independent journal of literature and opinion. This publication ceased in 1927 and Scott became one of the editors of its successor, the *Canadian mercury*, of which seven issues appeared (1928–9). He was also the moving spirit and an editor with Smith of the anthology *New provinces: poems of several authors* (1936) in which his own verse was included. In 1942 he shared in the founding of *Preview*, which merged in 1945 with *First Statement* to become *Northern Review*, of which he was an editor until 1947.

The success of Scott's satirical verse on Canadian society has distracted attention from the vigour and coherence with which he has expressed his belief in the evolution of man whose transient existence can be made whole by the renewal of contact with nature, by love, and through social justice. His poems, of which an excellent representation is available in *Selected poems* (1966), are fairly evenly divided between treating man as an individual and as a social being. They first appeared in three collections—*Overture* (1945), *Events and signals* (1954), and *Signature* (1964)—and show a steady development of thought and treatment. This development is reflected in his choice of form and diction as Scott progressed from the simple, direct language of *Overture*, through the richer expression of *Events and signals*, to the mythopoeic and metaphysical poems of *Signature*. There have been fewer developments in his satirical poems on Canadian life, of which the best known are 'The Canadian authors meet' and 'A Lass in Wonderland'. (*The eye of the needle: satires, sorties, sundries* (1957) was a selection from his satirical poems.) A collection of new poems and translations, *The dance is one*, appeared in 1973.

Scott is a skilful translator of poetry from the French. *St-Denys Garneau & Anne Hébert: translations/traductions* was published in 1962, and some of his translations are included in *The poetry of French Canada in translation* (1970) edited by John GLASSCO. In 1970 his correspondence with Anne HÉBERT on the art of translation was published under the title *Dialogue sur la traduction à propos du 'Tombeau des rois'*, with a preface by Northrop FRYE. Scott has also published a collection of 'found' poems: *Trouvailles: poems from prose* (1967). He collaborated with A. J. M. Smith in compiling *The blasted pine: an anthology of satire, invective and disrespectful verse: chiefly by Canadian writers* (1957; rev. 1967).

See *The McGill movement: A. J. M. Smith, F. R. Scott and Leo Kennedy* (1969) edited by Peter Stevens in the Critical Views on Canadian Writers series. NS

Scott, James. See HISTORY STUDIES IN ENGLISH 15.

Scott, Munroe. See DRAMA IN ENGLISH 4.

Séguin, Maurice. See HISTORY STUDIES IN FRENCH 2 and 7.

Séguin, Robert-Lionel (1920–). Born at Rigaud, Qué., he was educated at the Université de Montréal, at Laval, where he completed a Doctorat ès Lettres (Histoire), and at the Sorbonne where he received a second Doctorat ès Lettres (Sciences Humaines) in 1972. He is a pioneer in the field of material ethnographical studies. His always original and well-documented books focus on two dimensions of the French-Canadian experience: traditional ethnology and the technical context. His books include *L'équipement de la ferme canadienne aux XVIIe et XVIIIe siècles* (1955), *La sorcellerie au Canada français du XVIIe au XIXe siècle* (1961), *Les moules du Québec* (1963), *Les granges du Québec du XVIIe au XIXe siècle* (1963), *Le costume civil en Nouvelle-France* (1968), *Les jouets anciens du Québec* (1969), and *Les ustensiles en Nouvelle-France* (1972). In 1967 he published the important *La civilisation traditionnelle de l''habitant' aux XVIIe et XVIIIe siècles*, for which he received a Governor General's Award and the Broquette-Gonin Prix from the Académie française. This study, which synthesizes the material and ethnological environment with the mental and cultural climate, was followed in 1972 by a more detailed analysis of the moral attitudes and behaviour of French Canadians in the seventeenth and eighteenth centuries: *La vie libertine en Nouvelle-France* (2 vols, 1972).

Séguin has also written two studies dealing with the 1837 crisis: *Le mouvement insurrectionnel dans la Presqu'Île de Vaudreuil: 1837–1838* (1955) and *La victoire de St-Denis* (1968).

J-LR

Senior, Hereward. See HISTORY STUDIES IN ENGLISH 7.

Sewell, John. See POLITICAL WRITINGS IN ENGLISH 8.

Sewid, James. See INDIANS 2.

Sheffe, Norman. See INDIANS 6.

Shelton, George W. See HISTORY STUDIES IN ENGLISH 9.

Sheppard, Louise. See CHILDREN'S BOOKS IN ENGLISH 6.

Sheps, David. See LITERARY STUDIES IN ENGLISH 4.

Shipley, Nan. See CHILDREN'S BOOKS IN ENGLISH 6.

Shook, Lawrence K. See HISTORY STUDIES IN ENGLISH 15.

Shubert, Hilda. See FICTION IN ENGLISH 6.

Shumiatcher, Morris C. See INDIANS 6.

Siebert, Erna. See INDIAN LEGENDS AND ART.

Siebrasse, Glen. See POETRY IN ENGLISH 2.

Sigurdson, G. See INDIANS 6.

Simard, Jean (1916–). Born in Quebec City, he was educated at the École des Beaux-Arts, Montreal, and became a teacher there. He has since taught at the Université du Québec. A member of the Royal Society of Canada, Simard is one of the best satirists Québec has produced. His first novel *Félix* (1947; revised and re-edited 1966; Prix Korumain de l'Académie française) is a brief, spritely, semi-autobiographical portrait, spiced with the epigrams of such humorists as Oscar Wilde, Sacha Guitry, and Bernard Shaw. *Hôtel de la reine* (1949) is the satirical picture of life in a small south-shore town. It is a first-person confessional novel, like *Mon fils pourtant heureux* (1956; paperback ed. 1968; Prix du Cercle du Livre de France), in which the satire is tempered by serious religious preoccupations. In *Les sentiers de la nuit* (1959) Simard examines, half mockingly, half tenderly, the aspirations, dreams, and delusions of a pair of anonymities from the seething ant-hill of modern life, in this case Mr and Mrs George-Godley Roundabout, who, by their pathetic blindness, illustrate poignantly the near-hopelessness of the human search for happiness. In the 1960s Simard turned to the essay, presenting in *Répertoire* (1961) and *Nouveau répertoire* (1965) reflections on art, politics, travel, and writing. Two of his *13 récits* (1964) began as moral tales inserted into his *Répertoire*. He is also the translator of two of the novels of Hugh MACLENNAN, *Le matin d'une longue nuit* (*The watch that ends the night*) (1967) and *Le temps tournera au beau* (*Barometer rising*) (1966), and the author of a play, *L'ange interdit* (1961), and a monograph, *Marcel Braitstein, sculpteur* (1970). Simard's latest book, *La séparation*

(1970), is a long novel made up entirely of the letters two lovers, both married with children, write to each other during a lengthy separation, she in Portugal, he in Montreal. As in all his writing, Simard is here attempting to reveal the way in which we all try to decant from the raw material of our lives the essence we call happiness.

Simard seems to need to hide his attempts at self-objectification behind a set of masks: satirical distance; the conventions of the autonomous first-person narrator or the epistolary novel; the wisdom and wit of others, which is everywhere in his work; or the pen of the translator. He gives one reason for these masks in *Répertoire*, where he describes the risks the satirist once ran in the parochial society of a small town in Québec. Another reason lies in his proper fear that the mirror of Socrates can so easily become the pool of Narcissus. CRPM

Simeon, Richard. See HISTORY STUDIES IN ENGLISH 12 and POLITICAL WRITINGS IN ENGLISH 6.

Simons, Beverley. See DRAMA IN ENGLISH 2.

Simpson, Leo. See FICTION IN ENGLISH 4.

Sinclair, David. See ANTHOLOGIES IN ENGLISH 1.

Sirois, Antoine. See LITERARY STUDIES IN FRENCH 2.

Sissons, Jack. See HISTORY STUDIES IN ENGLISH 10.

Skelton, Robin (1925–). Born at Easington, Yorkshire, Robin Skelton was educated at Pockington Grammar School, at Christ's College, Cambridge, and at the University of Leeds, where he graduated in 1950. From 1951 until he immigrated to Canada in 1963, he was lecturer in English at Manchester University. Since 1963 he has taught at the University of Victoria, where he is now professor of english and director of the Creative Writing Program. In 1967, with John Peter, he founded the *Malahat Review*, which he still edits.

An industrious writer and editor, Skelton is represented by more than forty published volumes, including seventeen books and pamphlets of verse, of which the earliest is *Patmos and other poems* (1955) and the most important are *Third day lucky* (1958), *Begging the dialect* (1960), *The dark window* (1962), *The hunting dark* (1971), and *Selected poems 1947–1967* (1968).

Skelton edited two Penguin anthologies, *Poetry of the thirties* (1964) and *Poetry of the forties* (1968). His scholarly interests have been concerned largely with Irish literature and especially with J. M. Synge; he is the author of *The writings of J. M. Synge* (1971), *J. M. Synge and his world* (1971), and *J. M. Synge* (1972); he is general editor of the *Collected works of J. M. Synge* and personally edited the volume devoted to Synge's poetry (1962), while with Ann Saddlemyer he edited *The world of W. B. Yeats* (1965). His works of criticism and literary biography include *The poetic pattern* (1956), *The cavalier poets* (1960), and *John Ruskin: the final years* (1955). Skelton has also written as an art critic in *Painters talking* (1957) and in essays on contemporary painters that are so far uncollected.

While Skelton's verse remains his most characteristic expression, it reflects the analytical and strongly patterned frame of mind that dominates his critical work. The development from his early poems is out of the Movement manner of the British fifties into an individual style that is reflective and—in the later Canadian poems especially—marked often by a stoic melancholy. Narrative, especially of the emotional life—of exile and memory—is a mode that Skelton has particularly developed, but he has also written in a variety of lyric and satiric moods with a fine and continually experimental craftsmanship. His interest in the ambiguous frontier between translation and parody is shown in his *200 poems from the Greek anthology* (1971). GW

Slattery, T. P. See HISTORY STUDIES IN ENGLISH 7.

Sluman, Norma. See INDIANS 2.

Smallwood, Frank. See HISTORY STUDIES IN ENGLISH 12.

Smerek, John. See HISTORY STUDIES IN ENGLISH 14.

Smiley, Donald. See POLITICAL WRITINGS IN ENGLISH 4 and 6.

Smith, A. J. M. (1902–). Born in Montreal, Arthur James Marshall Smith was educated at McGill University and the University of Edinburgh. He taught English in several American colleges until 1936 when he was appointed to the English department of Michigan State University. Although an expatriate, Smith spends every summer in Canada and has been a vital force in Canadian literature as a poet and critic since his student days when he edited the *McGill Daily Literary Supplement* in 1924–5. When it was discontinued in 1925, he founded and edited, with F. R. SCOTT, the *McGill Fortnightly Review*, an independent journal of literature and opinion, in which his own critical articles and poems were included. Publication of this journal ceased in 1927 when Smith graduated. In 1966 the Royal Society of Canada awarded him the Lorne Pierce Medal for distinguished service to Canadian literature. Smith retired from teaching in 1972 and plans to spend five months of each year at his summer home near Magog in the Eastern Townships.

Smith's poetry shows careful craftsmanship. His earlier work includes some evocative landscape poems such as 'The lonely land', but his objection to provincialism and narrow nationalism in poetry led him to abandon this vein and to turn to symbolist and metaphysical poetry. As a metaphysical poet, Smith's logical mind has concerned itself with the essential meaning of life, love, and death. Freed from conflicting emotions by this intellectual approach, he has used his own idiom and that of other poets to express tolerant, frequently cryptic, and sometimes amused observations on the present-day world. His most distinctive characteristic is the use of sharp, clear imagery and symbol. He is the author of four collections of verse: *News of the phoenix and other poems* (1943), which won a Governor General's Award, *A sort of ecstasy: poems new and selected* (1954), *Collected poems* (1962), and *Poems: new and collected* (1967). His essays have been collected in *Towards a view of Canadian letters: selected critical essays 1938–1972* (1973).

Smith also compiled, and wrote an important critical introduction to, *The book of Canadian poetry: a critical and historical anthology* (1943), which he revised in 1948 and 1957. Widely used as a college textbook, it has done much to familiarize students with the merits and weaknesses of Canadian poets. Smith's other anthologies of poetry are *Seven centuries of verse* (1947; 3rd ed. 1966), containing English and American poetry; *The worldly muse: an anthology of serious light verse* (1951); *The Oxford book of Canadian verse: in English and French* (1960); *100 poems* (1965), which contains poetry from Chaucer to Dylan Thomas; and *Modern Canadian verse: in English and French* (1967). In collaboration with F. R. Scott he edited *New provinces: poems of several authors* (1936) and *The blasted pine: an anthology of satire, invective and disrespectful verse: chiefly by Canadian writers* (1957; rev. 1967). He also edited *The book of Canadian prose 1. Early beginnings to confederation* (1965); the long-awaited second volume appeared in 1973. The two volumes were re-titled as *The book of Canadian prose: Volume 1, English-Canadian writing before confederation* and *The Canadian century: English-Canadian writing since confederation.* A paperback abridgement of these two volumes has been published under the title *The Canadian experience: a brief survey of Canadian prose* (1973). Examples of Smith's critical essays are his introduction to *The Oxford book of Canadian verse* and to *Masks of fiction: Canadian critics on Canadian prose* (1961) and *Masks of poetry: Canadian critics on Canadian verse* (1962), two prose collections he edited for the New Canadian Library. He also co-edited with M. L. Rosenthal *Exploring poetry* (1955; rev. 1973), a textbook.

See *The McGill Movement: A. J. M. Smith, F. R. Scott and Leo Kennedy* (1969) edited by Peter Stevens in the Critical Views on Canadian Writers series. NS

Smith, Bernard. See POLITICAL WRITINGS IN FRENCH 4.

Smith, Denis. See HISTORY STUDIES IN ENGLISH 12 and POLITICAL WRITINGS IN ENGLISH 1.

Smith, Dorothy Blakey. See CHILDREN'S BOOKS IN ENGLISH 5 and HISTORY STUDIES IN ENGLISH 9.

Smith, James K. See CHILDREN'S BOOKS IN ENGLISH 5 and HISTORY STUDIES IN ENGLISH 3.

Smith, Ray. See FICTION IN ENGLISH: SHORT STORIES.

Smith, Waldo E. L. See HISTORY STUDIES IN ENGLISH 12.

Somcynsky, Jean. See FICTION IN FRENCH 3.

Sorestad, Glen A. See ANTHOLOGIES IN ENGLISH 2.

Souster, Raymond (1921–). Born and educated in Toronto, he served in the air force during the Second World War. While in service he co-edited *Direction* (1943–6), the first of three literary magazines he has been associated with: he was co-editor (with Jack Hersch) and then editor of *Contact: An International Magazine of Poetry* (1952–4) and editor of *Combustion* (1957–60). In 1952, with Irving LAYTON and Louis DUDEK, he founded a cooperative venture to publish the work of Canadian poets, Contact Press. Later he was associated with Dudek and Peter Miller as an editor of this press (Miller acted as the director) until it stopped publication in 1966. He was instrumental in forming the League of Canadian Poets in 1966 and was twice elected chairman, a position he held for four years. He is employed by the Canadian Imperial Bank of Commerce in Toronto.

Souster is thought of as a poet of Toronto—he differs from most of his contemporaries in his realistic acceptance and even enjoyment of urban life for what it is—but his poems also range widely over other places and subjects. He is both the poet-participator and poet-commentator. Many of his most effective poems are composed of a few colloquial, epigrammatic lines about an object, place, or building, an experience or a gesture, that record a pregnant insight, often ironically. A prolific poet, Souster is the author of *When we are young* [1946]; *Go to sleep, world: poems* (1947); *City Hall street* (1951); *Shake hands with the hangman: poems 1940–52* (1953); *A dream that is dying* [1954]; *Walking death: poems* (1954); *For what time slays: poems* [1955]; *The selected poems* (1956), edited by Louis Dudek; *Crêpe-hanger's carnival: selected poems 1955–58* [1958]; *A local pride: poems* (1962); *Place of meeting: poems 1958–60* [1962]; *The colour of the times: the collected poems* (1964), which won a Governor General's Award; and *Ten elephants on Yonge Street* (1965).

Souster's poetry has not changed radically over the years, though he has shown a recent interest in the longer poem, as in *As is* (1967). His other volumes—*Lost and found: uncollected poems* (1968), *So far so good: poems 1938–1968* (1969), *The years* (1971)—include unpublished poems from his early days as a poet together with new poems. In 1972 he published another survey of his career in *Selected poems*.

Souster had edited a number of anthologies: *Poets 56: ten younger English-Canadians* (1956); *Experiment: poems 1923–29* (1956) by W. W. E. Ross, a mimeographed booklet; and *New wave Canada: the new explosion in Canadian poetry* (1966). He is co-editor of *Shapes and sounds: poems of W. W. E. Ross* (1968) with John Robert COLOMBO; *Made in Canada: new poems of the seventies* (1970) and *One hundred Canadian poems from the nineteenth century* (1973) with Douglas Lochhead; and, with Richard Woollatt, of three textbooks: *Generation now* (1970), *These loved, these hated lands* (1973), and *Sights and sounds* (1973).

In 1949, under the pseudonym 'Raymond Holmes', Souster published *The winter of time*, a realistic novel set in England, Toronto, and New York. In 1973, under the pseudonym 'John Holmes', he is bringing out a novel of the RCAF called *On Target*. NS/PS

Sowby, Cedric W. See HISTORY STUDIES IN ENGLISH 15.

Spafford, Duff. See HISTORY STUDIES IN ENGLISH 8 and POLITICAL WRITINGS IN ENGLISH 8.

Spafford, W. See HISTORY STUDIES IN ENGLISH 5.

Sparshott, Francis (1926–). Born in Chatham, Eng., he was educated at King's School, Rochester, and at Oxford University. He served with the British Army Intelligence from 1944 to 1947 and came to Canada in 1950 to lecture in philosophy at the University of Toronto. He is now professor of philosophy at Victoria College in that university; he was chairman of the department from 1965 to 1970.

A philosopher and a poet, Sparshott has published in both fields. His books on philosophy have the elegant clarity, wit, and irreverance of many of his poems, while much of his verse—in *A divided voice* (1965) and *A cardboard garage* (1969)—has an unengaged, cerebral quality that suggests the academic and the thinker. His neatly turned poetry, much of it written in traditional forms, includes metaphysical poems and some clever light verse.

Sparshott has written four books on philosophy: *An enquiry into goodness: and related concepts; with some remarks on the nature and scope of such enquiries* (1958), *The structure of aesthetics* (1963), *The concept of criticism: an essay* (1967), and *Looking for philosophy* (1972), a mixture of essays, 'interludes', and two dialogues that form a lively and simulating investigation of the discipline of philosophy and the philosopher's task. *A book* (1970) by 'Cromwell Kent', which was privately printed, is a *jeu d'esprit*. WET

Speaight, Robert. See HISTORY STUDIES IN ENGLISH 12.

Spears, Heather. See POETRY IN ENGLISH 1.

Spencer, Loraine. See HISTORY STUDIES IN ENGLISH 17.

Spencer, Robert F. See INDIANS 6.

Spensley, Philip. See DRAMA IN ENGLISH 4.

Spettigue, Douglas. See GROVE, Frederick Philip and LITERARY STUDIES IN ENGLISH 4.

Spry, Irene M. See HISTORY STUDIES IN ENGLISH 8.

Stacey, C. P. (1906–). Born in Toronto and educated at the University of Toronto, and at Oxford and Princeton Universities, Charles Perry Stacey was a member of the history department at Princeton from 1933 to 1940, when he became the historical officer at Canadian military headquarters in London, Eng. In 1945 he became the director of the historical section of the Canadian army in Ottawa. When he retired in 1959 he joined the history staff of the University of Toronto, of which he is still a member.

Stacey is one of Canada's most distinguished historians and is a leading interpreter of Canadian military history. His writings are always fair, completely lucid, the result of painstaking research, and, considering the complexity of his documentation, very readable. *Canada and the British army: 1846–1871* (1936; rev. 1963) is unique in that it interprets Canadian history from the military point of view. Stacey concludes that the withdrawal of British forces in 1871 strengthened the concept of imperialism in Britain and encouraged self-respect and independence in Canada. He is also author of *The military problems of Canada: a survey of defence policies and strategic conditions past and present* (1940), an outline of the history of Canadian defence policy up to the early years of the Second World War. *The Canadian army, 1939–1945: an official historical summary* (1948), which won a Governor General's Award, studies the overseas operations and battles of the army. Stacey was the general editor of the three-volume *Official history of the Canadian army in the Second World War*, a series based on official documents and for which Stacey wrote volume I: *Six years of war: the army in Canada, Britain, and the Pacific* (1955) and volume III: *The victory campaign: the operations in north-west Europe, 1944–45* (1960). These works give a wide perspective to the achievements of the Canadian army by placing them against the background of the entire allied war effort. He also edited *Records of the Nile Voyageurs* (1959) for the Champlain Society and *An introduction to the study of military history for Canadian students* (2nd ed. 1960) in which nine examples, from 1690 to 1944, are given of Canadian military campaigns and serve to illustrate the development of the Canadian army. *Quebec, 1759: the siege and the battle* (1959) re-examines and re-evaluates the military reputations of Wolfe and Montcalm and the myths and legends surrounding them. *Arms, men and governments: the war policies of Canada, 1939–1945* (1970) critically appraises policy within the context of Canada's internal problems and international realities. Stacey concludes that Canada had little influence upon the higher direction of the war—the Americans being particularly insensitive to Canadian views. He is also the general editor of the Historical Documents of Canada series and has edited volume 5, *The arts of war and peace: 1914–1945* (1972), an authoritative collection of mostly government documents depicting the national scene. DF

Stamp, R. M. See HISTORY STUDIES IN ENGLISH 15.

Stanley, G. F. G. (1907–). George Francis Gilman Stanley was born in Calgary and educated at the University of Alberta and at

Oxford. In 1936 he joined the history department at Mount Allison University, where he became director of Canadian studies. In 1947 he moved to the University of British Columbia where he stayed until 1949, and to the Royal Military College, Kingston, where he was dean of arts and head of the department of history until 1969. He is now director of Canadian Studies and curator of the Davidson Collection at Mount Allison University. During the Second World War he served in the Canadian army overseas and from 1945 to 1947 was deputy director of the Historical Section, General Staff, Ottawa. He was a member of the Ontario Advisory Board on Historic and Archaeological Sites from 1953 to 1969, and of the Royal Society of Canada, from which he received its Tyrrell Medal for historical research in 1957. He was president of the Canadian Historical Association in 1955–6.

Stanley's *The birth of western Canada: a history of the Riel rebellion* (1936; rev. 1961) emphasizes the frontier nature of Métis society and attributes much of their resistance not to the personality and character of Louis Riel but to the environment and climate of opinion in the prairie communities. *Louis Riel* (1963) is a painstakingly fair analysis of the man in relation to his times. While Stanley reinforces the image of Riel as an enigma, he portrays him as a rebellious western patriot trying to thwart the American and Canadian expansionists. *Canada's soldier: the military history of an unmilitary people* (1954; rev. 1960) and *In face of danger: the history of the Lake Superior regiment* (1960) established Stanley as a lucid military historian. *New France: the last phase, 1744–1760* (1968), in the Canadian Centenary Series, places the military campaigns within the context of the international scene. Economic competition is said to be the motive of the French-English conflict, while victory was determined by chance actions rather than by superior strategy and tactics. Ultimately, however, the prevailing economic faith in France of continentalism and anti-colonialism convinced Versailles that America was not worth additional military commitment. The defeat meant that New France was smothered as a cultural community; the people were forced to turn to the land and the Church to survive as a peasant society. His study of the American invasion of Canada in 1775–6 will be published by the Canadian War Museum in 1973. Stanley appears as an exponent of the compact theory of confederation in *A short history of the Canadian constitution* (1969). He strenuously decries the centralizers—those who would give more power to Ottawa than to the provinces.

Stanley is also the author of *A short history of Kingston as a military and naval centre* (1950); *The story of Canada's flag: a historical sketch* (1965); *Manitoba 1870: a Métis achievement/une réalisation Métisse* (1972); and *Louis Riel*, a booklet in the Canadian Historical Association Series. He has edited and written introductions for: *In search of the magnetic north: a soldier-surveyor's letters from the north-west, 1843–44* (1955), the letters of Sir John Henry Lefroy; *For want of a horse: being a journal of the campaigns against the Americans in 1776 and 1777 conducted from Canada by an officer who served with Lt Gen. Burgoyne* (1961); *Canadian identity: a symposium held at Mount Allison University* (1969); and *Mapping the frontier: Charles Wilson's diary of the survey of the 49th parallel, 1858–1867, while secretary of the British Boundary Commission* (1970). He was co-editor of a symposium presented to the Royal Society of Canada in 1960, *Canadian universities today/Les universités canadiennes aujourd'hui* (1960) and editor of *Pioneers of Canadian science/Les pionniers de la science canadienne* (1964). DF

Steele, I. K. See HISTORY STUDIES IN ENGLISH 2.

Steele, James. See POLITICAL WRITINGS IN ENGLISH 2.

Stefanyk, Vasyl. See FICTION IN ENGLISH: SHORT STORIES.

Stein, David Lewis. See FICTION IN ENGLISH 4 and SHORT STORIES.

Stelmack, C. B. See HISTORY STUDIES IN ENGLISH 7.

Stelter, Gilbert A. See HISTORY STUDIES IN ENGLISH 17.

Stephens, Donald. See ANTHOLOGIES IN ENGLISH 2 and LITERARY STUDIES IN ENGLISH 4.

Stevens, James R. See INDIANS 2.

T

Tainturier, Jean. See HISTORY STUDIES IN FRENCH 6.

Takashima, Shizuye. See CHILDREN'S BOOKS IN ENGLISH 5.

Talman, James J. See HISTORY STUDIES IN ENGLISH 5.

Tarasoff, Koozma. See HISTORY STUDIES IN ENGLISH 14.

Tard, Louis-Martin. See HISTORY STUDIES IN FRENCH 10.

Tarver, Ben. See DRAMA IN ENGLISH 3.

Taylor, A. J. P. See HISTORY STUDIES IN ENGLISH 13.

Taylor, Alastair. See HISTORY STUDIES IN ENGLISH 12 and POLITICAL WRITINGS IN ENGLISH 7.

Taylor, Charles. See POLITICAL WRITINGS IN ENGLISH 4.

Taylor, James R. See POLITICAL WRITINGS IN ENGLISH 6.

Teeple, Gary. See POLITICAL WRITINGS IN ENGLISH 2.

Terrell, John Upton. See HISTORY STUDIES IN ENGLISH 2.

Tétreau, Jean. See FICTION IN FRENCH: SHORT STORIES.

Theall, Donald. See LITERARY STUDIES IN ENGLISH 3.

Thériault, Yves (1915–). Born in Quebec City, he claims to be partly of Montagnais Indian descent. While he was still very young the family moved to Montreal where he received his primary and secondary education (1921–9). At fifteen Thériault quit school. During the next four years he was a trapper, truck driver, nightclub employee, cheese salesman, tractor salesman, etc. Exhausted by the furious pace and suffering from tuberculosis, he spent a year and a half in the sanatorium at Lac-Édouard (1934–5). In 1935 he was engaged for a trial period as a radio announcer by station CKAC in Montreal. From 1936–9 he was an announcer for CHNC New Carlisle, CHRC Quebec, CHLN Trois-Rivières, and CKCH Hull, where he wrote his first radio sketches and published his first short stories in *Le Jour*, a newspaper edited by Jean-Charles Harvey. In 1942 he married Michelle-Germaine Blanchet, Harvey's secretary, and was named director of a newspaper in Toronto, but soon he became publicity manager for a factory producing war supplies. Between 1943–5 he worked as a script-writer and PR man for the National Film Board. From 1945 to 1950 he was a script-writer for Radio-Canada while also publishing anonymously or under pseudonyms an enormous quantity of 'ten-cent novels' (32 pages); at one point he was producing eleven of them a week and his wife three. In 1950 he was awarded a scholarship by the French government but was obliged by the pressure of work to refuse it. He made a trip around the world in 1952 aboard an Italian freighter and spent some time in Italy. Thériault was elected to the Royal Society of Canada in 1959. In 1961 he became a contributor to the *Nouveau Journal* and was invited by the Soviet government to the International Film Festival in Moscow. In 1965 he was elected president of the Société des Écrivains canadiens, then resigned and spent two years (1965–7) as cultural director for the Department of Indian Affairs in Ottawa. He received the Molson Prize in 1971. Thériault is also a member of the Association des auteurs dramatiques and the International P.E.N. Club. He lives on a small farm in the Richelieu River valley.

Thériault is the most prolific and versatile of contemporary Québec authors, a veritable prodigy. The quantity, quality, and variety of his writing have assured his popularity with the reading public in Canada; translations of *Agaguk* have made him known abroad; and he is widely studied in the CEGEPS and universities of Québec. Largely self-taught, animated by a driving dynamism, a bohemian restlessness, and a passion for liberty that caused him to revolt against conformism and convention, Thériault soon acquired a vast experience of the seamier and more violent sides of life that are reflected in the thirty books he has published since *Contes pour un homme seul* (1944). These unusual, captivating, and brutal stories (twelve of which had appeared in *Le Jour*) announced the themes that Thériault would later develop: naturalism, primitivism, exoticism, eroticism, and sublimated sexuality struggling for expression. Basic human instincts and passions, in conflict with the forces of tradition and repression, are the occasion for biting criticism of our civilization and of French-Canadian society in particular. Throughout his work, procreation, mutilation, and death take on special significance in his characters' desperate search for individuality. The importance of these acts is underlined by the role they play in the strivings for emancipation of the oppressed: Indians, Eskimos, Jews, immigrants, peasants —all the 'little people' who battle against the forces of moral, religious, social, economic, or ethnic domination that prevent them from becoming fully human. For Thériault refuses to confine himself to the narrow limits of French-speaking Québec. His characters inhabit the forests and tundra of the far north, or anywhere and nowhere—as in the case of Karnak, the isolated mountain village of his first novel, *La fille laide* (1950). Fabien, the hired hand, strangles the attractive widow Bernadette Loubron so that he and Edith, the ugly servant girl, may gain possession of their employer's rich farm. When their son is born deaf and blind, Fabien tries unsuccessfully to drown him, but he and Edith finally decide to rear the child in expiation of their sin. In 1951 Thériault published three novels: *La vengeance de la mer*, *Le dompteur d'ours*, and *Les vendeurs du temple*. In *Le dompteur*, the arrival of Hermann, a powerfully muscled and enigmatic vagabond who claims to wrestle with bears, unleashes among the women of a remote mountain hamlet a frenzy of pent-up sexual frustrations. On the morning of the promised combat, Hermann takes up a collection of money from the spectators, enters the church to pray, and disappears unseen out the back door. In spite of his deception, Hermann has nonetheless acted as a cathartic agent, purging the villagers of passions they dared not admit, even to themselves. In *Les vendeurs du temple*, a somewhat exaggerated political and religious satire on rural Québec, Father Alphose Bossé, priest of the parish of Saint-Léonide-le-Confesseur, finds himself embroiled in a scheme to relocate the village cemetery so that a road can be built to the advantage of the political party in power. Bossé unexpectedly discovers oil beneath the village, and to protect his poverty-stricken parishioners, he defies his bishop, the politicians, and the rapacious Inter Continental Oil Company. As punishment he is forced into retirement as chaplain of an isolated nunnery. *Aaron* (1954, Prix de la Province de Québec) is the story of a young orthodox Jew who is raised in Montreal by Moishe, his strict old grandfather who insists that Aaron follow the ancestral customs, work as a tailor, and become steeped in the rabbinic tradition. Under the influence of Viedna, a beautiful and emancipated Jewess, Aaron revolts against Moishe, rejects his cultural and religious heritage, becomes completely assimilated into the English-speaking business community, changes his name, and disappears. Moishe, his dreams shattered, can only await death in loneliness and desolation.

With the publication in 1958 of *Agaguk* (Prix de la Province de Québec, 1958; Prix France-Canada, 1961), Thériault achieved international recognition. This almost epic evocation of love and fatherhood among the Eskimos of the Canadian North has been translated into six languages (into English by Miriam Chapin, 1967). Agaguk's evolution towards maturity is the mainspring of the action and of the various conflicts he has with the whites, his own tribe, his father, and the harsh realities of the vast and hostile tundra. The gradual civilizing of Agaguk is the work of Iriook, his wife. Thanks to her courage, love, and shrewdness, she twice saves her husband's life: the first time when he is horribly mutilated by a monstrous white wolf and later when he escapes the police who are investigating the murder of the white bootlegger he has killed. The crux of the novel is when Iriook, in the face of the merciless Eskimo tradition that still governs her husband, demands at gunpoint that Agaguk spare the life of the daughter she has just borne him. In spite of the risks involved, she then succeeds in convincing Agaguk calmly and lucidly to accept his daughter and the responsibility that this decision involves. *Ashini* (1960; translated by Gwendolyn Moore, 1972), which won the Prix France-Canada and a Governor General's Award in 1961, is a sort of lyric poem to the glory of the Montagnais in which certain Indian myths are evoked with great beauty. Ashini is the last of the Montagnais to live in freedom in accordance with ancestral custom. Old and weary, he has lost his wife and his two sons; his daughter has disappeared. Death, his sole companion, constantly hovers around him. He despises the whites with their lies and their shoddy trinkets. He finally kills himself and with him dies a whole civilization. This book, a plea for justice, is also a work of art and Thériault himself ranks it as one of his best.

In 1960 Thériault also published *Roi de la côte nord*, the extraordinary life of Napoléon-Alexandre Comeau. The following year saw the publication of *Séjour à Moscou* (1961), an essay; *Le vendeur d'étoiles et autres contes* (1961), for which he was awarded the Prix Mgr Camille Roy; and three novels—*Amour au goût de mer* (1961), *Cul-de-sac* (1961), and *Les commettants de Caridad* (1961), set in Spain. In *Amour au goût de mer* a Sicilian immigrant couple, Pippo and Gina Martorama, succumb to the misery, sickness, and despair of their life alone in Montreal. Among other themes Thériault here criticizes the French-Canadian antipathy to foreigners or outsiders. *Cul-de-sac* is the story of the gradual disintegration of Victor Debreux, an engineer in his fifties who, after the death of Fabienne, starts drinking again. He falls and is trapped in a rocky crevice of the Manicouagan River. Lying helpless, and constantly attacked by a hawk that nearly eats him alive, he reviews the events of his life. After being rescued he has a leg amputated and learns that he is also suffering from cancer of the liver. He decides to hasten his doom by drowning himself in drink. The main theme of *Les commettants de Caridad* is universal, going back to biblical times, although the action is set in the once-idyllic mountain hamlet of Caridad in Andalusia. Herón the Magnificent, now become Herón the horribly mutilated scapegoat, has had all the sins of the village heaped on his head. Formerly Caridad was an earthly paradise where life was simple and carefree, crops abundant, and sexual delights fiery and frequent. All this is changed the day Herón tempts fate through his pride and foolhardiness, causes the death of Pilár, his fiancée, and brings down the wrath of the gods on the hamlet. This novel is included by Thériault in the list of his major works; structurally and symbolically it is more complicated than many of his other novels.

Experimenting with new techniques in 1962, Thériault published *Si la bombe m'était contée* in which he examines the frightening subject of the atomic bomb and its effects. Another experimental novel, *Le grand roman d'un petit homme* (1963), met with relatively little success. Returning to the primitivistic vein, Thériault recounts in *Le ru d'Ikoué* (1963), a sort of prose poem, how a young Algonkin Indian lad growing up in the forest falls in love with a stream he has discovered. The water symbolically becomes his mistress and guides him with tact and delicacy through the trials and conflicts of adolescence towards manhood. The development of Ikoué is extremely well handled: the author has succeeded in maintaining a delicate balance between primitive savagery and poetic sensitivity. *La rose de pierre* (1964) is a collection of nine short stories dealing with various aspects of love. In tone and setting they resemble *Contes pour un homme seul* and some, such as 'La main', reflect a strange and explosive violence. Géron, powerful and choleric, one day in a fit of rage strikes Marie, the wife he loves dearly. That night, in penance, with one swift stroke of his razor-sharp axe, he chops off the offending hand. In *Les temps du carcajou* (1966) violence and the obsession with degradation and destruction know no bounds. Bruno Juchereau, surly captain of the schooner Étoile de Natashquouanc, recruits a crew of sadists and perverts, each with a vice more vicious than the last. Annette, his mistress, has been unfaithful to him and he cold-bloodedly plots a horrible and brutal revenge. During a violent storm on the Gulf of St Lawrence, he has her gang-raped by his monstrous crew. In this orgy of sex and terror Annette is scalped, and while all the other members of the crew are washed overboard Bruno couples with her in a final explosion of love-hate that makes them feel like demonic gods. This novel, full of hatred and grotesque eroticism, is significant because it marks the antipode of *Agaguk*: the unity of the couple is shattered; the man and woman abhor each other, mutually destroying themselves and all those they come in contact with. The characters are portrayed as the ultimate in evil and because of their very excesses do not come to life as real literary creations. Vengeance is also the theme of *L'appelante* (1967). Henri l'Aveugle, blind for the last ten years, is a violent brute who terrorizes the villagers with his cane. Thanks to a potion that his sister-in-law Judith has obtained from a sorceress, Henri falls violently in love with Lisette Vaguerand. On their honeymoon in a strange hotel Lisette tells Henri that a year and a half previously he had come upon her and her lover in a thicket and in a fury of mindless violence he had disfigured her for life with his cane. She tricks her blind husband into plunging naked out of the hotel window and he becomes totally paralysed as a result of the fall. Back on their farm, she savours her revenge by slashing the helpless Henri across the face with his own cane.

In 1968 Yves Thériault accomplished a feat unequalled in French-Canadian letters by publishing six books in one year: *Le marcheur*, a play; *L'Île introuvable*, a collection of eighteen short stories; and four novels—*La mort d'eau*, *Kesten*, *Mahigan*, and *N'Tsuk*. Thériault himself has claimed to be more of a storyteller than a novelist and in *L'Île introuvable* he seems more at ease in exploring his own imaginary world, in creating characters and situations bordering on the epic, than in following the conventions of the novel. This collection reveals a serenity and a satisfaction in writing that contrasts with the tortured atmosphere of his recent novels. The tales illustrate all the different 'styles' in Thériault's writing—all his main themes and major tendencies. *La mort d'eau*, more a novella than a true novel, relates the story of Valère Babin, a fisherman from the Magdalen Islands, and of Eve-Angèle Comeau, his beautiful sister-in-law, who immigrates to Montreal in search of romance only to become disenchanted. *Kesten*, in contrast, is a brutal, violent novel where mythical monsters from the Middle Ages are reincarnated in the twentieth century to re-enact in unending cycles their unresolved feuds. Kesten the Swede, master of an immense ranch near Edmonton, has been living for the past ten years with Ingrid, a former prostitute. Their existence is shattered by the arrival of the great stallion Dragon, which Kesten has bought because the animal dared to challenge and defy him. Soon the conflict between man and beast becomes an obsession with Kesten, who has sworn to overcome Dragon and make him kneel before his lord and master. *Mahigan* also elaborates on the idea of eternal enmity between man and beast, but here Thériault reverts to the primitive life of the Indians as his source of inspiration. Mahigan is the name of both the wolf and the man in this novel and, like Kesten and Dragon, they seem to have been predestined to meet in mortal combat. The parallel evolution of the young Cree and the wolf is presented in alternating chapters until the clash in which each seeks vengeance against the other. *N'Tsuk* (translated by Gwendolyn Moore, 1972) has often been compared to *Ashini*. The main characters of both works are highly critical of modern civilization and castigate the unjust arrogance of the white man's technological society; both books are written in highly poetic language. N'Tsuk is a hundred-year-old Montagnais Indian woman who, on the threshold of death, undertakes to explain in all simplicity to a white woman what kind of existence she and her tribe have led. In conclusion she suggests that time is running out: unless man succeeds in re-establishing his shattered harmony with nature and living in accordance with its laws, both will be doomed.

In 1969 Thériault published two original works, *Tayaout, fils d'Agaguk* and *Antoine et sa montagne*, and adapted to novel form the film *Valérie* by Denis Héroux. For Thériault *Valérie* is a borrowed subject corresponding little to his real preoccupations and sources of inspiration. The action of *Antoine et sa montagne* begins in 1835 near Saint-Denis, a small village on the Richelieu River. Antoine is paralysed by an inexplicable fascination with a tiny mountain on the farm of his neighbour, Jusseaume, who refuses to sell. Things go to wrack and ruin until Rosanne Poulin, the new young schoolmistress, makes him understand the nature of his preoccupation with this hillock. They marry, and thanks to their profound love for each other they struggle along with very little and are truly happy. Some critics, because of references to political events of the day, see in this book an allegory on the situation of the French Canadians. In *Tayaout, fils d'Agaguk*, Thériault resurrects many of the characters of his earlier novel. But in the eleven years that separate the publication of the two works immense changes have taken place in traditional

Eskimo society. Once proudly independent, Agaguk and his wife have given up their liberty and gone to work for the whites. Tayaout, not yet sixteen, revolted by the degradation of his people, sets out alone on a series of endless wanderings. He discovers a vein of steatite, the sacred green soapstone so cherished by his ancestors. Suddenly realizing that he has been entrusted by the gods with a great mission, he encourages his people to venerate the spirits that live in these rocks by carving them after the manner of their forefathers. The Eskimos once again feel a sense of pride and accomplishment in their art until Jones, the government agent, convinces Agaguk to sell his holy statuettes and to carve others for sale. The other Eskimos follow his example and the wrath of the gods descends on their heads. To avenge this sacrilege, Tayaout is compelled to kill his father, making him the scapegoat that bears the guilt of the whole community—like Herón in *Les commettants de Caridad.* But Tayaout must also suffer for this deed. His fate is to be devoured by the huge white bear, which one year earlier he had successfully fought and escaped from. Agaguk, corrupted by the civilization of the whites, has provoked the gods and has died. Tayaout has tried to remain true to the old traditions and laws of primitivism and also has died. For man as portrayed by Thériault, no compromise between the ancient and the modern and no hope for the future appears possible.

The narrator of *Le dernier havre* (1970) is an eighty-year-old Gaspé fisherman who decides to embark on one final voyage on the Gulf. One day he discovers an old fishing boat run aground, which makes him reflect on his own situation. He conceives the plan of repairing it without anyone's knowing. But he also thinks about the meaninglessness of his existence and gradually comes to grips with the thought of death. All that really matters to him is death with honour and he chooses to go down with his boat once and for all. More than any other of Thériault's heroes, the old fisherman finally dies reconciled with life and, more importantly, with himself.

The characters in Thériault's latest novel, *La Passe-au-Crachin* (1972), are not extraordinary heroes but people with human weaknesses. This is a tale about the inability of a man to communicate; the loneliness, boredom, and revolt of a woman. Marie and Jean Dourmenec, born in France, have for the last ten years lived in the wilds of Labrador where Jean is a fisherman. After their marriage and immigration to Canada, a constant state of tension and incomprehension has existed between them: Marie is tormented by the silent and withdrawn nature of her husband and he cannot understand her urgent need to communicate orally. Unable to bear her frustrations any longer, Marie sets off on foot through the forest, carrying their baby Nicolas on her back, heading for civilization to the south. In the tragedy of the child's death and her own narrow escape Marie finally comes to understand the profound depth of Jean's love for her and the couple face the future on the basis of an imperfect albeit workable compromise.

Thériault has quite rightly been criticized by some for writing hastily and carelessly, but it is impossible at present to make any definitive assessment of his ultimate merit as a novelist. He has also written more than 1,300 radio and television texts of all kinds (by his own count). At one time he was producing thirteen dramatic programs a week for three different radio stations as well as a weekly rebroadcast of another text in Quebec City. Between 1950 and 1965 Thériault had more than sixty plays broadcast by CBF and CBFT alone. This vast production is virtually inaccessible to the reading public because only four of his plays have been made available in printed form. *Le samaritain* (1952) was published in volume four of *Écrits du Canada français* (1958). *Le marcheur* (1950) appeared in 1968 in the collection 'Théâtre canadien'. *Frédange* and *Les terres neuves*, both two-act dramas written earlier, were published in a single volume in 1970 but have not been performed. In fact only two of Thériault's plays have been put on stage: *Le marcheur* in 1950 and *Bérengère ou la chair en feu* by the Théâtre de la Fenière on the outskirts of Quebec City during the summer of 1965.

In addition to the radio and TV texts and the countless 'ten-cent thrillers' published under pseudonyms, Thériault is also the author of more than a score of science-fiction and adventure stories for children and adolescents. (See CHILDREN'S BOOKS IN FRENCH.) Most of these (*La revanche du Nascopie*, *La loi de l'Apache*, *Le rapt du lac Caché*, *Les aventures de Ti-Jean*, *Le petit tramway*, etc.) were published between 1959–67 and are still in print. LWK

Thério, Adrien. See ANTHOLOGIES IN FRENCH and FICTION IN FRENCH 2 and SHORT STORIES.

Thernstrom, S. See HISTORY STUDIES IN ENGLISH 13.

Thomas, Anna Rokeby. See CHILDREN'S BOOKS IN ENGLISH 6.

Thomas, Audrey Grace (1935–), *née* Callahan. Born in Binghampton, N.Y., she was educated at Smith College, Northampton, Mass., and at the University of British Columbia, having come to Canada in 1959. She has lived in England and spent two academic years in Ghana (1964–6), where her husband taught at the University of Science and Technology at Kumasi. During 1971 she travelled extensively in the former French West African colonies. She now lives on Galiano Island in the Gulf of Georgia, B.C.

Mrs Thomas writes polished, compelling fiction in which she pits her disturbed protagonists against people living normal lives in England, Africa, or Canada. Her feminine characters frequently suffer from a sense of inadequacy not understood by the men with whom they deal—men who take life casually. She sometimes reverses these attitudes with startling effect: a striking example of male suffering is given in 'Omo', one of the stories in her collection *Ten green bottles* (1964), which deals with African and English situations. Her novel *Mrs Blood* (1970) is a poignant revelation of the mental suffering of a white woman in hospital in Ghana where she fights to stave off a miscarriage. It was translated into French under the title *Du sang* (1972). Her interlocking novellas *Munchmeyer and Prospero and the island* (1972) recall *The tempest.* In the first of these novellas, Munchmeyer, an untalented writer who is a slave to his inordinate vanity and misanthropy, is a modern Caliban who suffers mental torment. In the second, Miranda, while writing the depressing story of Munchmeyer, lives on an island where she receives companionship and encouragement from an artist. She is inclined to be merciful towards Munchmeyer, but is given a more realistic view of the cruelty of human nature by the older artist, whom she calls Prospero. The setting of both stories is British Columbia. NS

Thomas, Clara (1919–), *née* McCandless. Born in Strathroy, Ont., she was educated at the University of Western Ontario. Her interest in Canadian studies dates from her student days in the forties when such an interest was not common; her M.A. thesis (Western, 1944), biographical and bibliographical notes on 122 writers, was revised and published in book form as *Canadian novelists: 1925–1945* (1946). Since 1947 she has been teaching and writing in the Canadian field. She received her Ph.D. from the University of Toronto in 1962 and is now a professor in the department of English at York University.

Her first biography was *Love and work enough: the life of Anna Jameson* (1967), a readable and thoroughly researched study of the nineteenth-century writer and visitor to Canada and of her works. Another biographical work, *Ryerson of Upper Canada* (1969), is a portrait of the man, of his careers as clergyman and educator and of the times he lived in. As well as many articles in the field of Canadian literature, Mrs Thomas has written *Margaret Laurence*, a monograph in the Canadian Writers Series. Her guide-book to English-Canadian literature, *Our nature, our voices: Vol. I* (1973) presents essays, bibliography, and pictures on the chronological development of Canada, its culture and its literature.

She contributed the chapter on the Strickland sisters (Mrs Moodie and Mrs Traill) to *The clear spirit* (1966) and introductions to four volumes in the New Canadian Library: Anna Jameson's *Winter studies and summer rambles in Canada*; Mrs Traill's *The backwoods of Canada* and *The Canadian settler's guide*; and Margaret LAURENCE's *The tomorrow-tamer.* She is editor of *John George Bourinot's 'Canada's intellectual strength and weakness'*; *T. G. Marquis' 'English Canadian literature'* and *Camille Roy's 'French Canadian literature'* (1973). WET

Thompson, Don W. See HISTORY STUDIES IN ENGLISH 13.

Thompson, Kent. See ANTHOLOGIES IN ENGLISH 2; FICTION IN ENGLISH: SHORT STORIES; and POETRY IN ENGLISH 2.

Thomson, Dale C. See HISTORY STUDIES IN ENGLISH 12; HISTORY STUDIES IN FRENCH 11; and POLITICAL WRITINGS IN ENGLISH 7.

Thordarson, Bruce. See HISTORY STUDIES IN ENGLISH 12 and POLITICAL WRITINGS IN ENGLISH 7.

Tivy, Louis. See HISTORY STUDIES IN ENGLISH 7.

Toews, John B. See HISTORY STUDIES IN ENGLISH 14.

Tougas, Gérard. See ANTHOLOGIES IN FRENCH and LITERARY STUDIES IN FRENCH 1.

Toye, William. See ANTHOLOGIES IN ENGLISH 3 and CHILDREN'S BOOKS IN ENGLISH 3 and 4.

Trait, Jean-Claude. See POLITICAL WRITINGS IN FRENCH 7.

Translations. From the translations of Philippe Aubert de Gaspé's *Les Anciens Canadiens* (1863) by G. M. Pennée in 1864 to Alan Brown's 1973 translation of Hubert AQUIN's *L'antiphonaire* (1970), some seventy French-Canadian writers and 110 works of literature have been translated into English. In the other direction only half-a-dozen English-Canadian authors and a dozen of their books have been put into French. The reason usually advanced to explain this discrepancy is that most French-Canadian readers are bilingual and can therefore read English works in the original. The fact is that English-Canadian writers have a severely limited circulation in Québec; that most Québec readers turn to France for literary nourishment outside their own province (and to French translations of American fiction); and that the only English-Canadian writers who are known at all to French-Canadian readers are those few who have been translated: MCLUHAN, FRYE, Kirby, MACLENNAN, RICHLER, and Mazo de la Roche.

On closer inspection, this cultural indifference is not so one-sided as it seems. More than half the 110 French titles mentioned above are now out of print; few of those available are in paperback; and only a handful of French-Canadian writers are well known in the rest of Canada: Hémon, ROY, Lemelin, CARRIER, and Marie-Claire BLAIS.

Forty titles have been translated since 1968 (thirty-five from French to English; five from English to French). A program of federal support announced in 1972 and administered by the Canada Council will certainly help individual translators in the future. Whether any farsighted national policy will emerge is another question.

The quality of translation has varied widely. So far Canada has produced no great translators, though some distinguished men of letters have been occasional practitioners of the art. Charles G. D. Roberts produced a second translation of Aubert de Gaspé's *Les Anciens Canadiens* in 1890 and translated Fréchette's *Noël au Canada* in 1900, and B. K. Sandwell englished Nantel's *À la hache* in 1937. More recently novelist Joyce MARSHALL has provided excellent translations of a variety of books, including a selection of Mère Marie de l'Incarnation's letters under the title *Word from New France* in 1967; an abridgement of Eugène CLOUTIER's *Le Canada sans passeport* (*No passport: a discovery of Canada*) in 1968; and two of Gabrielle ROY's latest novels: *La route d'Altamont* (*The road past Altamont*) in 1967 and *La rivière sans repos* (*Windflower*) in 1970.

Outstanding work has also been done by several English-Canadian poets. F. R. SCOTT's translations of Saint-Denys GARNEAU and Anne HÉBERT appeared in 1962 and his correspondence with the latter concerning his translation of *Le tombeau des rois* was published as *Dialogue sur la traduction* in 1970. Fred COGSWELL has published two volumes of translations, *One hundred poems of modern Quebec* (1970) and *A second hundred . . .* (1971), and John GLASSCO, who translated Saint-Denys Garneau's *Journal* in 1962, is the editor and chief translator of *The poetry of French Canada in translation* (1970), an anthology that includes poems by forty-seven French Canadians translated by twenty-two English Canadians, most of them poets in their own right.

Most translators, however, are not poets or novelists. Some have made a specialty of translating a single author. Glen Shortliffe was the translator of Gérard BESSETTE; Sheila Fischman of Roch Carrier; Harry Lorne Binsse of four novels by Gabrielle Roy, and Derek Coltman of five by Marie-Claire Blais. Others have been more eclectic: Alan Brown has translated Jacques GODBOUT, Naim Kattan, and Hubert Aquin; Philip Stratford has translated Jean LE MOYNE, Claire MARTIN, and André Laurendeau; and Felix Walter translated Ringuet's *Trente arpents* (with Dorothea Walter) and de Roquebrune's *Testament de mon enfance*.

Some translators of French-Canadian writers have been American: Derek Coltman/Blais's *Le jour est noir* (*The day is dark*) and *Une saison dans la vie d'Emmanuel* (*A season in the life of Emmanuel*); Samuel Putnam/Lemelin's *Au pied de la pente douce* (*The town below*). Others have been British: Barbara Bray/DUCHARME's *L'avalée des avalés* (*The swallowers swallowed*); Antonia White/Claire France's *Les enfants qui s'aiment* (*Children in love*). The classic example of mistranslation of Québec French is Hannah Josephson's rendering of *la poudrerie éclata* (an expression that means 'the blizzard struck') in Roy's *The tin flute* by 'the gunpowder works blew up'. The problems of translating *joual*, Québec's vigorous contemporary dialect, are not easy to resolve, but Gérald Robitaille in his translation of Jacques RENAUD's *Le cassé* (*Flat broke and beat*) and Alan Brown in his translation of Jacques Godbout's *Salut Galarneau!* (*Hail Galarneau*) have found some ingenious solutions. Harvest House, Montreal, publishes a translation series called French Writers of Canada that has some twelve titles of novels and short stories, and more have been announced.

Translations of scholarly and topical works by Québec writers have appeared with gratifying frequency since the middle sixties. Many of them are cited in the bibliographical entries HISTORY STUDIES and POLITICAL WRITINGS. New Press, Toronto, have begun an admirable policy of having outstanding French-Canadian plays translated for their series New Drama. Play translations are noted in DRAMA IN FRENCH.

Two Canadian periodicals are dedicated exclusively to translation: *Contemporary literature in translation* published in Vancouver and *Ellipse: writers in translation* published at the Université de Sherbrooke. The former only occasionally publishes Canadian material, though a special issue, Winter 1971–2, is entirely devoted to French-Canadian poetry. The latter translates works of two Canadian poets—one French, one English—in each issue. Since 1969 *Ellipse* has presented a dozen pairs of poets in translation.

Bibliographies of French-Canadian literature in translation are available in three places: in a short list in *Read Canadian* (1972) edited by Robert Fulford *et al.*; in a bibliography, 'French-Canadian fiction in translation', in Ronald Sutherland's *Second Image* (1971); and in a more complete bibliography (to 1968) by Philip Stratford in the Université de Montréal periodical *Meta: The Translator's Journal*, December 1968: 'French-Canadian literature in translation'.

The list of English-Canadian works in translation is so short that no bibliography has yet been compiled. It would include novelist Jean SIMARD's translation of Hugh MacLennan's *Barometer rising* and *The watch that ends the night* and Frye's *The educated imagination*; François Rinfret's translation of Frye's *The modern century*; Jean Paré's translation of McLuhan's *The Gutenberg galaxy*, *Understanding media*, and *Counterblast*; and René Chicoine's translation of Richler's *The street*. Major works by all these writers, plus numerous titles in Mazo de la Roche's Jalna series and *The fire-dwellers* by Margaret LAURENCE, have also been translated in France. There is renewed interest in translation in Québec, however, and more French-Canadian translations of English-Canadian works can be expected soon. PCS

Tremblay, Gemma. See POETRY IN FRENCH.

Tremblay, Gilberte. See CHILDREN'S BOOKS IN FRENCH.

Tremblay, Léo. See HISTORY STUDIES IN FRENCH 2.

Tremblay, Louis-Marie. See POLITICAL WRITINGS IN FRENCH 6.

Tremblay, Michel (1942–). Born and raised in the east end of Montreal, he won a scholarship to a classical college at the age of thirteen but left after three months 'because our professors told us that we were the intellectual cream of society. This was more than I could stomach.' He returned to secondary school, studied graphic arts, and became a linotype operator, like his father and brother. He wrote his first play, *Le train* (unpublished), in 1960, and four years later it won for him Québec's Young Authors' Award. The following year he embarked on *Les belles-soeurs* (1968), which was unanimously rejected on a first reading by the jury of the Dominion Drama Festival in 1966. Tremblay hawked the play round Montreal for two and a half years, before it received a public reading at the Centre d'Essai des Auteurs dramatiques. It was subsequently bought by the Théâtre du Rideau vert and in April 1973 was successfully produced in English at the St Lawrence Centre for the Arts, Toronto.

The production of *Les belles-soeurs* is probably the most important single event in the history of Québec theatre. Since then Tremblay has consolidated his position as the province's leading playwright. The wariness displayed towards this play is understandable, for it is written in *joual*. Although a debased form of language, its use on stage—a deliberate rejection of the domination of French culture in Québec—is a means of asserting the existence of an independent Québec culture. Tremblay's work for the theatre reflects the emergence of a colonized people after years of social and cultural oppression. Trying to sum him up in a few hundred words is a futile task, for his work, like that of Yvon Deschamps and Robert Charlebois, continues to develop in the same rapid rhythm as Québec itself develops culturally. For Tremblay puts the Québécois themselves on stage: in confronting his audience with them he effects a true interaction between stage and auditorium, as in all the great epochs of theatre. What Tremblay has brought to the Québec theatre is a combination of social realism and innovative theatrical techniques.

Les belles-soeurs is a pessimistic play: all the women (there are no men in it) are frustrated and vulnerable, malicious to one another, scathing of their men-folk. But Tremblay shows that this has nothing to do with some abstract 'human nature': these people are alienated because of the inhuman conditions in which they are expected to live (in working-class Montreal). In the end Germaine's neighbours steal the million trading-stamps she has won, for why should she be allowed to escape while they must go on living 'dans l'marde'? The one girl who got out of her proletarian surroundings has become a hostess in a dubious nightclub, but discovers that age has reduced her powers of attraction. Tremblay pursues this line of the one person who escapes in his subsequent work, *À toi pour toujours, ta Marie-Lou* (1971). After Léopold kills his wife and commits suicide, one of their daughters continues to live in 'la grande noirceur', but the other, Carmen, becomes a country-and-western singer. This play mirrors the break-up of the monolithic social structure that existed in Québec up to the time of the 'Quiet Revolution' through the break-up of a family 'ruled by the curé, crushed by ignorance'. Léopold is an intelligent man who sees the futility of spending his life working at the same machine, in the same factory, for the same boss. Marie-Lou, on the contrary, accepts the misery of her life as God's will. The husband and wife have made love four times during their marriage, and each time Léopold has almost had to rape Marie-Lou to achieve this. The only solution for them is suicide. This play, which has been translated into English by Bill Glassco and John Van Burek and published as *Forever yours, Marie-Lou* (1973), had an English production at the Tarragon Theatre, Toronto, in 1972. In the musical comedy *Demain matin Montréal m'attend* (1972), Louise chooses Carmen's way out. She dismisses her sister's self-interested advice and determines to become a nightclub singing star. She tells her mother: 'You're just going to go on doing what you started doing fifty years ago . . . You're going to go on moaning and not do anything till you take your dying breath.' Other possible means of escape are homosexuality (*La Duchesse de Langeais*) and madness (*En pièces détachées*, 1970). (*En pièces détachées* had its English *première* at the Manitoba Theater Center, Winnipeg, in January 1973.) Tremblay conveys, however, that none of these is a true means of liberation—the contradictions, brilliantly revealed in his use of language, continue to do battle within the individual. But thus far he is not concerned with offering solutions. This does not prevent his work from having a definite political importance, though it is frowned upon by the supporters of a more traditional 'French-Canadian' culture.

Tremblay has also successfully adapted works by other writers: Aristophanes' *Lysistrata* (1969—in collaboration with André Brassard, his friend and the director of most of his plays); two of Paul Zindel's Broadway successes (*L'effet des rayons gamma sur les vieux garçons*, 1970, and *. . . et Mademoiselle Roberge boit un peu . . .*, 1971); and a program of one-act plays by Tennessee Williams. *Trois petits tours* (1971) is a collection of plays originally written for television. *Les paons* (1971), which Tremblay himself describes as 'a very bad play', is in a completely different style. Instead of transposing the social and cultural reality of a particular sector of the Québec population, he has written here a symbolical drama.

In 1971 Tremblay received an award from the Canada Council that enabled him to rest and work in Paris for a year. He intends to concentrate on the theatre, with plans to write an opera, but he also wants to work in films. (A half-hour colour film produced by the National Film Board with a scenario by André Brassard and dialogue by Tremblay—*Françoise Durocher, Waitress*—was seen on CBC television in 1972.) He has, however, already attempted the fields of short-story and novel writing. Here Tremblay leaves everyday life behind and explores imaginary worlds. *Contes pour buveurs attardés* (1966) was written when he was seventeen. *La cité dans l'oeuf* (1969) tells of the finding of a manuscript that relates how Françoise Laplante discovered, explored, and inadvertently destroyed a fantasy world enclosed in a glass egg.

Hosanna was published and produced in 1973. It is the story of a male transvestite and 'her' homosexual 'husband', which suggests a symbolic diversion recalling Tremblay's statement that there are no real men in Québec. He also published in 1973 a novel, *C't à ton tour, Laura Cadieux*, which is reminiscent of *Les belles-soeurs* and presents a number of women who recount their lives to one another in a doctor's waitingroom.

The whole issue of *Nord* (No. 1, Autumn 1971) is devoted to Tremblay. JC

Tremblay, Renald. See DRAMA IN FRENCH 4.

Tremblay, Rodrigue. See POLITICAL WRITINGS IN FRENCH 3.

Trigger, Bruce G. See HISTORY STUDIES IN ENGLISH 2 and INDIANS 4 and 5.

Triggs, Stanley. See HISTORY STUDIES IN ENGLISH 7.

Trimborn, Herman. See INDIAN LEGENDS AND ART.

Trinel, Ernest. See ESKIMOS: BOOKS IN FRENCH.

Trobriand, Regis de. See LITERARY STUDIES IN FRENCH 2.

Troper, Harold M. See HISTORY STUDIES IN ENGLISH 8.

Trottier, Pierre (1925–). Born in Montreal, he studied law at the Université de Montréal and then entered the department of external affairs, serving abroad in Moscow, Djakarta, London, and then again in Moscow. In the 1950s he published three collections of much-admired verse: *Le combat contre Tristan* (1951), *Poèmes de Russie* (1957), and *Les belles au bois dormant* (1960)—the latter two written during his tours abroad. During a spell in Ottawa he published a poem, 'Le retour d'Oedipe', in *Écrits du Canada français* (XIII, 1962) and a collection of essays, *Mon Babel* (1963). 'Le retour d'Oedipe' and the commentaries on this poem and his earlier work contained in *Mon Babel* are the crystallization of a lifetime's reflection. The exiled Oedipus returns to his native land and views his life, his experience of the world, and his reading of the great universal myths—particularly those of love and the quest for identity—as a spiritual odyssey. His aim is twofold: first, to define his native land ('Te définir, terre natale') and second, to find in his experience elements in which 'quelque chose correspondit à mon être et me le révéla'. The two aims are complementary, a precise sense of location being an essential part of a sense of self. An elegant clarity, a playful detachment, and the deliberate search for universal values mark Trottier off from others who were treating these themes in the 1950s. It is, however, a Canadian experience that he is describing. The returning Oedipus-Trottier comes back to a Québec still in the repressive grip of a Creon-Duplessis, who is a slave to political expediency and reasons of state. The white virgin widow Jocasta-Maria Chapdelaine acquiesces in the situation and rival Laius-François Paradis is conveniently dead. There is no tragedy for Québec, which does not deserve one; no despair because there was never any hope. Yet Trottier salutes those Antigones who in the fifties kept memory alive, and sees the poets of Québec, who have belatedly made their own that ontological objective that has characterized French poetry since Baudelaire and have begun to shake off the effects of stultifying conformism, as winning for their country the title 'pays de poésie'. Trottier's almost total silence since 1963 is perhaps explained by the nature of his last works. The perfect myth has no sequel. His collected verse, which contained new material but marked no departure from his learned eclecticism, appeared in 1972 under the title *Sainte-Mémoire*. CRPM

Trudeau, Pierre Elliott. See BELLES LETTRES IN FRENCH; POLITICAL WRITINGS IN ENGLISH 1; and POLITICAL WRITINGS IN FRENCH 2, 3, 4, and 6.

Trudel, Marcel (1917–). Born in Saint-Narcisse, Qué., he was educated there and at Université Laval. After teaching in the Bourget College, Rigaud, Qué., from 1941 to 1945, he did postgraduate work at Harvard University. From 1947 to 1964 he was professor of history at Laval. In 1965 he joined Carleton University, Ottawa, and in 1966 was appointed chairman of the history department at the University of Ottawa. His thesis, *L'influence de Voltaire au Canada* (1945), provides a first survey of reading habits in Québec and of works by Canadian authors of the eighteenth and the first half of the nineteenth century.

Trudel's works can be classified in three categories. I. Political and institutional history: *Louis XVI: le congrès américain et le Canada* (1949); *Le régime militaire dans le gouvernement des Trois-Rivières 1760–1764* (1952); *L'affaire Jumonville* (1953); *Le régime seigneurial* (1956); *L'église canadienne sous le régime militaire, 1759–1764* (2 vols, 1956, 1957); *L'esclavage au Canada français: histoire et conditions de l'esclavage* (1960); *Histoire de la Nouvelle-France: Tome I: Les vaines tentatives 1524–1603* (1963) and *Tome II: Le comptoir 1604–1627* (1966); *Canada: unity and diversity* (1967), published in French as *Canada: unité et diversité* (1968); *Initiation à la Nouvelle-France: histoire et institutions* (1968), published in English as *An introduction to New France*; and *The beginnings of New France: 1524–1663* (1973), translated by Patricia Claxton for the Canadian Centenary Series. II. Biographies: *Chiniquy* (1955), *Champlain* (1956), and *Jacques Cartier* (1968). III. Documents: *Histoire du Canada par les textes: Tome I, 1534–1854* (1952; revised and enlarged 1972) with Guy FRÉGAULT. Trudel also co-authored with Geneviève Jain a study for the Royal Commission on Bilingualism and Biculturalism entitled *L'histoire du Canada: enquête sur les manuels* (1970), which was published in English as *Canadian history textbooks: a comparative study* (1970). He edited *Atlas de la Nouvelle France/An atlas of New France* (1968) and was associate editor of Volume I (1000–1700) of the *Dictionary of Canadian biography/Dictionnaire biographique du Canada* (1966). He is the author of *Vézine* (1946), a traditional novel of peasant life in the Saint-Maurice Valley.

By his vast knowledge of archival papers, his clarity of expression, and his abundant publications, Trudel has expanded our knowledge of the French period in Canadian history and the first years of the English régime. With great discretion he has presented an enlarged perspective of his subject: the fundamentals of Québec's co-existence in North America and of Canadian duality and diversity are always part of his substantial analyses.

In 1945 and 1951 Trudel was awarded the Prix David, the most important literary distinction conferred by the Québec government, and in 1967 he received a Governor General's Award for the second volume of his *Histoire de la Nouvelle-France*. J-LR

Trudel, Pierre. See HISTORY STUDIES IN FRENCH 4.

Tupper, Stanley R. See POLITICAL WRITINGS IN ENGLISH 2.

Turek, V. See HISTORY STUDIES IN ENGLISH 14.

Turnbull, Gael. See POETRY IN ENGLISH 1.

Turnbull, J. R. See HISTORY STUDIES IN ENGLISH 2.

U

Ullman, Victor. See HISTORY STUDIES IN ENGLISH 5.

Underhill, Ruth. See INDIAN LEGENDS AND ART.

Upton, L. F. S. See HISTORY STUDIES IN ENGLISH 4.

Usher, Peter J. See INDIANS 4.

V

Vac, Bertrand (1914–) is the pseudonym of Aimé Pelletier, a Montreal physician and surgeon. He was born at Saint-Ambroise-de-Kildare, a small village halfway between Rawdon and Joliette about forty-five miles north of Montreal. When he was very young the family moved to Joliette where his father, a doctor, set up practice. After completing medical studies in Montreal and Paris, Aimé Pelletier joined the Canadian Army and was attached to the general staff in northern France and Belgium. Upon returning to Canada he resumed his career in medicine while at the same time travelling widely and devoting part of his leisure to his writings.

Despite the fact that he has three times received the Prix du Cercle du Livre de France (1950, 1952, 1965), Vac's early works are relatively little known. His first novel, *Louise Genest* (1950), won the Prix the first year it was offered. Set in the village of Saint-Michel-des-Saints and the surrounding forest area north of Joliette, it relates the drama of a woman married at the age of seventeen to the owner of the village general store, Armand Genest, a coarse, brutal, miserly man who makes her life unbearable. In desperation Louise leaves her husband to seek happiness in the forest with Thomas Clarey, a young halfbreed hunter and trapper. To punish her, Genest withdraws Pierre, their sixteen year-old son, from the collège where he is studying and the boy winds up working in a logging camp. When he fails to return from a hunting expedition, his mother, tortured by guilt, remorse, and the conviction that she has abandoned him, sets out alone in search of him. All she ever finds is his rifle. Suffering from hallucinations, Louise succumbs to the elements and dies of exhaustion. Some critics have rightly insisted on the importance of the forest in this novel and on the myth of the noble savage living a life of freedom and contentment in the heart of nature. But the elements of social criticism are even more significant. The real tragedy of Louise Genest lies in the guilt complex from which she suffers as a result of her upbringing and the social and psychological pressures to which she falls victim.

In *Deux portes . . . une adresse* (1950), one of the relatively few French-Canadian novels based on the Second World War, Captain Jacques Grenon, a twenty-seven-year-old engineer, unhappily married and the father of two young sons, has been in the army for four years. He falls in love with Françoise Clair, a charming, cultivated, wealthy young widow. Much of the evolution of their love is revealed in the series of letters exchanged between their infrequent meetings during the course of one year. The captain finally decides not to return to his wife Berthe. But Berthe writes to Jacques' commanding general and has him repatriated against his will. Once back in Montreal, he is swallowed up in the quagmire of his former existence.

The tone of *Saint-Pépin, P.Q.* (1955) is considerably lighter. Satire and caricature play a large part in this story of political antics in a small Québec town. In his prefatory note, Vac takes pains to state that 'even the most grotesque situations in this novel have been lived; all we have done is interpret scenes which take place almost daily in our beloved province.' It is evident, however, that the events and characters, their foibles and absurdities, have been exaggerated for comic effect. The main character, Polydor Granger, becomes an election candidate in spite of himself, drawing along in his wake a colourful collection of local bigots, opportunists, malcontents, and hypocrites. The election campaign is preposterous and unleashes all sorts of passions, some shameful, some comic. The book ends on a cynical note, after the successful election of Polydor Granger, as Clara, Madame Granger's ambitious new maid, says: 'Now I've got to look after the deputy. If we want to keep him alive, we've got to take care of him, that fellow. A dead deputy don't do you no favours. . . .'

Bertrand Vac has successfully tried his hand at the detective story. In 1956 his novel *L'assassin dans l'hôpital* was awarded the Prix du Cercle du Roman policier but it has been out of print for some time. Vac's fifth book, *La favorite et le conquérant* (1963) is a historical novel whose action begins in 1397 during the reign of the famous Tartar chieftain Tamerlane, ruler of Samarkand. Based on painstaking and detailed documentation, this novel attempts to reconstruct, in a vast and exotic panorama of nearly 400 pages, the bloodthirsty triumphs, unbridled cruelties, and merciless rivalries that rent the empire of the great Mongol warrior during the latter years of his life. The action, which covers a period of about nine years, flags at times, but the narrative in general is deftly handled; it is interspersed here and there with passages of crude, erotic, and almost scabrous violence.

In 1965 Bertrand Vac was awarded his third Prix du Cercle du Livre de France for *Histoires galantes* (1965), a collection of eight short stories varying in length from six to thirty-six pages. Light and licentious, sometimes amusing, occasionally unpredictable, they constitute a series of variations on the theme, not of love, but of not-so-serious sex.

Appelez-moi Amédée, Vac's first play, was presented during the summer of 1967 by the Théâtre de l'Escale, an enterprising troupe of actors who renovated a decommissioned ferryboat to make it into an itinerant floating theatre plying the ports of the St Lawrence. Without being a major work, the comedy nonetheless enjoyed considerable success. Under the title *Mes pensées 'profondes'*, Vac also published in 1967 a tongue-in-cheek collection of maxims, aphorisms, and witticisms arranged chronologically from 1958 to 1966. The truths he serves up in capsule form are coated with humour or delicate irony; they are filled from time to time with biting sarcasm and on rare occasions are tinged with cruelty. But if he castigates vice and vanity, he avoids pedantry and moralizing. His readers may enjoy pondering such *bons mots* as: 'Vices are tightropes on which very few can dance elegantly'; or 'Every time you make love, it should be as if it were for the last time.'

LWK

Vachon, André. See HISTORY STUDIES IN ENGLISH 2 and HISTORY STUDIES IN FRENCH 3 and 11.

Vadeboncoeur, Pierre. See BELLES LETTRES IN FRENCH; FICTION IN FRENCH 3; and POLITICAL WRITINGS IN FRENCH 2 and 7.

Vallerand, Noël. See HISTORY STUDIES IN FRENCH 4.

Vallières, Pierre. See BELLES LETTRES IN FRENCH; HISTORY STUDIES IN ENGLISH 12; HISTORY STUDIES IN FRENCH 2; POLITICAL WRITINGS IN ENGLISH 1; and POLITICAL WRITINGS IN FRENCH 2.

Van Dusen, Thomas. See HISTORY STUDIES IN ENGLISH 12.

Van Schendel, Michel. See LITERARY STUDIES IN FRENCH 4.

Van Steen, Marcus. See HISTORY STUDIES IN ENGLISH 5.

Van Stone, James. See INDIANS 5.

Vaugeois, Denis. See HISTORY STUDIES IN FRENCH 3 and 4.

Veilleux, Gérard. See POLITICAL WRITINGS IN FRENCH 3.

Vernon, P. E. See INDIANS 6.

Vézina, Raymond. See HISTORY STUDIES IN FRENCH 8.

Viatte, Auguste. See ANTHOLOGIES IN FRENCH.

Viens, Jacques. See LITERARY STUDIES IN FRENCH 4.

Viger, Denis Benjamin. See HISTORY STUDIES IN FRENCH 11.

Vigneault, Gilles (1928–). Born in Natashquan, Qué., on the north shore of the St Lawrence, he was educated at Université Laval, where he was influenced and encouraged by Félix-Antoine SAVARD. He then taught at various high schools and at Laval, during which time he founded *Émourie*, a poetry magazine that ran for thirteen issues, and the publishing firm Éditions de l'Arc, with which he is still actively involved. In 1960 he made his debut as a chansonnier in Québec; his first triumphant Montreal concert was held later that year. The universal quality of his chansons and his individual and very versatile performing style—his voice sometimes almost raucous in exultation, at other times tender; his jigs and step-dances; and the wild semaphoring of his long arms, which can also achieve such gentle fluidity—have made him equally popular in English Canada and in Europe. His most famous chanson, 'Mon pays'—which he insists is not separatist or even nationalist as is generally believed but a personal lament for coldness and the inability to share love or experience—won an international award when sung by Monique Leyrac in Poland in 1965.

Vigneault's poems and chansons alike are carefully structured, the work of a highly disciplined writer. Some vividly describe his native region of Natashquan, its violent seasons and life lived precariously between the forest and the sea, and such characters as Jack Monoloy and Jos Monferrand, real persons from his youth whom he has raised to mythic proportions. Woman often appears in these poems as nature or explicitly as a river or some other aspect of the region for which he feels tenderness. More personal poems concern love and the difficulty of loving, solitude and the passage of time, and what man has done with his world. His collections are *Étraves* (1959); *Balises* (1964); *Avec les vieux mots* (1964); *Pour une soirée de chansons* (1965); *Quand les bateaux s'en vont* (1965), winner of a Governor General's Award; *Les gens de mon pays* (1967); *Tam ti delam* (1967); *Paroles de chanson* (1969); *Ce que je dis c'est en passant* (1970); *Les dicts du voyageur sédentaire* (1970); and *Exergues* (1971). He has also published *Contes sur la pointe des pieds* (1960) and *Contes du coin de l'oeil* (1966), two collections of brief prose pieces—more fables than stories—which make some comment on man's frailty or his alienation from nature and himself. The first of these collections has been published in a bilingual edition, translated by Paul Allard, as *Tales sur la pointe des pieds* (1972). Vigneault wrote the text for *Où la lumière chante* (1966), a book about Quebec City with photographs by François Lafortune.

Vigneault's poetry is discussed in *An outline of contemporary French-Canadian literature* (1972) by J. Raymond Brazeau. Studies in French are by Aline Robitaille (1968) and by Lucien Rioux (Paris, 1969) in the Chansonniers d'aujourd'hui series. *Fernand Seguin rencontre Gilles Vigneault* (1969), which is based largely on the transcript of a television interview, presents Vigneault's own thoughts about his life and work. English translations of some of his poetry have been published in *The poetry of French Canada in translation* (1970) edited by John GLASSCO. JM

Vigneault, Robert. See BELLES LETTRES IN FRENCH.

Vineberg, Ethel. See CHILDREN'S BOOKS IN FRENCH.

Virlaid, Arved. See FICTION IN ENGLISH 1.

Von Riekhoff, Harald. See POLITICAL WRITINGS IN ENGLISH 7.

Waddington, Miriam (1917–), *née* Dworkin. Born in Winnipeg, she was educated at the University of Toronto and at the Pennsylvania School of Social Work. She spent some years as a social worker in Montreal, taught social work at McGill University, and participated in the revival of poetic activity in Montreal during the 1940s, contributing poems to *First Statement* and *Preview*. She took a graduate degree in English at the University of Toronto and is now a member of the department of English at York University, Toronto.

Her first book was *Green world* (1945). This was followed by *The second silence* (1955) and *The season's lovers* (1958). These early poems are full of sensuous language, with some use of traditional metres, expressing a full-hearted response to people, especially in poems arising from her experiences as a social worker. There are also tender love lyrics and poems based on memories of her past. In her later verse, contained in *The glass trumpet* (1966) and *Say yes* (1969), the past is used as a measure to assess the poet's present situation. The poems investigate psychological states of disillusion, regret, and nostalgia, but her vision adjusts fearlessly and affirmatively in her quest for self-identity. She searches her past—'the snowblurred geography/of . . . childhood'—in Manitoba and her Jewish ancestry, recording her responses to travels back to her Winnipeg home and to other parts of the world, including England, Israel, and Russia. Often her poetry moves between polarities—love and betrayal, reality and fantasy, loss and discovery—in diction and structures that have been refined to a lucent sharpness while still retaining a fervent romanticism. It is language chosen from 'a red/passionate dictionary' and often drawn from fairy-tales and surrealistic elements. This more positive note of guarded affirmation about her own life is stated in the new poems in *Driving home: poems new and selected* (1972). *Dream telescope* (1972), a short collection published in England, contains mostly poems that appear in *Driving home*.

Mrs Waddington collaborated with a number of photographers in the National Film Board book *Call them Canadians* (1968), to which she contributed poems that match the moods and emotional content of the photographs.

In recent years she has shown a marked interest in her own Jewish background and in Jewishness in general. This has resulted in a critical study of the leading Canadian Jewish poet, *A. M. Klein* (1970), in the Studies in Canadian Literature series. She has also translated some of the Yiddish poems of Y. Y. Segal; a few of these translations appear in an anthology of poems written in Canada in languages other than French and English, *Volvox* (1971). She recently edited the writings of the critic and editor of *Northern Review*, the influential literary magazine of the forties and fifties: *John Sutherland: essays, controversies, poems* (1973). PS

Wade, Mason. See HISTORY STUDIES IN ENGLISH 1.

Wade, Scott. See HISTORY STUDIES IN ENGLISH 15.

Wainright, Andy. See ANTHOLOGIES IN ENGLISH 1.

Waite, Peter B. See HISTORY STUDIES IN ENGLISH 7.

Walker, David (1911–). David Harry Walker was born in Scotland, educated at Sandhurst, Eng., and became an officer of the Black Watch. He had served in India and the Sudan before coming to Canada in 1938 as aide-de-camp to Lord Tweedsmuir, the governor general. He rejoined his regiment in 1939 and was a prisoner of war from 1940 to 1945. He was controller to the viceroy of India in 1946–7, and on his retirement settled in St Andrews, N.B.

Walker's varied experience, his ability to tell a story, and the vividness with which he creates landscape as the natural environment of action contribute to the effectiveness of his comic novels and adventure stories. Light-heartedness characterizes *Geordie* (1950), the story of a stubborn Highlander who goes to the United States as a member of an Olympic team, and *Digby* (1953), the amusing adventures of an overtired businessman and his bored wife while on an uninhibited holiday in Scotland. *Come back Geordie* was published in 1966. *Digby* won the Governor General's Award for fiction as did *The pillar* (1952), a novel based on Walker's own experiences as a prisoner of war. *The storm and the silence* (1949) is the story of a manhunt in the Scottish hills; in *Harry Black* (1956) an attempt at symbolism is less effective than the events of a hunt for a man-eating tiger. Walker has given Canadian settings to *Where the high winds blow* (1960)—the story of a man who, having successfully met the challenge of the business world, encounters that of the North —and to *Mallabec* (1965), a melodramatic story set in an isolated fishing camp in New Brunswick. Other novels are *The devil's plunge* (1968), a detective story with exciting accounts of skiing in the Alps (published in the United States under the title *CAB-Intersec* (1968)) and *The Lord's pink ocean* (1972), science fiction that foresees the destruction of almost the whole world by the careless handling of noxious biochemical products. Walker sees the destructive pattern emerging among the survivors.

He has written four books for children: *Sandy was a soldier boy* (1957), *Dragon Hill* (1962), *Big Ben* (1969), and *Pirate rock* (1970).

NS

Walker, George. See DRAMA IN ENGLISH 3.

Walker, Russell R. See HISTORY STUDIES IN ENGLISH 9.

Wallace, Anthony F. C. See INDIAN LEGENDS AND ART.

Wallot, Jean-Pierre. See HISTORY STUDIES IN FRENCH 1 and 4.

Walsh, Gerald. See INDIANS 6.

Walton, Richard J. See HISTORY STUDIES IN ENGLISH 12.

Ward, Norman. See HISTORY STUDIES IN ENGLISH 8 and POLITICAL WRITINGS IN ENGLISH 8.

Warkentin, John. See HISTORY STUDIES IN ENGLISH 1.

Warner, Oliver. See HISTORY STUDIES IN ENGLISH 2.

Warnock, John W. See HISTORY STUDIES IN ENGLISH 12 and POLITICAL WRITINGS IN ENGLISH 7.

Warr, Bertem. See POETRY IN ENGLISH 1.

Warwick, Jack. See LITERARY STUDIES IN ENGLISH 1 and 2; LITERARY STUDIES IN FRENCH 2.

Waterfield, Donald. See POLITICAL WRITINGS IN ENGLISH 7.

Watkins, Melville. See POLITICAL WRITINGS IN ENGLISH 1 and 2.

Watmough, David. See DRAMA IN ENGLISH 2.

Watters, R. E. See ANTHOLOGIES IN ENGLISH intro. and HISTORY STUDIES IN ENGLISH 17.

Waubageshig. See INDIANS 1.

Weaver, Robert. See ANTHOLOGIES IN ENGLISH 2 and 3; ANTHOLOGIES IN FRENCH; and FICTION IN ENGLISH: SHORT STORIES.

Weaver, Sally. See INDIANS 5.

Webb, Phyllis (1927–). Born in Victoria, B.C., she was educated at the University of British Columbia and at McGill. She was on the staff of the department of English at the University of British Columbia for three years before becoming a program organizer in the public affairs department of the CBC, Toronto. She became the supervisor of the CBC series 'Ideas' and retained that position until 1969. She has lived since then in Vancouver or on one of the Gulf islands.

Phyllis Webb's collections of poetry are *Even your right eye* (1956), *The sea is also a garden* (1962), *Naked poems* (1965), and *Selected poems* (1971), which contains an essay on her poetry by John Hulcoop. Her early work was almost obsessively concerned with self, but later her poems began to develop more objectively as she moved between polarities of acceptance and denial in meditative stanzas and tightly structured verse paragraphs filled with images of an almost metaphysical weight. The themes of her poetry are love, history, time, public life, and they are expressed in images of bones, the sea, open landscapes, and nakedness—although paradoxically she includes in her poems many references to defined and enclosed areas such as gardens and briefly glimpsed scenes. The mood of her poetry is generally dark; the language is rigorously compressed, although there are occasional glimmerings of humour and ironic self-mockery, together with some eruptions of slang and colloquialisms. *Naked poems* is a sequence of haiku-like lyrics, each poem containing a 'bone-essential statement' about her experience of love. This whole sequence, together with selections from her other books, has been reprinted in *Selected poems*, which emphasizes the poet's continual concentration on the search for love in a world of loss. The poetry exists as a tension between the discipline of the poetic structures and the cries of unfulfilled desires that lie just beneath the surface of the language. She is presently working on a long sequence of poems related to the theme of imprisonment, 'The Kropotkin papers'. NS/PS

Weinman, Paul L. See HISTORY STUDIES IN ENGLISH 17.

Weiser, Elisabeth. See POLITICAL WRITINGS IN FRENCH 3.

West, Bruce. See HISTORY STUDIES IN ENGLISH 13.

West, Kent. See POETRY IN ENGLISH 3.

Westell, Anthony. See HISTORY STUDIES IN ENGLISH 12 and POLITICAL WRITINGS IN ENGLISH 5.

Wherry, Joseph H. See INDIAN LEGENDS AND ART.

Whitaker, Reginald. See HISTORY STUDIES IN ENGLISH 12.

Whittaker, Herbert. See HISTORY STUDIES IN ENGLISH 16.

Wichern, P. H., Jr. See INDIANS 6.

Widell, Helen. See CHILDREN'S BOOKS IN ENGLISH 5.

Wiebe, Rudy (1934–). Born near Fairholme, Sask., his family moved to Alberta when he was a child. He was educated at the Mennonite High School in Carsdale and at the Universities of Alberta and Tubingen, West Germany. Returning to Alberta in 1960, he took his M.A. at the University of Alberta and a theological degree at the Mennonite Brethren's College in Winnipeg. He has taught English at Goshen College, Indiana, and is now assistant professor of English at the University of Alberta.

Wiebe's religious views and his conviction that the development of the individual depends as much on his physical environment as on the economic, social, and spiritual pressures to which he is subjected give force and variety to his work. He is able to create in his novels vivid settings for the probing moral questions that he asks.

In his first novel, *Peace shall destroy many* (1964), Wiebe concentrates on a group of Mennonites who emigrated from Russia to the Canadian west in the late nineteenth century. By 1939 this group had partially succeeded in creating a pacifist rural theocracy that was easily manipulated by the richest farmer, a natural leader who becomes the local tyrant. But the outside world cannot be shut out. Education, modern technology, and the issues of the Second World War lead many of the younger generation to question communal values. The tensions of the novel rest primarily on the soul-searching of those who seek to reconcile their pacificism with their obligation to accept military service rather than hide behind the sacrifices of others. Liberation in one direction leads to liberation of human passion, and so to the downfall of the tyrant.

The blue mountains of China (1970) is a sometimes confusing saga of the descendants of those Mennonite families who remained in Russia when their relatives immigrated to Canada. Beginning with Soviet persecution and the escape of various groups to the Canadian west (and Paraguay), it follows their subsequent material successes and failures and their spiritual progress from simple piety to fanaticism or agnosticism as they become integrated into North American society. The tug of their roots is felt even by the most liberated when one of them makes a quiet but striking manifestation of his Christian beliefs. The title refers to one of the routes by which the Mennonites escaped from Russia.

In *First and vital candle* (1966), Wiebe's novel about the demoralizing effect of the white man on Indian culture, the religious theme is weakened by overemphasis on the too-evil independent fur-trader and the too-good missionary, his wife, and their assistant. Despite this flaw, the novel is spellbinding in its presentation of the principal Ojibwa characters—the Chief and the Medicine Man. There are notable descriptions of nature, particularly of the spring break-up of a northern river that culminates in a disastrous flood.

Wiebe's short stories have been published in various literary magazines. He has edited two short-story anthologies: *The story-makers* (1970), an international collection, and *Stories from western Canada* (1972), which includes his own 'Did Jesus ever laugh?', a chilling expression of fundamentalist fanaticism. NS

Wilgress, Dana. See HISTORY STUDIES IN ENGLISH 11.

Wilkinson, Anne (1910–61), *née* Gibbons. Born in Toronto, she moved to London, Ont., when a child and was educated in the United States and Europe. She was a founding editor of *The Tamarack Review*. She won distinction as a poet for the keen perception with which she treated the nature of sensuous experience and for the word music, grace, and wit of her verse. Because she used riddles and puns, some intellectual effort is required to grasp the full significance of her poems on life, love, and death. She was the author of two collections of verse, *Counterpoint to sleep* (1951) and *The hangman ties the holly* (1955). A. J. M. SMITH edited and wrote an introduction for *The collected poems of Anne Wilkinson* (1968), which includes some previously unpublished poems and a charming autobiographical fragment about her childhood, 'Four corners of my world'. Anne Wilkinson also wrote two books of prose: *Lions in the way* (1956), a history of the Osler family of which she was a member, and *Swann and Daphne* (1960), a fantasy for children. NS

Wilkinson, Doug. See HISTORY STUDIES IN ENGLISH 10.

Williams, Glyndwr. See HISTORY STUDIES IN ENGLISH 3.

Williams, Norman. See DRAMA IN ENGLISH 1.

Williamson, Moncrieff. See HISTORY STUDIES IN ENGLISH 16.

Wilson, Alan. See HISTORY STUDIES IN ENGLISH 5.

Wilson, Clifford P. See HISTORY STUDIES IN ENGLISH 10.

Wilson, D. See HISTORY STUDIES IN ENGLISH 15.

Wilson, James Reginald. See FOLKLORE: BIBLIOGRAPHY.

Wilson, Milton. See ANTHOLOGIES IN ENGLISH 1 and POETRY IN ENGLISH.

Wilson, V. Seymour. See HISTORY STUDIES IN ENGLISH 12.

Wilson, W. A. See POLITICAL WRITINGS IN ENGLISH 5.

Windsor, John. See HISTORY STUDIES IN ENGLISH 12.

Wingert, Paul. See INDIAN LEGENDS AND ART.

Winks, Robin W. See HISTORY STUDIES IN ENGLISH 12 and 14.

Winter, Jack. See DRAMA IN ENGLISH 3.

Wise, S. F. See HISTORY STUDIES IN ENGLISH 6.

Wiseman, Christopher. See POETRY IN ENGLISH 1.

Withrow, William. See HISTORY STUDIES IN ENGLISH 16.

Witney, Dudley. See HISTORY STUDIES IN ENGLISH 7.

Wolcott, Harry F. See INDIANS 6.

Wolfe, Samuel. See HISTORY STUDIES IN ENGLISH 8.

Wood, Kerry. See CHILDREN'S BOOKS IN ENGLISH 2.

Woodcock, George (1912–). Born in Winnipeg, Man., he went to England as a child and received a grammar-school education there. He was associated with the anarchist movement during the thirties and forties and edited two anarchist periodicals, *War Commentary* and *Freedom*, and founded a third, *Now*, a literary magazine that he edited from 1940 to 1947. He returned to Canada in 1949. In 1956 he joined the University of British Columbia, where he became associate professor of English literature and lecturer in Asian studies. He discontinued his regular teaching in 1963. Since its inception in 1959 he has been editor of the literary quarterly *Canadian Literature*. He won the Molson Prize in 1973.

Woodcock is a man of letters whose literary output—a veritable library of informed and lucid books—is remarkable not only for its volume but for its prodigious range: it embraces political movements and ideas, social communities, literature, history, travel, studies of seminal intellectuals, and poetry. During his anarchist period in England, Woodcock was influenced by such libertarian thinkers as Godwin, Proudhon, and Kropotkin, who became the subjects of three of his earliest books: *William Godwin: a biographical study* (1946); *The anarchist prince: a biographical study of Peter Kropotkin* (1950), which he wrote with Ivan Avakumovic; and *Pierre-Joseph Proudhon: a biography* (1953). (The last two were reprinted in paperback in 1970 and 1972.) At this time Woodcock began friendships with two contemporary thinkers and writers who are the subjects of two of his more recent books: *The crystal spirit: a study of George Orwell* (1966), which won a Governor General's Award, and *Herbert Read: the stream and the source* (1972), which Woodcock describes as an 'intellectual biography'. His other biographical studies are: *The incomparable Aphra* (1948), about the British novelist and playwright Aphra Behn (1640–89); *The paradox of Oscar Wilde* (1950); *Mohandas Gandhi* (1971); and *Dawn and the darkest hour: a study of Aldous Huxley* (1972).

Woodcock's travel books are enriched by his interest in cultures, political history, and the arts: *To the city of the dead : an account of travel in Mexico* (1957); *Incas and other men: travels in the Andes* (1959); *Faces of India: a travel narrative* (1964); *Asia, gods and cities: Aden to Tokyo* (1966); and *Kerala: a portrait of the Malabar coast* (1967). He has also written two books in the Great Travellers series, of which he is general editor: *Henry Walter Bates: naturalist of the Amazon* (1969) and *Into Tibet: the early British explorers* (1971).

Woodcock's cosmopolitan interests have not prevented him from giving his attention to the life and letters of his own country; indeed, they lend his Canadian studies an unusual and salutary perspective. The first book he wrote on Canada was *Ravens and prophets: an account of journeys in British Columbia, Alberta and Southern Alaska* (1952), which includes his impressions of the Doukhobors. Woodcock's interest in this sect continued over the years and with Ivan Avakumovic he wrote a definitive study, *The Doukhobors* (1968). He has also written *The Hudson's Bay Company* (1970), a brief history, and the most comprehensive and perceptive survey of our history, institutions, arts, cities, and politics, *Canada and the Canadians* (1970). An astute and objective critic of Canadian literature, Woodcock has written critical studies of two novelists—*Hugh MacLennan* (1969) in the Studies in Canadian Literature series and *Mordecai Richler* (1970) in the Canadian Writers Series—and a book of literary essays that is essential reading for students, *Odysseus ever returning: essays on Canadian writing* (1970). *The rejection of politics and other essays on Canada, Canadians, anarchism and the world* (1972) is a further compilation of Woodcock's writings on Canadian subjects that also has illuminating discussions of the political movement he was associated with. He has edited four books related to the magazine *Canadian Literature*: *A choice of critics: selections from 'Canadian Literature'* (1966); *The sixties: Canadian writers and writing of the decade* (1969), a symposium in celebration of the magazine's tenth anniversary; *Malcolm Lowry: the man and his work* (1971) and *Wyndham Lewis in Canada* (1971), both of which contain many essays that first appeared in the magazine.

Woodcock's other books, which collectively represent most of his interests, are: *The writer in politics* (1948), a volume of critical essays: *Anarchism: a history of libertarian ideas and movements* (1962), which remains an important book on the subject; *The Greeks in India* (1966) and *The British in the Far East* (1969), two historical studies; *Civil disobedience* (1966), seven talks for CBC radio; and *Victoria* (1971), an essay on the city with photographs by Ingeborg Woodcock. While living in England Woodcock wrote three small books of verse: *The white island* (1940), *The centre cannot hold* (1942), and *Imagine the south* (1949); his *Selected poems* was published in 1967. When he came to Canada he turned to verse drama, writing five plays of this kind for the CBC: *Maskerman, The benefactor, The floor of the night, The empire of shadows,* and *The island of demons.* He also wrote the libretto for one of the CBC's centennial operas, *The bride ship*, set to music by Robert Turner.

A symposium based on articles published in the *Canadian Forum* in 1972, *Nationalism or local control: responses to George Woodcock* edited by Viv Nelles and Abraham Rotstein, was published early in 1973. WET

Woodman, Ross G. See LITERARY STUDIES IN ENGLISH 4.

Woods, Herbert F. See HISTORY STUDIES IN ENGLISH 7.

Woodward, Lucy Berton. See CHILDREN'S BOOKS IN ENGLISH 2.

Worley, Ronald B. See HISTORY STUDIES IN ENGLISH 9.

Woycenko, Ol'ha. See HISTORY STUDIES IN ENGLISH 14.

Wright, Lawrence. See HISTORY STUDIES IN ENGLISH 7.

Wright, Richard. See FICTION IN ENGLISH 5.

Wuttunee, William. See INDIANS 1.

Wyatt, Rachel. See FICTION IN ENGLISH 4.

Wyczynski, Paul (1921–). Born in Poland, he had his education interrupted when he was deported to Germany in 1942. He is a graduate of Lille University, where he studied French and Slavonic literatures and linguistics. Since coming to Canada in 1951 he has taught at the University of Ottawa. Encouraged by Séraphin Marion and Guy Sylvestre, he studied French-Canadian literature and presented his doctoral thesis in 1957 on *Émile Nelligan: sources et originalité de son oeuvre* (Ottawa, 1960). In 1958 he was appointed director of the Centre de Recherches en Littérature canadienne-française, which became in 1969 the Centre de Recherches en Civilisation canadienne-française. He edited the four important reference works in the Archives des Lettres canadiennes produced by the Centre and made a major contribution to each: *Mouvement littéraire de Québec, 1860* (1961), *L'école littéraire de Montréal* (1963), *Le roman canadien-français* (1964), and *La poésie canadienne-française: perspectives historiques et thématiques, profils de poètes* (1969). A fifth volume on the theatre is in preparation. At a colloquium on the present state of French-Canadian studies organized by the Centre in 1968, the tenth anniversary of its foundation, just tribute was paid to the role Wyczynski played at an early stage in the promotion of the serious study of French-Canadian literature. The proceedings were published under the title *Recherche et littérature canadienne-française* (1969). The Centre is devoted to the study of the nineteenth century and, in this context, Wyczynski has pursued his work on Émile Nelligan in *Poésie et symbole* (1965), in which a general essay on symbolism is followed by chapters on Nelligan, Saint-Denys GARNEAU, Anne HÉBERT, and tree symbolism in French-Canadian poetry; in *Émile Nelligan* (1969); and in an ambitious essay, *Nelligan et la musique* (1971), in which the obscure complexities of the meaning of musicality in post-symbolist poetry are explored. Wyczynski inaugurated the Centre's projected collection of the works of François-Xavier Garneau with a critical edition of his *Voyage en Angleterre et en France dans les années 1831, 1832 et 1833* (1968) and edited a book of essays, including his own on the *Voyage . . .*, under the general title *François-Xavier Garneau: aspects littéraires de son oeuvre* (1966). Wyczynski combines the qualities of a dedicated and tireless scholar and a man of feeling. He has found the time to represent New Canadians on the Royal Commission on Bilingualism and Biculturalism. CRPM

Y

Z

GOVERNOR GENERAL'S AWARDS

The first Governor General's Awards were given in 1937. They were administered by the Canadian Authors' Association, which set up an Awards Board in 1944, until 1959 when the administration of them was taken over by the Canada Council. At that time the juvenile category was dropped and since 1959 the awards have carried with them a cash prize, which is now $2500.

1967

Eli MANDEL: *An idiot joy*. Poetry.

Alden NOWLAN: *Bread, wine and salt*. Poetry.

Norah Story: *The Oxford companion to Canadian history and literature*. Non-fiction.

Jacques GODBOUT: *Salut Galarneau*. Fiction (French).

Robert-Lionel SÉGUIN: *La civilisation traditionnelle de 'l'habitant' aux XVIIe et XVIIIe siècles*. Non-fiction (French).

Françoise LORANGER: *Encore cinq minutes*. Drama (French).

1968

Alice MUNRO: *Dance of the happy shades*. Fiction.

Mordecai RICHLER: *Cocksure* and *Hunting tigers under glass*. Fiction and essays.

Marie-Claire BLAIS: *Manuscrits de Pauline Archange*. Fiction (French).

Fernand DUMONT: *Le lieu de l'homme*. Non-fiction (French).

In addition, the selection committee chose Leonard COHEN's *Selected poems 1956–68* and Hubert AQUIN's novel *Trou de mémoire*. Both writers declined the award.

1969

Robert KROETSCH: *The Studhorse man*. Fiction.

George BOWERING: *Rocky Mountain foot* and *The gangs of Kosmos*. Poetry.

Gwendolyn MACEWEN: *The shadow-maker*. Poetry.

Louise Maheux-Forcier: *Une forêt pour Zoé*. Fiction (French).

Jean-Guy PILON: *Comme eau retenue*. Poetry (French).

Michel BRUNET: *Les canadiens après la conquête*. Non-fiction (French).

1970

Dave GODFREY: *The new ancestors*. Fiction.

Michael ONDAATJE: *The collected works of Billy the Kid*. Prose and poetry.

bp NICHOL: *Still water*, *The true eventual story of Billy the Kid*, *Beach head*, *The cosmic chef: an evening of concrete*. Poetry.

Monique BOSCO: *La femme de Loth*. Fiction (French).

Jacques BRAULT: *Quand nous serons heureux*. Drama (French).

In addition, the selection committee chose Fernand OUELLETTE's collection of essays, *Les actes retrouvés*. M. Ouellette declined the award.

1971

Mordecai RICHLER: *St Urbain's horseman*. Fiction.

John GLASSCO: *Selected poems*. Poetry.

Pierre BERTON: *The last spike*. Non-fiction.

Gérard BESSETTE: *Le cycle*. Fiction (French).

Paul-Marie LAPOINTE: *Le réel absolu*. Poetry (French).

Gérald Fortin: *La fin d'un règne*. Non-fiction (French).

1972

Robertson DAVIES: *The manticore*. Fiction.

Dennis LEE: *Civil elegies*. Poetry.

John NEWLOVE: *Lies*. Poetry.

Antonine MAILLET: *Don l'Orignal*. Fiction (French).

Gilles HÉNAULT: *Signaux pour les voyants*. Poetry (French).

Jean Hamelin and Yves Roby: *Histoire économique du Québec 1851–1896*. Non-fiction (French).